THE
NOBILITY
OF
FAILURE

ZW

Ivan Morris

THE NOONDAY PRESS
FARRAR STRAUS GIROUX
NEW YORK

THE NOBILITY OF FAILURE

TRAGIC HEROES IN THE HISTORY OF JAPAN

Suicide Submarine! by Yokota Yutaka, published by
Ballantine Books, a Division of Random House, Inc.,
copyright © 1962

*The Divine Wind: Japan's Kamikaze Force in World
War II*, by Inoguchi Rikihei, Nakajimi Tadashi, and
Roger Pineau, published by U.S. Naval Institute,
copyright © 1958.

"A Friend Whose Work Has Come to Nothing" and
"An Irish Airman Foresees His Death," poems by
William Butler Yeats reprinted with permission of
Macmillan Publishing Co., Inc., from *Collected
Poems of William Butler Yeats*, respectively
copyright 1916 by Macmillan Publishing Co., Inc.,
renewed 1944 by Bertha Georgie Yeats, and
copyright 1919 by Macmillan Publishing Co., Inc.,
renewed 1947 by Bertha Georgie Yeats.

Certain chapters of this book were first
published, in slightly different form, in the
following magazines: *Boston University Journal,
History Today* (London), *Horizon, The New Yorker,*
and *Sunday Times Magazine* (London).

This paperback edition first published in 1988 by
Farrar, Straus and Giroux in arrangement with
Henry Holt and Company, Inc.

Printed in the United States of America
Designed by Lynn Braswell
Published in Canada by HarperCollinsCanadaLtd

Library of Congress Cataloging in Publication Data
Morris, Ivan I
The nobility of failure.
Bibliography: p.
Includes index.
1. Japan—Biography. 2. Heroes. I. Title.
DS834.M64   952'.00992 [B]   73-3750

Contents

List of Maps

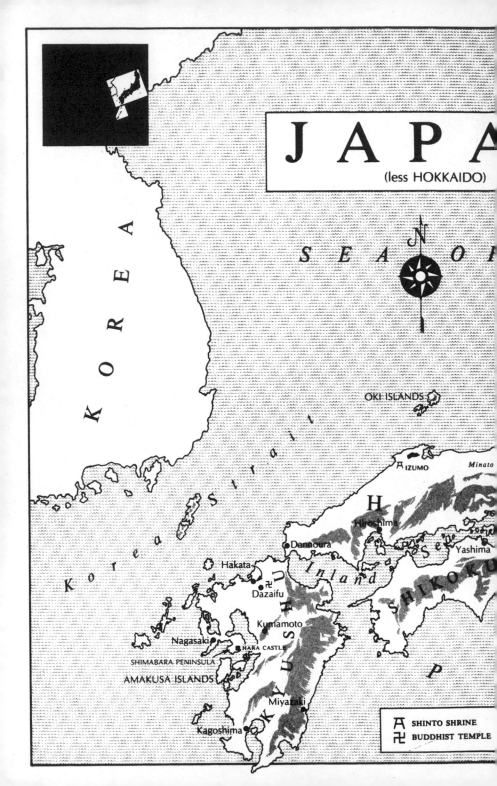

N

JAPAN

HOSHUU

Kotomo River

Hiraizumi

ATAKA BARRIER

Lake
biwa

Tokyo (Edo)

Kamakura

to
Kyō)

Sekigahara

THE PLAIN
OF NOBO

niwa)

Nara

KAWACHI

YAMATO

Ise

ISUMI
TOKAIDO

ashiro

KUMANO

PACIFIC OCEAN

The Islands

ŌSHIMA

TOKUNOSHIMA

OKINAWA

The Elbornest

0   20   40   60   80 STATUTE MILES

0 20 40 60 80 100 120 KILOMETRES

Dedication and Acknowledgements

Mishima Yukio once suggested to me that my admiration for the beauty of Japanese Court culture and the tranquil world of Genji might have obscured the harsher, more tragic side of his country. By concentrating my studies in recent years on men of action, whose brief lives were marked by struggle and turmoil, I have perhaps redressed the balance, and it is to Mishima's memory that I dedicate this book. He and I disagreed about many matters, especially politics, but this never affected my admiration or friendship.

In fact my fascination with the heroic tradition of Japan had already started during the Second World War, when I became interested in the special role of failures, which seemed to contradict the stereotype about the Japanese being exclusively "achievement-oriented." It was not until I came to know Mishima in 1957, however, that I began to understand its psychological significance. For all his own worldly success, the people he most admired were men like Ōshio Heihachirō (the perfervid Police Inspector who stabbed himself to death after the collapse of his uprising in 1837), the members of the League of the Divine Wind who were slaughtered in the rebellion of 1876, and the young suicide pilots who died in the war against America. This spontaneous sympathy with the courageous loser was no personal quirk of Mishima's but has deep roots among the Japanese, who since ancient times have recognized a special nobility in the sincere, unsuccessful sacrifice.

Mishima's own last act in the headquarters of Japan's Eastern Defence Forces in Tokyo on 25th November 1970 belongs squarely to the scenario of heroism as described in these chapters. Indeed the cause for which he declared he was killing himself was even more quixotic than those of Ōshio or the Divine Wind rebels; and, however we may interpret his motives, the moral and physical courage of his resolution was no less than theirs. Whether he comes to be generally accepted as a heroic figure or (in the terse description by the quondam Prime Minister, Mr. Satō) as "insane" *(kichigai)* can be decided only by future generations, and it will depend, at least partly, on the extent of Japan's break with her past.

The popular adulation and the outburst of nostalgia inspired by Lieutenant Onoda Hiro when he returned from his jungle hideout in the Philippines in 1974 after defying the reality of defeat for almost three decades suggest that certain traditional psychological patterns may have survived the massive postwar transformation. While a Western journalist described the case of Lieutenant Onoda as "an example of [the Japanese spirit] gone mad," a leading article in the *Mainichi Shimbun* lauded him as a hero, and observed: "Onoda has shown us that there is much more in life than just material affluence and a selfish pursuit. There is the spiritual aspect, something we may have forgotten." It had clearly not been forgotten by the vast crowds who stood observing him in awed silence during his visit to Yasukuni Shrine, where he closed his eyes and bowed long and deeply in honour of the legions of fellow soldiers who had been killed in Japan's disastrous war.

I take this opportunity to express my thanks for the various forms of assistance I have received during the years devoted to this study. Among friends, colleagues, and correspondents whose encouragement and strictures have been especially helpful are: Professor W. G. Beasley, Father Michael Cooper, Professor Alvin Coox, Sarah Cumming, Professor Yoshito Hakeda, Shirley Hazzard, Donald Hutter, Professor Marius Jansen, Dr. Constance Jordan, Professor Donald Keene, Karen Kennerly, Arne Lewis, Edita Morris, Muriel Murphy, Peter Nosco, Professor Moriaki Sakamoto, Professor Barbara Sproul, Professor Paul Varley, Professor Herschel Webb. The editors of Chūō Kōron Sha, Tokyo, helped to obtain the photographs and maps in this book. The Japan Foundation kindly gave me a grant to travel to Kagoshima, Shimabara, Koromo River, and other parts of Japan where my heroes fulfilled their fiery destinies.

Outline Chronology

(comprising some important dates in Japanese history and some signal events in the lives of the tragic heroes)

I c. 300 B.C.–c. A.D. 300 Yayoi (Late Neolithic) Culture

57 A.D. First recorded visit of Japanese envoys to the Chinese Court.

Late 3rd century Chinese visitors to Japan give the first detailed description of the "Queen Country," which is governed by Himiko, a shamaness chieftain.

II c. 300–552 Pre-Buddhist Period

4th century Reign of Emperor Keikō (12th Sovereign of Japan); his son, **Prince Yamato Takeru,** a composite, legendary hero, conquers dissident tribes but is killed by a mountain deity and dies alone on Plain of Nobo.

391 According to Japanese chronicles, a major invasion of Korea is ordered by Yamato Court.

c. 400 Korean scribe, Wani, reaches Japan: spread of Chinese written language, beginning of official records, edicts, etc.

III 552–710 Soga Family, Shōtoku Taishi, Great Reform

552 Traditional date for the official introduction of Buddhism to Japan.

562 Japan loses its last possessions on the Korean Peninsula.

587 Soga family gains paramount political power following their victory over the Mononobes.

Yorozu, a follower of the Mononobes, kills himself rather than suffer the indignity of capture.

593 Shōtoku Taishi becomes Regent for Empress Suiko until his death in 622: rapid advance of Japanese culture under continental influences, especially Confucianism and Buddhism.

607   First official Japanese envoy to China representing the sovereign of a united Yamato state.

645   Soga family overthrown by a conspiracy including Prince Naka no Ōe, Nakatomi no Kamatari, and others; beginning of the Great Reform (Taika) movement.

658   **Prince Arima** executed on dubious grounds of treason, probably at the instigation of Prince Naka no Ōe.

IV   710–1185 Nara, Heian, and Taira Periods

710   Capital established at Nara.

712, 720   *Kojiki* and *Nihon Shoki*, the earliest extant writings of their type, completed; they remain our main primary sources for Japanese myth, legend, and early history.

738   Tōdai Temple, headquarters of official State Buddhism, founded in Nara; 752 the Great Buddha dedicated in Tōdai Temple in a ceremony emphasizing the close ties between Buddhism and Shintoism.

c. 760   *Manyōshū* poetic anthology completed.

794   Capital moved to Heian Kyō (Kyoto).

805–06   Tendai and Shingon sects of Buddhism established.

812   Final subjugation of the Emishi tribes by the Imperial Shogun.

838   Last of the series of official Japanese missions to the Chinese Court (which started in 607). (N.B. Plans to send a further mission in 894 under Sugawara no Michizane were dropped.)

858   Establishment of hereditary civil rule by Fujiwara regents.

901   **Sugawara no Michizane,** having challenged Fujiwara hegemony by acquiring great power at Court, is ousted from the capital and sent to Kyushu where he dies two years later in virtual banishment.

935   First open revolt of a provincial warrior chieftain (Taira no Masakado) against the authority of the central Court.

c. 1020   *The Tale of Genji* completed (*c.* 990 to *c.* 1020 apogee of Heian culture).

1086   Beginning of attempt by Retired Emperors *(In)* to curb Fujiwara dominance.

1159   Taira no Kiyomori, a warrior chieftain, acquires effective control of central government and establishes himself in Kyoto.

V 1185–1333 Kamakura Period

1185 **Minamoto no Yoshitsune** wins his decisive victory at the Battle of Dannoura: final defeat of the Tairas by their military rivals, the Minamotos.

1189 **Yoshitsune,** having been hounded by his elder brother (Yoritomo), kills himself at Koromo River.

1192 Minamoto no Yoritomo is appointed Shogun; establishment of the Kamakura Bakufu.

c. 1200 Zen, having been established as a separate Buddhist sect, spreads rapidly, especially among members of the warrior class.

1205 Hōjō Yoshitoki appointed Regent (Shikken) for the Shogun: beginning of hereditary Hōjō Regency.

1274, 1281 Mongol invasions successfully repelled by typhoons *(kamikaze)* and warriors.

1318 Godaigo becomes Emperor.

1331 **Godaigo,** having been forced to flee the capital by the Kamakura Bakufu, is joined in the mountains by an obscure warrior called **Kusunoki Masashige.**

1333 Loyalist (pro-Godaigo) forces destroy Kamakura: end of the Hōjō Regency and of the Kamakura regime.

VI 1336–1600 Ashikaga (Muromachi) Period, Civil Wars, and Unification

1336 (1st Month) Ashikaga Takauji (a descendant of a branch of the Minamoto family) enters Kyoto, and Emperor Godaigo is again forced to flee.

(5th Month) Takauji defeats Nitta Yoshisada, Kusunoki Masashige, and the loyalist forces at the Battle of Minato River.

(12th Month) Emperor Godaigo flees to Yoshino, where he establishes his "southern" Court: beginning of the period of two Courts.

1338 Takauji is appointed Shogun by the Emperor of the "northern" Court in Kyoto: beginning of the Ashikaga shogunate.

1342 Resumption of active trade relations with China.

1378 Yoshimitsu (the 3rd Ashikaga Shogun) establishes the shogunal government in the Muromachi district of Kyoto (c. 1395 to c. 1467 apogee of Ashikaga (Muromachi) culture).

1392 The two Courts are unified, with imperial succession remaining in the Senior ("northern") Line.

1428 First large-scale peasant riot.

1467   Outbreak of Ōnin War; civil war becomes endemic throughout the Japanese islands; feudalism replaces the last remnants of organized central government.

1542   The first Western traders (Portuguese) arrive in Japan.

1549   (St.) Francis Xavier reaches Japan: official introduction of Christianity and beginning of large-scale conversions.

1568   Oda Nobunaga, the first of the great unifiers, starts bringing the great independent feudatories under his control.

1573   The last of the Ashikaga Shoguns is deposed.

1582   Assassination of Nobunaga; he is succeeded by Toyotomi Hideyoshi, who ruthlessly pursues his work of unification.

1587   Hideyoshi bans the Christian missionaries from Japan, but the order is not systematically enforced.

1592, 1597–98   Hideyoshi's campaigns in Korea; they are suspended owing to his death in 1598.

VII   1600–1868 Tokugawa (Edo) Period

1600   Battle of Sekigahara: victory of Tokugawa Ieyasu.

1603   Ieyasu appointed Shogun: beginning of the Tokugawa shogunate with headquarters in Edo Castle; Japan is reorganized under a form of centralized feudalism.

1615   Battle of Osaka: final defeat of Hideyoshi's supporters.

1617   Renewed efforts to extirpate Christianity from Japan: beginning of fierce, systematic persecution.

1624   The Spaniards are expelled from Japan.

1636   Closed Country (Sakoku) Edict, followed (in 1639) by the formal expulsion of the Portuguese; thereafter no one could enter or leave Japan except for a small number of Dutch and Chinese traders.

1637–38   Shimabara Rebellion under the leadership of the young Christian, **Amakusa Shirō**: the first and greatest rising against the government during the entire Tokugawa period ends in total slaughter.

1660   Beginning of the Mito (nationalist) school of historians, who paved the way intellectually for the movement that eventually led to Imperial "Restoration."

1688–1703   Genroku year-period: apogee of townsman (plebeian) culture in Edo, Osaka, etc.

Late 18th century   Growing incidence of famines, epidemics, and rice riots.

1791–92   American and Russian ships turned away from Japan: decrees against foreign intercourse are reissued.

1837   The greatest of all the insurrections *(ikki)* breaks out in Osaka under **Oshio Heihachirō** and is suppressed with draconian severity. Continued famines and economic difficulties combine with growing foreign pressure to weaken the shogunate.

1853   Commodore Perry reaches Japan and demands entry for American ships.

1854   Perry returns, and treaties are concluded between Japan and the Western powers: end of policy of national seclusion.

1867–68   Outbreak of fighting between imperial loyalists, who oppose concessions to the foreigners, and shogunal forces; the last Tokugawa Shogun resigns and the imperial monarchy is "restored" to power under Emperor Meiji, the capital being moved from Kyoto to Edo (Tokyo).

VIII   1868–present   Modern Period

1871   **Saigō Takamori,** a loyalist samurai from a poor family in Satsuma (southwest Kyushu) is appointed Chief Counsellor of State in the Meiji government; two years later he resigns owing to major disagreements with other members of the ruling oligarchy and retires to his home province.

1877   Outbreak of the Satsuma Rebellion, the last important national insurrection in Japan until the 1930s; it is defeated by the Imperial Army, and Saigō (its leader) commits suicide.

1889   Meiji Constitution promulgated; the 1st Imperial Diet is opened in the following year.

1894–95   Sino-Japanese War: Japanese victory.

1902   Anglo-Japanese Alliance.

1904–05   Russo-Japanese War: further Japanese victory.

1912   Death of Emperor Meiji: General Nogi (hero of the Russo-Japanese War) reacts by committing suicide.

1923   Great Kanto earthquake.

1926   Emperor Hirohito comes to the Throne: beginning of the Shōwa period.

1931   Outbreak of war in Manchuria (Manchuria Incident).

1936   February Incident in Tokyo: attempted coup d'état by zealous young Japanese army officers; the coup is promptly suppressed by the military establishment, who take advantage of the growing unrest to whittle away the power of the civilian leadership and to prepare for a further expansion of hostilities abroad.

1937   Outbreak of war in China (China Incident).

1941   Japan attacks Pearl Harbor: outbreak of war against the Allies in the Pacific and Southeast Asia.

1942   After a series of initial successes for Japan, the turning point comes with the Battle of Midway and thereafter Japan starts on its downhill course.

1944   Faced with imminent defeat, the Japanese armed forces officially adopt organized suicide (kamikaze) tactics, the first such units being directed by Vice Admiral Ōnishi Takijirō in the Philippines. Despite all their frenzied sacrifices the **kamikaze fighters** fail to avert disaster.

1945   Japan officially surrenders: the first defeat in its recorded history. Vice Admiral Ōnishi and many other wartime leaders commit harakiri. The Allied Occupation begins under the supreme command of General MacArthur.

1946   Emperor Hirohito issues his "nondivinity" rescript.

1947   New "peace" Constitution promulgated; Article IX outlaws Japanese war potential for all time.

1952   End of Allied Occupation of Japan.

1954   Japanese Self-Defence Forces established (despite Article IX of the new Constitution).

1970   Mishima Yukio commits harakiri following his failure to gain support from the Self-Defence Forces to revise the Constitution, legalize the military establishment, and "restore" power to the Emperor.

Introduction

Our red-toothed, red-clawed world, attuned to the struggle for survival and dominance, reveres success, and its typical heroes are men and women whose cause has triumphed. Their victory is never without travail, and often its price is the hero's life. Yet, whether he survives to bask in the glory of his achievements like a Mohammed, a Marlborough, or a Washington, or proudly dies in action like a Nelson or a Saint Joan, the effort and sacrifice will, in the most pragmatic sense, have been worthwhile.

Japan, too, has its successful heroes, from the founding emperor, Jimmu, who (according to legend) subdued the barbarians in 660 B.C. and established an imperial dynasty that has reigned until this day, through the Forty-Seven Rōnin, who died in the proud knowledge that they had avenged their lord's disgrace, to Admiral Tōgō ("the Nelson of Japan"), who in the Russo-Japanese War showed that the little island kingdom in the Pacific could defeat a major Western power, and more recently scientific geniuses like Yukawa and Noguchi, whose discoveries confirm that the Japanese can also match foreigners in peaceful, practical ways.

There is another type of hero in the complex Japanese tradition, a man whose career usually belongs to a period of unrest and warfare and represents the very antithesis of an ethos of accomplishment. He is the man whose single-minded sincerity will not allow him to make the manoeuvres and compromises that are so often needed for mundane success. During the early years his courage and verve may propel him rapidly upwards, but he is wedded to the losing side and will ineluctably be cast down. Flinging himself after his painful destiny, he defies the dictates of convention and common sense, until eventually he is worsted by his enemy, the "successful survivor," who by his ruthlessly realistic politics manages to impose a new, more stable order on the world. Faced with defeat, the hero will typically take his own life in order to avoid the indignity of capture, vindicate his honour, and make a final assertion of his sincerity. His death is no temporary setback which will be redeemed by his followers, but represents an irrevocable collapse of the cause he has championed: in practical terms the struggle has been useless and, in many instances, counter-productive.

While it is true that Western history also includes great men who have ultimately been unable to compass their aims, if indeed they become established as heroes it is only *despite* their debacle. Napoleon's panegyrists rarely dwell on the period after Waterloo, whereas if he belonged to the Japanese tradition his cataclysm and its bitter aftermath would be central to the heroic legend.

This predilection for heroes who were unable to achieve their concrete objectives can teach us much about Japanese values and sensibility —and indirectly about our own as well. In a predominantly conformist society, whose members are overawed by authority and precedent, rash, defiant, emotionally honest men like Yoshitsune and Takamori have a particular appeal. The submissive majority, while bearing its discontents in safe silence, can find vicarious satisfaction in identifying itself emotionally with these individuals who waged their forlorn struggle against overwhelming odds; and the fact that all their efforts are crowned with failure lends them a pathos which characterizes the general vanity of human endeavour and makes them the most loved and evocative of heroes.

Even we in our success-worshipping culture can recognize the nobility and poignancy of those eager, outrageous, uncalculating men whose purity of purpose doomed them to a hard journey leading ultimately to disaster. While historical heroes in the West are mostly winners and while we have no strong tradition of empathy with historic failures, our literature ever since the *Iliad* and *Oedipus Rex* has accustomed us to the concept of the "hero as loser"; and especially in recent times there has been a tendency to respect those individuals who cannot or will not bow to the bitch-goddess Success. "Now all the truth is out," writes Yeats to a friend whose struggle has come to nothing:

> Be secret and take defeat
> From any brazen throat. . . .
> Bred to a harder thing
> Than Triumph, turn away
> And like a laughing string
> Whereon mad fingers play
> Amid a place of stone
> Be secret and exult,
> Because of all things known
> That is most difficult.

The men who appear in this book belong to many different centuries and social systems and conform to no single pattern of behaviour or ideals; yet they were all "bred to a harder thing" and, taken together, they suggest the varieties of worldly defeat, the dignity it can bestow, and the reasons for its particular evocative appeal in the Japanese tradition.

"Oh, lone pine tree! Oh, my brother!"

Prince Yamato Takeru, the archetype of Japan's long line of poignant, lonely heroes, started his career in an unedifying style by murdering his elder twin brother in a privy. The Prince's father, Emperor Keikō, had summoned him one day and asked why his brother was no

longer appearing at mealtimes. Regular attendance at the imperial board was a token of loyalty, and the Emperor now ordered the young Prince to reprimand his delinquent twin.

Five days went by, but still the elder brother did not come. His Majesty accordingly asked, "Why has your brother not appeared for such a long time? Can it be that you did not give him my instructions?" "I have already instructed him," replied the Prince. "And how did you instruct him?" "Early in the morning," said the Prince, "when my brother went into the privy, I was lying in wait for him. I seized him, smashed him to pieces, tore off his limbs, wrapped them in a straw mat, and threw them away."

1.1

By any standards this was a severe penalty for missing some meals, and Emperor Keikō was shocked by his son's "rough, fearless nature." No doubt to prevent further mischief at Court he despatched the impetuous youth to Kyushu where he might put his zeal to better use by attacking the dissident Kumaso tribesmen.

The young man who burst on the scene with an act of such furious violence died fourteen years later on a solitary plain, a melancholy, romantic figure who, having been defeated in his last battle, had lost all desire to live. It is this final image of Yamato Takeru that has most appealed to the sensibility of the

1

Japanese people and established him as their *ur*-hero, not his "rough, fearless nature" as a lad or his subsequent military successes, which were frequently marred by trickery and vindictiveness. The cóntrast between Yamato Takeru's ferocity in his early career and his gentle, poetic quality towards the end confirms what is already clear from the chronicles: this many-faceted hero is no single historical personage but a composite figure who became the centre of an entire cycle of legends. "The Chronicles of Japan" gives his date of birth as a year corresponding to A.D. 72 in the Western calendar and describes his career during the following three decades as though he were an actual member of the imperial family who won a brilliant series of victories against the enemies of the Court until he was finally defeated in Ōmi Province and perished on the Plain of Nobo in the thirtieth year *1.2* of the reign of Emperor Keikō. In fact his story reflects the careers of numerous commanders who were sent from Yamato to subdue unreconciled tribes in Kyushu and the eastern districts and who died during their campaigns. The actual period is not the first but the fourth century A.D., the so-called "riddle century" in Japanese history. It was a time of strife and disorder, marked by bitter fighting in the provinces and a concerted effort by the ruling clan, which had established itself in the Yamato region, to consolidate the population of the main islands of Japan under its control. From numerous tales and traditions that originated during this misty period and from a gallimaufry of myths, poems, legends, and Chinese literary influences there evolved the figure of "the Brave of Japan," who is presented in the chronicles as the greatest man of the period.

In some ways Yamato Takeru is a standard folk hero that we can find in almost every culture on the boundary between legend and history. Yet he has a peculiarly Japanese appeal, and a study of his legend is a useful introduction to the mystique of the defeated hero. By piecing together the accounts in the chronicles, we can visualize him as a single person who actually lived and *1.3* suffered and died some sixteen centuries ago. Much of the story belongs to the familiar paradigm of the universal legendary hero, who recurs in all centuries and countries; but there are signifi- *1.4* cant variants, especially in the ending.

The hero's father, Keikō, was one of the semihistorical emperors who reigned during the troubled period of consolidation. He is listed as the twelfth Emperor of Japan (the present Emperor, Hirohito, who is theoretically his direct descendant, is the 124th); but like most of the early rulers he is a shadowy figure and, though he is said to have reigned for sixty years and to have lived to the venerable age of 106, almost nothing is known about his character or his practical achievements.

The most remarkable feat credited to Emperor Keikō is his marriage to his own great-great-granddaughter. This genealogical *tour de force* occurred when he took as wife a princess who was the great-granddaughter of his son, Yamato Takeru. Among Keikō's eighty children were two male twins, the younger being the boy who later became Yamato Takeru. The twins were "born on the same day with the same placenta." The Emperor, much impressed by this event, climbed on top of a large rice-mortar in the palace to announce it to the Court, and his offspring were accordingly dubbed Ōusu ("Great Mortar") and Ousu ("Little Mortar"). Prince Ōusu turned out to be a disobedient lad, who came to an untimely end. Concerning the younger twin the chronicles report that "while a child he was endowed with a brave spirit, and when he reached manhood he was of sublime beauty." The future hero was enormously tall, and strong enough—the hyperbole is Chinese—to lift a great tripod singlehandedly.   *1.6*

1.5

At the age of fifteen Prince Ousu was sent west to attack the Kumaso. The word "Kumaso," like "Emishi" for early inhabitants of the eastern and northern provinces, was a general term designating certain backward groups of tribesmen. Though belonging to the same racial stock as the main Japanese population, they were concentrated in remote regions and had been separated from the mainstream of cultural development for so long that they were regarded as aliens or aborigines who had to be forcibly subdued and brought under the civilizing control of the powerful Yamato clans; the campaigns against these rude, hirsute tribesmen started in the semilegendary period of Yamato Takeru and continued for some four centuries until they had all finally been killed, pacified, or assimilated by about A.D. 800.   *1.7*

The hero's first victory over the Kumaso exemplified the "successful" part of his career. Before setting out for the west, the boy-hero visited his aunt, the High Priestess of the Great Shrine at Ise, and she gave him a robe, a skirt, and a sword.

When he reached the house of the Brave of the Kumaso, he saw that it was surrounded by three ranks of warriors who had entrenched themselves in a pit dwelling by the wall. There was much noise and bustle in anticipation of a party that was to be held to celebrate the completion of the dwelling, and food was being prepared for the banquet. He wandered about the house, waiting for the day of the celebration. When the time came, he unfastened his hair and combed it down over his shoulders in maidenly style. Then he put on his aunt's robe and skirt and, having made himself look exactly like a girl, mingled with the women and *1.8* entered the pit dwelling.

1.9   The two Kumaso chieftains were much impressed when they saw the maiden and invited her to sit between them as they continued their carousing. Prince Ousu waited until the festivities were at their height, when he pulled out the sword from the breast of his robe and, seizing the elder Kumaso by the collar, pierced him through the chest. The younger Kumaso rushed from the room in terror. The prince chased him to the foot of the stairs, grabbed him from behind, and thrust his sword up his backside. Then the chieftain said, "Do not move your sword any further. I have something to say to you."

     The prince held him down and agreed to listen. Then the chieftain said, "Who may you be, my lord?" "I am the son of [the Emperor] who dwells in the palace of Hishiro and who rules the Great Land of the *1.10* Eight Islands. . . . Hearing that you two Kumaso chieftains were disrespectful and refused to submit to his commands, His Majesty sent me here with orders to kill you." "Yes, this must be true," said the chieftain. "For here in the West there are no strong, brave men except us two, but in the Great Land of Yamato there is one who excels us both in courage. I shall therefore present you with a name. Henceforth may you be *1.11* known as Prince Yamato Takeru!"

     As soon as the chieftain had finished speaking, the prince killed him, slashing him to pieces like a ripe melon. From that time forward he was *1.12* called Prince Yamato Takeru.

     His mission accomplished, the young Prince set off for Yamato. On his way home he stopped in the western province of Izumo to subdue the local chieftain. For this purpose he resorted to a remarkably unattractive ruse. Having first pledged friendship with Izumo Takeru (the Brave of Izumo) and thus established a form of bond that is regarded as sacrosanct in any early society, he secretly fabricated an imitation wooden sword which he wore at his side. One day he invited Izumo Takeru to go bathing with him in the river, and when they came out of the water he picked up his friend's weapon, saying, "Let us exchange swords!" This was a further pledge of comradeship and Izumo Takeru innocently put on the bogus weapon. The hero then invited him to cross swords in a friendly bout. The chieftain agreed but he was of course unable to unsheathe his wooden weapon and Yamato Takeru lost no time in slashing him to death. He celebrated this triumph by composing the first of his famous poems, a thirty-one-syllable verse in which he mocked Izumo Takeru for carrying a sword without a blade.   *1.13*

When Yamato Takeru finally returned to the capital, exhausted from his campaigns, he was not greeted as a conquering hero or allowed to bask in his success, but immediately sent on a new mission to subdue the Emishi in the eastern provinces. This was because his brother who by rights should have undertaken the next expedition was so terrified by the prospect that he ran away and hid in the grass. From an alternative account, however, one gets the impression that Emperor Keikō wanted to get his son out of the way as soon as possible, perhaps on the principle that there is nothing more dangerous than "a hero out of work." In any case, at this point in the narrative the figure of Yamato Takeru assumes a different cast: the callous, unprincipled bully gives way to a solitary, ill-starred wanderer who, for all his ardent loyalism and achievements in battle, is destined for defeat and early death.

On receiving his marching orders, Yamato Takeru addressed the Emperor as follows: "It is only a few years ago that I subdued the Kumaso. Now it is the Emishi in the East who have rebelled. When shall we finally have peace in the land? I am weary of fighting. Yet I shall exert all my powers to quell this new rebellion." Emperor Keikō then gave his son a symbol of military command (a Chinese-type axe in "The Chronicles of Japan" account, a giant spear in the more Japanese version of "The Record of Ancient Events") and delivered a long harangue about the importance of subduing "the rough deities in the mountains, the malicious demons in the plains, who bar the highways and obstruct the roads, causing much suffering to our people." Clearly there was little distinction between these super-   *1.14* natural creatures and the actual tribesmen who worshipped them; for the Emperor immediately went on to say, "Among the eastern savages the most powerful of all are the Emishi." He described their primitive state of culture ("men and women dwell together in promiscuity . . . they dress in furs and drink blood") and ordered Yamato Takeru to subdue them all so that the Imperial House might be preserved.

Before leaving for his final campaign, the hero once more visited the Great Ise Shrine. Keenly aware of the Emperor's shabby treatment, he unburdened himself to the High Priestess, Emperor Keikō's sister: "Is it because His Majesty wants me to die early? First he sent me to attack the wicked people of the West. Then hardly had I returned when he again sent me on a campaign, this time to subdue the wicked people of the twelve eastern districts, and he has not even provided me with troops. Why should he have done this if it is not that he wishes me to die at an early age?" The High Priestess responded to her nephew's *cri de coeur* by giving him a sword, which later became famous as Kusanagi ("the grass mower"), and also a bag that he was to open in case of emergency.

1.15

On his way east Yamato Takeru was betrothed to a princess in Owari Province, but decided not to marry her until he had carried out his mission for the Emperor. When he reached the eastern province of Sagami, a local chieftain deceived him with a story about a ferocious deity who dwelt in a marsh on the plain, and Yamato Takeru innocently set off for the attack. As soon as he was in the plain, the chieftain set fire to it; but the hero saved himself by mowing down the grass with his sword and by setting a "counter-fire" with a flint that his aunt had providently included in his emergency kit.

Yamato Takeru's next adventure in his "road of trials" is one of his most famous, no doubt because it is imbued with the type of pathos that has always characterized the hero in people's imaginations. While crossing the straits between Sagami and Kazusa (present-day Tokyo Bay), he aroused the enmity of the Deity of the Straits, who promptly stirred up the waves and set his boat adrift. Princess Ototachibana, who was accompanying him (and who is rather confusingly identified as his "empress"), knew exactly what must be done in such emergencies: "I will go into the water in your stead," she declared, "so that you, my prince, may carry out the sacred mission that has been entrusted to you and may return to His Majesty and report on it." Then eight layers of rush matting, eight leather mats, and eight silken carpets were spread on top of the waves, and the Princess lay on them and sank into the water. This immediately calmed the sea, and Yamato Takeru was able to cross the bay. Seven days later Princess Ototachibana's comb was washed ashore and carefully buried in a tomb.

1.16

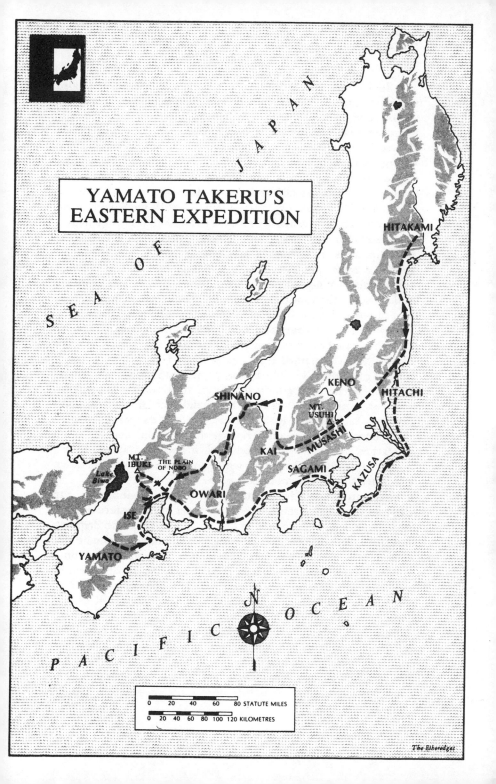

YAMATO TAKERU'S EASTERN EXPEDITION

SEA

OF

JAPAN

HITAKAMI

KENO

HITACHI

SHINANO

MT. USUHI

MUSASHI

KAI

MT. IBUKI

THE PLAIN OF NOBO

Lake Biwa

SAGAMI

KAZUSA

OWARI

ISE

YAMATO

N

PACIFIC OCEAN

0   20   40   60   80 STATUTE MILES

0   20   40   60   80 100 120 KILOMETRES

The Biberedges

In the earlier part of his career the hero was pictured as an unfeeling brute; now he became a different person—a man capable of being profoundly moved by a woman's self-sacrifice. "He was forever lamenting the death of Princess Ototachibana. One day when he had climbed to the top of Mount Usuhi and was gazing towards the southeast, he sighed three times and said, "Alas, my wife [*A tsuma*]." Accordingly the provinces east of the
1.17 mountains were named the Land of Azuma.

The hero's final encounters were not with the hairy Emishi but with a series of malignant local deities. It is as though he had now reached a stage where mere human enemies were unworthy of his powers. Entering the wild province of Shinano, he ascended a great mountain, "bravely making his way through the
1.18 smoky mist." When he reached the summit, he became hungry and sat down for a solitary repast. The god of the mountain took this opportunity to torment the Prince and, changing himself into a white deer, came and stood before him. Yamato Takeru, though startled by this apparition, had the wit to pick up a clove of garlic that remained from his meal and hurl it at the deer,
1.19 hitting the animal in the eye and promptly killing it. This was the act of a true culture-hero: by slaying the beast Yamato Takeru saved all future travellers from the maleficent effect of the god's breath, which in the past had always made it dangerous to cross the mountain. His encounter with the deer did not leave him unscathed, for he became dazed and, losing his way, wandered about helplessly until a kindly white dog came and led him down the other side of the mountain.

Yamato Takeru decided that the time had come to return to the capital and give the Emperor a report of his eastern expedition. On his way he stopped in Owari and married the Princess; but there was little chance for connubial dalliance, since he was now informed about a fierce god who was entrenched on Mount Ibuki near Lake Biwa. In an access of hubris he declared that he would subdue this particular deity with his bare hands, and he promptly set off by himself, leaving the invincible Kusanagi sword in his wife's keeping. When Yamato Takeru reached Mount Ibuki, the deity assumed the shape of a huge white serpent (or, in another account, of a white boar "as large as a cow") and lay across the road in front of him. Once again the hero was the victim of a ruse, since he was deluded into believing that the monster was not the actual deity but his messenger. A mere servant, he explained to the animal, was hardly worth the trouble of someone who had vanquished so many actual gods. Yamato Takeru then continued up the mountain. It was a fatal mistake. As "The Record of Ancient Events" specifies with Teutonic precision, "This was not a messenger of the deity; it was the deity himself." By addressing himself directly to this supernatural creature Yamato Takeru had violated a taboo. "Then the god of the mountain raised clouds in the sky and produced a hail storm. The top of the mountain was covered with mist and the lower part shrouded in gloom. Unable to find the path, Yamato Takeru wandered about, in confusion, but he forced his way onward through the mist and finally managed to escape."   *1.20*   *1.21*

Yet the hero had been mortally damaged by the supernatural fallout. When he reached the foot of the mountain, he was still in a daze "as though he were a drunken man." At this point in the story Yamato Takeru made the most striking of all his remarks: "I had always felt in my heart that one day I would soar high up into the sky. But now my legs will not move properly and have become all wobbly." Realizing that his ambitions had been thwarted and that he was now hopelessly earthbound, the exhausted hero hobbled along, supporting himself with a stick. For a while he recovered his senses thanks to the magic waters of a spring at the foot of the mountain. But the benign power that had protected the hero in his superhuman passage had now finally deserted him. His illness (which a modern medical scholar has rather prosaically diagnosed as beriberi) soon returned and, realizing that death was imminent, the young man did not even stop on his way through Owari to see his bride but pressed on for the capital, determined to make his last report to the Emperor in person. He failed. On reaching the Plain of Nobo in northern Ise, Yamato Takeru collapsed and, after reciting a final series of nostalgic poems, sent a farewell message concluding with the words, "I had hoped that the day and hour might come when I could report on my mission to Your Majesty, but my span of life has suddenly reached its end. Time passes as swiftly as a four-horse carriage flashing by a crack in the wall, and nothing will stay its course. So now I must lie down alone on this wild plain without a single companion to hear my words. Yet why should I repine at the death of this body? My only regret is that I shall never again behold Your Majesty."   *1.22*   *1.23*   *1.24*   *1.25*   *1.26*   *1.27*

This was the end. He died at the age of thirty. On hearing   *1.28* the news, the Emperor was shattered. He could not eat or sleep, and spent his days in tears and breast-beating. His former doubts about the Prince's "rough, fearless nature" were entirely forgotten as he recalled the young man's heroism:

When the Emishi arose in the East, there was no one else I could send to chastise them, and despite my deep love [for my son] I had to despatch him to the land of the rebels. Since then not a day has passed without my thinking of him; morning and evening I have paced these rooms, longing for the day of his return. What curse is upon me, what evil have I committed, that he should be snatched from me so unexpectedly? Who now can possibly undertake our great enterprises of state?

1.29 The Emperor ordered that an imperial tumulus be built on the Plain of Nobo, and thus (in accordance with universal custom) the hero was buried where he had died. The last part of the legend is perhaps the most remarkable:

1.30 Now Yamato Takeru was transformed into a white bird, and came out of the tomb and flew towards the Land of Yamato. The officials accordingly opened his coffin and, looking in, saw that the shroud was empty *1.31* and the corpse had vanished. Messengers were sent in pursuit of the white bird. It stopped first on Kotohiki Plain in Yamato, and so a tumulus was built there. Next the white bird flew to Kōchi, alighting in the village of Furuichi, where another tumulus was built. . . . Finally it soared high into the sky. Nothing of the Prince remained to be buried *1.32* except his robes and his Court cap.

1.33 The myth of the white bird may possibly reflect Taoist ideas *1.34* about immortal spirits. No doubt it is also connected with beliefs about the magical power of white animals. Its main significance in the story of Yamato Takeru, however, is surely the image of flying and escape: the hero, thwarted in his dreams of "soaring up high into the sky," that is, of transcending the worldly limita- *1.35* tions that lead to defeat and failure, finds eventual liberation in death. This accords perfectly with the romantic character of Yamato Takeru in the second part of his career: the melancholy young hero who makes his way through the wild eastern provinces, intrepidly attacking hostile deities and tribesmen until finally he is overcome by the wiles of a mountain god and dies on a barren plain, the victim of a typically romantic confrontation between fate and his own pride.

Yamato Takeru's status as the great romantic hero of the legendary period is confirmed by his love of poetry, the indispensable art for men and women of sensibility throughout Japanese culture. Military men in Japan, unlike their typical Western counterparts whose pleasures tended to focus on wine, women, and slaughter, have evinced a remarkable taste for poetry; and throughout the long centuries of warfare their respect for things artistic did much to redeem the pervasive brutality of samurai life. Unlike the West, where there has traditionally been a debate concerning the comparative virtues conferred on a man by arms and by arts, Japan has never regarded the two as incompatible. Far from it: a feeling for poetry was a confirmation of the warrior's sincerity. For all the conventional limits of its form, the little *tanka* verse with its rigid syllabic framework has been honoured as the supreme means of expressing deep emotion. The Japanese tragic hero, whose life is pitched at a higher emotional level than most men's, will often reveal his most powerful feelings in verse, especially as his career races towards its culmination. The tradition of farewell poems goes back to the country's most distant past, and hardly a single Japanese hero, from Yamato Takeru in legendary times until the kamikaze pilots in recent years, died without having first taken poetic leave of the world. This verse is rarely of the highest quality; yet, whatever such valedictions may lack in elegance and prosodic skill, they will always reflect the emotional sincerity that marks the true hero. *1.36*

With one unendearing exception Yamato Takeru's poems *1.37* belong to the romantic part of his career, which started with his departure for the eastern provinces. Shortly after the hero's lament for the drowned Princess there is an incident that exemplifies his respect for the ancient art of versification. Yamato Takeru had reached the land of Kai and, having evidently lost track of the time, he asked how long had elapsed since he passed Tsukuba (a mountainous district in Hitachi Province). He worded the question as the first lines of a poem, and the answer was provided in perfect metrical form (5–7–7 syllables) by an old man who was tending the fire. The hero was so delighted by this humble labourer's show of poetic dexterity that he appointed him to be Local Chieftain of the East. *1.38*

Among the romantic verses attributed to Yamato Takeru the following lines are said to have been composed during his final illness when he discovered a sword that he had left under a pine

tree. The personification of the tree, an unusual device for early
Japanese poetry, evokes the hero's forlorn state during his final
days:

> On the Cape of Otsu
> Directly facing Owari,
> There you stand,
> Oh, lone pine tree!
> Oh, my brother!
> Were you a man,
> Oh, lonely pine,
> I would gird you with a sword
> I would give you robes to wear.
> Oh, lone pine tree!
> Oh, my brother!

1.39

By far the most famous of Yamato Takeru's poems are the
final "homesick songs," of which the following are the first and
1.40 the last:

> Ah, Yamato, fairest of all lands,
> Girt with mountains like a many-layered hedge of green!
> How dear to me is the beauty of Yamato!

> Alas, the precious sword
> That I left by the maiden's bed!
> Ah, for that sword of mine!

1.41

"As soon as he had finished these poems," reports "The Record
of Ancient Events," "His Highness died."

It is above all the aura surrounding his end that established
Yamato Takeru, among the multifarious figures of myth and
legend, as the model hero. In most cultures, "if the monomyth is
to fulfill its promise, not human failure or superhuman success
1.42 but human success is what we shall have to be shown." The
Japanese tradition represents a departure from the monotony of
mankind's central ideas by *not* requiring a happy return for the
legendary hero. The ancient chronicles contain only one other
character whose individuality emerges as strongly as that of
Yamato Takeru. This is the tempestuous windstorm deity, Susanoo no Mikoto, who, owing to his unruly nature and abominable
conduct, was disgraced among the gods and banished from the

Plain of High Heaven. Susanoo, too, is pictured as an unhappy, isolated figure. Despite his wilfulness and bluster he has an unmistakable sincerity and even a certain outrageous charm; all this, combined with his poignant role as outcast who wanders about in a straw coat vainly seeking shelter, would have tended *1.43* to establish him as the perfect Japanese *ur*-hero. He was disqualified, however, by having flagrantly violated certain basic rules of society and, worse still, by having ended his career safely *1.44* and successfully ensconced in his great Izumo Palace among numerous wives and broods of deity-children. Yamato Takeru, on the other hand, had the advantage of capping his early success with failure when, after an uninterrupted series of victories, he suffered a touching defeat and died before he could return to Yamato for his last report to the Emperor. Here he sets the pattern for great historical figures like Yoshitsune and Saigō Takamori whose early triumphs led to glorious defeat. *1.45*

2

"The Emperor's Shield"

The Japanese warrior-hero has always known that, however many battles he may win and rewards he may receive, the fate that awaits him in the end is tragic—tragic not as a result of mistakes or lack of stamina or ill luck, though all these may be involved, but because of the karma of the man who embraces a painful destiny.

It is essential that the hero be prepared for this sublime end so that when the moment comes he will know precisely how to act and not be swayed by his instinct for survival or other human weakness. His final, blazing meeting with his fate is the most important event in his life. To continue fighting against all odds and to acquit himself properly at the end will give validity to his previous efforts and sacrifices; to die badly will make a mockery of everything that has lent meaning to his existence. "Think constantly of your death!" were the last words that the loyalist hero, Masashige, is said to have spoken to his son before commit-
2.1 ting harakiri in 1336; and twelve years later the young man, having fought on the same losing side as his father, was duly defeated and killed in battle.

2.2 The Western hero, too, is fearless in death; indeed, in any part of the world and at any time in history a hero who was scared of dying would be a somewhat absurd anomaly. For the Japanese warrior, however, death has a particular psychological significance, since it epitomizes the very sense of his existence. "One's way of dying," writes a famous samurai scholar, "can
2.3 validate one's entire life." Nobility in the face of certain defeat proclaims the magnificent tragedy of life, and the ultimate crite-

rion of heroic sincerity is the way in which a man confronts his end. This point of view is summed up in the most influential of all Japanese military treatises, which contains the seminal statement, "The way of the warrior is [finally] revealed in the act of dying."   *2.4*

Of all the possible bad deaths none is more odious to the warrior than capture and execution by the enemy; for this means intolerable humiliation not only for himself but, far more damaging, for the reputation of his family both retroactively and in generations to come. The most cataclysmic defeat will not mar the reputation of a hero or his kinsmen. Far from it: in the mystique of Japanese heroism nothing succeeds like failure. But, however hopeless the hero's situation may have become, to be held captive even for a short time is an irremediable disaster. The honourable status of prisoner of war, which was established at an early stage in Western warfare and included special understandings about the custody of important captives, ransom, and the like, was never accepted in Japan. The soldier who allowed himself to be captured automatically lost his dignity as a warrior and could expect only the most brutal treatment: savage torture, a humiliating form of execution, mutilation of his corpse, and, worst of all, the epithet of *toriko* ("prisoner").   *2.5*

Since defeat was such a likely outcome of the warrior's way and capture such an unthinkable disgrace, it is logical that suicide should have become accepted as the honourable death for the failed hero. Hardly a single hero in the Western world has ended   *2.6* his life by voluntary suicide. But since the earliest recorded pe-   *2.7* riod of Japanese history a warrior's self-destruction was accepted as a release from shame, an act of honour and courage, and an ultimate proof of integrity. From the time of the sanguinary civil   *2.8* wars in the twelfth century the particular method that became associated with the samurai tradition was harakiri, an excruciatingly painful form of self-torture which served as conclusive evidence that, though he had finally failed in his purpose, here was a man who could be respected by friend and enemy alike for his physical courage, determination, and sincerity. Long before the twelfth century, however, vanquished warriors resorted to suicide in order to avoid capture. The most common method was to stab oneself in the throat and sever the carotid artery with a short sword or dagger; this disagreeable but virtually foolproof method was also used in later times by solitary warriors who had

2.9   disembowelled themselves and wished to accelerate their departure.

Such was the death of Yorozu. He is the first hero who is
recorded as having committed suicide after defeat in battle, and
he is also the first of the full-fledged heroic failures. In a clash of
arms that took place in 587 and marked a turning point in early
Japanese history, he fought valiantly on the side that stood for
threatened national traditions, that lost the battle, and that was
irretrievably ruined.

Yorozu was not a famous man. It is only by the manner of
his dying that we know him. He came from a humble family, and
the chronicles give no details about his antecedents or career;
everything has been focussed on how he behaved during the day
of his defeat when he provided a coruscating display of military
virtuosity, a sort of bravura finale which occurs again and again
in the story of Japanese heroes.

The battle that became the occasion for Yorozu's glory was
the culmination of a drawn-out conflict between the two leading
clans of the day, the Mononobes and the Sogas. The tension
between them came to a head after the death of Emperor Bidatsu,
which occurred about two years before the battle. "The Chronicles of Japan" records an encounter between the chieftains of the
2.10   hostile clans, Mononobe no Moriya and Soga no Umako. It suggests a rather low level of political debate:

When His Majesty's body was lying in the palace of temporary burial
in Hirose, the Great Minister, Lord Umako, came to deliver his eulogy.
As he entered the hall, he was wearing a sword. Seeing this, the Great
Chieftain, Mononobe no Moriya, burst out laughing and exclaimed, "He
looks just like a little bird that has been pierced by an arrow." When it
2.11   was Lord Moriya's turn to deliver his oration, he was trembling so
violently that Lord Umako mocked him, saying, "He ought to have bells
tied to his limbs."

This exchange is said to have been the origin of the enmity
between Moriya and Umako; more probably it was the most
flagrant episode in the conflict that had smouldered for some
fifteen years, ever since they had succeeded, as headmen of their
respective clans, to the two leading civil posts in the land. The
political history of Japan in the sixth century was marked by the
rapidly growing power of a few great clans who, though theoretically inferior to the imperial clan, had acquired such influence

that they were able to decide crucial matters like policy in Korea, campaigns against the Emishi, and even the imperial succession. The contest for supremacy among the leading clan chieftains grew more intense from decade to decade, fatally weakening Japan's position in Korea and vitiating the secular authority of the imperial family, which towards the end of the century had become a mere tool in their struggle for power.

About the middle of the century the two leading contestants were the Mononobes and the Sogas. The former had risen to power in the previous century; at first their main official duty had been to superintend certain Shinto ceremonies at Court, but they shifted increasingly to judicial functions, and during the reign of Emperor Yūryaku in the middle of the fifth century Mononobe clansmen assisted the Throne as a sort of gendarmerie. Whereas the Mononobes had been particularly effective as an auxiliary force to powerful emperors who aimed at subjugating dissident factions and extending central control, the Sogas flourished in times when emperors were weak and could be dominated by outside clans. They were consummate politicians and knew how to manipulate individuals and groups to serve their family's own ends. It was they who initiated the brilliant system of "marriage politics" that was used in later times by the Fujiwaras and other families who ruled the country in the Emperor's name. The device of marrying Soga girls to imperial princes, thus ensuring that future emperors would have Soga mothers and (more important) Soga fathers-in-law, was started in the sixth century by Iname, the founder of the clan's greatness, and it proved more effective than their military power in preserving political supremacy.

The most important issue that the Sogas used in their struggle with the older, more conservative clans was whether Buddhism should be officially adopted in Japan. Since the fifth century, knowledge of the great Indian religion had been percolating into Japan by way of the Korean peninsula; but the traditional date for its actual introduction is the middle of the sixth century when the ruler of one of the Korean kingdoms presented the Court in Yamato with a gold and copper image of the Buddha, a number of sutras, and certain accoutrements used in Buddhist ceremonial. This momentous gift (which was said to have been motivated by the hope of obtaining military aid) forced the Court to take official cognizance of the religion, and inevitably the question became involved with existing clan rivalries. The Mononobes and other ancient clans, who from time immemorial had enjoyed special responsibilities concerning the

2.14 worship of the native Shinto deities, naturally wished to maintain the old order and opposed anything that might undermine the status quo. The rising Sogas emerged as the great antitraditionalist clan and the champions of Buddhism.

Owing to their knowledge of foreign conditions and their special connexions with Korea, the Sogas had undoubtedly been acquainted with Buddhism long before its official introduction

2.15 and some of their clan leaders may have been secret believers. Now they exerted their powerful influence at Court to persuade the Emperor to accept the foreign religion, which not only offered supernatural solutions to practical difficulties but addressed itself to the great problems of existence and death with which Shintoism was largely unconcerned.

A seesaw battle between the traditionalists and the innovators continued for several decades, each side exploiting natural disasters to discredit the opposing faith. In 585, for example, the Mononobes and Nakatomis persuaded Emperor Bidatsu to command that Buddhism be forbidden; a Buddhist statue that Soga no Umako had installed in his temple was thrown into a canal, the temple itself destroyed, and the nuns taken out and flogged in public. This ungracious behavior was followed by an epidemic of boils and sores, which the Sogas promptly attributed to the wrath of the Buddhas. Umako was accordingly permitted to resume the practice of Buddhism and the nuns were returned to him. A few years later he succeeded in introducing a Buddhist priest into the Palace where Emperor Yōmei lay dying of sores. The leaders of the traditional clans were horrified by this departure from precedent, but owing to Soga "marriage politics" (the Emperor in question was Umako's nephew) they were in a weak position at Court. Yōmei is said to have been converted *in extremis*, thus becoming the first Japanese Emperor to accept the Buddhist faith. The story may well be apocryphal, and the initial resistance to Buddhism at Court was probably far stronger than

2.16 the chronicles suggest; yet it is clear that in the long run the "new," advanced religion from abroad had far more to offer the Japanese, both spiritually and culturally, than native Shinto practices, and that in opposing it the traditionalists were fighting a hopeless struggle.

   As happened so often in early Japanese history, the spark
that produced the final explosion was a succession dispute. The
rules of succession were vague, and often an imperial illness or
death resulted in clashes between groups who supported different candidates among the Emperor's brothers or his sons. When
the Throne was weak and rival factions strong and embattled,
these clashes led to violence or even civil war. Such was the
situation in Japan at the death of Emperor Bidatsu in 585, which
was shortly followed by the death of his successor, Yōmei (a Soga
candidate), and the slaughter of Prince Anahobe (the choice of
the Mononobes). The Sogas played the political game with their
usual skill and soon Umako was ready to launch an all-out attack
against Mononobe no Moriya, the one remaining enemy who
blocked him and his clan from undisputed power. The Mononobes had evidently not expected that the final clash would come
so soon and they were taken by surprise. In the culminating
battle the forces were absurdly unequal. Umako had carefully
formed an alliance that included many of the important Yamato
clans; and, owing to astute Soga politics, he also enjoyed the
support of most of the young princes at Court, notably his grand-
nephew, Prince Umayado, who later (under the name of Shōtoku
Taishi) became one of the most impressive rulers in all Japanese
history.
   The main potential backing for Mononobe no Moriya came
from the old provincial clans, but by the very nature of traditional autonomy their strength was scattered and could not be
mobilized in time for the decisive battle. Deprived of outside
support, Moriya had to rely almost entirely on his own clansmen
and slaves. This force was no match for the Soga coalition, but
Moriya and his men fought bravely. At one point in the battle he
climbed into the fork of a tree and shot down arrows "like streaks
of rain." His troops filled a house occupied by the enemy and
overflowed into the plain. "The army of the Imperial Princes and   2.17
the troops of the high officials were terrified and fell back three
times."
   The turning point came when Mononobe no Moriya was
pierced by an arrow and killed. The main group of his followers
immediately lost heart and dispersed. Many of them disguised
themselves in servants' clothes so that they might avoid capture;
others changed their names and titles and escaped into the countryside. It was a complete rout. Though the engagement was   2.18

fought on a small scale (the battle has not even received an official name), this was one of the decisive clashes in Japanese history. The Sogas were totally victorious and, having eliminated all their rivals, could carry out their policies at will. Their candidate, Umako's nephew, promptly ascended the Throne as Emperor Sushun. The Buddhist religion, which could now be fully and freely practised, was given open support by the Court and the earliest of the great temples and pagodas were constructed as visible symbols of the new order. The ancient tribal system received its first great blow. No longer was the country to be divided among strong independent clans; instead there would be a coalition of forces centred about the Sogas, who would work in the name of the reigning Emperor to subjugate recalcitrant local magnates and tribal groups, to preserve what was left of Japan's position in Korea, to foster close relations with China, and to advance the country culturally with the help of Buddhism and other imports from the Asian continent. In almost every respect the Soga forces represented the wave of the future, and their victory paved the way for the Great Reform in the following

2.19   century.

Yet the most impressive figure to emerge from the battle of 587 is not Soga no Umako or one of the victorious imperial princes like Umayado but an obscure warrior who fought on the losing side. "The Chronicles of Japan," our only source for the story of Yorozu, is certainly not prejudiced in favour of the Mononobe cause, which ran counter to centralization, cultural advance, and the general trend of Japan's future development; the reason for Yorozu's preeminence is that his short career epitomizes the mystique of the failed hero. Here is the full account of how he fought and died:

A follower of the Great Chieftain Mononobe no Moriya, by name
2.20   Yorozu of the Totoribe, was in command of a large company of men guarding the [Great Chieftain's] mansion in Naniwa. When he heard that the Great Chieftain had fallen, he escaped on his horse in the middle of the night. He headed for the village of Arimaka in the district of Chinu and, having passed his wife's house, hid in the hills. The Court considered the matter and announced, "It is because Yorozu has treacherous intentions that he has concealed himself in these hills. Let his family be promptly put to death! These orders must be obeyed without demur."

Now of his own accord Yorozu came out alone from the hills with a sword by his side and a spear in his hand. His clothes were torn and filthy, and there was a look of great distress on his face. The officials sent hundreds of guardsmen to surround him. Yorozu was frightened and hid in a thicket of bàmboo, where he tied cords to several of the stems and pulled them to shake the bamboos to confuse the guards. As one of the bamboos began to sway, the guards were taken in by the trick and ran forward shouting, "Here he is!" Yorozu then shot his arrows and every single one found its mark. This terrified the remaining guardsmen and none dared approach him. He then unstrung his bow and, tucking it under his arm, ran towards the hills. The guardsmen pursued Yorozu, shooting arrows at him from the other side of a river, but no one managed to hit him. At this point one of the guards dashed ahead of Yorozu and, lying down by the river bank, strung his bow and shot him in the knee. Yorozu instantly pulled out the arrow and, fixing it in his own bow, shot it [back at the guard]. Then, prostrating himself on the ground, he called out, "The Emperor's shield, a man whose courage would be devoted to defending His Majesty—that is what I wished to be. But no one asked what my real intentions were, and now instead I find myself in these dire straits. Let someone come forward who can speak with me, for I wish to know whether I am to be killed or to be made prisoner." The guards raced towards Yorozu and started shooting at him, but he managed to ward off their arrows and, stringing his own bow, killed more than thirty of the men. Then, having taken up his sword and cut his bow into three pieces, he bent back the sword and hurled it into the river. Finally he seized the dagger that he had been carrying besides his sword and stabbed himself in the throat, and thus he died.

The Governor of Kawachi reported the circumstances of Yorozu's death to the Court who then issued the following sealed order: "Let his body be cut into eight pieces, and let each piece be sent to one of the Eight Provinces so that it may be exposed on a gibbet!" Just as the Governor was going to carry out the order and dismember Yorozu's corpse for exposure, there was a roar of thunder and it started raining in torrents.

Now the white dog whom Yorozu had kept with him looked up towards the sky and then looked down and walked howling round the corpse, and finally picked up his master's head in his mouth and placed it on an ancient mound. He then lay down next to the body and starved to death in front of it. The Governor of Kawachi, much impressed by the dog's strange conduct, reported it to the Court. The officials were deeply moved by the story and issued a further sealed order: "The dog has behaved in a way that is rare in this world and that should be made known even to later ages. Let Yorozu's relations be ordered to build a tomb where they may bury the remains!" The members of Yorozu's

2.21

family accordingly erected a tomb in the village of Arimaka and there
2.22 they buried Yorozu and his dog.

The story of Yorozu's death was written long before any specific warrior code had evolved in Japan; indeed it antedates by many centuries the formation of a distinct samurai class. Yet his behaviour in defeat is an almost ideal model of what was later prescribed for the fighter who has failed in his last battle. Clearly the ethos of the Japanese warrior far preceded any formulation of rules or principles.

Yorozu's initial hesitation—his escape into the hills and his terror when surrounded by the guards—serves only to accentuate the nobility of his last moments; for this reminds us that he is no supernatural hero, immune to human fear and hesitation, but an ordinary man who, like all other living creatures, wishes to survive, yet who in a crisis can draw on fantastic resources of energy and courage. Once he has decided his final course of action, Yorozu moves ahead unerringly, and from the moment in the bamboo grove until he plunges the dagger into his throat he seems, like so many of the defeated heroes in later Japanese history, to be propelled by the momentum of his own bravery.

Crippled by an arrow in his knee, he realizes that escape is impossible and, having despatched as many of the enemy as humanly possible, he destroys his two main weapons, the symbols of his military function, and stabs himself to death rather than incur the disgrace of capture. (If Yorozu had lived half a millennium later, he would almost certainly have preceded his death by disembowelment, but in 587 harakiri was not yet part of the warrior's repertory.) At this point the practical outcome of the battle no longer matters. What counts is not victory or defeat but the strength to pursue an honourable course of action until the finish.

Yorozu's brief, incandescent career establishes him as one of the earliest historical exemplars of *makoto*, the cardinal quality of
2.23 the Japanese hero. *Makoto* is usually translated as "sincerity," but its connotations reach far deeper and wider than the English word and come closer to the spiritual power to which Saint Thomas More (one of the noblest failures in Western history) referred when he prayed for the grace "to set thys worlde at noughte."

The focus of *makoto* varies in different periods of history, but its common denominator has always been a purity of motive, which derives from man's longing for an absolute meaning out of time and from a realization that the social, political world is essentially a place of corruption whose materiality is incompatible with the demands of pure spirit and truth.

Rejecting this grossly material world in which he finds himself, the man of *makoto* proceeds not by logical argument, pragmatic compromise, or a common-sense effort to attune himself to the "movement of the times," but by the force of his own true *2.24* feelings. Instead of depending on careful, rational plans and adjustments, he is propelled by unquestioning spontaneity. This aspect of *makoto* is reflected in that eager, undaunted strain which is common to Pure Land Buddhism, Zen, Wang Yang-ming philosophy, and other approaches to life that have been prominent in the Japanese tradition. "Sincerity" in the words of a modern Western observer "spells readiness to discard everything that might hinder a man from acting wholeheartedly on the pure and unpredictable impulses that spring from the secret centre of his being." *2.25*

Selfless dedication or, in more accurate psychological terms, belief in one's own selflessness, is a further mark of the sincere man. "I am intent on loyalty *(chūgi)*," declared a modern nationalist martyr (who did not conceal his courage with any false modesty), "while you gentlemen aspire to perform 'meritorious services' *(kōgyō)*." The sincere man has freed himself from the *2.26* besetting sins of "egoism" and worldly ambition and is undaunted by the danger of personal risk and sacrifice. The purity *2.27* of his intentions is revealed in action, usually of a dangerous nature; talk, unless reflected in deeds, is always a mark of insincerity and hypocrisy. *2.28*

Sincerity precedes not only the realistic demands of established authority but also conventional rectitude; for its ultimate criterion is not the objective righteousness of a cause but the honesty with which the hero espouses it. Thus even an executed felon like the famous nineteenth-century robber, Nezumi Kozō, can be esteemed as a hero, since his motives were believed to be pure. *2.29*

In his struggle against corrupt political power the hero's main weapon is sincerity of resolve. Though at first he may achieve impressive (even miraculous) results, his noble renunciation *2.30* of everything temporal and impure disposes him to defeat,

typically culminating in suicide. While sincerity is thus apt to
2.31 produce worldly disaster, the failed hero earns immortal respect
for that purity of spirit which his "successful" counterpart can
2.32 never attain.

Yorozu (like the prototypal Yamato Takeru) is described at
the end as being entirely alone. He has no faithful Achates to help
him while he is being hounded by the government troops or to
give him comfort during his last terrifying moments; his only
companion is his white dog, and this mysterious creature does
not enter the story until after his master is dead and has been
decapitated. The final loneliness of Yorozu is, of course, related
to the pathos that typically surrounds the failed Japanese hero
who ends his life as a solitary fugitive hunted down by the successful forces of law and order. By his bizarre behaviour the dog
dramatizes the poignancy of Yorozu's death and succeeds in stirring sympathy even among the enemy.

When Yorozu is introduced, the battle has already been lost;
from the outset he is cast in the role of loser and the only question
is how he will acquit himself in defeat. This defeat was not the
result of accident or bad luck. The cause that Yorozu supported
was doomed, not only owing to the unequal military balance, but
because the Sogas and their imperial allies represented forces that
in the long run were bound to prevail. It is significant that
Yorozu, the first of the historical failed heroes, should have
fought for a conservative clan representing the most ancient of
Japanese religious and social traditions in opposition to a more
enterprising, forward-looking group which aimed at changing
the status quo by introducing new ideas from abroad. Japanese
failed heroes were not necessarily on the "conservative" or "reactionary" side. Ōshio Heihachirō and the martyrs at Shimabara,
for example, fought the forces of authority in order to improve
an intolerable social situation. In most cases, however, they were
out of joint with the times and tended to associate themselves in
allegiance, thought, and style of life with traditional Japanese
ideals and patterns rather than with innovations and outside
influences. It is no accident that Yorozu should have fought for
a clan which had ancient connexions with Shinto ceremonial and
which bitterly opposed the introduction of a foreign religion.

As a staunch supporter of Japanese tradition, the hero will
almost automatically espouse the imperial cause. Among the

most illustrious of all Japan's heroes are those who supported the
Emperor in the fourteenth century against the Shogun's vastly
superior forces. It may seem strange therefore that Yorozu
should have fought against the side which represented the Imperial Court and which included Umayado (Shōtoku Taishi) and
most of the other imperial princes. Owing to their "marriage
politics," the Sogas had recruited nearly the entire imperial
family to their side, whereas after Prince Anahobe's death the
Mononobes did not have the support of a single important member. Yet in the conflict between the Mononobes and the Sogas,
as in so many clashes in subsequent Japanese history, it would
seem that both sides regarded themselves as loyalist. Moriya and
his adherents no doubt believed that they were protecting the
ancient Shinto, national traditions of the imperial family against
the corrupting Buddhist innovations of the Sogas. At the time of
the actual battle there was no reigning Emperor to give
legitimacy to either side, and it was only the outcome of the
fighting that could determine who the real loyalists were. In the   2.33
words of the old Japanese proverb, "Winners become the Imperial Army, losers become the rebels." This rather flexible concept of loyalism explains Yorozu's last lament in which he represented himself as "the Emperor's shield" (Ōkimi no mitate). The   2.34
hero could have had no specific Emperor in mind. By his final
words (or rather, by the words that the compilers of the chronicle
attributed to him) he was confirming his loyalty, not to any
particular, individual sovereign, but to the ancient traditions of
Japan as represented by the imperial family; and the fact that he
happened to have been fighting against the most prominent
members of this family made no difference. By losing the final
battle the Mononobes and their supporters automatically became
"rebels," as would of course have happened to the Sogas if they
had been defeated. Yet Yorozu, the most impressive adherent of
the Mononobe cause, is pictured as being a loyalist at heart, just
like Saigō Takamori who fought against the Imperial Army some
thirteen centuries later and is nevertheless regarded as a loyalist
hero. This existential loyalty was immediately recognized by the
Court itself when they allowed Yorozu (and his dog) to be buried
under a tomb, a privilege that could not conceivably have been
granted to a mere rebel.

3

The Melancholy
Prince

"Misfortune," said La Fontaine after the fall of Fouquet, "is a kind of innocence." In Japan, as the story of Prince Arima suggests, it can also be a kind of heroism. This strange, solitary young man who was accused of treason and strangled to death on his cousin's orders had no op-

portunity to perform a single noteworthy deed; and even the harebrained plot that provided the excuse for his execution was almost certainly a fabrication. At every point in his brief career Prince Arima appears as a victimized object rather than as a positive agent who makes decisions and incurs risks. Yet the tragic fate of this doleful prince and the nostalgic poems that he wrote shortly before his death made up for his ineffectuality and commended him to the Japanese imagination. He was lamented in verse by famous Court poets of the eighth century; in the 1960s he figured as the hero of a play by the well-known writer, Mr. Fukuda Kōson. Prince Arima's cousin, Prince Naka, who carried through one of the major Reform movements in the history of Japan, was far too efficient and successful to qualify as a romantic hero; no great poets mourned him, and in the drama he is cast in the role of the cold, calculating politician who plays his cards cleverly and survives.

When Prince Arima was born in 640, the Soga clan was still at the centre of political power, and it looked as if they were now so strongly entrenched at Court that they would continue ruling the country in the name of the imperial family from generation to generation. At about this time, however, the leaders of the clan appear to have been bedevilled by hubris which made them discard political manoeuvre in favour of direct action. Potential

3.1

3.2

opponents, including members of the imperial family who appeared to stand in their way, were eliminated. Worse still, the   *3.3*
Sogas now arrogated to themselves certain religious functions
like rain prayers that were traditionally reserved for the emperors. This was especially heinous in a society like Japan's that
attached the profoundest importance to ritual and precedent.
The Sogas gave the impression of actually planning to depose the
ancient clan that reigned over Japan and put themselves in its
place. In fact it is doubtful whether they ever had any such
intention: their aim was to control and use the emperors rather
than displace them. By their arrogant and precipitous policies,
however, they succeeded in antagonizing both the imperial
family and other important clans. In 644 a powerful anti-Soga   *√*
conspiracy was organized. The two main plotters, who are said
to have started their negotiations during a game of Court foot-
ball, were Prince Naka, the son of the former Emperor, and
Nakatomi no Kamatari, the chieftain of one of the old traditionalist clans that had vainly resisted the Sogas' rise to power in the
previous century. The conspiracy came to a head in 645 and was   *3.4*
a complete success. The Soga leaders were put to death, the
ruling chieftain being hacked to pieces in the Imperial Council
Chamber in the presence of Prince Naka's mother, the reigning
Empress.

With the precipitous fall of the Sogas, political power was
restored to the imperial family. To mark the beginning of the
new era it was decided that the Empress should abdicate in favour of her brother, Prince Arima's father, who now came to the
Throne as Emperor Kōtoku. A more likely successor would have
been Prince Naka himself, the son of the two previous sovereigns, but for reasons of his own he preferred to serve as Crown
Prince.   *3.5*

During his long period as heir apparent Prince Naka devoted his main energies to carrying out the Great Reform. This
ambitious attempt to remodel the Japanese state on Chinese lines
is one of the most important movements in Japanese history and
represents a fascinating example of a voluntary effort by one
country to take over political, economic, legal and military systems belonging to an entirely different society. The first, intense
phase of the movement lasted from 645 until 650, the so-called
Great Reform Year-Period; but there was not the slightest sense
of urgency such as existed in corresponding periods of reform

during the Meiji Restoration and the American Occupation, and
the movement continued for at least fifty years until the compilation of definitive codes in the eighth century.

It was a daring effort to reconstitute Japan on the model of
a country different in almost every material respect as well as in
social structure, traditions, and sensibility. Predictably enough,
the experiment proved abortive in the long run; yet the Siniciza-
tion of old Japan and its institutions, however superficial and
incomplete, helped postpone the development of a feudal structure. By undermining the authority of the local clans and assert-
ing the principle of a strong central government under the control of an Emperor who, as in China, was supposed to own all the
land and its people, the reformers laid the basis for a stable,
prosperous Court society that produced the magnificent flowering in Nara and Heian Kyō (Kyoto). None of this, to be sure, can
have had much effect on the great majority of the Japanese people, whose lives remained poor, nasty, brutish, and short; yet it
made possible one of the finest and most original cultures in
history.

During the most active period of the Reform, Crown Prince
Naka was the prime mover in planning and carrying out the
changes. Theoretically it would have been possible for him to
become Emperor at any time that he wished; yet he chose to
remain Crown Prince for over two decades. Several respectable
reasons have been given to explain this strange reticence. The
main traditional explanation is that like his great predecessor,
Shōtoku Taishi, he thought he could be more effective without
the burden of emperorship, which would lock him into ceremonial and religious functions that were the sovereign's principal
3.6   duty. Japanese historians have also suggested that he and his chief
adviser, Nakatomi no Kamatari, considered it unadvisable to link
any Emperor too closely with the reform movement until it
became clear that the measures would be reasonably successful;
furthermore Prince Naka's recent involvement in the sanguinary
destruction of the Sogas may have made him ritually impure and
therefore unqualified to become Emperor and officiate in the
all-important Shinto ceremonies.

A careful reading of the chronicle suggests that in addition
there was a strong personal factor which explains many of the
events during this period but which could never be openly men-

tioned. During a large part of his adult life Prince Naka was deeply involved in a love affair with Empress Hashihito, who was Emperor Kōtoku's consort and his own half-sister. The young Prince Arima, Emperor Kōtoku's only son, must have been tor- *3.7* mented by his knowledge (or suspicion) of this murky relationship.

Our first intimation of rot in the state of Japan is the strained relationship between Prince Naka and Kōtoku, the uncle whom he himself had helped onto the Throne after the fall of the Sogas. In introducing its account of the new reign, the chronicle gives an attractive picture of the old gentleman: "[Emperor Kōtoku] was of kindly disposition and had great love for learning. He made no distinction between people of noble and humble birth. He was forever handing down benevolent edicts." During the *3.8* first years of Kōtoku's reign, Prince Naka's attitude appears to have been loyal and respectful, but towards the end a rift developed between them. The main cause of the strain was probably Prince Naka's affair with Empress Hashihito, which was becoming too blatant to be ignored. Matters reached a head in 653 when Prince Naka suggested that the Court should remove from Naniwa (in the present Osaka region), where it had been established by Kōtoku early in his reign, to the ancient imperial centre in Asuka. The chronicle gives no reason for this unusual request, but it was evidently connected with Prince Naka's illicit liaison. *3.9* Predictably enough Emperor Kōtoku refused to change the capital, whereupon Prince Naka promptly moved to a temporary palace in Asuka, taking with him his mother, the Empress Dowager, several of the young imperial princes, and, of course, Empress Hashihito. Prince Arima stayed with his father, but most of the High Court nobles and officials, quick to recognize the future centre of power, deserted the old Emperor and followed Prince Naka to his new headquarters. In the next year even the rats, as though inspired by the Western proverb, decided to make the move: "Fifth Year, Spring, First Month: On the night of the first day the rats [deserted Naniwa] and betook themselves to Yamato." *3.10*

This mass defection may well have hastened Emperor Kōtoku's death. We are told that he was "overcome by bitterness and wished to abandon the Throne." In fact he did not abdicate but *3.11* moved into a new palace, perhaps in order to absent himself from

Naniwa and its bitter associations. From here he addressed the following plaintive lines to the young wife who had deserted him:

> The pony that I kept
> With a halter round its neck,
> Can any man have seen it—
> The pony that I never took outside?

3.12

In ancient Japanese the word "see" *(miru)* included the same sexual connotations as the English biblical "know," and Emperor Kōtoku is presumably using it to indicate his wife's relationship *3.13* with Prince Naka. In the following year Prince Naka heard that his uncle was gravely ill and visited him in his Palace, accompanied by a large retinue in which he included the Empress Dowager and, rather tactlessly, Empress Hashihito. Nine days later Emperor Kōtoku died.

Prince Naka was the logical candidate for the succession, but once again he declined. The next most likely choice was Emperor Kōtoku's son. Prince Arima, however, was only fourteen and there was still no precedent for enthroning boy emperors in Japan. Besides, as becomes clear from subsequent events, an imperial succession in Emperor Kōtoku's direct line was precisely what Prince Naka wished to avoid, since this would prevent him from eventually becoming Emperor himself. In the end the Prince and his advisers decided that his mother, the former Em- *3.14* press Kōgyoku, should reascend the Throne. She was now sixty-one years old, an advanced age for the time, and Prince Naka's decision was presumably a stopgap measure to keep the Throne in reliable hands until he himself was finally able to take over. Though the reaccession of a former sovereign was unprecedented in Japanese history, the chronicle does not provide a word of explanation or comment about the old Empress's return to the Throne that she had abdicated ten years earlier. This was probably because the real reason, though familiar to people at Court, *3.15* could not be officially stated. For many years Prince Naka and Hashihito had been living more or less openly as man and wife. The situation was no doubt painful for her stepson, Prince Arima, and embarrassing for many others at Court who had been close to the old Emperor. Yet there was nothing in the Japanese imperial tradition to prevent Hashihito from being appointed as

Prince Naka's empress if he ascended the Throne—nothing, that is, but the awkward fact that they happened to have the same mother. Ancient Japan was remarkably tolerant regarding de-   *3.16*
grees of relationship, and marriages between half-brothers and half-sisters were accepted in the imperial family (and presumably in society at large) so long as the shared parent was the father.   *3.17*
There was a strong interdiction, however, against marriages be-
tween offspring of the same mother, and Prince Naka was pre-   *3.18*
sumably unwilling to jeopardize his entire position by becoming Emperor and thus forcing an open decision about his relation-
ship with Empress Hashihito. The Prince's involvement with his half-sister was obviously a vital factor in his career: indeed it was only after her death that he finally decided to become Emperor.

With his uncle, the old Emperor, safely in his tomb and his mother safely back on the Throne, the Crown Prince continued to exercise the main political authority in Japan and to direct the numerous complicated measures involved in the Great Reform. Yet his position was far from impregnable. Apart from the delicate nature of his personal situation with Empress Hashihito, he was confronted with the potential opposition of numerous groups in the country who had not profited from the recent economic and administrative changes and who naturally resented his efforts to remodel Japan on foreign lines; there were   *3.19*
also immediate grievances arising from the expense of public works and construction. The Empress's new reign started with a building boom in the capital and surrounding regions, partly in order to impress the population with the strength and stability of the central government. This was bound to impose a great strain on an economy as primitive as that of seventh-century Japan, and the chronicle, though normally pro-government, records much popular discontent:

At this time [A.D. 656] the Government was greatly interested in public works. Navvies were employed to dig a canal from the west of Mount Kagu all the way to Mount Isonokami. Two hundred barges were loaded with rocks from Mount Isonokami and hauled with the current to a hill   *3.20*
at the east of the Palace where they were piled up to form a wall. People criticized [these enterprises], saying, "This insane canal has wasted the labour of more than thirty thousand men, and the construction of the wall has wasted the work of another seventy thousand. And think of the   *3.21*
timber for the Palace which rotted and the top of the hill which has been buried under rocks!" Others abused [the government] and said, "May

that pile of rocks they are building on the hill collapse as quickly as it
3.22   is put up!"

Popular opposition to the government's programme was evidently not limited to verbal abuse; during the Empress's reign
fires were repeatedly destroying the new buildings, and it is
3.23   unlikely that they were all accidental. The ensuing resentment
was naturally turned against the man most directly responsible
for both the unsettling reforms and the onerous public enterprises. Prince Naka, being endowed with a keen intelligence and
a suspicious nature, was obviously aware of the opposition that
his policies were arousing; and, since he was determined to press
forward with his reforms and other enterprises, it was essential
to avoid a situation in which dissident elements might join in an
attempt to topple him from power. During his period of rule as
Crown Prince he had often acted with speedy and ruthless determination to eliminate individuals who might become rallying
points for his opponents. In 645 he accused his half-brother,
Prince Furuhito, of plotting a rebellion and promptly ordered
that he be executed, though in fact Furuhito's only crime was
that he had been the Soga candidate for Emperor and might
therefore become a focus for anti-Reform elements. It seems unlikely that the remaining Sogas had any subversive plans. In each
case it was Prince Naka's policy to strike before potential opposition became an actual threat. If in the process it was necessary
to manufacture false evidence against innocent people, this could
be justified by the overriding importance of protecting the Reform movement during its early, critical phase.

In 658, as opposition to Prince Naka's policies again seemed
to be coming to a head, the only surviving member of the imperial family who was likely to serve as a rallying point for the
various antigovernment elements in the country was his cousin,
Emperor Kōtoku's son. Prince Arima was eighteen, the precise
age at which Prince Naka himself had launched his plot against
the Sogas. Though there was nothing to suggest that the young
man had any inclination to oppose, let alone overthrow, the
government, it was not hard to imagine that as he grew older the
malcontent elements in the population might choose him as their
candidate. Being the son of the former Emperor, he had by far
the strongest claim of anyone at Court apart from the Crown
Prince. In the long run there was no way for Prince Naka to keep

him from the Throne except to become Emperor himself, which was impossible for the time being, or to remove him from the scene entirely, which was very possible indeed.

In addition there may have been another, more personal consideration in the Crown Prince's mind: his young cousin might secretly be harbouring a bitter resentment. Prince Arima was obviously aware of the ignominious role in which his father, the old Emperor, had been placed by Prince Naka's affair with Empress Hashihito, and he had no doubt been informed about the highhanded way in which his cousin had removed her and other members of the Court to his palace in Asuka, thus causing the old Emperor much grief and possibly even hastening his demise. What could be more natural than that he might eventually decide to avenge his dead father and punish his peccant stepmother by supporting forces that wished to destroy Prince Naka and his Reform government?

Any such suspicions that the Crown Prince may have had about his cousin's future conduct must have been reinforced by the young man's peculiar temperament. An entry dated 657 describes Prince Arima as having a sly nature and adds that he "pretended to be mad" (*itsuwari taburete*). The chronicle, of   *3.24* course, is pro-government and does its best to justify Prince Naka's subsequent behaviour by building a case against Arima. In fact it seems probable that the young man, having lost both his parents at an early age and finding himself isolated in a Court that was dominated by an all-powerful and hostile elder cousin who was responsible for abducting his stepmother and humiliating his old father, had grown increasingly gloomy and neurotic with the years, and that his "madness" was not a ruse but a perfectly authentic dislocation of personality. Having observed the blatant misconduct of his father's consort and her royal paramour, Prince Arima had every reason to feel distrustful of his elders. His "slyness" may simply have been a defence against a world that seemed hostile and unsafe.

In the autumn he left the capital for a visit to Muro, a hot springs region on the coast of the Kii Peninsula, where he hoped to find a cure for his condition. The chronicle suggests that this   *3.25* was merely a pretext (*yamai wo osamuru mane shite*) and implies that Prince Arima had already decided on a coup against the government and was taking advantage of his feigned illness to meet his fellow conspirators in a safe, out-of-the-way place. Yet there is not the slightest evidence that the Prince had any such intention; it is far more likely that he was in a sad, troubled state of mind (a condition that might nowadays be described as an acute depression or nervous breakdown) and that he went to Muro to escape the tension at Court and find some mental relief. The visit seems to have helped him; on his return to the capital he praised the hot springs to his aunt, the old Empress, and told her that his illness had improved "from the very moment when I saw the place."

3.26

About a year later, when the Empress was in a state of great despondency over the death of her favourite grandson, she decided to visit Muro herself and travelled there with her son, the Crown Prince. Prince Arima stayed behind in Asuka, and it was now that he became enmeshed in the plot which ruined him. The following day-by-day account is from "The Chronicles of Japan":

3.27

3rd December (658) Lord Soga no Akae, who had been appointed as the official in Charge [during the absence of the Empress and the Crown Prince from the capital], spoke to the Imperial Prince Arima, saying, "There are three faults in the Empress's administration of her affairs of State. The first is that she builds great treasuries where she collects the wealth which has been gathered from her people. The second is that she wastes the revenue from the public produce to build long canals. The third is that she loads barges full of rocks which she transports to make into a hill." Prince Arima now realized that Akae had friendly feelings for him and he was delighted. . . .

3.28

5th December The Imperial Prince Arima visited Akae's house and went up to a high storey where they conspired together with Shioya no Muraji Konoshiro . . . [and others]. "First we shall set fire to the Imperial Palace," said Prince Arima. "Then with five hundred men we shall blockade the harbour of Muro for one day and two nights, immediately cutting off the island of Awaji with our fleet so that Muro will become like a prison. By these methods we shall easily succeed." Someone objected, saying, "This will not work. It is all very well to make plans, but you lack the power to carry them out. Your Highness is only eighteen years old and has not yet reached manhood. First you must reach manhood and then you will acquire the power that you need." "This year I have come to the age when I can lead an army," replied Prince Arima. [While they were talking,] an arm-rest suddenly broke of itself. The men recognized this as a bad omen and swore to each other that they would proceed no further in the matter. Then Prince Arima returned to his house in Ichifu.

In the middle of the night Lord Akae sent Mononobe no Enoi no

Muraji Shibi in command of a group of labourers who were working on the Palace, and they surrounded Prince Arima's house. Then he promptly despatched a mounted courier to inform the Empress.   *3.29*

9th December   The Imperial Prince Arima with Shioya no Muraji Konoshiro . . . [with two other prisoners] were arrested and sent to the hot springs in Muro. . . .

Immediately upon his arrival Prince Arima was questioned by the Crown Prince in person. "Why did you plot treason?" asked the Crown Prince. "Heaven and Akae know the answer," replied Prince Arima. "I myself understand nothing of this."

11th December   Lord Tajii was ordered to strangle the Imperial Prince Arima at Fujishiro Hill. On this same day Shioya no Muraji   *3.30* Konoshiro [and one other prisoner] were beheaded at Fujishiro Hill. As Konoshiro was about to be executed, he said, "May I request that I be allowed to use my right hand to make implements that will be treasures for the nation?"   *3.31*

The account in the chronicle conspicuously omits Prince Arima's two famous poems. The authors were determined to represent the young man as a traitor and did not wish to stir up any unnecessary sympathy for him by recording the type of poignant death verse that is usually associated with Japanese heroes rather than with enemies of the state. The editors of   *3.32* *Manyōshū*, the magnificent poetic anthology compiled about 760, had no such inhibitions and helped establish the young Prince as the great romantic-tragic hero of the seventh century by including:

Two Poems Composed by Prince Arima
as He Lamented His Fate and Bound the Pine Branches

Here on Iwashiro's shore
I bind the branches of the pine trees by the beach.
If only fortune favours me,
I may return to see this knot again.

Now that I journey forth, making the grass my pillow,
I no longer have a box to serve my rice
And so I place this offering to the gods
Upon rough leaves of oak.   *3.33*

Iwashiro, where the poems were written, is a desolate place on Kii Peninsula some ten miles from the Muro hot springs. Prince Arima was arrested on the 6th December and escorted from the capital on the same day. In three days he covered the ninety miles to Muro, where he underwent his official investigation by the Crown Prince. Probably the night of 8th December was spent at Iwashiro, about half a day's journey from his destination, and he therefore composed the poems shortly before hearing his doom. It was customary for people who were in trouble to bind pine branches as a charm to secure good fortune. In this particular case the charm did not prove effective, since Prince Arima was executed a couple of days later; but the bound pine became firmly linked in people's minds with the story of his last five days and helped to immortalize him. When the Court poet, Naga no Imiki Okimaro, visited Iwashiro some twenty-five years after the execution, he was shown the tree that was popularly associated with the unfortunate Prince, and this inspired him to write two elegiac poems that are included in the *Manyōshū* anthology. The first poem echoes the hero's own words:

> Ah, surely he has returned
> And seen this very knot
> That he bound here in the pine branch
> By Iwashiro's shore!

In the second poem the pine tree is personified as a symbol of the dead Prince:

> The bound pine that grows on Iwashiro's plain
> Does not forget the past,
> And its heart is still tied up in grief.

A few decades later Yamanoue no Okura, one of the finest of all the *Manyōshū* poets, wrote a verse in which the pine tree is again represented as remembering Prince Arima's fate:

> Though his spirit flutters overhead and still surveys this shore,
> People are unaware that he is here,
> Only the pine tree knows.

In fact he was far from forgotten. As the very inclusion of these poems in the *Manyōshū* suggests, Prince Arima had already caught people's imaginations, his role in seventh-century power politics having been established as that of the typical helpless victim whose innocence and purity lead to worldly disaster. The official chronicle, of course, presents him as a traitor, and this account could not be openly questioned. No doubt there was some sort of plot involving Arima; but from what we know of Prince Naka's methods it appears that the intended prey was not the government but the young Prince himself.

In the first place it is surely improbable that a youth who was so insecure and isolated at Court would seriously have thought of overthrowing the prepotent Crown Prince and his government. Arima's only close companion appears to have been the rather shadowy gentleman called Shioya no Muraji Konoshiro, a minor government official who certainly could not have provided the prestige and material support that would be necessary for the feeblest of uprisings. Though there were many disaffected elements in the country, notably local chieftains who opposed the Great Reform, even the official record does not suggest that Prince Arima had any contact with such potential supporters.

How then are we to interpret his dealings with Soga no Akae? From my reading of the record it seems that Akae was an *agent provocateur* who had agreed with the Crown Prince to ensnare Arima by involving him in a bogus plot against the government. Prince Naka had ample reason to fear that his young cousin might at some time in the future become a focus of opposition to himself and his policies, and it would be consistent with his previous measures against innocent men like Prince Furuhito that he should now use Akae to eliminate this last potential opponent. The *agent-provocateur* theory is supported by the fact that when Prince Naka finally came to the Throne (as Emperor Tenji) he made Akae his Minister of the Left, which was the highest post in the government and hardly an appointment that would be given to someone who had recently instigated an authentic conspiracy against the Throne.

One may wonder why Prince Arima should ever have trusted a man who was so close to the government that the Crown Prince had chosen him as Official in Charge during his absence from the capital. Possibly the Prince assumed that Akae was bound to loathe Prince Naka for his role in the destruction of the Soga clan and that, despite his own high position in the government, he would be prepared to risk everything in order to avenge his family. Furthermore, Prince Arima was a young, inexperienced man with no one at Court on whom he could rely;

consumed with bitterness against the overbearing cousin who had despoiled his father, he may have been naïvely receptive when Akae divulged his own pretended doubts about the government. Hence his delight on realizing "that Akae had friendly feelings for him": finally he had found someone—or so he thought—who resented the Crown Prince as strongly as he did and who was even prepared to take him into his confidence. It is therefore quite plausible that he should have gone to Akae on the following day.

Yet the actual plan that he is said to have proposed during his visit is a palpable fabrication. There were no "five hundred men" to blockade the harbour of Muro, nor was there any fleet *(funa-ikusa)* to cut off the island of Awaji. These and other details were probably invented by Akae, or even by the chroniclers, to bolster the flimsy case against Prince Arima. Amidst all the ambiguity and fabrication in the official record, Arima's reply to the Crown Prince's charge has a striking ring of truth: "Heaven and Akae know the answer. I myself understand nothing of this." Instead of explaining his alleged actions or trying to justify himself, Prince Arima expresses the bewilderment that anyone must feel when suddenly caught in an enemy's ingenious trap.

The full facts will, of course, never be known; but, whether or not Prince Arima was innocent of conspiring against the government, he certainly had the innocence of misfortune. His plot, if it ever existed, was a mere mockery and played perfectly into the hands of his enemies. Unlike his melancholy Danish counterpart, who eventually succeeded in shaming his mother and killing her royal paramour, the young Japanese hero failed utterly in any hope for revenge, and his early misfortunes led, not to splendid vindication, but to the executioner's noose; Prince Naka, the Claudius-equivalent in the drama, having successfully removed his worrisome kinsman from the scene, was able to live with his Empress Hashihito and to enjoy power and achievement.

3.34

3.35

Prince Arima belongs to a long line of ill-fated young heroes who through the centuries have had a particular appeal to the Japanese sensibility. Their misfortune is not merely "a kind of innocence" but central to their heroic status. This is connected with a general outlook on life, which in many ways is diametrically opposite to dominant Western attitudes. The Judaeo-Christian approach is based on the comforting idea that, so long as a man keeps faith, God will be on his side and he, or at least his cause, will eventually triumph. Thus a hero like Roland, though defeated in battle, is never abandoned by God and succeeds in contributing to the Christian victory over the Saracens.

This basically optimistic outlook has been especially conspicuous in the most western of all major Western countries, the United States of America, whose tradition has always tended to extrude any tragic sense of life and, often against cogent evidence to the contrary, to put its trust in the essential goodness of mankind, or at least that part of mankind which is fortunate enough to reside within its boundaries. "I know America," a recent President was fond of saying, "and the heart of America is good." The statement is not without a certain irony when one recalls the identity of its author; yet the sentiment reflects an underlying assumption that has been widely and confidently accepted. Americans, of course, are no strangers to despair, yet it comes not from any philosophical awareness of man's existential limitations but from disappointment that follows excessive hope in the possibility of compassing worldly happiness.

At the opposite end of the spectrum are the Japanese, who since ancient times have tended to resign themselves to the idea that the world and the human condition are *not* essentially benign. For all the country's vigour and ebullience, there is a deep strain of natural pessimism, a sense that ultimately things are against us and that, however hard we may strive, we are involved in a losing game. Sooner or later each individual is doomed to fail; for, even if he may overcome the multifarious hurdles set by a harsh society, he will finally be defeated by the natural powers of age, illness, and death. Human life—the *yo no naka* so repeatedly apostrophized by the poets—is full of sad vicissitudes, fleeting, impermanent like the seasons. Helplessness and failure are built into human enterprises, and (as the most common of all Japanese sayings reminds us) *shikata ga nai*: there is nothing to be done, it cannot be helped.

This underlying pessimism comes from a combination of Mahayana Buddhism (which remained the principal religious and emotional influence in Japan far longer than in any other major country) with a peculiar liability to earthquakes and other natural catastrophes. It is significantly revealed in the Japanese fascination with the extreme situation, which has produced a long literature of disaster extending from "The Tales of the

Tairas" and other ancient war chronicles to modern novels like

3.37 "Fires on the Plain."

Yet in the very impermanence and poignancy of the human condition the Japanese have discovered a positive quality. Their recognition of the special beauty inherent in evanescence, worldly misfortune, and "the pathos of things" *(mono no aware)* in many ways replaces the blithe Western belief in the possibility

3.38 of "happiness." This understanding of *lacrimae rerum* is reflected in an instinctive sympathy with the tragic fate of the failed hero, whose defeat by the forces of a hostile world exemplifies in a most dramatic form the confrontation of every living creature with adversity, suffering, and death. While we are all eventually doomed to go under, the pathos of worldly misfortune is especially evocative when the victim stands out as being young, pure,

3.39 and sincere. His fall represents in human form that quintessen-
3.40 tial Japanese image, the scattering of the fragile cherry blossom.

4

The Deity of
Failures

Japan's failed heroes ended their careers in many violent ways. Some stabbed themselves in the throat, others were burnt to death, garotted, beheaded, killed in battle by sword, spear, or bullet, or blown to pieces as human bombs or torpedoes; almost always their departure from the  world was early and painful, and usually they were their own executioners. Sugawara no Michizane died safely in his bed (or rather, on the straw matting of his curtained dais) at the age of fifty-eight. Yet only a few decades later his heroic credentials were so firmly established that he was enshrined as a Shinto deity.

Officially he was venerated as the god of poetry and scholarship, the fields in which he had excelled during his lifetime; but his contributions to literature and learning could never of themselves have brought the fame and popular devotion that his name has enjoyed through the centuries. The real reason that people have so long paid him homage in his shrines and that even now in the 1970s every schoolchild in Japan is familiar with the name of Sugawara no Michizane is that his cultural achievements and moral sincerity were confounded by the manoeuvres of his political opponents.

In almost any other period of Japanese history—indeed in almost any other part of the world—a man who had unsuccessfully pitted himself against the ruling forces of his country would have had little chance of a peaceful demise like Michizane's. He was fortunate in his enemies. One of the virtues of the much-maligned Fujiwara family, which controlled Japan's government during most of the Heian period (late eighth to twelfth centu-

4.1

√ *4.2* ries), was that they eschewed violence and physical cruelty. It was the established policy of the Fujiwara leaders to dispose of their enemies, not by imprisonment or execution, but by appointing them to distant provincial posts where they remained until they could safely be recalled to the capital or, as in Michizane's case, until death removed them permanently from the scene. This urbane form of exile was the fate of nearly all the famous victims of the Heian period, including Prince Genji, the most illustrious of Japan's fictitious heroes, who was exiled to the

4.3 Inland Sea by his Fujiwara rivals.

It was an age of civilians *par excellence* and the only time in Japanese history when the ruling class had no esteem for martial virtues; during this long, peaceful, slow-changing era when political power was centred in Heian Kyō ("The City of Peace and Tranquillity") militarism would have been totally incongruous with the prevalent cultural values. Such rivals as appeared from time to time presented a political not a military challenge and, though the Fujiwaras usually had the sanction of force in the background, their characteristic method was to avoid using it and to depend on peaceful means for eliminating outside threats. In this they were invariably successful; and the long rule of the "northern" branch of the Fujiwara clan attests to their remark-

4.4 able political acumen through successive generations.

This relatively benign nature of confrontation during most of the Heian period was not conducive to the outrageous, desperate type of heroism engendered by the succeeding era, and it is hardly surprising that Michizane, the prime failed hero of these calm centuries, should appear somewhat bland, even colourless, in comparison with fiery characters like Yoshitsune and Masashige whose short lives exploded in a suicidal blaze. The cardinal heroic virtue of sincerity was manifested by Michizane in the cultural, aesthetic realm of the Heian gentleman and lacked the excitement and tension associated with the *makoto* of activist, militant heroes in later periods.

√   When Sugawara no Michizane suddenly rose to prominence late in the ninth century, the Fujiwaras were established as the central force in Japanese politics, and had already evolved the various methods for controlling the administration and dominating the imperial family that were to serve them so admirably in

4.5 preserving and extending their influence. In the middle of the century Fujiwara no Yoshifusa, the clan leader at the time, had

created an invaluable precedent by securing the accession of
Emperor Seiwa, who in addition to being his grandson, was still
only eight and required a Regent to govern in his name. In 858
this vital post, which until then had always been held by members of the imperial family, was acquired by Yoshifusa himself,
who thus established the hereditary control of the Fujiwara clan
over successive emperors. In subsequent generations, when the
system had been fully developed, the ideal pattern was that the
head of the "northern" branch of the Fujiwaras would rule as
Regent during the minority of the child Emperor, who was usually his grandson or son-in-law, and would then continue ruling
as Chancellor after the Emperor came of age. To forestall the
danger that some recalcitrant sovereign might try to challenge
the system, it was usually arranged that the Emperor should
retire and take holy orders at an early age; the Throne and the
religio-magic aura of emperorship would then pass to his young
son, while political authority would devolve upon the new Regent, who would automatically be a close Fujiwara relation.

The full transfer of secular power to the Fujiwaras was not
accomplished until about a hundred years later. In the ninth
century there were still several non-Fujiwaras in high governmental posts and many families who, if the opportunity presented itself, might join in challenging the Fujiwara system
before it was fully consolidated. An even greater danger was that
a high official from some other clan might acquire the support of
an adult, independent-minded emperor who wished to weaken
Fujiwara control over the government.

And so, indeed, it happened. In 887 a learned and ambitious
young man came to the Throne as Emperor Uda. In allowing this
succession the Fujiwaras had departed from one of their cardinal
rules; for the new Emperor did not have a Fujiwara mother and
was virtually unrelated to the ruling Chancellor. Mototsune, the
energetic and strong-minded politician who succeeded Yoshifusa, was to regret this lapse, since it soon became evident that
Uda, unlike the five preceding emperors, was determined to rule
as well as to reign. He wished to return to the system of a mo-
narchically controlled bureaucracy that had existed in the early
decades of the Heian period. Though prepared to retain members of the Fujiwara family as high civil servants and advisers, he
was also determined to sabotage their monopoly of political
power by enlisting the support of eminent men from outside

families. The ensuing contest between the imperial family and the "northern" branch involved the Fujiwaras in the greatest danger they had faced since the capital was first founded in Heian Kyō; and it was to be their last serious challenge for about two centuries. But, as befitted the era, the struggle was carried out peacefully, even decorously: not a single person lost his life though many, notably Sugawara no Michizane, were ruined.

From the beginning of his reign Emperor Uda tried to reassert the position of the imperial family by enlisting the support of eminent men from non-Fujiwara families. His first close adviser was Hiromi of the Tachibana clan, whom he had long respected for his scholarship and integrity. Though Hiromi was not appointed to any important post, Mototsune was alert to the danger and now resorted to a typical Fujiwara stratagem. At the start of each reign it was customary for the great officers of state to resign their posts and then to be automatically reappointed by the new sovereign. The object of this ritual was to preserve the semblance of imperial independence, and when Mototsune duly submitted his resignation after Emperor Uda's accession no one at Court took the move seriously. The Imperial Reply on the following day, however, made no mention of the chancellorship and simply appointed Mototsune to be *Akō*. This term, which meant something like "He who rights the people's wrongs," had been used in remote Chinese antiquity to describe the chief minister at Court, and its precise significance in ninth-century Japan was moot.

Mototsune, realizing that the Emperor had deliberately chosen this ambiguous term on the advice of his scholarly friend, Tachibana no Hiromi, decided that the seemingly trivial departure from precedent could serve to create a useful crisis. Indignantly he argued that *Akō* described a rank rather than a specific post, that the appointment therefore demeaned his dignity, and that he could not possibly continue his governmental duties until the matter was clarified. Thus began the famous *Akō* controversy concerning the exact implications of the ancient Chinese word. The battle, which was waged with all the acerbity of the Swiftian dispute about how to crack a boiled egg, engaged the principal scholars of the day for the better part of a year. Owing to their jealousy of Hiromi and their awe of the Fujiwaras, the courtly savants tended to support Mototsune's interpretation. The Chancellor himself refused to conduct affairs of state and, since Uda had not yet reached the point where he could dispense with the services of the ubiquitous Fujiwaras, he was finally obliged to submit the matter to an official tribunal which, predictably enough, decided that the use of the term *Akō* had been a culpable error. This outcome was a triumph for Mototsune, who now resumed full sway as Chancellor. Hiromi, whose scholarship had ✓ been confounded by astute politics, received no punishment except shame; but he was obliged to retire from public affairs, and he died about a year later. For Emperor Uda the *Akō* controversy resulted in the first real setback of his career.

Fortunately for the new Emperor, his autocratic Chancellor did not have long to enjoy the triumph. He died in 891, about half a year after his defeated rival; and, since Tokihira, his son and putative successor, was still only twenty, it was possible for Emperor Uda to keep the post open while he tried to fill the resultant power vacuum in his own way. The new situation at Court provided the young Emperor with a rare and unexpected opportunity to reassert imperial authority. In the first place he refused to name any successor to Mototsune and kept the post of Chancellor vacant. Precedent demanded that Fujiwara no Tokihira become a Privy Counsellor and this appointment was made a few months after Mototsune's death; but to counter-balance Tokihira's influence the Emperor selected successive members of the Minamoto clan to serve as Privy Counsellors in the Great Council of State. A couple of years later Uda dealt a rude blow at the *4.6* "marriage politics" of the Fujiwara clan by choosing as Crown Prince his son, Atsuhito, whose mother did not belong to the main part of the "northern" branch. Tokihira, the new Fujiwara leader, was thus deprived of the important prerogative of being grandfather of the next Emperor. In the same year Emperor Uda promoted two important outsiders to the post of Privy Counsellor. The first of these was Yasunori, a vigorous, high-principled Governor who belonged to the unfashionable "southern" branch of the Fujiwaras; the second was the scholar-poet, Sugawara no Michizane.

These measures made a serious dent in the existing power system: two years after the imperial accession the Fujiwaras had so far lost their monopoly that less than half the seats in the Great Council of State were occupied by members of the "northern" branch of their clan. By balancing the distribution of families in the top echelons of the government Emperor Uda was in a better

position to assert his own influence and to direct the various administrative reforms that he considered essential for correcting local abuses and for restoring the old Chinese-style system of
4.7 central control under the imperial family.

The most decisive of Emperor Uda's appointments was his choice of Sugawara no Michizane to succeed the unfortunate Tachibana no Hiromi as chief adviser. By selecting yet another outsider as his mentor Uda made it insultingly clear that he was determined to exclude the Fujiwaras from his closest counsels and to prevent them from recovering the position they had enjoyed until Mototsune's death. Michizane had been the only prominent scholar to support Hiromi in his interpretation of the word *Akō*. Here he was clearly espousing a lost cause, since from the outset the issue had been political rather than academic, and in politics the Fujiwaras held the strongest cards. By his readiness to risk their enmity in the cause of truth Michizane no doubt impressed the Emperor with his idealism and sincerity.

In character Michizane was strikingly different from tough Fujiwara politicians like Mototsune, and this too must have endeared him to the young Emperor. When examining the personality of a god-hero who died more than a millennium ago it is hard to separate truth from legend; but, even if we discount the encomium that has been lavished on Michizane by generations of idolaters, there is every reason to believe that he was a gentle, kindly, serious man, somewhat introspective perhaps, and genuinely devoted to poetry and learning.

In many of these traits Michizane was similar to Uda himself, who despite his strong opinions and ambitions appears to have had a retiring nature and was certainly a great admirer of literary pursuits. Uda had lost his father, the incompetent Emperor Kōkō, at an early age, and it seems plausible that a wise, elderly scholar like Michizane should have become something of
4.8 a father figure. Their great common interest was classical studies, and over the years Michizane guided the Emperor in his study of the Chinese classics and his composition of Chinese verse. Uda for his part treated Michizane as a sort of Scholar Laureate, commissioning him to help edit "The True Record of Three Imperial Reigns," the last of the Six National Histories, and also to compile "A Classified National History," a major work in
4.9 which the history of Japan was arranged according to topics.

These books, like all important works at the time, were

composed in Chinese, the only respectable language for men of
learning. Michizane's family, though they traced their ancestry
to a legendary strongman who is said to be the originator of
sumō wrestling, had acquired a tradition of Confucian learning,   *4.10*
going back at least to the eighth century when the head of the
clan had been appointed tutor in Chinese classics to the Court.
Early in the ninth century Michizane's grandfather had founded
a family academy for Confucian studies; and his father, Koreyoshi, was a famous classical scholar who became head of the University in the capital.

The future god-hero, Koreyoshi's third son, is said to have
been a prodigy who lisped in verse from his infancy. Such attri-
butions of precocious genius are too common in the biographies
of heroes to be taken seriously; but there is no doubt that from
his youth Michizane was devoted to Chinese literature (his first
Chinese poems were written when he was ten) and that he estab-   *4.11*
lished his reputation as writer, teacher, and savant at an early age.
The ninth century was an excellent time for anyone interested
in such pursuits. A succession of Sinophile emperors had reinforced a tradition of respect for Chinese studies, and T'ang cultural influence remained strong in the Japanese Court throughout the century. Thus in the University the study of Confucian
classics took precedence over all other forms of learning; in the
Palace it was prescribed that gentlemen-in-waiting should wear
T'ang dress; and the most respected poets of the day concentrated
on producing anthologies of verse in Chinese, a language that few
of them had ever heard spoken.

The young Michizane, with his brilliant knowledge of Chinese composition, prosody, and calligraphy, was in his element.
After his coming-of-age ceremony at the age of fourteen he was
taken into favour at Court and commissioned by various high
officials as an elegant sort of ghost-writer to indite petitions and
other documents in limpid Chinese prose. He purveyed to the
Chancellor as a professional scholar and was consulted by Emperor Kōkō on such weighty matters as whether anything in
Chinese history corresponded to the Japanese post of Daijō Dai-
jin. In the University he became a popular and influential lec-
turer on Confucian texts, and at the remarkably early age of   *4.12*
thirty-two he was accorded the rank of Doctor of Literature,
which was the supreme academic degree in Japan and could be
held by only two men at any given time. Proudly recognizing his

son's talents, Koreyoshi ordered him to write the introduction to "The True Record of the Reign of Emperor Montoku," the fifth of the Six National Histories, which he had compiled in collaboration with Fujiwara no Mototsune. When his father died in the following year, Michizane inherited many of his duties, including the direction of the Sugawara family academy.

His career in the capital was interrupted at the age of forty-one when he was given a provincial appointment as Governor of Sanuki in the island of Shikoku, and he remained there for the full term of four years. It is said that he became extremely popular among the local inhabitants and that, when he left for the capital, people stood by the roadside weeping. Like so many of the touching stories about Michizane this is probably apocryphal: in actual fact, he was remarkably unsuited to the duties of local government and appears to have taken little interest in the prosaic details of administration. He preferred to give his time to Chinese literature. Among the poetry that he wrote during these years was a series of elegant verses with titles like "On Meeting a White-Haired Old Man on the Road" in which he lamented the plight of the esurient peasantry; yet never (so far as we know) did he try to improve local conditions or to institute the type of reforms that Fujiwara no Yasunori had carried out in his province.

Shortly after Emperor Uda's accession Michizane was summoned back to the capital to give his opinion on the *Akō* controversy, and there he presented an impressive written opinion supporting Hiromi's position. Though this document had not the slightest practical effect on the outcome of the case, it was the beginning of the close link between Michizane and Uda. In 893 Emperor Uda named his nine-year-old son, Prince Atsuhito, as Crown Prince. In reaching this crucial decision, which ran directly counter to Fujiwara interests, the Emperor consulted no one but Michizane, and shortly afterwards he appointed him as 4.13 official tutor to the young Prince. In the same year Michizane's daughter, Nobuko (Enshi) became one of Emperor Uda's consorts. This sealed the close relations between the Emperor and his adviser; but it was bound to exacerbate the Fujiwaras, who believed they had a monopoly in arranging marriages of this kind, and at the same time it provided them with a weapon that in due course they were to use most effectively against their rival.

In the following year Michizane was appointed to lead a

mission to China as Ambassador to the T'ang. The circumstances of this appointment is one of the mysteries in his career. Perhaps it was a personal decision by Emperor Uda, who wished to honour his close friend and adviser by putting him in charge of this important embassy and who also considered that Michizane, the Scholar Laureate of the day, would be the most appropriate leader of a mission whose primary aims were cultural. It is possible, on the other hand, that the appointment was initiated by the Fujiwaras in order to get their rival out of the way. In any case it seems that Michizane himself, despite his lifelong love of things Chinese, had no more desire to see the actual country than did the eminent modern scholar, Arthur Waley, when he consistently turned down invitations to visit the Far East.   4.14

Diplomatic missions to China, which had been regularly despatched since the seventh century, became intermittent after the capital was established in Heian Kyō. Though traders and priests still risked the crossing to the continent in order to obtain their respective commodities, no official envoys were sent after 838. This was part of the national withdrawal from outside contacts, a semiconscious process of concentrating upon indigenous Japanese culture and upon the Japanization of previous cultural imports, as opposed to direct borrowings from abroad.

More concretely, the growth of Korean piracy and the many other dangers involved in the long sea journey had made gentlemen at the Heian Court increasingly reluctant to be included in the China missions. The Ambassador who had been appointed in 836 was driven back to Kyushu in a terrible storm and did not set out again until three years later. When the mission finally did leave, the deputy Ambassador, a famous composer of Chinese poems, skulked in Kyushu, pretending that he was ill and could not risk the hardships of the journey. In consequence he was stripped of his rank and sent into exile; but he received full pardon a year later and returned safely to the capital, no doubt congratulating himself on his manoeuvre. For over fifty years there was no talk of further missions.

The main motives of Emperor Uda's sudden decision to send a new embassy in 894 were to secure literary materials missing from the collections in the Japanese capital and to satisfy leaders of the two main Buddhist sects who had long been urging the government to send an official mission to obtain certain sacred writings and arrange an exchange of priests. Only a month after the embassy had been appointed, however, it was cancelled on the advice of the Ambassador himself, Sugawara no Michizane, who wrote a memorial recommending that all further missions to the mainland be suspended. The ostensible reason was that conditions in China, where the T'ang dynasty was now reaching the end of its impressive span, were far too unsettled to justify a resumption of diplomatic relations and that it would be more politic to wait until the T'ang government reestablished its control or was succeeded by a new dynasty. This was a good argument; but in addition Michizane almost certainly had personal hesitations about proceeding to China.

Being the most eminent Sinologue of his day, Michizane may well have hesitated to expose himself to a situation in which his ignorance of spoken Chinese would be obvious both to his hosts and to the other members of the mission. A scholar who had been writing elegant Chinese poems since the age of ten might well find it embarrassing to depend on a common interpreter for his day-to-day communications. Besides, Michizane may have had a perfectly human fear of the practical dangers of the journey. For all his heroic reputation and posthumous ferocity he was not endowed with any unusual resources of physical courage, and the prospect of shipwreck, piracy, and attacks by armed bands in China itself, which would have been an exciting challenge to dynamic heroes of a later age like Saigō Takamori, were likely to daunt a Heian courtier who was acclimatized to the sheltered life of the capital and its environs. Most important of all, Michizane was now engaged in a decisive struggle with the Fujiwara family and any prolonged absence from Court (it often took several years before the envoys were able to return) could be disastrous.

Michizane's place in the government, and especially his relationship with the Emperor, were now so secure that he was able to abandon the mission without the slightest fear of reprimand. This turned out to be a milestone in Japanese history, for relations with the government of China were not resumed until many centuries later. During this long period Japanese culture moved steadily from Chinese tutelage and evolved on indigenous lines in almost every field. Thus from the tenth century most of the great poets wrote in Japanese, rather than Chinese, verse; prose fiction developed as a characteristically Japanese genre, culminating in *The Tale of Genji*, the world's first psychological

novel, which has no affinity with anything in early Chinese literature; and the tenth century produced the first of the *emaki* picture scrolls, whose style is Japanese through and through. It is
ironic (and typical of the failed-hero syndrome) that it should
have been Sugawara no Michizane, one of the greatest Sinophiles
in Japanese history, who took the step that symbolized his country's new independence from the continent.

So far as his political advancement was concerned, Michizane did well to stay in the capital. A few years after the China
mission was abandoned the government announced a round of
promotions. Tokihira and Michizane advanced in tandem, the
young Fujiwara leader being named Major Counsellor and Michizane receiving the same post on a supernumerary basis. Since
the chancellorship and all the top positions in the Great Council
of State were vacant, this meant that the two rivals were now the
foremost ministers in Emperor Uda's government. In addition
Michizane was appointed to be Minister of Civil Affairs. In the
Japanese Court, appointment to high rank and office had become
the prerogative of a favoured circle of families, and it was impossible to rise to the top by scholarship or intellectual qualities
alone. There was no strong body of literati such as flourished in   *4.15*
China and, though the ruling Fujiwaras were generous patrons
of art and learning, there was never any question of allowing
mere scholars to acquire political power. Yet, as the closest associate of the Emperor and as tutor of the Crown Prince, Michizane
now had the run of the Palace. He was regularly being summoned to the inner sanctum to provide not only academic in-
struction and advice on Chinese poetry but also his views on the
affairs of the imperial family and important matters of state. For
the Fujiwaras and their friends this represented an intolerable
violation of the unwritten rules, and it became clear that sooner
or later they would have to oust Michizane from the Court. In
this objective Fujiwara no Tokihira could count on the support
of most of the other nobles, since they were bound to resent the
rapid rise in the hierarchy of someone who had only recently
served in the humble post of Provincial Governor and who belonged to a family that had never enjoyed high rank. Michizane's
unpopularity in high Court circles was compounded by a report
that he had slapped Fujiwara no Sugane on the face; there is no
telling whether the charge was true (from what we know of his
personality, it seems unlikely), but we do know that Sugane was

one of the nobles who later joined in the accusations against the
hero.

Their opportunity came sooner than could have been expected and, strangely enough, it was an action by Michizane's
great supporter, Emperor Uda, that produced the situation in
which his enemies could topple him. Uda had frequently discussed the possibility of abdicating in favour of his son, Prince
Atsuhito. In the past, abdicated emperors and empresses had
usually removed themselves from affairs of state; but Uda had no
such intention and apparently believed that he could direct matters more effectively as Retired Emperor than while trammelled
by the duties of sovereignty. Withdrawal from the endless round
of palace ceremonies would also give him more time for poetry,
calligraphy, and other cultural pursuits which (as for so many
prominent men in Japanese history) were becoming increasingly
4.16   important as he grew older. Michizane did his best to dissuade
his friend from abdication, arguing that he should wait for a
more propitious time; but Uda was adamant and at the age of
thirty-one he hurriedly arranged a coming-of-age ceremony for
the thirteen-year-old Prince Atsuhito and ceded the Throne to
him forthwith. Shortly before abdicating, Uda prepared a written statement of advice for his young successor. This is the famous Kampyō Testament, which covers a variety of subjects
ranging from government policy and choice of advisers to
homely details such as how to guard against fires in the Palace
4.17   buildings. There are comments on the leading political figures of
the day, including Fujiwara no Tokihira, whose political acumen
is duly noted. By far the greatest praise is reserved for Sugawara
no Michizane, and probably the main object of the document was
to commend his scholarly friend to the new Emperor and make
sure that he would be retained as chief imperial adviser. Michizane's main virtue is represented as being loyalty to the Imperial House, and Uda implies that this far outweighs political
skill and administrative efficiency.

With the accession of Emperor Daigo, relations between
Michizane and Tokihira, still the two prime figures in the government, became more strained than ever, and it was clear that
things must soon come to a crisis. Tokihira's suspicions were
fanned by Michizane's visits to the residence of the former Emperor, who was forever consulting him on literary matters and
inviting him to poetry parties, as well as getting his advice about

how to guide the young Emperor Daigo and strengthen imperial authority. Finally in 899 Uda used his influence to secure Michizane's promotion to the post of Minister of the Right. This was a dangerously high position for an "outsider," and it is doubtful whether the former Emperor was doing his old friend any real favour. Michizane's situation in the Great Council of State was far from secure since he was sandwiched between his two chief opponents, Tokihira having received the top appointment as Minister of the Left, while Hikaru, who was the son of an imperial Prince and the leader of the warlike Minamoto clan, *4.18* became Major Counsellor. In the same year Uda took the tonsure, thus further diminishing the practical support that he could give to Michizane in an emergency.

Towards the end of 900 Michizane received a written warning from Miyoshi no Kiyotsura, another eminent scholar, who reminded him that the following year was astrologically dangerous and advised him to give up his post and withdraw to a life of safe retirement in the capital while there was time. It is not *4.19* clear whether this advice was inspired by jealousy (as is generally believed), or by Kiyotsura's genuine concern for the safety of a fellow scholar. Whatever the true motive may have been, Michizane chose to ignore the warning and continued to exercise his high functions as Minister of the Right and chief imperial adviser. During this time it is said that the young Emperor and his father were mooting the possibility of solving the current political impasse by combining the posts of Minister of Left and of Right and giving Michizane total control of the administration. Probably this was just a rumour, circulated by the Fujiwaras to drum up further resentment against Michizane. In any case his enemies struck early in the following year.

The coup against Michizane must have been planned carefully and in secret, for both he and Uda were taken by surprise. Since all the documents that detail the events were subsequently destroyed, we cannot tell precisely what accusations were made against Michizane. According to the most likely accounts, Tokihira clandestinely warned Emperor Daigo that Michizane, with the consent of the former Emperor, was planning to depose him in favour of his grandson, Prince Tokiyo, and that in order *4.20* to forestall any such mischief it was essential to remove the old Minister from the capital without delay. In typical Heian fashion Tokihira buttresses his argument by referring to an eclipse of the sun that had been observed a few weeks earlier. This, he is said to have told the young Emperor, was a harbinger of things to come: just as the moon (the female principle) had obscured the sun, so Michizane was going to use his daughter, Prince Tokiyo's mother, to displace the reigning sovereign.

The alleged plot was almost certainly a Fujiwara fiction. Michizane was a loyal servant of the Throne, and any notion of substituting his own son-in-law for the lawful Emperor, whom he had served faithfully as tutor and counsellor, would be totally out of character. A scheme of this sort might possibly be entertained by the Fujiwaras themselves if they found it essential for their position at Court, though even they preferred less blatant methods; that it should have been planned by a man with Michizane's temperament and beliefs makes no sense at all.

Yet the accusation worked. Somehow the Emperor, still an inexperienced youth of seventeen, was persuaded that the danger was imminent and, without even consulting his father, he agreed to Tokihira's proposal that Michizane be dismissed from the Great Council of State and appointed to the post of Supernumerary Governor-General in Kyushu, the standard sinecure for political exiles of the time. Tokihira had arranged with Minamoto no Hikaru that troops should be kept in readiness, and the Palace buildings were all carefully guarded. Since an elderly savant like Michizane hardly represented a military threat, the purpose of these steps was presumably to give verisimilitude to the "plot" by creating an atmosphere of emergency, and also to prevent communication with Uda and other potential supporters who might have rallied to his aid. In fact, several days elapsed before the former Emperor reacted to his friend's disgrace, and it was no doubt during this time that Michizane composed his poetic *cri de coeur* appealing for help:

> Now that I have become
> Mere scum that floats upon the water's face,
> May you, my lord, become a weir
> And stop me in my downward flow!

Michizane's banishment was announced on 16th February; it was not until the 21st that Uda proceeded to the Palace to remonstrate with his son, the young Emperor. On arrival he was refused admission by a high Fujiwara official, and after waiting all day on a straw mat by the gate of the Chamberlain's palace he returned disconsolately to his residence. The failure of Uda's intervention removed Michizane's last hope (a slim one at best), and he resigned himself to his lot. Though fully realizing that he was the victim of gross injustice, at no time did he make the slightest effort to resist the young Emperor's ukase.

Shortly after Uda's abortive visit, Michizane set off on his *via dolorosa* to the west, accompanied by an armed escort. At this *4.21* point he was forced to part with most of his family. Michizane had twenty-three children (a large number for even the most devoted Confucian patriarch), and to prevent any danger from this quarter the Fujiwaras ordered that his wife and daughters be detained in the capital and his sons removed from their official posts and rusticated. Only the two younger children were allowed to accompany their father in his exile, and it was to them that he addressed the following poem on the precariousness of worldly success. Though the ostensible purpose was "to comfort my little son and daughter," he chose to write the poem in classical Chinese, which must have reduced some of its consoling effect on the children:

> Your sisters must all stay at home,
> Your brothers are sent away.
> Just we three together, my children,
> Shall chat as we go along.
> Each day we have our meals before us,
> At night we sleep all together.
> We have lamps and tapers to peer in the dark
> And warm clothes for the cold
> Last year you saw how the Chancellor's son
> Fell out of favor in the capital.
> Now people say he is a ragged gambler,
> And call him names on the street.
> You have seen the barefooted wandering musician
> The townspeople call the Justice's Miss—
> Her father, too, was a great official;
> They were all in their day exceedingly rich.
> Once their gold was like sand in the sea;
> Now they have hardly enough to eat.
> When you look, my children, at other people,
> You can see how gracious Heaven has been.   *4.22*

In expelling Michizane from the capital the Fujiwaras proceeded with such despatch that he had no chance to take leave of his closest friend, the Retired Emperor. On arrival in his place of exile he wrote a wistful poem to Uda about his departure from the capital:

> Ah, how I gazed back on those treetops in your garden
> Which slowly disappeared from sight
> As I continued on my way!

4.23   He was, however, able to say goodbye to his plum tree. One of the more affecting scenes in the thirteenth-century picture scroll that depicts Michizane's life shows the defeated hero seated on the veranda of his residence in the Fifth Ward and gazing for the last time at his beloved plum tree, which has just burst into white
4.24   blossoms. It is this tree that he describes in his Chinese diary ("Notes from My Library") written during his palmy days as Privy Counsellor: "Near the gate [of the garden] grows a plum tree. Each time that it comes into bloom, each time that the wind wafts its fragrance towards me, its blossoms soothe and nurture
4.25   my spirit. . . ." Michizane apostrophized this same tree in the most famous of all the poems that he wrote after his fall from power:

> If the east wind blows this way,
> Oh blossoms on the plum tree,
> Send your fragrance to me!
> Always be mindful of the Spring,
> Even though your master is no longer there!

According to tradition, the faithful plum tree not only sent Michizane its precious fragrance but actually uprooted itself and flew all the way to Kyushu to accompany its unfortunate master into banishment. Known as Tobiume ("The Flying Plum Tree"), it still grows proudly outside Dazaifu Shrine in Michizane's place of exile, surrounded by thousands of other plum trees that devotees have planted in his honour.

The Government Headquarters in Dazaifu, some five hundred miles west of the capital, was in a rough, backward part of the country, totally isolated from the cultural activity that was central in the lives of the Heian aristocracy. For a well-born scholar like Michizane it was a sort of Siberia, and it must have been bitter indeed to realize that his long years of service at Court had culminated in an appointment to such a place. The official *4.26* residence, a dilapidated building with leaking roof and rotting floorboards, contrasted rudely with his patrician mansion in the Fifth Ward. The post itself entailed no official duties or powers whatsoever and, though the authorities maintained a polite pretence that the incumbent was still a high official (the dreaded governorship corresponded to the Third Rank in the Court hierarchy), he was in fact a virtual prisoner.

Little is known about Michizane's life during his last sad years in exile. He suffered from beriberi and stomach trouble, and his wife had to send him medicine from the capital, since nothing was available in the wilds of Kyushu. The death of his little son shortly after their arrival added to Michizane's woes. According to tradition, he found one of his few consolations in climbing up Tempaizan, a nearby hill, where he would face eastwards and offer prayers on behalf of the Emperor who had brought about his disgrace. The scroll shows the hero standing on top of the hill (which had turned into a steep, Chinese-style mountain) and gazing towards the capital. He is dressed in a black Court robe elegantly lined with crimson, and a peaked, lacquer cap perches above his plump, white, gourd-shaped face. He solemnly holds aloft a bamboo stick to which he has attached a document explaining his version of the charges that were used to banish him. A couple of dappled deer are grazing at the foot of the hill, and one of them looks up in surprise at the strange, solitary figure at the top.

Michizane took advantage of his enforced leisure to produce a final collection of Chinese poems, which includes a number of melancholy verses like the following:

Since I left home some three months have passed,
And a hundred thousand tears have fallen.
Everything is like a dream,
And time after time I gaze into the heavens.

On this same night one year ago
I attended the Emperor in his Palace
And poured out my heart in a poem called Autumn Thoughts.
Here lies the robe that Your Majesty bestowed upon me at that time.
Daily I lift it up and pay homage to its lingering scent.

> It was not the wind—the oil is gone.
> I hate the lamp that will not see me through the night.
> How hard—to make ashes of the mind, to still the body!
> *4.27*   I rise and move into the moonlight by the cold window.

The second of these poems inspired one of the paintings in the scroll. We see Michizane seated respectfully in front of a lacquered yellow box that is decorated with black chrysanthemum crests to show that it is an imperial gift; neatly folded inside the box lies the red Court costume that reminds him of happier days.

Michizane died exactly two years after his disgrace—of a broken heart, according to the legend. One of the great regrets during his years in exile was that his old friend Uda never sent a single word of consolation or replied to any of his poems. This seems a strange dereliction for a Heian gentleman, and it is possible that the former Emperor did in fact write to Kyushu but that his messages were intercepted by Fujiwara officials who were determined to forestall any possible effort to secure clemency for their rival.

The carriage transporting Michizane's remains is said to have stopped on the way to the burial grounds when the ox, in a sudden access of grief, lay down in the middle of the road. It *4.28* was decided that the body should be buried at that very spot, and the scroll shows a group of rough villagers sorrowfully preparing his grave, while the beribboned ox, still harnessed to the vast carriage, lies nearby and casts a baleful eye towards the sky.

Meanwhile in the capital the Fujiwaras had successfully regained control over the government. Their chieftain, Tokihira, had betrothed his daughter to young Emperor Daigo; and when, with usual Fujiwara efficiency, she gave birth to a boy, Tokihira arranged that the baby be named Crown Prince, thus ensuring *4.29* his family's control over the next emperor. Since Michizane's fall the Cloistered Emperor, Uda, had been effectively removed from the political scene and now he devoted himself almost entirely to literature and religion. His old hostility towards the Fujiwaras gradually diminished, and he even invited Tokihira to poetry parties and other entertainments where Michizane had once presided.

The Reform movement that had started under the aegis of Emperor Uda was now pursued far more vigorously and effectively by Tokihira, who was determined to implement the law of the land and to prevent the growth of independent, tax-free estates that were steadily sapping the strength of the central government. One of his first measures was to order a census and a new distribution of public rice land according to the old system of equal allotments. The so-called Engi Reform (named after the year-period that had started after Michizane's exile) was far more thorough than anything that had been attempted in the time of Uda and Michizane. Despite stubborn resistance in the provinces, Tokihira and his associates, with the encouragement of Emperor Daigo, started a concerted drive to correct abuses in regional administration and in particular to check the growing practice of commendation, which was encouraging the formation of illegal estates. Tokihira's death in 909, however, had a disastrous effect on the Reform movement; there followed a more or less steady decline in central control over the provinces, culminating eventually in a breakdown of the entire Heian system of government.

The man believed to be responsible for Tokihira's early demise was the former Minister of the Right, Sugawara no Michizane, now six years in his grave. Though they had effectively succeeded in ousting Michizane from the Court and restoring their own hegemony, the Fujiwaras were not allowed to forget their old rival. His posthumous career, in fact, was even more impressive than his live one. Though his actual death passed almost unnoticed in the capital, it was followed a few years later by a long series of mishaps—something like the collapse of the tower that is said to have recurred on the anniversary of Thomas à Becket's death but a great deal more damaging and frequent. *4.30* First came the unexpected death of Fujiwara no Tokihira when he was only thirty-eight and at the apex of his career. A few years later Michizane's other great enemy, Minamoto no Hikaru, who had supplanted him as Minister of the Right, was killed in a hunting accident. The next to succumb was Tokihira's grandson, Crown Prince Yasuakira, and a couple of years later the new Crown Prince (another of Tokihira's grandsons) died while still a baby. According to prevalent superstitions, this bizarre series of deaths must be the work of some vindictive spirit who was wreaking his posthumous revenge; and, since the principal victims all had Fujiwara connexions, it did not take long to determine that the perpetrator was the famous scholar whom they had driven into exile. To prevent further mischief it was essential that his furious spirit be appeased and, as the first step, Emperor Daigo's government decided in 923 that Michizane should be reappointed as Great Minister of the Right and given the Senior Second Rank. In the same year the Emperor ordered that the documents pertaining to Michizane's case should be burnt, thus permanently annihilating all evidence of his alleged plot.

These steps did not suffice to mollify the furious ghost. One day an ominous black cloud was seen approaching the capital from the west; it was accompanied by great peals of thunder, and shortly afterwards a thunderbolt fell directly on the Palace, killing a high Fujiwara Counsellor and badly scorching the face of a junior official. On this occasion Michizane's spirit appeared in the awesome form of the thunder god, putting Emperor Daigo and his courtiers into a state of abject terror. Of all the gentlemen present only Fujiwara no Tokihira rose to the occasion. With remarkable bravado he drew his sword and advanced on the ghost, addressing him as follows: "When you were alive your position in the state was lower than mine. Even now that you have become a spirit it is proper that you show me respect and keep your distance. . . ." On hearing this challenge the thunder god retreated. Emperor Daigo is said to have fallen ill as a result of this terrifying incident, and three months later he abdicated 4.31 the Throne.

After a series of fearful earthquakes and other natural disasters an oracle finally decreed that a shrine be erected in honour of the dead scholar. This order was duly carried out: in 947 the great Kitano ("Northern Fields") Shrine was built for Michizane 4.32 north of the capital. Here his spirit is enshrined together with all his literary works. The shrine attracted frequent imperial visits, and later became a popular resort for the ordinary inhabitants of 4.33 Heian Kyō.

Some forty years later, at the time of Murasaki Shikibu and Sei Shōnagon, the Emperor, acting on the advice of his Fujiwara Regent, bestowed the title of Heavenly Deity (Tenjin) on Michizane, thus making him the first subject in Japanese history to be officially recognized as a divinity. Through the centuries the Heavenly Deity of Kitano, as Michizane came to be called, has received offerings in the shrine as the patron deity of learning, literature, and calligraphy, and a famous Shinto festival is held there in his honour during the eighth month of each year. Heavenly Deity (Tenjin) shrines, usually surrounded by groves of plum trees, were subsequently built for Michizane throughout the country and attracted crowds of devotees and sightseers. There are more Shinto shrines consecrated to Tenjin than to any other deity in Japan except Hachiman, the god of war.   4.34

The dedication of Kitano Shrine laid the ghost to rest: the Fujiwaras had now salved their collective conscience and no longer attributed deaths and other disasters to Michizane's vengeful spirit. Ninety years after his demise they made a final gesture by having him raised to the Senior First Rank, an unprecedented distinction for all but royalty, and appointed to be Minister of the Left. As if this were not enough, he was promoted a few months later to be Prime Minister. This supreme post in the Chinese-style hierarchy was the terrestrial equivalent of his deification.

The Fujiwaras had good reason to honour their unfortunate rival; but the growing popularity and veneration that he received from the general public are less simply explained. Here the facts of Michizane's career must be distinguished from the legend that became entwined with them. In the legend he is a precocious genius, endowed with almost supernatural gifts, who developed as one of the supreme figures in the cultural history of Japan and became the god of learning, literature, and calligraphy. His meteoric public career was marked by unworldly idealism, selflessness, and steadfast loyalty to the Emperor, who used him to break the power of the arrogant Fujiwaras and restore authority to the Imperial House. By supporting Emperor Uda's policy Michizane bravely risked his career and even his personal safety, until finally he was outdone by Fujiwara machinations and died in lonely exile as a martyr to the cause.

In this legend the role of villain is naturally assigned to Michizane's chief adversary, Fujiwara no Tokihira. He is represented as an ambitious, unprincipled scoundrel who is jealous of his rival's brilliance and success and who schemes to ruin him in order to regain his own family's stranglehold over the government. In describing the events of 901 a famous twelfth-century historical work compares the two rivals as follows:

At this time, when Tokihira was about twenty-eight years old and Michizane about fifty-seven, they governed the country together. Michizane was a man of the most extraordinary talents, and his character too placed him above the common run. Tokihira was not only young but

also remarkably lacking in talent. In consequence Michizane had a magnificent reputation. This made Tokihira most uneasy and somehow he
4.35 arranged that things would go badly for Michizane. . . .

"The Secret of Sugawara's Calligraphy," one of the most popular plays in Japanese history, reinforces the legendary reputations of the godlike scholar and his devilish opponent.
4.36 Tokihira, the ruthless villain, not only contrives the great man's downfall but attempts to have him murdered by two secret retainers on his way to exile. In the end, however, it is Tokihira who is killed. After Michizane has died, lamenting that his enemy still controls the government, his sons avenge the old Minister by returning secretly to the capital and assassinating the fiend.

In fact, Tokihira was one of the outstanding products of a remarkably able family. Apart from his important scholarly activities, he was a vigorous, capable statesman whose talents were recognized by both Emperor Uda and his successor. During the fifteen years when he took the lead in the Kampyō-Engi movement to improve provincial and central government, he evi-
4.37 denced the highest administrative standards, and we know that his death had a disastrous effect on the Reform policy, which had largely depended on his guidance. It is true that he was relentless in destroying Michizane's career; but here he was simply carrying out traditional Fujiwara policy, and he certainly gave no evidence of the gratuitous cruelty that is attributed to him in the play. The banishment of Michizane was an unjust act but hardly the heinous crime that the legend pretends. Like most of the Fujiwara leaders, Tokihira emerges from the chronicles more as a public figure than as a living personality; but we know that he was intelligent, brave, and conscientious in fulfilling his responsibilities as head of the government.

If Emperor Uda's plan had worked and Michizane had permanently displaced Tokihira as his Chief Minister, it is doubtful whether there would have been any improvement in the administration of the country. Far from it—during the years when he enjoyed high office in the capital he gave no evidence of any particular administrative ability; during his periods of residence in Shikoku and Kyushu he appears to have been totally uninterested in the provinces except as a setting for his Chinese poems; and, when offered an opportunity to lead an important mission to China, he turned it down rather than risk his political position at home. Although he became Emperor Uda's closest adviser, he took hardly any part in the Reform movement, and his removal from office had no perceptible effect on practical matters of government. While Tokihira's death was a historical turning point, Michizane's banishment, although represented in the legend as a national tragedy, was in fact no great loss to the state.

Michizane's cultural reputation is far more soundly based, but even here legend outstrips reality. It is hard for modern Japanese readers, let alone for a modern Westerner, to judge his voluminous Chinese verse. However impressive this poetry may be, the fact is that hardly anyone, except a handful of scholars and specialists, would ever dream of reading it, and Michizane's preeminence in this field is largely accepted on authority. His Japanese *tanka*, though respectfully included in anthology after anthology, are mostly occasional verse of a banal nature, in which the poet compares white chrysanthemums with sea spray and maple leaves with brocade; only in the final poems written after his banishment does any real emotion show through the surface elegance.

Michizane's supreme gift as a calligrapher must again be accepted on authority, since not a single authentic example of his writing is extant. Calligraphy has been the art of arts in traditional Oriental culture, and it was almost automatic that a scholar-hero like Michizane would be credited with preternatural skill in this field and that a school of writing would be named after him. Whether or not his actual skill with the writing-brush deserved deification will always remain moot, except in the unlikely event that some verifiable examples of his work are discovered.

His major achievements are probably as a scholar and editor of official histories. Even here, however, the great man's reputation has not been invulnerable to the probing of modern experts, and his authorship of some of the important works that were traditionally attributed to him is now in question.

Concerning Michizane's much-vaunted loyalism, it is true that he served Uda faithfully, both when the latter was Emperor and after he abdicated; and there is little doubt that he would have continued working for Emperor Daigo had he been given the chance. This devotion, however, is surely not in the same sacrificial category as that of heroes like Kusunoki Masashige

4.38

4.39

4.40

4.41

4.42

who gave their lives to support their Emperor against fierce military enemies. Michizane risked none of the dangers incurred by the loyalists of a later period. And besides, his fealty to Uda was essential to his own advancement, since it was the Emperor's policy to elevate him to the position traditionally occupied by a Fujiwara leader. His connexion with the Palace was the key to his entire career and, if he wished to satisfy his political ambitions, there was no alternative to serving the Emperor loyally.

These ambitions brought about Michizane's downfall. If he had kept to his scholarship and left politics to the politicians, he could have continued safely in the capital, engaged in his literary pursuits, serving the Court as poetic adviser and Confucian tutor, enjoying his plum tree and his children and the other gentle delights of domestic life—and he might even have made the fascinating journey to China, the source of the culture that he valued so greatly. But then, of course, he would not have been enshrined as the Heavenly Deity of Kitano.

Why then did Michizane's legend become so fixed in the popular mind as to obscure the historical facts? Why, above all, did this scholarly gentleman, whose work is almost entirely in Chinese and hardly ever read, become so securely established in the pantheon of Japan's great heroes? He had none of the glamour and panache that attaches to the famous warriors in Japanese history, and he survived his normal lifespan without ever incurring real physical danger. It is true that he risked the wrath of the ruling family and suffered the pangs of exile. Yet this in itself would not have ensured him heroic stature; for Heian history is strewn with prominent men (including poets) who fell foul of the Fujiwaras and were banished. Michizane's great advantages were that he actually died in exile and, above all, that after the extraordinary success of his early career he was finally thwarted in the main purpose of his life and ended his days in the bitter knowledge that the Fujiwaras were back in power. The essence of Michizane's heroism, in other words, and the real basis for his lasting appeal are to be found in the nature of his ultimate failure. By virtue of his bitter exile and doleful demise in the wilds of Kyushu he became enshrined in the national pantheon.

Though Michizane was defeated in his lifetime, he enjoyed a posthumous victory by returning to high rank and office and even becoming a god. Michizane's vindication (whether or not he himself ever anticipated it) was impressive: having suffered un-

4.43

4.44

justly during his terrestrial life, he asserted himself after death by taking supernatural revenge on his enemies and receiving the adulation of posterity for over a thousand years.

The myth of the failed hero, as exemplified by Michizane during his lifetime and especially after his death, is the Japanese equivalent of the universal concept of a fallen god who is resurrected so that he may survive in a transcendent world—a world representing the perfection of those ideals for which he struggled on earth. While the Japanese hero is promised no paradise or elysium where he will receive compensation for his earthly travails, he does survive in the memory of his nation. The specific causes for which he suffered may not be those that his people have come to value historically; yet for that very reason he can personify the idea of unworldly, impractical selflessness. The failed heroes of Japan may thus be regarded as demigods. In the absence of any "official," central Christ-figure who dies to this world in order to realize his transcendence in the next, they express the human ideal of an unworldly perfection, one that by its uncompromising purity cannot under any circumstances survive the exigencies of this corrupt world.   4.45

The Japanese veneration of the hero as a demigod who is defeated by the world's impurity reinforces the emotional and aesthetic appeal of *mono no aware* ("the pathos of things"), and suggests that, if Michizane had succeeded in his practical enter- 4.46 prises by effectively supplanting the Fujiwaras at the centre of political power, he could not possibly have achieved his divine, heroic status.

In crass empirical terms it is clear that Michizane's rehabilitation was more apparent than real. For the Fujiwaras' appeasement of his spirit actually worked. Having thrown a sop to the old Minister's memory by according him honours that cost them nothing at all, their family flourished more than ever before, and Fujiwara politicians continued to dominate the Court for almost two more centuries, attaining their greatest glory about a hundred years after Michizane's death. When they fell from power 4.47 in the end, it was not because of any loyalist movement inspired by men like Sugawara no Michizane but because the entire system of central government (of which both Michizane and Emperor Uda had been part) finally collapsed. At this stage it no longer mattered whether the central government was controlled by the Fujiwara family, or by some other family or individual, or even by the Emperor himself; real power resided elsewhere.

Though Michizane's style of life differed diametrically from that of Japan's military heroes, the pattern of his failure was remarkably similar. By doggedly supporting a losing cause, he proved his moral sincerity. Furthermore, the cause that he espoused represented no political innovation or wave of the future; for it was in order to turn things back to the period before the Fujiwaras intruded on the scene—to that pristine period when (or so it was believed) the emperors ruled as well as reigned—that *4.48* Emperor Uda had tried to use Michizane's talents as a statesman. It is significant, too, that Michizane's best-known writing should be, not the impressive tomes produced at the height of his career, but poignant, simple verses, like the farewell poem to his plum tree, that he composed during his last years in Kyushu when he had been disgraced by the new Emperor and apparently abandoned by his old friend, Uda—poetry of a kind that almost invariably confirms the sincerity and emotional appeal of the failed *4.49* hero. Finally, the turpitude of Fujiwara no Tokihira, as established by the legend in utter disregard of the facts, belongs to the stock characterization of the successful survivors who "have their reward" in terms of worldly success but who traditionally serve as foils in the Japanese heroic scheme.

Victory
Through Defeat

Minamoto no Yoshitsune, who
after a series of brilliant military
victories spent his last years as a
fugitive implacably hounded by
his elder brother until he was
forced to commit harakiri at the
age of thirty, is the perfect exemplar of heroic failure. If he had
not actually existed, the Japa-

nese might have been obliged to invent him. Indeed, much of our
knowledge about this spectacular young man is invention, a rich
fabric of tales and legends woven during the course of the centuries to embellish the sparse historical facts of his career and to
create Japan's quintessential hero.

    Though Yoshitsune made not the slightest contribution to
the advancement of society or culture, he is one of the most
illustrious and beloved personalities in Japanese history. Even in
the 1970s, when samurai ideals are in eclipse, his story is relished
by schoolchildren, and the peculiar poignancy of his downfall
evokes an immediate response from people of every age.   5.1

    Yoshitsune's historical fame is due mainly to his military
achievements; but the real reason for his lasting popularity as a
hero is that his brief career was shaped in a dramatic parabola of
the type that most appeals to the Japanese imagination: after
suddenly soaring to success he was undone at the very height of
his glory and plummeted to total disaster, a victim of his own
sincerity, outwitted by men more worldly and politic than himself and betrayed by those whom he had trusted. So faithfully
does Yoshitsune conform to the ideal of heroism through failure
that the term *hōganbiiki* (which literally meant "sympathy with
the Lieutenant" and came from his rank in the Imperial Police)
has become fixed in the language to describe the traditional sym-

5.2   pathy with the losing side. By contrast his elder brother, Minamoto no Yoritomo, who happens to have been one of the most important leaders in Japanese history, paid for his worldly success by being relegated to the background of the legend, where he hovers murkily as a suspicious, vindictive character consumed with envy of the resplendent hero whom he ruthlessly pursues and destroys.

The two brothers belong to a decisive turning point in history when Japan was moving from the old Court-dominated government to a feudal society under the control of a military shogunate—a system that lasted in one form or another until the "opening" to the West seven centuries later. It is no coincidence that the most popular of all Japanese heroes should have lived out his short, tragic career during this seminal period.

Modern Japanese historians are at pains to clear away the tangle of legends on which almost all the subsequent literature about Yoshitsune is based and to concentrate on the scant documentary material that can be accurately verified. For the first twenty-one years of his life there is nothing authentic whatsoever, the factual vacuum being filled by a mass of fanciful tales and legends. Concerning the last four years we know the bare
5.3   historical events, but the rest is embroidery or outright fiction. This means that we have verifiable data for a mere five years of the hero's life, from 1180 when he joined Yoritomo's forces in preparation for the campaign against the Tairas until 1185 when he fled the capital and became an outlaw, having narrowly escaped assassination by one of his brother's henchmen.

This is a parlous state of ignorance for any historical work, but it is far from being an obstacle in the present study. Just as dreams, fantasies, and inventions often tell us more about an individual than the objective events of his life, so for the mystique of the failed hero, myth and legend are at least as important as
5.4   hard facts.

In the vast literature that recounts the story of Yoshitsune, the most famous source for the successful, military part of his life is the magnificent thirteenth-century epic known as "The Tales of the Tairas" (Heike Monogatari). These stories were spread throughout the country by minstrels, who accompanied their recitation with lute music. They reach their climax in the description of the three famous battles that brought the Taira clan to its ruin and established Yoshitsune as the greatest general in Japan. The most detailed source for the Yoshitsune cycle of legends, however, is "The Chronicle of Yoshitsune" (Gikeiki), which was written some two hundred and fifty years after the events, and which records all the important stories that had accumulated about the hero during the intervening centuries. By the time that this anonymous work was compiled the Yoshitsune legend, with its focus on the hero's tragic downfall, had already taken firm shape; and it is significant that "The Chronicle of Yoshitsune," though ostensibly covering his entire life, devotes only a few sentences to the military victories and concentrates overwhelmingly on his years as a fugitive. In "The Chronicle of Yoshitsune" the character of Benkei, the outrageous, swashbuckling priest who adheres to Yoshitsune throughout his misfortunes, emerges as a central figure and increasingly takes the lead in the action while his master grows gradually more passive, melancholy, and resigned to disaster. Both "The Tales of the Tairas" and "The Chronicle of Yoshitsune" provided inspiration and detail for a vast literature, including popular tales, dramatic dances, Nō, puppet, and Kabuki plays.   5.5

   The only definite date in Yoshitsune's early life is that of his birth, 1159. This was a memorable year in Japanese history; for it ended with the first outbreak of open violence between the two chief military clans, the Tairas and the Minamotos. The power structure in Japan was in a process of fundamental change. By the beginning of the twelfth century the Court aristocracy under the prepotent Fujiwara clan had long since wrested every vestige of real control from the theoretically supreme emperors; such powers as the imperial family retained were exercised mainly by the Retired Emperor (In), who had his own private governmental offices, independent both of the official imperial bureaucracy and of the well-entrenched Fujiwara administration.
   The late Heian system of government, cumbrous and inefficient though it was, looked as if it might lumber along by sheer inertia when suddenly in 1156 a brief explosion of violence, in which opposing Court factions unwisely enlisted the support of different military leaders, revealed that the entire structure of aristocratic rule was an anachronism. For all real power in the land had rapidly been passing to the samurai, those despised, boorish warriors whom the noblemen had for centuries used as

their lackeys to settle land disputes and to keep order in the provinces and the capital, but whose leaders were now determined and ready to take affairs into their own hands. Though the emperors were still regarded as the ultimate source of authority owing to their religious charisma as direct descendants of the sun goddess, and though members of the Fujiwara clan still kept an important position in the microcosm of the Court, such effective government as Japan might have would henceforth be directed by the class that during the past century had acquired by far the strongest force in the country and whose economic base was secured by its control of vast estates of rice land.

During the twelfth century the Court aristocracy had finally proved itself incapable of providing even a minimum of practical control and administration, not only in the unruly eastern territories but even in the home provinces and the capital city itself. While the military leaders were prepared to leave them with the trappings of prestige and to recognize the imperial family as the moral source of political power, there could be no question that a new era had started in Japanese history and that all important decisions would now be made by leaders of the samurai class, who alone had the power to enforce them.

The vital question that remained was which of the two main military clans would exercise power in the Emperor's name, or (in more personal terms) whether the dominant figure in the new period would be Yoshitomo, the leader of the Minamoto clan which was concentrated in the eastern plain (near present-day Tokyo), or Kiyomori, the clan chieftain of the Tairas whose main strength was in the home provinces to the west. Both clans were descended in collateral line from early Heian emperors, and this noble lineage was essential for their prestige; but during the past two centuries, while they had consolidated power in their respective provinces and formed a new society based on a feudal type of relationship between lord and vassals, they had dissociated themselves increasingly from the patterns of Heian Court life and developed a specifically military ethos that was almost diametrically opposed to everything represented by the world of *The Tale of Genji*. This new ethos, which came to be known as the "way of the bow and horse," was best exemplified by the eastern Minamotos, who both geographically and psychologically were far more distant from the capital than the Tairas and less susceptible to the supposedly enervating influence of the Imperial

Court. Yet in the fierce clash of 1159 it was the Tairas who triumphed decisively; and during the next quarter of a century it was Kiyomori and his family who from their headquarters in Kyoto exercised supreme rule in the Emperor's name.

Predictably enough—for the gentle mores of Heian were one of the first niceties to be sacrificed in this new, harsh age—Kiyomori's victory was followed by a series of killings and executions, in which the Tairas summarily disposed of their enemies and potential opponents. Yoshitomo, the chieftain of the Minamotos, had been treacherously slaughtered in his bath by one of his own retainers (the constant harping on loyalty in Japanese military treatises no doubt reflects the frequency of such lapses), and shortly afterwards his eldest son was captured and decapitated in the busy execution grounds of the Kamo River.

Taira no Kiyomori was not noted for his merciful disposition; yet for some unknown reason most of Yoshitomo's numerous sons were spared in the sanguinary aftermath of the Minamoto catastrophe. Of these the most famous were the senior survivor, Yoritomo, who was a lad of thirteen at the time of his father's assassination, and Yoshitsune, a mere infant less than one year old. Yoritomo was banished to an eastern province and put under the guard of two important vassals; Yoshitsune had been brought to the capital by his mother and, according to tradition, the first years of his life were spent with Kiyomori's own family. This act of magnanimity turned out to be fatal for the Tairas, since these two boys lived to compass the ruin of their clan. On his deathbed some twenty years later, Kiyomori's last request was that no Buddhist services be held for him but that someone promptly slay Yoritomo and cut off his head and lay it before his tomb—an empty wish, for the Minamotos were already in full resurgence and it was too late for simple solutions.

Yoshitsune, the ninth and last son of Minamoto no Yoshitomo, was far lower in the social hierarchy than his half-brother, Yoritomo, and this was no doubt an important factor in their subsequent relationship, since Yoritomo was never prepared to regard him as an equal. Lady Tokiwa, Yoshitsune's mother, was a minor lady-in-waiting at Court. She was a woman of outstanding beauty, and when Kiyomori met her after his victory he was so charmed that he made her his concubine and agreed to spare the life of her three young children. This story is no doubt apocryphal, but it is true that, while most of Yo-shitomo's adherents were being eliminated, Yoshitsune and his mother were allowed to remain safely in the capital and that subsequently she was remarried to a Fujiwara courtier.

As part of his condition for granting mercy, Kiyomori spec-ified that Yoshitomo's three youngest boys should be trained as Buddhist novices—an absurdly naïve precaution as it turned out —and at the age of six Yoshitsune was sent for religious training to Kurama Temple in the wild, mountainous region north of Kyoto. Everything was done to imbue him with a peaceful nature suitable to a priest; but, according to tradition, he would regu-larly sneak out of the temple and learn the use of arms from a 5.8 mysterious mountain hermit. The youthful Yoshitsune was vir-tually an orphan. He is pictured as a "wild child," untamed, solitary, and independent, with a great fondness for wanderings and adventures; and, though he lived in a temple as an acolyte, he obstinately resisted the discipline of monastic life and refused to let his head be shaved. Already we detect the lineaments of the future outlaw who was unable to submit to the control of his elder brother, the representative of established authority. Mean-while Yoritomo, exiled to his distant eastern province under a mild form of house arrest, was leading a relatively settled, disci-plined existence and impressing his guardians by his intelligence and rapid advancement. The contrast in character and style of life between the two half-brothers, the eldest and the youngest of Yoshitomo's sons, is established from the outset.

One of the most famous stories in the Yoshitsune legend 5.9 belongs to these early years. It describes a warrior monk, a great menacing mountain of a man, who has boasted that he will rob one thousand passersby of their swords so that he may contribute to the rebuilding of a temple. Having succeeded in stealing nine hundred and ninety-nine weapons, he posts himself one night by a bridge in Kyoto and is waiting for his final victim when he sees a slender young figure approaching alone in the dark. The youth is nonchalantly playing a flute and wears a silk cloak over his head and shoulders in a style common among temple acolytes. The monk first refuses to regard this effeminate stripling as a worthy opponent, but when they start fighting it becomes clear that Yoshitsune's secret lessons in the mountains have made him invincible. According to one version, Yoshitsune ends the final bout in a great triumph of skill over brawn when he discards his

sword and downs the gargantuan monk with his fan. Overawed   *5.10*
by this display of virtuosity (a typical example of the hero's life
as being a "pageant of marvels"), the monk offers to remain with
the lad as his sworn retainer. He is Benkei, who becomes prominent in the later, "downhill" part of Yoshitsune's career as his
most loyal supporter.

At the age of ten Yoshitsune happened to come upon a
genealogy of the Minamoto clan and thus discovered his true
identity. From then he was consumed with desire to fight the
Tairas and avenge his father's defeat; fixed in this objective, he
avoided taking the final Buddhist vows and pursued his military
exercises with redoubled energy. Unlike Yoritomo, for whom the
conquest of the Tairas was mainly a preliminary to establishing
a strong military government in the east under Minamoto rule,
Yoshitsune is shown from his early years as having been motivated by a moral imperative to defeat the enemies who had hu-
miliated his clan.

Some five years later Yoshitsune, assisted by a visiting gold
merchant, finally managed to escape from the temple and from
the surveillance of his Taira enemies. After many adventures and
narrow escapes he made his way to Ōshū, a remote territory in
the northeastern part of the main island where for several generations the so-called "northern Fujiwaras" (a distant branch of the
great Court family) had been established as virtually independent
rulers, secure in their vast wealth and military power. Hidehira,
their clan leader, offered the young man his protection, and he
remained for about five years, safe from pursuit by Taira troops.
It is said that on his way to the north, Yoshitsune stopped at a
post station for his coming-of-age ceremony. Since no members
of his family were present to officiate, he was obliged to perform
the solemn ritual himself. The anecdote serves, of course, to
emphasize the solitary nature of the young hero.

According to tradition, one of the reasons that Yoshitsune
enjoyed so much freedom during his years in the mountain temple was that his guardians underestimated him because of his
slight build and girlish looks and never suspected the lion that
lurked beneath the frail exterior. His physical appearance, which
is well established in the legendary accounts, may surprise Western readers, who are accustomed to somewhat sturdier heroes.
"The Tales of the Tairas" picture him as "a little man with a fair
complexion." From some of the descriptions it appears that the   *5.11*

natural pallor of his skin was enhanced by the use of white powder, a common custom among Heian aristocrats like Prince Genji but rather incongruous for a Minamoto warrior. In later accounts Yoshitsune appears as an etiolated youth with beautiful, feminine features; and the contrast between this delicate exterior and his powerful masculinity, as revealed in his military prowess
5.12 and active amorous life, is part of the hero's peculiar fascination. *Gempei Seisuiki* ("The Chronicle of the Rise and Fall of the Minamotos and the Tairas"), a detailed history of the struggle between the clans, gives perhaps the most reliable and unglamourized picture of Yoshitsune when it describes him as he joined Yoritomo's forces in the east to prepare for their all-out rebellion against the Tairas: "a small, pale youth with crooked teeth and
5.13 bulging eyes."

Now at the age of twenty-one this unlikely candidate for heroism embarked on his brief career as a soldier, which in a mere five years was to establish him as a prodigy. It is typical of the ironies that studded Yoshitsune's life that in his first campaign the enemy should have been not the hated Tairas but his own cousin Yoshinaka, one of the most illustrious fighters in Japan, whom he attacked on the orders of his elder brother and defeated with spectacular success.

Yoshinaka's brief, brilliant career in many ways adumbrates that of Yoshitsune himself. After a meteoric rise to fame when he led his fierce mountain forces in the first major victories against the Tairas, Yoshinaka incurred the suspicion and displeasure of Yoritomo; this was partly because of the unruly behaviour of his troops in Kyoto, but the underlying reason was his own independent attitude and unwillingness to submit to higher authority. Yoritomo ordered that he be "chastised" (the standard euphemism of the time) and, with typical disregard for
5.14 clan solidarity, used his younger brother for the job. The dramatic nature of Yoshinaka's downfall confirmed his status as one
5.15 of the heroes of the age; but his rough nature and the unruliness of his soldiery in the capital lowered him in popular esteem and provided a degree of justification for Yoritomo's decision to destroy him—a justification that never applied in the case of Yoshitsune, who was noted for his merciful treatment of the civilian
5.16 population.

Having established his credentials as a commander, Yoshitsune was eager to follow up his success by attacking the real

THE TRIUMPHANT CAMPAIGNS OF MINAMOTO NO YOSHITSUNE

ŌSHŪ

Hiraizumi

Kamakura

Fujikawa

Lake Biwa

Awazu

Kyoto

Ichinotani

Osaka

Dannoura

Yashima

SEA OF JAPAN

PACIFIC OCEAN

0 20 40 60 80 STATUTE MILES

0 40 80 120 KILOMETRES

The Etheredges

enemy. His opportunity came only one month later when he decisively defeated the Tairas at Ichinotani by the shores of the Inland Sea. The outcome of this famous battle was decided by a surprise attack in which Yoshitsune led a small body of cavalry down a precipitous mountain path (so steep, it is said, that even the local monkeys did not dare descend it) and attacked the enemy encampment from the rear, totally demoralizing the Taira forces and obliging them to flee to the island of Shikoku. This manoeuvre was typical of Yoshitsune's tactics, which were marked by panache, speed, and an uncanny ability to gauge the enemy's reactions. As part of these tactics he was prepared to take considerable risks and did not hesitate to override his fellow commanders who preferred a slower approach. The invariable success of his manoeuvres was bound to irk more cautious colleagues and to arouse their jealousy, and this was no doubt one reason for the damaging reports which Yoritomo, ensconced in his distant eastern headquarters, now began to receive about his headstrong young brother.

     Elated by his success at Ichinotani, Yoshitsune hoped to pursue the fight before the Tairas had time to recover, but Yoritomo's suspicions had already been aroused. Despite Yoshitsune's predominant role in the first great victory over the Tairas, the main honour went to Noriyori, an ineffectual but obedient half-brother, who was now despatched as commanding general of his forces in the west. Yoshitsune was obliged to linger in the capital, 5.17 and had to wait an entire year for his next opportunity to attack the Tairas. Once again he depended on surprise tactics: braving a fierce typhoon, he crossed the Inland Sea with a small body of troops and, by a brilliant and rapid manoeuvre, routed the vastly superior Taira forces who were entrenched in Yashima on the island of Shikoku. About one month later, on 25th April 1185, he dealt the Tairas a final, staggering blow at the great naval Battle of Dannoura fought off the straits that separate the main island from Kyushu. This famous victory established Yoshitsune at the age of twenty-six as the foremost military commander in Japan. It was all the more impressive in that his eastern forces were unaccustomed to naval engagements and were fighting in an area where the Tairas had particularly strong support. The early part of the battle went against the Minamotos; but the sudden change of the tide in the middle of the afternoon proved disastrous for the Tairas, and soon the sea was (as the chronicles tell us) dyed with their blood, and the red Taira banners flecked the surface of the water like maple leaves in autumn. Among the countless victims of the catastrophe was Taira no Kiyomori's widow who leapt into the waves clasping the child Emperor, Antoku. The victory announcement that Yoshitsune sent to the Court in Kyoto was impressively laconic: "On the twenty-fourth day of the Third Month at the Hour of the Hare at Dannoura in the Province of Nagato . . . the Tairas were annihilated. The Sacred Mirror and the Sacred Seal are being safely returned to the Capital."   5.18

    With their defeat at Dannoura the hegemony of the Tairas came to an abrupt end. During twenty-six years they had supplanted the Fujiwaras as the dominant power in the capital; their military strength had given them virtually dictatorial control over large areas of the country, and vast wealth accrued to them from their estates and from maritime commerce. Kiyomori's highhanded methods and intransigence, however, had made him increasingly disliked, not only at Court, where he was regarded as a bullying upstart, but in the Buddhist temples and, most damaging of all, among important elements of the warrior class in the provinces. Though widely resented during their years of prosperity, the Tairas acquired a sort of retroactive popularity thanks to their cataclysmic defeat. The traditional empathy with the loser—the psychology of *hōganbiiki*—inevitably evoked sympathy for a family that experienced the most dramatic rise and fall in all Japanese history. This, combined with Buddhist ideas of fatality and karma, underlies the famous Japanese adage, *Ogoru Heike wa hisashikarazu* ("The proud Tairas endure but for a little time"); and it inspired the opening threnody of "The Tales of the Tairas," one of the most affecting statements in literature about the uncertainty of human fortunes:

The toll of Jetavana's temple bell echoes the transience of all earthly things; the hue of the blossoms on the *sāla* trees displays the truth that those who flourish must surely fall. The proud ones of this world endure but for a moment like a spring night's dream. In the end the brave are brought low and scattered like dust before the wind.   5.19

The speed and totality of the Tairas' fall were the measure of Yoshitsune's success. Though the Minamoto victory was the outcome of Yoritomo's statecraft and careful preparations, the war

might have dragged on for many years after the Tairas entrenched themselves in their base at Shikoku had it not been for
Yoshitsune, who by his Napoleonic verve and imagination broke
the stalemate and brought the conflict to an end in a mere five
weeks. Now the young conquering hero returned to Kyoto, the
cynosure of general admiration and praise, with a degree of
popularity and prestige at Court that no member of the military
class had enjoyed for centuries. Yet this moment of Yoshitsune's
culminating triumph was the turning point in his career, which
now abruptly started on its downhill course. The key to this
amazing peripetia is, of course, Minamoto no Yoritomo, whose
personality and long-term objectives made a clash with Yoshitsune inevitable, and whose political acumen ensured that in this
sort of battle he would be the victor.

The estrangement between Yoritomo and Yoshitsune is
typical of the dissensions that bedevilled the Minamoto clan and
that caused them to spend almost as much time in fighting each
other as in opposing their common adversary. Originally the
hostility between the two men was one-sided; it was only after
extreme provocation, culminating in an assassination attempt,
that Yoshitsune resigned himself to the knowledge that his
brother was a mortal enemy. The legendary accounts suggest
that one of the main causes for Yoritomo's ire was jealousy arising from the dazzling military successes and consequent adulation of Yoshitsune. In particular, we are told, he was enraged by
Yoshitsune's attitude that the final victory at Dannoura was due
to his own prowess rather than to divine favour and to the combined efforts of the Minamoto warriors. This may be part of the
explanation, but we must be wary of sources that deliberately
paint Yoritomo in dark colours. It has been said that his character
was flawed by a streak of cruel perversity which he directed most
5.20   fiercely against members of his own family. Over the years, it is
true, Yoritomo managed to destroy almost every close relation
who showed any real talent or originality; but whether this was
due to a "cruel nature" or to cool political calculations remains
a moot point, since there are no relevant documents and all the
existing works are tendentious.

Apart from any possible psychological compulsions, Yoritomo's hostility to his brother can readily be explained as a by-
product of his fundamental political objectives. He envisaged a
new system of law and order under the control of a warrior class

dominated by the Minamoto clan in which he would be the unquestioned overlord and in which all the other clansmen, including his closest relations, would obey him as vassals. It was partly in order to consolidate this new ruling class and to impose discipline and cohesion upon his contentious subordinates that in 1180 he established his military headquarters in the eastern encampment of Kamakura, several hundred mountainous miles (and a fortnight's hard journey) from Kyoto. Here, in a rugged Spartan atmosphere, diametrically opposed to the ease, sophistication, and aestheticism of the ancient capital, he succeeded in forming an entirely new type of administration based primarily on the needs of the samurai class; and it was his firm principle that all military vassals owed their allegiance exclusively to Kamakura and must never take orders from the Court or from any other authority in the land.

Yoritomo proceeded with quiet deliberation. To overthrow the Tairas he appointed successive members of his own clan as military commanders, while he himself remained in Kamakura, securing the eastern base and strengthening the new military administration. When a general like Yoshinaka proved to be obstreperous and threatened the success of his overall policy, Yoritomo did not hesitate to eliminate him regardless of blood relationship; and for such purposes he was quite prepared to use other members of his family. His great fear was not dissension among his Minamoto clansmen but rather that two or more of his unruly relatives might join against him and, possibly in collusion with the Court, challenge the authority of Kamakura. So far as the Tairas themselves were concerned, Yoritomo always took their eventual defeat for granted. From the outset of the civil war he looked beyond the day when his clan would win the final battle, and concentrated on establishing a settled system under firm, efficacious Minamoto rule in Kamakura.

To ensure the loyalty of his vassals Yoritomo made it clear that no members of the military class might receive favours directly from Kyoto. He alone had the right to reward his followers for their service and, if such rewards were to take the form of Court appointments (appointments which, though devoid of content, still had all the heady prestige of titles in modern England), they must be recommended by him. It was his younger brother's flagrant violation of this rule that first roused Yoritomo's anger against him. As a reward for Yoshitsune's victories the Retired

Emperor appointed him Lieutenant in the Imperial Police (a much-coveted sinecure) and, more important, granted him the privilege of waiting in attendance upon the Emperor in the Senior Courtiers' Chamber. According to one account, Yoritomo resented that this honour, an unusual one for military men, should have been accorded not to himself but to a younger brother of far lower birth. Perhaps so; but the main reason for Yoritomo's suspicions was that Yoshitsune had deliberately violated the code of the lord-vassal relationship by accepting honours that had been neither recommended nor approved by himself. In Yoritomo's scheme of things this relationship superseded any ties of blood or friendship. Since his overriding aim was to consolidate his strength in the new peacetime conditions that would follow the defeat of the Tairas, he could not tolerate any individual or group that refused to submit totally to his rules. Rightly or wrongly it appeared that Yoshitsune represented a potential threat to the new order, a nucleus round whom dissident anti-Kamakura elements at Court, in the temples, and among the military might gather to cause renewed disruption and civil conflict. It was this fear, rather than the cruel, vindictive character of the legendary Yoritomo, that explains his implacable
5.21   attitude to the young hero.

What were the personal relations between these two remarkable brothers? Tradition has it that they first met in Yoritomo's eastern headquarters at the outbreak of the anti-Taira uprising in 1180, and there are stories of later encounters; but in fact it is
5.22   uncertain whether they ever saw each other at all. Clearly Yoritomo never shared the general enthusiasm about his brother, whom he doubtless regarded as an unreliable young hothead, corrupted by his upbringing in the capital and his close association with Court circles, and woefully lacking in obedience, discipline, and the other essential qualities of the eastern samurai. In his mind Yoshitsune was something of an anachronism, who, for all his military prowess, was unable to understand the fundamental changes that were taking place in the country. Furthermore, he was never prepared to accept Yoshitsune as a social equal. One
5.23   of the chronicles recounts an incident (dated 1181) during a ceremony outside Hachiman Shrine in Kamakura when Yoritomo instructed his young brother to hold a horse by the reins. When Yoshitsune balked at this menial task, Yoritomo tartly ordered him to do as he was told. The story reflects Yoritomo's general

attitude: Yoshitsune may have been his half-brother, but above all he was a vassal and must be made to behave like one.

The difficulties between the brothers, which sprang from a combination of historical circumstances and personal temperament, were exacerbated by two very different men, Goshirakawa and Kajiwara no Kagetoki. In the year of the Tairas' final defeat the reigning Emperor was a boy of five, and such influence as the imperial family retained was exercised principally by Goshirakawa, who since his brief reign some three decades earlier had consolidated a position of authority in the capital as Retired (or Cloistered) Emperor. The growing ascendancy of the military class made this position increasingly difficult; but Goshirakawa was a subtle man, much addicted to intrigue and conspiracy, and, though the last vestiges of real power were rapidly slipping from the Court, he managed to stay afloat in a period of stormy change. Having no military strength of his own, he was obliged to steer a careful course in his dealings with the warrior class. His policy towards the various commanders who were competing for supremacy was vacillating and at times ignominious; but the Court had neither the power nor the will to risk a confrontation with the military. In dealing with the victorious Minamotos, the Retired Emperor took advantage of the rivalries within their quarrelsome clan to play one member off against the other, hoping that eventually he would emerge on the winning side or at least retain some influence in an uneasy balance of power. It was no doubt in line with this policy that after the Battle of Ichinotani, and again after the final victory at Dannoura, he decided to reward Yoshitsune directly, fully realizing that such unprecedented honours would provoke Yoritomo's anger and keep the two Minamoto leaders at loggerheads.

The Retired Emperor appears to have developed a sincere personal regard for Yoshitsune during his period of residence in the capital; it is also likely that he considered this somewhat naïve young general to be less of a threat to the Court than Yoritomo, who in his new headquarters at Kamakura was planning to alter the power structure of Japan, relegating the Court to a position of irremediable impotence. These were probably the considerations in Goshirakawa's mind when at the end of 1185 he agreed to make Yoshitsune the Chief Steward of all the manorial estates in Kyushu and to entrust him with the task of "chastising" his elder brother as an enemy of the Court. Whatever devious motives the

Retired Emperor may have had, his machinations after the fall of the Tairas were certainly one of the main factors in the rupture between the two brothers and played an important part in the events that led to Yoshitsune's downfall. The Retired Emperor's support was short-lived: once Yoshitsune was a fugitive, Goshirakawa reversed his former order, explaining that it had been issued against his will, and now commissioned the elder *5.24* brother to chastise the younger.

In addition to suffering from Goshirakawa's friendship, Yoshitsune was bedevilled by a series of reports and rumours that found their way to Kamakura. Some of these calumnies appear to have emanated from his envious half-brother, Noriyori; but the main source was Kajiwara no Kagetoki, one of Yoritomo's closest retainers, who originally endeared himself to his master by saving his life in an early battle against the Tairas. From all that we can reliably tell, Kajiwara was typical of the hard-working, loyal, somewhat dour warriors who were the backbone of Yoritomo's eastern regime; but in the legend, especially as it developed in later centuries, he is represented as a sort of super-villain, a man whose consuming envy and hatred of Yoshitsune *5.25* made him goad his master into committing his worst injustices.

Thanks to his abilities and to Yoritomo's support, Kajiwara rose rapidly in the martial hierarchy and was appointed Assistant Director of the Warriors' Office. As the war against the Tairas approached its climax, Yoritomo despatched him to the western front to assist in the final attack; according to traditional accounts, however, his real function was to observe Yoshitsune and report anything suspicious to Kamakura. He did not have to wait long for an opportunity to traduce the young general. At a council of war on the eve of the Battle of Yashima the two men became involved in a furious quarrel, the so-called Reverse Oars controversy, which almost led to blows and which allowed Kajiwara to send Yoritomo a damning report about his hotheaded young brother. The following account, quoted from "The Tales of the Tairas," evokes the high-spirited, disrespectful character of the hero as he is traditionally pictured in the "successful" part of his career, and incidentally suggests why he was eventually bound to incur his brother's enmity:

The greater and lesser lords of the Eastern Provinces gathered at Watanabe. "We have not yet had any experience of fighting at sea," said one of them. "How shall we manage?" "I think that for this particular battle we had better fit our ships with reverse oars," suggested Kajiwara no Kagetoki. "And what may they be?" asked Yoshitsune. "On horseback one can ride in either direction," explained Kajiwara, "since it is a simple matter to turn one's steed left or right. But a ship cannot be swung round so easily. I therefore suggest that we fit oars at both the bows and the sterns of our ships . . . so that we can readily change direction if necessary." "What an inauspicious thing to suggest at the beginning of a fight!" exclaimed Yoshitsune. "A soldier enters battle with the intention of never retreating. It is only after things have gone badly that he [even] thinks of turning back. What good can come from preparing one's retreat in advance? Your Lordships may fit these "reverse oars" or "turn-back oars" to your ships by the hundreds or thousands as you please. I myself am quite satisfied with the ordinary oars that have been used in the past."

"A good general," said Kajiwara, "is one who advances at the right time but who also knows when to retreat, thus preserving his life to destroy the enemy. A fighter who cannot adapt himself to circumstances is called a wild-boar warrior, and no one respects such a man." "Wild boar or wild deer—it's all the same to me," said Yoshitsune. "The way to win a battle is to push forward and attack the enemy."

The greater and lesser lords of the Eastern Provinces [were amused]. They did not dare laugh openly since they were afraid of Kajiwara, but their feelings showed in their expressions. On that day Yoshitsune and Kajiwara were on the verge of coming to blows, but the matter was settled without an actual fight.   *5.26*

Yoshitsune's sensational victory at Yashima did not endear him to Kajiwara, and shortly afterwards, at the outset of the Battle of Dannoura, the two men were again embroiled in a clash of wills:

"I should like to lead today's attack," said Kajiwara. "Yes," said Yoshitsune, "but I am here for that job." "Outrageous!" exclaimed Kajiwara. "Surely you are the commander-in-chief."

"Not so," said Yoshitsune. "Our commander-in-chief is the Lord of Kamakura. I am simply his deputy in battle just as you are."

Kajiwara, unable to press his request any further, muttered, "This man is unsuited by nature for leading warriors." Yoshitsune overheard the remark and, putting his hand to his sword, shouted, "And you are the greatest fool in all Japan."

"I have no master but the Lord of Kamakura," said Kajiwara, also reaching for his weapon.   *5.27*

Once again the two men were about to cross swords; they were
barely restrained by their fellow warriors, who reminded them
that a quarrel like this could help only their common enemy and
would certainly displease Yoritomo. According to "The Tales of
the Tairas," this latest flare-up inspired Kajiwara to transmit
further calumnies "which finally succeeded in bringing Yoshitsune to his death."

5.28

After the triumph at Dannoura, Kajiwara did his best to
detract from Yoshitsune's role by emphasizing in his despatch to
Kamakura that the victory was due to divine succour and not to
the skill of any particular commander. Later in the same year,
when relations between the two brothers had deteriorated still
further, Kajiwara no Kagetoki, who had now returned to the
eastern headquarters, informed Yoritomo that his younger
brother, far from obeying the recent orders to "chastise" his
uncle, Yukiie, was in fact conspiring secretly with him in Kyoto
and planning joint action against Kamakura. This rumour
aroused Yoritomo's worst suspicions about collusion between
members of his family and led directly to his decision to order
Yoshitsune's assassination. Thus the super-villain, having systematically fostered resentment against the hero, provided his
enemy with an ideal pretext to destroy him.

5.29

Though Yoshitsune was slow to realize it, the sad truth was
that his final victory over the Tairas had largely eliminated his
raison d'être in Yoritomo's overall scheme. From Kamakura's
point of view the young man's courage, resourcefulness, and
military prowess had served their purpose and now threatened
to become a nuisance. In the words of the old Chinese proverb,
"Once the cunning hare is killed, the swift hound will be
cooked." Yoshitsune had accomplished his main function, the
destruction of the enemy clan, and it now required little provocation for Yoritomo to dispose of him entirely. The theme of
worldly ingratitude adds to the poignancy of Yoshitsune's career
as we move into the final and most important part of the story.

A few weeks after his triumphant entry into Kyoto, the hero
set out for Kamakura to make his victory report in person to
Yoritomo and to hand over the principal Taira prisoners whom
he had captured in his last battle. He was not allowed to reach
his destination. On arrival at a nearby post station he was instructed to await further orders, and there he remained for about
a week in a state of increasing anxiety. Evidently realizing that

his brother had heard damaging rumours about him, he sent repeated protestations of loyalty, all of which went unanswered. Finally he grew desperate, and from the little post station of Koshigoe about a mile from Kamakura he addressed his famous "Koshigoe letter" to one of his brother's chief ministers. Though Yoshitsune probably sent some sort of emotional appeal to Kamakura at this time, the particular document that has come down to us is full of additions and embellishments that are deliberately designed to build up sympathy for the mistreated hero. *5.30* This final appeal, however, is a most important part of the Yoshitsune legend; with its mixture of bravado and an almost masochistic indulgence in misfortune, it gives valuable insights into the psychology of heroic defeat:

5th day of the 6th month of the 2nd year of Genryaku [1185]   *5.31*
    I, Minamoto no Yoshitsune, Lieutenant of the Outer Palace Guards, respectfully venture to address Your Excellency. Having been chosen as His Lordship's [Yoritomo's] deputy and being entrusted with an Imperial commission, I overthrew the enemies of the Court by a display of those military arts that have been passed down from generation to generation in our family, and thus did I expunge the disgrace that we have suffered by our defeat. I had thought to receive special commendation for these deeds of mine, but to my astonishment I became the object of the most damning slanders, in consequence of which my great exploits have been ignored. I, Yoshitsune, though innocent of all offence, have incurred blame; though worthy of honour and guilty of no mistake, I have fallen into His Lordship's disfavour.
    So here I remain, vainly shedding crimson tears. . . . I have not been permitted to refute the accusations of my slanderers or [even] to set foot in Kamakura, but have been obliged to languish idly these many days with no possibility of declaring the sincerity of my intentions. It is now so long since I have set eyes on His Lordship's compassionate countenance that the bond of our blood brotherhood seems to have vanished.
    Is this misfortune the outcome of fate, or is it retribution from some previous existence of mine? Woe is me! Unless the venerable spirit of our dead father should be reborn into this world, what man will reveal [to his Lordship] the anguish that afflicts my mind, and who will bestow any pity upon me?
    I hesitate to write this further letter lest it appear to be another [idle] declaration of personal feelings, but I am bound to tell you that shortly after my parents gave me life His Excellency, my father, passed to another world and I became an orphan and was carried to [the capital] clasped in my mother's bosom, and that thereafter my mind has never

been at peace for a single moment. Though I managed to drag out my useless existence, I could not move about the Capital in safety and had to wander from province to province, hiding myself in many an obscure village, being obliged to make my nesting place in distant parts of the land and to serve common people and peasants.

Then suddenly fortune came my way and I was sent up to the Capital to overthrow the Taira clan. Having first chastised Yoshinaka for his offences, I set about destroying the Tairas and for this purpose I spurred my horse on craggy precipices, heedless of my life in the face of the enemy; at other times I braved the fierce winds and waves on the great sea, not caring that my body might sink to the bottom and be devoured by monsters of the deep. My armour and helmet were my pillow; my bow and arrows were my trade. . . .

Concerning my promotion to be Lieutenant of the Fifth Rank [in the Imperial Police] I welcomed this appointment as the greatest possible honour for our Minamoto clan. Yet now I am plunged into this state of profound grief and bitter lamentation. Realizing that only through the help of the Buddhas and the Gods could I hope that my appeal might succeed, I inscribed oaths on talismans of various temples and shrines, swearing by the Gods of the great and small shrines in Japan and by the spirits of the underworld that I had never for a moment harboured any [evil] ambitions; and all these pledges of loyalty I submitted [to Kamakura]. Yet have I received no pardon.

This is the land of the Gods, but it appears that the Gods have not heeded my petition; and so, having nowhere else to turn, I now throw myself upon Your Excellency's great mercy and entreat you to bring my declaration to His Lordship's notice on a suitable occasion, so that he may be persuaded of my innocence. . . .

It is impossible to express myself fully in writing, but I have tried to inform Your Excellency on the main points and respectfully beg you to give your attention to this letter that I now most humbly submit.

Minamoto no Yoshitsune

The hero's resourcefulness and prowess on the battlefield contrast with the childlike simplicity that he showed in his personal relations—a type of innocence and naïveté that in the Japanese tradition is so often associated with *makoto*. For even at this late stage he seems to have believed that all his difficulties would disappear if only he could meet Yoritomo face to face and declare the "sincerity of his intentions." His hopes for a reconciliation were shattered when he received the humiliating order to return directly to the capital without entering Kamakura. Yoritomo compounded the insult by repossessing the Taira estates that his

5.32

brother had received as a reward for his military services and, worse still, by dropping him from the ranks of the Minamoto liegemen. Within a week of writing his Koshigoe letter, Yoshitsune set out despondently for his journey back to Kyoto.

A few months later Yoritomo followed up this rebuff by trying to have his brother removed from the world entirely. For this purpose he despatched a warrior monk to the capital with orders to assassinate Yoshitsune. The monk and his henchmen carried out a night attack on the hero's mansion; but they were driven off, and the ringleader himself, having fled to the northern hills of Kurama, was tracked down by Yoshitsune's friends in the monastery, brought back to the city, and executed. This crude attempt on his life was enough to convince even Yoshitsune that there was no longer any hope for a reconciliation and that he would have to seek allies if he was to survive. It was now that he obtained the document in which the Retired Emperor instructed him to "chastise" his elder brother as an enemy of the Court.

Goshirakawa's order may have conferred official legitimacy on Yoshitsune's future enterprises, but it failed to give him the material support that he needed for a campaign. Instead of striking at Kamakura, he and his uncle, Yukiie, accompanied by a couple of hundred men, now proceeded to the west in the hope of collecting new recruits to their side. This caution seems *5.33* strangely out of character for Yoshitsune, who had always been noted for his bold tactics, and it is clear that Yoritomo himself expected his impetuous young brother to launch an immediate attack against the east. We can only guess the reasons why at this juncture Yoshitsune should have changed to such careful behaviour. Possibly he had been unnerved and depressed by Yoritomo's hostility and had lost the derring-do and optimism of his early period; possibly, too, he still hesitated to launch an attack against his elder brother, whom he had obeyed for so many years as head of both the Minamoto clan and of his immediate family; also his uncle may have persuaded him that it would be madness to confront the might of Kamakura without first recruiting a reasonable force of men.

In any case the luck that so often favoured Yoshitsune in his more dynamic days had now run out. Shortly after leaving Kyoto and embarking on the Inland Sea, his little troop was almost entirely destroyed in a sudden storm, which (as Yoritomo was informed) had arisen from the will of the gods. By some extraordinary chance Yoshitsune and his uncle survived the shipwreck, which killed nearly all their men; but any hopes of raising armed support—a feeble prospect from the outset—had now vanished, and the most they could hope was to avoid capture by the hostile troops who surrounded them on all sides. After the shipwreck the two men parted forever, and some months later Yukiie, the inept uncle, was run to ground and killed.

Yoshitsune was now an isolated outlaw, proscribed by the Court and ferociously pursued by his brother, who ordered what was to become the greatest manhunt in the history of Japan. After a series of narrow escapes, Yoshitsune managed to hide his tracks entirely. It was thought that he might make his way back to Kyoto (which in fact he did), and there was a door-to-door search in the city; troops were also sent to many of the temples where it was believed Yoshitsune might take refuge; warriors in every province and at all the barriers were put on the alert and directed to follow each possible clue that could reveal his whereabouts. But twelfth-century Japan, with its poor communications and slow transport, was an immense country; and the complicated, mountainous terrain made it an ideal hiding place for an ingenious fugitive, especially for one like Yoshitsune who must have had many secret well-wishers.

Month after month the great hunt continued. Even the Buddhas and the gods were enlisted in the cause: prayers for Yoshitsune's capture were recited in many of the temples; and on the orders of Kamakura similar appeals were made at the Ise Shrine. On one occasion the Intendant of a certain temple dreamt that he had met Yoshitsune in the eastern province of Kōzuke. He dutifully reported this event, and a special searching party was sent there; but in fact Yoshitsune was near Kyoto several hundred miles to the west. Yoritomo's desire to track down his brother appears to have become obsessive, and he was enraged by the failure of the hunt. He obviously suspected that the Court was not doing its share, and about a year after launching the search he wrote as follows to the Retired Emperor in Kyoto:

[Yoshitsune] has sympathizers in every part of the land, and we cannot possibly effect his capture with the present half-hearted measures. It is therefore my intention to despatch a force of some twenty or thirty thousand men to make a thorough search of every hill and temple in the country. Since this may lead to certain untoward eventualities, I request that, if the Court can propose some sure method of capturing [the enemy], this should be communicated [forthwith to Kamakura].   *5.34*

The Retired Emperor, now thoroughly cowed by the Lord of Kamakura, reacted to this ill-concealed threat by issuing additional search orders. It was shortly afterwards that Yoshitsune, realizing he could not longer remain in the region of the capital, decided to escape to the domain of the "northern Fujiwaras" in Ōshū.

There has been much speculation about the exact route that Yoshitsune followed on his dangerous journey through the central and eastern provinces (now all under the sway of Kamakura) to his final destination in the remote northeastern part of Japan, where he arrived towards the end of 1187 after some six months of travel. Since even his brother's frantic search could not uncover the hero's whereabouts, we can hardly expect, seven centuries later, to find out anything accurate about his fugitive period. He probably received considerable protection from monks and warrior-priests in temples near the capital and along his route— men who had known him in palmier days and who sympathized with him in his misfortune. According to the legend, both he and his followers disguised themselves as "mountain monks" *(yamabushi)* travelling through the eastern provinces to collect subscriptions for rebuilding a temple. The route traditionally ascribed to Yoshitsune for his escape to the east is identical with the one followed in later centuries by ascetic pilgrims from the Kumano district south of the capital; and many of the stories about the fugitive period may well have been invented by these monks and recited by them during their long travels. This is perhaps one of the ways in which the Yoshitsune legend spread through Japan, and it may also explain the particular route that was chosen for him in the ballads.   *5.35*

By far the most famous of the escape adventures took place at the newly erected barrier of Ataka on the Japan Sea, where Yoshitsune barely evaded detection and capture owing to the resourcefulness of his chief follower, the stalwart priest Benkei. This story, which inspired two of the best plays in Japanese literature, the fifteenth-century Nō drama *Ataka*, and the nineteenth-century Kabuki play *Kanjinchō*, or "The Subscription List," is of course fictitious. Yet it may well be based on actual events in which Yoshitsune was saved from disaster by people who recognized him as "the most wanted man in Japan" but were moved by such personal sympathy, such a sense of *mono no aware* ("the pathos of things"), that they were prepared to incur risks on his behalf.

The drama, which brings into focus some of the main aspects of Yoshitsune's downhill career, is important for a study of heroic failure. The various presentations agree in their general approach to the events, though the Kabuki version is a great deal more elaborate than the Nō play. The three main characters in *Ataka* are Benkei, the swaggering warrior-priest; Lord Togashi, an important vassal of Yoritomo's who has been appointed to guard the strategic barrier; and Yoshitsune, the quarry whom all Japan is hunting. The play starts, in typical Nō style, with a succinct account of the situation by Togashi:

I am the officer in charge of the barrier at the port of Ataka in Kaga Province. Now Yoshitsune has incurred the enmity of his elder brother, Lord Yoritomo, and can no longer remain in the Capital. He and a dozen followers, all disguised as mountain priests, are said to be on their way to Ōshū to seek the protection of Lord Hidehira. Hearing of this, Lord Yoritomo has ordered that new barriers be erected in every province, and he has instructed us to subject all mountain priests to close investiga-
5.36   tion.

Next Yoshitsune and his small band of followers enter the stage disguised as itinerant monks. They are dismayed to hear about the new barrier that has been erected at the nearby harbour of Ataka. Some of the men want to break through, but Benkei explains that this will endanger the rest of their long journey and advises that they resort to a trick:

Yoshitsune: Suggest a plan for us, Benkei!

Benkei: Very well, my lord. Allow me to propose the following course of action. I and these other men all look like rough mountain-priests, but your noble appearance is hard to disguise. May I respectfully suggest that you give your brocade stole to the porter and instead put his pannier on your back? Then, if you follow behind
5.37   us at a slight distance, you will surely be taken for a real porter.

By now Yoshitsune, having become almost entirely passive, is prepared to accept all Benkei's suggestions, and he willingly changes places with the lowly porter. The party then proceeds towards the barrier of Ataka, where the blackened heads of some recently executed monks can be seen under a tree. Undeterred by this grisly sight, they walk up to the barrier. The dramatic climax is Togashi's confrontation with Benkei, who angrily insists that they are a group of innocent monks on their way to raise subscriptions for rebuilding Tōdai Temple in Nara. Togashi says that he cannot possibly let them pass, and it turns out that three suspect monks were decapitated by the barrier guards on the previous day. Yoshitsune and his followers have walked straight into the lion's mouth, but Benkei is unshaken. He starts a fierce argument with Togashi, after which he and the other "priests" try to browbeat the guards with loud Buddhist chants. Togashi challenges Benkei to read the subscription list that monks would normally carry on such a mission. Of course Benkei possesses no such list, but he rises splendidly to the occasion by taking a scroll from the porter's pannier and improvising a history of Tōdai Temple full of erudite theological references. The guards, hypnotized by Benkei's recital, allow him and his party to pass the barrier without further demur:

> *Chorus:*   . . . [Benkei] reads the scroll in such a booming voice that the heavens themselves resound. The terrified guards
>
>> In fear and trembling let them pass,
>> In fear and trembling let them pass.
>
> *Togashi:*   Hurry and cross the barrier!
>
> *Sword-Bearer:*   Pray pass, pray pass!   *5.38*

The party is almost out of danger when suddenly Togashi's sword-bearer recognizes that the pretended porter, who has been lagging behind, is none other than Yoshitsune himself. Togashi orders him to halt. Benkei, realizing that the situation is desperate, furiously berates the porter for having caused this delay; then he snatches his staff and beats him furiously. His purpose, of course, is to convince the barrier-keepers that, despite the physical resemblance, the porter cannot possibly be Yoshitsune, since no retainer would dare raise a hand against his lord under any circumstances. Togashi admits that he was wrong to suspect the porter and gives the party final permission to cross the barrier.

When they are safely on the other side, there is an emotional scene in which Benkei tearfully begs his master for forgiveness;

Yoshitsune, also weeping, thanks Benkei for having saved his life
and (much as in the Koshigoe letter) bemoans the world's injustice that has brought him to his present state:

Chorus: I, Yoshitsune, was born of a warrior's line and dedicated my
life to Yoritomo. I submerged the bodies [of the enemy] beneath the
waves of the western sea. In the hills and fields and on the shore I
slept, using the sleeves of my armour as a pillow. At times I drifted
in a boat, entrusting my life to the wind and waves; on other days
I made my way across the mountain ridges, with my horse half sunk
in snow. By the sea at dusk I fought in Suma and Akashi, and within
three years I defeated the enemy. Yet my loyalty was all in vain.
Alas, what a wretched fate is mine!

Yoshitsune: This is indeed a sorry world
Where nothing happens as one hopes.

Chorus: . . . It is a world where the sincere man suffers,
While the slanderer goes from strength to strength. . . .
Are there no Gods or Buddhas [to protect us]?
How wretched is the life of man in this sad world!
5.39   How wretched is his life!

The play ends on a somewhat merrier note as Lord Togashi
offers wine to the departing pilgrims by way of apology for his
unjust suspicions. Benkei pretends to become drunk and per-
forms an energetic "manly dance" *(otokomai)*. Shortly afterwards
the party proceeds on its journey, while the chorus chants,

. . . Let us hasten from this place!
Strung tight as a bow,
Do not relax your care,
Guards of the barrier,
We bid you now farewell.
Shouldering their panniers,
They make their way towards the land of Ōshū,
Feeling as though they had trod on a tiger's tail
5.40   Or escaped from a serpent's mouth.

This time Yoshitsune has escaped; but every reader and spectator
knows that the hero is heading ineluctably towards his doom.
Much of the play's impact comes from the fact that Lord
Togashi has actually suspected Benkei's deception from the outset; the reading of the fraudulent subscription list, though delud-

ing the common guards, simply confirms his doubts. Togashi's role is by far the most complicated in the story. Torn between loyalty to Yoritomo, his overlord, and sympathy with the unfortunate young fugitive, he is so moved by Benkei, in particular by the agony he endured when he was forced to beat his master, that he lets the party pass the barrier. In other words, by pretending to be deceived by the ruse, he sacrifices his feudal loyalty in favour of a higher, emotional loyalty inspired by a sense of the "pathos of things" (mono no aware), deep sincerity (makoto), and sympathy with the loser (bōganbiiki).   5.41

During most of the play Yoshitsune is inactive: though nominally the hero, he makes no decisions and simply does as Benkei instructs. To emphasize the unmasculine nature of his role, Yoshitsune in the Nō drama is played by a child actor (kokata) and on the Kabuki stage by a female impersonator (onnagata). This is part of the transformation in Yoshitsune's character as the legend developed during the centuries after his death. All the later accounts emphasized the losing part of his career and suggest that Yoritomo's enmity and the subsequent setbacks transmogrified his brother from a stalwart warrior into a melancholy, ineffectual aristocrat, a supine victim of fate so numbed by his misfortunes that he can scarcely function without Benkei's support and initiative. Nothing remains of the fighting spirit that won the great battles against the Tairas; instead, Yoshitsune figures as a cultured member of urban society, closer in spirit to Prince Genji and the Heian ideal than to fellow members of his rough provincial clan. His appearance, too, is altered: more and   5.42 more he assumes a feminine or childlike beauty, pale, slender, delicate, in contrast to the gigantic, super-masculine figure of the warrior-monk who protects him.

The name of Musashibō Benkei appears now and then in the historical records as one of Yoshitsune's retainers, but it is not until later versions of the legend, notably "The Chronicle of Yoshitsune," that he becomes central to the story and bursts forth as an overpowering character, typifying the energy, optimism, and resourcefulness which have deserted his master during the losing years. Everything about Benkei is larger than life,   5.43 from the time of his remarkable birth (he stayed for eighteen months in his mother's womb), through his childhood when he was reputed to be eight feet tall and as strong as a hundred men, until the climax of his career as Yoshitsune's loyal follower, a terrifying colossus of a man with his black armour and murderous battle club, who is capable of fantastic feats. Nor was he a mere brainless bully: apart from his physical strength Benkei displayed humour, wisdom, and (as we can tell from his *tour de force* at Ataka barrier) an impressive erudition. For all his blustering violence, he was capable of much charm and even gentleness. Above all he was a paragon of loyalty, whose devotion to his

5.44   master became ever greater as the situation grew more desperate.

The relationship between the two men is reminiscent of the friendship between Sancho Panza and Don Quixote, the woebegone Spanish gentleman who is one of the full-fledged heroic failures in Western literature. In twelfth-century Japan, as in sixteenth-century Spain, the ineffectual, failure-prone knight is supported by a crude, resourceful companion with irrepressible spirits and gusto. And one of the most attractive aspects of both Yoshitsune and Don Quixote is the way in which each man accepts, even enjoys, the antics of his low-born retainer, knowing that underneath is a bedrock of strength and fidelity. There are other parallels between the roles of the two retainers and their masters. Both Sancho Panza and Benkei become increasingly important as their respective stories progress, and both grow steadily in stature. As Don Quixote's fantasies come to be more and more debilitating, his servant's earthy common sense changes into a mature wisdom; similarly, Benkei makes up for his master's increasing passivity and pessimism by revealing unex-

5.45   pected resources of intelligence and learning.

Another character who becomes prominent in the later legends and who also represents an ideal stereotype of loyalty and courage is Yoshitsune's favourite mistress, Shizuka, famous as the most beautiful woman in Japan and also as the greatest dancer of her time. Shizuka's legendary quality is emphasized by the supernatural power of her performances. In "The Chronicle of Yoshitsune" she dances in the presence of the Retired Emperor and miraculously ends the terrible drought that has afflicted the country for a hundred days. During Yoshitsune's downhill period, Shizuka clings with passionate devotion to her ill-starred lover and insists on accompanying him when he leaves the capi-

5.46   tal. In the Nō play, *Yoshino Shizuka* ("Shizuka at Yoshino"), when Yoshitsune is being pursued by Yoritomo's forces, Shizuka distracts the hostile soldiers by performing one of her magnificent dances and telling them about her lover's fine character. On this occasion she enables the hero to escape; but, after the disastrous shipwreck on the Inland Sea, Benkei insists that she will slow down their flight and must return to Kyoto. Yoshitsune, who has now entered his passive phase, is obliged to agree and the two lovers have an agonizing last farewell. Almost immediately after their separation Shizuka is betrayed by the men who were supposed to escort her to the capital.

She is arrested and sent to Kamakura. Here she is interrogated about her lover's whereabouts but staunchly refuses to betray him. When it is discovered that she is pregnant, the Lord of Kamakura decrees that any male child must be killed, since no potential heir of Yoshitsune's may be allowed to survive. Predictably enough, Shizuka gives birth to a baby boy. The infant is promptly seized and taken to the beach at Yuigahama, where his brains are dashed out against a rock. Later the distraught mother is asked to dance at the shrine of Hachiman, the god of war, in the presence of Yoritomo and his attendants. She complies with *5.47* the request, but only so that she may have the opportunity to challenge her enemies by improvising defiant love songs in Yoshitsune's praise. Despite this insult she is allowed to return to Kyoto on the following day. There the beautiful young girl cuts off her hair and becomes a nun. She dies in the following year at the age of twenty, unable to endure the sad burden of her worldly memories, and in due course she becomes established as the great romantic figure in the Yoshitsune cycle of legends. Though most of Shizuka's story is fictitious and though her role is always subordinate to her lover's, she may be regarded as the first (and one of the very few) of Japan's failed heroines. *5.48*

Apart from Benkei, Shizuka, and three other stalwart followers, Yoshitsune was almost entirely isolated during his fugitive period. Why should a leader who had acquired such immense popularity after his military victories suddenly become so feeble and abandoned? Since Yoshitsune's lack of support is the main reason for his spectacular collapse, this is an important question for understanding his heroic career. One fundamental weakness in Yoshitsune's position was that the military support he enjoyed during his victorious years depended entirely on his role as Yoritomo's deputy. The younger brother, being himself a vassal of the Lord of Kamakura, had no important feudal adherents of his own. The captains who fought with him in the battles against the Tairas were all basically loyal to Kamakura and, once it became clear that he had fallen foul of Yoritomo, they were not prepared to intercede on his behalf. When the break became open and Yoshitsune tried to recruit his own military supporters in the provinces, his efforts were hopeless. "The warriors of Ōmi Province would not join Yoshitsune," says a diary of the time. "... Though he hunted everywhere for samurai [supporters], few *5.49* agreed to help him."

Many of the samurai whom Yoshitsune tried to enlist probably sympathized with the young general, but being members of the Minamoto clan they recognized Yoritomo as their overlord and saw that Yoshitsune's prospects of success were far too slim to justify their turning against Kamakura. Not only were they reluctant to back a losing cause, but now after a prolonged period of disruption they were no doubt ready for the stability promised by Yoritomo's regime. As happens so often after years of strife and bloodshed, there appears to have been a decline in what Professor Gaston Bouthoul describes as *l'impulsion belliqueuse* and a general desire for peace and security, even among professional fighters. Much as some of his fellow warriors may have admired Yoshitsune for his courage, sincerity, and other personal qualities, they saw that his resistance to Kamakura would keep the country in turmoil, whereas a final victory for Yoritomo would consolidate an efficient military government that could finally restore order to the country and guarantee their own positions.

Apart from all this, Yoshitsune's quest for followers was hampered by his own impulsive, impractical, individualistic character. He totally lacked his brother's skill at manoeuvre and ability to use other people for his own purposes. Though a good leader of soldiers, he appears to have had little talent for getting along with his fellow commanders, and we know that many of Yoritomo's generals came to resent him. In other words, Yoshitsune was a hopeless politician, temperamentally incapable of the manipulation, cool planning, and compromise that are necessary for lasting worldly success. Consequently, when it came to a crisis, he could gain no support from captains with large bodies of men under their command, and had to depend on a small group of loyal followers, many of them mountain bandits, warrior-priests, and outlaw types, who were bound to him by strong personal connexions. One by one his supporters were brought to bay by the forces of Kamakura and tortured, killed, or driven to suicide, until Yoshitsune was left with only a pathetic handful of survivors. With this motley little band he reached his final refuge in the northeast.   5.50

On arrival in Ōshū, Yoshitsune was given shelter and promise of lasting support by Hidehira, the clan leader of the northern Fujiwaras, who had already befriended the hero in his youth when he was fleeing from the Tairas. Hidehira was the supreme   5.51 ruler of the north, and his autonomous territory of Ōshū may be regarded as the first major fief in Japanese history. Its strategic   5.52 position in a wild, remote region, where it was defended by an army of tough and disciplined fighters, had made it virtually impregnable, and now in 1187 it represented the last serious obstacle to the hegemony of Kamakura. Here Yoshitsune was securely installed in a new residence that Hidehira built for him between his own mansion and Koromo River.

As it turned out, the hero's decision to stay in Ōshū suited Yoritomo perfectly. First he demanded that Hidehira hand over the fugitive, but (as he had no doubt expected) his threats produced no effect on the doughty old chieftain. Then, on the pretext of "chastising" his rebellious brother, the Lord of Kamakura pressed the Court for an order to attack Ōshū. Even at this late stage, when Kyoto was thoroughly demoralized by the overpowering might of Kamakura, the Retired Emperor demurred before issuing the crucial edict. Meanwhile an event had taken place in Ōshū that helped Yoritomo in his plans and accelerated the hero's catastrophe. When Yoshitsune arrived to seek Hidehira's protection, the chieftain was already ninety-one years old (a fantastic age for the time), and only a few months later he died. His final command to his sons was that they continue to shelter Yoshitsune from the wrath of Kamakura. Presumably he knew how Yoritomo would take advantage of his death and wanted to forestall any betrayal of the youth he had agreed to shelter.

On hearing the fateful news Yoshitsune galloped frantically to Hidehira's house. The death of the old chieftain was not only a practical blow but an emotional disaster; for Yoshitsune was virtually an orphan and Hidehira had become a substitute for both father and brother. "The Chronicle of Yoshitsune" emphasizes his archetypal sense of isolation:

"Alas," declared Yoshitsune, "I should never have travelled this great distance had I not put all my trust in [Lord Hidehira]. I lost my father,

Yoshitomo, when I was only one year old. Though my mother remained in Kyoto, our relations became strained since she sided with the Tairas. I also had many brothers, but they were so widely scattered that I never saw them as a child. And [then] Yoritomo became my enemy. Ah, no

5.53 parting between parent and child could be sadder than this!"

On the day of the funeral Yoshitsune appeared at the burial grounds clad in the white clothes of mourning: "So great was his sorrow that he wished he might leave the world together with [Lord Hidehira]. There on the desolate moor Yoshitsune bid his last farewell; then he turned away, a solitary, pitiful figure."

The old chieftain's last fears turned out to have been fully justified. As soon as the news of his death reached Kamakura, Yoritomo saw his opportunity and sent a message promising to spare Ōshū on condition that his brother be handed over for

5.54 punishment. Yasuhira, the new chieftain of the northern Fujiwaras, blatantly ignored his father's wishes and decided that it would be foolish to continue alienating Kamakura for the sake of

5.55 a helpless fugitive. In the fourth month of 1189 he violated Yoshitsune's trust by ordering a surprise attack against his stronghold.

In the Battle of Koromo River, as it is somewhat euphemisti-

5.56 cally described, Yoshitsune and his small band of nine followers were confronted by an attacking force of some thirty thousand men. In such an unpromising situation the aim of the Japanese warrior is to sell his life as dearly as he can and to take the largest possible number of enemy officers with him to the next world. According to the legend, Yoshitsune's supporters acquitted themselves with fantastic courage and skill until one after another was killed or so seriously wounded that he had to commit suicide.

"The Chronicle of Yoshitsune" gives the most detailed version of the first part of the legend. As the fighting rages outside, the hero himself, ensconced in his stronghold with his wife and

5.57 two children, sits calmly intoning the scriptures. This may seem rather peculiar behaviour at such a juncture, but it agrees perfectly with the elegant, inactive role that is attributed to Yoshitsune during his last phase. He has reached the eighth book of the Lotus Sutra when Benkei rushes in and informs his master that only he and one other retainer remain alive. "Now that things have reached this pass," adds Benkei, "I wish to come and bid you

5.58 my last farewell." Yoshitsune replies that, though they long since

agreed to die together, this has now become impossible since he
cannot go outside and risk facing unworthy enemies. He there-   *5.59*
fore begs Benkei to return to the fray and hold off the attackers
a little longer lest some of the ruffians break in and intrude on
his suicide: "I have only a few more lines of the sutra to recite.
Protect me with your life until I have finished."   *5.60*

After a tearful exchange of poems Benkei strides out for his
last fight, which turns out to be the most coruscating display of
his career. His fellow retainer has finally succumbed and Benkei
must face the horde alone. He charges the enemy again and again
like one possessed, slaughtering them by the dozens, until no one
dares approach him. Then there is a lull as he stands in their
midst, a vast, solitary figure whose black armour is bristling with
the arrows that have been shot at him from all directions. His last
moments are reminiscent of El Cid's posthumous attack on
horseback:

"Look at that monk!" said one of the soldiers. "He keeps gazing over here
as if he's about to attack. And how strangely he smiles! Don't let us go
near him or he will surely kill us." They all kept their distance. Then
another of the men said, "I have heard that in the past heroes have died
while still on their feet. Someone should go up and take a look at him."
No one volunteered for the task, but just then a warrior happened to
gallop past. The wind from his horse caught Benkei, who had in fact
been dead for some time, and he crashed to the ground. He was still
grasping his halberd . . . and as he collapsed he seemed to lunge forward
with the weapon. "Look out! He's running wild again," cried the soldiers, retreating rapidly. . . . It was only after Benkei lay completely
motionless that the men rushed to his side in an absurd effort to reach
him first.   *5.61*

Meanwhile Benkei's delaying tactics have given his master
time to finish his recitation and prepare for his own death. Seated
in his Buddhist chapel, Yoshitsune turns to his wife's guardian,
a valiant warrior named Kanefusa, and asks him how he should
commit suicide. Kanefusa recommends the method used by
Tadanobu, one of Yoshitsune's staunchest retainers who had
killed himself in the capital in order to avoid capture. "People are
still praising him after all this time," explains Kanefusa. "Yes, it
is an acceptable method," says Yoshitsune. "I had better make a
wide wound." When it comes to the horrifying deed itself, he
shows no trace of hesitation or passivity. As in the careers of so

many Japanese heroes, this seems to be the great moment he has awaited, and one has the impression that the ritual has been carefully rehearsed. Having once made his decision, he produces a famous sword that was given to him as a lad by the abbot of Kurama Temple and that he has secreted under his armour ever since his campaigns against the Tairas.

Seizing the sword, Yoshitsune plunged it into his body below the left breast, thrusting it in so far that the blade almost emerged through his back. Then he cut deeply into his stomach and, tearing the wound wide open in three directions, pulled out his intestines. He wiped the sword on the sleeve of his robe, which he then draped over his shoulders, and *5.62* leant the upper part of his body on an arm-rest. . . .

Though still alive, the hero is now immobile, and the agonizing task of killing Yoshitsune's wife, his son, and his seven-day-old daughter is left to the unfortunate Kanefusa, who hesitates at *5.63* first but is urged on by his mistress. Surrounded by the inert bodies, he staggers to his feet, intoning a prayer to Amida Buddha.

Yoshitsune was still breathing and now, opening his eyes, he asked about his wife. "She lies dead by your side, my Lord," replied Kanefusa. Yoshitsune stretched out his hand. "And who is this?" he said. "Is it the boy?" He reached over the child and touched his wife's body. At the sight Kanefusa was pierced with grief. "Quickly now," said his master, *5.64* "burn down the house!"

These were Yoshitsune's last words. He expired in his chapel at the age of thirty—precisely the age at which Japan's prototypal *5.65* hero, the Brave of Yamato, had died on the Plain of Nobo. As soon as Kanefusa saw that his master was dead, he set fire to the entire stronghold in grand Wagnerian style, and then completed his own career by running into the flames, dragging one of the enemy generals with him to his death.

The events immediately following Yoshitsune's death are unclear, but it appears that Yasuhira's men managed to recover the hero's corpse before it was destroyed by the flames and that he was posthumously beheaded. Yasuhira immediately informed Yoritomo that he had carried out his part of the bargain, and a messenger was despatched to Kamakura carrying a black lacquer

box in which the hero's severed head was preserved in sweet rice
wine for official inspection and identification. In the middle of   *5.66*
the Sixth Month the messenger reached the posting-station of
Koshigoe, the very place where Yoshitsune had written his last
pathetic letter to his brother, and here the grisly trophy was
examined by an official inspection party, which included the
hero's old enemy, Kajiwara no Kagetoki. It is said that even this
hardhearted villain was so overcome by emotion on seeing the
severed head that he was obliged to turn away and that other
members of the party (all military men) were reduced to tears.

The head in the black box was identified as being Yoshitsune's, and this was duly reported to Yoritomo. Here the matter   *5.67*
of his death was allowed to rest until in later centuries the hero's
growing popularity led to the fabrication of several bizarre survival theories. It was suggested that a false head had been substituted in the box to deceive the inspection party and that Yoshitsune himself had managed to escape from his burning
mansion and fly to the north. According to a legend that grew up   *5.68*
in the Tokugawa period, when there was particular interest in
the development of Hokkaido, the hero fled to the northern island, where he led a campaign against the enemies of the local
Ainus; they gratefully chose him as their leader and he ruled over
them benevolently. Another survival story is that Yoshitsune fled   *5.69*
from Ōshū and travelled north through Hokkaido and the island
of Sakhalin, eventually reaching Mongolia where he started a
new career as Genghis Khan. This theory, concocted in the late
Meiji period, was no doubt related to current Japanese ambitions
in northern Asia. If Genghis Khan was indeed a thirteenth-century Minamoto warrior, the Japanese could claim an impressive
precedent for their expansion on the continent. Proponents of
the theory stress the agreement in dates and the facts that both
warriors were renowned horsemen and skilled in attack; they
also note that Minamoto no Yoshitsune's name can be read "Gen-
gikei," which is indeed close to "Genghis Khan." Unfortunately
the circumstances that do *not* fit are somewhat more numerous
and persuasive. Still another theory is that Yoshitsune crossed to
China and became the ancestor of the Manchu Dynasty. These   *5.70*
stories about Yoshitsune's later life reflect profound folkloric
impulses and also have an undeniable charm; but they were never
accepted as part of the main legend, whose central theme is that

the hero, far from surviving or succeeding, is fated by his sincerity and lack of political acumen to die at an early age as a glorious failure.

Out of this mixture of fact, half-fact, and legend, what is one to make of the actual characters and historical roles of Yoshitsune and his elder brother? From what is known of the objective circumstances it seems clear enough that Yoshitsune's downfall was propelled by certain tragic flaws in his own nature which not only made a clash with Yoritomo inevitable but ensured that in any such encounter he would be the loser. From his wild childhood years in the mountains of Kurama he seems to have developed as a high-spirited, impetuous, headstrong young man with little respect for established order and authority. The accounts describing the dynamic part of his career before he lapsed into the elegant passivity of the later legends suggest that he could be blunt, irascible, and tactless in his dealings with fellow commanders. In battle he was brave and resourceful; but he insisted on taking the lead and on doing everything in his own way, leaving little possibility of glory for the other generals. His remarkable record of military success made him overconfident and unwilling to accept advice; and, though he never openly questioned the authority of Kamakura, he tended to exceed his instructions and to act with a degree of independence that was *5.71* bound to infuriate the authoritarian Yoritomo. If he had faithfully submitted himself to instructions like his lacklustre brother Noriyori, he could never have been a hero but he would undoubtedly have enjoyed a longer and more successful career. As it was, he became a perfect exemplar of the old Japanese adage about the dangers of individualism: "The nail that sticks out is knocked on the head."

Yoshitsune had a warm, spontaneous nature, which is said to explain much of his popularity among ladies and courtiers in the capital and among priests in the mountain temples. Having been deprived of parental guidance and affection as a child, he evidently hoped for a close relationship with his elder brother; but in the end these aspirations were betrayed and he had to turn for support to the old Fujiwara chieftain, Hidehira, whose death therefore came as a culminating blow. Affectionate, trusting, naïve, and pure, Yoshitsune was temperamentally incapable of the realistic calculation and planning that are necessary for mundane success, and he was no match for manipulators like Yukiie, the Retired Emperor, Kajiwara, and (above all) the Lord of Kamakura. Yoshitsune's impracticality and political innocence were disastrous weaknesses that led to his downfall; but from a Japanese point of view they count among his most admirable qualities, being natural concomitants of the sincerity *(makoto)* that denotes the true hero.

Considering his vast prestige through the centuries, Yoshitsune's historical accomplishments are modest. It is true that the decisiveness and speed of his military manoeuvres greatly accelerated the defeat of the Tairas; but by 1184 the balance of force in the country was such that a final Minamoto victory was certain with or without Yoshitsune's contributions. Ironically enough, the hero's main historical role was that he helped establish Yoritomo's hegemony. First and most obviously, he and other Minamoto relatives conducted Yoritomo's military campaigns against his troublesome cousin, Yoshinaka, and then against the Tairas. This allowed Yoritomo himself to remain safely in 5.72 Kamakura and consolidate his control over the east.

After the Tairas had been destroyed, Yoshitsune was no longer needed for his military talents but acquired a new usefulness by becoming a fugitive and official enemy of the Court. The great manhunt provided Yoritomo with an ideal pretext to extend his control over large parts of Japan beyond the eastern provinces. By representing Yoshitsune as a dangerous rebel whose prompt capture was essential for restoring order in the country, the Lord of Kamakura forced the Court to agree to a national levy in the form of a rice tax, which ostensibly was to pay for the campaign. He also imposed a system of appointing Minamoto constables and stewards to represent the authority of Kamakura in different regions and to supervise the great manorial estates that produced the main wealth of the country. These measures mark the real beginning of feudalization and were infinitely more important in Japanese history than the hunt for a single doomed fugitive.

The prolonged search for his brother also allowed Yoritomo to find out who were his real friends at Court, in the temples, and elsewhere. Members of the nobility who had supported Yoshitsune were dismissed from their posts and sometimes banished, and the Imperial Government in the capital was reorganized on lines favourable to Kamakura. All this was part of what Yoritomo himself rather grandiloquently described as "the beginning of the country" *(tenka no sōsō)*, in other words, a new order for Japan. The hero's final service was to take refuge with the northern Fujiwaras and thus give Yoritomo the pretext he needed for eliminating his last potential opponents and for incorporating the vast Ōshū territories into his own domains.

5.73

Already during his residence in the capital Yoshitsune became the victim of political intrigue by the Retired Emperor, who tried to play him off against Yoritomo. It is now evident that at each stage of his career he was used to further the aims of the brother who eventually destroyed him. But again, this very innocence and victimization, far from diminishing Yoshitsune's stature, only add to his heroic poignancy.

In contrast to his unfortunate young brother, whose main practical contribution was the way in which he was exploited by others, Yoritomo established himself as one of the truly creative leaders in Japanese history, who put together new systems of administration, law, and discipline that largely superseded those in force during the past many centuries. Though the old civilian government in Kyoto, deriving its mandate from the prestige of the imperial family, theoretically continued to be the supreme authority in the land, the Minamoto centre in Kamakura, which Yoritomo had originally established as a purely military headquarters, became the second centre in the land and the source of all real power. From the outset of the uprising against the Tairas in 1180, Yoritomo concentrated on politics and administration, directing everything from his distant eastern base and never leading an army. Finally in 1192, when his regime had been consolidated and he was the undisputed political master of the country, he chose the title of Shogun, or Generalissimo. This was a relatively low rank in the Court hierarchy, but it ensured his control of the all-important warrior class. Though actual military rule did not remain long with Yoritomo's immediate family, the shogunal form of government that he created in the late twelfth century continued in one form or another for almost seven hundred years.

5.74

Though Yoritomo is recognized by historians as one of Japan's most influential statesmen, his role in the legend (and in the numerous plays and other literary works derived from it) is one of almost unmitigated villainy; for here he is cast as the "successful survivor," whose machinations cause the downfall of the lovable, pathetic hero. While the gallant Yoshitsune and his little band of followers occupy the centre of the stage, the Lord of Kamakura lurks in the wings, a coldblooded, heartless man obsessed with hatred of his enemies and lust for personal power. After the defeat of the Tairas he is said to have ordered that the young children of the enemy clan be drowned or buried alive and the older ones stabbed or strangled. We are told that even some of his tough eastern captains hesitated to carry out these hideous commands, yet that finally they had no alternative but to obey. Then, according to the legend, Yoritomo's cruel, jealous nature made him turn against the popular young hero, Yoshitsune, and hound him to his death. In actual fact the Lord of Kamakura had sound reason to resent his insubordinate brother as a source of continued disunity and confusion in the country; but in the legendary version he is inspired entirely by envy and vindictiveness.

Yoshitsune, on the other hand, lives securely in people's imaginations as the ideal Japanese hero whose person and career, especially as developed in the legend, embody almost every characteristic that appeals to the national sensibility. In battle he was imaginative and daring, in private life spontaneous, trusting, and sincere. But above all he was loved for his misfortune and defeat. A peculiarly Japanese type of pathos marks his career from the time of his early youth when he wandered alone through the streets playing his melancholy flute until his last years as a 5.75 hunted fugitive, the innocent victim of men more powerful, realistic, and cunning than himself, abandoned by everyone but a handful of outlaw followers, and finally betrayed and forced to kill himself at an early age. Yoshitsune's brilliant success during his fighting years was a prerequisite for his greatness, since it made the subsequent collapse all the more impressive and poignant. As Japan's quintessential hero, he maintained his prestige through the centuries by the nature of his tragic failure, which established his name as a byword for emotional identification with the loser.

"Seven Lives for the Nation"

Yoshitsune, for all his military achievements, is endowed with the pale, delicate lineaments of a young aristocrat, and in dramatic representations the victor of Ichinotani, Dannoura, and other epic battles is actually portrayed as a woman. No such echoes of the elegant world of  Heian can be detected in the robustious, swashbuckling hero from the wilds of Mount Kongō, who delighted in action and ruses and risks, who disdained melancholy and despair, and who (in legend if not in history) towers above his contemporaries at the end of the Kamakura period.

Now, one and a half centuries after the establishment of a military regime in Kamakura, the samurai ethos had spread throughout Japan and had come to dominate the contemporary imagination. While Minamoto no Yoshitsune and Kusunoki Masashige both failed with noble grandeur and stand out as the two most evocative heroes in mediaeval history, the differences in their personalities and styles of life as depicted in the respective legends indicate what immense changes had affected the Japanese sensibility during this first long era of military rule.

Masashige, the paragon of failed loyalist martyrs, is often depicted beneath his fluttering war banner by Minato River near the coast of the Inland Sea. Seated on a folding chair, he wears the elaborate panoply of a fourteenth-century samurai, and there is a look of desperate determination on his face. Nearby a great drum is being beaten to summon his followers for the decisive 6.1 battle against the Emperor's enemies.

The Battle of Minato River, a fierce, seven-hour engagement fought in 1333 on the site of the present-day city of Kobe, was a turning point in mediaeval history and its repercussions lasted for centuries. In almost any other country the hero of such an engagement would be the brave conqueror who led his troops to glory and who, though he himself might be killed on the field of honour, would have secured victory for his cause. Being Japanese, however, the hero unerringly chose the losing side. Masashige anticipated that Minato River would be a disaster, and he was correct. The battle resulted in failure for Masashige and for everything he had supported; and to avoid the humiliation of capture he was obliged to commit harakiri in a nearby farmhouse.

This defeat and this death ensured Masashige's lasting popularity as a national hero. Some three centuries after the catastrophe, Tokugawa Mitsukuni, a cousin of the ruling Shogun and an eminent nationalist scholar, visited the site of the battlefield at Minato River, and on the hero's reputed burial-place he planted a marker with a simple inscription conveying his sense of loss and poignancy: "Ah, here lies Kusunoki, the [Emperor's] loyal subject!" Masashige's prestige reached new heights *6.2* during the nineteenth century. In 1872 an important Shinto shrine was erected on the site of the farmhouse where he is believed to have killed himself; and there the defeated hero is worshipped as the supreme exemplar of devotion to the imperial dynasty.

Predictably enough, Ashikaga Takauji, the victor of Minato River, who successfully founded a new shogunate and who by any objective standards must be ranked as one of the truly creative men of his time, was vilified by later generations and his name became a byword for treachery. During the Restoration period statues of him in Kyoto were decapitated by loyalist warriors, and in the 1930s a cabinet minister was actually obliged to resign from the government because he had written a pro-Takauji article in a magazine. Such are the posthumous rewards *6.3* of failure and the perils of success in Japan.

When Kusunoki Masashige was born towards the end of the thirteenth century, the centre of real power in Japan was still the eastern capital of Kamakura, where Minamoto no Yoritomo had established his headquarters one century earlier and organized the first Bakufu (military government) in the country's history.

Actual control, however, had long since passed from the Minamotos to the Hōjōs, a relatively obscure warrior family, who efficiently consolidated the system that Yoritomo had improvised with such brilliance in the twelfth century. During their generations of rule the Hōjōs, though noted for frugal ways and high standards of probity, which contrasted with the opulence and aesthetic hedonism of the ruling class in earlier centuries, managed to accumulate immense wealth and personal power. Inevitably this led to resentment among less favoured members of the warrior class and also among the aristocracy in Kyoto, whose fortunes had steadily waned as those of Kamakura rose.

The Mongol invasions in the late thirteenth century culminated in a sensational victory for Japan but imposed a serious
6.4 strain on the Bakufu. The defeated invaders left no booty with which Kamakura might reward its warriors, and the need for continued preparations in case of a further attack involved expenses that gravely weakened the military government. Such compensation as could be provided was random and inadequate. Japanese mediaeval samurai, for all their protestations about selfless, disinterested service, usually fought in the knowledge that their sacrifices and valour would be noted by their overlords and duly rewarded in the form of land grants or other material advantages. Any failure to bestow such rewards or any inequity in the
6.5 distribution was bitterly resented. Discontent with the Bakufu spread widely among the warriors, many of whom were in straitened circumstances, and there was growing unrest in the provinces. The Hōjōs, who had originally established themselves as paragons of integrity, were now charged with corruption and unjust authoritarianism. Though still firmly in control, they no
6.6 longer enjoyed the overwhelming support of the warrior class.

The doubts and dissatisfactions about Hōjō rule came to a head early in the fourteenth century. As so often in Japanese history, the immediate issue was a succession dispute. The imperial family, though long since bereft of all practical power, was still the unchallenged source of legitimacy for warriors and aristocrats alike. Although the Court's financial difficulties had made it necessary to abandon the Imperial Palace itself, the military government still based its ultimate authority on imperial commissions given to successive shoguns. Since Kamakura was inevitably involved in difficulties concerning the imperial succession, the Hōjōs did their best to prevent rifts that might lead to the creation of a hostile faction at Court. In this objective they failed. The death of the Retired Emperor Gosaga in 1272 led to the fiercest succession dispute in the country's history, and by the time it was resolved, more than a century later, the Hōjōs had long since been toppled from power, Japanese feudalism had undergone fundamental changes, and the government was in the hands of a new dynasty of military rulers.

Gosaga's two sons, who followed him in turn as titular emperors, became the ancestors of two lines of imperial succession, the Senior and the Junior, each having its own influential supporters at Court. In 1300 it was decided that representatives of these lines would occupy the Throne in alternate succession. *6.7* This peculiar system, which was accepted by Kamakura as the best way to avoid civil disruption, was reasonably successful during the seven short reigns that followed Gosaga's demise; but there was always the danger that some ambitious, refractory emperor might try to disrupt the arrangement by passing the succession to his own son rather than to a cousin from the other line. Such an emperor emerged in the person of Godaigo, a member of the Junior Line, who was determined not only to acquire a degree of independent power that had long since lapsed from the reigning sovereigns but to bequeath such power to his son in disregard of Gosaga's will and of Kamakura's policy. In pursuing these aims Godaigo was ready to mobilize the growing sentiment against the Bakufu and to take advantage of its many economic difficulties.

Most of the recent emperors had been children or youths at the time of their accession, and usually they were still in their teens or twenties when the Hōjōs obliged them to abdicate. *6.8* Godaigo, however, was in his early thirties on his accession to the Throne in 1318, and he soon established himself as the first Emperor to reign personally in more than two centuries. *6.9*

In textbooks and historical writings Godaigo, the ninety-sixth sovereign of Japan, has traditionally been pictured as a "good thing"; and during the nationalist period until 1945 any attempt to denigrate this unfortunate monarch would have been regarded as a breach of patriotism and good taste. Even to this day texts used in history classes reflect a pro-Godaigo bias, and it is generally assumed that he was the victim of unfortunate events and disloyal subjects rather than the foolish perpetrator of his own mistakes. Any objective study of his career, however, detracts from the traditional image and points up the confused and rather inglorious nature of his role. It is true that Godaigo was a man of independent spirit, that he had the originality and assertiveness to promote people of talent in disregard of hierarchical considerations, that he was a serious scholar with a deep interest in Sung Confucianism and its applicability to affairs of state—and also that he was a good poet. His salient characteristics, however, were stubbornness and vanity. He was a proud, arrogant ruler who would let nothing stand in his way, yet who, for all his intelligence and learning, pursued his ambitions with a remarkable lack of realism. He had all the cunning and callousness of his imperial ancestor, Goshirakawa, but little of his political acumen. What more suitable type of emperor could a Japanese hero have chosen to support?

6.10

From early in his career Godaigo deliberately set himself up against the hegemony of the Kamakura government, and as time passed he became more and more determined to challenge the military upstarts in the east and eventually to reassert the prestige and power of the reigning sovereign. To designate his momentous reign he chose the name Godaigo ("Daigo the Second") in memory of the Heian Emperor who had resisted the encroachments of the Fujiwara family some four centuries earlier.

6.11

If Godaigo was to remain Emperor beyond the usual brief period and to pass the Throne to a son who could pursue his objectives, it was essential to break away from the policy of early abdication and alternate succession. Since the Bakufu categorically refused the request that Godaigo's son (rather than a Prince of the Senior Line) be designated as Crown Prince, and since no Crown Prince could be appointed without the sanction of Kamakura, it was clear that, if the Emperor was to realize his guiding ambitions, the Hōjō regime would sooner or later have to be destroyed.

A plot to overthrow the "eastern savages" was being hatched in Kyoto as early as 1324 by an anti-Bakufu group with the rather improbable name of the Free and Easy Society. Godaigo was almost certainly privy to the conspiracy. During the following years he entered into secret anti-Bakufu negotiations with some of the large Buddhist temples and certain dissident members of the warrior class. Before he could carry out any of his plans, however, his manoeuvres were treacherously revealed to

6.12

Kamakura by one of his most trusted advisers. Threatened with *6.13*
persecution by the Bakufu authorities, Godaigo rather inglori-
ously quit the capital in 1331. He escaped to the mountainous
region west of Nara, where he took refuge in a monastery at the
summit of Mount Kasagi, a picturesque eminence which from a
height of some nine hundred feet overlooks the magnificent val-
ley of Kizu River. Here he was given protection by soldier-monks *6.14*
who did their best to prepare for the mighty attack that was
bound to come from Kamakura.

The Emperor was in serious difficulties, since he had no
troops of his own and since none of the local warriors who joined
him commanded any significant bodies of men. It was at this
critical juncture that Godaigo had the famous dream which inspired him to recruit Kusunoki Masashige to his side and eventually led to his restoration. Gravely concerned about how he will *6.15*
resist the onslaught of the Bakufu, the Emperor dozes off and
dreams that he is back in the courtyard of his palace in Kyoto.

His Majesty saw a huge evergreen tree with dense foliage and with
branches stretching out in rich profusion towards the south. Beneath the
tree were the Three Great Ministers and all the other high officials, each
seated according to his rank. The chief seat faced south and was piled
high with mats, but there was still no one sitting on it. "For whom can *6.16*
this seat have been prepared?" wondered the Emperor as he stood there
in his dream. Suddenly two children appeared with their hair divided
and braided on both sides. Kneeling before His Majesty, they wept into
their sleeves and said, "There is no place in the entire land where Your
Majesty may hide even for a short time. Yet beneath that tree there is
a seat facing south. This is an imperial throne that has been prepared
for you. Pray sit there for a while!" The Emperor then saw the children
ascend into the sky and disappear, and immediately he awoke.

It occurred to His Majesty that some heavenly announcement was
being conveyed to him in the dream. He considered it carefully and
realized that if one placed the character for "south" (南) next to the one
for tree (木) it produced "camphor tree" or *kusunoki* (楠). "When those
two children asked me to sit under the tree facing south," thought the
Emperor, "it must have been a sign from the Bodhisattvas Nikkō and
Gakkō telling me that I shall once again have authority over this realm
and rule its people." Such was the auspicious interpretation that the *6.17*
Emperor put on his own dream. *6.18*

In the morning His Majesty summoned the Master of Discipline,
a priest of Kasagi Temple by the name of Jōjubō, and asked him whether
there was any warrior called Kusunoki in those parts. "I have heard of

nobody near here with such a surname," replied the priest, "but west
of Mount Kongō in the province of Kawachi there is indeed a renowned
warrior called Kusunoki Tamon Masashige of the Middle Palace
6.19   Guards. He traces his line back to . . . the Minister of the Left, Lord
6.20   Tachibana no Moroe, a descendant in the fourth generation of Emperor
Bidatsu, but his ancestors left the capital a long time ago and settled in
the provinces. It is said that when his mother was young she made a
hundred-day retreat to Bishamon Temple on Mount Shigi and that there
she dreamt of the son who was later born to her and who was therefore
6.21   given the childhood name of Tamon."

The Emperor understood that it must be this man who had been
announced to him in his dream and he ordered his attendants to summon Kusunoki Masashige at once. . . . When the imperial messenger
arrived at Kusunoki's stronghold and transmitted the Emperor's summons, Masashige realized that this was the supreme honour that could
be given to a warrior and, without considering the advantages or disad-
6.22   vantages, he immediately set out in secret for Kasagi.

His Majesty addressed Masashige through [Lord Fujifusa]: "Having
decided to rely on you in order to subdue the eastern barbarians, we sent
a messenger to summon you here, and it pleases us greatly that you so
promptly responded to our call. Tell us now what plan you can devise
so that we may start bringing the country together under our control!
How may we win a swift victory and extend the great peace to the four
seas? Speak freely and explain whatever ideas you may have!"

Then Masashige respectfully replied to the Emperor: "Of late the
eastern barbarians have incurred the censure of heaven for their rebel-
6.23   lious ways. Now the time has come to take advantage of their weaknesses
and visit them with heaven's punishment. This will be no difficult task.
Yet to bring the realm under Your Majesty's control will require artifice
as well as military force. If we merely pit strength against strength, it
will be hard to secure victory even if the soldiers of your entire realm
6.24   are matched against just Musashi and Sagami provinces. But if our
battles are guided by skilful stratagems, the eastern barbarians will be
easily deceived and we shall have nothing to fear, for their strength
consists merely in smashing sharp blades and crushing heavy armour.
In warfare we can never tell the outcome of each battle, and Your
6.25   Majesty must not attach importance to any single engagement. But so
long as you hear that Masashige still lives, be confident that your sacred
cause will prevail!"

Having spoken in these confident tones, Masashige returned home
to Kawachi.

This speech, like most of what we know about the hero, is
part of the legend that was elaborated in later years to glorify his

career. There is ample historical evidence, however, that at this point in Godaigo's career, when things seemed almost totally hopeless, he was joined by a man called Kusunoki Masashige, who for one reason or another decided to devote himself whole-heartedly to the imperial cause. Godaigo appears to have put absolute trust in his new supporter as the man who could take the lead in salvaging the loyalist cause.

Who was this mysterious fighter whose brief career established him as the greatest hero of his turbulent age? Our information is scanty. Indeed no famous character in all Japanese history is quite as obscure as Kusunoki Masashige. Dogged efforts by generations of scholars and present-day specialists have still not determined his origins; writings on the subject are full of such cautious formulae as "There may possibly be a shade of truth in this account." Masashige, like Yoshitsune, is more a creature of *6.26* legend than of history; and in his case too we have verifiable data for a mere five years—from 1331, when he first joined Godaigo, until 1336, when he committed suicide. Much that is known about Masashige is invention—that unconscious process of creating fiction which informs the psychology of hero worship more than any historical facts. *6.27*

Masashige started life auspiciously after his mother was told about his birth in a dream during a visit to a Buddhist temple. *6.28* He was generally regarded as descending from the Tachibanas, who had imperial antecedents, and his family claimed that their ancestor was Moroe, the eminent eighth-century statesman. A *6.29* copy of the Lotus Sutra, which is proudly preserved in Minato River Shrine, has an inscription signed "Lord Tachibana Masashige." This is said to be in the hero's own hand, and the writing may well be authentic. Yet the document proves nothing, since successful warriors of the time frequently claimed aristocratic descent in order to enhance their prestige and to justify the rank and other honours that they received at Court. *6.30*

About the Kusunokis themselves there is no positive knowledge. Since they fail to appear in any of the numerous genealogies of the time, they were clearly not one of the important warrior families, nor can they have belonged to the Kyoto nobility. Masashige's father was an obscure provincial known as *6.31* "Kusunoki, the Lay Priest of Kawachi," who, despite his priestly cognomen, was at one time reported to be involved in local rowdyism including raids on nearby properties. Tradition sug- *6.32* gests that (like Yoshitsune) Masashige was educated in a temple. Until the age of fifteen he is said to have been a student-acolyte in a Shingon (Esoteric) monastery in Yamato Province. Here he became a serious scholar and (again like Yoshitsune) evinced particular interest in martial arts. On one occasion he borrowed a rare Chinese treatise on strategy and from its thirty tomes acquired such erudition that the superior of his temple, in a rather un-Buddhist access of fear, jealousy, and pique, attempted to have him assassinated in the neighbouring woods.

The vacuum of knowledge about Masashige's career until the age of thirty-seven is filled by many theories. It has been surmised that he was a scholarly member of the well-to-do provincial gentry who spent most of his life in Kawachi, either supervising his own acres or serving as overseer in some other manorial estate or as a tenant of Crown property. One bizarre theory is that Masashige had commercial connexions and that he travelled about the country purveying (of all things for a samurai hero!) red mercuric sulphide, or cinnabar. The most plausible set of suggestives, however, is that his military studies as a youth led him to become a professional warrior; having established a reputation for courage and ingenuity, he served as a retainer, either to the Bakufu in Kamakura or to the imperial family in Kyoto or to one of the great temples nearby.

From what is known of Masashige's temperament and later guerrilla activities, it appears that if he was indeed a professional warrior, he did not serve as the vassal of any specific overlord but functioned more or less independently, maintaining his headquarters in some stronghold in the mountainous region of Kawachi Province where he was supported by a small band of followers, who no doubt were more like armed bandits than soldiers. This accords with many postwar writings about Masashige 6.33   which describe him, rather disrespectfully, as an *akuto*. The word is best translated here as "outlaw" or "swashbuckler" and suggests the type of independent, outrageous samurai that is familiar to cinema-goers from the roles of Mifune Toshirō.

Among the first documentary references to Masashige is a report dated 1332 in which "the *akuto* Kusunoki, Lieutenant of the Middle Palace Guards" is accused of having broken into a certain 6.34   imperial estate where he committed acts of violence. This incident, though important as one of the earliest verifiable facts in his life, is judiciously omitted from most prewar accounts. Though details are scarce, there seems to be good evidence that Masashige and his armed followers occasionally indulged in the type of estate-raiding for which his father, "the Lay Priest of Kawachi," made a reputation and which had perhaps become something of a tradition in the Kusunoki family. "The Pellucid Mirror" (*Masukagami*), a famous history of the period, presents the hero as a bold, independent, loyalist warrior based in the mountainous region of Kawachi:

There was a man called Kusunoki Masashige, Lieutenant of the Middle Palace Guards, upon whom His Majesty relied from the very outset of these events. Bold and stalwart by nature, he elaborately fortified his own stronghold in the province of Kawachi [so that] in case His Majesty's present headquarters [Mount Kasagi] should become too dangerous he would be able to proceed there [for safety].   6.35

Shortly after the Emperor's flight from the capital, Bakufu forces attacked his refuge on Mount Kasagi and captured it without much difficulty. Godaigo escaped from the beleaguered monastery and fled towards Kawachi, presumably in the hope of reaching Masashige's stronghold near Mount Kongō. He was accompanied by a handful of high-ranking noblemen, with whom he exchanged dolorous verses about the hardships of the journey and the sorrows of his lot. Rather typically the little party of courtiers managed to lose its way, and before long the Emperor was caught and escorted back to the capital as a prisoner of the Bakufu. At the time of Godaigo's capture his hair was in disorder (an appalling humiliation for any member of the aristocracy, let alone an Emperor) and he was wearing a simple hempen robe. "The Chronicle of the Great Peace" comments   6.36
elegiacally on Godaigo's return:

As the imperial party was hurriedly escorted east along the Seventh Avenue and north along the bank of the river on its way to Rokuhara, all those who saw shed tears and those who heard felt pain in their hearts. Alas, how sorrowful! Only yesterday His Majesty was seated high on the imperial dais . . . surrounded by his hundred officials all attired in their ceremonial robes; today he has descended into the rude, reed-thatched dwelling of the eastern barbarians and is wretchedly exposed to the stern gaze of the myriad men of war who guard him. . . . Just like a dream [is the life of man].   6.37

With the troublesome Emperor safely in their custody, the military authorities hastened to depose him and to place a member of the Senior Line on the Throne. This was Emperor Kōgon, to whom Godaigo was now obliged to cede the imperial regalia. The Bakufu, though always pictured as the villains of the piece, were in fact acting in accord with precedence and complying with the rule of alternate succession that Godaigo had so blatantly flouted. As if to emphasize the correctness of their procedure, they concurrently approved a member of the Junior Line as Crown Prince who would in due course succeed Emperor Kōgon on the Throne.

Godaigo's fortunes had reached their nadir. His attempted coup against the military had miscarried, and the Bakufu now decided to relegate him to a place where he could do no further mischief. In the Third Month of 1332 he was banished to a small volcanic island some fifty miles off the rough coast of the Japan Sea. On the journey to his place of exile Godaigo is said to have been impressed by the evidence of friendly feelings towards himself and hostility against his military captors. This may well have strengthened his belief that the Bakufu regime was insecure and that before long he might make a comeback. Despite his defeat Godaigo obdurately refused the suggestion that he retire from the world and become a monk.

At this point in the story the illustrious warrior Kojima Takanori first makes his appearance. Kojima, a loyalist chieftain from the province of Bizen, had become discouraged after hearing about the fall of Mount Kasagi. When he learnt about Godaigo's exile, however, he gathered his followers and decided to stage a desperate last attempt to rescue the Emperor at the border of Bizen Province. Unfortunately for Kojima the route of the imperial party was changed, and by the time he and his men reached the correct highway it was far too late. Nothing daunted, Kojima later crept into the courtyard of the house where Godaigo was spending the night under heavy guard, and on the side of a large cherry tree he carved a poem in bold characters. It was based on an erudite reference to Chinese history and cryptically assured the Emperor of his undying devotion. The ignorant eastern guards were unable to understand the carving, but Godaigo himself immediately recognized the allusion and was delighted to realize that he still had such staunch (and cultured) supporters in the country. Kojima frequently reappears in

later chapters of "The Chronicle of the Great Peace" as a brave
warrior who, until his final defeat and death, persevered in the
hopeless struggle for the loyalist cause.   *6.41*

The Bakufu victory at Mount Kasagi and the capture of the
Emperor left Kusunoki Masashige almost entirely alone to carry
on the fight against Kamakura, and he rose gloriously to the
occasion. Having managed to escape from the fastness of Kasagi,
he circulated a rumour that he had committed suicide to avoid
capture. This was a ruse that he used several times during his
fighting career to put the enemy off his track. Disappearing from
view for a while, he reemerged after Godaigo's exile and
launched a campaign of sporadic guerrilla raids against Bakufu
forces in the Kawachi-Yamato region south of the capital. Many
of his sorties in 1332 were carried out in cooperation with Prince
Morinaga, one of Godaigo's young sons, who proved to be a
remarkably effective guerrilla fighter and whose imperial name
added lustre to Masashige's company. During this campaign
Masashige probably had no more than about a hundred followers; yet because of skilful surprise tactics, detailed knowledge of   *6.42*
the mountainous terrain, and support from local warriors, he was
able to score successes against thousands of organized and well-
armed Kamakura troops. Owing to the vast numerical discrepancy, Masashige had to avoid pitched battles and other conventional engagements and to depend on hit-and-run raids carried
out from fortified positions in the hills and mountains—a type of
fighting that was no doubt familiar from earlier days when he
and his followers took part in attacks of a less legitimate nature.   *6.43*

Though this guerrilla campaign inflicted no serious damage
on the enemy forces, it was effective in giving new hope to the
Emperor's sympathizers at a time when loyalist fortunes were
dim: the small-scale successes of Masashige and his irregulars
showed that, even though the Emperor was now a helpless prisoner in exile, his cause was still alive. The Bakufu itself clearly
took the threat seriously, for in the end they sent a large army
to deal with Masashige and his elusive band of followers. At the *6.44*
same time Kamakura somewhat contemptuously offered a reward of rice land to anyone, regardless of rank, who could prove
that he had killed either Masashige or Prince Morinaga.   *6.45*

Meanwhile Masashige, encouraged by the success of his
forays, was shifting to more ambitious tactics. To resist the growing pressure from Kamakura he decided to raise a small loyalist

army in the region of Akasaka west of Mount Kongō. The fighting between the loyalist troops and the army from Kamakura was mainly concentrated on Masashige's stronghold in Akasaka, which became the centre of a network of small fortresses that he established in the area of Mount Kongō.

In these and subsequent engagements the loyalist forces were always absurdly small in comparison with the attackers. During the fighting at Akasaka Castle (as it was rather grandiloquently called), Masashige probably had no more than a thousand followers while the Bakufu army numbered over ten thousand.

According to the famous account of the Battle of Akasaka Castle in "The Chronicle of the Great Peace," the attackers from Kamakura were shocked and even disappointed when they approached Masashige's position and saw the pathetic nature of his defences. Having arrived too late for the capture of Mount Kasagi, they had hoped to find a worthy (and profitable) opponent in the hills of Akasaka.

After crossing the Plain of Ishikawa River, the soldiers got their [first] sight of [Kusunoki Masashige's] castle. It looked as if it had been built in a hurry. There was no proper moat; and the fortifications, which were less than two hundred yards in circumference and contained only about two dozen hastily constructed towers, were surrounded by a single wooden wall. Looking at the castle, the soldiers thought, "Ah, what a pathetic enemy! One could pick up that castle of theirs in a single hand and throw it on the ground. Let us hope that somehow Masashige manages to hold out for at least a day so that there will be time to capture some booty and win honour that will bring us future rewards!"

Thereupon . . . the attacking forces approached the fortifications and, after dismounting, jumped into the ditch and gathered below the towers, each man hoping to lead the way into the castle.

This was Masashige's first head-on encounter with massed divisions from Kamakura. Despite the disparity in numbers he won the opening round by methods that were to establish his reputation as the master tactician of his age.

Masashige was by nature a man who planned how to defeat an enemy while he was still in his camp a thousand leagues away; and his schemes were as ingenious as if they had sprung from the brain of Ch'en-p'ing or Chan-kuo Liang. He now posted some two hundred highly skilled archers inside the castle and assigned three hundred horsemen to his

brother, Shichirō, and to Wada Gorō Masatō, who were waiting on a hill   *6.51*
outside the encampment. The attackers, being unaware of this and having only one thought in mind, rushed down the steep slopes of the
ditches on all four sides, determined to overwhelm the castle in a single
fierce assault. Then from the towers and embrasures the archers let fly
a mighty hail of arrows so that in an instant more than a thousand of
the enemy had been killed or wounded. "Oh no," cried the attackers,
"this castle is certainly not going to fall in a day or two. We had better
camp here for a while . . . before returning to the charge." Accordingly
they all fell back a short distance from the line of attack, unsaddled their
horses, took off their armour, and rested in their tents.

Meanwhile Kusunoki Shichirō and Wada Gorō Masatō, who were
surveying the scene from their distant hill, decided that the time was
right and, having divided their three hundred riders into two groups,
sent them from the shelter of the trees on the eastern and western slopes.
Each group carried a banner with the floating chrysanthemum crest
which fluttered in the wind. . . . Stealthily the horsemen made their way   *6.52*
through the mountain mist and rode down towards the enemy. As the
eastern warriors saw them approach, they hesitated for a while, wonder-
ing whether they were friends or enemies. Then suddenly the three
hundred attacked from both sides in wedge-shaped formations, letting
out great battle cries as they charged into the vast, cloud-like mass of the
three hundred thousand [*sic*] [Bakufu] warriors. The horsemen broke
through the enemy lines from every direction, cutting them down on all
sides and so astounding the eastern warriors that they could not form
ranks.

At this point three of the castle gates were flung open simultane-
ously and out charged a company of two hundred horsemen in close
formation, shooting great volleys of arrows as they approached. Despite
their huge numbers the Bakufu troops were thrown into utter confusion
by the small force of defenders. Some of them leapt onto tethered horses
and vainly spurred them on, while others fixed their arrows to unstrung
bows and desperately tried to shoot. Two or three men would fight over
a single suit of armour, each claiming that it was his own. When a lord
was killed, his retainers paid no attention; when a father was shot down,
his sons did not go to the rescue. Instead they all scurried back towards
the Plain of Ishikawa River like so many little spiders. For several miles
along their way the ground was strewn with the horses and arms they
had abandoned in their flight. For the villagers of Tōjō District this was
indeed a windfall.   *6.53*

Despite this initial disaster the Kamakura forces attacked
Akasaka again and again during the days that followed. Masashige, however, was invariably prepared. Both in his first big

battle and in subsequent engagements he had recourse to ruses which not only weakened the enemy materially but shook their morale. Masashige became famous for this "ingenious scheming." At one stage in the Battle of Akasaka "two hundred thousand" enemy troops gathered round the castle "like dense stalks of bamboo" in preparation for an all-out assault. Masashige ordered his archers to hold their fire, and not a sound was heard from the castle. Deceived by this silence, the attackers started scaling the wall. Though they did not know it, this was a special outside wall, and at a given signal from Masashige the defenders cut the supporting ropes so that it suddenly collapsed. The attackers plummeted to the ground where they lay dazed "with only their eyes moving." The men inside the castle then hurled down logs and boulders, killing more than seven hundred of the enemy.

About a week later the Bakufu forces decided to destroy the inner wall and laid hold on it with grapnels. They were about to pull it down when Masashige's men took wooden ladles with immensely long handles that they had prepared for such an occasion and poured boiling water on the attackers. The scalding liquid passed through the holes in the tops of their helmets, ran down their shoulder guards, and burnt them so badly that they could no longer fight and fled in terror.

And so it continued: "Whenever the enemy came forward with new methods of attack, [Masashige and his men] defended the castle with new tricks." Finally the Bakufu commanders resigned themselves to starving out the castle by a siege, and they surrounded it completely. The defenders resisted for about three weeks. When their supplies and good spirits were almost exhausted, Masashige made a famous speech to his men, explaining why he had decided to escape rather than face death in the castle:

During the past weeks we have overcome the enemy in one engagement after another and killed countless quantities of his soldiers. Yet so great are his numbers that these setbacks mean nothing to him. Meanwhile we have used up all our food, and no one is coming to our rescue.

Being the first warrior in the land to enlist himself in His Majesty's great cause, I am not likely to begrudge my life when virtue and honour are at stake. Nevertheless [it is said that] in the face of danger the courageous man chooses to exercise caution and to devise stratagems. I therefore intend to abandon this castle for a while and to make the enemy believe that I have taken my life. If they are convinced that I have killed myself, those eastern soldiers will no doubt return to their provinces rejoicing. If they leave, I shall return; and, if they come back here, I shall withdraw deep into the mountains. After I have harassed them a few times in this way, they are sure to grow weary. Such is my plan for fulfilling my [mission] and destroying the enemy. What do you all think of this?   6.58

As might be expected Masashige's followers agreed to his suggestion, and he now put his latest scheme into effect by ordering that a huge hole be dug within the Akasaka encampment. When the hole was completed, it was filled with the corpses of soldiers who had been killed and fallen into the ditches, and a mass of charcoal and firewood was piled on top. The defenders then waited for a dark, rainy night when the Bakufu troops would be off their guard. On the first such night they threw off their armour, disguised themselves as besiegers, and calmly left the castle in little groups, passing directly in front of the enemy lines. As Masashige himself was making his escape, one of the Bakufu guards, thinking that he was a horse-thief, shot an arrow at him. It hit Masashige full on the chest, but suddenly turned round and flew back again without wounding him. The reason for the missile's unusual behaviour was that its head had struck an amulet containing a sutra which the hero had always carried since his days in the monastery, and it had been deflected by a passage that said, "Wholeheartedly invoking the Buddha's name." When the defenders, including Masashige and Prince Morinaga, were out of danger, one man who had been left behind for the purpose lit a fire, and soon the castle was ablaze.

The attackers were amazed by the flames. "Ah, so the castle has fallen!" they cried and raised a shout of victory. "Let none of the enemy escape! Let every man be put to death!" When the flames died down, they entered the fortification and saw the huge hole piled high with charcoal and filled with burned corpses. "Alas, how pitiful!" they exclaimed. "So Masashige has taken his own life! Though he was our enemy, he died nobly as befits a warrior." And there was not one of them who did not praise him.   6.59

One might suppose that by now the Bakufu forces would be familiar with this particular ruse. But they were still gullible:

believing that their chief enemy was now safely incinerated, they
left only a token force to guard Akasaka, and this in due course
enabled Masashige to return to the attack.

At Akasaka and in all his subsequent engagements Masashige regarded the righteousness of his cause and the spirit of his
troops as far more important than numbers. On one occasion he
warned a fellow officer who was urging him to attack a small
enemy detachment that it was precisely such little groups of men
fighting with united hearts under a brave commander who were
most to be feared in battle, since they had the overwhelming
6.60 strength of sincerity. Masashige, like Yoshitsune, was respected
6.61 for sparing the lives and property of the peasants, and he is said
to have treated his men with unusual fairness and consideration.
His reputation for combining courage in battle with careful planning and ingenious trickery spread rapidly, and more and more
warriors galloped forth to join him in his crusade.

After the final collapse of Akasaka early in 1333, Masashige
established his headquarters in the stronghold of Chihaya a few
miles to the south. This became the key position for the entire
struggle, and the Bakufu immediately launched an all-out attack.
The famous Battle of Chihaya Castle climaxed the successful part
of Masashige's career, and one modern scholar has been inspired
to compare his brilliant resistance at Chihaya with that of Mar-
6.62 shal Pétain in the Battle of Verdun. Once again Masashige was
defending a small, weak encampment, but this time the attacking
forces were far greater. The Hōjōs had decided to commit the
overwhelming majority of their troops to the subjugation of Chihaya, and three entire divisions were sent from Kamakura. According to "The Chronicle of the Great Peace," the attackers
numbered no less than one million men. This is of course preposterous; but even the more probable figure of 100,000 was enor-
6.63 mous for the time. Against this avalanche of samurai from the
east Masashige probably had about one thousand supporters to
defend his last stronghold. By various ingenious devices he
managed to decimate the attackers during the two months of
siege. When they tried to defeat Chihaya by depriving its defenders of water, he made use of secret springs and conduits. At one
stage of the battle his followers rolled huge rocks down the hills,
killing "more than five thousand" of the enemy each day.

Masashige now resorted to his famous ruse of the dolls:

"Let us play a little trick on the enemy," said Masashige, "and rouse them from their sleep!" He ordered his men to make a couple of dozen life-size human figures out of dirt and, having clothed them with helmets and armour, equipped them with weapons and in the night placed them behind folding shields at the foot of the castle. In the rear he stationed his five hundred finest warriors, who when the mist began to lift at dawn let out a great battle cry.

"Ah!" cried the besiegers when they heard this. "So they are [finally] coming down from the castle! Their luck has run out and now they are desperate." Then they rushed forward, each man trying to lead the attack. According to the prearranged scheme, [Masashige's archers] came out and fired a volley of arrows; then, as the great [enemy] host approached, they all retreated into the castle, leaving the dolls in the shelter of the trees. Thinking that these were real warriors, the attackers charged ahead to strike them down.

Masashige, seeing that the enemy had been drawn near the castle as he had planned, ordered his men to drop dozens of huge rocks all at one time. The rocks fell on them as they stood gathered near the dolls, killing over three hundred soldiers outright and gravely wounding more than five hundred.

When the fighting was finished, the attackers saw to their dismay that what they had taken for tough, stalwart warriors were merely dolls. What glory could there be for their companions who had been pierced or crushed to death while attempting to attack these figures? And how ignominious were those who had been too scared to advance against such opponents!   6.64

One reason for Masashige's success at Chihaya is said to have been the poor morale of the attackers. As the long siege continued, there appears to have been growing boredom and dissatisfaction among the Bakufu troops. Masters of *renga* (linked verse) were summoned from the capital to arrange poetry meetings which might divert the warriors; other amusements included tea-judging contests, *sugoroku* (a type of backgammon), and *go* matches. Most of the samurai, however, probably preferred the excitement of brisk combat to an elegant linking of poems about the beauties of the season; before long they began to show signs of the weariness that Masashige had predicted at Akasaka, and there were many defections. Masashige, on the other hand, managed to buoy up the defenders with the ebullience of his command. Despite the vast investing force Chihaya remained unreduced till the end. This was undoubtedly his greatest contri-

6.65   bution to Godaigo's restoration. As the famous Tokugawa historian, Arai Hakuseki, observed, if Masashige had not held out at Chihaya, the imperial cause would surely have failed; and it is the combination of this brilliant success with the final cataclysmic failure that makes Masashige such a perfect Japanese hero. His determined defence of the last mountain stronghold immobilized a large part of the Bakufu army and stripped many important provinces of their troops. This encouraged imperial partisans to attack Hōjō forces in various parts of the country, including Kyushu, the northern part of the main island, and the capital itself. Though the attacks were beaten back, they had an important psychological effect by underscoring the Bakufu's vulnerability.

In the Second Month of 1333, while Chihaya was still under siege, Masashige urged Godaigo to escape from his island. The Emperor responded and safely reached the mainland, where he received the protection of a loyalist warrior near the Japan Sea. This flight from Elba threw the Bakufu into great consternation and they promptly dispatched a fresh expeditionary force from Kamakura to forestall any attempted seizure of Kyoto. Two further divisions were sent to suppress the disorders in the west and to attack Godaigo's new headquarters by the Japan Sea. One of these divisions was under the command of the young Kamakura general Ashikaga Takauji; shortly after reaching the home provinces, his fellow commander was attacked and killed, and Takauji found himself in sole command of the main Bakufu forces in the west.

The Ashikagas, of whom Takauji was chieftain, were direct descendants of the Minamoto clan. Related to the ruling Hōjōs by marriage, they had for well over a hundred years enjoyed prestige and widespread influence as one of the leading military families in the east. The Ashikagas had the reputation of being extremely ambitious, and it is said that for some time they had aspired to supplant the Hōjōs, whom they scorned as their social

6.66   inferiors. Takauji, who was twenty-eight years old at the time of Godaigo's escape, was a particularly energetic and brilliant member of the family, and the Hōjōs had put him in charge of their expeditionary force to stem the tide in the west. Yet they must have been uneasy about this ambitious young general, for they insisted that before quitting Kamakura he leave hostages behind in their headquarters.

They had good reason to be wary. A fortnight after reaching the capital, Takauji, who had been making secret overtures to Godaigo's headquarters and had received an imperial commission to "chastise" the Bakufu, suddenly announced that he had changed sides and would now fight for the Emperor. He promptly drove the Hōjō garrison out of Kyoto, and then sent envoys throughout the country to recruit military allies for a final assault against his former overlords. Though Takauji couched his statements in loyalist terms, the underlying motive for his defection was a belief that the time had come to overthrow the Hōjōs and to secure control for his own family as the legitimate descendants of the Minamotos. It was in order to make his cause seem worthier and to gather wider support that he presented himself as a devoted supporter of the Emperor.

6.67

6.68

Takauji's *volte-face* was catastrophic for the Hōjōs, whose weaknesses now came to the surface. The collapse of their Kyoto garrison forced them to raise the siege at Chihaya. Many of the Bakufu commanders were killed or executed, and most of the troops went over to Takauji.

A few weeks later Nitta Yoshisada, a loyalist cousin of Takauji's, led a hastily assembled army in an attack against Kamakura. The recent collapse in the west had hopelessly demoralized the Hōjōs, and they were too feeble to offer any serious resistance. Kamakura, the military capital founded by Yoritomo a century and a half earlier, fell rapidly to the loyalists, and much of it was destroyed. Seeing that all was lost, Takatoki (the Regent) and other Bakufu leaders committed mass suicide rather than risk capture, and thus nine generations of Hōjō rule came precipitously to an end.

6.69

The way was now clear for Godaigo to return to the capital, which he entered triumphantly at the beginning of the Sixth Month in 1333. He promptly displaced Emperor Kōgon, his rival of the Senior Line whose succession he had never recognized, and cancelled all Court appointments that had been made during his absence. Much like Louis XVIII after his return to Paris in 1815, Godaigo considered his restoration to real power to be a *fait accompli* and rapidly proceeded to reimpose what he regarded as the legitimate order. His aims were, in the fullest sense of the word, reactionary. The motive that underlay all his measures was to revive direct political rule by the imperial family as represented by the Junior Line to which he belonged. The fact that such direct rule had rarely existed in Japanese history, except perhaps in remote antiquity, did not deter Godaigo from his objective; and certainly none of his courtly advisers was likely to 6.70 inform him that he was harking back to a fiction.

In the month of his return the Emperor made a number of important appointments. His son, Prince Morinaga, was given the supreme military post of Shogun. This was the title that the victorious Takauji had wanted for himself, but it was against Godaigo's principles to accord such a distinction to someone from a warrior family. Instead Takauji was appointed Commander-in-Chief of the eastern provinces and Governor of Musashi. Even this was considered too great an honour by many of Godaigo's aristocratic advisers, who regarded the Ashikagas as mere eastern parvenus. The relationship between Godaigo and Takauji, however, was still in its honeymoon phase and, though the Emperor never really trusted the turncoat general, he was 6.71 determined to reward him. Among other of Godaigo's first measures was the establishment of the Settlements Board, a vitally important department responsible for deciding claims and rewards, and the revival of the Records Office, which had been formed almost three centuries before in order to regulate manorial estates. In 1334 the Emperor changed the year-period to Kemmu (which subsequently became the name for the entire Restoration movement) and gave orders that the Imperial Palace should be rebuilt, an expense that the exchequer could ill afford.

Masashige does not appear to have played a prominent part in affairs of state at this time. Being a Japanese hero, he thrived on difficulties and disasters rather than on propitious resolutions. Traditional accounts, however, stress the Emperor's immense gratitude to the hero at the time of his return to Kyoto. The following exchange is reported in "The Chronicle of the Great Peace":

Kusunoki Tamon Masashige of the Middle Palace Guards came to meet [the Emperor] with seven thousand horsemen. He was a most impressive figure. His Majesty raised the blinds [of his palanquin] high and, having summoned Masashige to approach, addressed him gratefully: "The rapid triumph of our Great Cause is due entirely to your loyal fighting." Masashige made obeisance and modestly declined the Emperor's honour: "Were it not for Your Majesty's wise governance of the realm and his godlike skill in quelling disorder, how could the feeble schemes of this poor servant have enabled us to break through so mighty an enemy?"   *6.72*

Fortunately this reply does not sound quite so fawning in the original Japanese, which has a far greater tolerance of "humble me!" locutions than English. According to the chronicle, Masashige was permitted to ride in the forefront of the retinue that escorted the Emperor back to Kyoto. In 1333 Godaigo made him   *6.73* Governor of Settsu and Kawachi, the mountainous provinces where he had done most of his fighting, and he was promoted to the Fifth Rank; later he was appointed to both the Records Office and the Settlements Board. These favours do not compare with those accorded Prince Morinaga or Takauji, but they were generous for a warrior of Masashige's social standing and caused considerable resentment among the Court aristocracy and the Ashikagas. Despite such demurs Godaigo included Masashige in his close entourage and continued to favour him, both in recognition of his singular loyalty and in the belief that a man of Masashige's humble origins was least likely to challenge the Emperor's personal rule.   *6.74*

Emperor Godaigo's Restoration, which was intended to change the entire course of Japanese history, turned out to be an unmitigated fiasco. The immediate reason was the chaotic policy of distributing rewards to the men who had participated in overthrowing the Kamakura Bakufu. Most of the warriors who had switched to the loyalist side did so in the expectation of substantial compensation. As George Sansom has eloquently expressed it, "Through the heraldic battle cries and the lofty speeches of the feudal warriors there can be heard the persistent murmur of Property! Property!" Under the new royalist regime, however,   *6.75* land rewards were given mainly to members of the Court nobility, who had contributed virtually nothing to Godaigo's victory. This and similar injustices were bound to anger the armed men who, having thronged into the capital with their claims, were now confronted with bureaucratic delays and corruption. Because Godaigo believed that he should rule as well as reign, he insisted on personally confirming all the new land holdings. While indignant warriors were being denied their deserts, he himself did not hesitate to indulge in conspicuous luxuries such as rebuilding the Palace. This shabby treatment of the Emperor's

military supporters soon weakened their confidence in the new
government; and the absurd arrogance of the restored aristocracy
must often have made them regret their defection from
6.76 Kamakura.

Quite apart from such practical mismanagement, the Restoration never had the slightest chance of working. Failure was
inherent in its very concept. Godaigo's ideal of going "back to
Engi," that is, to the supposedly benign conditions that prevailed
in the early tenth century, could only be a fantasy. Most of the
high-ranking nobles proved to be helpless in dealing with economic matters that had long been the responsibility of the
Bakufu, and in the Records Office and similar departments the
government was increasingly obliged to use warrior personnel
even though this contravened the ideal of aristocratic rule. The
nobility' had long since lost the power and ability to govern and
could continue existing only by the tolerance of the military
whom they so blatantly scorned. Thus the only significant question in fourteenth-century Japan was not whether government
would be in the hands of the aristocracy or of the warrior class
but what particular form the new military rule would take.

Godaigo's policy was not only a total anachronism but
showed that he had never understood why so many members of
the warrior class had swung to his side and restored him to
power. In the case of a few remarkable individuals like Masashige
and Yoshisada, this support may indeed have betokened an upsurge of loyalist spirit; but most of the warriors had sided with
him because of dissatisfaction with a particular military regime.
As Takauji knew very well, he and his fellow warriors had not
destroyed the Kamakura Bakufu in order to restore power to the
Court but to further their own objectives, and in the long run few
of them would back an imperial government, however legitimate, if it ignored their demands. In obstinately clinging to the
illusion that loyalism rather than self-interest was the guiding
motive of his warriors—an illusion that was undoubtedly fostered by men like Chikafusa and Masashige—Godaigo misread
both the spirit of the times and human nature in general. He thus
doomed himself and his handful of true supporters to ultimate
collapse.

As Godaigo's disastrous Restoration entered its second year,
there were growing rifts between important personalities in the

capital. Ashikaga Takauji, the most powerful representative of the warrior class, had become estranged from most close supporters of the Emperor and notably from his son, Prince Morinaga, who held the coveted post of Shogun. The antagonism between Takauji and the young warrior-prince came to a head at the end of 1334. It appeared that Morinaga had been intriguing at Court against the Ashikagas, possibly with the encouragement of his old companion in arms, Masashige. Whatever his plans may have been, they were signally unsuccessful; for in the Tenth Month, when Masashige was away from the capital, Prince Morinaga was suddenly arrested and banished to Kamakura, where he was delivered into the custody of Takauji's brother. Emperor Godaigo had been on poor terms with his son, and despite all the young man's contributions to the loyalist cause, his father did nothing to prevent his ruin. In the following year the twenty-seven-year-old Prince was ignominiously executed in Kamakura, and we are told that not a single person came forward to bury his corpse. Morinaga's short, tragic career fits perfectly into the familiar Japanese pattern, and in due course he became established as one of the many failed heroes of this fierce period. The 6.77 Emperor's unsavory role in this episode did not pass unnoticed, and it was even suggested that his acquiescence in his son's banishment portended a collapse of imperial rule. 6.78

Meanwhile the provinces were in a state of turmoil. This reached a climax in the Seventh Month of 1335 when the son of the former Hōjō Regent staged a sudden comeback which en- 6.79 abled him to attack and capture Kamakura. At this critical point Ashikaga Takauji decided that he should leave the capital with his troops and restore order in the east. Flagrantly ignoring the Emperor's refusal to appoint him to the post of Shogun, he joined forces with his brother and recaptured Kamakura. Once entrenched in the former Bakufu headquarters, he established himself as a *de facto* Shogun, assuming the power that had been held by his ancestor, Minamoto no Yoritomo. In alarm the Court ordered him to return to the capital, but Takauji refused to budge. The rift with Godaigo had become complete, and Takauji was again on the enemy side. The Emperor responded by sending Nitta Yoshisada to "chastise" the recalcitrant general.

Widespread dissatisfaction with the Restoration played into Takauji's hands at every stage, and he was now stronger than ever. He decisively defeated Yoshisada's army near Mount Fuji,

then marched on the west. As he approached the capital, more and more anti-Restoration warriors flocked to his side. Masashige, having of course remained staunchly loyal, sallied out of Kyoto in a desperate attempt to check Takauji's advance. There was fierce fighting outside the city and Masashige scored a temporary success with a new type of light shield that he is said to have
6.80   devised for this occasion. Takauji's forces, however, were overwhelming and soon they were flooding into the city. When Masashige saw that the situation was hopeless, he resorted to his usual ruse and circulated a rumour that he had died in the fighting. Once more Emperor Godaigo was rudely dislodged from his Palace and took refuge in the Buddhist centre of Mount Hiei.

Only three days later, Yoshisada, Masashige, and other loyalist generals counter-attacked and, having forced Takauji to fly to the west, escorted Godaigo back to the capital. The imperial forces were again in control. Before leaving Kyoto, however, Takauji had shrewdly obtained a commission from Kōgon (the puppet Emperor of the Senior Line) ordering him to "chastise" Yoshisada. This gave him a façade of legitimacy that was essential for anyone who aspired to govern the country. Since he was theoretically acting under the orders of a former Emperor, he could resist the charge of being an "enemy of the Court."

In the Second Month of 1336 Takauji reached Kyushu and subjugated most of the island. A couple of months later he and his troops were ready to embark from the port of Hakata for their assault on the east.

The loyalist commander, Nitta Yoshisada, was encamped by the estuary where Minato River flows into the Inland Sea, and it was expected (correctly as it happened) that Takauji would launch his attack here. The Court accordingly ordered Masashige to proceed immediately with his troops to join Yoshisada. Masashige demurred. He realized that the approaching Ashikaga forces vastly outnumbered the loyalists and that a pitched battle should be avoided at all costs. He instead advised Godaigo to withdraw once more to Mount Hiei, temporarily abandoning the capital to Takauji, while he himself would gather his forces at the old stronghold in Kawachi. The loyalists could then cut off Takauji's lines of supply and attack him in force from Kawachi and Mount Hiei. This was probably a sound plan, but Masashige's advice was rejected out of hand, owing to the opposition of the courtiers and to the obstinacy of Godaigo, who absurdly

overrated the loyalists' strength and, besides, had no desire to go
scurrying off again to Mount Hiei. Once the Emperor had *6.81*
spoken, the hero dutifully accepted the Court's disastrous orders
and left the capital to join Yoshisada by the Inland Sea, knowing
full well that Minato River would be a death trap for him and his
men. *6.82*

One of the most famous episodes in the Masashige legend is
his parting with Masatsura, his young son. This touching event
took place at the posting station of Sakurai on the hero's way
from Kyoto to the coast. He had allowed Masatsura to accom- *6.83*
pany him from the capital, but now insisted that the boy must
go home to his mother. Before saying farewell, he gave him a
book on military strategy, a sword that he had received from
Emperor Godaigo, and also some final instructions. He pointed
out that the coming engagement would be decisive for the future
of Japan. "If you hear that I have died in battle," he told his son,
"you will know that our country has definitely entered the age
of the Shogun's [i.e., Ashikaga] rule." In this event Masatsura
should withdraw to the region of Mount Kongō with any remaining loyalist survivors and resist the enemy to the end. Such
would be the true course of filial piety. It was weighty advice for *6.84*
a boy of ten.

The parting between Masashige and his son used to be included in all elementary school readers and was the subject of a
patriotic song which was popular in Japanese schools before the
war. The song, though prohibited by the Occupation authorities
in 1945, is still well known and has particular evocations for
people of an older generation, since it epitomizes the sense of
resignation, poignancy, and *aware* that surround the defeated
Japanese hero:

> Evening draws nigh at Sakurai's leafy ford
> As in the shadow of the trees [the hero] stops his horse
> And deeply ponders what the future holds in store.
> Are they tears or drops of dew
> That spatter on his armour's sleeve?
>
> Wiping away his tears, Masashige calls his son.
> "Your father," says he, "is bound for Hyōgo Bay,
> And there he will lay down his life.
> You, Masatsura, have come with me thus far,
> But now I bid you hurry home."

"Dear Father," replies the boy, "whatever you may say,
How can I leave you here and go back home alone?
I may indeed be young in years,
Yet shall I come along with you
On your journey to the world beyond."

"Not for *my* sake do I send you hence," the father says.
"Soon, when I no longer live,
This land will be in Takauji's hands.
You, my son, grow quickly and become a man
So that you may serve our Emperor and his realm!

"Here is the precious sword
That His Majesty bestowed upon me many years ago.
Now I am giving it to you
In memory of this, our last farewell.
Go, Masatsura, back to our village,
Where your aging mother waits!"

Father and son exchange sad looks as they wend their separate ways,
And through the early summer rain
They hear the mournful call of the *hototogisu*,
Who, when he cries, sheds tears of blood.

6.85   Ah, who would not be moved by such a song?

After they had said their last farewell, the son reluctantly returned home to his mother, while Masashige and his men continued their march to the Inland Sea.

The Battle of Minato River was fought on a sweltering summer day in 1336 and lasted from ten o'clock in the morning until
6.86 about five in the evening. As Masashige had expected, his loyalist
forces were hugely outnumbered. The traditional accounts say
that he had only seven hundred men under his command
whereas the Ashikagas had tens of thousands. No doubt the im-
balance in numbers was exaggerated in order to enhance the
hero's *bōganbiiki* appeal. Yet the disparity was overwhelming:
modern studies suggest that the Ashikaga generals led some
thirty-five thousand men (twenty-five thousand having come by
sea with Takauji and ten thousand by land under the command
of his brother) while the loyalists had about half that number.

Takauji's fleet, which had sailed up the Inland Sea from
6.87 Kyushu, comprised about five hundred craft of all kinds. We are
told that on the eve of the battle the whole sea from the Awaji
Island to Hyōgo was ablaze with lights and that as the ships

neared land to unload their troops they looked like high-crested waves. On the 4th of July the two loyalist commanders, Yoshisada and Masashige, sighted the great fleet as it approached through the morning haze; at the same time the troops led by Takauji's brother were closing in from behind as part of a skilfully coordinated attack in which the forces at sea paralleled those on land. It was decided that Yoshisada would fight the seaborne troops, while Masashige, whose men stood with their backs to the dry bed of Minato River, would confront the land army.

The climax of the battle came when Yoshisada, threatened with attack from behind by a wave of troops that had landed from the ships, hastily withdrew from the field. This left Masashige encircled and isolated. Though fully realizing that the situation was hopeless, he never quailed. Exposed to mighty assaults from both front and rear, he fought for several hours with desperate courage. By evening Masashige's force had been almost entirely wiped out; he himself was covered with wounds (eleven is the traditional number) and to avoid capture he retired with his younger brother, Masasue, to a nearby farmhouse for the final deed.

6.88

The parting exchange between the two brothers is probably the most famous conversation in the Japanese loyalist tradition. As they were about to commit suicide, Masashige asked his brother what his last wish might be. "I should like to be reborn seven times into this world of men," replied Masasue, laughing loudly, "so that I might destroy the enemies of the Court." Masashige was delighted with this answer and said that, although he knew it was a sin to kill, he too would like to be reborn so that he might continue destroying the Emperor's enemies. The two brothers then disembowelled themselves and, having stabbed each other with their swords, lay down "on the same pillow." Fifty of Masashige's closest followers who had survived the holocaust at Minato River promptly followed their master's example "and all cut open their stomachs at the same time."

6.89

6.90

The disposal of severed heads keenly interested the chroniclers of early Japan, and the last notable passage about Masashige in "The Chronicle of the Great Peace" is devoted to this grisly subject. This is the only picture of his wife that we find in the traditional accounts, and it also tells us something about the son to whom he bequeathed his heroic spirit:

6.91

6.92   [Masashige's] head was exposed in the river bed at Rokujō. . . . Subsequently Lord Takauji sent for the head and despatched it to Masashige's home [in Kawachi] with a message saying, "It really grieves me when I think how long he and I were close associates both in public life and privately. I am sure that his widow and child would like to see his face once more even in death." Admirable indeed was His Lordship's com-

6.93   passion!

When Masashige set out for Hyōgo, he had given all kinds of instructions and told Masatsura to stay behind, saying that he would certainly be killed in the coming battle. Both his widow and his son were therefore resigned to the idea that he would never return. Yet, when they saw the head which, though unmistakably Masashige's, was totally altered with the eyes closed and the colour all drained, grief filled their hearts and they were convulsed with tears.

Masatsura, who was [still only] ten years old, gazed at his father's face which had been so completely transformed, and observed his mother's inconsolable sorrow. Then, pressing his sleeve to his eyes, he left the room and went to the Buddha Hall. His mother became suspicious and, following him to the hall, entered through a side door. At once she realized that he was about to kill himself. In his right hand he held an unsheathed sword with a floating chrysanthemum crest, the very weapon that his father had given him as a keepsake when he left for Hyōgo, and his trouser-skirt was unloosened at the waist [to expose his stomach].

His mother rushed up to the boy and, catching hold of his arm, spoke to him through her tears: "It is said that sandalwood is fragrant

6.94   even in seed leaf. You are still young but, if you are really your father's son, how can you stray so far from your duty? Though you have a child's mind, consider the matter carefully! When your father left for Hyōgo and sent you home from the Sakurai posting station, it was certainly not so that you might say masses for the repose of his spirit or that you might commit harakiri. Surely you cannot have forgotten his last instructions, which you even repeated to me. 'If my luck has run out and I am killed on the field of battle,' he told you, 'as soon as you hear of His Majesty's whereabouts, you must pay stipends to our surviving kinsmen and retainers and, once having raised an army, vanquish the Emperor's enemies and restore him to the Throne.' If now you take your life, you will not only destroy your father's name but fail in your duty to His Majesty."

Having thus tearfully admonished the boy, she took away his drawn sword. Masatsura, who was now unable to kill himself, collapsed from the altar and, bursting into tears, joined his mother in her lamenta-

6.95   tions.

Masatsura's mother is presented as the ideal samurai wife—high-minded, self-effacing, and dutiful. Inspired by her lecture, the boy thereafter concentrated on developing his fighting powers. Indeed he went about it with such gusto that the chronicle comments, "His spirit was truly terrifying." He would knock down *6.96* other boys and, while pretending that he was about to decapitate them, would shout, "Thus do I take the head of an enemy of the Court." On other occasions he would thrash a bamboo horse with great cries of "Now I am [chastising] the Shogun." In due course *6.97* he would have a chance to confront more substantial opponents.

As a result of the debacle at Minato River the loyalist army was destroyed as an effective fighting force. Godaigo, bereft of military support, was obliged to fly once again to Mount Hiei, where he was given sanctuary by the loyal monks. The triumphant conqueror, Takauji, reoccupied the capital and put the fifteen-year-old Kōmyō, a member of the Senior Line, on the Throne. Under Takauji's direction the new puppet Court rapidly undid most of the measures of the past three years. A few months later Godaigo came down from his retreat and handed over the regalia to his successor, Emperor Kōmyō. The Kemmu Restoration had totally failed.

Godaigo suffered from many weaknesses, but supine acceptance of misfortune was not one of them. Only a couple of months after his return he suddenly fled the capital, once more claiming that the surrendered regalia were false. His destination was Yoshino, a beautiful, mountainous district some sixty miles to the south, which was especially noted for its magnificent cherry blossoms. Here he established a rival "southern" centre, thus inaugurating the so-called period of the Northern and Southern Courts, which lasted for half a century and was marked by almost constant fighting and disorder throughout the country.

In 1338 the "northern" Emperor, Kōmyō, gave Takauji his long-coveted appointment as Shogun. This marked the official beginning of the Ashikaga Bakufu, a new dynasty of military leaders who from their headquarters in Kyoto prepared to rule the country in the name of successive emperors on the general pattern that had been established by the Kamakura regime. *6.98*

Godaigo died soon afterwards in Yoshino, surrounded by his courtiers and clasping the imperial sword in his hand. His last words are said to have been an expression of regret for his capital

to the north and an injunction that his followers continue the
6.99   good fight. In 1347 Masatsura led a group of loyalist partisans in
a rising against the Ashikagas, whom they still regarded as traitors to the true (that is, the "southern") Emperor. After some
initial successes, he and his men were overwhelmed by Bakufu
troops. Masatsura, who is said to have been twenty-two when he
died, ended his short, heroic career by committing harakiri, and
6.100   three dozen kinsmen followed him in mass suicide. Other descendants of Masashige continued to attack the Ashikaga "usurp-
6.101   ers," but their cause was lost and they were all destroyed.

In 1358 Takauji died in his Kyoto headquarters, basking in his
success, and was duly succeeded as Shogun by his son. The struggle between the two Courts continued, but the Yoshino loyalists
had been gravely weakened by the prolonged fighting and were
unable to secure a sufficient number of new adherents from the
warrior class. Their decline was slow but steady, and by 1383
loyalist resistance had virtually ceased.

The succession dispute finally came to an end in 1392. By now
the Ashikaga shogunate had become stabilized and was able to
impose its rule on most of the country. The new Shogun (Takauji's grandson) persuaded the reigning "southern" Emperor to
return from Yoshino to Kyoto, where he transferred his regalia
and abdicated in favour of the "northern" line. It was understood
that future emperors of the two lines would succeed each other
alternately; but the Ashikagas probably never intended to honour this agreement, and in fact succession has passed consistently
in the "northern" line, to which the present Emperor, Hirohito,
6.102   belongs. Thus, after so many decades of struggle and sacrifice, the
loyalist cause finally went down in defeat. Godaigo's movement
to recover the imperial prerogatives had ended in total failure,
and no future Emperor of Japan ever held the type of real power
6.103   to which he aspired. The idea that the Emperor should rule as
well as reign had proved to be a chimera, and for the next five
centuries authority remained firmly in the hands of the military.

From this complex and important period Kusunoki Masashige and Ashikaga Takauji emerge as the great hero and the
great villain. Masashige's posthumous popularity was slow to
develop. Following his suicide at Minato River the grieving
Godaigo (who was, of course, largely responsible for the disaster)
promoted Masashige to the Third Rank; but, after the final vic-

tory of the Ashikagas, members of the Kusunoki family were for a long time held in low repute, being regarded as fire-brands and disturbers of the new order. It was not until the sixteenth century that the general attitude towards Masashige began to shift decisively in his favour: in 1563 he was officially accorded a posthumous pardon, and thereafter his rise was rapid. This is related to the growing fame of "The Chronicle of the Great Peace," which, despite its modest literary merits, became established as one of the most popular and influential books in Japan. Its supreme hero is Kusunoki Masashige, and its best-loved passages are those that describe his tragic career.   6.104

During the Tokugawa period there was increasing sympathy with the "southern" cause. Respect for its self-sacrificing adherent, Masashige, reached such a pitch that it became known as *nankō sūhai* ("the worship of Lord Kusunoki"). Eminent Con-   6.105
fucianists described him as an exemplar of the most important moral virtues, and the famous scholar-statesman Arai Hakuseki elevated him to a higher level than Emperor Godaigo himself.   6.106

In the second half of the nineteenth century, when once again there was an attempt at imperial restoration (this time successful), Masashige's heroic status was officially reconfirmed. Some five hundred years after his death he was raised to the Junior First Rank. This was a fantastic promotion for a mere commoner and would certainly have shocked his traditionalist contemporaries like Kitabatake Chikafusa. The new school textbooks honoured Masashige as a loyalist paragon, and his story was impressed on the mind of every young Japanese child as a shining example of patriotic virtue and the Bushido ethic. One of the early acts of the young Meiji government was to build the Minato River Shrine in his honour. As a further mark of esteem   6.107
a huge equestrian statue of Masashige was erected outside the Imperial Palace in Tokyo; with typical Meiji syncretism this statue in honour of the most Japanese of heroes was built entirely in Western style.

The glorification of this obscure warrior from Mount Kongō reached new heights during the ultra-nationalist period, and in the 1930s the state-directed educational system presented him as the worthiest samurai in Nippon's long, hero-studded history. Among the kamikaze pilots in the Second World War, Masashige was the most revered hero in history, being a far more appropriate model for young fighters than the somewhat eti-

olated, asthenic figure of Yoshitsune; and the desperate suicide
attacks in Okinawa were named *Kikusui* in reference to his chrys-
6.108 anthemum crest. The abrupt collapse of militarism and the emperor system in 1945 put an end to Masashige's official apotheosis,
but he remains a famous and beloved figure for all of traditional
bent.

Inevitably, however, Masashige has his debunkers. Already
in the Meiji period historians questioned many parts of his leg-
6.109 end, and more recently it has been suggested that Masashige may
simply have been an opportunistic swashbuckler *(akuto)* who
was posthumously fitted into a heroic mould in order to gain
sympathy for the "southern" cause and to provide an ideal model
6.110 for loyalism. According to this point of view, Masashige was a
scheming provincial ruffian who supported Godaigo not because
of any devotion to the legitimate dynasty but because he thought
it would raise his family's political and economic status; for a
time his designs were successful, and he rose from being an
obscure outlaw-type in Kawachi Province to one of the chief
imperial advisers in the capital. In the end, it turned out that he
had backed the wrong horse and he was obliged to kill himself.
Legend-makers of later centuries obnubilated the facts and portrayed Masashige as a pathetic, tragic figure, anachronistically
crediting him with loyalist ideals *(chūshin)* that were in fact not
formulated until long after his time. Thus posterity invented a
hero who had little, if any, connexion with the living man.

The revisionist theory has been presented here in rather
extreme terms, not so that it may be more easily refuted but to
emphasize that the paucity of objective information about Masashige allows an amazing variety of constructions. What is important is the way in which the sparse historical data were obscured
or distorted to create a particular type of legend.

How then should one interpret this mysterious samurai
whose story has come down to us through the mist of the centuries? There will probably never be any definite facts about his
background, but it seems likely that Masashige's claim to aristocratic descent was fictitious and that he started his career as a
6.111 rough, independent mountain fighter. Concerning his military
prowess there seems little doubt. Even when full allowances have
been made for the exaggerations and inventions in "The Chronicle of the Great Peace," it seems clear that he was an inspiring
commander and a canny strategist who, being constantly out-

numbered by the enemy, resorted to skilful guerrilla tactics and unconventional devices. *Baishōron*, which is a strongly pro-Ashikaga work, comments on Masashige's death: "Truly there could be no one, enemy or friend, who failed to regret the death of such a talented warrior." *6.112*

Masashige's character and motives are more problematical. There is evidence that, for a military man, he was modest by nature and ready to praise others for their accomplishments. We *6.113* are also told that he was merciful to helpless peasants and considerate for his soldiers. But all this may be conventional embellishment designed to present the hero as a true gentleman who knew the meaning of *aware*. On the crucial question of Masashige's loyalty it must surely be admitted that, whatever his original motives for joining Godaigo, it was not a promising side to support in 1331, and still less in 1336, and that he stuck to it doggedly until the end even though he could conveniently have defected like Takauji and many others, thus ensuring his safety and prosperity. At a time of shifting allegiances he remained implacable in his opposition to the Emperor's enemies, first the Hōjōs and then the Ashikagas. Even when he realized that the situation was desperate and that his advice was being ignored, he never hesitated to carry out the Court's orders but threw himself into his hopeless Waterloo at Minato River. Fierce, obstinate determination does indeed appear to have been Masashige's salient quality: once he had decided to resist the Bakufu, he could never be swayed. *6.114*

Whatever the motive of his frenzied career, one thing is certain: he failed to achieve his ultimate objectives. And it is Masashige's defeat, marked by the cataclysm of 1336, the inauguration of the Ashikaga Bakufu two years later, and the eventual downfall of the "southern" Court that established him as the supreme samurai hero. If Masashige had been on the winning side, no amount of courage or loyalty would have qualified him for the adulation he received from later generations. Masashige's *6.115* failure was all the more significant in that it came not from fortuitous bad luck but from his resolute support of a "loser." By attaching himself to a stubborn and unrealistic master like Emperor Godaigo, Masashige ensured that all his years of effort, all his brilliant ruses, all his sacrifices, would ultimately be of no avail.

The Kemmu Restoration and its aftermath produced the

richest crop of failed heroes in Japanese history, including Kitabatake Chikafusa, Godaigo, Prince Morinaga, Nitta Yoshisada, Kojima Arinori, and Kusunoki Masatsura; and it is noteworthy that they, rather than the victors, were the most respected figures of this period. The reason that Masashige stands out from among the others is that his career most perfectly exemplified the Japanese heroic parabola: wholehearted effort on behalf of a hopeless cause, leading to initial achievement and success but ending in glorious failure and a brave, poignant death.

The heroic image of the vanquished Masashige is enhanced by his foil, the villainous and successful Takauji. For his life there is a mass of historical material; and the contrast between his actual career and the legendary accretions is therefore far more patent than in the case of Masashige. He was a fearless and remarkably efficient commander who, by giving his support to Godaigo at a crucial juncture, secured victory for the loyalists. It was he (not Masashige) who captured Kyoto for the Emperor; and it was he too who made it possible to destroy Kamakura and the Hōjō "usurpers." In addition he was a consummate organizer and political leader. When things were going badly for his side (whichever side it happened to be), he was adaptable and persuasive enough to gain crucial support from warriors who owed him and his family no allegiance. He was attuned to the times and realistically comprehended the needs of the military class. All of this enabled him to found the Ashikaga Bakufu, a new "dynasty," which remained in power for about a century.

By temperament Takauji appears to have been a warm, generous man with a keen interest in cultural pursuits, especially the composition of *tanka* poems. He was known for his piety and sponsored the construction of the important Zen temple, Tenryū Ji, which in 1339 he dedicated to the memory of his imperial enemy, Godaigo. For many years he was on close terms with the famous Zen prelate, Musō Kokushi, who wrote about him in glowing terms. After his triumph at Minato River he submitted a written vow in which he prayed for forgiveness to Kannon, the Buddhist goddess of mercy; he compared the present life to a dream and looked for reality and salvation in a future world. Takauji's spiritual protestations should perhaps not be taken very seriously, for they did nothing to curb his worldly drives; but, regardless of his religious sincerity, there can be no doubt that he was one of the few really constructive statesmen of his age. Historically he was infinitely more important than the glamorous loyalists, and in most other countries it would probably be he, rather than Masashige, who would figure as the leading hero.

Yet Takauji came to be regarded as the most heinous of traitors in Japanese history. While Masashige was being apotheo- *6.121* sized, his successful rival was damned as an ambitious, self-seeking villain. "Though he received rewards far in excess of the value of his services to the Crown," wrote Arai Hakuseki, "his purpose had always been to promote his own interests." And Rai *6.122* Sanyō, another eminent Tokugawa scholar, spluttered that Takauji was a "dog, sheep, fox, and rat" who had stained the history of the Japanese Throne by seizing power. For Confucian- *6.123* ists his unforgivable crime was to have changed sides, first turning against his overlords, the Hōjōs, and then—most monstrous of all—against the legitimate Emperor. In fact side-changing was *6.124* a common practice in mediaeval Japan and, though Takauji (like the contemporary Scottish hero, Robert the Bruce) went about it rather more blatantly than most, he no doubt felt that his position in the capital had become untenable in 1335 and that he had ample provocation for refusing to leave Kamakura. As his priestly friend, Musō Kokushi, explained:

During the disorders of the Genkō era [1331–34] the Shogun [Takauji], acting promptly on the imperial command, swiftly subdued the foes of the state [the Hōjō Regents], as a result of which he rose higher in the ranks of government day by day and his growing prestige brought a change in the attitude of others towards him. Ere long slander and defamation sprang up with the violence of a tiger, and this unavoidably drew upon him the imperial displeasure. Consider now why this should have happened. It was because he performed a meritorious task with such despatch and to the entire satisfaction of his sovereign. There is an old saying that intimacy invites enmity. That is what it was. *6.125*

Takauji was also accused by Tokugawa scholars of being a warmonger who for decades kept the country in a constant state of turmoil. This traditional criticism is repeated by George Sansom when he writes about Takauji:

Today a butcher, tomorrow a penitent, he presents contradictions which cannot be resolved, since frank contemporary statements about him are scarce. That he was a great figure in his country's history cannot

6.126 be denied, but it is doubtful that he did his country good service by plunging it into decades of incessant and needless war.

Ashikaga Takauji was certainly no pacifist; but there is not the slightest evidence that he was more bellicose than the other military commanders of mediaeval Japan, and it could well be argued that, if any single man was responsible for disrupting the peaceful status quo and for stubbornly prolonging a "needless war," it was Emperor Godaigo.

What really confirmed Takauji as the legendary super-villain was that he so ideally fitted the role of the successful survivor, the cool politician who is motivated not by sincerity but by self-interest and who, like Fujiwara no Tokihira in the story of Michizane and Minamoto no Yoritomo in the Yoshitsune legend, methodically compasses the ruin of the noble hero.

The Japanese
Messiah

One of the few objects to have survived the holocaust at Shimabara in 1638 is the flag of the young insurgent leader, Amakusa Shirō. On a three-foot square of white silk two rather stolid, Western-looking angels are worshipping a huge, black chalice that rises between them.

Above the chalice hangs a circular white host adorned with a black cross, and across the top are inscribed the Portuguese words, LOVVAD° SEIA O SACTISSIM° SACRAMENTO ("Praised be the Most Holy Sacrament!"). A strange device for the banner of a Japanese hero. But then almost everything that is told about Amakusa Shirō, the obscure lad from Kyushu who at the age of sixteen is said to have commanded some forty thousand country people in a campaign against the feudal authorities of Tokugawa Japan, is bizarre and incongruous.

There is a wealth of material about the explosive Christian rebellion, but its youthful hero is still shrouded in factual obscurity. Owing to the annihilation of his headquarters in Hara Castle, the slaughter of his supporters and family, and the destruction of all the rebel archives, there are hardly any contemporary records about him except some brief, imprecise references in official reports. In consequence, while Amakusa Shirō belongs to a well-documented period, and while there is no question about his historical existence, he remains a mysterious figure, poised, like Yoshitsune and Masashige, on the borderline between fact and legend.

The fabulous aspect of the hero's career is epitomized by a famous poem, the so-called "Divine Revelation," which was secretly circulated among Japanese Christian communities in Kyu-

7.1

7.2

143

shu during the months before the revolt. These prophetic verses were supposedly written by a foreign Jesuit priest who had been expelled from Japan some twenty-five years earlier; but they may well have been a later concoction produced by organizers of the revolt who wished to ensure that, despite his youth and obvious inexperience, Amakusa Shirō would be accepted as leader of the insurgents. The poem, which is composed in Chinese and in a deliberately cryptic style, goes as follows:

> Hereafter, when five years have passed five times,
> A God will come into this world [in the guise of] a boy aged twice
>   times eight.
> This youth, endowed by birth with every gift,
> Will effortlessly show forth his wondrous power.
> Then Heaven will cause the clouds to flame in East and West,
> And Earth will make the flowers bloom before their time.
> The counties and the provinces will rumble then and roar,
> And the dwellers of this realm will see their trees and plants
>   consumed by fire.
> All people shall wear the nine-jewelled Cross about their necks,
> And suddenly white banners will be fluttering in the fields and hills.
> All other faiths will be engulfed by the True Creed,
> And Our Heavenly Lord will save the people of this world. . . .

7.3

When the rebellion broke out, five years had indeed passed five times and, by a more remarkable coincidence, Amakusa Shirō had precisely reached the age of "twice times eight." In that year Kyushu had also experienced a number of natural disturbances that seemed to validate the prophecy. A strange red glow, a sort of heavenly flame, had been seen on the horizon at early dawn and again just before dusk; and, far more significant in a country so obsessed with the seasons as Japan, untimely cherry blossoms were said to have been observed in the autumn. It cannot have been hard to convince the gullible and desperate peasants, who had long been the victims of fierce religious persecution, that the other parts of the prophecy would now also be fulfilled: under the leadership of Amakusa Shirō, the lad of "wondrous power," they would soon be freed from their oppression and white Christian banners would flutter in the fields and hills.

The young man's heroic credentials were buttressed by reports of miraculous powers. It was said that, like St. Francis, Amakusa was able to call down flying birds and make them alight on his hand; in fact, he went even further and persuaded them to lay eggs in his palm. He could also run over the waves, and on one memorable occasion he was seen walking on the sea off Shimabara Peninsula near a great burning cross that rose from the waters. From this it was only a short step to proclaiming that Amakusa Shirō was an incarnation of *deusu (Deus)*, the Lord himself, who had been sent down to establish the rule of Christianity and thus save Japan.

7.4

Introduced in the middle of the sixteenth century, Christianity enjoyed a great initial success in certain parts of Japan, especially Kyushu; but once the new Tokugawa rulers began to suspect it as a threat to social stability and a possible precursor of foreign invasion, they stamped it out with merciless efficiency. By about 1640 the foreign religion had been virtually extirpated, Shimabara being in a sense its dying convulsion. When the prohibitions were removed some two centuries later, Christian missionaries again became active in Japan; but today, after more than a hundred years of proselytism and good works, it would appear that their efforts have on the whole been nugatory. Less than one percent of the population is even nominally Christian, and the spiritual influence of Christianity in Japan is minimal. Yet, despite general indifference to the foreign creed, the story of the great rebellion, in which Christianity played a central part, has a strong appeal for many present-day Japanese, and its young Christian leader, Amakusa Shirō, ranks as a national hero. He was especially admired during the antimilitarist period after the Pacific war when he became a symbol of youthful resistance to "feudal" oppression and injustice. Several popular films have been made about him and his disastrous uprising. In one version the rebel leader is depicted as an attractive youth with the smooth, delicate features of the romantic Yoshitsune. Two young Christian girls whose families have joined the rebellion pine after the handsome young chief; the hero, of course, is far too ethereal and idealistic for any carnal dalliance, but this reserve only adds to his fascination. Amakusa Shirō is also the hero of a play (*Ranun* = "Scattered Clouds") by a left-wing theatrical group who used his story as a paradigm of unsuccessful revolution. A famous female impersonator, Maruyama Akihiro ("the most beautiful man in Japan") focused popular attention on Amakusa Shirō by claiming to be his reincarnation (*umarekawari*). In 1972 a popular

7.5

7.6

7.7

historical magazine started publishing a serialized version of an "autobiography" in which the hero describes his brief, dramatic career from the time when he was obliged to witness the public torture of Japanese Christians in Nagasaki and Unzen Hot Springs and first came to realize the horrors that were being
7.8 perpetrated by the feudal authorities. Interest in the hero has also been fostered by the recent "Song of Amakusa Shirō" (*Amakusa Shirō no Uta*), which has had particular appeal for student protesters resisting the conservative government:

> Now they have risen—the Christian farmers who did groan
> Under the tyranny of Shimabara's lord.
> Strike down [Lord] Matsukura and, in the echoes of Mount Unzen,
> Ah, [proclaim] Amakusa Shirō and the resistance of Shimabara!
>
> Now by the thousands and tens of thousands they are besieged in
>   Hara Castle,
> Overwhelmed by the government's encircling troops
> [Yet] firmly joined beneath their Christian Cross.
> *7.9*   Ah, Amakusa Shirō and the resistance of Shimabara!

Amakusa Shirō qualifies as a Japanese hero because, armed with the courage of sincerity, he and his followers struck out against the overwhelming might of the feudal levies and, after an initial period of brilliant success and months of brave but hopeless resistance, went down in tragic defeat. The totality of their collapse emphasized the purity of their motives, and earned them the *hōganbiiki* sympathy that is traditionally accorded to the loser. In one of the great massacres of premodern history the insurgents were all slaughtered; the ancient castle by the sea where they had entrenched themselves and fought with such zeal was razed to the ground, and soon nothing was left but the wind blowing through the ruins to remind passersby of the transience,
7.10 poignancy, and *aware* of human effort.

The setting of the great rebellion was the peninsula of Shimabara and the nearby islands of Amakusa some forty miles across the bay from the city of Nagasaki. It is one of the most dramatic parts of Kyushu's wild, craggy coast. The beauty of the riant seascape, with its hundreds of rugged islets and its bright white sand bordering the clear waters of Shimabara Bay and Amakusa Sea, all set against a background of gentle, pine-green

hills, contrasts strangely with the hideous events that were
enacted there during the early decades of the seventeenth century, and it is hard for the modern visitor to imagine that, like
Conrad's Congo, this had indeed been "one of the dark places of
the earth."

Western Kyushu was always a painfully poor part of the
country, and even at the best of times the farmers in the little
villages in the hills of Shimabara and by the shores of the
Amakusa Islands lived close to subsistence level. A prolonged
drought or an unexpected increase in tax levies meant disaster for
them and their families. It was also a very remote area. When a
commanding general was despatched from the shogunal headquarters in Edo (present-day Tokyo), it took him over a fortnight
to reach Shimabara—six days for the land journey to Osaka and
a further ten days by sea to Nagasaki. One reason for the difficulty in suppressing the rebellion was the initial delay in receiving orders from the Shogun, who alone had the power to issue
the necessary instructions.

Though the uprising in Shimabara was far from being
purely Christian in its origins, most of the insurgent peasants and
their leaders, including Amakusa Shirō, were in fact believers,
and the religious inspiration was vital. Since the arrival of Francis Xavier and his fellow Jesuits about a century earlier, Christianity had taken deep roots in this wild and distant corner of
Japan. Kyushu was the centre of proselytism, and the unremitting work of the Catholic missionaries produced remarkable results in poor, backward regions like Shimabara. In 1577 the Lord
of Amakusa, having been converted to Christianity, ordered all
his subjects to accept the true faith or leave the islands at once;
and there were few families that did not comply. Thirty-five
years later, despite the Shogun's repeated edicts against the foreign religion, almost all Shimabara Peninsula was Christian,
from the daimyo himself, Lord Arima, down to the poorest peasant; the Amakusa islands, which until the turn of the century had
belonged to the domains of another converted daimyo (the famous General Konishi), were also overwhelmingly Christian.

The Tokugawa government, alarmed by the political and
military implications of the spread of Christianity, finally decided in 1612 to enforce their long-standing edicts: Christianity
was definitively prohibited and all missionaries were ordered to
leave. Christians, foreign and Japanese alike, continued to flout

the regulations; but now the authorities, as if to make up for lost
time, launched a reign of terror to eradicate the alien creed for
7.11 once and all. During the following two decades almost all the
foreign missionaries who remained in the country were tracked
down and killed; and some ninety percent of the 300,000 Christians in the country were arrested and either forced to apostatize
7.12 or painfully put to death. Inspired by faith and desire for martyrdom, the Christian community endured its ordeal with incredible patience and made no attempt to resist by force. Kyushu,
being the centre of Japanese Christianity, witnessed the most
savage persecution of all. Nearly every form of torture that human ingenuity and savagery could devise was used to ferret out
information from Christian prisoners or to obtain recantations.
A list of standard methods employed by the Chief Commissioner
of Nagasaki includes: the water torture, the ordeal of the snake
pit, branding on the face, slicing with a bamboo saw, the torture
of the wooden horse (in which heavy weights were attached to
the feet of the straddling victim), roasting alive, and (one of the
few imports from the West that the authorities accepted with
undiluted enthusiasm) crucifixion.

In a further effort to prevent foreign intrusion the
Tokugawa Bakufu issued a series of edicts banning most foreigners from Japan and forbidding all Japanese from leaving the
country on the pain of death or, if they had already left, from
returning. The first of these orders was a seventeen-article edict
issued in 1633; still stricter regulations were promulgated in 1635
and 1636; and, as one aftermath of the Shimabara Rebellion, a final
exclusion edict in 1639 prohibited Portuguese ships from entering
7.13 Japanese ports. These rules put an end to foreign trade and tour-
ism for over two centuries and effectively severed the remaining
Christians in Japan from outside contact and support.

Lord Matsukura, who succeeded to the domain of Shimabara
Peninsula after the final Tokugawa victory in 1615, was at first
deceptively mild in controlling his subjects; but soon he resorted
to tougher methods, and after a decade of rule he had acquired
the dubious reputation of being one of the two most successful
persecutors in all Japan. He was noted for the fiendish ingenuity
of the torments inflicted on his Christian prisoners. A favourite
place of torture was Unzen Hot Springs (mentioned in the "Song
of Amakusa Shirō") in the central mountainous part of
Shimabara. At Unzen, which has now become a popular tourist

resort, victims who refused to apostatize were slowly boiled to death in the scalding, sulphurous waters under the horrified gaze of their families and fellow villagers.

In the Amakusa Islands a few miles to the south the Tokugawa Bakufu had transferred rule from the former Christian daimyo to the Terazawa family. A large number of refugees, including many *rōnin*, had tried to escape persecution in Nagasaki and other parts of Kyushu by fleeing to the islands, where they became part of the Christian farming and fishing communities. It proved to be an unfortunate move. Though Lord Terazawa may at one time have been a secret adherent, he exposed his Christian subjects to the harshest treatment, notably ordeal by burning; his son, who succeeded as overlord in 1633, enthusiastically kept up the tradition. By 1637 the policy of official terror and repression had outwardly succeeded: the majority of believers in the region had publicly recanted by treading on holy images *(fumie)* or signing oaths of apostasy. As events were to show, however, persecution had only made the local adherents more determined. Most of them, including Amakusa Shirō and his family, remained Christians at heart and still practised their faith in secret.

A number of incidents in 1636 and 1637 suggest the desperate situation of the local Christians. Late in 1637 a devout farmer in the village of South Arima at the tip of the peninsula examined an old picture of *Deus* that he had kept hidden in a chest for fear that it might be discovered and reported to the authorities. To his amazement and joy he saw that the picture had been provided with a border while still lying in the chest. A miracle! He promptly announced it to his co-religionists, including his elder brother who was the village headman, and a few days later they all congregated secretly in his house to worship the picture and give praise to God. News of the meeting had, however, leaked out and a posse of constables hurried in a small boat from the fief headquarters at Shimabara. They broke in while the subversive ceremony was underway and arrested sixteen of the celebrants, including the two brothers. The prisoners were roped up and sent to Shimabara, where they were promptly executed as a warning to others. On the day after this grim news reached the villagers they celebrated the feast of the Ascension and defiantly hung up their white Christian flags. When the bailiff tried to interfere, the indignant participants put him to death. The be-

7.14

lievers of South Arima realized that they would now be subject
to fearful reprisals, and rather than wait for the sword to strike
they rapidly joined forces with co-religionists in nearby villages
and made plans to seize the local government offices. A few days
7.15 later the momentous rebellion broke out.

Most contemporary Japanese accounts ascribe exclusively
religious origins to the revolt. Modern scholars, however, give
overwhelming importance to economic factors and insist that
Shimabara was not essentially a Christian uprising but a furious
protest by peasants in a poor, backward region of Japan against
extortionate taxation by their feudal overlords. Rather surprisingly, the economic motive was also stressed by European observers, including Duarte Correa, a Portuguese Familiar of the
Holy Inquisition, who at the time of the rebellion was languish-
7.16 ing in a Kyushu prison waiting to be burnt at the stake. Correa
was hardly an economic determinist, but in his account of the
uprising he stressed the miserable conditions that drove the local
population to despair and quotes a Japanese gentleman who remarked that "the rebellion could not be due to the rebels being
Christians, since in times when there were many such, including
7.17 famous captains, they never had rebelled."

Naturally the shogunal authorities had good reason to emphasize the religious nature of the revolt, since this provided
concrete justification for their anti-Christian policy; and for the
local officials it was obviously preferable to represent Shimabara
as a result of religious fanaticism rather than as a desperate revolt
of starving people against their oppressors. "L'on attribuait la
révolte à la raison réligieuse," writes Pagés in his famous history
of Japanese Christianity; "mais telles n'étaient pas les véritables
causes." The Japanese government, he points out, stressed the
religious motive "pour couvrir ses méfaits et sauver son hon-
7.18 neur."

The economic hardships of the Kyushu peasantry cannot be
blamed entirely on the iniquity of local officials. There is no
evidence that overlords like Matsukura or Terazawa were venal
or inefficient in governing their territories. They were, however,
subject to increasingly onerous and unrealistic levies that the
7.19 central Bakufu government was imposing on "outside daimyos"
and naturally they transferred impositions to the ultimate source
of agricultural wealth, the hard-working peasants in the rice

fields. To aggravate the situation the harvests had been poor in   *7.20*
western Kyushu since 1634, and there was a major crop failure in
1637. Normally local taxes would have been abated in such hard
times, but this was impossible because of the obligation to remit
rice payments to the Bakufu treasury. On the peninsula there
was the additional expense of constructing the new Shimabara
Castle. Far from reducing the burden on his peasants, Lord
Matsukura now imposed fresh levies. In addition to the basic
produce tax they were subject to impositions such as a door tax,
a hearth tax, a shelf tax, a tax on cattle, and even special taxes
when there were births or deaths in the family. Since the levies
were normally payable in rice and other grains, the result was
widespread undernourishment and starvation. This reached its
height in 1637 when, according to contemporary accounts, peasants were reduced to eating mud and straw.

In these grim conditions the regular collection of revenue
obviously presented difficulties. Sometimes the peasants concealed food in order to save themselves and their families from
starvation; more often they had little or nothing to hide and were
simply unable to meet the collectors' demands. The authorities
in both Shimabara and Amakusa decided that harsh methods
were necessary; for peasants were like sesame seeds—"the harder
you squeeze them, the more they give." Lord Matsukura, already
known for his rough handling of Christians, now used his expertise to harass tax-defaulters. The following account of his Mino
Dance torture is contained in a letter from Nicolaus Couckebacker, the chief of the Dutch factory off Nagasaki, to the Governor-General in Formosa:

Those who could not pay the fixed taxes were dressed, by [Matsukura's]
order, in a rough straw coat made of a kind of grass with long and broad
leaves and called *mino* by the Japanese, such as is used by boatmen and
other peasantry as a rain-coat. These mantles were tied round the neck
and body, the hands being tightly bound behind their backs with ropes,
after which the straw-coats were set on fire. They not only received
burns, but some were burnt to death; others killed themselves by bump-
ing their bodies violently against the ground or by drowning themselves. This tragedy is called the Mino dance *(Mino-odori)*.   *7.21*

In order to make the victims burn more brightly and further to
terrify their fellow villagers, who were forced to watch the

ghastly spectacle, the officials in charge ordered that the straw coats be rubbed with lamp-oil; and often the punishment was carried out after sunset like some macabre display of fireworks.

When direct methods of this kind did not produce the desired payments, the authorities arrested the wives or daughters of tax-defaulters as hostages and subjected them to painful and humiliating ordeals such as being suspended upside-down and

7.22   naked. We are told that in many cases husbands, especially those who had formerly belonged to the warrior class but had now become farmers, would actually kill their wives and children with their own hands rather than let them undergo such shame. Frequently women were seized and kept immersed in icy water until they died or, as the authorities hoped, until their families disgorged the tax payments. In December 1637 the pregnant wife of a village headman in Amakusa was held in a "water prison" for six days and nights and died while giving birth to her child. Correa recounts another outrage that took place in Shimabara in the same month:

The daughter of a village headman was seized; and, young and beautiful as she was (*moca donzella, e fermosa*), they exposed her nude and branded her all over the body with red-hot irons. The father, supposing that his girl would simply be kept as a hostage until his debt was paid, had accepted the separation; but, when he heard about the barbarous treatment to which she had been subjected, he became mad with grief and,

7.23   summoning his friends, attacked the local bailiff and killed him.

According to Pagés, this was the incident that led to the general revolt. It would be a mistake, however, to identify any particular event as decisive. The Shimabara Rebellion resulted from a combination of economic and religious motives. In its origins the economic causes were probably more compelling; but once the movement got underway and the oppressed peasants had rallied under predominantly Christian leaders and slogans, the rebellion assumed an increasingly religious character. Though the economic suffering of the peasantry was a crucial motive, Amakusa Shirō and the others insisted that their aims were exclusively religious. The leaders of the Shimabara Rebellion sought to inspire their supporters by concentrating on ideological beliefs rather than material issues. In a statement addressed to the authorities some months after the outbreak they declared:

It is simply because the Christian sect is not tolerated as a distinct sect. . . . Frequent prohibitions have been published by the Shogun, which have greatly distressed us. Some among us there are who consider the hope of future life as of the highest importance. For these there is no escape. Because they will not change their religion, they incur various kinds of severe punishments, being inhumanly subjected to shame and extreme suffering, till at last, for their devotion to the Lord of Heaven, they are tortured to death. Others, men of resolution even, solicitous for the sensitive body, and dreading the torture, have, while hiding their grief, obeyed the [Shogun's] will and recanted. Things continuing in this state, all the people have united in an uprising in an unaccountable and miraculous manner. Should we continue to live as hitherto, and the above laws not be repealed, we must incur all sorts of punishments hard to be endured; we must, our bodies being weak and sensitive, sin against the infinite Lord of Heaven; and from solicitude for our brief lives incur the loss of what we highly esteem. These things fill us with grief beyond our capacity. Hence we are in our present condition.   *7.24*

   During the first months of the movement, the non-Christians among the insurgents were increasingly swayed by the religious professions of their leaders, which must have seemed nobler and more inspiring than economic grievances, and by the end of the rebellion most of them had probably been converted to the faith that prevailed in the rebel camp and that was so proudly announced on their banners.

   The rebellion broke out in Shimabara on the 17th December (1637) and, like a flame among dry kindling, rapidly fanned out to the rest of the peninsula and then across the straits to the Amakusa Islands. The rank and file among the insurgents were poor, weaponless peasants and fishermen, the *Lumpenproletariat* of agricultural Japan. Being mainly Catholic converts or the children of converts, they had been harassed for decades, and now they were prepared for action. Entire villages in Shimabara were abandoned as their inhabitants—men, women, and children— went over in mass to join the rebels.

   The very first to revolt, however, were not the small peasants but the relatively secure village headmen (*shōya*). Many of these men were of warrior stock, having formerly been in the service of Catholic daimyo like Lord Arima and General Konishi, and having fought under them in the civil wars or in Korea. In the new regime they had become squires or gentleman farmers;

yet their style of life was hardly different from that of the ordinary farmers, and now many of them were goaded to fury by the daily exactions and humiliations they were forced to endure.

The effective organization and leadership of the rebellion appears to have been in the hands of half a dozen such former samurai who, having been cut off from their overlords, were now classed as *rōnin*. Typical among them was a sixty-year-old ex-warrior called Ashizuka Chūemon whose father had been Governor of Udo Castle, the feudal headquarters of Higo Province at the time of the former Christian daimyo, General Konishi. After the death of his father and the appointment of the new anti-Christian overlord, Ashizuka moved to Shimabara Peninsula and became a farmer. Appalled by the cruelties and injustice of the Matsukura regime he collaborated in December 1637 with other *rōnin* to lead a revolt by his villagers, and soon he became famous for his prodigies of courage in fighting government troops. According to one version, it was Ashizuka who first recommended that the youthful Amakusa Shirō be made Commander-in-Chief of all the rebels.

Contemporary official documents scornfully describe Amakusa Shirō as "having no pedigree" (*yuisho mo naki*), but in fact we know that his father, Masuda Yoshitsugu, was a respectable Christian samurai-turned-farmer who had been born in the little island of Ōyano in Amakusa and who was originally a retainer of General Konishi. Masuda, who later became famous as a rebel leader under the name of "Amakusa Jimbei," remained on his island until 1600; after the change of regime he and his younger brother, a physician called Gensatsu, moved to the hamlet of Ebe on the mainland of Higo Province. There he was appointed headman and there, about 1621, his son, Amakusa Shirō, was born. Jimbei appears to have been a fearless proselytizer; on several occasions he preached Christianity in Nagasaki and Amakusa, a risky venture in seventeenth-century Kyushu; and sometimes he took along his precocious son, who from an early age was thus exposed to the joys and perils of Christianity.

There are various accounts about Amakusa Shirō's boyhood and youth, and often they contradict each other. One set of stories is patently designed to emphasize his fabulous attributes. We are told that without any formal study he acquired preternatural knowledge (he could read and write at the age of four) and also that he was endowed with the convenient gift of performing

7.25

7.26

7.27

miracles. When Amakusa Shirō was twelve years old, he worked   *7.28*
as a servant for some Chinese merchants in Nagasaki; an eminent
physiognomist from China was surprised to see the lad in this
menial capacity, for he recognized in him the lineaments of future greatness.The story, which remains uncorroborated, is typi-   *7.29*
cal of those told about heroic figures in the Far East. Somewhat
more plausible is the account that Amakusa Shirō was employed
as a pageboy by one of Lord Hosokawa's vassals but that, owing
to his precocious love of learning, he asked to be excused from
service so that he might pursue his studies; he then joined his
father in Higo.

A somewhat different version was given by his mother when
she was being interrogated by the authorities. According to Martha (as she was called after her baptism), Amakusa Shirō spent
most of his childhood in Ebe. At the age of eleven he embarked
on serious studies, having refused to take service with his feudal
overlord until completing his education. From the age of about
twelve he made frequent study trips to Nagasaki. Shortly before
the outbreak of the rebellion, according to Martha's confession,
he had gone with his father to stay at the house of his brother-in-
law in Ōyano (Amakusa). He had never travelled to Osaka or to
any other part of Japan beyond western Kyushu. Martha's statement may not be entirely reliable, since she obviously had to be
careful not to inculpate her son. The story about his visits to
Nagasaki, however, seems authentic, and it was probably on one
of these occasions that he was secretly baptized and given the
Christian name of Hieronimo (Jerome).   *7.30*

The great mystery, of course, is why a lad of Amakusa
Shirō's age, with no special knowledge of military affairs or organization, should have been chosen as Commander-in-Chief of the
insurgents. Admittedly no one can have suspected that the rebellion would grow as it did and that the young man would eventually be in command of almost forty thousand people. Yet why
should experienced ex-samurai like Ashizuka have regarded him,
of all possible candidates, as an appropriate military leader? The
circumstances of the choice are unclear. One possibility is that
Amakusa Shirō was intended as a figurehead and that real leadership of the rebellion was to remain in the hands of a small number of *rōnin*, including his father, who would act in his name, just
as powerful political and military leaders in Japanese history
have so frequently exercised power that was "delegated" to them

by a child Emperor or some other nominal ruler. It is also possible that the *rōnin* leaders were divided into numerous factions, each supporting different strategies and objectives, and that Amakusa Shirō was chosen as a compromise candidate precisely because he was so inexperienced and did not belong to any particular group. Besides, he no doubt possessed unusual personal qualities. Making full allowance for legendary accretions, we have reason to believe that he was a gifted young man (this is confirmed by the Hosokawa Family Records, which are unlikely to have been prejudiced in favour of a rebel leader); and, whether or not he was quite as impressive a figure as is popularly believed, he may well have been endowed with some of Yoshitsune's youthful glamour and also possessed that mysterious attraction which Weber defines as charisma.

7.31

7.32

7.33

Perhaps there were also religious reasons behind the choice. The *rōnin* organizers may have thought—and, if so they were correct—that the religious peasants of Shimabara and Amakusa would be more likely to rally to the cause of a pure, innocent youth, who could be represented as a Heavenly Child *(Tendō)* or a Son of God than to some grizzled ex-samurai. General plans for the rebellion had probably been mooted for at least six months before the outbreak, and during this time the *rōnin* leaders did their best to spread Amakusa Shirō's reputation as a Messianic figure whom God had sent to redeem his suffering people. By December the ground was prepared and it was possible to put him forward as the natural leader under whose divine inspiration the peasants of Shimabara and Amakusa—later of all Kyushu and even of all Japan—would throw off their shackles. The extent to which this young Japanese Messiah actually made the day-to-day military decisions and handed out the orders will never be known. It is quite probable that the practical direction of the revolt was mainly in the hands of elder *rōnin* leaders like Jimbei and Ashizuka. In the legend, however, Amakusa Shirō has always been *the* leader and *the* hero of Shimabara, while the other commanders are mostly unknown.

7.34

Shortly after the outbreak of the revolt an alert fourteen-year-old village youth provided the local constables with information that led to the arrest of Amakusa Shirō's mother and sisters and also of his elder sister's family. The authorities were impatient to get information about Amakusa Shirō and to find out whether he was in fact the central figure in a coordinated plan of revolt. The prisoners were accordingly put to the question. Under interrogation they stated that Amakusa Shirō had lived entirely in his native village of Ebe, that recently he had suffered from a bad case of scabies (a homely touch which certainly has the ring of authenticity), and that, though he had visited the islands, he had *not*, as suggested by the investigators, preached the Christian gospel in either Amakusa or Nagasaki. Though probably subjected to fierce torture, Kozaemon and the others stalwartly tried to cover up for Amakusa Shirō and his father.   7.35

After their interrogation was completed, the hostages were forced to write letters begging the two men to leave the rebel camp in Amakusa and to join them on the mainland. It is not known whether Amakusa Shirō and Jimbei ever received these letters, but if so they clearly recognized this as a trap (one can imagine the kind of treatment they would have received at the hands of Lord Terazawa's henchmen) and there was no reply. The authorities then got wind of a rumour that the father and son had gone to Nagasaki, and a careful but unsuccessful search was made in the Christian quarter of the city. Subsequently the hostages, who were obviously under heavy pressure, sent message after message imploring Amakusa Shirō and his father to return home and renounce Christianity, thus saving countless innocent farmers from further agony. None of these appeals was ever answered. By this time the revolt was well underway and the two men were no doubt busily engaged at the rebel headquarters.

Once news of the rebellion spread in the peninsula and the nearby islands, revolts broke out more or less spontaneously in various towns and villages. These usually took the form of attacks on the headquarters of the local feudal authorities *(ryōshu)* and led to the seizure of weapons and ammunition, which would make it possible to confront government troops. In Shimabara 23,000 out of a total population of 45,000 are said to have joined the rebellion, and in the Amakusa Islands the proportion was even higher (14,000 out of 21,000); there were other areas where virtually all the inhabitants participated. In their initial skir-   7.36
mishes with official forces, Amakusa Shirō and his fellow leaders were almost invariably successful. With growing self-confidence the newly armed peasants under their command were able to repel trained samurai troops, and plans were made to capture Shimabara Castle and other local strongholds that would afford

them a secure military base. Before long the southern part of the peninsula and all the Amakusa Islands were under rebel control.

One reason for this initial success was the sluggish reaction of the feudal authorities. In view of the Bakufu's vast military power and its ability to use troops from the western fiefs, a quicker response could surely have stopped the rebellion from spreading. As it was, the forces of law and order wasted invaluable time. News of the outbreak reached Edo, appropriately enough, on Christmas Day. It was well over a month before any effective counteraction was taken in Shimabara, and by then the rebels were entrenched.

The immense distance (in terms of travel time) between Edo and western Kyushu only partly explains the delay. More damaging was the Bakufu's own rule that the fiefs must not cooperate in any military venture without specific instructions from Edo. Two years earlier the shogunal government, in its fear of collusion between the "outside daimyos," had included a clause among the Regulations for the Military Class (*Buke Shohatto*). This ill-advised measure now served to impede precisely the type of joint action by nearby fiefs, like those of Lord Hosokawa and Lord Nabeshima, that might have nipped the rebellion at the outset. When faced with an emergency, each fief had to look to its own defences until the Shogun issued his orders. Consequently in December 1637 the feudal armies in neighbouring provinces stood by idly and refused to join the fight against the rebels until a decision came from Edo. As Lord Hosokawa remarked in a letter to a fellow daimyo in the east, "Even if [Shimabara] Castle were about to fall tomorrow, we should simply have to stay here and watch unless we received instructions
7.37 from the Bakufu."

Furthermore, not only the shogunal government but even the local daimyos in Kyushu tended at first to underestimate the seriousness of the rebellion, regarding the insurgents as a peasant rabble who would scatter in terror at the first sight of a samurai army. Here the attitude of the Japanese rulers was much like that of the Roman authorities at the outbreak of the Servile Revolt
7.38 under Spartacus. Evidently they did not realize that many of the rebel leaders were themselves professional warriors; nor did they suspect what courage and fanaticism had been aroused in the persecuted peasants by their religious faith or what enthusiasm they felt for the "boy of divine power" who led them. When the

Shogun's chief adviser was asked whether it was not dangerous
to delay action when the number of insurgents was growing day
by day, he replied that the more people who joined the revolt the
better, since they were all bound to be killed. Lord Matsukura of   7.39
Shimabara happened to be in Edo when news came that a rebellion had erupted in his territory; though hardly blameless for the
events, he was filled with righteous indignation and declared that
he himself would lead a punitive attack against the outlaws.

Itakura Shigemasa was appointed to coordinate the forces of
the various Kyushu daimyos and to suppress the rebellion. The
selection of this elderly general, who was in ill health and temperamentally unsuited for such a job, is further evidence that at
this stage the government underestimated its difficulty. He set
out from Edo with no particular sense of urgency and took three
full weeks for the journey to Shimabara, arriving there in mid-
January with a force of cavalry and foot-soldiers at the same time
as Lord Matsukura.

The shogunal authorities were much disturbed by the news
that the uprising had spread to the islands of Amakusa, and as the
fighting continued they were increasingly alarmed by its possible
repercussions. Since the despatches from the west all stressed the
religious nature of the revolt, the government realized not only
that they had failed to get rid of the "evil faith" in Kyushu but
that the rot might infect other backward parts of the country like
the northeast (Tōhoku) where Christianity still had many supporters. All daimyo residents in Edo were accordingly ordered
to return to their provinces in order to forestall further trouble.
The Bakufu also feared that the rebels in Kyushu must be receiving help from the "southern barbarians," that is, the Portuguese.
How else could peasant riffraff have dared confront the might of
armed samurai? The suspicion was totally unfounded; in fact, the
only recipient of European assistance in the rebellion was the
government itself.   7.40

The revolt continued to spread week after week, and the
rebels defeated the troops of both Lord Matsukura and Lord
Terazawa. To Amakusa Shirō and the others it must have seemed
too good to be true—and of course it was. The first setbacks came
in January when repeated mass attacks by the rebels failed to
capture Shimabara and Tomioka castles. We are told that at this   7.41
point Amakusa Shirō was preparing to lead a force of twelve
thousand men to Nagasaki; there he would send in messengers

to demand arms and ammunition, whose scarcity was always the
Achilles' heel of the rebels, and in case of refusal he would attack
7.42   the city. He was diverted, however, by news of an attack on one
of his villages in Amakusa and was obliged to go to its defence.
Thereafter Amakusa Shirō and his advisers decided that, in view
of the rapidly growing strength of the government divisions and
the recent arrival of the shogunal commissioner, General
Itakura, it was essential to change their strategy. They would
withdraw entirely from the Amakusa Islands while there was
still time and join forces with their fellow rebels on the peninsula
where they could immure themselves in the abandoned castle of
Hara. This new defensive plan was immediately put into effect:
Amakusa Shirō and all his thousands of followers in the islands
crossed the straits to Shimabara and started to fortify themselves
in their new headquarters. A report from one of Lord Hosokawa's envoys describes the scores of boats traversing the narrow
straits, each with a crucifix erected in its prow.

With the rebels safely in their castle, all the boats but one
were broken up and the wrecks used to reinforce the ramparts.
Now there could be no return. Much of Amakusa had become a
wasteland, with the rebel villages virtually abandoned. On General Itakura's instructions these villages were burnt to the
ground. The inhabitants who could not escape were destroyed in
the flames or put to death; among those captured were a number
of children whom Itakura ordered to be burnt alive at the stake
—a move as foolish as it was cruel, for it merely stimulated the
ire and resistance of the defenders in Shimabara.

Old Hara Castle (Hara Kojō), where Amakusa Shirō, his
lieutenants, and all the insurgents now gathered for a determined
stand against their oppressors, had been abandoned some twenty
years earlier after the completion of Shimabara Castle in the
northern part of the peninsula. Though rapidly falling into
ruins, it remained a natural fortress, ideal to defend. The castle
stood on a windy plateau, on three sides surrounded by the open
sea and protected by steep cliffs about one hundred feet high. On
the landward side the attackers were impeded by a large marsh,
and the level ground made them easy targets as they approached
the outer moat. As in most Japanese castles of the time, there
were three large defence circuits: the outer circuit, which was
about one and a half miles in perimeter (1,200 × 200 yards), a
middle circuit, and an inner circuit or main citadel (*honmaru*)

where Amakusa Shirō was ensconced with his principal advisers. Vast, cellarlike trenches were dug inside each of the circuits, and this is where most of the defenders lived after the bombardments started. Under the direction of Amakusa Shirō the essential repairs were made so rapidly that about ten days later the dilapidated fortress was ready for occupation. On 27th January a flag with a great crucifix was raised above the ramparts, and the thousands of defenders and their families streamed into the place that in a few months would become their execution grounds.

It will never be known how many insurgents actually inhabited Hara Castle. Estimates vary between twenty thousand and fifty thousand men, women, and children. The number given in most Japanese sources is thirty-seven thousand, of whom about twelve thousand were men of fighting age; but this may well be an exaggeration designed to explain the Bakufu's difficulty in subjugating the peasant revolt. Among the occupants of the cas- 7.43 tle were some two hundred former samurai who provided military expertise and leadership of the peasants. Several of these men had probably been on the losing side in earlier battles against the Tokugawas at Sekigahara (1600) and Osaka (1615) and were now looking for another chance to resist the hated Bakufu. Overall strategy for the defence of the castle was in the hands of Amakusa Shirō and a group of five or six elderly Christian *rōnin*. 7.44

The military hierarchy within Hara Castle was based, rather pathetically, on that of the huge feudal force outside. It comprised the Commanding General (Amakusa Shirō), a Chief of Staff (*jitaishō*), a Commander of Artillery, a Commander of Engineers, Battle Commanders, Captains (*hatagashira*), and numerous aides-de-camp (*tsukaiban*). Despite these impressive titles the de- 7.45 fenders were poorly accoutred and armed mainly with sickles, scythes, and homemade spears together with such weapons as they had managed to capture during the weeks before they entered Hara Castle. There were also several hundred matchlock 7.46 men, whose skill accounted for much of the rebels' success during the early months. Though both arms and bullets were forged inside the castle, there was a serious shortage of ammunition from the beginning, and as time passed it became desperate. Since they could not afford to waste a single bullet, the insurgent artillerymen developed remarkable accuracy in firing their matchlock guns, and so long as the ammunition held out they wreaked havoc among the attacking samurai, who were trained principally in sword fighting. To save on guns and bullets the insurgents collected stores of large stones which could be shot at the enemy with special catapults. We are told that on one occasion a party of over a hundred men clambered down the steep rocks to the beach to collect stones; government ships fired at them, but the men managed to climb back unscathed.

Notwithstanding the shortage of food and ammunition and the ultimate hopelessness of their situation, morale among the defenders appears to have been high. One reason was the popularity of their Messianic leader, Amakusa Shirō. Even the deserters who left the castle and crossed over to the enemy lines during the final month impressed government interrogators by their continued personal devotion to this unconventional young
7.47   Shogun. Amakusa Shirō was an embodiment of the faith that was proudly emblazoned on their flags and banners. "All round the parapet," reported the Dutch factor, Mr. Couckebacker, "one could see countless banners with red crosses; there were also
7.48   many [wooden] crucifixes, both large and small." The rebel banners were dedicated to Sanchiyago (St. James), and in their battle cries the insurgents called on the Spanish patron saint as well as on Iesu (Jesus) and Maria. Throughout the siege, religious services were regularly held within the castle precincts, and twice a week the occupants gathered to hear sermons preached by Amakusa Shirō himself.

The high spirits of the defenders resound in the numerous
7.49   battle songs and pasquinades that mocked the Bakufu troops for their ineffectuality, and also in their stirring declarations of purpose. These statements were fired into the enemy camp in the form of "arrow letters" (yabumi), written messages attached to the shafts of flying arrows, and are recorded in the official accounts of the campaign. Again and again the defendants insisted in their "arrow letters" that they had no material demands whatsoever and that the only reason they had walled themselves in Hara Castle was to escape persecution and practise Christianity freely. Their aims, they explained, were not of this world. If they had been merely concerned with the present life, they would never have dreamt of rebelling; their regard was for the future life (goshō) and they were sacrificing themselves in the knowledge that their sufferings in this world would be rewarded by joy in Heaven. Being Christians, they were assured of Paradise if they died in defence of their faith. In "normal" times, said one of the

letters, they would not have hesitated to come to the help of government troops who were putting down enemies of the Shogun; but now they were fighting under the orders of "Heaven's messenger" *(ame no tsukai)*, Amakusa Shirō, who superseded any worldly authority.

Gathered on the landward side of the castle were the official forces who had been mobilized by the Kyushu daimyos on orders from Edo. In terms of material strength they vastly outweighed the defendants. By the end of February more than one hundred thousand government troops were besieging Hara Castle, and they were greatly reinforced in March. This was a huge army for the time—considerably greater, in fact, than the number engaged at the Battle of Sekigahara, which had secured victory for the Tokugawas in 1600. The government forces were well equipped, and during the early stages of the siege General Itakura concentrated on building up supplies. In addition—an interesting sidelight on warfare during this period—enterprising merchants from Kyoto and Osaka were free to circulate among the besieging units selling extra food and provisions to the troops. No such supplements were available to the defenders, whose supplies were almost entirely limited to what they had brought into the castle when they first entered.

7.50

7.51

Yet the attackers suffered from many weaknesses that prevented them from achieving an easy victory. In the beginning they were incompetently led and their morale was poor, so that they displayed far less skill and courage than the insurgents. Most of their guns were too small to fire effectively across the distance of five hundred yards that separated their lines from the castle; and, since the commanding general insisted on completing all the equipment of his forces before advancing or launching an attack, they failed to take advantage of the defenders' initial vulnerability. Above all, the attackers were not a united force but comprised seven main units from different fiefs. As the impatience and tension mounted, there was growing antagonism, notably between the Hosokawa and the Kuroda forces, which erupted in internecine quarrels and even killings. The Shogun himself was obliged to issue a reprimand insisting that they concentrate on fighting the common enemy.

To increase their fire power the attackers built movable siege engines and huge towers *(yagura)* with emplacements for their heavy artillery. A contemporary diary relates a lively exchange

between the insurgents and a group of labourers who were working on a siege engine near the castle walls. When the defenders
began hurling down stones from the parapets, the workmen
shouted to them that this was unjust, since they were mere labourers whose masters had forced them to work on the siege
engines against their will. The argument had the desired effect
and the men were able to continue their work without further
interruption. After they had finished, one of them shouted, "You
poor fellows there in the castle! You're living in holes in the
ground with nothing to eat but soy beans and dried cod. Why
don't you have done with it and surrender?" Thereupon one of
the insurgents leaned through an embrasure in the wall and
shouted, "You're right about our living in holes, but look at the
delicious fish we get to eat every day!" And he proudly held up
7.52 a fresh mullet for the workmen to see.

Rather than risk the casualties of a frontal attack across the
open marsh, the besiegers decided to excavate a tunnel that
would lead directly from their lines into the castle itself. The
work was carried out as surreptitiously as possible, but soon the
defenders heard the sound of the digging and counteracted by
filling the tunnel with smoke and also by pouring in large quantities of faeces and urine. This incommoded the workers, and the
7.53 plan had to be abandoned. The next stratagem was to destroy the
castle walls with huge cannon balls. The balls were brought to
the front lines, each being lifted by twenty-five men, but for some
reason (perhaps no adequate cannon was available) they were
7.54 never fired. A further scheme was to engage specialists known as
"invisible men" *(ninjutsuzukai)* who would sneak into Hara Castle and return with information. These spies appear to have been
quite effective, and several dozen were used. Late in March two
"invisible men" made their way into the castle with cords attached to their bodies so that they could be hauled out if they
7.55 were killed or wounded. It might be expected that their cords
would have given them away, but they both returned safely with
detailed reports about the castle's defences and new construction
work. On one occasion an "invisible man" from the province of
Ōmi near Kyoto got into the outer citadel but was nonplussed by
the Kyushu dialect of the occupants and by their use of Christian
terms. He did not dare speak to anyone for fear that his Ōmi
dialect might give him away. Finally the silent stranger began to
arouse suspicion; but he managed to escape in time, and as he ran

away from the castle amid a hail of stones he was even able to take along one of the rebel banners as a souvenir.

The shogunal government in Edo, increasingly alarmed by the possible repercussions of the revolt, decided to send a second general with reinforcements to Shimabara. The commander *7.56* chosen for the job was Lord Matsudaira Nobutsuna, a leading member of the Great Council in whom the Shogun had particular confidence. With five thousand men, three hundred horses, and a force of heavy artillery he promptly set out for the west, first marching to Osaka and sailing from there to Kyushu in a fleet of sixty ships. As soon as the shogunal commissioner, General Itakura, heard of the new appointment, he resolved to storm the castle in the hope of taking it before Matsudaira arrived. One reason appears to have been a letter that he had just received from a cousin in Osaka. His correspondent referred to the rebels as *7.57* "mere peasants," and warned that Hara Castle would be attacked and captured on the very day after Matsudaira appeared with his new forces. Determined to forestall such a disgrace, Itakura ordered a preliminary assault on 3rd February. The attack was poorly prepared and, despite heavy losses, the samurai troops failed to force an entry into the outer precinct. When the defenders saw that the enemy had been beaten back, they jeered loudly from the castle walls, accusing the local samurai of being cowards who were more adept at torturing poor farmers than at storming a fortified position. *7.58*

Appalled by this debacle and determined to vindicate his honour, Itakura decided to launch a general attack at dawn on New Year's Day (14th February in the Western calendar). This was an even greater disaster. Some four thousand government troops were killed or wounded as they advanced on the castle. General Itakura, who in a sudden access of derring-do led the charge himself, was shot dead. He had evidently sensed that he would be killed, for on the eve of the engagement he is said to have written a gloomy farewell poem asking that "When only the name remains of the flower that bloomed on New Year's Day, remember it as the leader of our force [*sakigake to shire*]!" *7.59*

The news that their commanding general had been killed by the peasant rabble shocked the government leaders in Edo. It was an appalling humiliation and could badly damage their prestige both in Japan and abroad: if mere farmers could successfully flout the Bakufu, what might not happen if some of the stronger dai-

myos rose against them? Itakura himself was posthumously criticized for the daredevil tactics that had caused the disaster. At the
same time several daimyos from Kyushu were ordered to join
forces with Lord Matsudaira in the next part of the campaign
against the insurgents.

Matsudaira profited from his predecessor's fiasco by putting
off all plans for general attack and concentrating on a blockade
of the castle. Rather than risk further heavy losses by trying to
rout the defendants, he would starve them out of their fortress
and meanwhile get time to rest and reequip his own forces. For
a samurai army engaged in subjugating a peasant rebellion this
was not a particularly noble strategy, but the Bakufu gave its full
approval. Matsudaira, much concerned by the possibility that the
defendants might attempt a sortie, took numerous precautions
such as constructing palisades and ditches and keeping flares lit
at night. He also ordered that the official passwords be changed,
since the rebels had found out the previous ones: in future anyone challenged with the question "A mountain?" must establish
his credentials by replying "A river."

The new commanding general also resorted to psychological
warfare by promising a free pardon to all rebels who came out
of the castle and surrendered; furthermore they would be excused from their tax obligations and even given special grants of
rice land. By these temptations he hoped to sow dissension
among the defenders, but his offers were promptly rejected. Replying by means of an "arrow letter," the insurgents ridiculed
Matsudaira's suggestions, pointing out that they were "devoted
Christians" *(omoikiritaru Kirishitan)* whose religion was so powerful that the attackers' bullets were incapable of wounding
them. They could never consider accepting a free pardon if it
implied any compromise of their beliefs; for their only concern
was the right to practise Christianity freely. This, however, was
precisely the concession that Matsudaira could not make, and the
exchange ended in an impasse.

In the middle of February the Chief Commissioner of
Nagasaki, acting on instructions from Lord Matsudaira, demanded that the Dutch and Chinese should aid in suppressing
the Shimabara rebels. Chinese help was never actually used, but
the Dutch manager, Nicolaus Couckebacker, became involved in
the campaign. In his final report to Holland he stressed that the
Japanese authorities had compelled him to participate against his

7.60

will. No doubt he and the other Dutch officials were reluctant to join overtly in the extermination of their fellow Christians (albeit Roman Catholics); on the other hand, the rebellion had seriously damaged their trade in Nagasaki and they must have been anxious to see it crushed. In any event Couckebacker complied with the Japanese instructions: on 24th February he arrived off Shimabara in *de Ryp*, a Dutch ship of twenty guns, and started bombarding the insurgents. During the fortnight it rode at anchor before Hara, the ship fired several hundred shells at the castle. For obvious reasons Couckebacker reported that the barrage had been of little use; in fact, it appears to have inflicted considerable damage to the walls and outer defences and may have hastened the final catastrophe. In the course of this unheroic engagement, two Dutch sailors lost their lives, one having been shot down from the topmast onto the deck of *de Ryp*, where he crushed a shipmate to death.

7.61

7.62

7.63

On 12th March Lord Matsudaira suddenly informed the Dutch that they might withdraw and thanked them for their help. Now that the attacking forces were so near the castle walls, he explained rather unconvincingly, their ship might be damaged by cross-fire and their men injured.

7.64

The reason for Lord Matudaira's decision to call on the Dutch for help is one of the minor mysteries of the Shimabara Rebellion. Possibly he overestimated the fire power of the Dutch ships, and underestimated the embarrassing effect of foreign participation (which suggested that the Bakufu needed outside help to quell local disorders). According to Matsudaira's own account, his aim was to test the Hollanders by finding out whether they would accept the authority of Japanese officials to the point of attacking fellow Christians. If such was indeed his purpose, the Dutch passed the test brilliantly. Their inglorious role in firing on the hard-pressed Japanese Christians (whom, if anything, they should have been trying to help) was quickly noted in Europe and compared with their recent action in attacking Huguenot co-religionists at La Rochelle. Nor was the significance of the foreign participation lost on the defenders, who now shot a hail of "arrow letters" out of the castle with pasquinades mocking the enemy as incompetent cowards who preferred manipulating account books and dunning poor people for taxes to risking their lives on the field of battle, and who therefore had to rely on foreigners when it came to a real fight. According to Correa (the

7.65

Portuguese Familiar), pasquinades in which the samurai were ridiculed for having abandoned the profession of arms to commoners were found scattered all over the surrounding country-
7.66   side.

Later in the same month Matsudaira, still hoping to avoid the immense losses that were bound to result from an all-out attack, made a few final attempts to persuade the rebels (or at least certain groups among them) to leave the castle peacefully. In an effort to induce Amakusa Shirō and his father to surrender, he ordered that Martha, Regina, and the other hostages be removed from their prison and brought to Shimabara by ship under heavy
7.67   armed escort. Since no prison was available near Hara Castle, the hostages were kept bound on the ship and taken from there to Lord Matsudaira's camp for interrogation. In the middle of March, Amakusa Shirō's little nephew was sent into the castle with a letter informing the insurgents that the Bakufu's policy was to exterminate them all, down to the last babe in arms. Matsudaira was, however, prepared to make an offer: if the rebels would liberate those people in the castle who had been forcibly converted to Christianity or who now wished to abjure their faith, then, in exchange, Amakusa Shirō's mother, sister, and other captive relatives would be released and allowed to enter the castle where they could share the fate of the defenders and satisfy their frequently expressed wish to die for the Christian faith. The letter also stated that, since Amakusa Shirō was still only fifteen years old, he himself could hardly be the leader of such a huge rebel force; the commander who represented himself as Amakusa Shirō must therefore be an impostor acting in his name; if the "real" Amakusa Shirō would now leave the castle, Lord Matsudaira would immediately give him a free pardon.

Further letters were addressed to the rebel leader by his mother and elder sister. They implored him to accept the exchange plan, since their great wish was to die together, and they also begged to be allowed to talk to him, if only through a crenel in the parapet. These and subsequent letters from the outside were skilfully concocted by the government officials to weaken the morale of the defenders; yet, if anything, they had the opposite effect and merely steeled their determination. Kohyōe was sent back with a letter containing a staunch reaffirmation of faith, a polite refusal of the offer, and a statement that there were no forced converts in the castle. He was also given a large parcel of food (honey, oranges, bean-jam buns, and yams) to take to Amakusa Shirō's family. This was partly to console the unfortunate prisoners, but it also served to persuade the attackers that there were still plenty of provisions in the castle.

On his next visit Kohyōe was accompanied by Amakusa Shirō's little sister, Man. He carried letters in which Martha and Regina, obviously writing on the dictates of their captors, refuted the contention that there were no forced converts; recent deserters, they said, had confirmed that there were in fact many people who had been obliged to become Christians and who now wanted to surrender; they at least should be allowed to leave the castle safely, if only for humanitarian reasons. The mother's letter contained a somewhat unconvincing reference to the traditional magnanimity of the Bakufu and again begged for a meeting with her son.

Amakusa Shirō, mindful perhaps of Jesus' reply, "Who is my mother and my brethren?" was unswayed by his family's appeals. The two little messengers were sent back with a letter stating that the defendants were acting in accordance with God's will (*Deusu-sama no on-hakarai shidai ni sōrō*), and were protected by Santa Maria-sama, Sanchiyago-sama, Sanfuranshisuko-sama (St. Francis), and all the Blessed Saints. They were seen off at the castle gates by a company of more than two thousand rebels; his little sister carried in her hand a ring and two soap-berries that Amakusa Shirō had given her as a parting gift.

Realizing that the emotional appeal of family hostages had proved ineffective, Lord Matsudaira next ordered that an "arrow letter" be fired into the castle proposing a cease-fire and negotiations. The letter, which was addressed to "the Honourable Masuda Shirō" (Masuda Shirō Tayū-dono), suggested that a negotiating party representing the government should be admitted into the castle or that, alternatively, the talks could take place at the castle walls. After some difficulty a cease-fire was arranged and negotiations were held on Ōe Beach below the castle in full view of the attacking armies and of the defenders. Their positions were irreconcilable, however, and the talks broke down almost immediately.

7.68

Negotiations, blandishments, threats, and maternal pleadings had all failed to weaken Amakusa Shirō and his fellow rebels, who knew that compromise would eventually lead to surrender and to abandonment of all the beliefs for which they had

suffered and fought. Though their position was patently hopeless, they would stay in the castle and go down in a blaze of glory
that would proclaim the sincerity of their faith to the entire
world.

By the beginning of April the rebels' provisions were almost
exhausted. There had always been far too many people in the
castle to feed adequately, and now the situation was critical. Deserters reported that most of the defenders were so weak that
they could not stand up even while doing sentry duty, and the
labour of repairing the damaged fortifications would soon be too
exhausting to continue. In their desperate hunger (which must
often have reminded them of pre-rebellion days) several people
from the castle were slipping into the besiegers' camps in the
hope of finding food and then returning; others were climbing
down the cliffs to the beach and searching for edible seaweed.
Finally Lord Matsudaira's strategy was producing the desired
results.

At this stage an inauspicious incident cast further gloom
over the defenders. A cannon ball fired by the besiegers tore into
the main citadel, where Amakusa Shirō was calmly playing a
game of *go*. Several onlookers were killed outright; the rebel
commander himself survived, but the right sleeve of his robe was
ripped. The story, which spread quickly through the castle, made
many people wonder whether their young leader was not begin-
7.69   ning to lose the protection of *Deus*.

On the night of 4th April the defenders decided on a sortie.
One of the castle gates was suddenly thrown open and a body of
defenders, led by Amakusa Shirō himself, charged the besiegers'
camp, inflicting heavy casualties on the government troops. Warriors of the Kuroda division continued firing on each other pell-
mell in the dark even after the raid was over. Yet despite initial
success the sortie miscarried; Amakusa Shirō and his men were
forced to retire to the castle, leaving behind over three hundred
of their own killed and wounded.

When the corpses of some of the slain rebels were examined,
it was found that their stomachs contained seaweed and barley,
and that most of them were in an advanced stage of malnutrition.
This confirmed the reports of recent prisoners and deserters that
food supplies in Hara Castle had run out. Even to the cautious
Lord Matsudaira it was clear that the rebels' situation was critical
and that at last the time had come for a general assault. Now the

password for the attack was fixed: *Question:* "A province?" *Answer:* "A province." Yet there were further delays, partly owing to heavy rain and partly because it was necessary to coordinate plans among the numerous daimyo forces.

When the attack finally came, it was by mistake. On 12th April one of the fire-signals was accidentally lit, and men of the Nabeshima division rushed forward to the assault in disregard of Matsudaira's careful plans. They were rapidly joined by the other divisions in a confused but successful attack on the outer defences, each of the daimyo forces trying to gain as much glory as possible for itself by being first into the castle. An illustration   *7.70* in the Shimabara Camp Screen shows the attackers in their heavy samurai armour clambering up the steep castle walls like so many black armadillos. Despite fierce resistance and appalling confusion, which often led the attackers to fight among themselves, they forced their way into the outer circuit, cutting down everyone in sight, and then steadily advanced over great mounds of corpses to invest the middle and inner circuits. The starving defenders, having run out of ammunition, fought with stones, beams, cooking-pots, and anything else that came to hand. During two days and nights of frenzied fighting they held out against thousands of well-armed, well-fed samurai.

On 14th April the defences began to crumble. The attackers systematically set fire to the huts and trenches, and occupants were burnt to death by the hundreds. Others, including large numbers of women with their children, hurled themselves into the flames rather than be taken alive. This, of course, was highly unorthodox behaviour for Christian believers; but many of the rebels were Japanese above all, and in this last moment of crisis they were impelled by national traditions rather than the strictures of a foreign religion. "Large numbers [of rebels]," writes a contemporary daimyo observer, "would cover their hands with their clothes and force up the burning [beams] so that they could enter the buildings. They also pushed in their children and then lay down on top of them and all were [burnt to] death." And he adds a revealing comment about these brave peasant fighters who preferred suicide to surrender, "For people of their low station *(shimojimo)* this was indeed a praiseworthy way of dying. Words cannot express [my admiration]."   *7.71*

The massacre began on 15th April. By this time the huge ditches in the castle were filled with rebel corpses; often, accord-

ing to Correa's account, the wounded were thrown into the
ditches while still alive and struggled helplessly to get out. There
were still thousands of survivors, however, and the government
forces now set about exterminating them. In order to prove their
assiduity and to obtain rewards, they lopped off the heads of men
and the noses of women and brought these grisly trophies to the
collection centres set up by the respective fiefs, where the numbers were tallied by special "head count" officials. One greedy
samurai from the Nabeshima division was so eager to impress his
superiors that he actually bought a severed nose from a soldier
7.72 and presented it as his own trophy. The offence was discovered
however, and he was ordered to disembowel himself, thus bringing his career to an abrupt end.

By far the most important prize, of course, was the head of
Amakusa Shirō, and special glory was bound to accrue to the clan
that captured it. Since the young rebel leader was not known by
sight, and since it was rumoured that he had somehow managed
to escape, it was no easy task to bring in his head. After the
campaign there was an unseemly squabble (between the
Hosokawa and the Kuroda divisions) about who was actually
responsible. Among the numerous conflicting accounts the most
detailed (though not necessarily the most reliable) is that of the
7.73 Hosokawa clan. A Hosokawa retainer by the name of Sasaemon
was wandering about the burning ruins of the inner citadel. He
already had two severed heads, and was hoping to add a third to
his collection. Looking inside one of the burning huts, he caught
sight of a handsome youth who had evidently been wounded and
who was now lying on the floor arrayed in silk robes. On hearing
footsteps the youth began to rise, but Sasaemon promptly cut
7.74 him down and sliced off his head. As he ran out of the hut with
his new trophy, the beams collapsed in flames. On his way to the
great ditch where heads taken by the Hosokawa forces were
being collected, he happened to pass Lord Hosokawa himself,
who was seated on a campstool surveying the carnage. Noticing
one of Sasaemon's heads, Lord Hosokawa remarked with characteristic acumen that it probably belonged to "the rebel general,
Shirō" and should "not be handled negligently" *(soryaku
subekarazu)*. The head was therefore carefully washed and
combed before being brought to the place of inspection, where
it was placed among several others that had been tentatively
identified as belonging to the rebel general. Amakusa Shirō's

mother was now summoned and told to point out her son's head.   *7.75*
She proudly replied that he could not possibly have been killed;
he had been sent from Heaven and had now either returned
there, or changed form and escaped to some place like Luzon in
the Philippines. Head after youthful head was presented to her,
but she rejected them all until they held up the one recently taken
by Sasaemon. Then finally she broke down and said, "Can he
really have become so thin?" And she clung to the head and wept.
At this point the inspectors knew, without even asking her, that
they had found their quarry. Head-inspection scenes *(kubi-jik-*   *7.76*
ken), with their mixture of horror and poignancy, were of absorb-
ing interest for Japanese writers during the feudal period, and are
included in the stories of many famous failed heroes, among them
Yoshitsune and Masashige. The present account of Amakusa
Shirō adds a Christian overtone to this traditional theme by pic-
turing the hero's mother as a Japanese *mater dolorosa* in a macabre
version of the *pietà*.

Though Hara Castle fell more rapidly than anyone had expected, the attackers' losses were considerable. The final assault
cost them some fifteen thousand casualties, of whom more than
three thousand were killed. Estimates of the total number lost in
the campaign vary considerably. According to Pagés, some seventy thousand government troops succumbed to illness during
the siege, or were killed or wounded in the fighting. Since there
were only two general attacks in the course of the entire campaign, this figure is probably exaggerated, but even the more
modest estimates of government casualties confirm the fierceness
of the resistance. From his prison, Correa saw innumerable
wounded samurai being carried on litters; he also observed the
doleful sight of hundreds of horses whose masters had been killed
at Shimabara being led through Omura by servants with heads
shaved in sign of mourning.   *7.77*

The rebels themselves were wiped out. The few who
managed to escape from Hara Castle were hunted down and
decapitated. The slaughter on 15th April was one of the greatest
in all Japan's sanguinary history. The nearby rivers and inlets
were clogged with decapitated bodies; vast ditches were filled to
overflowing with severed heads, and heads were strewn thickly
over the fields. A total of 3,632 rebel heads was counted in the
Hosokawa ditch; we are told that the actual number taken was
far greater, since many had been removed (presumably as souve-

nirs) or destroyed by fire. Another official source states that 10,869
heads were severed and stuck on wooden spikes which were
erected in the fields in front of the castle and all the way down
7.78   to the beach. Another 3,300 heads were loaded onto three ships
and taken for burial in a mass grave in Nagasaki. These numbers
are suspiciously exact, but there is no evidence that they are
exaggerated.

The only known survivor of the holocaust was Yamada
Emonsaku, the painter and Christian renegade, who from the
outset had served as one of Amakusa Shirō's chief captains and
7.79   also as the "war artist" of Hara Castle. His role in the story is that
of the Judas Iscariot who betrays his young master to the enemy
and receives his thirty pieces of silver. Soon after the siege began,
Yamada was realist enough to see that the situation was hopeless.
Having decided to communicate secretly with the attackers, he
shot the following letter into the enemy camp:

Yamada Emonsaku addresses you with true reverence and respect. I
desire to obtain your forgiveness, and restore tranquillity to the empire,
by delivering up [Amakusa Shirō] and his followers to be punished. We
find that, in ancient times, famous rulers ruled beneficently, proportion-
ing their rewards to the merit of the receiver, and the punishments to
the demerit of the offender. When they departed from this course, for
any purpose soever, they were unable to keep the control of their countries. This has been the case with hereditary lords; how much more will
it be the case with villagers who rebel against the Government. How
will they escape the judgement of Heaven? I have revolved these truths
in my mind, and imparted them to the eight hundred men under my
command.

These men, from the first, were not sincere Christians; but when
the conspiracy first broke out they were beset by a great multitude and
compelled to support the cause. These eight hundred men all have a
sincere respect for the [samurai] class. Therefore speedily attack the
castle, and we having received your answer, without fail, as to time, will
make a show of resisting you, but will set fire to the houses in the castle,
and escape to your camp. Only I will run to the house of [Amakusa
Shirō] and make as if all were lost; and having induced him to embark
with me in a small boat, will take him alive, bring him to you, and thus
manifest to you the sincerity of my intentions. For this purpose I have
prepared several boats already, having revolved the matter in my mind
from the time I entered the castle. Please give me your approval immediately, and I will overthrow the evil [rebels], give tranquillity to the
empire, and, I trust, escape with my own life. I am extremely anxious

to receive your orders. Yamada Emonsaku thus addresses you with true regard. 20th of 1st Month [5th March]. To the commanders of the [shogunal] army.   *7.80*

This was a risky plan and, not surprisingly, it misfired. One of the "arrow letters" sent to Yamada from outside the castle was intercepted, and the rebels were thus alerted to his treachery. Yamada was bound up and sentenced to death. While he awaited execution, however, the castle was stormed and he was promptly rescued. Later Yamada was taken to Edo by Lord Matsudaira and safely installed in his mansion, where he served as Matsudaira's assistant. Though he had failed to deliver Amakusa Shirō to the enemy, he justified his rescue by providing Bakufu officials with the only detailed account of the uprising from the rebels' side.   *7.81*

Before returning to Edo, the commanding general made certain final dispositions. Amakusa Shirō's head was sent to Nagasaki, where it was publicly gibbeted together with those of his elder sister and Kozaemon. His mother and little sister were executed, and his remaining relatives sent to a village in Shimabara where they were all subsequently put to death. Finally Old Hara Castle, the scene of so much courage and pain, was razed to the ground in order that it might never become a rallying point or a place of pilgrimage for future troublemakers.   *7.82*

The rebellion ended in unmitigated failure. Not only were the tens of thousands of participants all slaughtered (with the exception of the treacherous Yamada), but the uprising made conditions far worse than before. Just as Yoshitsune's futile resistance had played directly into the hands of his brother, so the Great Christian Rebellion of 1637–38 proved immensely useful to the government in several different ways. This indeed was its main historical result. For one thing, almost all the ex-samurai Christians in Japan and all the main dissident elements in western Kyushu had been conveniently massed in Hara Castle, and all were exterminated in a clean sweep that is the dream of any repressive regime. Moreover, potential rebels in the rest of Japan had been offered a grim warning. For the shogunal government in Edo and for the local authorities in the west, the uprising was the last major challenge for well over two centuries, and its suppression led to an era of law and order under a remarkably effective form of central feudalism. Only occasionally was the long Tokugawa peace troubled by plots and riots, and these were promptly quashed by the overwhelming forces of the military authorities.

New local overlords and officials were appointed to govern Shimabara and Amakusa, and some of the worst horrors of the previous administrations were abated. Yet the rebellion brought *7.83* little real improvement to the lot of the peasants, who continued to toil hard and lose much of their produce in taxes. It did, however, have a definite effect in increasing the severity of religious persecution, especially in western Kyushu. All suspected believers were done to death, and apostates were forced to confirm their renunciation of Christianity by repeating the ritual of stepping on holy images. On Bakufu orders the decimated regions of Shimabara and Amakusa were resettled by compulsory migration from different parts of the country where Christianity had not gained a foothold. Special measures were taken *7.84* to foster Buddhism. The Bakufu, which now assumed direct control of the Amakusa Islands, encouraged the building of new temples and Shinto shrines, and promoted indoctrination against the subversive faith that had caused them so much trouble and *7.85* expense.

The collapse of Amakusa Shirō's rebellion marked the end of overt Christian worship in Japan. The Bakufu, having become thoroughly alarmed by the uprising, now enforced the anti-Christian edicts more rigidly than ever before, and the results *7.86* were overwhelming. The largest wave of arrests took place about twenty years after the rebellion in a rural district near Nagasaki. A visiting farmer mentioned an extraordinary Christian boy of thirteen who had even greater supernatural powers than Amakusa Shirō. The authorities lost no time in rounding up some six hundred villagers, of whom 411 were executed, seventy-seven died in prison, and ninety-nine were freed after taking the *7.87* oath of apostasy. The time for Christian resistance had long since passed.

Another unintended, and still more important, effect of the rebellion was to reinforce the shogunate's antiforeign policy. The Christian uprising had made the government more nervous than ever about foreigners and had stimulated xenophobic feelings among many members of the ruling samurai class. Conservative elements in the government found it an ideal pretext to

strengthen *sakoku*, the policy of foreign exclusion, which now
assumed its most extreme form. In 1639 a new Bakufu edict dealt
a death-blow to the century-old trade with Portugal. For the next
two hundred years the only Western traders allowed in Japan
were the Dutch, who by their ignominious role at Shimabara had
proved that they were unlikely to abet local Christians. The edict
was enforced with draconian severity. In 1640 a Portuguese ship
from Macão reached Nagasaki with envoys who had come to
plead with the government to modify its ban. They were
promptly arrested, bound, and imprisoned, and their ship was
burnt. On 1st August the chief shogunal commissioner addressed
them with some acerbity:

You villains! You have been forbidden ever to return to Japan on pain
of death, and you have disobeyed the command. The former year you
were guilty of death but were mercifully granted your lives. Hence you
have earned this time nothing but the most painful death; but since you
have come without merchandise and only to beg for something, this will
be commuted to an easy death.   *7.88*

An executioner was assigned to each of the sixty-one envoys and
they were all beheaded on Martyr's Hill in Nagasaki. Thirteen
crewmen were allowed to return to Macão to report on the fate
of their masters and to carry an official message with the warning: ". . . [even if] King Felipe himself, or even the very God of
the Christians, or the great Buddha contravene this prohibition,
they shall pay for it with their heads!"

Japan's exclusion policy was perhaps bound to reach this
final stage in any case; but the catastrophic rebellion at
Shimabara was certainly the immediate cause of measures that
not only removed any hope of outside support for Christianity
but in one way or another affected almost every aspect of Japanese life. It was hardly the outcome that Amakusa Shirō and his
fellow insurgents had anticipated.

Amakusa Shirō's career, bizarre and nebulous though it was,
fits at almost every point into the pattern of Japanese failed
heroism. He fought bravely for a doomed cause and after the
usual period of early success led his followers to unconditional
disaster. The fantastic *élan* and courage of the Shimabara rebels,

which contrast with the cautious, lacklustre calculation of the enemy, could never prevail in the world of sober reality. Amakusa Shirō appears in the legend as a pure, idealistic youth, endowed with the preternatural gifts and romantic charm of a Yoshitsune, who led the downtrodden peasants of Kyushu in an absurd act of defiance against the forces of authority. His heroic sincerity is reflected in a failure to lay careful, realistic plans and in a refusal to vitiate the ideals of his crusade by negotiation and
7.89   compromise. The conquering general, Lord Matsudaira, survived to enjoy the rewards of his success, but never came to be adulated as a hero and has been almost totally forgotten except by students of Tokugawa history; for the great man of Shimabara
7.90   was, inevitably, the loser.

Unlike most of Japan's failed heroes, Amakusa Shirō refrained from taking his own life; this, however, was not due to any lack of resolve but because of his adherence to a faith that forbade self-slaughter. Here, of course, we come to the greatest incongruity of all: this most Japanese of heroes was fighting for a faith that was completely alien to his country's traditions. Despite the underlying economic motives of the rebellion, Amakusa Shirō and the other leaders invariably expressed their objectives in religious terms. And the religion they professed was a foreign creed supported by only a small minority of the population and
7.91   rigidly interdicted by the government. To this forlorn cause they gave their lives as martyrs. They differed entirely from Christian martyrs in the West, however, in that their suffering and violent death did not lead to any posthumous success; indeed, the uprising produced exactly the reverse of the effect they had intended, since it led to the final suppression of Christianity in Japan. In this sense the Shimabara insurgents correspond less to our Christian martyrs than to heretic groups like the Albigensians or to the peasants who rebelled under Wat Tyler in fourteenth-century England; for their failure was total and irremediable.

Despite its violent history, Japan had had no tradition of religious persecution or martyrdom. Buddhism, Shintoism, and Confucianism had managed to coexist with remarkably little friction; and, though there were conflicts between the various Buddhist sects, they were based mainly on material, rather than doctrinal, differences, and rarely took the form of the intolerant *odium theologicum* that caused so much horror and misery in the
7.92   West. Not until the late sixteenth century, when the spread of

Christianity made the government decide that this subversive, foreign creed had to be suppressed, did large-scale persecution and martyrdom make their grim appearance in Japan. It is typical that Amakusa Shirō and the majority of his countrymen who suffered and were killed because of their faith should have been martyrs for a failed religion.

"Save the People!"

In 1837, a year of famine in Osaka, an eminent Confucian scholar, who had formerly distinguished himself as a police official of the city, led an uprising in protest against the conditions of the starving townspeople. Ōshio Heihachirō's rebellion was an unmitigated fiasco.  The main participants were hunted down by the forces of Tokugawa law and order and their lives brought to an end in various painful ways; nor was the misery of the populace alleviated one iota by the sacrifices of Ōshio and his followers.

It is hardly surprising that this furious opponent of economic injustice should be respected by left-wing radicals as a prototype of the modern revolutionary fighter who gives his life for the people in the struggle against an intolerable status quo. Ōshio, however, cannot be pigeonholed as a social reformer or a champion of the downtrodden masses; rather, he embodies characteristics that are common to the general tradition of the Japanese hero, and his admirers are far from being restricted to one end of the political spectrum. In recent years his philosophy and heroic example had a decisive effect on Mishima Yukio, a writer who was hardly noted for his commitment to left-wing politics. I recall that during one of our last conversations Mishima mentioned Ōshio Heihachirō as the fierce type of hero that Westerners would do well to study if they wished to understand the essence of the Japanese spirit, which, as he gently pointed out, was not exclusively represented by diaries of Heian Court ladies, elegant poetry exchanges, or ritual tea ceremony. Shortly afterwards he composed an essay examining the revolutionary implications of Wang Yang-ming and also the lessons that present-day Japanese could learn from the hero who organized the revolt of 1837.   *8.1*

This carefully written and deeply felt article was published only a few months before Mishima staged his pseudo-coup in the Eastern Corps Headquarters in Tokyo and committed harakiri at forty-five—precisely the age at which Ōshio Heihachirō, having failed in his rebellion, stabbed himself to death in Osaka. Mishima's essay stressed that the intense, "demonic" aspect of Wang Yang-ming philosophy had always made it suspect among more conventional types of Confucianists, who were inclined to pragmatism and compromise. Owing to its stress on action, as opposed to mere study and observation, it was a philosophy, or rather an approach to life, that accorded with revolution and with unquestioning dedication to a righteous cause however visionary it might seem to common-sense empiricists.   *8.2*

Wang Yang-ming, the sixteenth-century scholar-official who founded the Idealist School of Ming Confucianism, had set an   *8.3* example in his own dramatic career by shaking himself free from intellect and "taking the leap from knowledge into action." His   *8.4* followers in both China and Japan were men who were forever mindful of their own deaths, knowing that their sincerity and refusal to compromise with the world's injustice would almost certainly lead them to a violent end; but, far from fearing this outcome, they welcomed it as the supreme token of their rejection of worldly selfishness. This, according to Mishima, is a far cry from the ethos of present-day Japan. Ever since the end of the Pacific war, he wrote, the Japanese people have been determined to "play it safe," attaching overwhelming importance to security and material ease and ignoring what is unique and most precious in their country's heritage. In consequence their bodies go on   *8.5* living longer than before but their spirits die an early death. Ironically enough, the outstanding exceptions to this drab, conformist *modus vivendi* have been members of the radical student movement, who have not shirked risks and sacrifices in their dedication to the seemingly hopeless cause of destroying the conservative Establishment. Though Mishima was one of the most outspoken adversaries of Zengakuren and other left-wing groups, whose specific objectives were diametrically opposed to his own, and though he conceived his Shield Society (*Tate no Kai*) as a symbolic force to protect the Emperor from their depredations, he had a certain grudging admiration for these young zealots who, like the traditional heroes of earlier times, were prepared to *act* rather than simply study and talk.

8.6   Ever since the noble suicide of General Nogi in 1912, says Mishima, the philosophy of Wang Yang-ming has been largely ignored in Japan, where intellectuals have ostracized it as a form of "dangerous thought" that should be hidden not only from

8.7   foreigners but from the Japanese themselves. Yet this philosophy was a central inspiration of the most eminent heroes in modern Japanese history. Mishima refers to its influence on Saigō

8.8   Takamori and General Nogi; but the major part of his essay is focused on the way in which Wang Yang-ming's philosophy determined the heroic climax of Ōshio Heihachirō's life. As Mishima points out, Ōshio's continued fame and prestige in Japan are due, not to his official career or even to his scholarly achievements, but to the action he took in pursuance of his ideals—an action that was totally unsuccessful.

The hero of the second volume of Mishima's final tetralogy is Isao, a dedicated youth who risks his life in a harebrained rightist coup during the 1930s and who, after the plot had been betrayed and wrecked, slashes himself to death with a dagger. Isao is deeply affected by Ōshio Heihachirō's philosophy and by the story of his revolt, which he reads in prison while awaiting

8.9   trial. Later in the courtroom Isao (like so many of the actual young ultra-nationalists during the 1930s) fervidly explains his *Weltanschauung* to the judge. He starts by quoting the famous dictum of Wang Yang-ming: "To know and not to act is the same

8.10   as not knowing at all." Then he elaborates on his own motives, which he now recognizes as being akin to those of Ōshio Heihachirō one hundred years earlier:

It was this philosophy that I strove to put into practice. To know of the decadence of Japan today . . . to know of the impoverished state of the farmers and the despair of the poor, to know that all this is due to political corruption and to the callous contempt for the people shown by the financial combines [Zaibatsu] who turn this corruption to their own profit . . . such knowledge automatically makes it incumbent upon

8.11   one to take action. . . .

The culminating act in Mishima Yukio's life was also determined, at least on the conscious level, by the philosophy of Ōshio

Heihachirō. In a letter that Mishima wrote to me just before his death he said:

. . . You may be one of the very few people who can understand my conclusion. Influenced by Yōmei [Wang Yang-ming] philosophy, I have believed that knowing without acting is not sufficiently knowing and the action itself does not require any effectiveness.   *8.12*

Despite Mishima's generous assumption, I confess that at the time I did not fully understand his explanation. Subsequently, however, my study of Ōshio and other representatives of the Japanese heroic tradition has made it abundantly clear: Mishima was referring to the inherent value of the sincere, self-sacrificial act, a value which is entirely irrelevant to its practical effectiveness and which may, on the contrary, be given additional validity by failure. Truly "it is the journey not the arrival that matters."

Ōshio Heihachirō is a complex, controversial figure. For all his idealism and sympathy with the unfavoured people of the world, he was an inflexible, humourless, and even cruel man, who as a police official harshly persecuted Christian believers in Osaka, and who later did not hesitate to order the assassination of one of his own followers when he thought (incorrectly as it appears) that he might compromise the plot. Yet the failure of his uprising and his dramatic suicide instantly elevated him to the status of hero—the perfect hero, in fact, whose personality is idealized and whose shortcomings, however blatant, are all forgotten. Moreover, like so many of Japan's tragic heroes whose worldly careers terminated in catastrophe, Ōshio Heihachirō was not allowed to die but was given a fictitious continuation in legend: instead of ending his life gorily in a towel merchant's house in Osaka, he escaped to China where, having been transmogrified into Hung Hsiu-chü'an, he led a new (and even more disastrous) uprising, the Taiping Rebellion.   *8.13*

The common denominator of Ōshio Heihachirō's diversified admirers was their loathing of the political and moral status quo and their determination to confront the existing power structure by whatever dangerous and violent methods might be necessary, and however hopeless their efforts might appear. The 1837 rebellion stimulated similar riots *(ikki)* and "smashings" *(uchikowashi)* both in the Osaka region and in other parts of the country. Though these risings differed greatly in scale and objectives, they

8.14 were identical in one respect—all were ineffective. Sometimes
the leaders were the remnants of Ōshio's own band who had
survived the disaster of 1837. Most of the rebellions, however,
were headed by men who had no direct connexion with Ōshio yet
regarded themselves as his spiritual successors; and in their declarations and manifestoes they proudly proclaimed the name of
8.15 "Lord Heihachirō." Despite all his rigidity, intolerance, and impracticality, the failed philosopher was a charismatic figure, idol-
ized by the poor townsfolk and simple peasants of the time. The
indigent inhabitants of Osaka and its environs had certainly
derived no material benefit from Ōshio's insurrection, whose
main practical result had been the incineration of their dwellings
and meagre belongings; yet after his death they regarded him as
their champion, and we are told that they would secretly copy his
8.16 Summons (Gekibun) and use it for practicing calligraphy.
Ōshio's admirers were not restricted to the downtrodden members of society; he was also much respected by late Tokugawa
loyalist thinkers who (quite mistakenly) represented him as a
dedicated anti-Bakufu revolutionary intent on demolishing the
existing political system.

   After Japan's opening to the West in the Meiji period and the
consequent transformation of the sociopolitical structure, Ōshio
Heihachirō's fame underwent a temporary eclipse; but as dissatisfaction with the central government began to grow in the
1870s he became the hero for many elements who opposed the
new oligarchy. He was particularly admired by men of the
League of the Divine Wind, a society of nationalist zealots in
Kyushu who violently opposed the government's policy of encouraging Western ways and abolishing old customs like the
wearing of swords. In 1876 there was a typical confrontation of
"Japanese spirit" *(Yamato-damashii)* against material power when
members of the League, furiously wielding their samurai swords,
slashed their way into an imperial garrison, whose defenders
were equipped with modern weapons, and after a few prelimi-
8.17 nary successes were totally exterminated. Ōshio was also a hero
for the leader of Japan's last important national insurrection, the
8.18 Satsuma Rebellion. Saigō Takamori, whose disastrous uprising
occurred exactly forty years after the Osaka revolt, was, as
Mishima points out, much influenced by Ōshio's form of neo-
Confucianism; and one of the books he most frequently read and
quoted in his own writings was a collection of Ōshio's philosoph-

ical lectures. At about the same time members of the burgeoning *8.19*
"people's rights" movement, whose campaign for democratic reform led them to oppose the imperial absolutism of the Meiji
oligarchy, referred to Ōshio as a precursor in their struggle—not,
of course, because they shared any specific objectives (Ōshio
could hardly be pictured as a believer in political democracy) but
because they defied established injustice with the same fierce,
self-sacrificial approach. *8.20*

During the present century Ōshio Heihachirō has had a
similar diversity of admirers. In 1918 he was represented as an
inspiration for the participants in the "rice riots" that swept
Osaka and other large cities. In the 1920s Ōshio was taken up by *8.21*
the dialectical materialists and pictured as a heroic pioneer whose
rebellion represented the first act of conscious resistance in the
class struggle against the old feudal order. During the period of
ultra-nationalism that started in the following decade Ōshio was
much esteemed by right-wing intellectuals, and he also had an *8.22*
influence on the "young officers" and ultra-nationalists, whose
sanguinary coups during the 1930s almost invariably failed to
achieve their objectives. With the reversal of the political climate *8.23*
after 1945, Ōshio once again became a hero for members of the
left; yet he was at the same time a model for Mishima Yukio.

Such a protean hero inspires a rich and varied literature.
Apart from extensive historical documentation of Ōshio, there
are books and plays of a more popular nature. In the Tokugawa
period his revolt had hardly been suppressed before it was taken
as material by playwrights and professional storytellers, who
rapidly spread his fame through the country. Later in the nineteenth century he was much respected by Meiji writers as a
model of idealism and self-sacrifice. By far the most eminent *8.24*
Japanese author to use Ōshio as a hero was the novelist Mori
Ōgai. As Donald Keene has pointed out, Ōgai was inspired by
General Nogi's suicide in 1912 to abandon his successful career as
a writer of fiction in the German romantic tradition "to devote
himself exclusively to painstaking, historically accurate accounts
of virtuous samurai, considering that they represented the essence of what it meant to be a Japanese." Among these works is *8.25*
a short, exciting novel that focuses on the two last days of
Ōshio's life. During the "liberal" era of the early 1920s a success- *8.26*
ful play was produced in which Ōshio figures as a great humanitarian leader; and in the postwar period he has been the hero of

a number of stage and television dramas where he appears as a brave idealist pitting himself hopelessly against a callous, conservative Establishment.

In the life of the Japanese failed hero, there usually arrives a moment when he suddenly realizes that his early upward course of success has reached its limit and that from this point forward the emotional logic which determined his career—the sincerity, the courage, the refusal to compromise with the evil forces of reality—will ineluctably plummet him to defeat and disaster. Thus the prototypal hero, Yamato Takeru, having returned from his victories in the west, is promptly despatched on a new mission to the eastern provinces and senses that his father, the Emperor, wishes him to die at an early age. In the legendary account of Yoshitsune, the hero has his awakening at the post station of Koshigoe when his last appeal to Yoritomo is rebuffed and he understands that his all-powerful brother is determined to destroy him. For Masashige the fatal hour comes when the Court rejects his advice and orders him to proceed to the Inland Sea, where he knows he will meet his defeat. In the career of Saigō the Great the corresponding turning point is when he hears about the precipitous action of his hot-headed young followers, who have broken into the government armoury, and realizes that now he has no alternative but to confront the might of the Imperial Army. After these crucial moments of truth the hero, far from losing heart, becomes fully aware of his calling and draws on inner resources that will enable him to stay the hard course until the end.

In the story of Ōshio Heihachirō the knowledge that all is lost comes a few hours after the uprising has started. The massive support that he expected from the nearby villages has not materialized, and the townspeople to whom he distributed weapons have been more inclined to use them for pillaging coins and looting *sake* warehouses and silk shops than for fighting the government troops. Surrounded by a handful of confederates, Ōshio sits on a campstool at the end of Naniwa Bridge and meditatively munches a rice ball as he gazes at the flaming buildings across the river and listens to the roar of the government cannon. Shortly afterwards he withdraws to a new position and orders that the great drum be sounded for retreat. The fight will continue, but there is no longer a scintilla of doubt concerning its outcome.

8.27

8.28

8.29

8.30

8.31

Like the other heroes Ōshio has experienced a total peripetia; and it is at these key moments that one most keenly realizes the contrast between the preceding success and the catastrophe that is to ensue. Much of the appeal of the *hōganbiiki* type of hero derives from this contrast: it is because he has such a great distance to fall that the hero's failure stirs the emotions.

Though Ōshio Heihachirō never approached the worldly heights of a Michizane or a Yoshitsune, any objective observer at the beginning of 1837 would have pronounced him a successful man. Scholar, official, and gentleman-samurai, he epitomised in his career all that was most respected by contemporary society. The city where he was born and where forty-five years later he met his dramatic end was Osaka, the commercial centre, seaport, and money mart, which enjoyed an economic importance in Tokugawa Japan comparable to that of Manchester in Victorian England. Though the population had fallen since the middle of the eighteenth century as the centre of economic and cultural activity steadily shifted to Edo, the western market-city retained its prestige. Mitsui, Kōnoike, and the other huge merchant houses grew steadily in wealth and power. Osaka continued as the "kitchen of Japan," and if conditions in the city became dislocated there were bound to be national repercussions.

In the early nineteenth century the country was still very much a self-contained, isolated unit. To be sure, the Tokugawa era was reaching its end, and there were increasing presages of challenge from the Western powers. Yet the established order of centralized feudalism was still in force, and the government protected itself from foreign contamination by preserving its two-hundred-year-old policy of "chaining off the land" (*sakoku*). When a small vessel, the *Morrison*, chartered in China by American missionaries, brought home some Japanese castaways for repatriation, the Tokugawa officials ordered their batteries to open fire upon her. By this unhospitable gesture, which occurred in 1837 (the year of Ōshio's insurrection), the government served notice on foreigners and Japanese alike that the status quo was to be rigidly maintained.

It was into such a closed and seemingly stable world that Ōshio was born in 1793, the eldest son of a samurai family of intermediate rank. Despite all the social changes during the long Tokugawa period, the samurai class, which numbered less than

8.32

8.33

8.34

ten percent in most of the fiefs, still retained a virtual monopoly,
not only of military power, but of administrative and judicial
functions. Ōshio's father held a hereditary post as Police Inspector in the Magistrate's Office in Osaka, and according to the
contemporary system of appointments this was the office that
would in due course accrue to his eldest son. For all his
egalitarian professions, Ōshio was inordinately proud of his lineage and made a point of tracing his ancestry back to a vassal house
of the Tokugawas.

Having lost both his parents at an early age (his father died
when he was six and his mother in the following year), young
Heihachirō was brought up by his grandparents; later he was
adopted by two successive foster families, the second of whom,
the Ōshios, held the same type of hereditary post in the Osaka
8.35 Magistracy as his own father. According to Mishima, this unsettled childhood accounts for the hero's fierce, tense, hot-tempered
8.36 nature. Such quasi-Freudian speculations about personality
traits are apt to be facile and suspect; but it is surely significant
that Mishima, who was himself brought up largely by his grandmother, should have explained his hero's character in this way.

In his youth Ōshio evinced a special fascination with philosophical studies. As a member of the samurai class he also devoted
himself to the military arts, especially spear-throwing; but he had
little interest in firearms, perhaps because of their foreign, unheroic connotations, and we are reminded that one of the immediate reasons for the failure of his revolt was the inability of
his followers to make good use of their guns and cannons. In 1818
at the age of twenty-five he defied social convention by marrying
the adopted daughter of a rich farmer. Such "downward" marriages were generally discouraged in samurai circles, and the
young man's decision is often cited as an example of his headstrong, iconoclastic nature. A portrait of Ōshio Heihachirō that
8.37 must have been made about this time shows a slender, handsome
young man with samurai topknot and shaven head; he is seated
in formal robes with his two swords neatly in position, a white
fan in his hand, and a solemn expression on his long, oval face.
Descriptions made at the time say that he was five and a half feet
high (quite tall for the period); his arched, narrow eyebrows
surmounted a pair of tense, acute, penetrating eyes; and on his
wide, pale forehead one could make out the delicate blue veins.
Maliciously he was nicknamed "green gourd" (aobyōtan) in refer-

ence to his pallid complexion, a result of weak lungs. He frequently suffered from haemorrhages, but managed to surmount
his physical handicap by unremitting will-power.

At the age of twenty-three Ōshio automatically succeeded to
his father's office as Police Inspector under the jurisdiction of the
Municipal Commissioner for Eastern Osaka, a high shogunal
official from Edo. There was a total of sixty such Inspectors
(thirty each under the eastern and western Commissioners), and
between them they were responsible for day-to-day judicial and
administrative functions in the city. Though they occupied a
fairly low rung on the feudal ladder, their position could be
extremely lucrative, since traditional perquisites included "gratitude money" from merchant-class litigants and others who
sought their favours. Ōshio made it clear that he would have no
truck with this particular tradition. From the outset the future
rebel distinguished himself by his rigid adherence to the rules.
Such rectitude might seriously have hampered Ōshio's career,
but his position was solidified a few years after his appointment
when an elderly dignitary named Takai, Governor of Yamashiro,
arrived from Edo as Municipal Commissioner for Eastern Osaka.
Takai was immediately impressed by his zealous young subordinate and gave him full backing in his campaign to fight corruption and impose the law.

Ōshio's first important achievement came at the age of
thirty-four when, after painstaking investigation, he uncovered
a number of hidden Christian believers in Osaka and ordered
their mass arrest. Having sent these luckless individuals to their
doom, he turned his energies to a more challenging problem,
corruption in the municipal administration. Thanks to Takai's
patronage he was soon able to make himself a scourge of dishon-
est officials and merchants. After only a couple of years Ōshio had
become famous for his drive against bribery. Often he called
attention to his campaign by unconventional tactics. On one
occasion, in a move that adumbrated the last part of his career,
he ordered that the wealth accumulated by a certain venal official
be confiscated and distributed among the poor people of the city,
whose appalling condition had already begun to incite his indignation. Ōshio made particular efforts to expose corruption in the
courts. A typical incident occurred when Takai instructed him
to settle a certain lawsuit that had dragged on for several years.
The plaintiff, hearing that Ōshio was now in charge of the case,

8.38

visited him late at night, bringing along a box of sweetmeats as a gift. On the following day Ōshio, who had carefully examined the evidence (and also the box), declared that the plaintiff was in the wrong and that his plea must fail. At a subsequent meeting with his colleagues he produced the box of delicacies and remarked with an acerbic smile, "It's because you gentlemen have such sweet teeth that it has taken so long to settle this case." He then raised the lid, revealing a glittering pile of gold coins. We are told that the other inspectors blushed crimson and did not say a word.

This was hardly the type of behaviour to endear Ōshio to his less principled fellow officials, and before long many of them came to resent him for "excessive integrity." Yet his intelligence, his learning, and above all his honesty in performing judicial duties won him widespread popular regard as well as the respect of successive shogunal representatives from Edo.

Ōshio's attentions were not limited to secret Christians and venal officials. His ire was also aroused by corruption in the Buddhist establishment; in 1830 he prosecuted a number of Buddhist priests who had been breaking their vows, and in consequence many of them were derobed and banished from Osaka. It was in this year, when his reputation was reaching its zenith, that Ōshio suddenly resigned from public life, bequeathing his post as Police Inspector to his adopted son, Kakunosuke, and resolving to devote himself entirely to teaching, scholarship, and the correction of social evils. Why at the age of only thirty-seven should an intelligent and energetic man like Ōshio have cut short his promising career to become an *inkyo* ("retired person")? The fact that his old patron, Takai, also resigned in that year and returned to Edo may explain the timing of his decision. But a more important reason was that he had become discouraged by the rampant corruption in the municipal administration and by the indifference of his fellow officials to the sufferings of the poorer townspeople; like Saigō the Great some forty years later, he retired from office so that he might reinvigorate himself spiritually, develop his own thinking, train a group of disciples, and try to rectify the unjust system from outside.

Not long after his retirement Ōshio experienced a spiritual trauma which appears to have had a profound influence on the rest of his life and which, according to Mishima, was analogous in its effect to Saigō's attempt to drown himself with his friend,

the priest Gesshō. He had made a pilgrimage to the school in   *8.39*
Ōmi where Nakae Tōju ("The Holy Man of Ōmi") had expounded the teachings of Wang Yang-ming some two centuries
earlier. On his return to Osaka he was crossing Lake Biwa when
a fierce storm arose and it seemed almost certain that he would
be drowned. As water filled the boat, he entrusted himself to
Heaven and started contemplating his death. At this moment he
had an "awakening" and realized that a certain philosophical
poem about failure to attain intuitive knowledge *(ryōchi)*, which
he had written during his recent visit, applied not to mankind in
general but specifically to himself. "I now understood," wrote
Ōshio, "that, unless I was able to find fault with myself, all the   *8.40*
learning I had accumulated in my life was of no avail. As I sat
there immobile, with the waves raging about me, I had the vision
that I was being directly confronted with Wang Yang-ming himself. If only I could negate [lit. forget] my own identity, how
could the roaring waves have the slightest effect upon me? At that
moment all fear and regret vanished like snow melting in the
sun. . . ." Shortly afterwards the storm abated and Ōshio was
saved. He returned frequently to the school in Ōmi, where he
gathered the local villagers and lectured to them about the attainment of intuitive knowledge and self-clarification. This mystical   *8.41*
experience on the lake may well have propelled Ōshio to total
emotional commitment and prepared him for his final action and
death in a way that no amount of study or abstract reasoning
would have achieved.

   After his retirement Ōshio could devote ample time to study
and writing. Of his numerous philosophical works the most famous was his collection of lectures, which was compiled in 1833
and soon spread his scholarly reputation through the country.   *8.42*
Ōshio (like his spiritual successor, Mishima Yukio) was far from
shunning literary publicity. When his lectures were published,
he took one section of the book to the top of a hill near the Great
Ise Shrine and burnt it as a dedication to the sun goddess; shortly
afterwards he placed another copy in a cave on the sacred Mount
Fuji. Mishima suggests Ōshio's aim may have been to immortalize his spirit by informing the gods that he had completed his
work; also he may have foreseen the conflagration of 1837 and
wished to make sure that at least one original manuscript of his
book would be preserved. In any case his behaviour here, as in   *8.43*
so many other ways, was unprecedented among Japanese writers.

Despite his impressive attainments as a Confucian scholar, Ōshio gave his main energies during the last period of his life to the private school he had founded in Osaka. The Senshindō Juku (Cleansing-the-Heart-to-Obtain-Insight Academy) was open to all students, regardless of class, so long as Ōshio considered them suitable subjects for his philosophical and moral training; and the Academy may well have influenced Mishima Yukio's decision a few years before his death to create his Shield Society, where he recruited high-minded, patriotic young men from different social milieux. Ōshio's emphasis was on inculcating his particular form of neo-Confucianism; but students were also trained in calligraphy, fencing, and other traditional subjects. His lectures were terse and aphoristic, consisting mainly of categorical conclusions rather than analysis and argument, and depending to a large extent on the emotive repetition of certain central ideas. Ōshio's approach as a teacher was very much that of a samurai, and he relied greatly on zeal and discipline. The curriculum was severe, usually involving four hours of concentrated study at a stretch, and the puritanical rules, as set forth in eight articles, or "oaths" (*meisei*), were imposed with terrible severity, including liberal use of the whip for delinquents.

8.44

In view of these austere conditions it may seem surprising that Ōshio was able to recruit (and retain) a schoolful of voluntary students. Evidently he was a brilliant teacher, whose inspiring personality and vigorous samurai spirit could inspire young people with readiness for self-sacrifice.

His strong will and idealism were combined with a wild, hot-tempered nature that bordered on the frenetic. During one of his lectures he worked himself into such a state of fury concerning the iniquities of the government that he abruptly seized a gurnard that was baking on a grill in the corner of the room and gobbled up the entire fish from head to tail with a loud crunching of bones. Sometimes Ōshio's righteous wrath was turned against members of his own family, including his wife. Despite her humble social origins she was well versed in the Confucian classics, and when her husband was busy she often substituted for him by lecturing on *The Great Learning* and other texts. On one occasion someone sent her a decorative comb. Knowing her husband's principles against accepting gifts of any kind, she decided to hide the object until she had an opportunity to return it. Ōshio happened to discover the comb. In a livid rage

8.45

he ordered his wife to shave off her hair in the style of a nun. Like so many famous men in history who have championed the down-trodden elements of society, he seems to have had little tolerance, humility, or gentleness in his actual dealings with individuals. Ōshio's intolerance may well remind us of Him who drove the money-changers from the Temple; but he was the very opposite of the man who washed His disciples' feet or who allowed Mary to anoint Him with costly ointment of spikenard.

The philosophy that came to dominate Ōshio's life and that finally drove this loyal samurai to rebel against the government he had served was perfectly suited to his complex personality. Its founder, Wang Yang-ming (1472–1529), combined an energetic ca- *8.46* reer as soldier-statesman with that of philosopher. He spent much of his time campaigning successfully against rebels; but he appears to have been a poor politician, and partly owing to slan-der at the Court in Peking, his services received scant recognition from the government. Despite this lack of worldly success, Wang Yang-ming's school became a centre of reformist activism, and his ideas were seminal for later generations in China.

The individualistic philosophy of Wang Yang-ming took root in Japan about one century after his death, and since then it has had an important, though intermittent, influence. During *8.47* the early decades of the Tokugawa period, his form of neo-Confu-cianism was established as an independent school, whose main founder, the famous philosopher and teacher Nakae Tōju, had exemplified his filial piety by giving up an important official position to look after his aged mother in a village near Lake Biwa. In his determination to spread the truth Nakae did not hesitate to address himself to the humblest members of society, who were largely neglected by exponents of the more orthodox forms of Confucianism. The most famous of Nakae's disciples was *8.48* Kumazawa Banzan, an energetic *rōnin* philosopher-official who was much concerned with the plight of the esurient peasantry and who, though persecuted for his unorthodox ideas, tried to apply Wang Yang-ming's principles to the field of political action by instituting a practical programme of reform in the fief near Osaka where he served.

Though Wang Yang-ming's basic tenets will hardly strike the modern reader as inflammatory, in Tokugawa Japan his philosophy was regarded as a subversive heterodoxy. The official form of neo-Confucianism, which under Bakufu tutelage came

close to being a state religion, was based on the teachings of Chu
Hsi, who in the twelfth century had evolved a synthesis of Confucianist teachings that put overwhelming stress on knowledge as
a preparation for correct conduct and that came to be known as
8.49   the School of Reason, or Principle. The official school of Chu Hsi
philosophy as established in Japan during the early decades of the
Tokugawa period emphasized traditional loyalties to state and
family. Attaching great importance to external, mechanical pro-
priety, it tended towards a narrow and conventional formalism,
which like the Church of England in the days of Queen Victoria
supported the social and political status quo at almost every
point.

By contrast the adherents of Wang Yang-ming favoured an
individualistic approach to the human condition. They believed
that the truth was to be found by intuition rather than cold
8.50   reason. Nakae Tōju and subsequent Japanese followers of Wang
Yang-ming differed among themselves in many respects, but all
agreed on the primacy of introspection, independence of mind,
and a pure conscience. Clearly this approach had much in common with that of Zen Buddhism, which for many centuries had
exerted a most powerful influence on the emotional and aesthetic
lives of the upper class; and one reason that Wang Yang-ming's
form of neo-Confucianism appealed to many thinkers and activists in modern Japan was that it corresponded to the Zen strain
8.51   in the national tradition. Like Zen Buddhism, Wang Yang-ming
Confucianism rejected conformism and pedantry in favour of a
direct perception of the truth attained by self-command. The
understanding and control of the self were regarded as more
important than any type of formal reasoning. Proper behaviour
in society came not from adherence to traditions and precepts or
from fear of punishment but from the individual's intuitive
moral sense, which would prompt him to act in a sincere and
generous way. The philosophy of Wang Yang-ming had a strong
antischolastic bent. Certain outstanding adherents such as
Kumazawa Banzan were largely self-taught and gave their energy overwhelmingly to practical action rather than book-learn-
ing; but even the more scholarly representatives of this school
tended to denigrate the authority of written works and support
a subjective morality leading to sincere action. In this respect
there is an obvious similarity with the approach of Zen. As part
of the Buddhist religious tradition, however, Zen was always

more concerned with the individual's ability to achieve enlightenment for himself by meditation and other means, whereas Wang Yang-ming philosophy, being a form of Confucianism, focused on the individual's actions in society.

The Tokugawa Bakufu, with its strongly conservative approach and devotion to rules, precedents, and established authority, was bound to look askance at such a nonconformist, individualistic philosophy. The Chu Hsi type of neo-Confucianism received all official support, and finally in 1790 the Shogun's chief adviser published an edict forbidding the dissemination of "different doctrines." The measure, though conferring a monopoly on the teachings of Chu Hsi, did not prevent scholars of Wang Yang-ming persuasion from advocating their ideas in writing or from maintaining their private academies.

In the 1830s, when the edict was still in force, the most eminent of such philosophers was Ōshio Heihachirō. Though he had started his intellectual career as a believer in Chu Hsi's form of neo-Confucianism, he gradually abandoned it in favour of the rival, heretical school of Wang Yang-ming, which was more compatible with his own independent, activist temperament. Thus, many years before Ōshio even remotely envisaged the possibility of a revolt, he had adopted a stance of intellectual opposition to the Establishment.

Ōshio's system of metaphysics, which profoundly influenced his own career and that of many a heroic successor, was based on Wang Yang-ming's concept of *taikyo*. This term can be variously translated as Absolute Spirit, Absolute Ideal, or Absolute Principle. *Taikyo* is the fundamental creative force and the source of all things in the universe. To explicate the notion of Absolute Spirit, Ōshio frequently used metaphors in a manner reminiscent of Taoist and Zen teachers. In one of his lectures he evoked the image of a jar. If the jar is broken, the empty space that has filled it immediately returns to the outside space; thus is the human body automatically merged with the Absolute Spirit. It is eternal and stable; even a great mountain, said Ōshio, can be moved by an earthquake, but the Absolute Spirit can never be dislodged. Being universal and preceding all things—objects and senses and reason—it cannot be grasped by mere scholarship; being absolute and including all things, it transcends form, time, history, and change; admitting no opposites, it rejects all categories of distinction. According to this approach, social injustice, a subject that

8.52

8.53

increasingly exercised Ōshio, could be traced to the Chu Hsi type
of dualistic analysis, in which one group of people is judged as
being intrinsically different from another.

In order to rid our minds of the false, conventional categories of distinction it is essential that we reidentify ourselves with
the Absolute Spirit. Only by returning to the Absolute *(ki-taikyo)*
can we clarify ourselves and all things, rectify our false notions
about the human condition, and attain stability *(fudō)*. As a samurai philosopher Ōshio was much concerned with the theme of
death, and in his lectures he stressed that both time and death
were negated by a return to the Absolute Spirit. Again and again
he emphasized the unimportance, indeed the meaninglessness, of
physical death: "What is this thing called death? . . . We cannot
possibly begrudge the death of the body; but the death of the
8.54   spirit—that indeed is to be dreaded." By reidentifying oneself
with the Absolute, one attains purity of spirit and sincerity of
motive; and then life, in the classical samurai phrase, becomes
8.55   "lighter than the feather of a bird."

In Wang Yang-ming's philosophy, as in Zen, self-under-
standing and control of the mind are the most important forms
of learning. All men must recognize their true nature and, by
means of meditation, self-discipline, and sincere action, must
8.56   clean away the rust that has accumulated through false thinking.
Our goal, wrote Ōshio, is innate, intuitive knowledge *(ryōchi)*,
and only by attaining such knowledge *(chi-ryōchi)* can we remove
8.57   the mist from the mirror and see things clearly.

Ōshio applied the concept of Absolute Spirit to the realm of
ethics by stressing that one of its main aspects was sincerity
(makoto), and thus he provided a philosophical basis for the concept that was always central to the Japanese heroic ideal. In
Ōshio's sense *ki-taikyo* ("return to the Absolute") meant a return
to sincerity and goodness and an imperative need to "rectify
injustice" *(fusei wo tadasu)*. Since *taikyo* comprised Absolute
Truth, error and wickedness were impermanent and could, just
like time and death, be overcome by reidentification with the
Absolute.

This sanguine approach to the world's evils was related to
the classical Confucian doctrine of man's original goodness as
expressed in the famous dictum, "Men by nature are fundamen-
8.58   tally good; by nature they share this quality." According to
Ōshio, we are all potentially receptive of the celestial light, which

enables us to distinguish good from bad, and by a transformation of personality *(kishitsu henka)* we can return to the Absolute. The rigid, formalized class distinctions, which were so important in the official Tokugawa concept of society, were invalidated by the criterion of the sageliness inherent in the heart of every man. The potentiality to return to the Absolute applied to all human beings, regardless of their station in life and (a significant concession for a Confucian samurai-scholar) regardless of their sex. The meanest peasant woman toiling in the rice fields could *in theory* become a sage.

I emphasize the theoretical aspect of this rather startling egalitarianism. For Ōshio Heihachirō, as for the porcine rulers of Orwell's animal farm, everyone may be equal but some are more equal than others. Despite his insistence that all men have the potentiality of sagehood, he was by personality a fierce elitist, very conscious of his own samurai status, and he treated his followers with all the paternalistic authoritarianism of a feudal overlord. While insisting that the possibility of returning to the Absolute was inherent in all people, he recognized that in practice very few would be able to perfect themselves to the point of actually attaining sageliness. The sage-hero as conceived by Ōshio—and certainly no false modesty inhibited him from attributing the role to himself—was a passionate, single-minded man, who had achieved intuitive knowledge of himself and of all things *(chiryōchi);* he was thus no longer restrained by any worldly fears and could devote himself with self-sacrificing sincerity to the rectification of evil and injustice. Ōshio pictured the sage as a belligerent, iconoclastic rebel whose action in society was "like that of a madman"; and one is reminded of Baudelaire's 8.59 prescription, quoted by Lytton Strachey in his account of General Gordon's heroic catastrophe, "Il faut être toujours ivre . . . il faut vous enivrer sans trêve." 8.60

The aim of the sage-hero is *kyūmin* ("Save the people!"), and these were the characters blazoned on Ōshio's banners when his theories eventually led him to open revolt. It is incumbent on those who have succeeded in reidentifying themselves with the Absolute to make other people realize their own sagely potential. By the sincerity and morality of his position the sage will attract a group of devoted followers and with their help he will carry out selfless action in the public domain. This brings us to the aspect of Ōshio's philosophy that made the greatest impression upon

later followers, including Mishima Yukio: "The way of the sage
is in the public realm alone. . . . Knowledge must be united with
action *(chigyō gōitsu)*. . . . Even the superior man *(kunshi)*, if he
knows the good but fails to act upon it, is transformed into a
8.61   pygmy." As opposed to Chu Hsi's form of neo-Confucianism,
which taught that we must first acquire knowledge and then act
upon that knowledge as appropriate, Ōshio insisted that "to
8.62   know without acting means that we still do not know. . . . If we
do not immediately transform our moral truths into action, our
actual understanding [of those truths] is nullified." This, of
course, goes a great deal further than the truism about action
speaking louder than words. Return to the Absolute *(ki-taikyo)*
includes the clarification of society; and the attainment of intuitive knowledge *(chi-ryōchi)* impels the sage to carry out the dictates of his conscience directly in social and political action.
Ōshio put these ideas into effect by refusing to rest content with
an official career or, later, with a safe life of teaching and scholarship. As an eminent Japanist writer observed in the Meiji period,
Ōshio Heihachirō was even more consistent in his activism than
8.63   the great master Wang Yang-ming himself.

Ōshio's philosophy of action automatically made him direct
his attention to the practical crisis before his eyes. It was lucky
for a man with his ideas that he should have been presented with
an eminently suitable cause: the "rectification" of economic injustice by saving the oppressed people of his city. Had he lived
about half a millennium earlier, Ōshio's philosophy and personality would no doubt have made him direct his energies to the
hopeless but "righteous" cause of loyalism espoused by his hero,
Kusunoki Masashige; and in the Meiji era he might well have
belonged to one of those groups of doomed zealots who tilted
against Westernization with their antiquated samurai weapons.
But in a calm period of prosperity he would have been hard put
to give a concrete sense to his philosophy. That was Mishima's
tragedy: he espoused the philosophy of Ōshio Heihachirō at a
time when no suitable field was available for his energies and was
therefore obliged to act out his ideas and psychological impulses
in a cause that lacked any worthy objective.

In choosing the goal of justice for the common people Ōshio
had knowingly set himself upon a course that would lead to
headlong collision with his acknowledged overlords, the Bakufu
authorities. He himself, having been trained as a loyal member

of the samurai class, was well aware of this contradiction; but he resolved it—at least to his own satisfaction—by insisting that loyalty to the Absolute Spirit must precede loyalty to one's lord (*chū*). Faced with the moral imperative to "clarify society" by obtaining justice for the common people, he was prepared to jettison the conventional loyalism that prescribed obedience to his feudal superiors. For this reason he could confidently proclaim that his action, far from being a "rebellious uprising" (*zokuran*) as it was called by the government, was a "righteous undertaking" (*gikyo*).

    Ōshio's defiance of the feudal authorities on behalf of the "wretched of the earth" has led some modern observers to describe him as a revolutionary leader and even as an incipient socialist. It is true that the Osaka insurrection of 1837 had far wider social implications than the numerous local risings which preceded and followed it during the Tokugawa period. But, despite the scope of his challenge, Ōshio was far from having any revolutionary intent, and to categorize him as an "incipient socialist" involves the same oversimplification of motives and distortion of objectives that has allowed Mishima to be dubbed a "fascist." Ōshio was a religious leader whose philosophy of moral activism happened to take the form of social protest. In none of his writings or pronouncements does he criticize feudalism per se. Far from it: Ōshio implicitly accepted the social system that gave preeminence to his own samurai class. His indignation was directed against the abuses of the system and specifically against the corruption and misgovernment of officials who ignored their moral responsibilities. If only these rogues could be swept from power, and righteous officials (like himself) put in their place, it would be possible to rectify patterns of evil and to "establish a timeless order of justice." This is the stance of the utopian reformer fighting for moral justice, not of the revolutionary who wishes to demolish an irrational or outmoded socioeconomic system. A succinct explanation of Ōshio's seemingly radical position was given by Maeda Ichirō in 1952 at a time when the hero was widely being touted as a precursor of the modern socialist revolutionary:

He was a consistent supporter of the feudal order who, as a member of the class that stood at the head of the four social estates, was determined to correct the evils and misgovernment which were responsible for the

8.64

8.65

8.66

8.67

8.68

8.69

universal distress of his time. . . . But in order to put his plans into effect he was obliged to call on members of the lower, oppressed classes who were confronting feudal [authority].

8.70

Ōshio, the samurai-philosopher, did not think in mundane terms of systematic reform or organized social revolution. Rather, his mission—idealistic, romantic, and eminently impractical—was "to rectify evil in a moment" so that he might "save the people from the hell of the past and . . . establish paradise before their very eyes."

8.71

Ōshio's "hell" referred primarily to the economic misery of the poorer elements of the population. The peasants were the principal victims in the long period of famine that recurrently afflicted the entire nation during the Tokugawa period. But the urban masses also suffered cruelly from the food shortages and sudden increases in the price of rice. The ease and opulence of the Floating World as reflected in Kabuki theatre, *ukiyoe* colour prints, and literature of the "pleasure" quarters can give a somewhat misleading picture of the actual life of most city dwellers during the centuries of Japan's glorious isolation. In fact the majority of the inhabitants in the great cities like Edo and Osaka lived close to the economic margin, and any abrupt inflation in the cost of staples made their situation desperate. Much of the urban population consisted of recent migrants who had been driven from their villages by economic pressure and subsisted precariously as servants and day labourers. Such people were the immediate victims in periods of famine.

8.72

The direct cause of these scourges was, of course, poor harvests and crop failures; but their effects were vastly aggravated by the unrealistic and ungenerous economic policy of the Bakufu. The ruling samurai class, whose wealth was measured in terms of rice income (*koku*), was forever increasing pressure on the villages to produce more and consume less, firmly convinced that the aim of the peasant's existence is "to stay alive but not to enjoy life"; yet by the eighteenth century the poorer farmers had reached their maximum productive capacity and there was little more to be squeezed out of them by taxes or sumptuary edicts. Naturally they could accumulate no reserves to tide them over hard times.

The underlying cause of the famines and other disasters was demographic. In a closed, isolated economy like that of

Tokugawa Japan, any steep increase in the population was bound to be dangerous, and it could be argued that the recurrent famines served as a short of Malthusian check. It is probably no coincidence that the economic crises of 1782 and 1832 both occurred at a time when Japan had exceeded its "safe" population threshold of about twenty-seven million. The fact remains that the intensity of human suffering could have been mitigated by a more rational and beneficent administration.

Faced with intolerable hardships and a callous, ineffective officialdom, the Japanese population, for all its tradition of resignation and obedience, periodically exploded in outbursts. Historians count a ten-yearly average of uprisings during the Tokugawa period, and they become increasingly frequent from the beginning of the nineteenth century as the long period of Bakufu rule nears its end. The overwhelming majority took place in rural areas, where most of the working population lived; but, as the cities grew in size, they too became the scene of large-scale riots, mainly triggered by food shortages and rising prices. Most dramatic were the "smashings" (*uchikowashi*), desperate outbursts of violence in which day-labourers, small shopkeepers, unemployed artisans, vagrants—the *Lumpenproletariat* of Tokugawa Japan—joined in wrecking the houses of rich merchants, *sake* dealers, and money-lenders. Osaka, the nation's granary, was noted for its "rice-dealer smashings" (*komeya-kowashi*), but all the large cities experienced outbreaks of one kind or another. Among these the most violent occurred in Edo in 1732, and in Edo, Osaka, and other cities between 1783 and 1787; the last major outbursts of the Tokugawa period took place in 1836 and 1837, Ōshio's insurrection thus being the culmination of a long trend.

The feudal authorities reacted to these troublesome symptoms with an efficiency that they never managed to display in attacking the causes. Owing to poor planning by the peasants and townsmen and to the immense repressive power of the government, the uprisings invariably failed in their main objectives. Each abortive outbreak was followed by reprisals and a rash of new edicts. In 1721 farmers were forbidden under pledge from making leagues (*totō*) and were ordered to join official five-man groups that would take joint responsibility for infractions; in 1741 the punishment for appeal to the authorities, for making leagues, or for deserting one's village was stipulated as being confiscation

of fields, increase in taxation for the villages, and death for the
8.73   leaders. Crucifixion, that precious import from the West, was a
favourite punishment for violators. Thus after an uprising in 1749
to protest against high taxes following a crop failure, the local
officials were sentenced to a few weeks of house arrest for ne-
glecting their duties, but the farmers who had presumed to defy
the authorities were treated less leniently. Three of the leaders
were trussed up and exposed outside the town limits and then
killed on the cross; two others were burnt at the stake, three were
8.74   beheaded; and over two hundred received lesser sentences.

The final years of the long shogunate of Tokugawa Ienari
(ruled 1787–1837) were marked by natural disasters and famines,
which, however, did nothing to curb the notorious extravagances
of the Shogun himself and the consequent drain on the Bakufu
treasury. From 1832 there was a series of poor harvests, especially
in 1833; and in 1836 there was a major crop failure which reduced
the production of rice and other cereals to barely half the normal
yield. This resulted in a steady increase in the price of rice, which
8.75   in 1837 reached catastrophic levels. The famine affected the poorer
rural regions and all the large cities. As usual the authorities were
both unable and unwilling to take the necessary emergency
measures to protect the population, and the misery spread rapidly. Even in Nagoya, where an attempt was made to provide
8.76   relief, some 1,500 corpses lay unburied in the spring of 1837.

Osaka, whose economy was now largely controlled by Kōnoike and a few other large merchant complexes in close cooperation with municipal officials, was seething with unrest. Atobe,
the Municipal High Commissioner, with a callousness reminiscent of the English government at the time of the Irish potato
famine a few years later, did not hesitate to comply with Bakufu
directives that rice be shipped to Edo from the depleted store-
houses of Osaka, thus driving up the price still further and bringing the urban populace to the verge of starvation.

As the situation in the city deteriorated, Ōshio observed the
people's misery with growing indignation and in a vitriolic attack on the authorities declared that the famine was not, as the
official Confucianists would have it, an "act of Heaven" (tensai)
but an "act of the government" (seisai). Appalled by the suffering
he witnessed in the alleys of Osaka and the dilapidated huts of
the surrounding villages, he wrote a series of poems in Chinese
style where he described the wretches who foraged for the bodies

of dead birds or who, unable to feed their children, abandoned
them to die of cold. His sympathy with the suffering masses   *8.77*
turned directly into fury against the corrupt, faineant officials
and the callous merchants, whom he pictured, in the censorious,
puritanical terms of the Confucian scholar, as disporting themselves at expensive banquets with wine, fine food, and dancing
girls. Yet words were not enough. Now in early 1837 Ōshio finally
had a perfect field for the type of action that his philosophy
prescribed.

As the famine in Osaka worsened and it became clear that
the authorities were not going to take any remedial steps, Ōshio
filed a petition with Atobe asking that rice be released from the
government granaries to feed the sufferers; at the same time he
approached Kōnoike, Mitsui, and other large merchant houses
urging that they lend money for relief. After some hesitation the   *8.78*
merchants, evidently acting on Atobe's orders, turned down the
request. Atobe himself not only refused to open the granaries but
scornfully threatened Ōshio with prosecution for having submitted a "direct petition" (gōso) and for meddling in public affairs
when he no longer had official status. The failure of his appeal
and the fact that a mediocrity like Atobe should be in charge of
the government at such a critical time are said to have convinced
Ōshio, if he still had any doubts, that nothing could be gained by
legal, nonviolent methods.

Shortly afterwards Ōshio made one of the gestures that most
endeared him to his supporters and later admirers. In order to
raise funds he sold the possession that as a scholar he treasured
most in the world—his library of some fifty thousand volumes.
This precious collection realized a sum of about one thousand
gold *ryo* (approximately $6,000 in present-day values), most of
which Ōshio distributed among the destitute people of the city.
His largesse, though ridiculed by Atobe as an act of undignified
self-advertisement, earned him widespread popularity in Osaka.
In addition to giving money to the poor, Ōshio secretly used the
proceeds of his sale to buy a cannon, a dozen rifles, and several
hundred swords; he also hired a gunnery expert to train his
followers in the use of firearms. The knowledge that he had
acquired from his books was now being fructified by action in the
public domain.

In March 1837 Ōshio ordered that his Summons (Gekibun) be
distributed to the "people and farmers" in the four districts sur-

rounding Osaka. This was an open incitation to revolt, and now there could be no turning back. Printed copies of the famous Summons were delivered to the villages in saffron-coloured silk bags inscribed with a Shinto litany from the Great Ise Shrine and bearing on the front the modest inscription, "Given down from Heaven" *(ten yori kudasarusōrō)*. Since the document was written in complicated Chinese, it cannot have conveyed very much to the majority of its intended readers; but such practical questions were the least of Ōshio's concerns.

8.79

The Summons starts by referring to the recent series of earthquakes and other natural disasters which, as Ōshio pointed out in good Confucian style, were signs of Heaven's anger with corrupt, self-seeking officials of the Bakufu government. The warnings, however, had not been heeded. Rice was being shipped to Edo while the populace in Osaka starved; and the authorities who were responsible for the people's hardships continued to indulge in worldly pleasures with rich merchants, actors, and wicked women.

Then came the call to action. It was impossible, said Ōshio, to continue bearing this injustice in silence. The time had come for all sincere people to revolt and "visit Heaven's vengeance" *(tembatsu)* on the corrupt officials and greedy merchants who were battening off the poor by hoarding rice and other foodstuffs for their selfish profit. The guilty, including the Municipal High Commissioners, must be chastised and the food immediately distributed to people in distress.

In launching his armed "rectification of injustice" Ōshio called on the farmers to break into the local government offices and burn all registers of annual tribute and other documents on which the authorities depended for taxation. If any officials in their area had got wind of the plans for revolt, they should be killed forthwith. As soon as the villagers heard that the uprising had started in the city, they should flock to the support of the insurgents and help destroy the rogues who were responsible for their misery. Then finally it would be possible to wash away the centuries of accumulated corruption and return to the pristine, moral government that Japan had enjoyed in the days of Jimmu, the founder of the imperial dynasty.

8.80

We do not know exactly when Ōshio decided on armed insurrection. The reason traditionally given for the revolt was his fury with the government, in particular with Atobe, for failing to cope with the famine of 1836–37. But the theoretical decision had likely been taken several years before, probably when he was first teaching at his Cleansing-the-Heart-to-Obtain-Insight Academy. In the Summons he stressed the moral basis of his revolt, pointing out that he and his followers had no ambition to seize the country and obtain political power but, like the Chinese heroes of the late Ming Dynasty, were motivated exclusively by sincerity—sincerity that obliged them to visit Heaven's punishment on the wicked.

8.81

The practical objectives of the revolt, beyond the immediate plan to kill some of the more egregious officials and merchants and to distribute food to the starving, were left vague in the Summons, and probably Ōshio himself had no clear idea about them. He specified that this was not to be another ephemeral uprising but would be sustained until justice for the people had been fully realized. It is doubtful whether he had any specific programme in mind. His aims almost certainly did not include an overthrow of the Bakufu feudal structure, but rather, the correction of its injustices by the appointment of virtuous officials.

The detailed plans for the revolt itself are also unclear. The evidence subsequently presented by the authorities is unreliable, having been obtained mainly from defectors who hoped to receive leniency by traducing their former leader or from prisoners who were undergoing torture and were willing to say anything in order to end their torments. We do know, however, that Ōshio decided to launch his uprising by attacking the two Municipal High Commissioners during their tour of inspection on 25th March, when they would be resting in a house opposite his own at three o'clock in the afternoon. Immediately afterwards his followers would set fire to the houses of rice merchants, break open the granaries, and distribute food. The fires would be a signal to the peasants in nearby villages to stream into the city and join the revolt. To prepare for the great day, Ōshio's followers had been meeting regularly in his house. With its rooms stripped bare since the sale of the library, it had been turned into a secret armoury for storing cannons and firearms and for manufacturing ammunition.

8.82

In planning and carrying out his insurrection Ōshio was assisted by a group of about twenty confederates. Of these the most important was his twenty-six-year-old adopted son,

Kakunosuke, one of the few people in Ōshio's life with whom he ever maintained a warm relationship. His other principal supporters were mainly old colleagues from the Eastern Magistracy, whose morale had deteriorated since Atobe's appointment and who held Ōshio in respect as a guide and moral mentor; he had also managed to recruit a handful of idealistic young samurai who had come under the spell of his personality. Here Ōshio's revolt differs from almost all previous *ikki* in the Tokugawa period: since the Shimabara Rebellion two centuries earlier, his was the first important uprising in which members of the warrior class made common cause with the afflicted masses.

8.83

Ōshio's popular support, such as it was, came mainly from the surrounding villages. During the months preceding the revolt he despatched several of his lieutenants to recruit "able men" *(kitoku aru hito)* who were to be chosen in the villages regardless of their social status and education. They in turn would order the peasants to flock to the support of the insurgents once the uprising started in the city—or so at least was Ōshio's plan. He himself had close connexions with local headmen and yeomen, many of whom had become his disciples and who had contributed funds to him and his Academy. It will be recalled that he had defied convention by choosing a wife from precisely such a family, and this may have helped him win the confidence of village people. In Osaka itself his rank-and-file supporters consisted mainly of city paupers and *burakumin* ("outcasts"), who belonged to the very bottom of the socioeconomic hierarchy and had little to lose by joining the revolt. On one occasion he pointed out, with characteristic lack of realism, that by treating the despised and oppressed *burakumin* like human beings he could make them into staunch allies who would gladly give up their lives for the cause. Yet on the whole Ōshio, with his typical samurai approach, had more faith in the villagers than in townspeople and, though his insurrection was centred in the city, he looked mainly to the countryside for manpower. His doubts concerning support from the urban masses turned out to be entirely justified; but he fatally overestimated the backing he might expect from the countryside.

8.84

8.85

Ōshio was at pains to maintain secrecy, and he even ordered the coldblooded murder of one of his own loyal followers lest he betray the plot. Yet despite his precautions there were traitors in the rebel camp, one of whom sent a warning to Atobe on the eve of the uprising. Fortunately for Ōshio, the High Commissioner

8.86

was sceptical about the report, which he thought was motivated by personal animosity resulting from Ōshio's notorious temper. As at the time of Shimabara two centuries earlier, the officials failed to take the prompt action that could have nipped off the revolt from the outset. It was not until dawn on the 25th, when a second traitor sent a letter confirming news of the impending outbreak, that the authorities finally decided to act. They started by ordering the arrest of two police officials who were involved in the plot. One of them was hacked to death in the guard house, but the other managed to escape through the window of a lavatory in the Magistrate's Office and rushed to Ōshio's house to warn him that he had been betrayed. As a result Ōshio was obliged to advance his timetable by eight full hours. At seven o'clock in the morning a posse of constables was sent to seize him in his house. But they arrived too late: the insurrection was already underway.

According to plan, Ōshio and his followers first set fire to his own house as the starting signal. They then marched out into the streets in different directions, carrying banners emblazoned with the devices, "Save the People!" and "The Great Shrine of the Goddess Amaterasu." As they advanced along the city streets, they systematically set fire to the houses of police inspectors and other officials who were known for their unjust dealings. Ōshio and his men also fired large numbers of dwellings in the section of Osaka that was occupied by the big merchant houses. Owing to the wooden construction of the buildings the flames spread rapidly, and by the time they were brought under control at the end of the second day almost one-quarter of the huge city had been burnt to the ground.

A central part of the programme was to seize the warehouses of the rich merchants and "liberate" foodstuff and other hoarded wealth. This is where Ōshio's inadequate planning and overoptimistic assessment of his rank-and-file supporters produced the most damaging results. The motley rabble that broke into the depots of Mitsui and Kōnoike made not the slightest attempt at organized distribution of the silver, rice, and other booty; instead each man grabbed what he could secrete on his person and scampered off to safety. And, in the ancient tradition of looting mobs, many of them broke into the wine stores and drank their fill, thus rendering themselves even less effective as a fighting force. This 8.87 was hardly the type of conduct that the sage-hero had expected from his followers; nor can Ōshio have derived much comfort from the thought that this mob comprised the very people he was attempting to "save" by his action.

When it came to the actual fighting, Ōshio's men proved remarkably ineffective in using firearms and cannon to confront the Bakufu forces. One of the few satisfying moments during the rebels' disastrous day, however, occurred when their cannonfire scared the horse of Lord Hori, the Municipal High Commissioner for the Western Magistracy, who, together with Atobe, was leading an attack on Ōshio and his partisans. The horse reared and Hori promptly fell off, causing great consternation among his men, who thought that he had been killed. A few moments later Atobe dismounted in a similar undignified fashion. These two mishaps afforded great delight to Ōshio's men, and provided material for numerous malicious jibes among the townsmen of Osaka. Shortly afterwards the morale of the insurgents was shaken by the death of their chief cannoneer, a tall, elegantly dressed samurai, who was mowed down by Bakufu gunfire. On Atobe's orders his head was promptly severed, stuck on the end of a spear, and paraded through the city streets as a grim warning of the fate that awaited all rebels.

Though the initial vacillation of the authorities gave Ōshio a few hours of success, the weakness and disorganization of his forces in the city and the nonappearance of the expected peasant army doomed his revolt to early disaster. The turning point occurred about four o'clock in the afternoon when Ōshio, realizing that everything had gone awry, ordered his men to escape while there was still time. As hundreds of dazed townsmen wandered through the streets trying to salvage a few remaining possessions from their blazing houses, Ōshio and his companions hurried along the banks of Yodo River, stopping only to set fire to granaries they passed on their way. Before commandeering a boat and escaping downstream to a deserted spot on the other side of the river, he took out his scroll of the Summons and also a copy of his marching orders and hurled them into the flames. The revolt had been crushed after less than a day of fighting, and the "philosopher in action" had failed to inflict a single serious casualty on the Bakufu forces.

Now the vast repressive forces of the government moved inexorably into action. Information about the revolt took a full week to reach Bakufu headquarters in Edo. By this time Ōshio's uprising had been quashed; yet the news caused much alarm, and instructions were issued that the guilty be hunted down and promptly brought to justice. Meanwhile the commander of Osaka Castle, whose garrison had taken virtually no part in the fighting on 25th March, ordered that the participants be seized with all despatch. A close watch was put on roads and river traffic, and rewards were offered for the capture of Ōshio and the other main culprits, who, it was feared, might try some new deviltry if not quickly arrested. During the early days of the suppression many of Ōshio's adherents anticipated their capture by committing suicide. Thus when his uncle, a Shinto priest who had been deeply involved in the conspiracy, heard that the police were approaching he tried to disembowel himself. The wound was shallow and the priest was still alive when the posse arrived; he desperately forced his way out of the house and rushed to a nearby irrigation pond, where he succeeded in drowning himself.

Ōshio fled the city with fourteen companions and some seventy-five other supporters. At this point the failure of his revolt was irremediable and he was prepared to die; but, having been persuaded to delay the final act, he headed into the mountainous region of Kii Peninsula. He now admitted that he had no concrete plan of escape (as he had earlier pretended) and declared that he would await further news from Osaka before ending his life with dignity. In order to give his followers a better chance to make good their escape, he ordered them to throw their swords and other weapons into the river and to set off on their own in different directions. Soon he was left with only three companions —his son, Kakunosuke, and two devoted police officials from the Eastern Magistracy who had been given the privilege of accompanying him on his last flight.

There are no historical records of the route followed by the four hunted fugitives as they made their way down the peninsula in the freezing cold, but scholars have offered a plausible reconstruction. The flight of the little band is reminiscent of Yoshitsune's famous escape to Ōshū, and it is unlikely that the analogy was lost on Ōshio. One of the police officials, who had begun to lag behind, decided to commit harakiri rather than slow down the others. Ōshio, far from dissuading him, acted as *kaishaku* ("second") and chopped off his head. Shortly afterwards the second official (the young man who had originally warned Ōshio of

8.89

8.90

8.91

his betrayal) became so exhausted that he sought shelter in a farm house; on waking from a deep sleep, he realized that his dagger had been stolen and that the farmer was on his way to alert the authorities; rather than risk being captured alive, he ran out of the house and hanged himself from a tree. Now only Ōshio and his son were left. As if to imitate the great twelfth-century hero, they both shaved their heads and disguised themselves as mountain priests.

Meanwhile the government forces were hunting down Ōshio's followers one by one. Even people who had been involved only indirectly were being pursued and arrested. The main objective, of course, was to capture the ringleader himself, and for this purpose the net was spread wider and wider. The authorities were impeded, however, by receiving several false reports about the direction of Ōshio's flight, and futile searches were made in the Kyoto region. He could probably have hidden his traces in the mountainous countryside of Yamato for a considerable time; but five days after the revolt he suddenly decided to return to the city—perhaps because he was curious to observe developments at first hand, perhaps because with his apocalyptic sense of mission he sensed it was in Osaka that he must meet his fate. At dawn on 31st March an aged towel-merchant named Gorōbei, who for many years had enjoyed the patronage of Ōshio's family, was rudely awakened by knocking at his gate and found two mountain priests urgently demanding admittance.

When he recognized who they were, Gorōbei found himself in a dilemma of a type that is peculiarly painful for the Japanese and that has racked many a character in puppet and Kabuki plays: either he had to harbour the two most wanted outlaws in the country and risk the fierce penalties of the law, or he must violate his obligation (*on*) to Ōshio's family by refusing protection to him and his son. In the event he did not have much choice, since the fugitives soon forced their way unceremoniously through the front door. Gorōbei decided to hide them in a detached building separated from the main house by a garden. Terrified of discovery, he carefully concealed their presence from everyone in the household except his wife. During the weeks that followed the elderly couple took turns in surreptitiously bringing food and other essentials to the fugitives.

All went well until one of the maids, who had gone to visit her family in a nearby village, mentioned that an unusually large

8.92

amount of rice was lately being consumed in her master's house. This news found its way to the local magistrate. The authorities summoned the terrified Gorōbei and his wife, who under questioning confessed the identity of their famous guests. Immediately the commander of Osaka Castle gave orders that Ōshio and his son be captured alive. The constables appointed to make the arrest drew lots to determine who would be first to enter the narrow entrance leading to Ōshio's hiding place and thus acquire fame and honour.

At dawn on 1st May a posse of fourteen constables surrounded the building. They had worked out a scheme according to which Gorōbei's wife would be forced to lure Ōshio out of the house so that they might take him alive. The plan failed when Ōshio spotted one of the officials outside the gate and realized that the fatal moment had arrived. The constables next challenged Ōshio to come out and fight, but he would not respond to their taunts, and they decided on an immediate attack. Ōshio instantly set fire to the straw and other combustibles that he had laid round the house for such an emergency. As the constables broke in, he drew out an eighteen-inch blade and thrust it directly into his throat, severing the carotid artery. He then pulled out the weapon and hurled it at one of his assailants; but, typically enough, he failed to inflict any serious injury. For a moment he stood near the entrance, and the constables had the flickering vision of his tall, priestlike figure surrounded by the flames. Then he collapsed and died in the burning house like Yoshitsune in his stronghold at Koromo River.

The rapidly increasing heat made it impossible for the police to advance. When the flames had been brought under control, they entered the room and identified the charred corpses of Ōshio and his son. Kakunosuke had acquitted himself courageously during the street fighting in Osaka five weeks earlier; but when the end came he had evidently hesitated to kill himself, and his father had been obliged to stab the lad to death in order to save him from capture. According to one account, Ōshio had been heard shouting, "Coward! Coward! [*Hikyō, hikyō*]" to his son as the police prepared to attack. Perhaps failure had gone to his head. In any case, if the report is true, it was a sad leave-taking from the son for whom he had felt such affection. After being pulled out of the house, the two cadavers were washed and placed in litters to be transported to the Magistrate's office. Meanwhile

8.93

a huge crowd had gathered in the street. As Ōshio was carried out, it was observed by some of the onlookers that his head had been so swollen and distorted by the heat that he looked like a great toad.

The dramatic deaths of Ōshio and his son were followed by a detailed investigation into the circumstances of the revolt. Official hearings by the Bakufu started in Edo on 4th September, but the law's delays were such that judgment was not pronounced until 28th September of the following year. The court's verdict reflected the full ferocity of Tokugawa law and the gruesome nature of punishments reserved for those who dared challenge

8.94 the established order. The twenty men who were judged to be mainly responsible for the uprising were allotted the supreme penalty of crucifixion; other participants were sentenced to

8.95 decapitation, imprisonment, or exile to distant islands. As a mark of special leniency the court decreed that Kakunosuke's infant child, who would normally have been executed for his father's crime should simply receive life imprisonment.

The punishment of the main culprits, Ōshio and his son, presented some difficulties, since they had already been dead for sixteen months when judgment was pronounced. In its final decree the court condemned Ōshio for having "criticized the government" *(seidō wo bihan itashi)* and for having taken advantage of his role as a teacher to browbeat a group of followers, including police officials, into staging a rebellion. "In view of these nefarious deeds," concludes the order, "let it be known that the pickled corpses of Ōshio Heihachirō and of [his son, Kakunosuke,] shall be led round for public exposure and shall be cru-

8.96 cified in the city of Osaka." As a final disgrace it was ordered that no tombstone could be built to mark his place of burial, which might otherwise have become a place of pilgrimage for admirers.

Of the twenty-nine other conspirators sentenced to the heaviest penalties only five were alive to hear the verdict. Most of the others had died in Osaka Gaol, where the conditions were so terrible that prisoners rarely survived for more than a few

8.97 months. The salt-pickled bodies of those who had been sentenced to crucifixion but who had succumbed in prison were paraded through the streets and duly attached to crosses at the Osaka

8.98 execution grounds.

Though the main function of the court was to punish the guilty, the government was also mindful of the Confucian pre-

cept that the virtuous be rewarded. Payments were made broadcast to turncoats and informers, and a special emolument was
given to a conscientious Police Inspector called Sakamoto who
had distinguished himself by destroying the rebel cannon. Nor   *8.99*
were the legal officials themselves forgotten: their arduous inves-
tigations and judicious sentences earned them commendation
from the Bakufu and respectable grants of money.

"Ōshio Heihachirō's enterprise ended in total failure,"   *8.100*
writes Mishima Yukio, his foremost modern admirer. The injustices that Ōshio had intended to abolish continued unabated, and
such results as his action produced were the opposite of those
intended. It is true that the critical shortage of food in the cities
was somewhat alleviated, but this was due to improved harvests,
rather than any efforts of the sage-hero. Ōshio himself was obviously aware that the revolt had been a disaster, but his nature
would never have allowed him to admit the fact.   *8.101*
    The leaders of the revolt had perished in the flames; the men
who had betrayed him were promoted, and the corrupt officials
and "greedy" merchants continued to flourish. Meanwhile thousands of the inhabitants suffered cruelly as a result of the fires and
of the epidemic that followed shortly after. Though the famine
came to an end, the condition of the poorer townsmen remained
precarious. "Last year," writes a contemporary chronicler,
"those who were hunted down by famine have fallen to the status
of beggars, good-for-nothings. They came and went, not being
able to tell night from day, plaintively calling out with tears in
their eyes. Most of them have disappeared through death, it
seems, because the number of beggars has greatly diminished."   *8.102*
    Although initially checked by the revolt, the Tokugawa
Bakufu did nothing to alleviate the conditions that had caused it.
The shogunal reforms that were initiated a few years later were   *8.103*
aimed mainly at reinforcing order and increasing the government's military power rather than at creating the type of changes
that Ōshio had demanded, and they were always carried out in
terms of orthodox (Chu Hsi) Confucianism. The minister who
was chiefly responsible for the reforms dramatized the importance of thrift by appearing in cotton clothes instead of the customary silk; but, despite this edifying example, governmental
economies failed to mitigate the plight of the masses, and the
harsh new programme of national austerity often made condi-

tions worse for the very people Ōshio had been trying to help. Traditional restrictions were confirmed, and taxation and other burdens increased. One objective of the reformers was to check inflation; but this failed completely, and after a few years the price of rice and other staples resumed its upward course, with *8.104* the usual cruel consequences for the working classes.

Despite its spectacular failure the Osaka uprising inspired *8.105* numerous other *ikki* throughout the country. One of the first major risings of this kind was an outbreak in the remote northern province of Echigo against the high price of rice. On this occasion the banners of the insurgents proclaimed that they were "disciples of Ōshio" and wished to "strike down the robbers of the country." During the brief remaining period of Tokugawa rule there were some three hundred uprisings in the towns and cities and well over a thousand in the villages. In every case these *ikki* were suppressed and the participants punished: they were a symptom of important defects in the Bakufu's economic policy, but they were by no means a cause of its downfall.

Ōshio's posthumous failure was confirmed by developments after the Meiji Restoration. The replacement of the Tokugawa Bakufu by an imperial bureaucracy merely involved a change of masters: the Restoration proved to be a mockery of Ōshio's idea that the imperial institution should be reshaped into a symbol of justice for the people. The land and tax reforms instituted by the new officialdom were disastrous for the mass of the poor people whose conditions had inspired Ōshio's uprising, and from 1873 *8.106* there was a new succession of *ikki*. The punishments were less horrifying than in Tokugawa days, yet the revolts all failed to accomplish their purpose, and Ōshio's admirers in later years could never comfort themselves with the thought that their master's philosophy and action had set precedent for successful resis- *8.107* tance to unjust authority.

Ōshio's failure was not fortuitous but resulted from funda- *8.108* mental weaknesses in his approach. He hopelessly misjudged the balance of strength between his supporters and the Bakufu. Be- *8.109* sides, he was an absurdly poor planner. Though he fancied himself as an efficient man of action, he was incompetent in devising a unified strategy and had little grasp of practical detail. Owing to poor organization, even his simple plan to destroy records in village offices was not carried into effect. In addition he seems to have had only the vaguest idea about what would come after the insurrection if it should succeed; nor had he prepared any contingency plans in case of a setback. Concentrating as he did on philosophical principles, moral denunciations, and religious slogans, Ōshio spurned concrete programmes of practical action to follow the revolt. Here again we are reminded of certain other men of action in modern Japanese history, including Saigō Takamori, the young officers in the 1930s, and, in more recent years, Mishima Yukio, whose approach and temperament allowed them to give scant thought to the concrete, practical sequel of their confrontation with established authority.   *8.110*

This is clearly related to the nature of the nonconformist philosophy that inspired Ōshio and his admirers in later decades. In Japan, as Abe Shinkin has pointed out, Yōmeigaku (Wang Yang-ming philosophy) is not so much a philosophy of action as a philosophy of failure in action. And, as Mishima himself observed, Ōshio and later Japanese believers in the doctrines of Wang Yang-ming were alike in "their eagerness to assert their own wills while failing to see things through to a conclusion."   *8.111*   *8.112*
Ōshio's personal philosophy, with its pronounced mystical strain and its hubristic emphasis on achieving immortal fame as a sage-hero, provided little scope for the mundane details of organizing realistic reforms. He inhabited an entirely different emotional realm from pragmatic Western contemporaries like Jeremy Bentham and William Wilberforce. For this individualistic, essentially solitary man, sincerity of purpose always took precedence over realistic planning; and he eschewed the type of practical compromise that would have allowed him, for example, to seek material support from the lord of one of the powerful anti-Bakufu fiefs or to ally himself with underground groups of disaffected *rōnin*.   *8.113*

In a tight-knit, conformist society like Japan's, in which the greatest value is attached to achieving success within a conventional and carefully defined framework, there is a special fascination about an individual whose idiosyncratic personality and commitment to a set of abstract ideals impel him to break out of the "web society" and confront the overwhelming force of established authority in an outburst of desperate defiance *(yake no yanpachi)*. Not only is such a man admired for his physical courage and readiness to risk everything for a worthy cause (qualities that are regarded as heroic in almost any culture), but his life becomes a symbolic expression of the resistance to practical restrictions that thousands of other people must feel yet dare not bring to the surface. Accordingly, his sacrifice provides them with a vicarious release from frustration. The old Japanese proverb warns that the nail which sticks out will ineluctably be

8.114 knocked on the head; yet such refusal to conform with practical realities is the very stuff of heroism. Ōshio Heihachirō gave up a secure, promising career as a samurai official and espoused a heterodox philosophy that drove him from the safety of his study into the hurly-burly of the outside world where, in a quixotic crusade against the government, he tried to challenge the unchallengeable. Yet for all his stress on action, Ōshio made no positive accomplishment in the practical domain. His brief life perfectly exemplifies "the spirit of idealism flying triumphant over the

8.115 prostrate body of its terrestrial champion."

The Apotheosis of Saigō the Great

Near the entrance to Ueno Park, only a few minutes' walk from the smog-drenched hubbub of the Tokyo streets, is a small plateau called Sakuragaoka, the Hill of Cherry Blossoms. Here, surrounded by souvenir stalls and the ubiquitous photographers, stands a monument to the  adherents of the Tokugawa shogunate who fell near this site after being decisively defeated by the loyalists in a battle that led to the Meiji Restoration. In front of the monument and totally overshadowing it rises the bronze statue of a loyalist hero who killed himself in Kyushu almost exactly one century ago. Dressed in an informal summer robe and shod in straw sandals, he clasps a samurai sword in his left hand, while his right hand holds a hunting dog by the leash; during much of the day his head and body (and also his dog) are festooned with dingy city pigeons. In a proud yet natural pose he stands on a pedestal that bears the epitaph: THE SERVICES THAT OUR BELOVED SAIGŌ TAKAMORI RENDERED TO THE NATION REQUIRE NO ENCOMIUM; FOR THEY HAVE WITNESSES IN THE EYES AND EARS OF THE PEOPLE. . . .

The famous statue in Ueno Park is far from belonging to the world's great pieces of monumental sculpture; yet it conveys much about the hero and his legend. A pair of bronze pillars supporting the sturdy edifice of a body that for sheer weight and strength of muscle overwhelms one—such are the legs of Saigō Takamori. His hands are fists, and each finger is a tool for action. He has no neck; the bomb that is his head rests squarely on a chest as solid as a launching-pad. His huge, staring eyes fly at one: two tigers burning with the power of will and demonic energy.

The hero had been dead for over twenty years when his

9.1   statue was completed at the end of the nineteenth century, most of its expense having been defrayed by small contributions from devotees all over Japan. During the next fifty years Sakuragaoka was a place of pilgrimage for hundreds of thousands of visitors, who paid their respects to Saigō Takamori and the spirit he represented and who, duly inspired by their encounter, left with photographs of themselves posed against his gargantuan bulk. In the Occupation period the American authorities decided to demolish the statue as being a symbol of Japanese nationalism, militarism, and other ideologies that were unfashionable at the time. Popular opposition, however, was sufficiently widespread

9.2   to make the Supreme Command relent. The bronze image remains intact, and the camera shutters still click away tirelessly in its vicinity.

The foreign visitor to Ueno Park may find it hard to believe that this venerated figure ended his life under official proscrip-

9.3   tion as a traitor. Yet such is the case; for Saigō the Great climaxed his career as a leader of the Meiji Restoration by heading the last and most sanguinary revolt against the very imperial government he had helped create, and challenged a force commanded by an Imperial Prince, a cousin of Emperor Meiji himself. His armed defiance was on a vastly larger scale than Ōshio's attempt some forty years earlier—more a civil war than an insurrection —but, like the Osaka Rebellion, it ended in disaster and the hero was constrained to take his own life in acknowledgement of defeat.

Saigō Takamori's career exemplifies the entire gamut of the national ethos, as well as the vertiginous changes that were occurring in Japan during the early Meiji period. It has the same parabolic form as the careers of Michizane and Yoshitsune; but the curve is even sharper, and the drama was enacted not in the dim past but in recent history. Until the age of twenty-seven Saigō served as a minor clan official in a remote part of Kyushu; at forty-five he bestrode Japan like a colossus, serving Emperor Meiji not only as a leading member of the national government but as Chief Counsellor of State, Commander of the Imperial Bodyguard, and Marshal; five years later he had plummeted to the status of rebel and was escaping from the imperial forces he had once led. The man who had until recently been the cynosure of both official and popular admiration was formally designated as guilty of high treason and condemned by a Counsellor of State (his erstwhile friend and supporter) as the blackest villain in Japan, "an enemy of the Court, for whom there is no place in heaven or on earth."   9.4

Only a few years after his defeat and decapitation, however, Saigō Takamori was rehabilitated by the same government that he had tried to topple. A Shinto shrine, dedicated to the worship of his spirit, was built near his grave and named after him. In 1890 he received a posthumous pardon from Emperor Meiji and was restored to his former rank and dignity. In 1902 his son received the title of Marquis—not in recognition of any services of his own, but as a further mark of respect for his father.

Such a series of peripeteias is rare even in Japan; if transposed to a Western context, it enters the realm of the fanciful. Saigō's fame, popularity, and power after the Restoration were comparable to those of the Duke of Wellington when he returned to England following his victory at Waterloo. If the career of the Iron Duke had followed a course similar to Saigō's, he might have left England a few years later in disgust with the country's domestic corruption and liberal foreign policy, returned to his birthplace in Ireland, and led a force of young rebel hotheads in a hopeless uprising in which he would have been defeated and killed by the British army; but only a dozen years later he would have received a royal pardon for his act of treason, his dukedom would have been restored, statues would have risen to honour him in London, Dublin, and other parts of the empire, and legends would grow up that he had miraculously survived and would soon return from the continent to rescue his country. The analogy is, of course, approximate, but it certainly does not exaggerate the vicissitudes in the official standing of the Japanese hero.

The government's rehabilitation of Saigō Takamori—an easy measure now that he was safely dead—was not simply an attempt to heal old wounds but reflected his repute among the Japanese people. It is as if the rulers of the country had realized, somewhat belatedly, that they had a full-fledged hero on their hands and must rise to the occasion by granting him the proper honours. For not only was he by far the most popular of the men who had led the Restoration movement, but he became established as the quintessential hero of modern Japanese history, a man who belonged to the same emotional tradition as Yoshitsune and Masahige and who, owing to a peculiarly Japanese combination of qualities, could be loved, not merely respected.

His close associates and followers worshipped him as a superman, and his final failure in battle certainly did nothing to diminish their enthusiasm. The following typical description was written by a lad who accompanied him on his disastrous retreat from Kumamoto when it was clear that the rebellion had miscarried:

When I was walking along a path, [someone] stopped me suddenly and said, "Wait a minute, boy."

"What is the matter?" asked I, turning back.

"You must get out of the way, for the Master [Sensei] is coming along."

We two got out of the way to the left-hand side. Dai-Saigō-Sensei [Saigō the Great] was walking along quietly, with a cap . . . on, and wearing a sword at his side. He seemed as if he were hunting at ease over a peaceful field, forgetting the presence of the enemy. When I thought that this accounted for the stately mien and magnanimity of the greatest hero the world had ever seen, I could not help revering him.

"How great a man the Master is!"

9.5   "Yes, he is a god."

It was not only Saigō's supporters who were moved by the force of his personality. Even an enemy like General Yamagata, who was responsible for crushing Saigō's rebellion, recognized
9.6 his stature while deploring his poor judgement. After the pacification a leading article in a staunchly pro-government newspaper stressed Saigō's lack of skill and generalship, but admired his honesty and courage, and conceded that he was "in some respects a remarkable man":

What sort of man was Saigō Takamori? In his house there was neither wealth nor a retinue of servants. But he was able to so secure the confidence of the people that he could lead a great army into rebellion against the Imperial forces, and though only three provinces joined him in the revolt, by successive battles and retreats he held out against the government for more than half a year. Finally . . . when surrounded by Imperial troops, he cut his way out and escaped to his native place in Kagoshima, and there he was killed in battle. If we carefully consider his course, we see that he fully sustained his fame until the last. He died without shame
9.7 and closed his eyes in peace. . . .

Shortly afterwards, when the time came to compile Saigō's "Post-humous Words," the editor was none other than the steward of a northern clan that had fiercely resisted the hero during the fighting in 1867–68. The preface to this collection ends with the threnody, "Alas, why did you leave the world so hastily, Lord Saigō?"   *9.8*

In the subsequent glorification of Saigō Takamori there are two principal lines of descent, one represented by people of strong nationalist or "Japanist" persuasion, who stressed his traditional samurai ethos and his intransigent attitude towards Korea, the other by liberals, democrats, and socialists, who responded to the hero's bold confrontation with the conservative Establishment of his day. Among Saigō's earliest adherents were   *9.9* members of the "people's rights" movement, including revolutionary opponents of the Meiji regime. These men adulated him as a symbol of freedom and resistance *(jiyū to teikō);* he was their great hope who, like George Washington, would lead his people   *9.10* in the struggle against unjust oppression by a ruling oligarchy.

The eminent liberal thinker, Fukuzawa Yukichi, who probably did more than any other single person in Japan to introduce political democracy and Western ideas, was profoundly impressed by Saigō Takamori despite the latter's suspicion of foreign innovations. The difference in viewpoints between the two men never diminished their mutual admiration. Fukuzawa described Saigō as *the* great hero of the Meiji Restoration and as a man who stood not just for one segment of Japan but for the entire people *(tenka no jimbutsu).* In a book written only one month after the rebellion (but, owing to government censorship, not published until twenty years later) he expressed his resentment at the way in which Saigō had been transformed from a national idol into "the great traitor," and reserved special indig-   *9.11* nation for those lickspittle journalists who presumed to criticise the former hero because it had now become respectable and politic to do so. It is significant that during the period of Saigō's official disgrace a liberal Westerniser like Fukuzawa should have been the only famous writer to defend him publicly. He went so far as to justify the rebellion itself, explaining that it was the despotism of the Ōkubo regime which had driven Saigō "into a difficult situation" and had finally killed him. The uprising was   *9.12* caused by the "dark, unjust policies of the government," which had tried to take over the country from the people and to treat

the populace like slaves. Saigō's sincerity in upholding the cause
of justice must never be impugned, and to suggest that this most
loyal of Japanese could actually have been a traitor to the Em-
9.13   peror was a travesty of the truth. The day might well come when
Saigō would again be indispensable. "Though Japan is a small
country and the national law is severe, yet surely it is big enough
9.14   for the one and only Saigō Takamori."

Another seemingly incongruous admirer was Uchimura
Kanzō, Japan's leading Christian thinker, who had been forced
to resign from his academic post in 1891 for refusing to bow before
a copy of the Imperial Rescript on Education, and who became
a pacifist after the Sino-Japanese War. On most important questions the two men differed widely (Saigō had not the slightest
interest in Christianity and could hardly be described as a
pacifist); yet in a book entitled "Representative Japanese"
Uchimura devotes the opening chapter to the hero from Kyushu,
whom he describes as the last and greatest in Japan's long line of
9.15   eminent samurai. He pairs him with Commodore Perry as one
of the two men who did most to awaken Japan from her long
9.16   slumber, and points out that, though neither knew about the
other, they worked in the same direction, the Japanese hero carrying out what the Westerner had initiated. Later in his essay
Uchimura points out that many of Saigō's most important sayings were identical, at least in spirit, with passages from the New
Testament, and he comes close to representing the Kyushu samu-
9.17   rai as a sort of unconscious Christian.

In terms of ideological objectives it would be hard to imagine
anyone more different from Saigō than the famous socialist journalist Kōtoku Shūsui, an organizer of the Social Democratic
Party, who was prosecuted for his writings against the Russo-
Japanese War and was finally hanged, in an apparent miscarriage
of justice, for his complicity in a plot to assassinate Emperor
Meiji. Yet, like many of the early Japanese socialists, Kōtoku
venerated Saigō Takamori—not, of course, because of his political or social ideas but as a "public-spirited man of virtue" (*shishi-*
9.18   *jinnin*), a "candle that lights others and consumes itself." When
Kōtoku was sentenced to death, his fate was compared with that
of Saigō Takamori, "another tragic hero who had been inveigled
[into a plot] by his companions," and pleas for clemency referred
to the fact that Saigō, who was now officially recognized to be a
9.19   national hero, had once been condemned as a rebel.

At the other end of the spectrum, believers in "Japanism" and right-wing nationalism were almost unanimous in regarding Saigō Takamori as the supreme hero of modern times. The first in this influential category was the superpatriot, Tōyama Mitsuru, a founder of numerous jingoist societies, a powerful advocate of Japanese expansion on the continent, and in his later years the recognized doyen of the ultra-nationalist movement. During the entire course of his long, hectic career Tōyama was a fervent admirer of Saigō Takamori, whose life and character he commended to his followers as the ideal examples for Japanese patriots. Also in the "rightist" category was the famous revolutionary   9.20 and writer Kita Ikki, who because of his advocacy of national socialism in the 1930s and of a new order in Asia under Japan's aegis, had been dubbed the "founder of modern Japanese fascism." In his study of Meiji history Kita analyzed Saigō's rebellion as an abortive nationalist revolution; with Saigō Takamori's failure the attempt at revolution came to an end and power lapsed into the hands of "new-rich daimyos" *(narikin daimyō)* who were more concerned with preserving their own authority than with the national welfare. Kita, like his hero, inevitably fell afoul of the established authorities, and in 1937 he was executed by a firing squad because of his alleged influence on the "young officers" who participated in the 26th February incident. For these "young   9.21 officers," and for many of the ultra-rightists during the chauvinist period that culminated in the defeat of 1945, Saigō was a revered figure; and army officers made a point of explaining that the struggle in China was an implementation of his policy to assert Japan's influence on the continent.   9.22

With the discredit of samurai ideals and other traditional values in the postwar period, Saigō's standing became ambiguous. Yet, despite the vast change in the ideological atmosphere and the new freedom of historians to separate fact from legend and to puncture the inflated reputations of certain national heroes, he remained an immensely popular figure. A public-opinion poll taken shortly after the Pacific war among young Japanese people included Saigō as one of the ten most respected figures in Japanese history; in a poll twelve years later he was   9.23 recognized as one of the eighteen "most splendid personalities" *(rippa na jimbutsu)* in Japan. In order to maintain Saigō's image   9.24 in the changed atmosphere, his advocates have usually emphasized the magnanimous, liberal side of their hero and his efforts to limit the bloodshed in the civil war of 1867–68, while playing down, or even indignantly denying, any authoritarian or imperialist proclivities that seemed reminiscent of unpopular prewar values. Thus a modern expert on Saigō Takamori, writing in 1948, represented him as Japan's first great democrat, and identifies his famous "Revere Heaven, Love Humanity" slogan with *9.25* the democratic ideals of Abraham Lincoln.

This many-faceted popularity of Saigō Takamori has inspired a vast "Saigō literature" in which writers have used his career and legend as material for biographies, historical studies, and romantic narratives. He is also an ideal dramatic hero. The first of many plays about Saigō, produced in 1878 when he was still officially in disgrace, had such an immediate success in Tokyo that the producer was able to rebuild his theatre on the *9.26* proceeds.

In general the writers are laudatory and uncritical in their approach and make little attempt to plumb the hero's psychological complexities; yet cumulatively they provide ample factual information about most aspects of Saigō's life, except his early childhood and his family relations. A number of famous songs and poems reflect contemporary emotional reactions to Saigō Takamori and his disaster. The earliest, which was later set to music and used as an army marching song, was written just after the rebellion and referred to a crucial battle in which Saigō's rebel army was defeated. Though the poet spoke from the point of view of the government forces, his sympathies were obviously divided:

> We are the Imperial forces,
> While our enemy is the enemy of the Court,
> For whom there is no place in Heaven or on earth.
> He who leads the enemy forces
> Is the bravest hero who ever lived [*kokon musō no eiyū*],
> And all the men who follow him
> Are intrepid, death-defying warriors,
> Who can stand without shame before the fiercest gods.
> Yet since ancient times those who have defied Heaven and
>   risen in rebellion
> Have always met bad ends.
> So now, until the foe is vanquished,
> Charge forward, one and all,

Charge forward!
Draw out your flashing swords (with one accord),
And be prepared to die
As you rush [against the enemy]!   *9.27*

The author of the famous "autumn wind" poem imagines the hero's state of mind as he is about to die:

With my forlorn band [of loyal fighters]
I have cleft my way through the besieging enemy
And marched a hundred leagues back to these ramparts [of Kagoshima].
Now my sword is broken, and my steed has fallen dead.
The autumn wind will bury my bones
Here in the hills of my native town.   *9.28*

The long ballad of Shiroyama, named after the "castle hill" in Kagoshima where Saigō's life came to an end, emphasizes the parabolic aspect of his career. It starts by describing the scene of Saigō's death; then

The men of the government forces who had observed these [sad events]
Said, "He who until yesterday was revered as the leader of our Imperial
    Army,
He who basked in His Majesty's favour and enjoyed the world's esteem
As the greatest hero of them all [*tagui nakarishi eiyū*]—
Today, most pitifully, has he vanished like the dew . . .
How full our hearts have grown
From the deep sense that naught endures in this world of ours [*yo no
naka no mujō wo fakaku kanji*]. . . .   *9.29*

In addition to this "Saigō literature" there is a large quantity of pictorial representation, including formal portraits, statues, popular prints, and an assortment of thermometers, toys, teapots, and other trinkets decorated with the corpulent figure of the hero from Kyushu. Perhaps the most remarkable examples are con- *9.30* temporary prints in which he is depicted sitting cross-legged on Mars with an afterglow emanating from the planet like a sort of heroic effluvium. When adulation for Saigō soared to new heights *9.31* a few years after his death, he was actually identified with Mars, and the planet came to be called "the Saigō star" (*Saigōboshi*). As part of the popular deification he was fitted into the Buddhist cosmology: in the Saigō Nirvana Painting (Saigō Nehan Zu), though still attired in army uniform, he is frankly portrayed as a Buddha.

The cult of Saigō led to a body of survival legends, according to which the hero had not died in Kagoshima but had escaped to a foreign country and would soon return home. Theories of survival are common to many heroes in Japan and elsewhere. What is remarkable is that fabulous legends of this type should have become attached to a recent historical figure who died a few years after Disraeli. The first theory, which circulated shortly following his downfall, is that he had fled in a ship from Kyushu and reached a certain "Indian island," whence he would return to save his country. In 1891 there was an upsurge of such legends connected, rather improbably, with the forthcoming state visit of the Russian crown prince. It was bruited that Saigō, having escaped from Kyushu and crossed over to Russia, would shortly be arriving in Japan on a Russian warship in the company of the crown prince. Once back in Tokyo he would clean out the Augean stables of Meiji corruption, revise the unequal treaties with the Western powers, and lead an invasion against Korea. One enterprising newspaper took advantage of the widespread excitement to conduct a primitive public-opinion poll:

Is He Alive or Is He Dead?

Readers, both those who believe [Saigō Takamori] is alive and those who think he actually died, are invited to fill in a ballot stating their opinions and itemizing their reasons. Ballots should be placed in a box at this office or else sent by post not later than the 15th of the month. . . . The person whose answer is closest to the opinion given by the majority of our respondents will receive as First Prize a three months' subscription to the Hokushin News. . . .

Saigō came from Satsuma, a proud, pugnacious province, noted for its beautifully rugged nature—a province whose relation to Japan is not unlike that of Ireland to Great Britain. Though its inhabitants constituted no separate race like the Celts, they clung proudly to their native dialect, which was virtually incomprehensible to other Japanese, and in a period of rapid change they stubbornly preserved their traditional mores. This was partly because of Satsuma's geographical isolation from the political and cultural centre of the country. Even today it takes

almost twenty-four hours by the fastest express train to travel
from Tokyo to the provincial capital of Kagoshima; in Saigō's
time the most rapid mode of transport was ship, and the journey
to Osaka normally required about ten days. Satsuma was the
second largest province in Japan and by far the most independent, closed, and clannish. The Shimazus, its hereditary rulers,
descended from ancestors who had been defeated by the Tokugawas in a crucial battle in 1600, and Satsuma was traditionally one
of the bitterest foes of the ruling shogunate. Though obliged to
recognize the Tokugawa regime in Edo as the principal political
authority in Japan, the Shimazus kept their province aloof for
some two centuries; and even after the Meiji Restoration, when
Satsuma was reorganized as Kagoshima Prefecture, it remained
in many ways a semi-independent fief, often retaining old feudal
practices and blithely ignoring such innovations as tax reform,
the regulation against carrying swords, and the new Western
calendar.   9.37

The poor condition of the peasantry in Satsuma was aggravated by the fact that an unusually high proportion of the
population consisted of samurai—about forty percent of the six
hundred thousand inhabitants, and over seventy percent in
Saigō's native town of Kagoshima. To support this numerous and   9.38
largely unproductive class, the workers in the fields suffered
harsh exploitation in the form of taxes and corvée. According to
a contemporary Satsuma saying, "Peasants are expected to do
thirty-five days of public service (buko) each month." To escape   9.39
their crushing burden they frequently tried to abscond to neighbouring provinces but were almost invariably caught and fiercely
punished.

Poverty was by no means limited to the peasant class. Most
of the samurai, except those on the highest rungs, lived in Spartan conditions, their economic situation being hardly different
from that of farmers in more prosperous parts of Japan. They
made up for such hardship by pride in their ancient military
tradition and by inculcating their sons with the values of the
hayato, the ideal Satsuma samurai who combined dignified frugality with valour, agility, and independence.   9.40

It was into such a warrior family that Saigō Takamori was
born towards the end of the Tokugawa period, and throughout
his life he remained keenly conscious of his status as a Satsuma
samurai. He was the eldest of seven children. His father, a minor 9.41

9.42 clan official who served the Lord of Satsuma as head of the Accounts Department, was renowned for stern integrity. The
9.43 Saigō family ranked low in the samurai social hierarchy, and they were poor even by the prevalent standards of the Satsuma *hayato*. As was common among petty samurai in Satsuma, the father is said to have eked out his stipend by agricultural work, being assisted by Takamori and three other sons. When Takamori was sixteen, he completed his studies at the clan school, and immediately started work as an assistant clerk in the County Magistrate's Office, contributing his modest salary to the family budget. A keen sense of thrift and duty were inculcated into the future hero from an early age.

One of the best-known facts about Saigō Takamori is his
9.44 size. He would have been an imposing figure in any country, but in nineteenth-century Japan he was a veritable Gargantua. Many affectionate (and often spurious) anecdotes are based on his corpulence, which was said to have made it impossible for him to mount a horse; and he also became famous for his voracious appetite. Takamori's physique was inherited from several generations in the Saigō family, his father being a burly man over six feet tall and a powerful *sumō* wrestler. Takamori is said to have been a huge, wide-eyed baby, and at school he was known for his bulk. As an adult he was just under six feet tall and weighed over two hundred and forty pounds. He had a bull neck (his collar size was 19 1/2 inches) and immensely broad shoulders. People who met him were invariably struck by his large, piercing eyes (the British diplomat Satow described him as having "an eye that
9.45 sparkled like a big black diamond") and by the great, bushy eyebrows. A recent biographer adds that he was endowed with huge testicles *(idai naru kōgan)*, though the source of this particu-
9.46 lar detail is not specified. In a country whose historical figures have tended to conform in size to a somewhat modest pattern, he stands out larger than life. This unconventional physical stature of Saigō the Great later became associated with certain inner qualities, notably a strong nonconformist nature, that are especially admired in Japan because they tend to be so rare.

During most of his life this behemoth from the west overflowed with vigour. At school, where he acquired the nicknames of *udo* ("huge gawk") and *ōmedama* ("big eyes"), he was a powerful fighter; later he put his weight to use as a *sumō* wrestler, and during the final years in Kyushu he worked off his physical energy by tramping tirelessly through the hilly countryside with his dogs. One painful effect of his weight was a recurrence of filiariasis, an obscure illness associated with obesity. In his bad attacks Saigō was obliged to purge himself daily and to remain indoors. He took advantage of these periods of enforced seclusion to write letters to his associates; and the historian can therefore thank the hero's fatness for the voluminous correspondence that has come down to us.

Concerning the personality enveloped within this vast frame, it is harder to separate fact from legend. As a child he appeared somewhat slow-witted, and at the clan school he became known as a stolid and inarticulate lad. One day, according *9.47* to a typical (and perhaps apocryphal) story, he was walking down a lane on his way to deliver a huge tray of cakes when another boy, who had decided to play a practical joke on his corpulent schoolmate, jumped out from an alley with a piercing yell; the young Saigō carefully placed the tray on the ground and turning to the boy said in his slow Satsuma accent, "Goodness, how you startled me!" Saigō Takamori's apparent slowness, of course, concealed the overabundant energy which inspired his frenzied career; but the "provocative silences that could pass for contempt or wisdom" continued throughout his life. *9.48*

As a youth he was headstrong and disrespectful of authority; and these qualities carried over into his later years when he displayed a frankness and unorthodoxy that Japanese people are traditionally warned to avoid lest they be hammered on the head. A wild, mischievous boy, Saigō in due course won the respect of his schoolmates for his pluck and enterprise. He became the leader (*nisegashira*) of a group of boys from local samurai families, including Ōkubo Toshimichi, who was to have such a vital, and indeed fatal, influence on his career. Until the end of Saigō's life, *9.49* moral intrepidity and disdain for physical danger were salient in his personality, and even contemporaries who regarded his objectives as confused and his methods as unwise never questioned the man's courage. Beneath his reticence and silences lurked an enthusiastic, passionate nature, which sometimes erupted in outbursts of violence. The following incident occurred in 1860 during his first period of exile. One day news reached the island where he lived that the chief shogunal Minister, whom he had himself intended to kill as an enemy of the Court, had been assassinated in Edo:

"They have done it at last," said Saigō to himself. He could not keep still. Taking his wooden sword from the alcove, he rushed out of the house to the garden and began to strike an innocent old tree, shouting at the top of his voice, as if he were taking the tree for a man upon whom to wreak his furious passion. His shouts echoed through the stillness of the night. The sound of his blows on the tree was heard too. People wondered what had happened, but he did not mind, for he was quite beside himself with fury.

It was not until this nocturnal fencing exercise with the old tree had refreshed him that he took off his sandals, washed his feet, and entered the house.

9.50   He had already regained his usual calm. . . .

But the rage remained, and was soon to explode in more momentous ways.

From his youth he possessed a fundamental moral fastidiousness, marked by forthright honesty, modesty of speech and taste, a repugnance for display, and a total lack of avarice. He was unique among the Meiji leaders in appearing almost entirely uninterested in honours and awards. According to one of his eminent admirers, this is because he did only what he believed *9.51* to be right in the national interest. Perhaps so; but it would be naïve to overlook the possibility that desire for a noble reputation played its part and that, consciously or not, he pursued this goal throughout his life.

About Saigō's personal magnetism there can be no question. The man's charisma was evident to all who met him, from the young camp-follower who recognized him as a god to the shrewd English diplomat who was instantly struck by the power of his *9.52* character. Saigō's peculiar charm depended on the combination of a mighty physique with an apparently open, radiant, human quality (so different from the cold, self-centered fanaticism of an Ōshio Heihachirō), a simple, almost childlike enjoyment of the moment, and an immediate, earthy humour. Unlike most grand men of his time, he was direct and natural with his equals, gentle, considerate, and forbearing towards inferiors. Above all it was the dynamism of his will and energy that made him, as a modern historian has put it, "the most potent personality in Japanese *9.53* history."

Yet between the lines of contemporary panegyrics and later hero-worshipping biographies are hints of a darker side to the hero's nature. One of the few striking details in Saigō's early life was his reaction to the disembowelment of a Satsuma samurai, who was closely associated with the Saigō family and who, in his efforts to ensure the succession of Shimazu Nariakira as lord of the clan, had become involved in an abortive plot and was condemned to commit ritual suicide. According to one version of the story, Saigō witnessed the gory scene himself. At the moment when the samurai was about to plunge the sword into his stomach, he turned to the young man and explained that he was offering his life for his lord and his province. This dramatic experience is said to have first awakened the hero to a sense of duty and self-sacrifice. In a more probable version Saigō was not actually present at the suicide but later received a blood-stained under-kimono, which the samurai had worn while disembowelling himself and which he bequeathed to the young man as a parting gift. "As he gazed at this sad and gruesome memento of his friend," speculates one biographer, "Saigō vowed vengeance upon those who were corrupting Clan affairs and swore that Nariakira should succeed to his just and proper position as their Lord." Whatever lofty resolutions this event inspired in the young man, it may well have aroused a fascination with the image of noble self-destruction and have contributed to a death-wish—a wish that he first acted out in his attempt to drown himself at the age of thirty, that later influenced his decision to go to Korea "in order to be killed," and that finally led him into a rebellion which was, quite-literally, suicidal.

Intimations of the darker side of the hero's personality—the side which was largely obscured by his serene, radiant impression—can be found in much of his poetry. Frequently he expresses uneasiness about living fellow humans, as in this poem written on the anniversary of the death of one of the samurai plotters who were sentenced to commit suicide:

> I do not mind the bitter cold of winter;
> What fills my heart with fear is the cold hearts of men. . . .

Or again,

> . . . Such joys as [then] I knew came not from living men,
> But from those who had long since died.

In a letter from his island of exile Saigō wrote, "Now I have finally discovered that human beings cannot be trusted. They are as changeable as the rolling eyes of a cat. To my amazement some people on whom I had relied as kindred spirits have made un-

9.57   founded accusations against me."

In a later poem Saigō remarks that he would not be scared by even a million devils, but that the sight of "that pack of wild beasts called human beings" *(ningen-korō no gun)* makes him want

9.58   to escape from the world. At other times, and more significantly, Saigō's painful doubts are directed towards his own nature:

> I sit and study far into the bitter night.
> My face is cold, my stomach empty.
> Again and again I stir the embers to give light.
> One's selfish thoughts [*shii*] should melt away like snow before
> [this] lighted lamp.
> Yet, when I gaze deep within my heart,
> I am humbled by abundant shame [*hazuru koto ōshi*].

Beneath the hero's bluff, ebullient exterior there appears to have lurked a deep sense of personal unworthiness; but, lacking details about his early years, we are unlikely ever to be in a position to probe its origins and full implications.

Little is known about Saigō's years as a Magistrate's assistant. He was trained as a scribe-copyist, and it may well have been during this period that he developed his skill in calligraphy, the supreme art for the Japanese gentleman. His job also brought him into close contact with the indigent Satsuma peasantry. On one occasion the Magistrate despatched him to the countryside on a tour of inspection for tax assessment. The clan authorities had just refused an appeal by the peasants that levies be reduced owing to a recent crop failure. During his tour Saigō came across a farmer sadly taking leave of his cow, which he had been obliged to sell in order to pay his taxes. The young official was moved by the man's plight and, having gone to some trouble to examine his case, managed to reduce the assessment. The anecdote fits nicely into the Saigō legend as an illustration of his benevolence and of

9.59   his typically heroic sense of *nasake.*

In 1849, when Saigō was twenty-one, the Shimazu clan was split by an involved succession dispute of the type that has always plagued Japanese politics. The crisis had an important influence on Saigō's career, for he sided wholeheartedly with the "progressive," anti-Bakufu candidate, Shimazu Nariakira, who wished to modernize and reform the fief. In cooperation with his old school companion, Ōkubo Toshimichi, Saigō helped to secure victory for the "progressive" faction, and in 1851 Shimazu Nariakira was appointed the twenty-sixth Lord of Satsuma at the age of forty-two. In the long, secret manoeuvres that led to the final decision, Saigō forged an alliance with Ōkubo (the man who would later compass his ruin); the negotiations also brought him close to his great hero, Nariakira.

9.60

A few years later, Saigō had the honour of being included in Nariakira's suite on the occasion of the daimyo's annual procession to Edo, a journey of several months. This experience intensified Saigō's adulation for his overlord. Nariakira for his part appears to have been impressed by his energetic young vassal, and a few months later he appointed him to be head gardener in the magnificent grounds of his residence outside Kagoshima. It was a modest position in the hierarchy, but afforded frequent opportunities for private meetings, during which the daimyo and his retainer are said to have exchanged views on the future of Japan. In the same year Nariakira introduced Saigō to a famous Confucian nationalist scholar, who made a great impression by inveighing openly against the Bakufu's weak-kneed policy towards the foreign powers and the lack of a proper patriotic spirit in high places.

9.61

As Nariakira developed increasing confidence in his retainer's talents, he began using Saigō for confidential political missions, including manoeuvres against the Bakufu and complex negotiations concerning the shogunal succession. Officially Saigō held the somewhat incongruous post of birdkeeper at the Shimazu mansion in Edo, but his actual functions were considerably more impressive. During Saigō's late twenties, one of the most active and apparently happy periods in his life, he travelled frequently to the imperial capital in Kyoto and to the shogunal headquarters in Edo, covering these huge distances with his usual indefatigable vigour. On one of his journeys, when he happened to be in Kyoto during an outbreak of cholera, his energy extended to organizing a successful campaign against the epidemic, thus making him a sort of samurai equivalent to the contemporary Western heroine, Florence Nightingale.

9.62

9.63

Saigō's thirtieth year, a turning point in his life, started auspiciously with his employment in Edo as the daimyo's confidential agent. Only a few months later, however, Nariakira suddenly fell ill and died. At one stroke Saigō was bereft, not only of his main political support, but of an adored friend. This disaster plunged him into a state of acute misery and was one of the direct reasons for his attempted suicide. In traditional accounts Saigō is said to have reacted to the news by immediately deciding to follow Nariakira to the grave according to the ancient Japanese practice of *junshi* (self-immolation of an attendant on the death of his lord) but was dissuaded by a friend in Kyoto, the loyalist priest called Gesshō, who insisted that the young man stay alive for his country's sake.

9.64

A few months later, when Gesshō reached Kagoshima as a fugitive from the Bakufu police, Saigō arranged that they would escape at night by boat and end their lives together in the sea. When the boat was about a mile into Kagoshima Bay, the two friends went to the prow. The other men on board supposed that they had gone to admire the magnificent moonlight scenery, but in fact they were exchanging farewells and writing their obligatory death-poems. These preliminaries completed, Saigō and his friend leapt off the gunwale. A contemporary print shows the white-robed priest and his young samurai companion as they are about to hit the water; their grim, determined faces are brightly illuminated by the full moon, while further back in the boat a companion sits playing the flute, serenely unaware of the tragedy that is being enacted a few feet away. Shortly after the loud splash was heard, the crew sighted the two bodies and, having hauled them out of the water, brought them to a hut near the shore. The priest did not respond to attempts at artificial respiration; the burly young samurai, however, was still alive, and the little straw-thatched hut, which has been carefully preserved and now stands by a main road opposite the coastal railway line, remains a place of pilgrimage for Saigō's admirers. The two *tanka* poems which were found on Gesshō's body and which, rather incongruously, had been indited on toilet paper, referred to the "cloudless moon of his heart" which would soon sink into the waters of Kagoshima Bay, and ended by affirming his joy at dying for the Emperor (Ōgimi).

9.65

Saigō's biographers have suggested various motives for his frantic deed. Nariakira's recent demise was almost certainly a proximate cause. This was probably combined with a desire to

die with his loyalist friend, Gesshō, who was doomed for execution within a matter of days unless he forestalled the authorities
by taking his own life. According to Uchimura Kanzō, Saigō's   *9.66*
famous Christian admirer, the hero decided to kill himself as a
"mark of friendship and hospitality to his friend" *(yūjin ni taisuru
jōgi to kantai no shirushi)*, and the act was inspired by his "excessive compassion" *(amari tsuyosugiru nasake)*. Such explanations   *9.67*
may all contain an element of truth (though "hospitality" seems
a rather feeble motive); but the pent-up fury and violence revealed in Saigō's attempt at self-destruction must certainly have
come from deep wellsprings in his personality that actuated his
irrational and erratic behaviour during later crises.   *9.68*

Long after he had become recognized as the grand hero of
the Meiji Restoration, Saigō often harked back to the climactic
moment when he had tried to die with his friend and regretted
that the attempt had failed. He solemnly celebrated each anniver-   *9.69*
sary of the drowning, and seventeen years after the event addressed this Chinese poem to the spirit of the dead priest:

> Clasped in each other's arms we leapt into the abyss of the sea.
> Though we both jumped together, Fate foiled my expectations and
>   brought me back alive above the waves [*ani hakaramu ya hajō
>   saisei no en*].
> Now more than ten years have followed like a trail of dreams,
> And I stand here before your grave, separated by death's great wall,
> While my tears still flow in vain.   *9.70*

This desperate attempt to die at the age of thirty must have
profoundly influenced Saigō's psychological development and
outlook on life. The fact that, however unintentionally, he had   *9.71*
outlived the suicide pact, while his friend had drowned, was
bound to stimulate the sense of guilt that classically haunts survivors and may have led to subsequent attempts to bring his life to
an end in a violent manner. The crisis in Kagoshima Bay is
undoubtedly connected with those later writings in which
Saigō stressed that one must free oneself from all fear of death
and be constantly prepared for its advent as an indispensable
condition for that selflessness *(jiko-fuchūshin-shugi)* which is essential for the cultivation of a true heart *(shinjō)*. As he absorbed the
teachings of Zen Buddhism and Wang Yang-ming Confucianism,
his attitude towards his own death became increasingly mystical,

and in one of his last works he stated that he had already died
9.72 with Gesshō twenty years earlier.

Saigō had hardly recovered from the shock of his attempted
drowning when the new ruler of Satsuma issued an order for his
indefinite banishment to an island some two hundred and fifty
miles south of Kagoshima. This was part of a purge which was
being directed against anti-Bakufu elements and included a
9.73 number of Nariakira's close associates. The next five years of
Saigō's life—years during which the Tokugawa regime was hastening towards its final crisis—were spent almost entirely in
exile. In 1862 he was pardoned and allowed to return to Kagoshima where he was briefly restored to his old post of birdkeeper.
But soon by his blunt, undiplomatic ways he managed to irk Lord
9.74 Hisamitsu (the conservative who had succeeded Nariakira as
ruler of the clan) and only six months after his release he was
banished once again—this time to a small island further south
where the conditions were harsher; later he was moved to a still
9.75 grimmer islet near Okinawa. Traditional accounts all refer to
Saigō's patience and dignity in misfortune. When the ship set sail
on a tropical August day to take him to the last island of his exile,
he calmly entered the little cage that had been built for him, and
when informed by a kindly official that he need not remain in the
cage once they were at sea, he is said to have replied, "Thank you,
but whatever happens I have to obey the Lord [of Satsuma]. I am
9.76 a convict, and I must be where a convict should be. . . ." During
the stormy journey through the East China Sea he composed a
poem defying the winds to blow their hardest and the waves to
rise like mountains, since he, being dedicated to the Imperial
9.77 Cause, would always remain imperturbable. He showed the same
sangfroid when he reached the bleak island where he was to
spend the next several years. Far from complaining about his
treatment, he used his imprisonment as an exercise in self-discipline and forced himself to sit immobile and bolt upright in his
prison cell for hours at a time.

The island of Saigō's first exile was a centre of the Satsuma
sugar industry, and he soon witnessed the sufferings of the slave-
workers, who lived in a sort of *Nacht und Nebel* condition, being
subject to fierce punishment for any infraction of the rules.
These unfortunates were literally unable to taste the fruit of their
own labours; for, with a severity reminiscent of conditions in the
gold mines of South Africa, workers who presumed merely to

lick the sugar were shackled and punished by flogging or even by execution. Poor harvests were never taken into consideration when it came to assessing taxes. The zealous local officials frequently arrested islanders and put them to the torture so that they would reveal whether they had any hidden produce. Some suspects actually tried to kill themselves by biting out their tongues rather than undergo further torment. Horrified by these conditions, Saigō (though himself a convict) remonstrated with the chief inspector, pointing out that such rapacious and pitiless folly was a disgrace to the name of Satsuma, and that, if the officials refused to lower taxes in years of bad harvest, they might as well murder the islanders outright. When the inspector, in the usual manner of officials dealing with meddlesome reformers, ordered him to mind his own business, Saigō insisted that matters affecting the honour of the clan *were* his business and threatened to make a detailed report to Kagoshima. As a result of his intervention the treatment of prisoners was somewhat mollified and a number of island-slaves *(bisa)* were set free.

Apart from his humanitarian activities, Saigō used the years in exile to read voluminously and to further his skill in calligraphy and Chinese poetry. Many of his most famous poems were written during this long period of seclusion; these include "New Year's Day in Exile" *(Takkyo toshi wo mukauru)* and "Feelings in Prison" *(Gokuchū kan ari)*, in which he points out that, although good fortune may continue to elude him, this will only confirm the sincerity of his intentions.

With the permission of the island authorities Saigō used some of his ebullient physical energy to indulge in his favourite sport of *sumō* wrestling. It was also during this exile that he took the daughter of a humble islander as his mistress, and she soon gave birth to his first son. His new family, however, was not allowed to accompany him in his subsequent exiles.

After Saigō had been banished for five years, Ōkubo and other friends interceded with the ruler of Satsuma to permit his release. Ōkubo himself (somewhat ironically in view of his later role in Saigō's career) threatened to commit harakiri unless a full pardon were granted. Lord Hisamitsu signed the order, but he is said to have been so vexed by this evidence of Saigō's popularity that he gnawed his silver tobacco pipe and left a permanent mark on the stem.

Despite the querulous tone of some of the poems from this

9.78

9.79

9.80

9.81

9.82

9.83

9.84

period, Saigō appears to have come through his long exile in surprisingly good spirits. On one occasion he even declared that he intended to stay in the islands permanently. For all the physical hardships of these years, they may well have been the most restful and spiritually invigorating period in the hero's turbulent life. Before leaving the island near Okinawa and returning to the hurly-burly of national politics, he wrote a tearful poem to his chief gaoler, thanking him for his kindness and saying that the

9.85   pain of this parting would remain with him throughout his life. Whatever inner effect Saigō's banishment may have had—and it is surely significant that in subsequent years he periodically retired from public activity in a sort of self-exile—there is no doubt that it helped establish him among dissenting samurai as the great loyalist, the man who had suffered for the Imperial Cause in a way that more practical politicians managed to avoid. In Saigō's career, as in those of Gandhi, Nehru, Kenyatta, and other national heroes, unjust imprisonment served as invaluable testimony to the fortitude of his character and the sincerity of his beliefs.

The four years that followed Saigō's return from exile represent the steep upward curve of his parabolic career and correspond to the periods of Yoshitsune's victories over the Tairas and of Masashige's early battles against the forces of Kamakura. These years culminated in the downfall of the Bakufu and the establishment of a new regime under the nominal authority of Emperor Meiji. In 1864 at the age of thirty-six, Saigō was appointed to be the Satsuma War Secretary as well as the clan's principal emissary in Kyoto, and thus he became a central figure in the last feverish manoeuvres to topple the Edo regime. Much of his energy was devoted to negotiations with other "outside" clans, notably the militantly anti-Bakufu fief of Chōshū at the extreme west of the main island. Though his first actual military experience was as commander of the Satsuma troops in a successful engagement against the insurgent Chōshū, Saigō was always reluctant to fight this staunchly loyalist clan. He insisted on sparing the lives of the principal captives, a rare act of clemency in Japanese warfare, and finally helped arrange a Satsuma–Chōshū coalition that, with the support of the Tosa domain in

9.86   Shikoku, succeeded in overthrowing the enfeebled Bakufu. It is typical of the ironies that studded Saigō's career that representatives of these powerful fiefs, whose alliance he had worked so hard to establish, should later have become the very clique that dominated the Meiji government and pursued policies which he detested. Saigō was also engaged in foreign diplomatic negotiations, particularly with England. In 1866 he arranged the reception in Kagoshima of the first British Minister, Sir Harry Parkes, and persuaded him that the future of Japan lay in the hands of an imperial government and that the Bakufu was no longer competent to carry out the treaties with foreign powers. Subsequently he met the brilliant young English secretary-interpreter, Ernest Satow, at an inn in Kobe, and politely parried his offers of British aid, which he feared might involve Satsuma in unwelcome obligations.

9.87

9.88

The climax came at the beginning of 1868 in a decisive battle when some four thousand loyalist troops, mainly from Satsuma and Chōshū, engaged a Bakufu army of twenty thousand. Their resounding victory led to the official surrender of Bakufu headquarters in Edo Castle—the famous *akewatashi* that was pictured in all primary school textbooks before the war as a scene to inspire nationalist fervour in young minds. Saigō followed up these triumphs a few months later by mopping up remaining Bakufu supporters in the north and east.

Traditional panegyrics, apart from glorifying Saigō's military genius and representing him as the only indispensable figure in the Restoration movement (both rather questionable propositions), stress his magnanimity in victory. This admits no cavil. Saigō not only demanded amnesty for his enemies, the defeated Shogun and high Bakufu officials, but took every possible step to spare the innocent population from the type of carnage that had followed similar upheavals in the past. Though large forces took part in the fighting in Edo (almost the same number of men as in the Sino-Japanese War), the actual loss of life was small. Indeed, there can be few violent transformations in history that were accomplished with so little actual bloodshed, and even Saigō's detractors are bound to admit that he was at least partly responsible for this benign outcome.

9.89

9.90

The most obvious effect of the Restoration was to terminate the military government, which had persisted in one form or another during almost the entire time since Yoritomo's victory some seven centuries earlier. The insurrection of 1867–68 was the first all-out effort to "restore" the Emperor since the time of Kusunoki Masashige in the fourteenth century. The system of

Bakufu rule in the Emperor's name had been durable and, especially during the Tokugawa centuries, remarkably effective. Simply because we know that the Bakufu did finally collapse in 1868 we must not underestimate its apparent power of survival in the 1850s and '60s nor the risks incurred by the loyalists who presumed to defy it. What was their official objective? One of the clearest statements is contained in an agreement signed by representatives of the Satsuma and Tosa domains (including Saigō Takamori) in July 1867:

[Our purpose] is to restore Imperial Rule and to deal with affairs, taking the situation of the world into consideration, in so reasonable a manner as to leave nothing to be desired by posterity. The main point of the reform is that the powers of administration and judicature shall pass into the hands of the Emperor. Though our country has had an unbroken line of Emperors, it happened a long time ago that, the feudal system once adopted, the reins of government fell into the hands of the Shogunal Government. The presence of the Sovereignty that ought to rule the land has been ignored, a state of affairs which cannot be found in any other country in the world. We must, therefore, reform our political system, restore the reins of government to the Imperial Court, hold a conference of the Daimyos, and in concert with one another work for the purpose of lifting the prestige of the nation among the Powers of the world. Thus we shall be able to establish the fundamental character of our Empire. . . .

9.91

The real objective, in fact, was not to restore power to the person of the sovereign (in 1867 Emperor Meiji was a youth of fifteen who was hardly in a position to assert his country's prestige in the world) or even to the imperial family and Court nobility, but to bring about certain reforms that seemed urgently necessary if Japan was to avoid the fate inflicted by Western powers on India and, more recently, on China. For this purpose actual authority in the new government was not given to the Emperor but assumed largely by a group of young samurai who represented a balance of leadership from four "outside" clans, including Satsuma, and who were determined to carry out policies necessary for Japan's national survival and emergence as a modern power. In the process they brought about many reforms that were not necessarily part of their original aims. Japan opened its doors to the Western world; the domains into which the country had been divided all disappeared; the warrior class lost its traditional privileges; a predominantly feudal society was largely replaced by industrial capitalism; and a powerful national army was created —an army manned not by samurai but by peasant conscripts and supported by a new system of national taxation. These momentous changes and the fact of popular participation have led many writers to describe the Meiji Restoration as a "revolution." It is *9.92* largely a question of how we define the term; but, since the Restoration did not fundamentally alter the system of property-holding, we can hardly regard it as revolutionary in the full modern sense of the word. *9.93*

After the loyalist triumphs of 1868 Saigō insisted on returning to his native province, and the next three months were spent in peaceful, semimonastic retreat in the countryside near Kagoshima. His prestige and popularity were now at a high point, not only in Satsuma, but in Edo and Kyoto. In recognition of his services to the Imperial Court he was offered a generous financial reward and, far more important, the First Grade of the Third Court Rank. Saigō startled the government by declining these honours, an act at least as remarkable as if an English general turned down the sovereign's offer of a country seat and a peerage. In his letter of refusal Saigō implied that it was inappropriate for him to receive a distinction of this kind which was beyond the authority of the clan that he served. With conventional humility he added that, while such ranks were obviously important for courtiers in the capital, they could have no meaning for a rustic boor like himself. Saigō was asked to reconsider, but in the end *9.94* the government had to accept his refusal—a refusal that redounded to his popularity but hardly endeared him to officialdom in Tokyo.

A few years later Ōkubo and other high officials visited Kagoshima in a concerted effort to induce Saigō to join the central government. Saigō's younger brother, Tsugumichi, who had *9.95* now become a successful Establishment figure and had recently returned from a mission to Europe, tearfully pleaded with him to accept the offer, and finally he agreed. Before leaving Satsuma, he wrote a poem predicting his own sacrificial death. He re- *9.96* turned to Tokyo in 1871 and a few months later became a leading member of the government with the post of Counsellor (Sangi), a sort of Minister without Portfolio. Real power in the new *9.97*

regime was now held mainly by a small group of able and energetic men belonging to the lower strata of the samurai class from
Satsuma and other "outside" clans.

For a country where age was traditionally regarded as a
criterion of wisdom these leaders were amazingly young, the
oldest among them (Saigō Takamori) being only forty-three. In
addition to his civilian duties, Saigō exercised supreme military
power in the new government: in 1872 he became Commander-in-
Chief of all the armed forces and in 1873 was appointed to the
unique rank of Field Marshal, a rank corresponding to that held
by the Duke of Marlborough after his victories. On this auspicious occasion Saigō, as if embarrassed by the plethora of worldly
success, stated once again that he knew he was destined to be
9.98 killed.

Towards the end of 1871 some fifty high government officials,
including Ōkubo, left Japan for a lengthy tour of Europe and
America, the so-called Iwakura Mission. Saigō and two other
leaders remained in Tokyo to head an unofficial caretaker government. By this time Saigō's dissatisfaction with the regime and its
leaders had crystallized. The caretaker government had virtually
no authority to make important decisions during the absence of
the Iwakura Mission. Saigō evidently resented the idea that the
politicians travelling to the West were leaving him as a sort of
cipher, and when seeing off his colleagues at Yokohama he is said
to have remarked, in his typically blunt style, that he wished
9.99 their boat might sink on the way.

The main causes for Saigō's disaffection with the regime he
had helped put in power and for his break with the Meiji government and his final rebellion were of a moral nature. Though an
avid reader and student, he never thought of himself as a scholar.
He wrote a wealth of poems, essays, and letters, but his only
complete book is a posthumous collection of miscellaneous say-
9.100 ings. The main intellectual influence in his life was undoubtedly
the neo-Confucianism of Wang Yang-ming, which he admired
9.101 from an early age. After Saigō left the clan school and was serving as an assistant clerk, he and some of the other young samurai
met regularly to study the writings of Wang Yang-ming and his
9.102 followers. Particularly relevant was Ōshio Heihachirō, the sage-
hero of Osaka who had killed himself about a decade earlier; and
until the end of his life Saigō invigorated himself by rereading

Ōshio's philosophical lectures. The influence of Wang Yang-ming and of Ōshio pervades Saigō's own scattered writings. Mishima Yukio stresses the effect of their philosophy on Saigō's career and suggests that the Absolute Spirit *(taikyo)* which he envisaged may have been the motive for his rebellion.   *9.103*

Like Ōshio, Saigō vigorously indoctrinated his young disciples with the notion that deeds were more important than any amount of knowledge acquired by study or observation, and the word "sincerity" *(shisei, makoto)* recurs with plangent regularity in his writings.

However seriously systems and measures may be discussed, they cannot be put into practice unless there is the right man to do it. There is no deed without a doer. To have the right man is the greatest blessing. One must aim at being that man.   *9.104*

His philosophical poems stress the importance of cultivating a "pure heart"; and in a famous saying he points out that instead of finding fault with others we should forever be looking for flaws in ourselves. "What is achieved by depending on one's *9.105* ability," he writes, "is so uncertain that we cannot regard it with any satisfaction. Only sincerity can accomplish an enterprise." *9.106* To show that mere physical force is useless unless backed by moral power he cites an example from the recent Franco-Prussian War when three hundred thousand French soldiers, who still held a vast supply of provisions, surrendered to the enemy "simply because they had too mercenary a spirit."

Saigō frequently expressed his disdain for "worldly wisdom" *(ningenteki no chie)*, which is concerned simply with practical achievement; and while true wisdom is likely to produce present misfortunes it assures success in another, more impor- *9.107* tant way:

A man of true sincerity will be an example to the world even after his death. . . . When an insincere man is spoken well of, he has, so to speak, got a windfall; but a man of deep sincerity will, even if he is unknown in his lifetime, have a lasting reward: the esteem of posterity.   *9.108*

Clearly it was this form of success—a success born of worldly failure—to which Saigō aspired during his life and which he reaped so abundantly after his death.

The greatest of all dangers to sincerity is love of self, and the

overriding rule in personal life, family relations, and official dealings must be to slough off one's natural selfishness. One of
Saigō's best-known passages gives his prescription for the national saviour:

He who cares neither about his life, not about his fame, nor about rank
or money—such a man is hard to deal with [*shimatsu ni komaru*]. Yet it
is only such a man who will undergo every hardship with his companions in order to carry out great work for the country.

And in a late poem, written "to be shown to my pupils," he
returns to the theme of self-sacrifice:

Those things that common men all shun
Are not feared by the hero but held most precious [*eiyū kaette
kōshin su*].
When confronted with difficulties, never escape them;
When faced with worldly gain, never pursue it. . . .

He who would conquer himself and attain sincerity must
exercise extreme control. The first requisite, according to Saigō,
is "self-watchfulness": "To attain the holy state of sincerity, you
must begin with *shindoku*, which means care of your own conduct
or behaviour when alone, out of the sight and hearing of others."
Here he was referring to a Confucian precept; but in his efforts
to master himself, and in particular to curb his "excessive compassion," Saigō also had recourse to Buddhist discipline, and he
took advantage of his periodic retreats from active life to study
and practise Zen.

Saigō's main philosophical slogan—the slogan that he indited again and again in his powerful calligraphy, presenting
copies to the various private schools that had been established
under his aegis—was Confucian through and through. Its four
characters, "Revere Heaven, Love Mankind" (*Keiten Aijin*), occupied the same place in his campaign for righteousness as did
"Save the People" (*Kyūmin*) in that of Ōshio Heihachirō. Here
Saigō's thinking may impress some readers as fuzzy. The Way,
he writes, is the way of Heaven and Earth, and it is our duty to
follow it with all our efforts. In so doing we should not make man
our partner but Heaven, and it must be the object of our life to
revere Heaven. Yet, since Heaven loves everyone in the world
equally, we too must love others as we love ourselves. These are

no doubt fine and unexceptionable sentiments, but they are sufficiently vague so that writers like Uchimura and Nitobe were able
to associate them with "the law and the prophets" and with the
Christian rule to love one's neighbour as oneself.   9.116

How were Saigō's ideas about "loving others" *(hito wo aisuru)*
translated into practice? During much of his life he exhibited to
a remarkable degree the "warrior's compassion" *(bushi no nasake)*,
a genuine sympathy with the weak and unfortunate people of the
world; and this is one reason for his continued popularity as a
national hero, since it showed that he had the human talent,
prized in Japan since ancient times, of entering into the feelings
of others. While serving as a Magistrate's assistant, Saigō learnt   9.117
at first hand about the poverty of the toiling masses in Satsuma,
who often lived little better than animals; he saw how the situation was exacerbated by grasping officials and tried to alleviate   9.118
it. During his exile he showed a genuine concern for the workers   9.119
in the sugar plantations, and gave most of his own rice ration to
the poverty-stricken inhabitants of the island. Later, as a military
commander, Saigō did his best to minimize the sufferings of the
common people who were caught in the cross-fire of war.

Yet Saigō's humanitarian sentiments were limited by his
social attitudes. For one thing, they were directed almost entirely
to the peasantry, and his slogan of *Aijin* ("Love Mankind") was
really equivalent to "Love the Peasants." In his view of society
the population was divided into two immutable categories: those
who worked with their bodies *(chikara wo rōsuru mono)* and those
who used their minds or hearts *(kokoro wo rōsuru mono)*—that is,
the farmers and their samurai masters. Though the new national
leaders were increasingly aware that Japan must be industrial-
ized if she was to survive, and though Saigō himself recognized
the importance of industry and trade, he continued to regard
agriculture as the country's economic base and the peasantry as
its mainstay. It was the duty of the samurai officials to provide
benevolent social leadership: they should love and protect the
peasants as a lord cherishes his vassals and a father his children.
There was, however, no question of changing society so that the
peasants might become the equals or partners of the officials and,
in the end, class barriers disappear entirely. Saigō's paternalism
was rooted in a traditional Confucian outlook which was essentially the same as that of Ōshio when he spoke of "saving the
people." Later admirers who represented Saigō as a radical re-

9.120   former or believer in egalitarianism were blinding themselves to the staunchly conservative nature of his social ideas.

Beyond his constant protestations about the importance of the peasantry, Saigō generally exemplified the traditional rural ethos of Japan. He loved the land and country life and people who spent their time close to nature; conversely he distrusted and despised cities and all they represented. In a typical poem he complained about life in the capital, where the clamour of the traffic alarms one's soul *(mukon odoroku)* and where one's clothes are soiled by the dust and grime of the streets, and extolled life *9.121*   in the country, which allows one to regain purity and innocence.

A major aspect of the rural samurai ethos was an emphasis on frugality and a dislike of luxury and ostentation. The traditional samurai respected thrift, not as a means of economy but as an exercise in abstinence and a sign that his life was devoted to more important values than the acquisition and enjoyment of material commodities. Saigō's lack of personal greed and acquisitiveness became proverbial; and the contrast between his Spartan approach and the opulent style of many of the Meiji Establishment leaders, who used connexions with business tycoons to indulge their taste for newfangled Western luxuries, was a fur-*9.122*   ther reason for his popularity. Coming from a strict samurai family, Saigō had been brought up with a seignorial disregard for *9.123*   money, and throughout his career, during a period when finance was becoming more and more important in the country's life, he remained magnificently uncontaminated. His material needs were minimal, and even when he had become a high government functionary in Tokyo he managed to live on fifteen yen a month, *9.124*   a modest sum by any standards. For months at a time he did not bother to collect the salary that was due to him as Counsellor of State, and when an anxious official reminded him about this oversight he replied that he still had money from previous payments and needed no more. He loathed the idea of accumulating funds for himself or his family, and whenever he had a surplus he gave it away to friends or to his private Academy in Kago-*9.125*   shima.

While his colleagues in the Meiji government were luxuriating in the perquisites that attend political success, Saigō inhabited a humble dwelling for which he paid three yen a month in rent. On one occasion when he heard that his old schoolmate Ōkubo, who was now serving as Minister of Finance, had or-

dered a splendid jewelled sabre, he managed to obtain the valuable weapon and gave it away to a young student; Saigō's aim, of
course, was to admonish his colleague for unseemly extravagance, but it is doubtful whether Ōkubo appreciated the lesson.

He was especially revolted by the intimate relationship that
government leaders had formed with the rapidly growing Mitsui
and other zaibatsu. When invited to a party given for Prince
Iwakura by the famous Chōshū loyalist, Inoue Kaoru, who was
serving the Meiji government as Vice-Minister of Finance, he
expressed his sentiments with characteristic brusqueness: "Pouring a cup of *sake*, he offered it to his host, saying loudly: 'This is
for you, Inoue, the *bantō* [clerk] of Mitsui.' Inoue seemed not to
be offended, but the remark alarmed others. . . ."

After reaching the summit of power, Saigō still dressed in
simple country clothes, disdaining the frock coats and top hats
that were favoured by many of his colleagues. Even when he
visited the Imperial Palace he wore the typical Satsuma robe of
cotton woven with mottled thread (Satsumagasuri) and encased
his huge feet in a pair of sandals or clogs. Once on leaving the
Palace grounds in the rain he removed his clogs and walked
barefoot; this unprecedented lack of decorum incited the suspicion of a guard, who detained him until Prince Iwakura happened to pass in his carriage and was able to identify the apparent
intruder as Field Marshal and Counsellor of State.

His taste in food was equally plain. Rather than attend elaborate Western-style banquets or elegant entertainments with gei-
sha, he preferred eating in the company of his secretaries and
military retainers, with whom he would share noodles and other
simple fare from a large earthenware pot. Altogether he eschewed fuss and formality, and in his dealings with servants and
other social inferiors he showed none of the haughtiness that was
common among his colleagues. "There was an innocent, easy-
going quality about him," wrote one of his close associates, "that
reminded one of a child." Saigō had pride in abundant measure;
but it was the inner pride of an idealist.

This summary of Saigō's philosophy and style of life will
suggest why, sooner or later, he was bound to fall afoul of the
Meiji oligarchy. Much of his opposition to the new regime was
nebulous and unformulated, being based more on psychological
incompatibility than on objective political issues, but there were
also several specific grievances. The most important concerned

9.126

9.127

9.128

9.129

9.130

its treatment of the warriors. During the post-Restoration years the samurai, Japan's traditional rulers, were systematically stripped of their exclusive rights to office. The stipends on which the rank-and-file samurai had depended were all cancelled by government decrees, and the daimyos received bonds in exchange for the fiefs that they and their ancestors had ruled for centuries. They were not removed from political power, for the new Meiji regime was controlled largely by ex-samurai; but as a class they no longer enjoyed the hereditary right to govern. In 1872 a universal military conscription law deprived the samurai of their monopoly of military function, and a few years later, as if to symbolize all these deprivations, the government issued an edict cancelling their age-old privilege of carrying swords.

These measures dealt a painful blow to the samurai class and resulted in widespread poverty. The conscription law and the creation of a new national army recruited from the general population robbed the samurai of their justification for special status; and the antisword edict seemed a crowning indignity that emasculated the very "spirit of the warrior" *(bushi no tamashii)*—evoking, in a far more virulent form, the type of instinctive suspicion and hostility that efforts at gun control have produced among traditionally minded elements in the United States.

Powerless to stem the wave of the future, the former samurai looked to some powerful figure who might represent their multiple grievances and frustrations, and in many ways Saigō Takamori appeared to answer their needs. Though he had agreed to become a member of the new government, it was clear from his writings and statements that he believed the ideals of the civil war were being vitiated. He was opposed to the excessively rapid changes in Japanese society and was particularly disturbed by the shabby treatment of the warrior class. Suspicious of the new bureaucratic-capitalist structure and of the values it represented, he wanted power to remain in the hands of responsible, patriotic, benevolent warrior-administrators who would rule the country under the Emperor. It was for this purpose and not to preside at the official disbandment of the samurai class that he had joined the central government. Edicts like the interdiction against carrying swords and wearing the traditional topknot seemed like a series of gratuitous provocations; and, though Saigō realized that Japan needed an effective standing army to resist pressure from the West, he could not countenance the social implications of the

9.131

9.132

9.133

9.134

9.135

military reforms. For this reason Saigō, although participating in   *9.136*
the Ōkubo government, continued to exercise a powerful appeal
among disgruntled ex-samurai in Satsuma and elsewhere.   *9.137*

Apart from his objections to the downgrading of the samurai
class, Saigō had grave doubts about the way in which the government was implementing its crucial policies of centralization and
Westernization. Concerning the decision to disestablish the fiefs
and to replace them by prefectures under the administrations of
Governors and other officials directly appointed by the central
government (a policy that was put into effect only one month
after he became Counsellor of State), Saigō's feelings were bound
to be ambiguous. By temperament he always remained the most
provincial of Japan's national leaders. In his younger days his
emotional attachment had, like that of most samurai, been to his
clan and daimyo, rather than to the somewhat abstract entity
known as Japan or to that remote, shadowy figure, the Emperor,
who was its theoretical ruler. During the hectic years that led to   *9.138*
the Restoration many of the strongest anti-Bakufu elements
looked forward to replacing Tokugawa rule with a new form of
feudalism that would preserve local autonomy under a federal
samurai council, which would be directly responsible to the Emperor, and where all the clans would be represented; and Saigō
himself probably envisaged government by some such council of
great lords from the clans (in which Satsuma, of course, would
play a dominant role) rather than a centralized bureaucracy in
Tokyo that would abolish the clans entirely.   *9.139*

In the event, Ōkubo and other members of the new oligarchy
came to the conclusion that antidomanial policy of centralization
must be carried out thoroughly. Realizing that Saigō was the
main focus of the widespread samurai opposition and a natural
rallying point for any possible uprising, Ōkubo was at pains to
convince him that in the national interest it was essential to
abolish the domains; and with characteristic political acumen, he
used Saigō himself to implement the controversial measures.
Since the domain of Satsuma was a hotbed of resistance to the
Meiji policy of centralization, it was logical that Saigō, who retained such strong provincial ties, should be induced to take the
lead in persuading his clansmen to give up the struggle and bear
the unbearable. When he made his triumphal tour of Satsuma in
1872 as a representative of the central government he was therefore trying to reconcile the clan leaders to the loss of their limited

autonomy—an autonomy that he himself had favoured only a few years before. The role was incongruous but the mission successful, and when he returned to Tokyo the main territorial *9.140* centre of opposition had been neutralized.

Saigō's views on Westernization were equally ambiguous, but ultimately contributed to his disaffection with the new regime. During his early years the most urgent question in the country was whether to open Japan to the West and, if so, under what conditions. The failure to solve this problem in any satisfactory fashion was the most immediate reason for the downfall of the Tokugawa regime. As one of the leading members of the anti-Bakufu movement, Saigō started his career as a convinced xenophobe, who rarely missed an opportunity to chide the government for its weak-kneed attitude to "foreign barbarians." Observing the depredations of Western imperialist nations, he impugned their claim to be the champions of civilization:

Civilization is the upholding of justice; it has nothing to do with outward grandeur, palatial magnificence or gorgeous clothing or general ostentation of superficial appearances. . . . Once I got into an argument with a man. He refuted my argument that the Westerners were uncivilized [and] . . . asked me to give him reasons for my belief. I explained to him that truly civilized countries would have led the uncivilized ones to enlightenment by adopting a policy of benevolent and well-meant teaching, but that, far from this being the case, they have been barbarous enough to benefit themselves by conquering weaker countries by force of arms and treating them with a ruthlessness which becomes the more *9.141* intense the greater the ignorance of the conquered.

Ironically enough, it was the punitive bombardment of *9.142* Saigō's home town by the English navy in 1863 that convinced *9.143* him to change his position. For all his idealism and adherence to traditional ways, he was enough of a pragmatist to know that there were times when Japan must use Western methods to combat the West. Thus he grudgingly accepted the idea that, if his country was to survive the foreign onslaughts, it would be obliged to adopt modern industrial technology. The outmoded Bakufu regime, which was obviously unable to deal with the challenge, must be swept away in order that the necessary changes might be implemented under the aegis of samurai from Satsuma and other loyalist clans.

And so it happened. The new imperial government took over the necessary technology with a speed and ruthless efficiency reminiscent of Japan's "miraculous" economic resurgence in the 1950s and 1960s. For Saigō and many fellow samurai, however, the process of Westernization was too rapid and indiscriminate. Though fully recognizing the need for foreign techniques, Saigō remained resolutely Japanese, and in the context of this quickly changing period he came to seem old-fashioned to the point of eccentricity.

Of the dozen leading figures in the Meiji government, Saigō was one of the only two who neither visited the West nor evinced any interest in doing so; indeed, apart from his exile, he never once left the main islands. Until the end of his life, Saigō's cultural orientation was totally Asian. He doggedly resisted Western innovations unless they were essential for the nation's survival. Not only were such innovations connected with the commercial, urban values that he conspued, but they involved an undignified aping of foreigners and, above all, a corruption of the Japanese spirit. His growing distrust of what he regarded as the government's surrender to foreign influences is summarized in his "posthumous words":

As to adopting the system of every other country to improve our own way of life, it is necessary first to base our country on a firm foundation, develop public morals and after that consider the merits of foreign countries. If, on the other hand, we blindly follow the foreign, our national policy will decline and our public morals decay beyond rescue —and in the end we shall be under their control. . . .

To develop human understanding is to open the heart to patriotism, loyalty and filial piety. When the way of serving one's country and working for one's own family is clearly understood, then from this all kinds of enterprise are developed accordingly. For the purpose of developing human intercourse, a telegraph service is established, a railway is laid and a steam engine is constructed, things startling enough to create a sensation. But if the people, without asking themselves why a telegraph service or a railway service is indispensable, instead squander national funds by indulging in luxury, by imitating European styles from building a house to selecting toys without considering their merits and demerits, merely envying the prosperity of foreign countries, then surely will come a decline in national power, a frivolity in public feeling and at last the inevitable bankruptcy of Japan.   *9.144*

His doubts about excessive Westernization were related to his ire at the mercenary politicians who, as he believed, were betraying the cause for which so many brave men had sacrificed themselves. On one occasion he declared with tears in his eyes (the Western platitude according to which the Japanese never show their emotions is particularly untrue in the case of Saigō) that "[the struggle against the Bakufu] seems to have been fought in the selfish interests of government officials, a thing which will undermine our dignity not only in the presence of the people but also of the departed spirits of those who lost their lives in the war."

9.145

With his traditional samurai scorn for finance, Saigō loathed the new emphasis on commerce and other forms of business. Above all he was incensed by the corruption and moral degeneracy, which he regarded as an inevitable result of the close ties between government officials and businessmen, and he attacked the "meeting-place of robbers" (as he dubbed the Meiji regime) with all the moral fury that Ōshio Heihachirō had directed

9.146

against the municipal administration in Osaka forty years earlier. In 1870 a patriotic samurai from Satsuma committed harakiri in front of the National Council Building as a protest against the corruption of the central government, having publicly posted a letter of remonstrance with ten points that included "Evil practices which prevailed in the Tokugawa Government remain unchanged in the new Government, discriminating right from wrong not in accordance with reason and justice but with personal feelings and interests" and "Sensual pleasures are thought

9.147

much of, while a sense of duty is ignored." Saigō, much moved by this "sincere" deed of his fellow clansman, wrote an epitaph which started in typical Confucian style with the words,

Many of the Government officials, addicted to dissipation and debauchery, are living in such extravagance that they fall into error and public

9.148

opinion is in turmoil.

Saigō's suspicion of bureaucrats in the central government —a suspicion that probably had its origins in his youthful resentment against grasping local officials in Satsuma—grew stronger with the years, and when he referred to "that pack of wild beasts

9.149

called human beings," he was thinking primarily of those ambitious civil servants and politicians who (in his view) had unjustly gained control of the Meiji government. In a long letter to some northern clansmen he compared the present government to a wheel that had become stuck with rust. It is not enough to oil the wheel; first it must be hit with an iron hammer to start it moving —and Saigō made it clear that when the time came he would be ready to apply the blow. Certainly his own career was entirely   *9.150* untainted, and in death he became a symbol of that human purity for which people looked in vain among their actual leaders.

Saigō's ideas contain many ambivalences, of which he himself was no doubt unconscious. Though emotionally attached to his clan and to its tradition of autonomy, he was adamant in his insistence that Satsuma must accept the new policy of centralization. Though a firm believer in the old type of military forces that were based on domanial samurai armed with traditional weapons, he resolutely modernized the army in Satsuma and elsewhere so that Japan need not kowtow to the foreigner. Though convinced that agriculture was the only worthy foundation of the national economy, he came to support the official policy of "enriching the country and strengthening the army" *(fukoku kyōhei)*, which depended on rapid industrial development. Above all, this ardent loyalist, who devoted the first part of his career to "restoring" the Emperor, became the outstanding critic of the new imperial government and eventually led the greatest rebellion against it. One of Saigō's most eminent admirers described him as "a stupid hero" *(muchi no eiyū)*, and this comment is no   *9.151* doubt justified if logic, foresight, and sensible planning are the criteria of wisdom. But Saigō, like all Japan's failed heroes, lived in a different emotional climate, where sincerity takes precedence over logical consistency, and where men are guided by intelligence of another kind.   *9.152*

The year 1873 was a second turning point in Saigō's life. While the other leaders of the government were still abroad with the Iwakura Mission, relations with the kingdom of Korea began to deteriorate rapidly. The Koreans issued an edict forbidding trade with Japan, and compounded the insult by refusing to accept the new forms of address contained in official Japanese documents. Saigō and certain other members of the caretaker   *9.153* government chose to regard this as an intolerable provocation that demanded forceful action. The militants favoured immediate invasion of the peninsula, but Saigō insisted that first a high-

ranking envoy be sent from Japan to bring the recalcitrant Koreans to heel, and that only if this miscarried should there be an
invasion. In fact, he was well aware that the diplomatic approach
would fail and that an invasion was therefore inevitable. The
army high command was opposed to attacking Korea for the
present; but this did not deter Saigō since, according to his plan,
the invading force would comprise the Imperial Guards and
battalions of loyal samurai from Satsuma. Nor did the choice of
an envoy present any difficulty, for this was the sacrificial role
that he had ascribed to himself. Not only would he cross the
Japan Sea to remonstrate with the Korean government but he
was determined to undertake this dangerous mission without a
9.154   single soldier to escort him.

Historians have given many reasons to explain why Saigō
should have favoured a tough policy towards Korea. It is frequently suggested that he regarded an invasion of Korea as a last
9.155   resource for the dispossessed and frustrated military class. Fighting on the continent would turn the energies of the unemployed
samurai in Satsuma and other domains away from intractable
domestic issues and provide them with honourable employment
and a new *raison d'être*. In addition a foreign war would help
unify the country, stop the moral decline as represented by rampant materialism and loss of traditional values, and lead to the
fundamental reforms that the present government was unable or
9.156   unwilling to put into effect.

Saigō has also been represented as an ultra-patriot who, cha-
grined by the failure of the Iwakura Mission to revise the unequal
treaties with the Western powers, was determined to assert Ja-
9.157   pan's national pride by a glorious victory. His bellicose attitude
in 1873 was based (according to this argument) on his belief that
the time had come for the military class to show its mettle and
to chastise the insolent peninsulars by direct action. In addition
an expansionist Japanese policy would help curb the steady en-
9.158   croachment of the Western powers on the Asian continent. In
fact, though many of Saigō's later admirers were out-and-out
jingoists, there is not the slightest evidence in his writings or
statements that he himself had any such inclination. On at least
two earlier occasions he had resolutely opposed plans to invade
Korea; and, if he now favoured a strong policy, it was not from
any chauvinist tendencies but from concern with the deteriorat-
ing domestic situation. In addition—and this point has been gen-

erally overlooked—there appears to have been a strong psychological motive: his wish to compass in Korea the death he had missed in the waters of Kagoshima Bay fifteen years earlier.

Saigō's writings make it clear that, rightly or wrongly, he was convinced the envoy to Korea would be killed. Thus in July 1873 he ended a letter to one of his influential colleagues whom he had asked to intercede on behalf of his proposed mission:

> If it is decided to send an envoy officially, I feel sure that he will be murdered. I therefore beseech you to send me. I cannot claim to make as splendid an envoy as [the Prime Minister], but if it is a question of dying, that, I assure you, I am prepared to do.   9.159

Quite apart from any practical value the proposed mission may have had, it is clear that Saigō aspired to a martyr's death. As he wrote in one of his early poems,

> I am a boat cast on the rough water [*suteobune*]
> For my country's sake.
> If the winds blow, let them blow!
> If the waves rise, let them rise!   9.160

Once again Saigō's attempt was foiled. The Korean issue threatened a major governmental crisis, and the members of the Iwakura Mission were urgently summoned back from Europe.   9.161 They turned out to be unanimous in rejecting Saigō's policy, the most vehement opposition coming from his old friend Ōkubo. He   9.162 and his colleagues who had recently observed the technological strength of the Western powers at first hand were now thoroughly convinced that Japan must press ahead with the policy of "enriching the country and strengthening the army" before she could possibly risk a foreign war. It was not that the Meiji leaders opposed aggression in principle—twenty years later, when Japan was properly armed, they and their successors in the oligarchy were only too ready to strike out—but in 1873 they knew that their country was not yet equipped for a major military operation of this kind. With characteristic sagacity Ōkubo argued that an invasion would be premature, since even a successful occupation of the peninsula would not make up for the vast expense of the venture or for the risks that Japan would incur vis-à-vis Russia and the other great powers. Prince Iwakura   9.163

summed up the opposition views in a judicious letter to the
Emperor which stressed that the time was not ripe for an invasion since the army was unprepared and the most urgent need
was to consolidate the domestic reforms.

These cool-headed arguments made no impression upon
Saigō, whose determination to go to Korea and "meet his death-
9.164 situation" *(shisho wo uru)* had now become obsessive. In August,
a few weeks before Prince Iwakura's return from Russia,
Saigō's efforts succeeded: an Assembly of Counsellors decided
that he should shortly proceed to Korea with the title of Ambassador. On hearing the news he was transported with joy and
wrote to a colleague that the decision had instantly cured him of
9.165 the painful illness from which he had been suffering.

Though the plan to send Saigō to Korea had been approved
by the young Emperor, the government made no official announcement until Prince Iwakura's return. Meanwhile Ōkubo
and the other members of the anti-Saigō faction, who were exert-
ing all their political expertise to reverse the decisions of the
caretaker government, succeeded in delaying the mission. The
long-smouldering antagonism between Saigō and Ōkubo had
now burst into flames, and years of accumulated resentment
became focused on the Korean issue. Ōkubo openly berated his
former friend for having decided a major matter of foreign policy
during the absence of the Iwakura Mission; Saigō defended himself by replying that certain urgent issues brooked no delay; and
in his fury he went so far as to call Ōkubo a coward, the supreme
9.166 insult in the samurai vocabulary. After the return of Prince
Iwakura the balance of power swung decisively in favour of
Ōkubo. Realizing that he was being outmanoeuvred, Saigō sent
the Prime Minister a frantic letter, which ended with the following ultimatum:

As for my dispatch as an envoy, which was already approved by you, if
such treachery should ensue as to cause the instructions already issued
to be altered, it would be tantamount to making light of an Imperial
Command. Though I am given to understand that you are sure to remain
firm in your attitude concerning the matter, I am obliged to mention my
fear in order to call your attention to my humble request, as I hear such
a rumour is current in some quarters. It is with great awe that I should
say such rude things beforehand, but if the decision should be vetoed,
I should profoundly regret it and should have no alternative but to

apologize to the country for my failure to do my duty, at the cost of my life. Such being the case, I beg you to understand me.   *9.167*

At this crucial moment the Prime Minister resigned on the grounds of ill health and was succeeded by Prince Iwakura, a resolute opponent of Saigō's policy. Whether or not this was (as some of Saigō's devotees suggest) part of a master plan by Ōkubo, it promptly clinched the matter: on 14th October the decision to despatch an envoy to Korea was rescinded.

Ōkubo had succeeded to perfection and Saigō had suffered an unmitigated political defeat. Ten days later he gave up all his official posts, except that of army general, and returned to Kagoshima in dudgeon, informing the Emperor that he would never resume public service. As a face-saver the government "allowed"   *9.168* Saigō to resign on the grounds of ill health.

Saigō's impetuous departure from Tokyo not only marked the end of his career in the government but signified a final break with the Meiji oligarchs, whom he now regarded as hopelessly corrupt and misguided and with whom he could no longer possibly cooperate in good conscience. Following Saigō's resignation all his main supporters left the government. The outcome of the Korean crisis was therefore a total victory for the Ōkubo faction and for the principle of central bureaucratic power that it represented. In a manner typical for the Japanese failed hero, Saigō's long struggle in the corridors of power had produced the opposite effect of what he had intended. Such an outcome was no   *9.169* doubt inevitable considering Saigō's personality and ideas. In the political atmosphere of the 1870s this hero of the Restoration had become an anachronistic misfit, and if the Korean crisis had not arisen some other issue would soon have impelled him to break with the regime in Tokyo.

In psychological terms Saigō's return to a simple, bucolic existence in Satsuma marked one of his periodic retreats from the turmoil of public life and from the harsh modern world of ambitious men, political chicanery, and noisome city streets. Back in his birthplace of Kagoshima, he shed all the trappings of worldly success and resumed the existence of a gentleman farmer, working in the fields and tramping through the countryside. Saigō's poems written at this time express his joy at returning to country life. The following was composed shortly after his retirement:

. . . Since ancient times misfortune has been the usual price of
      worldly fame.
   Far better then to trudge home through the woods, carrying a
9.170   spade upon my shoulder.

A few months later and in a similar vein he wrote:

   I have shaken off the dust of the world,
   I have taken leave of rank and fame.
   Now I can give myself wholeheartedly to joy in Nature,
9.171   The great creator [of all things].

For all his apparent conviviality there was a solitary streak in
Saigō's nature, and his recent embroilment with the politicians
of Tokyo aggravated this to the point of misanthropy. After the
babble of the city he relished nature's silence:

   Here deep in the hills near the ancient pond it is quieter than in
      the middle of the night.
9.172   Instead of listening to people's voices, I gaze towards the sky.

   He spent more and more time with his dogs, happily sharing
9.173 his loneliness with these guileless, affectionate creatures. In a
country where politicians were (and are) none too squeamish
about receiving expensive presents Saigō had made a point of
refusing all *douceurs* except dogs. In his house he kept a large box
with pictures and lithographs of these animals whom he chose as
his lifelong companions. There is no poem from this period that
mentions his family, but there are many references to his canine
friends. Here is one of his famous Chinese verses:

   Through these steep hills that soar towards the clouds
   I wander with my dogs,
   Whose lusty barking echoes now from peak to peak.
   Look, I pray you, at the craggy hearts of men,
9.174   Harder to follow than these crooked mountain paths!

One of Saigō's companions describes a day spent walking with
him and his dogs across the fields and hills near Kagoshima. In
the evening they stop at a farmer's cottage; after his bath Saigō
settles down comfortably and remarks that his present feeling of
9.175 serenity must be close to that of a sage *(seijin)*.

Saigō's new life in Kagoshima was not devoted exclusively to rustic pleasures. He also organized a number of independent private schools, where he trained Satsuma boys in the military arts, agriculture, and moral principles. For this purpose he used the government stipends that he and his associates had accumulated and also the annuity he still received for past services. The schools varied in size and nature, with the total number of pupils eventually reaching several thousand. Some concentrated on artillery and military techniques; others were more in the nature of rural communes whose members (often assisted by Saigō himself) did farm work during the day and spent their evenings reading or listening to lectures.

At one point the Ōkubo regime, possibly hoping to keep their unpredictable ex-colleague under closer watch, invited him back to Tokyo and suggested that he might make an official visit to Europe. Saigō, still thoroughly disgusted with the ruling oligarchy, declined the offer, preferring to continue a simple life in Satsuma and to prepare his young men for future developments. When a special envoy from Prince Sanjō arrived in Kagoshima to request that Saigō return and work with the central government, he is said to have sent the brusque message, "You are really a fool, aren't you, Prince Sanjō?" The envoy remonstrated with Saigō, pointing out that he could not possibly deliver such a disrespectful answer to his master, but Saigō insisted that it was his function to transmit the message as given.

During the years of Saigō's retirement in Satsuma there was a series of violent outbreaks in different parts of the country, many of them organized by groups of ex-samurai who had been driven to fury by governmental measures such as the antisword edict and the commutation of stipends. The first major rising, which took place in 1874 in the northern Kyushu province of Saga, was directed specifically against the government's "weak" policy towards Korea, the leader being Etō Shimpei, a fiery young official who had resigned at the same time as Saigō. A force of some two thousand samurai rebels succeeded in capturing the former domanial capital, but were rapidly suppressed by the government's firm military action. Etō himself fled to Kagoshima, hoping that Saigō would help him resume the revolt. Though their views were similar in many ways, Saigō tried to dissuade Etō from continuing. Shortly afterwards the Saga leader was captured by government forces and, at the special insistence of Ōkubo, was condemned to the ignominious punishment of being decapitated and having his head publicly exposed on a

9.176   pillory as a deterrent to other potential rebels.

This gruesome warning had little effect. A couple of years later one of the most dramatic rebellions occurred in the castle town of Kumamoto in central Kyushu, where about two hundred former samurai, enraged by the policy of abolishing Japanese customs and encouraging foreign ideas at the expense of the native Shinto religion, formed a League of the Divine Wind and attacked the imperial garrison, killing the commander and many of his men. They were quickly crushed by an imperial force of some two thousand, and almost every survivor committed

9.177   harakiri rather than risk the indignity of capture. In conjunction with the uprising by the League of the Divine Wind a similar revolt took place in the old Chōshū castle town of Hagi in the western part of the main island. This effort had even less success: the leader (also a former high official) was seized and executed, and most of his main followers committed suicide.

This series of samurai uprisings, combined with numerous

9.178   peasant revolts, alarmed the central government and made them keep a close watch on Kagoshima, which they feared might become the centre of a major rebellion. They had good reason for suspicion. At the time of the uprising in Hagi some of Saigō's militant supporters tried to persuade him that this was the ideal time to strike against the government. Indignantly he turned

9.179   down the suggestion as being foolish and irresponsible, but the atmosphere in Kagoshima was obviously becoming explosive.

At this stage the Tokyo government, on the urging of Ōkubo and General Yamagata, sent police spies to Kagoshima to observe whether Saigō's followers were in fact fomenting an armed uprising. Members of the Academy soon discovered the identity of the agents and managed to elicit the sensational information

9.180   (which may well have been correct) that the central authorities intended not only to dissolve the Academy but to assassinate Saigō and his main advisers. Appalled by this discovery, some of the pupils started keeping watch over their master. For a time Saigō was unaware of this, but before long he realized that he was being guarded. The following incident has a prophetic ring:

... One day ... the pupils [who were keeping watch over their master] went to Saigō's lodging, where one of them, playing with a double-barrelled gun, carelessly pulled the trigger, thinking it unloaded, when, all of a sudden, the gun went off and a shot which had remained in the barrel pierced the ceiling. The frightened pupil told his master that he wanted to atone for his fault by committing harakiri. Saigō roared with laughter saying that he would find cutting his belly a most painful process.   *9.181*

Later Saigō informed his pupils, who had decided to execute the government spies, that he did not mind in the slightest if he himself was assassinated and that it was "meaningless to kill the policemen from Tokyo," since the real culprits were the leaders of the central government. As tension mounted among Saigō's   *9.182* followers, the government decided (in January 1877) to forestall trouble by chartering a ship of the Mitsubishi Company to transport arms and ammunitions from Kagoshima under cover of darkness. This crucial decision, far from solving any difficulties, triggered the disaster. While Saigō was away on a hunting expedition with his dogs, the pupils in his Academy got wind of the plan. The news confirmed their worst fears about the government's intentions, and in a wild fury a group of young hotheads attacked imperial arsenals in the suburbs of Kagoshima and removed the gunpowder and other supplies. This was an open act of rebellion, and now there could be no turning back.

When Saigō was told what had happened, he reacted with the laconic exclamation, *Shimatta*, which means something like "That does it!" or "Damnation!" He instantly returned to Kago-shima for a meeting with representatives from the Academy. After listening to their report in silence, he suddenly exploded with a roar of fury. Fifty years later Saigō's son, who was seven-teen years old at the time, recalled that he had never in his life heard anyone shout so loudly as his father did on that day when he berated the students for their irresponsibility and bellowed at them, "What a monstrous thing you have done!" Once his first   *9.183* anger had abated, however, he reconciled himself to the inevitable and declared to his lieutenants that they should proceed with the necessary military operations, since he was now prepared to offer his life for them. It is as if he had realized that once again   *9.184* he was being given the opportunity to compass a noble death.

Saigō was now the leader of a major rebellion whose out-

break he had profoundly influenced though never actually con-
doned. He knew that the final prospects were hopeless; but once
the die was cast he threw himself into the enterprise with characteristic verve, no doubt welcoming the opportunity for an open
military confrontation with Ōkubo, Iwakura, and the other
9.185 politicians who had thwarted him for so long. At no time did he
regard himself as a rebel against Emperor Meiji; rather, like the
ultra-rightist rebels in the 1930s, he was a loyal subject who was
trying to save his master from "evil counsellors." In a letter to
Prince Arisugawa he pointed out that His Majesty must be protected from the ruling politicians, whom he described as the
9.186 "great criminals of the universe."

Though relieved that things had finally come to a head,
9.187 Ōkubo and his government knew that they now faced their most
dangerous challenge since the Meiji Restoration. They reacted by
stripping their former colleague of all his military ranks and
other remaining honours, and declaring him to be an enemy of
the Court. Emperor Meiji, who was on a visit to Kyoto when the
fateful news came, issued a rescript ordering that the rebellion
be crushed promptly. Prince Arisugawa and General Yamagata
were appointed to lead the imperial forces, and they immediately
proceeded to headquarters in northern Kyushu. There is a typical irony in the fact that the army which now had the duty to
crush Saigō, the former loyalist hero, should be commanded by
a Prince who only ten years earlier had fought by his side in the
campaign against the Tokugawa Bakufu.

The government, which had obviously been prepared for
the military crisis, promptly mobilized an army of some forty
thousand men, which was later increased to sixty thousand. This
was backed by the national police force, the Imperial Guards
(formerly under the direct command of Saigō himself), and a
naval force consisting of eleven warships. About eighty percent
of the army consisted of peasant conscripts, who had been organized by General Yamagata after the passing of the national
conscription law five years earlier. Saigō and his generals made
the great mistake of underestimating these peasant conscripts,
whom they regarded as incapable of standing up in battle against
professional samurai with centuries of military tradition. The
rebel army, despite its initially high morale and the advantage of
fighting near home territory, was always far inferior in numbers
and at its very height did not exceed twenty-five thousand men;

in addition it was handicapped by an immense discrepancy in ammunitions, money, and supplies. Though at first the outcome may have seemed in doubt, the sheer physical power of the imperial forces was bound to tell.

Saigō started his operations with a major strategic blunder. This was the decision to attack the town of Kumamoto, a key point in central Kyushu, and to capture the castle before the main government forces had time to arrive from the main island. On 17th February he and his men marched out of Kagoshima in a heavy snowstorm. In Japan snow is symbolically associated with pure, heroic enterprises (the "forty-seven *rōnin*" carried out their climactic vendetta in a snowstorm, and in more recent times the mutiny of the young officers in February 1936 was heralded by a heavy fall of snow), and the fact that the Satsuma army set forth under a snowy sky must have seemed a sort of heavenly confirmation that their cause was just. The banner carried by the pupils from his Academy was inscribed with the proud device, "Respect Virtue! Reform the Government!" As Saigō advanced the hundred miles north to Kumamoto, disaffected samurai from various parts of Kyushu flocked to his side, and he was also joined by supporters from many distant regions in Japan.   9.188

Kumamoto Castle, the object of their initial assault, had been built in the early part of the seventeenth century and ranked as one of the three mightiest fortresses in Japan. It was a sturdy edifice, solemnly dominating the town and its environs. The design of the castle and the steep slope on which it stood made it ideal for repelling invaders. When first invested by Saigō's army, it was guarded by some four thousand men of the local garrison, who managed to hold out against wave after wave of frantic attack. "Arrow letters," of the type used two and a half centuries earlier at the time of the Shimabara Rebellion, were fired into the castle urging the defenders to surrender, since they were overwhelmingly outnumbered, but the imperial troops were determined to resist.

Finally the main government forces reached Kumamoto. This was the turning point. The siege of the castle was raised, and after twenty days of bitter fighting, during which Saigō lost many of his best officers, the Satsuma army was obliged to withdraw from Kumamoto Castle and retreat to the south. The costly, drawn-out siege had been disastrous for the rebels and deprived Saigō of the remotest possibility of success.   9.189

9.190

By concentrating all his strength on the assault against Kumamoto, Saigō had left his home base of Kagoshima undefended. This was another serious miscalculation, for in due course the town was attacked by imperial troops and warships, and fell into the government's hands. The Satsuma forces continued to fight fiercely after their withdrawal from Kumamoto, moving south to Kobayashi and up the eastern coast of Kyushu, and there was a series of sanguinary engagements, but the government's overwhelming superiority in manpower, weapons, and transport was now obvious. Saigō's remaining troops were soon surrounded at Nabeoka. With a small contingent of followers he managed to break through the encircling lines, inflicting heavy losses on the enemy. On 1st September he and his men forced their way back into the town of Kagoshima, where they were welcomed by a scared and somewhat bewildered population.

9.191

Saigō's army had now dwindled to a pathetic band of a few hundred men, of whom only about a third were properly armed. As in most civil wars, the casualties had been terrible on both sides. In his seven-month struggle against the Imperial Army, Saigō had lost approximately half his men, including almost every pupil from his Academy. The government's rate of casualties was about twenty-five percent, including sixty-three hundred killed and ninety-five hundred wounded. Altogether some thirty thousand men had fallen as a result of the rebellion.

Though Saigō and the remnants of his force had finally succeeded in returning to Kagoshima, their material situation could hardly have been worse. They were devoid of munitions and supplies, and thirty thousand government troops surrounded the town. Ineluctably the trap began to close. After the siege had continued for a couple of weeks, Saigō moved his headquarters to a little cave behind Shiroyama, a hill in the north of the town. From here he and his men could enjoy the resplendent view of Kagoshima Bay and its famous volcanic island of Sakurajima. With the imperial forces poised for the coup de grace, Saigō and his closest followers spent their last five days in the cave preparing for their end. After all the exhaustion and disappointments of the previous months, this was a serene period for Saigō Takamori. He appears to have been in high spirits, content no doubt in the knowledge that the death which had eluded him so often was now imminent; and he spent much of

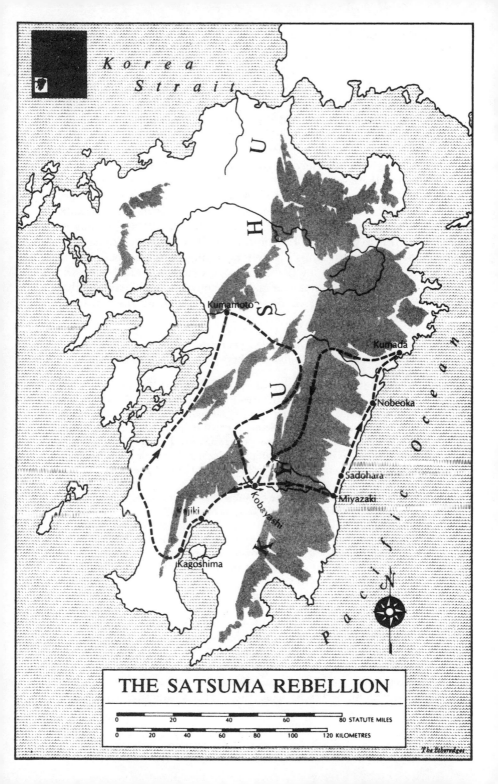

THE SATSUMA REBELLION

his time playing *go*, exchanging poems, and joking with his companions.

On the last day, 23rd September, a messenger arrived in the cave with a missive from Yamagata, the commanding general of the imperial forces and Saigō's former colleague in Tokyo. This moving and intensely Japanese document used to be quoted in school textbooks, both for its fine prose style and as an example of "sincerity." The letter starts by addressing the rebel leader with the term *kun*, a form used only between close friends: "Yamagata Aritomo, your intimate friend, has the honour of writing to you, Saigō Takamori Kun." The burden of Yamagata's message was to stress his understanding of Saigō's position, to recall the futility of the drawn-out struggle, and (though the shameful word "surrender" is never actually used) to suggest that he prevent further needless carnage by ending his resistance forthwith:

9.192

> . . . How worthy of compassion your position is! I grieve over your misfortune all the more intensely because I have a sympathetic understanding of you. . . .
> Several months have already passed since hostilities began. There have been many hundred casualties every day. Kinsmen are killing one another. Friends are fighting against one another. Never has there been fought a more bloody internecine war that is against all humanity. And no soldier on either side has any grudge against the other. His Majesty's soldiers say that they are fighting in order to fulfill their military duties, while your Satsuma men are, in their own words, fighting for the sake of Saigō. . . .
> But it is evident that the Satsuma men cannot hope to accomplish their purpose, for almost all the bravest of your officers have been killed or wounded. . . . I earnestly entreat you to make the best of the sad situation yourself as early as you can, so as, on the one hand, to prove that the present disturbance is not of your original intention and, on the other, to see to it that you may put an end to the casualties on both sides immediately. If you can successfully work out remedial measures, hostilities will soon come to an end.

The letter closes with a typically Japanese appeal for reciprocal understanding: "I shall be very happy if you would enter a little into my feelings. I have written this, repressing my tears, though writing cannot express all that is in my mind." It is doubtful whether General Yamagata, knowing his old colleague as he did, expected his letter to have the slightest practical effect. The drama had to be played to its emotional conclusion. Saigō, having read the long document in silence, informed the messenger that he would send no reply.

There was a bright moon on the night of the twenty-third. Saigō's companions took advantage of its light to make music on the Satsuma lute, perform the *kenbu* (an ancient sword dance), and compose some final poetry. Typical of their verses, which have all, of course, been carefully preserved, are the two following:

> If I were a drop of dew, I could take shelter on a leaftip,
> But, being a man, I have no place in this whole world [*waga mi no okidokoro nashi*].

And, in a more patriotic vein:

> Having fought in the Emperor's cause,
> [I know my end is near.]
> What joy to die like the tinted leaves that fall in Tatsuta
> Before they have been spoiled by autumn rains!   *9.193*

Finally Saigō exchanged farewell cups of *sake* with his chief officers and other followers.

The general attack by government forces started at four o'clock on the morning of the twenty-fourth. Under heavy fire from all sides, Saigō and his companions began descending Shiroyama. Before long Saigō was hit in the groin by a stray bullet and could walk no further. Beppu Shinsuke, one of his *9.194* most devoted retainers, had the honour of lifting his master's weighty bulk onto his shoulders and carrying him down the hill. When they stopped for a rest outside the gate of a Shimazu mansion, Saigō uttered his last words, "My dear Shinsuke, I think this place will do." He then bowed in the direction of the *9.195* Imperial Palace and cut open his stomach, whereupon Beppu, who was standing behind him, drew out his sword and slashed off his head with one clean stroke. The rest of the little band continued down the path. Most of them were killed, but a few managed to reach the bottom. Among them was Beppu, who, having cried out in a loud voice that their master was dead and that the time had now come for those who wished to die with him, rushed towards the enemy's line and was mown down by rifle fire.

The one-sided engagement was over by nine o'clock in the morning. Government soldiers soon discovered Saigō's body, but his head was nowhere to be found. Since the identification of the enemy general's head had a traditional importance in Japanese *9.196* battles, there was a careful search and eventually it was dug up in the place where Beppu had ordered that it be buried after the decapitation. The remains of the rebel leader were treated with unusual deference. One of the government generals roared out an order to his troops that no disrespect must be shown to *9.197* Saigō's body, and this was scrupulously obeyed. The large head was washed clean in pure water from a spring and brought to the commander, General Yamagata, for his inspection. Holding the enemy's head in his hands and bowing respectfully, Yamagata *9.198* murmured, "Ah what a gentle look you have upon your face!" It is said that the soldiers who had been posted in the place from where the fatal shot was fired went into mourning and that they all wept profusely when the time came for Saigō's burial.

The famous Saigō Cemetery (Nanshū Bochi) in Kagoshima, one of the most poignant necropoles in the world, was completed long before the official rehabilitation of the rebel leader. Seven hundred and forty-nine tombstones of many sizes and shapes are clustered about the plain, oblong monument erected in Saigō's honour shortly after his death. The remains of two thousand and twenty-three of his followers are buried with him. Among the names commemorated on the stones, the visitor can read those of Beppu Shinsuke and Saigō's brother, Kōhei; of men who had journeyed all the way from distant provinces in the northeast to join his campaign; and of his two youngest adherents, both thirteen years old when they were killed in the rebellion.

The government had won a total victory: almost every single rebel was killed or committed suicide, and after the fighting many others were imprisoned and executed. A leading article published in a Japanese newspaper one week after the fall of Shiroyama starts with the following paean:

Saigō Takamori is dead, and the war in the southwest is ended. The time for the return of the soldiers with songs of triumph has come. The clouds of trouble that have so long hung over the west have all been dispelled by the wise and energetic measures of the government and the *9.199* courage and zeal of the army.

Later the article stresses the futility of the entire rebellion:
". . . the only consequence . . . has been a vast destruction of life
and property and large expenditures of money on both sides.
Excepting these sad ends, nothing has been attained."

In fact Saigō's effort had many significant consequences—all
of them diametrically opposed to what he had intended. For one
thing it made rebellion against the ruling oligarchy virtually
impossible. In future no group opposing the Meiji government
could resort to arms in the name of the Emperor or of traditional
values. "If, hereafter, new demonstrations against the supreme
authority are attempted," writes a contemporary Japanese observer, "they must be started upon other grounds, for this old
spirit of the rule of the sword over constitutions and laws must
now be regarded as defunct." Subsequent confrontation took   9.200
the form of individual action, mainly the assassination of "iniqui-
tous politicians," or of efforts to organize opposition political
parties on a Western model, which Saigō would certainly have   9.201
disliked.

The Satsuma *coup* was, in fact, the last organized attempt
until the 1930s to oppose the government by force. One reason
was that the struggle of 1877 had demonstrated the strength of a
conscript army. In battle after battle the new imperial force,
manned largely by peasants, had defeated an elite army of gentle-
man-warriors; and their victory symbolized the end of the long
age of the samurai. Saigō's rebellion was drowned in the blood
of his samurai followers, and he himself has been described as the
last true samurai in Japanese history. There is a further symbol-   9.202
ism in the fact that Satsuma, the final bastion of domanial resistance to the new national order, should have been decisively
crushed by a central army of peasant recruits.

The Satsuma Rebellion destroyed the class of ex-samurai as
a potential source of organized resistance, and thereafter the
Meiji oligarchy was free to pursue its policy of "enriching the
country and strengthening the army" without any threat of internal resistance from conservative diehards. After Saigō's defeat   9.203
the oligarchy in Tokyo, working in close concert with the zaibatsu and other big-business interests, could proceed apace with
heavy industrialization and other Westernizing efforts that men
like Saigō had regarded with misgivings. The uprising in Satsuma, like the Shimabara Rebellion two and a half centuries

earlier, had played perfectly into the government's hands by making it possible to identify, concentrate, and finally crush a major source of opposition.

Of all the politicians in Tokyo to welcome the defeat of Saigō's cause, none can have been more jubilant than Count Ōkubo Toshimichi, now the effective head of government. Ōkubo has figured frequently in the course of this chapter, first as a childhood companion and schoolmate of Saigō's, later as a fellow official in the domanial government of Satsuma and as a staunch supporter who actually threatened to commit harakiri unless his friend was freed from exile; then came the confrontation between the two men, and they ended their careers as implacable enemies. Their complex relationship and respective reputations throw considerable light on what makes a hero in Japan. Ōkubo was born three years after Saigō into a similar lower-samurai family in a nearby part of Kagoshima. Though closely linked throughout their youth (both of them, for instance, belonged to the group of young samurai who met to study the philosophy of Wang Yang-ming) and though their careers ran parallel in many ways, Ōkubo usually stayed on the winning side; thus he managed to avoid the exile and other hardships that Saigō underwent when he fell afoul of the new daimyo.

The two boyhood friends had been closely bound by their common determination to overthrow the Tokugawa Bakufu; but the initial success of the Meiji Restoration soon altered their relationship. The intrinsic differences in their characters and points of view were bound to lead to disagreement and, given Saigō's uncompromising nature, to a final break. Ōkubo looked realistically to the future in a way that his former ally could only regard as unworthy and insincere.

9.204

When the emotional logic that determined Saigō's career eventually brought him to lead the greatest of all uprisings against the Meiji regime, it was his old colleague Ōkubo, who, from special headquarters in Kyoto, directed the war against the rebel army. In this enterprise he demonstrated his customary skill and efficiency, and as usual he was successful.

Count Ōkubo's career came to a sudden end less than six months after the suicide of Saigō. Travelling in his carriage one spring morning in 1878 he was attacked and murdered by a small

group of fanatic ex-samurai, who, among other things, were determined to avenge Saigō's death. Owing to this unexpected set-   *9.205*
back, Ōkubo was unable to complete the great tasks that he had
set himself. Yet in almost every practical sense his career was a
triumph. He had been the driving force in the policy of abolishing the domains and other feudal institutions and of consolidat-
ing an efficient central government under a modern bureaucracy.
He had striven for technological modernization so that Japan
might rapidly transform herself from a backward conglomera-
tion of agricultural fiefs into an industrial nation capable of confronting the great powers on their own tough terms. He had
pursued a rigid policy of law and order to combat the anarchic
trends of the Restoration period; in 1875 he promulgated a crucial
censorship law, and he was draconian in suppressing opposition
to the Meiji regime. That these general policies were pursued by
his survivors and that Japan's fantastic accomplishments culminated in the victory over Russia in 1905 can be regarded as
posthumous testimony to his brilliance and foresight.

Yet for all his far-reaching attainments in helping Japan to
modernize and survive as a nation, Ōkubo never achieved real
popularity. He inspired awe but not affection. One important
reason was his personality and style. Attired in fashionable Western clothes, with carefully groomed hair and neat sidewhiskers,
adorned with medals, cordons, sashes, and other impressive in-
signia of worldly success, he presented a formal, cosmopolitan,   *9.206*
somewhat chilling image to his fellow Japanese and entirely
lacked the ebullience and rustic simplicity that made Saigō so
attractive. We can hardly imagine him visiting the Imperial Pal-   *9.207*
ace in wooden clogs, still less leaving barefoot in the rain.

More important disqualifications for heroic stature were his
pragmatism and his judicious accomplishment of political goals.
At school he was articulate and skilled in argument, in contrast
to the slow, silent Saigō. In later years he developed into a   *9.208*
shrewd, pragmatic politician, more concerned with practical results than with means, and always ready to compromise in order
to achieve his ambitions. As Ōkubo advanced from strength to
strength, he became the personification of Meiji bureaucratic
virtues, and represented the very antithesis of Saigō's wild, impractical "sincerity." Though the careers of both men were cut
short by violent deaths, Ōkubo's role in the legend is inevitably

that of the foil, whose practical success serves to enhance the beauty of the hero's debacle.

There are times in the history of many countries when growing internal discord and fear of dangers from the outside create a special need for some unifying symbol in the form of a national hero who will give the people a sense of pride and cohesion and help them confront their common difficulties. Such a need became paramount in Japan during the early 1890s, a time of acute domestic and international tension, and it was recognized by leaders of the government and by others who had the power to influence public opinion. As one newspaper writer in 1891 expressed it rather bluntly, "We are all becoming fed up with 'clever people.' What we need now is some brave, vigorous figure. . . ." Since the epic events leading to the overthrow of the Tokugawa shogunate and the "restoration" of the Emperor were still fresh in the national memory, and since the present imperial government in Tokyo was a historical consequence of these events, it was logical that the figure to emerge as a supreme symbol of national self-esteem and unity should be one of the Restoration heroes who had fought to make the new order possible.

9.209

The need to establish one particular historical figure as a unifying symbol leads to the creation of a body of legend surrounding that figure and to a sloughing away of facts that seem inappropriate, so that the fallible human being who actually lived in this world may become a fit object of unquestioning respect or even of worship. This process is similiar in every part of the world and in every period, applying equally to Mohammed in seventh-century Arabia, to El Cid in eleventh-century Spain, to Jeanne d'Arc in fifteenth-century France, and to Saigō Takamori in nineteenth-century Japan. In the course of time the historical personage is moulded to fit the requirements of the legend; and the resultant factual distortions are all the more effective in that they are usually performed unconsciously in response to a special national ethos.

Saigō the Great became an object of popular veneration less than fifteen years after his death, but the authorities were faced with the awkward fact that he was still officially a traitor. This necessitated his formal rehabilitation, which as we have seen took place in 1891 when he was posthumously pardoned by Emperor

Meiji and appointed to the Third Court Rank, a position in the hierarchy that was normally reserved for high nobles. Legendary accretions about Saigō developed apace during the half century after his suicide, and in my account of his life I have frequently had to make the qualification that what is widely believed about the hero may result from the distorting process of legend-making.

9.210

Since the hero is created in the image of a people's ideals, he tends to be all things to all men. This is particularly striking in the case of Saigō, who immediately became an ideal for Japanese belonging to both extremes of the political spectrum, as well as for the moderates in between. Created in response to deep popular needs, the legendary hero survives long after his death; in fact, his full heroic existence does not begin until his historical career has terminated. As if to dramatize this need to keep the hero alive after the physical man is dead, people frequently come to believe, against all concrete evidence to the contrary, that he is not dead but has temporarily departed and will return in due course to save his own people or all mankind. Thus we have the fantastic survival legend according to which Saigō would reappear in Japan in 1891 on a Russian warship in order to rescue his country from foreign danger. It has the same psychological basis as the idea in the later Middle Ages that Charlemagne would return from the dead to participate in the Crusades and also the central Christian belief in the second coming of Him who would "stand at the latter day upon the earth."

While the positive aspects of the hero's life and character come to be emphasized (or even created out of whole cloth), less attractive features are passed over in silence and remain forgotten until they are eventually exhumed by debunking historians of later generations. Thus in the legend of Martin Luther, nothing is said about his vicious opposition to the Peasants' Revolt that he himself had so greatly influenced; and in the case of Saigō Takamori, we hear about his pleas for the wretched workers in the sugar plantations, but not about his failure to help them when he actually had the power to do so. One result of legend-making, with its complicated process of accretions and excisions, is to produce a psychologically incomplete and unbelievable personality. Thus the "darker side" in Saigō's nature, which involved feelings of guilt, a need for self-exile, much pent-up rage, and an inclination to direct this rage, not only against "corrupt" enemies but against himself by willing his own destruction, has been overlooked in legend and history alike. Yet the evidence is cogent.

Granted that a unifying national hero was required at a particular point in Japanese history, and that this hero soon became the stuff of legend, the central question remains: Why, among all the possible great men of the Restoration years, should a defeated rebel most appropriately have filled the need, and how could a man like Saigō Takamori, who came to represent premodern, "feudal" values and who was admired by old-fashioned Japanists and chauvinists, have remained popular despite the total change in the *Zeitgeist* during the past decades? The reasons, of course are not primarily his practical talents. Saigō had none of the political and economic acumen of an Ōkubo or a Kido, nor the military skill of generals like Yamagata or Nogi. In the successful fight against the Bakufu he was only one among many impressive leaders, and his forceful personality was matched by those of several colleagues in the Meiji government. When finally he broke away from these colleagues and struck out on his own, the result was a catastrophe, which produced the exact opposite of what he intended. Yet it was he, and not any of the successful founders of the modern Japanese state, who became the idol of the period, the very symbol of resistance to unjust power.

9.211

Perhaps the life of Kusunoki Masashige provides the most telling analogy. According to the legends, both Masashige and Saigō led the fights to overthrow the wicked Bakufu and succeeded in "restoring" the respective emperors (Godaigo and Meiji) to their rightful power; later, however, both men fell afoul of their former allies (Takauji and Ōkubo) and suffered conclusive defeat at their villainous hands. Significantly enough, the password used by Saigō and his followers was *Kikusui*, the floating chrysanthemum that had been Masashige's crest half a millennium earlier. And the legendary parting scene between Saigō and his son at the time when the hero set out on his last fatal venture is clearly analogous to the farewell between Masashige and Masatsura as immortalized in the Sakurai song:

The streets swarmed with people when Saigō set out. Most of them were confident of his victory. Toratarō, Saigō's son of twelve, was brought to see his father off. On seeing him there, Saigō said, "Oh, you are here." Toratarō had followed him a few hundred yards when he said, "Go home, my good boy," and Toratarō had to obey. Prepared for death, Saigō seemed undisturbed by the most touching scene of life.   *9.212*

It has been said that the Satsuma Rebellion was the final war with a purely national image, marking the end of the heroic phase of Japanese history; and Saigō Takamori himself has been described as the last true hero of Japan. There have certainly   *9.213* been changes in the modern world that make the traditional form of Japanese heroic failure an anachronism, and it is hard to imagine any significant revival of the earlier pattern. Yet many of the psychological fundamentals have continued into the twentieth century: during the Pacific war the kamikaze suicide pilots were given the name *Kikusui*, and these young men revered the "death-defying Saigō" as their spiritual ancestor.   *9.214*

"If Only We Might Fall . . ."

If only we might fall
Like cherry blossoms in the Spring—
So pure and radiant!

*Haiku by a kamikaze pilot of the Seven
Lives Unit, who died in combat in
February 1945 at the age of twenty-two*

10.1

. . . The aircraft was of simple design and construction without refinements and appropriate for its use. Three solid-fuel rocket motors were installed in the rear fuselage and operated for the final phase of the flight. The [aircraft] was usually carried by a twin-engined Mitsubishi bomber and released at high altitude some distance from the target. When within striking distance the rocket motors were ignited for the final high-speed dive through the defensive screen of the target.

Description: Single seat, mid-wing monoplane. Wood and mild steel construction. Span 16'15"; length 19'18 1/2"; weight empty 970 lbs., loaded 4,700 lbs.; weight of high explosive in nose 2,650 lbs.

Performance: The aircraft could glide 50 miles at 230 m.p.h. after release from mother aircraft at 27,000'. With motors operating the aircraft dived at 570 m.p.h.

Power plant: 3 solid-fuel rocket motors giving a total thrust of 1,764 lbs. for 9 seconds.

10.2

Thus the visitor to the Science Museum in London is introduced to one of the strangest and most poignant weapons in the history of warfare. Suspended by three slender cables, it hovers inconspicuously in the back of the third floor, where it is overshadowed by sturdy-looking Hawker Hurricanes, Supermarine Spitfires, and Gloster Turbojets—a delicate green cocoon, smaller and frailer and simpler than the nearby V-1 flying bomb,

yet, unlike its German counterpart, equipped to carry a human
warrior to his fiery destination.   *10.3*

"Ōka" it was named by the Japanese—"cherry blossom," the
ancient symbol of purity and evanescence. The Americans,   *10.4*
against whom this diminutive craft was designed, dubbed it the
"*baka* [idiot] bomb," as if by denigrating this eerie weapon they
might neutralize the unease it instinctively evoked.   *10.5*

From any common-sense viewpoint it was indeed something
of an absurdity. That hundreds of young pilots should have clambered into these contraptions—mere wooden torpedoes with toy-
like fuselage and stubby wings—to pit themselves against the
leviathan carriers and battleships of the American navy would
truly appear idotic, even incredible, to those unfamiliar with
Japan's ancient heroic tradition and the nobility that tradition
attributed to forlorn ventures inspired by sincerity.   *10.6*

The principle was simple enough: as conventional methods
of aerial warfare were rapidly becoming ineffective, Japan would
have recourse to a one-way glider which would be transported at
high altitude close to the target and would then dive down at
enormous speed to detonate its warhead onto the enemy ship.
The use of such dirigible manned bombs would thus allow the
transporting aircraft, the mother plane, to return safely to base
and be available for future missions. The suicide craft itself with
its ton of tri-nitro-anisol would sink, or at least incapacitate, the
ships of the enemy navy, which were now slowly strangling the
home islands; in addition, the use of this new secret weapon
would overawe and demoralize the foreigners, who were psychologically unprepared for such methods.

The Ōka was designed so that it could be tucked snugly
under the fuselage of the mother plane, usually a converted Mitsubishi G4 M.2e bomber or, in the homely nomenclature of the
enemy, a "Betty." During the main part of the flight towards the
target, the kamikaze fighter would sit with the pilot of the carrying plane. As they neared the area where American ships had
been sighted, he would briskly make his last farewell, exchange
salutes, then climb through the bomb bay of the mother plane
into the cramped cockpit of the flying coffin where he would
spend the remaining minutes of his life. His equipment, limited
to bare essentials, included a steering device and a voice tube that
allowed him to communicate with the bomber pilot until the
moment of separation. When the target was verified, usually at

a distance of some twenty-five miles, the kamikaze fighter would pull the release handle. His craft would then drop from the belly of the mother plane and glide downwards at a gradual angle gaining a speed of about two hundred and thirty miles an hour. Approaching the enemy ship, a rapidly growing dot in the ocean, he would activate the booster rockets, which were installed directly behind his seat without any protection. They instantly increased his velocity, which soon approached six hundred miles an hour (a fantastic speed for the time) and helped protect his precious cargo from enemy fighters and antiaircraft fire. Preparing for his suicide dive, the pilot would increase his downward angle to about fifty degrees; and, as he plummeted towards his prey, he was supposed to keep his eyes wide open until the last second, for a final adjustment in course could determine the outcome of his sacrifice.

The first Ōka attacks were launched towards the end of March 1945 as the American navy prepared to invade Japan's last line of defence, the island stronghold of Okinawa. At dawn on the 21st a mighty force of enemy ships, including seven aircraft carriers (the prime kamikaze target), had been sighted three hundred miles southeast of Kyushu. Vice Admiral Ugaki, the zealous commander of the Fifth Naval Air Fleet, who had been involved with kamikaze tactics since their inception, decided that the time had come to use the new weapon and to launch the Divine Thunder Unit on its first operation. Almost immediately there was a dispute, of a type common in the annals of samurai warfare, to decide who should lead the attack. After some heated wrangling the honour was awarded to Lieutenant Commander Nonaka, an expert on torpedo bombing. The force consisted of eighteen twin-engine Mitsubishi bombers, of which all but two had Ōka dirigible bombs attached to their bellies, escorted by fifty-five Zero fighters (an absurdly inadequate defence for such a momentous mission). Soon the roll of drums, the sound that traditionally precedes the hero's departure for battle, announced that the planes were ready to take off. The bomber crews hurried onto the field, and the sixteen Ōka pilots ran towards the mother planes that were to transport their little craft. Under the standard flight uniforms all wore white scarves, and in conformity with samurai custom each man, as he prepared for his last sortie, tightened round his helmet a white *hachimaki* cloth—the antique symbol of determination and derring-do. Above them fluttered the unit's

10.7

10.8

pennant, a white banner emblazoned with the slogan HI RI HŌ KEN TEN. These characters referred to a favourite saying by Kusunoki Masashige:

> Wrong [*Hi*] cannot prevail over Truth [*Ri*];
> Nor Truth conquer the Law [*Hō*];
> The Law cannot prevail over Power [*Ken*];
> Nor Power conquer Heaven [*Ten*].   *10.9*

Masashige's disastrous last battle, in which the Emperor's forces were routed by the enemy, was clearly in Nonaka's mind as he prepared to board his lead plane: "This," he said with a smile, "is my Minatogawa." While Admiral Ugaki watched from his com-   *10.10* mand post, the young Ōka pilots climbed into the cockpits of the mother crafts, shouting their farewells and their thanks for being included in the momentous mission. Led by Nonaka's plane, the bombers started taking off at half past eleven. As the last craft left the ground, the beat of drums ceased abruptly.

Almost at once it became clear that this might indeed be a Battle of Minato River. So defective was the equipment at this stage of the war that only about half of the escorting planes were able to accompany the mission. Many of them could not take off at all, while others had to turn back owing to engine trouble. Next it was learnt from reconnaissance reports that the enemy force was a great deal more powerful than originally believed, and thus it would be harder than ever to break through their defence screen. Vice Admiral Ugaki could still have called back his planes but he evidently decided that after so many months of feverishly preparing this first Ōka venture, such a move could have a devastating effect on morale.

The fatal hour came at two o'clock in the afternoon, when the mother planes, now some fifty miles from target, were suddenly intercepted by fifty Grumman fighters. In an attempt to gain speed the pilots jettisoned their Ōka craft; but they were still not sufficiently manoeuverable, and there were far too few fighters to provide adequate protection. The Americans furiously assaulted one bomber after another. As each of the huge planes caught fire and broke formation, the pilot would wave a final salute to his leader, Lieutenant Commander Nonaka, before spiralling down to the ocean. Soon every single bomber had been destroyed, and only a few Zero fighters remained to return to base with details of the disaster. Nonaka's bomber had disappeared behind a cloud bank, but one of the fighters reported that he later saw it burst into flames and plunge into the water like a meteor. The attack of 21st March was a gloomy augur for the final weapon that was to save Japan: not a single Ōka craft had even approached its target, let alone caused any damage. When Ugaki, the commanding admiral, heard the news, he is said to have wept openly.

After American forces started their invasion of Okinawa, further Ōka attacks were launched from the same airfield in the desperate hope that this time the new tactic might justify all the effort it had entailed. A major operation of 12th April included 333 aircraft and was designated as "Kikusui Number 2" in typical reference to the chrysanthemum emblem used by Masashige. With its eight Ōka-carrying bombers the force headed south towards Okinawa, the planes choosing different courses in order to approach their targets from various directions and confuse the enemy. In the base headquarters the senior officers listened anxiously to radio messages from the mother planes. Commander Nakajima, an expert on kamikaze operations, was particularly interested in the fate of a certain Lieutenant Doi, an Ōka pilot who had recently graduated from normal school in Osaka. Doi had distinguished himself at the base by organizing an energetic house-cleaning operation to improve the sordid conditions in the barracks, and his immediate reaction on being informed that he had been chosen for the next day's mission was to tell Commander Nakajima, "I have ordered six beds and fifteen straw mats. They are supposed to arrive today. May I ask that you watch for them and make sure they go to the billet?"

Messages came in rapid succession from the mother plane that was now carrying Doi and his green flying bomb to their target: "Enemy fighters sighted" was the first report, shortly followed by the encouraging news, "We have bypassed enemy fighters"; next came the messages, "Standing by to release Ōka ... Targets are battleships," and, a few seconds later, "Released!" "I visualized the scene," writes Commander Nakajima "as Doi plummeted toward a great battleship, his speed boosted by rocket thrusts, and the final successful direct hit." The reality was somewhat different. Only one of the eight mother planes succeeded in returning to base. As it happened, this was the bomber that had transported Lieutenant Doi, and the crew was able to provide detailed news of his last hours. Shortly after take-off the young man announced that he wanted to take a nap and asked that he be called half an hour before reaching the target area. He stretched out on a makeshift canvas cot and despite the noise and the rather tense nature of the situation, promptly fell asleep. On being awakened, he remarked with a smile, "Time passes quickly, doesn't it?" Lieutenant Doi then shook hands with the commander of the mother plane and climbed through the bomb bay into his Ōka craft. Approaching the battleship that had been selected as his target, he waited for the optimum position (altitude twenty-thousand feet, distance fifty thousand feet), then pulled the release handle. In accordance with Ōka tactics the mother plane was obliged to withdraw rapidly from the scene of action, but the crew reported that they had seen Doi's bomb hurtling down towards its target and afterwards a pillar of heavy smoke had risen some fifteen hundred feet from the general position of the battleship. It was not a signal of success: from official United States Navy reports we know that Lieutenant Doi missed his target, for not a single capital ship was hit by a piloted bomb on that day. The sortie did, however, provide at least an intimation of hope, since one American destroyer was damaged. Destroyers were certainly not the most worthy targets for suicide bombs, but without this scintilla of encouragement the Imperial High Command might well have abandoned the entire Ōka venture. *10.16* *10.17*

Ōka bombs, though the most dramatic manifestation of Japan's suicide tactics in the Pacific war, by no means dominated the kamikaze epic. The history of organizing suicide units as a major part of military strategy had started about half a year before Ōka bombs were first used. On 17th October 1944, as Japanese forces in the Philippines prepared to meet an all-out American attack, a new commander, Vice Admiral Ōnishi, arrived from Tokyo to take over the First Naval Air Fleet in Manila. Two days later he visited Mabalacat, a little town some fifty miles northwest of the capital, and the headquarters of the 201st Air Group. The base at Mabalacat now became the scene of one of the most fateful conferences in the Pacific war. *10.18* *10.19*

The central figure, Ōnishi Takijirō, had made a name for himself from the outset of hostilities when he had cooperated with the eminent Admiral Yamamoto in planning the attack on

Pearl Harbor. In the Imperial Navy he and Yamamoto were the two most fervent exponents of aviation as the key to Japan's strategy in the Pacific, and they had worked in close partnership
10.20 until Yamamoto's sudden death in 1943. Ōnishi himself flew every type of aircraft, and during the early, successful part of the war he exercised personal command as Chief of Staff for land-based air operations in action over the Philippines and in the sea battle off Malaya. When Japan's situation became critical in 1944, he was appointed to a key position in the aviation department of the Munitions Ministry and soon came to realize his country's hopeless inferiority in the production of aircraft compared with the enemy's boundless capacity. Like Yamamoto he had a resourceful and imaginative mind, and it was no doubt during this time that he began to seek some new form of aviation strategy that might help offset the absurd material discrepancy between Japan and America.

Considering his key role in the latter part of the war, remarkably little is known about Vice Admiral Ōnishi. The few published pictures show a large, kindly-looking man with round, somewhat puffy features. He certainly does not resemble the impassive, grim-looking Japanese officers who glare at us from most photographs of the time. In the Imperial Navy he was a controversial figure with a "maverick" reputation much like Admiral Yamamoto's. A poor politician, blunt, straightforward, uncompromising, he was endowed with the type of simple-hearted sincerity so often encountered among heroic nonconformists in Japanese history. Like Saigō Takamori and earlier representatives of the tradition, he stressed the importance of resolute ac-
10.21 tion as opposed to talk, and of spirit over "systems." Again like Saigō, he became known as a masterful calligrapher; he was also a keen (though not especially talented) composer of haiku.

Ōnishi's soft appearance belied the toughness of a man who demanded much from others and still more from himself. He was noted for his dynamic energy and for a courage that bordered on foolhardiness: Vice Admiral Ōnishi was the first military man in Japan to practise parachuting and often during the war he seemed to court physical danger. In almost every respect he was the ideal leader for organized kamikaze strategy.

Though recognized as Japan's foremost officer in naval aviation, Ōnishi was not altogether popular in the corridors of power. Owing to his outspoken, somewhat tactless nature, many regarded him as aggressive, arrogant, even dangerous—the typical "nail that sticks out" and needs a sharp knock on the head.   *10.22*

Among his own men, however, especially the young pilots, he appears to have been loved, and he reciprocated their admiration by extolling them as "the treasure of the nation" and declaring, in his powerful calligraphy, that "The purity of youth will usher in the Divine Wind."   *10.23*

These were the young men whose deliberate and systematic sacrifice he was to propose at the meeting on 19th October. The Admiral was tired and in poor health when he reached the headquarters at Mabalacat, and the extraordinary nature of the conference must have added to the strain. Facing the assembled officers, he started by rehearsing the all too familiar facts about Japan's material shortages. Having presented a seemingly insoluble problem, he offered the idea that had been forming in his mind during the past months: "In my opinion, there is only one way of assuring that our meagre strength will be effective to a maximum degree. That is to organize attack units composed of Zero fighters armed with two-hundred-fifty-kilogram bombs, with each plane to crash-dive into an enemy carrier. . . . What do you think?"   *10.25*

Captain Inoguchi, a senior staff officer who was present at the conference, has described the moment: "The Admiral's eyes bored into us as he looked around the table. No one spoke for a while, but Admiral Ōnishi's words struck a spark in each of us."   *10.26* The decision had to be made at once, for time was rapidly running out. Responsibility devolved upon Commander Tamai, the executive officer of the 201st Air Group, who now excused himself and left the room with an aide in order to assess the probable reactions of the pilots themselves. Tamai returned shortly and said, "Entrusted by our commander with full responsibility, I share completely the opinions expressed by the Admiral. The 201st Air Group will carry out his proposal. May I ask that you leave to us the organization of our crash-dive unit?" Not a single   *10.27* officer at the meeting demurred.

The decision to adopt organized suicide tactics had been made in a matter of minutes, though the psychological groundwork had been laid during many centuries. In less than a week the first kamikaze planes took off from Mabalacat to attack the American navy. Captain Inoguchi ends his description of the meeting as follows: "I well remember Admiral Ōnishi's expres-

10.28   sion as he nodded acquiescence. His face bore a look of relief coupled with a shadow of sorrow." Ōnishi was indeed the father of the kamikaze units, but he had mixed feelings about his progeny. He knew, of course, that with ordinary tactics there was no longer the slightest chance of stopping the enemy. In addition he attached great importance to the "spiritual" aspect of the operations, quite apart from any practical effect they might have. In a speech delivered a few months later to members of the first kamikaze unit in Taiwan he declared, "Even if we are defeated, the noble spirit of the kamikaze attack corps will keep our homeland from ruin. Without this spirit, ruin would certainly

10.29   follow defeat."

These might appear surprising sentiments for a commanding officer at a period when "defeatism" was officially considered the most heinous of crimes; yet clearly they belong to the Japanese heroic tradition that places sincerity of purpose above practical efficacy. At the same time we know that Ōnishi regarded the kamikaze operations as a tragic necessity rather than a source of satisfaction. One morning shortly after the formation of the first units, when he was crouching in an air-raid shelter with Captain Inoguchi, he recalled that similar tactics had been mooted earlier in the war but that he had then refused to countenance them. "He stared fixedly at the wall during the burst of machine-gun fire and continued, 'The fact that we [now] have to resort to [such a method] shows how poor our strategy has been since the begin-

10.30   ning.' " Ōnishi paused for a moment, then suddenly let drop the remark, "You know, this really is a violation of [proper] com-

10.31   mand."

If Ōnishi, the single man in Japan most responsible for initiating the suicide strategy, could harbour such hesitations, it is hardly surprising that more conventional military leaders should have had their doubts. Imperial Headquarters in Tokyo, though giving official approval to the organization of kamikaze units, tended at first to view the plan with misgivings. This was not, of course, due to any humanitarian scruples, but because they were frankly sceptical about Ōnishi and the feasibility of his new tactics and, perhaps more important, because these tactics represented a disturbing departure from orthodox principles and procedures, which were still based on the principle of "great

10.32   warships and big guns" (taikan-kyobō-shugi).

As the months passed and kamikaze attacks became an established way of warfare, Japan's leaders increasingly accepted their necessity. The practical advantages were obvious. Now that the Imperial Navy was crippled and the air force rapidly dwindling, here was a method that allowed pilots with minimal experience, flying almost any kind of craft, to damage, perhaps even sink, the seemingly impregnable carriers, the core of the American threat. The young men in their disposable planes merely had to take off on their one-way missions, follow their flight leader, and steer their lethal cargo straight onto the target. Youth, speedy reactions, and, above all, zeal were the prime requirements, and there was no need for special skills or elaborate training. The Americans, being unprepared for such unconventional methods, had not yet invented antiaircraft batteries capable of destroying a plane as it hurtled down in a full-throttled dive, and they therefore had to improvise zigzagging manoeuvres and other evasive tactics which were far from foolproof. There was also a psychological element. Japan's military leaders managed to convince themselves that their enemy would be daunted by the spiritual strength of the kamikaze. As it turned out, they grossly misjudged American reactions and overestimated the demoralizing effect of Ōka and other suicide weapons. But in the last desperate *10.33* phase of the war the idea that the Japanese spirit (*Yamato-damashii*) was the trump card that could counter the enemy's material force had become an article of faith. Thus when General Ushijima addressed his troops in Okinawa he insisted that their ultimate strength lay in moral superiority. And the eagerness of *10.34* young kamikaze volunteers to make an oblation of their lives served as dramatic evidence of this supposed advantage.

The initial doubts of the men in high places were certainly not shared by the pilots in the Philippines, who appear to have responded to Ōnishi's challenge with spontaneous enthusiasm. We are told that every single member of the 201st Air Group volunteered for the new kamikaze units in a frenzy of elation; and, while the outsider may be permitted to wonder what would have happened to the rare dissenting pilot who preferred to continue orthodox operations, there can be no doubt about the general reaction. Once it was clear that the candidates for self- *10.35* sacrifice were available, a leader had to be chosen for the historic first mission. Captain Inoguchi and the Executive Officer of the 201st Air decided on a fervent young Lieutenant called Seki, who had frequently volunteered for dangerous missions, and the young man was promptly summoned. Inoguchi's description evokes the highly charged atmosphere of the time:

The Philippine night was dark and quiet. We sat silently in the officers' lounge as the sound of the orderly's footsteps faded upstairs. I thought of Seki, deep in slumber, and wondered what his dreams might be. Quick steps soon descended the stairs and the tall figure of the lieutenant appeared in the doorway. It was evident that he had hurried, for his jacket was still not completely buttoned. He addressed Commander Tamai: "Did you call me, sir?"

Beckoned to a chair, the young man sat down facing us. Tamai patted him on the shoulder and said, "Seki, Admiral Ōnishi himself has visited the 201st Air Group to present a plan of greatest importance to Japan. The plan is to crash-dive our Zero fighters, loaded with 250-kilogram bombs, into the decks of enemy carriers. . . . You are being considered to lead such an attack unit. How do you feel about it?"

There were tears in Commander Tamai's eyes as he ended.

For a moment there was no answer. With his elbows on the table, hands to his head, jaws tight shut and his eyes closed, Seki sat motionless, in deep thought. One second, two seconds, three, four, five. . . . Finally he moved, slowly running his fingers through his long hair. Then, calmly raising his head, he spoke, "You absolutely must let me do it." There was not the slightest falter in his voice.

10.36   "Thank you," said Tamai.

During the following hectic week four kamikaze units were formed in Mabalacat, and detailed arrangements made for their maiden sortie on 25th October. As the news spread among other pilots in the area, further units were rapidly created, notably by members of the Second Air Fleet, who in less than a week managed to organize several Special Attack units of their own. In these early days most of the initiative and detailed planning came from the pilots themselves, the principal role of the superior officers being to coordinate and supervise the new tactics.

10.37 Early on the morning of the 25th the two dozen men chosen to take part in the first attack from Mabalacat ate a quick breakfast and lined up on the airfield, with Lieutenant Seki a step ahead of the others, to hear their first and final instructions from Vice Admiral Ōnishi. According to Inoguchi's description, the Admiral looked pale and, as he started to speak, his words were slow and troubled:

"Japan is in grave danger. The salvation of our country is now beyond the powers of the ministers of state, the General Staff, and lowly commanders like myself. It can come only from spirited young men such as you. Thus, on behalf of your hundred million countrymen, I ask of you this sacrifice, and pray for your success." He paused for a while and tried to regain his composure, then continued, "You are already gods, without earthly desires. . . . I shall watch your efforts to the end and report your deeds to the Throne. You may all rest assured on this point." His eyes were filled with tears as he concluded with the words, "I ask you all to do your best."   *10.38*

Just before take-off, Lieutenant Seki pulled out a handful of crumpled bank-notes from his pocket and handed them to an officer who was staying behind, asking that they be sent to Japan and used to build new planes. A few minutes later the twenty-four pilots started on their one-way journeys. Seki's plane was in the lead, and his was the first to crash into its target. The unlucky victim was the American escort carrier *St. Lo*, which, after being hit in the flight deck by another suicide plane, sank following a fierce succession of internal explosions. On this opening day, altogether the most encouraging in the entire history of kamikaze operations, half a dozen other American escort carriers were struck by suicide planes and damaged. The sensational news of the attack—the one favourable development for Japan at a time of almost unrelieved setbacks—was instantly signalled to Tokyo and conveyed to the Emperor. His reaction, as reported to Ōnishi and members of the kamikaze units, was typically ambiguous. Captain Nakajima describes the scene at Mabalacat when he ordered all his men to assemble at the command post: *10.39* *10.40* *10.41*

As they gathered I could see that their spirit and morale were high, despite the intense day-and-night effort demanded of them. Holding [Vice Admiral Ōnishi's cablegramme] in my hand I addressed them: "I relay to you His Majesty's words upon hearing the results achieved by the Kamikaze Special Attack corps." Everyone snapped to attention, and I read the message from Admiral Ōnishi: "When told of the special attack, His Majesty said, 'WAS IT NECESSARY TO GO TO THIS EXTREME? BUT THEY HAVE CERTAINLY DONE A GOOD JOB.' His Majesty's words suggest that His Majesty is greatly concerned. . . . We must redouble our efforts to relieve His Majesty of this concern. I have pledged our every effort toward that end."   *10.42*

10.43   It appears that Ōnishi himself interpreted the Emperor's comment as a criticism of the new tactics. The doubts that he inferred from the Imperial words echoed his own earlier hesitation regarding Special Attack methods, and they must have been painfully vivid in his mind when the time came to carry out his

10.44   own slow and painful suicide.

Whatever reservations about the kamikaze may have lurked in the Emperor's mind, at this stage there could be no question of abandoning the hopeful new venture. In the weeks following the first attack the pilots in the Philippines established a regular kamikaze procedure. It was during this time also that the nomenclature for the new type of warfare was fixed. Many of the names that were chosen are worth examining for their symbolic references. Previous suicide attacks during the course of the war usually resulted from individual, spontaneous initiative and were designated by rather literal, even crude, terms like "body-smash-

10.45   ing," "flesh-bullets," and "self-blasting." But now that deliberate self-immolation was officially accepted as a part of Japan's general strategy, it was felt that something more impressive and evocative was needed. One night, shortly after the historic meeting at Mabalacat, two of Vice Admiral Ōnishi's officers visited him in his room. One of them was Captain Inoguchi, who describes the scene as follows:

> I went upstairs where Admiral Ōnishi was resting to report that the organization of the unit had been completed. I knocked and then opened the door.
> There were no lights burning in the room, but starlight filtered through the window and I could see a form on the canvas cot near the door. During the several hours since meeting us Admiral Ōnishi had remained in the darkened room, alone with his thoughts and his anxieties.
> He arose as I began my report: "There are 23 men for the special mission, and Lieutenant Seki, an Academy man, has been chosen to lead them. Since this is a special affair, we wish you to [name] the unit.

10.46   Commander Tamai and I suggest that it be called the *Shimpū* Unit."

Shimpū ("divine wind") referred to the momentous typhoons of 1274 and 1281 which (according to tradition) rescued Japan from the fury of the Mongols. The invasions in the thirteenth century were by far the greatest threat from overseas in the country's past. In 1944 there was a new and even graver danger; and just

as the Japanese had once prayed for divine intervention and were
saved by a storm that destroyed the invader's fleet, so now, some
six and a half centuries later, they would again look to a spiritual   *10.47*
force, this time manifesting itself in the self-sacrificial sincerity
of the young pilots who would crash themselves and their planes
into the enemy's ships to protect their beleaguered homeland
from the foreign hordes. Recognizing the term as inspiring and
historically appropriate, Ōnishi adopted it immediately. At first
shimpū referred specifically and exclusively to aerial attack forces
under his command in the Philippines, but as the new tactics
spread it came to be used far more widely. Suicide pilots were   *10.48*
never called *kamikaze* at the time. This term, which has become
so familiar in the West and is also current in Japan as a metaphor
for breakneck skiers, taxi drivers, and other assorted daredevils,
is an early reading of the characters 神風 that in Sino-Japanese   *10.49*
are pronounced *shimpū. Kamikaze* lacked the solemn, dignified
ring of the Sino-Japanese equivalent and would have been quite
unsuitable for the heroic exploits of 1944 and 1945.   *10.50*

The new name was first officially used in an order dated 20th
October: "The 201st Air Group will organize a special attack
corps and will destroy or disable, if possible by 25 October, the
enemy carrier forces in the waters east of the Philippines. The
corps will be called the *Shimpū* Attack Force. . . . " The full   *10.51*
designation was "Divine Wind Special Attack Force" (*Shimpū
Tokubetsu Kōgekitai*), which was usually abbreviated to "Special
Attack Force" (*Tokkōtai*). Here the word "special" (*toku*) is a
euphemism which obviated the use of "suicide."   *10.52*

The names chosen for the first four aerial attack units also
carried powerful symbolic associations and, like the word *shimpū*,
served to stress the emotional and cultural continuity involved in
this unorthodox type of warfare. "The Attack Force," said the
order of 20th October, "will be divided into four units, designated
as follows: Shikishima, Yamato, Asahi, and Yamazakura." *Shiki-*   *10.53*
shima (the unit to which Lieutenant Seki belonged and which
sank the *St. Lo)* is an old poetic name for Japan; *Yamato* is another
traditional name for the country and has strong patriotic associations (reflected, for example, in the name of the prototypal hero,
Yamato Takeru); *Asahi* is the rising sun; and *Yamazakura* are the
wild cherry blossoms, which are so important in samurai symbolism. The four words are the framework of a poem by a famous
eighteenth-century nationalist writer:

> What is the spirit of Yamato's ancient land?
> It is like the wild cherry blossoms,
> Radiant in the rising sun.

10.54

"The wild cherry blossoms," comments Lieutenant Nagatsuka, an army kamikaze volunteer, "spread their radiance and then scatter without any regret; just so must we be prepared to die, *10.55* without regret, for Yamato—such is the meaning of this verse."

10.56 The traditional image of the cherry blossom also came to designate the human bombs, which were put into production some months later. Many other names and terms in the vocabulary of suicide tactics had historical connexions, notably with Kusunoki Masashige, the failed loyalist hero of the fourteenth century. Thus Masashige's chrysanthemum crest, the *Kikusui*, gave its name to several Special Attack groups and to a number of individual operations; later it became a general term referring to almost all land, sea, and air operations in the Battle of Okinawa, which more and more assumed the character of a cul-*10.57* minating suicidal explosion.

In the Philippines, kamikaze operations were standardized with amazing rapidity, and until the end of the war procedures conformed closely to the pattern set at this time. Despite the frantic nature of these tactics, there was nothing chaotic or slipshod about their execution. As a rule the pilots who had been selected for a particular suicide mission were informed on the previous day, though occasionally they were given somewhat longer notice. The announcement of names triggered powerful emotions. Those chosen few knew that their great moment was at hand and could now pride themselves on being full-fledged heroes, "gods without earthly desires"; the other pilots, who had keyed themselves up for the same self-sacrifice but were now condemned to wait for some future mission, often reacted with *10.58* bitter, even hysterical, disappointment. Normally the men who were leaving had completed their brief training and technical preparation, and during the last day, or days, they stayed quietly in their barracks, reading, playing cards, listening to music, and writing their final letters and farewell poems. The pilots had seldom reached the age of being married, and the few who had wives were normally disqualified from suicide operations. The men's last messages were almost invariably addressed to their parents; sometimes they added an informal will and, in accordance with the tradition of samurai leaving for their last battle, they would enclose locks of hair and nail parings—all that was to remain for their burial.

Lieutenant Nagatsuka, one of the rare survivors, describes the scene in his barracks when he and his companions had received their flying orders for the following morning. After joining in a lighthearted discussion about what would become of them after their deaths, Nagatsuka went to his bunk and tried to write his last letter. Nine hours of life remained—or so he thought. For some time he was overwhelmed with past memories and unable to put his ideas together. Then he took up his pen:

"My dear parents, [tomorrow morning] 29th June 1945, at seven o'clock I shall be leaving this earth for ever. Your immense love for me fills my entire being, down to my last hair. And that is what makes this so hard to accept: the idea that with the disappearance of my body this tenderness will also vanish. But I am impelled by my duty. I sincerely beg you to forgive me for not having been able to fulfil all my family obligations.

"Please convey my thanks to all those who have shown me friendship and goodness. Dear sisters, farewell. Now that our parents will no longer have a son, you must show them all possible consideration as long as they live. Always remain kind and worthy of being Japanese women."

I should have liked to go on writing endlessly, but instead I simply signed my name and added the date: "10 P.M. on 28th June 1945." I put my Will, together with the paper containing my lock of hair and nail parings, into an envelope. After I had sealed it, I realized that everything was finished.

10.59

Before retiring to bed, the pilots usually collected their money, books, and other personal possessions that would not be needed on the flight and presented them to friends who were staying behind. On their final night most of them slept peacefully. They rose from their bunks shortly after sunrise, washed carefully, and put on their flight uniforms for the last time; round their helmets they tied a white cloth decorated (depending on their unit) with a *Kikusui* chrysanthemum, a rising sun, or some evocative slogan like SEVEN LIVES. "On our last sortie," wrote Lieutenant Hayashi to his mother, "we shall wear regular flight uniforms and a headband bearing the rising sun. Snow-white scarves [will] give a certain dash to our appearance." Sometimes the pilot would remove his white scarf just before take-off and

10.60

10.61

give it to a companion as a farewell memento. Many kamikaze fighters also wore *senninbari*, "thousand-stitch belts." These waistbands had been lovingly prepared by their mothers, who would go out into the streets and ask a thousand young girls—maidens whose purity would contribute to the ritual value of the belt—to make one stitch each. The *senninbari* served as comforting talismans during the pilots' last hours. Thus Lieutenant Matsuo Tomio, an Ōka flyer who crashed his "cherry blossom" bomb at the age of twenty-one, wrote in a final poem:

> Now that I set off on my last attack
> I can never feel alone,
> For my mother's band
> 10.62   Is safely tied about my waist.

The brief departure ceremonies usually took place outside the barracks or on the "landing" field itself, where long tables with white cloths were set with flasks of cold *sake* and plates of austere dishes like dried cuttlefish. The commanding officer of the unit would pour ceremonial cups for each of the departing pilots in turn. As the pilot took his cup, he would bow, lift it respectfully in both hands to his lips, and drink; for what he had received was no Western-style stirrup cup but something closer 10.63 to a Last Communion. In addition the pilots were often given a small lunch box *(bentō)* to take along in their airplane—presumably more for psychological comfort than to provide a last-minute snack. "We shall be given a package of bean-curd and rice," explained Lieutenant Hayashi. "It is reassuring to depart with such good luncheon fare. I think I'll also take along the charm and the dried bonito from Mr. Tateishi. The bonito will help me 10.64 to rise from the ocean, Mother, and swim back to you."

In 1945 a story about this last meal became current among kamikaze pilots and, though the details may well be apocryphal, it appears to have moved many of them deeply. Here is Lieutenant Nagatsuka's version:

According to our commanding officer, this year the Emperor refused to celebrate New Year's in the usual way. The government officials and high military leaders who usually appeared in their grand uniforms to pay their respects on this occasion were not invited to come. At noon a military aide brought His Majesty a white wooden platter with a bowl of boiled rice and red beans, a piece of grilled sea-bream, and a flask of *sake*. Meagre fare indeed! "Your Majesty," he said respectfully, "this is what is given to our kamikaze pilots at the moment of their glorious departure." The Emperor looked at him eyes filled with tears. Then he stood up abruptly and left the room without touching any of the dishes. For an hour he walked by himself in the garden, which had now fallen into decay and was covered with weeds. Surely he was contemplating the future of his country and also the sincere patriotism of his kamikaze pilots. "This year" our commanding officer told us, "it is only the spirits of the kamikaze fighters that have paid their respects to His Majesty. . . ." 10.65

Before the pilots boarded their planes for take-off the commanding officer would make a brief farewell speech, usually ending with an exhortation that they do their very best. Their fellow pilots, who were standing by to see them off, joined in some military anthem like the one that starts: 10.66

> If I go away to sea,
> I shall return as a brine-soaked corpse. . . . 10.67

As the kamikaze flyers climbed into their cockpits, the ground crew would wave and salute. These men had usually been working through the night under appalling conditions to get the planes ready for their mission. Owing to constant American strafing, the suicide craft often had to be concealed in forest revetments until the time came to remove the camouflage and rapidly haul them out for action.

Captain Nakajima has described one devoted mechanic at Mabalacat airfield, whose attitude seems to epitomize much of the spirit that flowered in Japan during these emotionally heightened months:

There was one maintenance man who made a point of meticulously scouring and polishing the cockpit of each kamikaze plane he tended. It was his theory that the cockpit was the pilot's coffin and as such it should be spotless. One recipient of this service was so pleasantly surprised that he summoned and thanked his benefactor, saying that the neatness of the plane meant a great deal to him. The maintenance man's eyes dimmed with tears, and, unable to speak, he ran along with one hand on the wing tip of the plane as it taxied for its final take-off. 10.68

After the pilots had waved goodbye from their cockpits, they took off in rapid order. The standard formation for a kamikaze attack consisted of five aircraft—three suicide planes, one escorting fighter, and one "evaluation" plane. The duty of the escorts was to protect the suicide pilots from enemy interceptors by every possible stratagem, including dodging and bluffing, and to get them safely to their target. Until the attackers approached the American ships, their bombs normally remained unarmed, so that pilots who could not find their target might return to base and wait for better conditions; later in the war, however, even this theoretical possibility of survival was removed since as a rule the bombs were armed immediately after take-off and the planes 10.69 could not possibly land without exploding.

Approaching their targets, the attackers would scatter tinfoil to jam enemy radar and then pull a toggle which set the propel- 10.70 lers in the bombs spinning. When the ships were clearly in sight, the lead pilot would bank slightly, raise his arm, and signal "All planes, attack!" Each of the men would identify his respective target and come in for attack, at either an extremely high or an 10.71 extremely low altitude. Steering with the greatest possible accuracy, he would set his sights on the most vulnerable part of the ship. For those fortunate pilots whose target was an aircraft carrier the crucial spot was the flight-deck elevator, but it was rare indeed that the final impact was this precise.

Death came instantaneously upon impact, when both plane and pilot disintegrated in a mighty explosion. This was the blaze of glory, the "splendid death" (rippa na shi), to which they so 10.72 often referred in their letters and diaries. The actual physical aftermath, however, was less beautiful. Typical of the gruesome scenes that followed an attack was that aboard the light cruiser Montpelier which on the morning of 27th November 1944 became the target for no less than eight kamikaze planes from Mabalacat, yet somehow managed to stay afloat. As soon as the all-clear was sounded, the crew set about the grisly task of cleaning the decks.

After the sailors had thrown overboard the hunks of metal that remained from the attacking planes, they began hosing down the decks, and soon the water was red with blood. Here and there they found shreds of flesh and other remains from the bodies of the Japanese pilots—tongues, tufts of black hair, a brain, some arms, a leg. One sailor triumphantly hacked 10.73 off a finger and removed a ring. Before long the decks were clear.

Meanwhile the escorting planes, having done their best to assess the results of the attack, tried to race back to their base through a barrage of antiaircraft fire and interceptors. A detailed report of the mission was promptly forwarded from the base to the Commander-in-Chief of the Combined Fleet, who, regardless of the results of the mission, would recommend the dead pilots for promotion in rank. From a Western point of view such post-   *10.74* humous honour might seem a rather unsatisfactory form of compensation for a life, especially since none of the kamikaze pilots had received awards or decorations of any kind before their missions. Yet the young men's knowledge that they would be officially recognized after death assured them of their heroic status and no doubt served as an added incentive during their final hours.

Kamikaze sorties continued from Mabalacat and other airfields in the Philippines until January 1945, at which point not a single operational aircraft remained. From 20th October until 6th January there had been daily raids involving altogether some five hundred suicide planes. The surviving pilots were in a state of agonized frustration as they realized that no more missions would be possible and that they would now be reduced to fighting a rearguard action in the mountains as ordinary infantrymen. On the morning of the sixth, however, it turned out that the maintenance crews, having worked throughout the night, scrounging bits and pieces from damaged hulks round the field, had miraculously put together five Zero planes. Captain Nakajima, who was faced with the unenviable task of choosing the pilots for this last mission, recalls the sortie:

In view of the special circumstances now that the 201st Air Group was practically disbanding . . . instead of simply designating the day's fliers . . . I decided to call for volunteers.

I ordered all of the pilots to assemble in front of the shelter. When they had gathered I addressed the group, reviewing our situation and explaining how the splendid work of the maintenance men had provided an additional five planes.

"They are not in first-class condition," I pointed out. "In fact, two of them cannot carry a 250-kilogram bomb, so they have each been loaded with two 30-kilogram bombs. . . . When these planes have been dispatched, our air battle will have ended and the rest of us will join in the fight as land troops. In making plans for this last special attack I want to know your wishes."

With this I paused to give them a chance for reflection. When it was clear that they had understood my message, I continued, "Anyone who wishes to volunteer for today's sortie will raise his hand."

The words were scarcely uttered before every man had raised his arm high in the air and shouted, "Here!" as they eagerly edged forward. . . . I breathed deeply and tensed my facial muscles into a scowl to keep from betraying the emotion that flooded over me.

"Since you all want so much to go, we will follow the usual procedure of selection. You are dismissed."

As I turned to enter the shelter, several of the pilots reached out to grab at my arms and sleeves saying, "Send me! Please send me! Send me!"

I wheeled about and shouted, "Everyone wants to go. Don't be so selfish!"

That silenced them, and I entered the shelter to confer with the air group commander about the composition of the final list.

We were in complete agreement as to who should lead this unit. Lieutenant Nakano had recently been hospitalized with tuberculosis in Manila. Upon his release he had said to me, "I have now recovered, but there is no telling when I may have a relapse. If this recovery were complete I could wait my turn for duty at the regular time. But if the illness returns there would be no chance for me to serve. Therefore, please send me on a mission at the earliest opportunity."

Remembering his plea, I had kept him in mind for some short-range mission that would not tax his strength. This flight would not be long, and this was the last chance. Considering all the factors, I decided that Nakano was the ideal man for leading the mission. . . .

Enemy air raids continued all this while, so that we hardly dared risk showing our heads. Enemy ships were swarming at Lingayen Gulf, and a landing there was imminent.

In preparation for a 1645 take-off, the five planes, hidden at various points around the Mabalacat airfield, had their camouflage removed and engines warmed up. Now the training which had been practised so enthusiastically proved valuable. The pilots moved swiftly. As the first plane started to roll, the others followed in close order.

The field was pock-marked with bomb holes, but following my hand signals, the planes were skilfully taxied to their starting places without mishap. As I waved my right hand in the signal for taking off, Lieutenant Nakano raised himself in the cockpit and shouted, "Commander Nakajima! Commander Nakajima!"

Fearing that something had gone wrong, I ran to the side of his plane to learn what troubled him. His face was wreathed in smiles as he called, "Thank you, Commander. Thank you very much. . . ." Realizing that enemy raiders might appear at any moment and that there was not an instant to lose, I wordlessly gave the signal for take-off.

Nakano's plane started forward with a roar. As the second plane passed in front of me the engine was revved down momentarily as the pilot screamed, "Commander! Commander!" I flagged him on with a vigorous wave of my arm, but through the din came back his shrieked farewell: "Thank you for choosing me!" I pretended not to hear these messages, but they tore at my heart. The scene repeated itself as each smiling pilot passed my position and I waved on the next: No. 3 . . . No. 4 . . . No. 5—each did the same. . . .

10.75

This was the coda of kamikaze operations in the Philippines. All five planes managed to break through enemy interceptors and reach a powerful American naval force in Lingayen Gulf. They were accompanied by a single scout plane, which took photographs of the attack. This evidence disappeared, however, and the Imperial High Command allowed themselves to believe that the sortie had been a triumph; in fact, only a single American ship was sunk by Nakano and his companions—and that was a humble minelayer, the DMS *Long*.

The hundreds of kamikaze sacrifices had not succeeded in saving the Philippines, and now Vice Admiral Ōnishi was ordered to transfer his headquarters to Taiwan. He took all documents pertaining to the kamikaze with him so that they might be preserved for posterity. With enemy forces moving ever closer to the home islands, Ōnishi was determined that what had failed in the Philippines would be tried with even greater determination in Taiwan. There was a growing sense of urgency: the first kamikaze force took off from Taiwan only two days after it was formed, and sorties continued in rapid succession thereafter. The training of pilots for suicide attacks was reduced to the modest period of ten days. All attention was now devoted to take-off and crash procedures, no time could be expended on the luxury of learning how to land the plane.

10.76

10.77

10.78

Like a dying patient whose enfeebled body is beset by one new assault after another, Japan was rapidly losing the last defences that might save her from total collapse or at least delay the fatal hour. All-out kamikaze tactics were a desperate recourse. Vice Admiral Ōnishi's Special Attack groups in the Philippines were the first officially organized suicide units, but deliberate

self-destructive tactics had frequently been used in earlier stages
of the war, notably at the very outset when Admiral Yamamoto
sent five pocket submarines into Pearl Harbor as part of the
attack on 7th December. Though these underwater midgets were
not actually described as suicide weapons, there was little question about the fate of their crews. Four of the five were sunk
promptly and (as it turned out) uselessly. Pocket submarines
were later employed in the abortive attack against Sydney Harbor, and it was after the collapse of this venture that the Imperial
Navy decided to abandon underwater suicide craft. As the war
suddenly took a turn for the worse, however, the Japanese once
more resorted to suicide tactics and weapons. At first the exploits
were individual and usually improvised on the spur of the moment when it became clear that conventional methods would not
avail. Long before kamikaze units were even imagined, pilots of
the Imperial Navy were using "body-smashing" tactics in air-to-
air combat against B-24s and other enemy bombers. The first
recorded ramming attack took place in May 1943 when a Sergeant
Oda deliberately crashed his little Ki-43 fighter plane into a B-17
and by this sacrifice succeeded—or so tradition has it—in saving
an entire Japanese convoy, a heroic feat for which he was posthumously given a double promotion.

10.79

When head-on ramming attacks seemed ineffective, navy pilots, acting on their own initiative, would strike at the huge
enemy plane by shearing off its rudder with their own propellers.
Despite the fantastic difficulty of approaching the rudder at high
speed while avoiding the enemy's gunfire and propellers, this
"shearing" method enabled a number of Japanese pilots to down
enemy bombers in midair.

Suicidal crash-attacks on American ships date back to the
Battle of Santa Cruz Islands in September 1942 when the commander of a squadron of Japanese bombers deliberately dived at
the stack of the aircraft carrier *Hornet* and plunged onto the flight
deck where his two bombs exploded; the *Hornet* sank some hours
later, though this was probably the result of a torpedo attack

10.80

rather than of the suicide plane. The first planned assault of this
type did not occur until two years later (12th September 1944)
when a group of army pilots decided on their own that they
would crash their planes into American carriers near Negros
Island. A pair of fighters armed with two-hundred-pound bombs
took off before dawn, but they were never heard of again

and were presumably shot down before reaching their target.   *10.81*

It was not only pilots, or even military men, who responded with suicidal desperation to the agonizing course of events. In battle after battle, from the Aleutians to Guadalcanal, Japanese soldiers avoided surrender by participating in fierce suicide attacks, which the Americans described as "*banzai* charges." Probably the most fearsome scenes of all took place on the island of Saipan in July 1944. When organized military resistance became   *10.82* impossible, some three thousand Japanese soldiers, most of them armed with nothing but bayonets or sticks, charged into the concentrated machine-gun fire of the American marines and were mown down to the last man. At times the Japanese corpses were piled so high that the marines had to move their machine-gun emplacements into an open line of fire as new waves surged forward. A particularly macabre note was provided by a contingent of wounded soldiers, many of them swathed in bandages and leaning on the shoulders of their comrades, who staggered out of the hospitals and infirmaries to take part in the last suicide attack. Subsequently entire units of Japanese soldiers knelt down in rows to be decapitated by their commanding officers, who then in turn committed harakiri; hundreds of other soldiers shot themselves through the head or, more frequently, exploded themselves with hand-grenades. As the marines advanced through the blood-drenched island, they witnessed one mass suicide after another, culminating in the terrible last scene when hundreds of Japanese civilian inhabitants, including large numbers of women with children in their arms, hurled themselves off the cliffs or rushed out of caves by the sea and drowned themselves rather than risk the indignity of capture. The self-slaughter, probably the ghastliest in world history since the mass suicide of the Jews in Masada, continued for three days and nights; when finally Admiral Spruance was able to announce that the island was "secure," less than one thousand Japanese survived from the original thirty-two thousand, and hardly a single soldier remained to be taken prisoner.   *10.83*

The cataclysm at Saipan led to the resignation as Prime Minister of General Tōjō, the single leader most directly responsible for having brought Japan to its present predicament. He was succeeded by another military man, General Koiso. A few months later the new Prime Minister publicly admitted, in one of the classic understatements of the war, that "military develop-

10.84

ments in the Pacific theatre are in a state which does not necessarily admit of optimism." In case this could be interpreted as
defeatism, however, he hastened to add that "the greatly extended supply lines of the enemy on all fronts are exposed to our
attacks and in this fact, I believe, is to be found our golden
opportunity to grasp victory. Now indeed is the time for us, the
one hundred million, to give vent to our flaming ardour, and
following in the footsteps of the valiant men of the Special Attack
Corps, demonstrate even more spirit of sure victory in the field

10.85

of production."

In response to the pressing military situation a number of
new weapons had rapidly been designed and put into production. Almost all depended on suicide tactics. Among the naval
craft were tiny launches with wooden hulls and ordinary motor-
car engines, which were given the grandiloquent name of
shinyō or "ocean shakers." Each was manned by a single young
officer, who sat in the stern and whose aim was to ram his craft
and its two tons of high explosive into an enemy ship. The first
mass attack by these Lilliputian vessels took place in January 1945
and was a total disaster, since the approaching craft were detected by radar and obliterated by American firepower like a
swarm of troublesome gnats. Altogether some six thousand of

10.86

these launches were built during the last phase of the war, and
they carried large numbers of seagoing kamikaze fighters to their
thunderous and useless deaths.

By far the most promising of the nautical kamikaze weapons
were the fifty-foot manned torpedoes known as Kaiten. Closely
corresponding to the flying cherry blossoms (Ōka), they travelled
on "mother submarines" in groups of four or six and were
released at a short distance from the target. The pilot would steer
with the help of a small periscope and try to crash his warhead
of three thousand pounds of TNT. The units operating the
Kaiten, whose name came from an old word meaning "to remedy
an unfavourable situation with a single blow," were greatly inspired by Vice Admiral Ōnishi's men in the Philippines. Though
there was provision for the pilot to eject himself before actually
striking his target, this safeguard was almost entirely theoretical
and the operator's chance of survival was similar to that of his

10.87

airborne counterpart.

The sailing of the mother submarines with their human
torpedoes was accompanied by much the same ceremony and

emotion as attended the departure of the airborn kamikaze
fighters from their bases. As the large submarines began to move
slowly towards the open sea, dozens of motorboats and launches,
decorated with patriotic banners, swarmed nearby to escort them
out of the harbour. The occupants of the smaller craft waved   *10.88*
Rising Sun flags and chanted the names of the Kaiten pilots one
by one in a last farewell; when they had gone through the heroic
list, they again started shouting out the names, and this strange
chorus continued until the submarines had glided out of sight.
Meanwhile the young officers who were squeezed in their torpedo cabins stuck their white-draped heads out of the hatches,
and as their names were called they bowed and waved their
swords in acknowledgement.

Once the mother submarines were underway and submerged, the Kaiten pilots spent their time with the regular crew,
studying navigational procedures and frequently offering to help
with routine tasks—offers that were almost invariably refused
since such work was deemed unworthy of "living gods." Shortly   *10.89*
before they approached the target area, the captain of the submarine would invite the torpedo pilots for a simple meal during
which he offered them the usual libations of *sake*. When the time
came to enter their torpedoes, the senior pilot would make a short
speech, thanking the captain for having brought them safely to
their destination and wishing him and his crew long life and
good luck.   *10.90*

On the night of 11th January 1945 the captain of a huge I-58,
one of a fleet of six Kaiten-bearing submarines which were navi-
gating at full speed above water, informed the suicide pilots that
they were approaching the American target ships off the island
of Guam. When they had finished their ceremonial last supper   *10.91*
and exchanged farewells, two of the pilots went up on deck and
ensconced themselves in their cigar-shaped coffins. Shortly after
eleven o'clock, the dark silhouette of Guam loomed in the distance, all hatches were battened down, and the submarine
plunged. At two o'clock in the morning the two remaining pilots
clambered up through a special passage, entered their Kaiten,
and completed preparations for attack. All watertight doors were
now closed, and the only remaining link between the pilots and
the mother submarine was a telephone line. As Kaiten No. 1 was
about to be launched at three o'clock, the pilot shouted his last
words into the telephone: "Long live the Emperor!" Then the

line was cut and there was complete silence. The remaining
Kaiten were released in rapid succession, while the mother submarine remained in deep water. Shortly afterwards the occupants heard a tremendous roar, and the captain immediately
ordered his ship to surface. They cruised about for several hours,
but saw no sign that any American vessel had been hit; evidently
10.92 one of the Kaiten had exploded "spontaneously." Nor could they
discover what had become of the three other torpedoes. After a
few hours of futile search, orders were given for the submarine
to head back to Japan. The doleful results of the combined operation were not known until several days later when it turned out
that the Kaiten pilots had all lost their lives without damaging a
single American ship; to make matters worse, one of the mother
submarines had been sunk on its way home, with all hands on
board.

Despite their variety and ingenuity, the maritime suicide
craft did "not necessarily admit of optimism," and although they
continued to be launched until the end, increasing effort was put
into aerial tactics, which on the whole seemed more promising.
Among the many bizarre types of aircraft designed exclusively
for suicide purposes only the Ōka "cherry blossoms" were ever
actually used in combat, but others were planned and even put
into construction. With almost all essential materials in short
supply (and sometimes nonexistent), economy was a prime consideration, and some of the contraptions thrown together for the
suicide candidates seem absurdly primitive. The Tsurugi
("Sword"), for instance, was a flimsy, wooden monoplane, loaded
with a thousand-pound bomb and so constructed that immediately after take-off the pilot could press a button and release the
undercarriage, which was now useless for his own purpose but
10.93 could be retrieved and attached to the next plane.

One type of aerial Special Attack unit, about which very
little is known, was organized towards the end of the war in
10.94 response to the expected American invasion of the home islands.
Small, single-mission craft, heavily loaded with high explosive,
would be catapulted from mountains and steered by their pilots
into nearby enemy ships which by that time would have forced
their way into the Inland Sea and other territorial waters. The
main training was on top of Mount Hiei, the Buddhist sanctuary
near Kyoto. This incongruous site was cleared of almost all its
priestly inhabitants, and the monsteries and cells converted into

a headquarters for suicide pilots. Since hostilities ended without the expected invasion, none of the young men had a chance to put their strange expertise into practice.

In March 1945, as the war entered its last phase, suicide tactics and psychology lost their "special" character and were accepted as the principal Japanese method of defence. In accordance with Vice Admiral Ōnishi's prediction, the kamikaze approach, which had at first been associated mainly with the Imperial Navy, now became central for all the armed forces; and, as defeat followed defeat in conventional engagements, nearly every remaining unit in the Pacific adopted kamikaze tactics of one kind or another. It was specifically after the invasion of Okinawa that Japanese military operations took on this broadly suicidal aspect. The fortress of Okinawa now appeared to be the home islands only protection from invasion, and its defence was the key to whether Japan would survive as an independent nation. When the Americans finally launched their attack on 1st April, they encountered surprisingly little conventional resistance; instead imperial forces—land, sea, and air—depended overwhelmingly on suicide methods, so that Okinawa, Japan's last important stand in the war, became virtually synonymous with kamikaze. The dominant emblem was Masashige's chrysanthemum crest.

In earlier months the Imperial Army, perhaps owing to its traditional rivalry with the navy, had looked askance at organized kamikaze operations, but now they made haste to adopt them. Special Attack groups were formed by the army air force in March and first used in the defence of Okinawa. Most dramatic were the suicide attacks by which the infantry tried to resist the American advance. Thousands of soldiers became "living grenades" and, totally oblivious of any instinct for self-preservation, hurled themselves against the enemy. When finally it was clear that no amount of determination or self-sacrifice could prevent the American success, the defenders obliterated themselves with guns and hand-grenades rather than risk capture. On one memorable occasion, shortly after the fall of the capital, a Japanese delegation requested that the Americans hold their fire and give the officers time to commit suicide according to traditional ritual. The last of the many thousands of suicides on Okinawa were those of the two commanding generals, Ushijima and Chō, whose harakiri on 22nd June brought the long battle to its symbolic

10.95

10.96

close. The stronghold was conquered and its defenders annihilated, but they had never deigned to surrender.

As part of the *Kikusui* strategy for saving Okinawa, the Imperial Navy decided early in April to send the last of its important ships to attack enemy task forces. Included in this operation
was the mightiest of Japan's battleships, the *Yamato*, the pride
and hope of the Imperial Navy. There was never any doubt about
the suicidal nature of the mission. Thus Rear Admiral Komura,
the captain of one of the participating cruisers, informed his crew
that they and other ships of the Second Fleet were now proceeding towards Okinawa without any aerial cover and without even
sufficient fuel for the return journey. "In short," he pointed out,
"we are involved in a *shimpū* (kamikaze) mission, but unlike those
carried out by our airforce it has not the slightest chance of
destroying an important target. I have taken the liberty of telling
Admiral Kusaka [Chief of Staff of the Combined Fleet] that this
10.97   is a suicide mission pure and simple. . . ."

The operation ended in a holocaust. Every single important
ship was sunk, including the *Yamato*, which went down with its
captain, Admiral Itō, and almost all hands on board. In this most
momentous Battle of Bonomisaki, which virtually destroyed
what was left of the Imperial Navy, the Americans lost a total of
twelve men. The final sortie of the Imperial Navy was not only
suicidal (as Rear Admiral Komura had predicted) but, from any
10.98   practical point of view, utterly useless.

Until the very end of the war, pilots, both navy and army,
continued individual suicide attacks against American bombers.
The first devastating air raids on Tokyo and other centres of
population, which had started at the end of November 1944 after
the fall of Saipan, inspired Japanese aviators with renewed determination. As the mammoth B-29s, now virtually immune to conventional forms of interception, roared imperturbably towards
their metropolitan targets, the small Japanese planes tried to
down them by ramming, shearing, and other improvised tactics;
but it was rare indeed that they were able to delay, let alone
destroy, the attackers. More hopeful were the combined kamikaze attacks launched from Kyushu as part of the all-out struggle
for Okinawa. The first major offensive of this kind took place on
6th April with several hundred suicide planes from both the navy
10.99   and the army, and in the following weeks the High Command
ordered further vast *Kikusui* attacks. As aircraft and fuel dwin-

dled, the scale of kamikaze operations had to be reduced; but suicide attacks, which during Japan's death throes had become the principal manifestation of the country's will to resist, were never abandoned. With the termination of kamikaze operations all active fighting in the Pacific area came to an end.

Aircraft became so scarce during the last months of the war that the most rickety flying-machines were being patched up and despatched on suicide attacks, yet there was never any shortage of pilots to fly them. Even at this late point no one was ever ordered or forced into a kamikaze operation against his will. Not only would such compulsion have been pointless (it is hard to imagine anyone less effective than a reluctant suicide pilot), but it was unnecessary since in practice the imperial forces never experienced the slightest difficulty in recruiting kamikaze fighters and until the very end of the war had at least twice as many volunteers as available planes. Who were these men that made it possible to carry out the multifarious suicide operations? For outsiders perhaps the most remarkable thing about them is their youth. Few were over twenty-six years old, and even the unit commanders were sometimes in their early twenties. This was by no means fortuitous. Since the actual suicide missions required relatively little technical training, it was obviously practical to assign young men to the attacks and keep the older, more experienced pilots to train future candidates and to fly the escort planes, which demanded far greater skill. No less important were   10.100
the psychological reasons. From the outset of suicide operations in the Philippines, Vice Admiral Ōnishi had insisted, "If Japan is to be saved, it is up to these young men—men of thirty and younger. It is they with their self-sacrificing spirits and deeds who may be able [to rescue our country]." Most of the men   10.101
chosen for the *shimpū* and other Special Attack operations were between twenty and twenty-five.

The typical kamikaze fighter was a university student whose education had been interrupted when military deferment came to an end and who subsequently joined one of the Special Attack units. It is significant that far more of them had been students of the humanities and law than of engineering, science, and other more "practical" subjects. Very few had any military background whatsoever and, though they threw themselves wholeheartedly into their intensive training, many of them ex-

perienced moments of nostalgia for their studies, to which they now had scant chance of ever returning. Thus during his months in training camp, and even when he left on what he believed would be his last flight, Lieutenant Nagatsuka clung to his two thumbworn volumes of George Sand's *Maître sonneurs*, which
10.102   served to evoke a gentler past. Owing to their "bookishness" and their relatively free, unmilitary approach, the kamikaze candidates were frequently resented by professional soldiers, especially NCOs, who knew that these young, inexperienced ex-students would soon become officers and godlike heroes while they themselves lingered in the ranks.

Though one must obviously avoid generalizing about personality types when thousands of individuals are involved, most material about members of the kamikaze units shows that they were far from being the fierce, superstitious, jingoistic fanatics that foreigners have usually imagined. From all available records, diaries, letters, and photographs it appears that the principal type was quiet, serious, and above average in both culture and sensibility; Japanese descriptions of them frequently include the word *reisei*, which means "serene" or, in the best modern sense,
10.103   "cool."

Were these kamikaze fighters in fact volunteers, or had they (as most non-Japanese tend to imagine) been somehow dragooned or "brainwashed" into joining the suicide squads? No simple answer is possible, but there seems little doubt that, at least during the early stage of kamikaze operations in the Philippines and Taiwan, the pilots were all volunteers in the full meaning of
10.104   the word. Though there must have been many a hesitant young man who succumbed to the psychological pressure exerted by his fellow pilots and by the febrile wartime atmosphere, they were certainly never coerced by recruitment boards or superior officers. On the contrary, it often happened that young men who feared they might *not* be accepted for suicide duties wrote earnest requests and even signed them in their own blood according to
10.105   ancient tradition.

As army and navy units increasingly came to adopt kamikaze methods, existing members of these units would be given the choice of continuing "conventional" operations or of joining in the new suicide enterprises. On these occasions the men were not subject to any formal pressure to volunteer, and there appears to have been no discrimination against those who declined the honour. Thus in a training centre for torpedo-boats near Shimonoseki the director summoned four hundred recruits to inform them of new types of naval suicide warfare that were being planned in late October 1944:

10.106

In this particular matter I have no orders to give you. . . . You are [in this school] to be trained for orthodox torpedo-boat operations and these new tactics are so different from your specialty that I cannot possibly oblige you to participate. You may opt for the exploding launches [shinyō] or for the frogman operation [fukuryū], or again you may continue with conventional torpedo-boats. You must make this choice in all freedom, and I promise that no influence or pressure will be exerted on those men whose conscience prevents them from subscribing to the new forms of attack. You will come one by one into my office to let me know your decision, and I give you my word that I shall put no question to you nor ask for any sort of explanation.

From early afternoon until four o'clock on the following morning the young men visited his office in turn to give their answers. Half of the students selected cerain death, one hundred and fifty choosing the exploding launches and fifty deciding to become suicide-frogmen; and this provided more than enough manpower for the two ill-fated operations.

It is true that as aerial kamikaze attacks grew in scale, the somewhat informal system of spontaneous volunteering initiated in the Philippines was no longer adequate, and from about the time of the Battle of Okinawa men were increasingly "requested" to join the suicide units. Captain Nakajima describes the effect of this new form of "volunteering":

Many of the new arrivals seemed at first not only to lack enthusiasm, but, indeed, to be disturbed by their situation. With some this condition lasted only a few hours, with others for several days. It was a period of melancholy that passed with time and eventually gave way to a spiritual awakening. Then, like an attainment of wisdom, care vanished and tranquility of spirit appeared as life came to terms with death, mortality with immortality.

An example of the achievement of this spiritual calm was seen in the case of [sublieutenant] Kuno, who was extremely perturbed upon arrival at the base. Then suddenly, after several days of sulking about, he came with jaunty step and a spark in his eye, asking permission to divest his plane of all unneeded equipment, saying that it was inconsiderate to homeland workers to take non-essentials along on a kamikaze mission.

10.107

In the army, where Special Attack units started far later than in the navy, there was a greater sense of urgency about finding the proper pilots, and more overt pressure was probably exerted *10.108* to obtain candidates. Yet even here the principle of voluntary enlistment was never abandoned. Lieutenant Nagatsuka describes the scene on the night of 31st March 1945, when he and his two dozen fellow pilots were summoned to the quarters of their commanding officer:

He looked at each man in turn, and his usually gentle eyes seemed to pierce through us. "As you know," he finally said in a solemn voice, "our army lacks pilots, fuel, planes, ammunition—in fact everything. We are therefore in a deadlock, and only one method remains for us: to crash into aircraft carriers, as so many of your comrades have done in the past. Two hours ago our unit received orders to form a Special Attack corps. I am now obliged to ask you to. . . ." He hesitated before continuing, "to volunteer for this mission. But you are free to choose. You have twenty-four hours to think it over, and will give me your reply before 8 P.M. *10.109* tomorrow. Each of you will come separately to my office."

What most struck Nagatsuka at the moment was that his commanding officer had used the word "ask"; for, as he points out, "in the army a superior always *ordered*, never *requested.*" On the following morning, when Nagatsuka was in the canteen eating breakfast with his companions, one of them blurted out, "We're all of us ready to accept the mission, aren't we? So let's go at once and give him our answer!" The men all nodded in agreement, but one of them lightheartedly suggested that they might at least *10.110* finish their meal.

What influenced large numbers of serious, well-educated young men to make such a dramatic sacrifice of their lives? Certain general ideas run through the collections of letters, diaries, and poems that constitute our primary source for studying the *10.111* kamikaze personality; and, though there are many individual variations and exceptions, these themes are important for understanding the Japanese heroic tradition as it has survived into our century.

Hatred for the enemy and a desire to avenge dead comrades —motives so often adduced to explain (or condone) the soldier's fury in battle—do not appear to have dominated the psychology of kamikaze fighters. Often they mention their duty to protect

Japan's sacred soil from foreign pollution and to offer their lives in defense of their families. Yet this never takes the form of visceral loathing for enemy soldiers or of racial antagonism against Westerners. Rather, it expresses a keen sense of obligation to repay the favours bestowed on them since birth. Such recognition of a debt of gratitude *(on)* and the determination to requite it with whatever sacrifice may seem necessary are basic to the Japanese moral sense and for many centuries have been a powerful inspiration in both peacetime and battle. During the Pacific war the *on* motivation was certainly not peculiar to kamikaze fighters, but it seems to have inspired them in an especially intense form, and the deliberate totality of their self-sacrifice was a measure of their gratitude.

They were grateful, first of all, to Japan, the country of their birth, and to the Emperor who embodied its unique "national polity" *(kokutai)* and virtues. In description after description of suicide attacks we read that the pilot's last words refer to the Emperor, who, despite his somewhat lacklustre personality, was the supreme father figure in the Japanese nation-family. The following is an extract from the last letter that Lieutenant Yamaguchi Teruo of the Twelfth Air Flotilla wrote to his father just before his suicide mission:

. . . It is of no avail to express it now, but in my twenty-three years of life I have worked out my own philosophy.

It leaves a bad taste in my mouth when I think of the deceits being played on innocent citizens by some of our wily politicians. But I am willing to take orders from the high command, and even from the politicians, because I believe in the polity of Japan.

The Japanese way of life is indeed beautiful, and I am proud of it, as I am of Japanese history and mythology which reflect the purity of our ancestors and their belief in the past. . . . That way of life is the product of all the best things which our ancestors have handed down to us. And the living embodiment of all wonderful things out of our past is the Imperial Family which, too, is the crystallization of the splendour and beauty of Japan and its people. It is an honour to be able to give my life in defence of these beautiful and lofty things.   *10.112*

More frequently the pilot's sense of obligation was focused on his family, specifically on the favours received from his own parents who had given him the gift of life and twenty years of upbringing, rather than on abstractions like king and country.   *10.113*

Many letters express regrets at not having been able to repay the parents' kindness and apologies for leaving the world before them. This hasty last letter by Lieutenant Nomoto Jun of the White Heron Special Attack Unit was actually dictated from the plane just before his take-off:

Dearest Parents:
   Please excuse my dictating these last words to my friend. There is no longer time for me to write more to you.
   There is nothing special that I can say, but I want you to know that I am in the best of health at this last moment. It is my great honour to have been selected for this duty. The first planes of my group are already in the air. These words are being written by my friend as he rests the paper on the fuselage of my plane. There are no feelings of remorse or sadness here. My outlook is unchanged. I will perform my duty calmly.
   Words cannot express my gratitude to you. It is my hope that this last act of striking a blow at the enemy will serve to repay in small measure the wonderful things you have done for me. . . .
   . . . I shall be satisfied if my final effort serves as recompense for the heritage our ancestors bequeathed.

                                                              Farewell!
10.114   Jun

   Most often the gratitude of the kamikaze fighter is directed equally to family and Emperor, and his death appears as a sort of combined repayment for all the favours he has received in his life from both personal and impersonal sources. In a typical diary entry Lieutenant Adachi of the True Spirit Special Attack Unit writes that it is because of his parents' love that he can now give his life for the Emperor, and he rejoices that in this last attack he
10.115 will be able to fight *together with* his father and mother. Similarly Lieutenant Kaijitsu Susumu of the Seven Lives Unit writes to his family:

   Words cannot express my gratitude to the loving parents who reared and tended me to manhood that I might in some small manner recipro-
10.116 cate the grace which His Imperial Majesty has bestowed upon us.

   The last letter of Matsuo Isao of the Heroes' Special Attack Unit also represents his death as a combined repayment to his own family and to the larger, national family, and he even has some additional *on* to spare for his superior officers:

Dear Parents:

Please congratulate me. I have been given a splendid opportunity to die. This is my last day. This destiny of our homeland hinges on the decisive battle in the seas to the south where I shall fall like a blossom from a radiant cherry tree. . . .

How I appreciate this chance to die like a man! I am grateful from the depths of my heart to the parents who have reared me with their constant prayers and tender love. And I am grateful as well to my squadron leader and superior officers who have looked after me as if I were their own son and given me such careful training.

Thank you, my parents, for the twenty-three years during which you have cared for me and inspired me. I hope that my present deed will in some small way repay what you have done for me. . . .   *10.117*

Another recurrent theme in the writings of the kamikaze fighters is "sincerity" (*makoto* or *shisei*), that traditional concept which looms so large in the history of Japanese heroes. Nagatsuka reports the following typical conversation between two army air force officers that he overheard shortly before volunteering for Special Attack duties. Captain Sanaka, the leader of the Second Aerial Attack Group, was trying to persuade his commanding officer that, since Ki-45 Kai attack planes were now in short supply, the army should use the smaller Ki-27s to intercept American B-29 bombers:

"But how can a Ki-27 possibly take on a plane with the speed and armament of a B-29?"

"I beg your pardon, Sir," replied Captain Sanaka . . . "but under the circumstances I think we are obliged to use every available plane in our base to destroy the greatest possible number of American bombers."

"And what about our pilots? They still aren't properly trained."

"What counts, Sir, is neither the skill of our pilots nor the quality of our planes but the spirit and morale of the fighters. Everything depends on that."   *10.118*

Kamikaze fighters were repeatedly assured that suicide tactics were the only remaining way to stave off defeat and preserve Japan from catastrophe. My reading of their letters and diaries, however, and my conversations with survivors suggest that few of the actual participants believed that at this late stage their attacks would materially alter the outcome of the war. Especially after the disaster at Okinawa most members of the suicide units, and certainly the more clear-headed among them, seem to have realized that, while their forthcoming sacrifice was not without honour, it was almost certainly without hope. Thus Lieutenant Nagatsuka recalls his last rambling thoughts as he sat in the cabin of his Ki-27 fighter:

> Do I really believe that suicide attacks are effective? Aren't they, in fact, a foolhardy enterprise for flyers like us without any escort planes or any armaments of our own? . . . Is it true that self-sacrifice is the only thing that gives meaning to death? To this question the warrior is obliged to reply "yes," while knowing full well that his suicide mission has no
> *10.119* meaning.

Such doubts, however, never impaired their morale; nor did the countless stories of comrades who had exploded themselves and their craft without any practical effect lead to discouragement or despair. The repeated setbacks seem, if anything, to have added to the verve of the young volunteers. This is the spirit of the popular kamikaze song:

> Never think of winning!
> Thoughts of victory will only bring defeat.
> *10.120* When we lose, let us press forward, ever forward!

While sincerity takes precedence over the question of victory or defeat, this does not mean that the volunteer regards his efforts as ultimately pointless. The sacrifice may not save Japan from losing the war, but it can lead to some form of spiritual rebirth. A student of literature from Kyoto University, whose plane was shot down one moonlit night only a fortnight before the end of the war, wrote in his last poem:

> Cease your optimism,
> Open your eyes,
> People of Japan!
> Japan is bound to be defeated.
> It is then that we Japanese
> Must infuse into this land
> A new life.
> A new road to restoration
> *10.121* Will be ours to carve.

The idea that a sacrificial act which produces no practical effect on the war may nevertheless have precious spiritual repercussions is discussed in one of the last entries of the diary by Sublieutenant Okabe, the author of the cherry blossom poem quoted at the head of this chapter:

> 22nd February 1945
> I shall die watching the pathetic struggle of our nation. My life will gallop in the next few weeks as my youth and life draw to a close.
> . . . The sortie has been scheduled for the next ten days.
> I am a human being and hope to be neither saint nor scoundrel, hero nor fool—just a human being. As one who has spent his life in wistful longing and searching, I die resignedly in the hope that my life will serve as a "human document."
> The world in which I lived was too full of discord. As a community of rational human beings it should be better composed. Lacking a single great conductor, everyone lets loose with his own sound, creating dissonance where there should be melody and harmony.
> We shall serve the nation gladly in its present painful struggle. We shall plunge into enemy ships cherishing the conviction that Japan has been and will be a place where only lovely homes, brave women, and beautiful friendships are allowed to exist. *10.122*

Material victory in the war, far from being the primary goal, may even act as an impediment to spiritual regeneration: "If, by some strange chance," writes Sublieutenant Okabe, "Japan should suddenly win this war it would be a fatal misfortune for the future of the nation. It will be better for our nation and people if they are tempered through real ordeals which will serve to strengthen." The same theme is elaborated by an officer in a *10.123* Kaiten (suicide-torpedo) unit who had recently amazed a young volunteer by telling him he expected Japan to be defeated:

> I couldn't believe my ears, an officer talking like this! "What was that you said, Sir?" I asked.
> "Japan will be defeated, Yokota," he told me.
> I was shocked. I didn't know what else to say at the moment, for I had never heard anyone in the military discuss this possibility before, so I came back with, "Then why do you volunteer to die?"
> "A man must do what he can for his country," was his simple answer. His death meant nothing, he added. "Japan will be defeated, of that I am sure. But she will be born again, and become a greater nation

than ever before." [He] went on to explain that a nation had to suffer and be purified every few generations, so that it could become stronger by having its impurities removed. Our land was now being bathed in fire, he said, and she would emerge all the better because of it.

10.124

Ideas and sentiments that had germinated in the country's distant past and become fixed during the long centuries of military hegemony were still alive and inspiring in 1944, and they recur again and again in the conversations and writings of the kamikaze fighters. Thus when Lieutenant Nagatsuka ventures to express some doubts concerning a proposal by one of his colleagues that they should ram their Ki-27 fighters into American B-29s despite the minimal chances of success, the young man evokes the samurai principle of honour:

> You attach too much importance to life. Imagine that the whole world were to disappear except for you. Would you really want to go on living? If a human life has any important meaning, it is because of some relationship with other human beings. From this springs the principle of honour. Life rests on this idea, as exemplified by the conduct of our ancient samurai. That is the essence of Bushidō [the Way of the Warrior]. . . . If we cling to our own lives, we actually lose self-esteem.
> There are two types of existence in this world: that of animals, who simply obey their instincts, and that of men, who consciously devote their lives to serving something outside themselves. . . . If man merely *existed*, what a burden it would be! It is not reason that can tell us the meaning of life or of death. . . .

10.125

Nagatsuka's companion, like many of the young kamikaze volunteers, expresses himself in a somewhat disjointed, naïve fashion; but his general attitude is derived from a coherent body of thought which had been explicated in manuals of samurai philosophy and which played an important part in "moral training" (*shūshin*) during the modern nationalist period. Among historical figures the man most revered by kamikaze pilots was the loyalist warrior, Kusunoki Masashige, who committed harakiri in 1336 after the predictable failure of his last-ditch battle for Emperor Godaigo. In their letters, diaries, and conversation Masashige is repeatedly cited by kamikaze pilots as a model of honourable conduct, and the defiant statement about "seven lives" was quoted by them again and again. "I shall be the Emperor's shield," wrote Matsuo Isao on 28th October 1944, "and die

10.126

10.127

cleanly with my squadron leader and other friends. I wish that
I could be reborn seven times, each time to smite the enemy." *10.128*
The following jovial conversation during a pilots' gathering at
the Cebu kamikaze base is reported by Commander Nakajima:

One pilot, who was getting his share of the drinks, surprised me when
he walked up and said, "When can I make a special attack? Why don't
you let me go soon?"

This inspired another to join in, "I've been a member of the Special
Attack Corps from the very first, and yet later volunteers have already
gone. How long must I wait?"

Momentarily I was at a loss to answer these sudden questions, until
an idea suddenly came to me. "Do you recall how the most loyal of all
Japan's great warriors, Kusunoki Masashige, on the eve of his last battle
summoned his warrior son and told him to go home to his mother?
Sooner or later the time comes for each of us. Special attacks of one kind
or another will continue until peace comes to the whole world. You
fellows should think of yourselves as being among the first of many, and
not complain that you are a couple of days later than someone else."

They nodded, and the first man spoke again. "Yes, I understand
what you mean, but I think it would be better to be the *elder* Kusunoki." *10.129*

The lone kamikaze pilot, squeezed into the cockpit of his
Ōka bomb or his Kaiten torpedo and hurling himself against
overwhelming enemy forces, belongs to a familiar Japanese tradition in which the embattled hero is propelled by confidence in
his own sincerity and by the knowledge that his cause, however
hopeless, is a true one. Of his own free will he has assumed a task
"beyond the limits of human might," a task that common sense
can only judge as being absurd, even insane. *Hagakure*, the most
influential of all samurai treatises ever written, combines the
characters for "dying" *(shini)* and "going mad" *(kurui)* into a *10.130*
single word, *shinigurui* ("death-frenzy"), and enjoins this ardent
state on the warrior; for he cannot hope to accomplish any great
deed until he has first "surmounted himself" by discarding the
cautious dictates of reason and self-interest. The single-minded, *10.131*
solitary aspect of the kamikaze warrior emerges in the writings
of Miyanoo Bunbei, a young poet who joined an aerial Special
Attack unit and exploded near Okinawa in April 1945. In a collection, edited posthumously with the title of "A Single Star," Miyanoo foresees his death, and though he belongs to a totally different tradition from that of Yeats's airman whom

> A lonely impulse of delight
> *10.132*   Drove to this tumult in the clouds

He too is free of rancour ("Those that I fight I do not hate") and
can observe his own state of mind with a similar lyricism and
purity of vision: "When I think of it," he writes in an introduc-
tory note to the poems, "a great chill comes over me. . . . [Soon]
I shall vanish for good. I shall quietly become nonexistent, like
10.133   a nameless star that fades away at dawn."

The kamikaze volunteers were conditioned by the Japanese
metaphysics of death as expressed both in traditional samurai
philosophy and in religion. Since mediaeval times the samurai
10.134   had been taught that he must "hold life lighter than a feather"
and must subordinate all desire for personal survival to "the just
cause" *(gi)*. During the short training period allowed the kamikaze pilots there was little time for indoctrination. Nor was there
much need for it, since already on joining their suicide units they
were imbued with an ideology of death that belonged to the ethos
of the Japanese warrior. During their months in the barracks this
ideology was dramatized by the fact that *dying* was constantly
before their eyes. In *Hagakure* they were eloquently told how to
confront this daunting prospect:

One should expect death daily so that, when the time comes, one can die
in peace. Calamity, when it occurs, is not so dreadful as was feared. It
is foolish to torment oneself beforehand with vain imaginings. . . .
Tranquillize your mind every morning, and imagine the moment when
you may be torn and mangled by arrows, guns, lances, and swords,
swept away by great waves, thrown into a fire, struck down by thunder-
bolts, shaken by earthquakes, falling from a precipice, dying of disease,
or dead from an unexpected accident: die every morning in your mind,
10.135   and then you will not fear death!

Death for these youthful volunteers would not come from
the outside by chance or ill luck, but from within by a deliberate
act of their own volition. Ever since the shadowy times of the
prototypic Yorozu, the warrior was always ready to cut off his
own life rather than risk dishonour to himself, his family, or his
overlord. Suicide, far from being the "coward's way out," was the
only honourable course of action for the hero in extremity; it was
no impulsive gesture of despair but a proud act that had been
carefully pondered and prepared.

Buddhism, with its stress on non-ego and self-denial *(muga)*, teaches that we can escape the sufferings inherent in the human condition only by surmounting the illusion of the self and its desires, above all the desire to survive. This reinforced the sacrificial aspects of the samurai ethos and helped the warrior accept physical hardships and eventual destruction. For many of the suicide recruits an initial period of unease was followed by a sort of Buddhist *satori* or spiritual awakening as they came to terms with their impending deaths. The kamikaze volunteers, unlike pilots in most other countries, were given no special privileges or luxuries, and the material conditions in the barracks until the very day of their take-off were as austere as those of a Buddhist ascetic. Yet their letters and diaries never contain a hint of dissatisfaction or any inkling that they might have appreciated some extra food or comfort during their last months. These Spartan living conditions, far from being a painful deprivation, helped them attain that "tranquillity without inner resistance"   10.136 which comes from denying the ego and its desires, and thus prepared them for the final self-effacement on the day of their last sortie.

While religious influences were important in the psychological preparation of the kamikaze fighters, this certainly does not mean, as non-Japanese readers might suppose, that most of them were comforted (let alone motivated) by any idea that they would survive after death and reap the benefit of their sacrifice in some paradise or pantheon. Buddhism not only posited a goal of total annihilation but, being an eminently pacifist doctrine, was hardly going to offer rewards to men who had died while deliberately inflicting violence on themselves and others. The state Shinto religion, it is true, promised that those who had given their lives in the service of the Emperor would return as divine spirits to be worshipped in Yasukuni Shrine; yet Shintoism had only the most nebulous concept of an afterlife and from its very origins shunned metaphysical speculations. As recent university students, most of the kamikaze pilots whose writings have been preserved tended to be somewhat dubious about the popular forms of religion that assured the believer of happiness in some future existence. Even when faced with imminent death, few of these young men appear to have accepted the consolation of a possible afterlife. Typical is Nagatsuka's conversation with his friend, a fellow pilot called Fujisaki, whom he visited two hours before leaving for his attack. Fujisaki smilingly asked him whether he believed in an afterlife.

"No," I replied, "I suppose I am something of an atheist."

"I expect you're right," said Fujisaki. "After we die there's only emptiness. . . . Everything comes to an end for us, and even our spirits disappear without a trace. Yes," he continued cheerfully, "for more than twenty years we have been receiving joy and affection from our families. Surely that's enough. I don't care in the slightest what happens to me after death. In any case it's utterly unthinkable that we'll meet in the beyond, not even through the medium of our spirits. . . . So now I'm saying goodbye to you forever."

10.137

Despite all the nationalist propaganda about the spirits of the glorious war heroes being venerated in Yasukuni Shrine, the prevailing attitude among the actual kamikaze pilots appears to have been a somewhat lighthearted scepticism. During the gathering at Cebu airbase one of the men asked Commander Nakajima whether there was any discrimination at Yasukuni according to military rank:

"There is no discrimination in Yasukuni Shrine," I replied. "Precedence is determined entirely by time of arrival."

"I will outrank you then, Commander, because you will have to send out many more pilots before you can go yourself."

"Look, what shall we do with the Commander when he reports in at Yasukuni?"

"Let's make him the mess sergeant!" This was greeted with roars of approving laughter.

"Can't you do better by me than that?" I pleaded.

"Well then, perhaps mess officer," the last speaker conceded, and they all roared again.

10.138

Being human, many of the kamikaze fighters must have had moments of doubt, even terror, about their forthcoming destruction; but a peculiarly Japanese combination of traditions and influences helped them surmount these natural impulses. On the day before leaving for his sortie, Lieutenant Nagatsuka lives through a dark night of the soul as he contemplates his annihilation; but he is buoyed up by a belief in the positive meaning of his deed:

10.139

The rapid approach of my death made me try to find some justification for it by denying the value of human life. I knew what I was doing. Besides, my death was entirely different from one caused, for example, by an illness. I [now] owed it to myself . . . to remain fully lucid so that I might be in control of my actions until the very last moment; a dying patient, on the other hand, has to await death passively in his bed. My own death had a meaning, a value. As time passed, I was amazed to discover that these reflexions had restored my calm.   *10.140*

Despite the highly charged nature of their predicament, the suicide pilots never (except in certain special situations that will shortly be described) indulged in displays of hysteria or dramatics, and it was widely recognized that from the inception of kamikaze units in 1944 theirs was the highest morale in the Japanese armed forces. Even pilots who had the minimum experience were full of enthusiasm as they took off on their one-way missions; and this joyful approach made up for their lack of training. In the descriptions of daily life in the kamikaze bases and in the personal writings of the pilots there is rarely a trace of gloom or pessimism; and on the day of their departure, as they prepared to soar up like Icarus on his flight towards the sun, their usual mood was one of eagerness and exaltation that seems to have voided all instinct for survival. In a typical photograph of a kamikaze fighter tightening the Rising Sun *hachimaki* round the helmet of a fellow pilot who is about to sortie, the young man is smiling with relaxed self-possession as if he and his companion were getting ready for a wedding ceremony or a graduation. Lieutenant Suga Yoshimune of the True Spirit Special Attack Unit describes his pride at being given a chance to prove his sincerity by defending Japan with this "final trump card." "Life has now become a true pleasure for me," he says. "How genial is the springtime for us who belong to a [Special Attack] unit— so much warmer and softer than in the sad world outside!" A Kaiten suicide-torpedo pilot describes his state of mind as he prepared for his final sortie: *10.141 10.142 10.143*

On April 20 [1945], the day of departure for the Tembu Group, the six of us were like new men, all filled with confidence. As each held a cherry blossom branch in his hands and posed for our souvenir photo, I looked at my bit of blossom tree with the blooms still on it and say to myself, "How fortunate, Yokota Yutaka, that you were born a boy! A woman

could have no adventure such as this!" We were bubbling with eagerness. Shinkai and I swore to each other we would sink the largest ships
we could find. I thought of my age, nineteen, and of the saying, "To die
while people still lament your death; to die while you are pure and fresh;
this is truly Bushidō." Yes, I was following the way of the samurai. My
eyes were shining as I stepped on board I–47 once more. I remembered
with pleasure Ensign Anzai Nobuo's quoting from a poem and telling
me I would "fall as purely as the cherry blossom" I now held. More
banzai cheers sent us on our way. My mind was full of what Lieutenant
Fujimura Sadao, one of the Tsuchiura instructors, had said so many
times to me: "Never shirk facing death. If in doubt whether to live or
die, it is always better to die. . . ." We stood atop our Kaiten again,
waving swords until the trailing, well-wishing boats turned back. Then
I climbed down inside the Kaiten and placed the ashes of Yazaki and the
10.144   cherry blossom branch near the seat.

Often in their farewell letters, kamikaze pilots try to comfort
their parents by transmitting some of this calm joy. Lieutenant
Hayashi tells his parents to continue living happily after he is
dead. "Mother," he writes, "I do not want you to grieve over my
death. I do not mind if you weep. Go ahead and weep. But please
realize that my death is for the best, and do not feel bitter about
10.145   it." When his sortie has been delayed for one day, he adds a
postscript describing a beautiful walk he took in the evening
between the nearby paddy fields, listening to the croak of the
frogs and lying down in a field of *rengesō* clover, which filled him
with memories of home. "The cherry blossoms have already
fallen. . . . It appears that we will go to make our attack tomorrow.
Thus the anniversary of my death will be 10th April. If you have
a service to commemorate me, I wish you to have a happy family
10.146   dinner." Matsuo Isao starts his last letter by asking his parents
to rejoice in his fate and hopes that they will smile when they
watch the newsreel film that has recently been taken of himself
and fifteen other members of the Heroes' Special Attack Unit.
He ends, like so many of the pilots, by praying that he will die
beautifully. "May our death be as sudden and clean as the shatter-
10.147   ing of crystal!"

One of the few times that tension among kamikaze volunteers came to the surface was when they realized that they had
not been included in a particular mission on which they had been
counting, or when by some peculiar circumstance they actually

survived a sortie and underwent the appalling anticlimax of returning safely to base. For commanding officers of kamikaze   *10.148*
units the process of selection must have been hard, at times
agonizing. Most of their men were determined to be sent out as
soon as possible, and the effusive gratitude of the few who had
been picked was often outweighed by the ill-concealed bitterness
of the others. This was not because the pilots wanted to get their   *10.149*
job over with, though such motives may sometimes have lurked
in the background, but because they had keyed themselves up to
their extraordinary task and feared that, if the kamikaze operations were called off or if hostilities suddenly ceased, they would
be permanently left behind after thousands of comrades had
accomplished their resolution to its end. A typical sense of "abandonment" was revealed by a subordinate when Vice Admiral
Ugaki, who had been in charge of kamikaze operations from
Kyushu, left for his own suicide sortie on the very last day of the
war. The senior officer of the Fifth Air Fleet staff, Captain
Miyazaki, had tried to dissuade Ugaki on the grounds that such
an attack was now inappropriate, but the Admiral was adamant
and told him to follow his orders. Shortly afterwards Ugaki went
to the airfield, carrying only his short samurai sword and a pair
of binoculars:

Captain Miyazaki had been standing by quietly and solemnly, but
finally, unable to restrain himself any longer, he stepped forward and
said, "Please take me with you, Admiral."
    Ugaki answered him sternly, "You have more than enough to at-
tend to here. You will remain."
    This refusal was too much for Miyazaki. He stopped in his tracks
and burst into tears, crying openly and unashamed as the others walked
past.   *10.150*

    From among the thousands who volunteered for suicide du-
ties of one kind or another only a handful lived through the war.
The reaction of these men to their bizarre fate throws further
light on kamikaze psychology. Among the survivors were members of the Katsura Unit of the Army Special Attack Force who
took off in twelve fixed-landing-gear fighters one May morning
in 1945. By this time most of the planes were rickety crates in a
hopeless state of disrepair. Only three of the fighters came any-
where near their targets; one by one the other nine were forced

to ditch or crash-land, and the pilots were waiting for replacement aircraft when the war ended in August. The seven men who had survived the attack gathered twenty-one years later in a temple near their old airfield. After a standard kamikaze "last meal" consisting of rice and dried cuttlefish, they exchanged cups of *sake* to toast the old heroic days. One of the survivors, now a middle-aged agricultural official, said that the reunion had inspired him with a "burning nostalgia for those days when I was so pure that I thought nothing of dying for the glory of my nation," and he wistfully expressed a desire to "meet his past."

The immediate reaction of kamikaze fighters when they realized that their missions had been abortive, or that they would never have a chance to undertake any mission at all, was usually a compound of crushing disappointment and self-disdain, which often took years to overcome; far from experiencing any pleasure at being alive, many of them did their best to escape the unexpected reprieve by killing themselves. Sakai Saburō, an ace flyer who took part in an attack on Iwo Jima, reports a scene one night when he stumbled over a pilot who had survived a suicide attack; the young man was hiding by the runway, in the darkness, and had to be picked up and marched to the office of their commander. When Watanabe Sei was informed, only two days before he was due to leave on his aerial suicide attack in Ulithi, that the war had ended and that he could soon return home safely, "I cried and felt hurt. I was deprived of death." Describing the reaction of his fellow volunteers, Watanabe informed a newspaper reporter, "We were shocked and stunned, and many cried. We had prepared so hard for our mission and now it was to be aborted." The termination of the war had, as he observed twenty-five years later, saved his life; but if he could be a kamikaze pilot again today, he would not hesitate.

The survival rate among the human torpedoes and "ocean shakers" was almost nil. An American naval officer, however, recalls his rescue of three kamikaze fighters whose suicide torpedo had developed engine trouble and drifted into the open ocean outside Manila Bay in January 1945. Much later the strange little craft was sighted by an American pilot, who reported its position to a nearby destroyer. The torpedo had become ineffective and, as the enemy ship approached, the Japanese tried to commit harakiri. They no longer had sufficient physical strength to carry out the act, however, and the American officer was able

10.151

10.152

10.153

10.154

to disarm the men and bring them aboard his destroyer, where he helped nurse them back to health and finally persuaded them not to take their lives. A similar story concerns a twenty-two-year-old navy pilot, Sublieutenant Aoki Yasunori, whose lumbering old plane hit the water as he tried to crash into an American destroyer off Okinawa in May 1945. Rescued against his will, he *10.155* spurned all offers of food and cigarettes. Since escape was impossible, Aoki realized that there was only one honourable solution and attempted suicide by biting his tongue and choking on the blood. When this proved ineffective, he tried to strangle himself with a strand of twisted string, but was interrupted by a guard. Now it became clear that death was determined to elude him and that he was fated to remain in this world. In several other cases *10.156* pilots who had miraculously survived their crash attacks begged their captors to kill them or to give them the possibility of suicide —requests which as far as is known were invariably refused.

It does not require any great effort of the imagination to understand these reactions by kamikaze survivors. After they had forsaken life and prepared themselves psychologically to follow their predecessors into annihilation, the idea that they had (both literally and figuratively) missed the boat must have been a disgraceful anticlimax, and the prospect of having to wait for another chance to make their "final" departure must often have seemed intolerable. Such reactions are common among people who, for whatever reason, have seriously tried to commit suicide and failed in the attempt; but for kamikaze fighters they were reinforced by samurai traditions and by their country's heroic ethos. The pilot who, having prepared himself for self-destruction and gone through the multifarious rituals of leave-taking, was then obliged to return to base without having found a target suffered from the most intense form of spiritual frustration, and it would not be surprising if many of them deliberately crashed their planes without ever approaching a target rather than undergo such agonizing bathos. One is familiar with the disaffection that can occur in everyday life when someone who has made his elaborate adieus unexpectedly returns—or, worse still, fails to leave. How infinitely greater must it have been among living gods in wartime Japan!

A painful account of such a return from beyond is provided by Lieutenant Nagatsuka (the only kamikaze survivor to have written about his experiences with any psychological detail)

when he describes his abortive attack against an American task
10.157   force on 29th June 1945. Heavy rain and fog had removed the
slightest possibility of sighting the warships, and the leader of the
attack unit decided that they should return to base while they
still had sufficient fuel, and await a more propitious day to repeat
their sortie. When Nagatsuka saw the signal to turn back, he was
filled with mixed emotions:

Beyond those clouds certain death had been awaiting me at every point;
it was those clouds that had stopped us from continuing our last flight.
Now I had been given a chance to go on living in this world a little
longer. Should I thank the sky, or curse it for having interrupted my
mission?

Perhaps he should pursue the attack alone, even though the other
planes followed their leader back to base. But that would be
insane: he could not possibly navigate through those heavy
clouds by himself. Yet what if he returned?

Would I have a chance to set out again? I knew very well that our base
had run out of fuel, and there was no telling when we would get more
supplies. . . . No, this was my first and last opportunity to attack. I had
left base with the firm intention of sacrificing my life. How ignominious
it would be to return like this!

A moment or so later he saw ahead of him that the second and
third planes in the formation were following the leader and bank-
ing for a turn. As if he had become an automaton, Nagatsuka felt
his left foot kick the rudder-bar while his right hand moved the
joystick. Heading back for the mainland, he was overcome with
further doubts:

How can I have done this? . . . Until I get another chance to sortie I shall
be suffering both from myself and from others. Since I decided to sacrifice my life, I should have gone all the way to the end. To plead that
I could not sight the American ships is merely an excuse. People will say
that I preferred humiliation to a heroic death. Shame on me!

Nagatsuka's fears about what awaited him at the base proved
more than justified. After making a safe landing, he and his
fellow pilots went to the commanding officer and reported what
had happened. They were in a state of shocked misery and their

anguish was soon increased when they learned that six other pilots in their attack unit had persevered despite the weather conditions and must by this time have plunged, uselessly but heroically, into the rough waters of the Japan Sea. Nagatsuka vividly evokes the condition of acedia that characterizes the rare and incongruous phenomenon which he had now become—the kamikaze survivor:

I experienced no real sense of having had a narrow escape. Still less did I feel the slightest joy on finding myself back at base. With an empty soul I followed the path that led to the underground barracks. I made no effort to avoid the puddles, but tramped right through them, vacant, distracted, totally unaware whether I was walking or reeling like a drunkard. The wet cornfields stretched out far into the distance. I saw their green tapestry without looking at it—that green which I had never expected to see again. Yesterday it had been friendly and familiar, but now it was almost hostile. Surely it was reproaching me for having failed in my mission. At this thought a great sadness filled my heart: the corn had the right to continue growing, at least until autumn, whereas my own existence was undeserved and provisional.

After this somewhat dispiriting stroll in the fields Nagatsuka returns to the barracks. Here he meets a group of volunteers who have not yet been assigned to a mission:

I saluted them without a word, and they silently returned my salute. Probably they could not decide whether to try and distract me from my state of confusion or to reproach me for my cowardice. I thought I could detect a look of compassion in their faces. . . .

To escape their presence he goes into the officers' hall.

It was a hall in name only; in actual fact it was more like a dingy cave. My sword, the envelope containing my Will—all was lying there on my cot. I had written, "The late Captain Nagatsuka." Now the piece of paper filled me with disgust, it defied me, it insulted me. In a rage I picked up the envelope and tore it into tiny pieces. Then I threw everything off my cot. No one dared say a word. Even Lieutenant Tanaka, who was usually such a chatterbox, stayed silent. We were all crushed by shame, tormented by remorse. Stretched out on my cot, I tried to doze off, but could not manage. My state of agitation gave way to a great physical and spiritual fatigue. *10.158*

Until now the main agony for Nagatsuka and his fellow survivors has been inner guilt; but worse is to come in the form of public humiliation. Shortly after lying down on his cot, he and the eleven other members of his attack unit are summoned before the commanding officer, who addresses them in a hollow voice:

"You men are the first pilots in the Special Attack corps of our squadron. Six members . . . pursued their mission to the end though they were not fortunate enough to sink any enemy ships. Clearly they were ready for death before they took off. But you—you were incapable of preparing yourselves. And so you have returned on the pretext of bad weather conditions. Contemptible cowards! . . . You never became real officers. You are still only students. . . . We have no more fuel and you've wasted the little we had. . . . Why couldn't you have died courageously?" His lips were trembling as he finished: "Shame on you! It is as if you had deserted in the face of the enemy. You have disgraced our squadron and demoralized my men. . . . I put you under arrest and order you to copy out His Majesty's sacred words until further notice."

10.159

When the commander strode out of the room, Lieutenant Uehara, an army officer who had risen from the ranks and who already resented the kamikaze pilots as unreliable upstarts, approached each man in turn and with a look of implacable hatred slapped him on the face.

After Nagatsuka had been copying the "sacred words" for several days, the weather began to clear, and his spirits rose at the thought that another sortie might now be possible. But he was rapidly disabused: on 8th July news reached the base that the American task force had moved away. "Soon [the ships] would be beyond our range, and other units would take over our responsibility for suicide attacks. I was in despair, for all my inner efforts to achieve a patriot's death had been shattered." From then until the end of the war—and even beyond—Nagatsuka and the other members of his suicide unit, were condemned to the slow agony of survival.

Since remotest antiquity there have been innumerable instances of men who knowingly sacrificed their lives in battle; yet as a rule there has always been at least a theoretical possibility that they might survive. Without that scintilla of hope, the sacrifice would be equivalent to premeditated suicide and therefore unacceptable in countries (like those of the "Christian" West) whose religions or mores condemn such a deed. In Japan, how- 10.160 ever, where suicide was integral to the warrior's way of life, there could be no scruples about acts in which soldiers not merely risked themselves in battle but opted for certain death.

Official suicide tactics were adumbrated in modern warfare when Admiral Tōgō ordered his "death-defying unit" (*kesshitai*) to blockade Port Arthur in 1905. Yet there was at least a *pro forma* attempt to provide a means of survival for the participants. As the 10.161 situation in the Pacific deteriorated, attacks involving deliberate self-destruction by *individual* Japanese military men became increasingly frequent; but it was not until Vice Admiral Ōnishi's arrival in the Philippines that suicide fighting was officially adopted as a strategy. His formation of kamikaze units was unprecedented, not only in Japan but in the entire history of human warfare.

During a last visit to his family, Lieutenant Nagatsuka tried to explain the rationale of kamikaze tactics: "Listen carefully!" he said. "You have nothing in your hand but a pebble, and you want to hit a tree. What is the best method? To throw the pebble, or to strike it against the tree yourself?" The trouble was that, by 10.162 the time suicide warfare had been officially adopted, neither method of using the pebble was likely to succeed. The course of the war had long since been decided and, as it now rushed to its conclusion, a startling new strategy, which might have had considerable impact if initiated in 1942, could not possibly affect the outcome.

The organized use of suicide tactics was indeed startling and new, but from every practical point of view it was an unmitigated failure. Ironically enough (in view of the nomenclature of the strategy), a typhoon that struck the United States Third Fleet east of the Philippines on 18th December 1944 caused more losses to American men, ships, and planes than even the most successful of the mass kamikaze attacks. 10.163

In order to enhance morale at a time when almost everything was going awry, the government clutched at the straw of supposed kamikaze triumphs and gave them the greatest possible publicity. Official propagandists not only made it appear that the imperial forces had developed a decisive new method to counter the enemy but used this dubious evidence to reinforce their pet theory about the superiority of the Japanese spirit. Thus contemporary reports concerning American ships sunk by suicide planes in the Philippines give double the actual figure; in the case of the Okinawa campaign a few months later, the rate of exaggeration is over six hundred percent.

10.164

The main practical difficulty in reporting the effect of kamikaze sorties was that the suicide plane was, by definition, unable to describe the results of his crash; indeed not a single Special Attack fighter ever knew the practical outcome of his sacrifice. The Japanese therefore depended almost entirely on information from the "evaluation" planes—information that was highly inaccurate and always erred on the side of optimism. Often the pilots reported (and believed) that aircraft carriers or battleships had been sunk when the only evidence was huge columns of water and spectacular pillars of smoke, which had in fact been produced by their own exploding planes as they crashed near the warships. Since there was no reliable way to confirm these reports, the commanding officer of the Special Attack unit would usually give his men the benefit of the doubt and transmit the information to Tokyo in all its glorious inaccuracy.

10.165

The blithe optimism of Japanese officials about the kamikaze had its origins in the remarkable results of the maiden attack by the Shikishima Unit on 25th October, when a mere two dozen Japanese pilots and their planes were exchanged for an American aircraft carrier sunk and six others grievously damaged. Such initial success is typical of the heroic parabola, in which it serves as an essential preliminary to the subsequent fall. In fact, from the very outset the war had been a struggle between David and Goliath—in which, however, the giant was bound to be victorious. By the time it came to its explosive conclusion in August, about five thousand suicide volunteers had died in kamikaze craft of one kind or another. For all their frenzied efforts, they had succeeded in destroying only three capital ships, and this did not include a single fleet carrier or battleship. In the entire Okinawa campaign no American ships were sunk by an Ōka and only four were damaged. It is true that almost three hundred vessels were damaged in kamikaze attacks, and many of them had to be withdrawn from the combat areas for repair. Usually, however, they were soon able to return to the fray, and such damage did little to slow down the American advance. Suicide operations and the

10.166

10.167

entire war ended in unconditional surrender, a unique disgrace in Japan's history. The kamikaze effort was a microcosm of the practical futility inherent in the war effort from the very outset, and in the end Divine Wind became a symbol of ineluctable failure.

Far from accomplishing its objective the Special Attack strategy may well have contributed to one of the greatest catastrophes that ever befell the disaster-prone Japanese people, namely, the destruction of Hiroshima and Nagasaki by the first (and only) nuclear bombs every used in warfare. This is hardly what the air-borne samurai had envisaged as the fruit of their dedication, yet such ironic outcomes are familiar in Japanese history where heroic efforts have often led to results totally at variance with those intended. Suicide tactics, instead of overawing the Americans as had been confidently expected, produced indignation and rage out of all proportion to their practical importance and had much the same psychological effect as did the German V-1 and V-2 rockets in England, which were similarly regarded as "unfair" weapons. This probably helped remove such qualms as President Harry Truman and his close associates may have felt about dropping atomic bombs on huge population centres at a time when Japan was already on the verge of surrender and busy with peace feelers. Furthermore, the ferocity of kamikaze tactics seemed a logical culmination of Japan's wartime "fanaticism" and no doubt served to warn the Americans of the immense casualties they could expect if they proceeded with their plans to invade the home islands in the autumn of 1945. It is possible that Japan, faced with the dual threat of atomic attack and the full participation of Russia in the grand alliance, might have capitulated without any invasion at all, and that the obliteration of Hiroshima and Nagasaki was therefore not only immoral but gratuitous. This we shall never know. Clearly, however, America's decision to use nuclear weapons obviated the need for an invasion—an invasion during which the Japanese would have resorted to mass suicide tactics on a far greater scale than ever before.

The connexion between kamikaze and nuclear bombs is of course a hypothesis and one that can never be proved. Yet there is no question about the incongruity of their juxtaposition at the end of the Pacific war, when one side resorted to suicide tactics,

10.168

10.169

10.170

10.171

whose psychological origins lay in the country's remote past, and
was defeated by the most modern and impersonal of all weapons,
the weapon that ushered in the atomic age.

At eleven o'clock on the morning of 9th August the B-29
bomber *Bock's Car* dropped the "Fat Man" over Nagasaki, killing
and wounding some 75,000 people in one terrible blow; on the
very same morning the Japanese government received the news
that Russia had declared war. Six days later, in the first public
address ever made by a Japanese sovereign, Emperor Hirohito
informed millions of astounded subjects (including hundreds of
kamikaze pilots who were awaiting their missions) that Japan
was taking the unprecedented step of surrender and that they
must "endure the unendurable and suffer what is insufferable":

10.172

> After pondering deeply the general trends of the world and the actual
> conditions obtaining in Our Empire today, We have decided to effect a
> settlement of the present situation by resorting to an extraordinary
> measure.
>   We have ordered Our Government to communicate to the Govern-
> ments of the United States, Great Britain, China, and the Soviet Union
> that Our Empire accepts the provisions of their Joint Decla-
> ration. . . .
>   . . . now the war has lasted for nearly four years. Despite the utmost
> that has been performed by everyone—the gallant fighting of military
> and naval forces, the diligence and assiduity of Our servants of the State,
> and the devoted service of Our one hundred million people—the war
> situation has developed not necessarily to Japan's advantage, while the
> general trends of the world have all turned against her interest. More-
> over, the enemy has begun to employ a new and most cruel bomb, the
> power of which to do damage is indeed incalculable, taking the toll of
> many innocent lives. Should We continue to fight, it would not only
> result in an ultimate collapse and obliteration of the Japanese nation, but
> also it would lead to the total extinction of human civilization. Such
> being the case, how are We to save the millions of Our subjects; or to
> atone Ourselves before the hallowed spirits of Our Imperial Ancestors?
> This is the reason why We have ordered the acceptance of the provisions
> of the Joint Declaration of the Powers. . . .

10.173

On the evening of the broadcast Vice Admiral Ōnishi, who
had recently been appointed Vice Chief of the Naval General
Staff, invited several staff officers to his official residence in
Tokyo. During the past four days Ōnishi had done his best to

persuade the leaders of the government that surrender was unthinkable and that, however hopeless the prospects might be, the
only honourable course was to continue fighting until the end,
using whatever suicidal tactics might be necessary. During his
final meeting with the Navy Minister, Admiral Yonai, Ōnishi is
said to have wept openly as he vainly urged the Minister to
persevere. On the final day, shortly before the decision for un-   10.174
conditional surrender had been announced, he had tried to gain
time by suggesting to Prince Takamatsu that a representative of
the Emperor should journey to the Great Ise Shrine and report
on the situation. Foiled in one effort after another, Vice Admiral
Ōnishi became desperate. "Knowing that his own time was running out," writes Captain Inoguchi, who was closely associated
with the Admiral during these feverish days, "and that he was
dealing with men who were not planning to die, he must have
been infuriated at the idea of their accepting the humiliation of
defeat. Their complacence must have been galling to this man
who was so firm in his resolution not to survive the defeat of
Japan."   10.175

Now, on the night of the 15th, Ōnishi knew that all his
endeavours had ended in failure. He stayed talking with his
guests until about midnight. Then everyone went home, and he
retired to his study on the second storey. Shortly before three
o'clock in the morning he unsheathed the sword that he had
borrowed on the previous evening from a young friend named
Kodama, and disembowelled himself with the traditional cross-   10.176
wise cuts (jūmonji) that Mishima Yukio was to use in his own
deed twenty-five years later. After completing the ritual, he
turned the sword round and stabbed himself in the throat and the
chest. But death was in no hurry to release him. Perhaps (as he
told Kodama later) the weapon was not very sharp; more probably he wished to draw out his agony as long as possible and
therefore did not stab deep enough.

Shortly before dawn an employee in the official residence
noticed a faint light coming from the study. He opened the door
and found the Admiral lying on a blood-sprayed *tatami*. Mr.
Kodama and two naval aides were promptly notified and hurried
to the residence accompanied by a fleet surgeon. Despite his
gaping wounds the Admiral was still conscious. The doctor was
amazed by the man's physical endurance, but realized that he was
far beyond help. In any case Ōnishi categorically declined medi-

cal attention. "Do nothing that may keep me alive!" he said as soon as he saw the doctor. Then, turning to Kodama, he wryly observed that it was only because his sword was so dull that they had been able to meet again. At this point Kodama frantically seized another sword and was about to stab himself in an act of *junshi* when Ōnishi said in a surprisingly loud voice, "Don't be a fool! What good would it do to kill yourself now? Young people must go on living and build up Japan again."

The Admiral began vomiting blood and was obviously in great pain, but he refused the traditional coup de grace that would have provided his immediate quietus. Shortly afterwards Kodama suggested that he should bring Ōnishi's wife from the country for a last meeting and begged him to stay alive until she arrived. "You silly fellow!" said Ōnishi with a smile. "What could be more foolish than for a military man to cut open his stomach and then wait for his wife's arrival before dying? Instead take a look at that poem!" He pointed to his final haiku, which he had written on a square of thick paper:

> Refreshed and clear, the moon now shines
> After the fearful storm.

"Not too bad for an old man!" he commented, and these appear to have been his final words. He lingered in agony for several hours and died about six o'clock in the evening. Mr. Kodama, who stayed with him until the end, has described the dismal funeral:

The casket to contain the remains of Vice Admiral Ōnishi was made by soldiers, but because of a shortage of planks, the casket was five inches too small for the body of the admiral. The naval authorities, who had lost all their dignity and presence of mind as a result of the defeat, did not have the sincerity to provide a casket for one of their own comrades who had committed suicide out of a realization of his responsibilities. Neither did they have the magnanimity to provide him with a funeral hearse.

On the way to the crematorium in a truck carrying his body, I saw one naval plane flying towards Tokyo from the direction of Atsugi Air Base. It circled slowly over our heads dipping its wings. This was the last tribute being paid by one of Vice Admiral Ōnishi's men. Incidentally, this was the last time that I was to look upon a Japanese plane.

Ōnishi's two last letters, which he had composed on the previous night with his usual bold brush-strokes, were found in his study. One was a simple farewell note to his wife, written somewhat in the style of departing kamikaze pilots. In it he made his final dispositions and ended with the haiku:

> Now all is done,
> And I can doze for a million years.

The other was a posthumous expression of gratitude to the kamikaze pilots and a testament to the country's youth:

I wish to express my deep appreciation to the spirits of the brave special attackers. They fought and died valiantly with faith in our ultimate victory. In death I wish to atone for my part in the failure to achieve that victory and I apologize to the spirits of these dead flyers and their bereaved families.

I wish the young people of Japan to find a moral in my death. To be reckless is only to aid the enemy. You must abide by the spirit of the Emperor's decision with utmost perseverance. Do not forget your rightful pride in being Japanese!

You are the treasure of the nation. With all the fervour of spirit of the special attackers, strive for the welfare of Japan and for peace throughout the world.

(signed) Vice Admiral Ōnishi Takijirō,
[died] at the age of fifty-four   *10.180*

Despite Ōnishi's outstanding courage and efficiency as a commander, he never expected glory, or even recognition, after his death. According to an old Chinese proverb, a man's true worth can be judged only when his coffin has been covered by the earth, but Ōnishi once remarked to an aide that in his case there would be no one, even after he had been in his coffin a hundred years, to justify what he had tried to do. While believing in the nobility   *10.181* of the kamikaze venture, he seems to have had a profound sense of its practical hopelessness. From every point of view—personal, historical, and aesthetic—his suicide was an inevitable culmination. "It would be wrong to think that it was merely an atonement," Captain Inoguchi has written. "I believe that his life was dedicated from the moment he organized the Kamikaze Corps. Thereupon he had resolved to take his own life, and

would have carried out that resolve even if Japan had won the
war. In imagination he must have journeyed with every pilot of
10.182   his command as each made his last special attack."

> Today in flower,
> Tomorrow scattered by the wind—
> Such is our blossom life.
10.183   How can we think its fragrance lasts forever?

Notes

Chapter 1

1.1 *Kojiki* ("The Record of Ancient Events"), Nihon Koten Zensho (Tokyo, 1963), II: 128. (Unless otherwise specified, all translations of Japanese texts are my own.) *Kojiki*, the earliest extant chronicle in Japan (and indeed the oldest extant Japanese book of any kind), was presented to the Court in A.D. 712. See note 1.3 below.

1.2 Plain of Nobo: for this and all subsequent place names see maps, pp. x–xi, 7.

1.3 The main primary sources are *Kojiki* ("The Record of Ancient Events," A.D. 712) and *Nihon Shoki* ("The Chronicles of Japan," A.D. 720). In *Nihon Shoki* the hero's father, Emperor Keikō, is given a far more important role in the campaign against the "rebels" than the *Kojiki* allows; there are also far more foreign touches, for example the Emperor's commission to his son (VII:22), which is in pure Chinese style. The *Kojiki* account, which is both briefer and more vivid, emphasizes the sacred aspect of the hero's mission and describes his principal enemies as deities (e.g., "mountain gods, river gods, and gods of the sea straits," *Kojiki*, p. 119); frequently it uses verbs (e.g., *idemashiki*, p. 128, and *kamuagaritamaiki*, p. 143) which suggest that Yamato Takeru is in fact an Emperor. His character is somewhat more ardent and romantic in *Kojiki*, more subdued, dignified, and "Chinese" in *Nihon Shoki*. In my account of Yamato Takeru, I combine elements from the two main sources, mentioning discrepancies only when they appear significant. *Hitachi Fudoki*, an 8th-century gazetteer, briefly mentions Yamato Takeru as the conqueror of the eastern Emishi; this is the only primary source in which he is actually styled as an Emperor: Yamato Takeru no Sumeramikoto, see *Hitachi Fudoki*, ed. Musashino Shoin (Tokyo, 1956), p. 2.

In the traditional chronologies Yamato Takeru, though not counted as an Emperor, is a link in the direct line of imperial descent that extends from the mythological founding ruler, Jimmu, to the present Emperor, Hirohito. According to a confusing passage in *Kojiki* (p. 148) Yamato Takeru had six wives and one child by each; he does not appear to have lived with any of them, and indeed his career was far too short and hectic for any domesticity. The first and principal wife (the daughter of Keikō's father, Emperor Suinin) was the hero's aunt; she gave birth to a beautiful, ten-foot Prince who became Emperor Chūai. This appears to be the chronology:

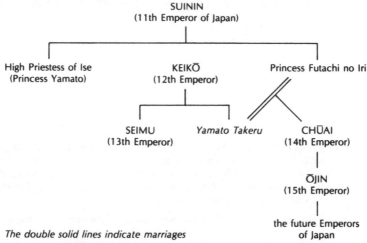

The double solid lines indicate marriages

1.4   For an explication of the "universal myth," see Joseph Campbell, *The Hero with a Thousand Faces* (New York, 1956).

1.5   In the *Nihon Shoki* version, which omits the undignified murder in the lavatory, Prince Ōusu is pictured as a cowardly survivor who shuffles off his military responsibilities upon his younger twin (see p. 5).

1.6   "... the tendency has always been to endow the hero with extraordinary powers from the moment of birth, or even the moment of conception. The whole hero-life is shown to have been a pageant of marvels with the great central adventure as its culmination." Campbell, *Hero*, p. 319.

1.7   It is only recently that historians have reached a fairly clear understanding of the Emishi and the Kumaso. Formerly the Kumaso were described as primitive migrants from Borneo and other southern islands. The Emishi caused still greater confusion, and even Sir George Sansom, the most distinguished of all historians to have written about Japan in English, identified them with the hairy Ainus, the Caucasoid aborigines of the north, who of course belong to an entirely different race from the Japanese.

1.8   The word *tawayame* ("soft, gentle women") is used to provide contrast with the hero's *araburu* ("rough") nature. *Kojiki*, p. 127.

1.9   Both were called Kumaso Takeru (Brave of Kumaso) and they appear to have been brothers. In the *Nihon Shoki* version, however, there is only one chieftain.

1.10   One of the many ancient poetic names for Japan.

1.11   Yamato Takeru = the Brave of Japan. Yamato originally referred to the particular region where the first imperial government was established in Honshu; later it came to be used for the entire land of Japan, and in this sense it still appears in poetic and rhetorical contexts (e.g., *Yamato-dama-shii* = "the soul of Japan"). *Takeru* ("Brave" or "Hero"), which is here applied to Prince Ōusu for the first time, was evidently a title given to warrior chieftains in Izumo, Kyushu, and other western parts of Japan.

1.12   *Kojiki*, pp. 128–29.

1.13   In *Nihon Shoki* this story is placed in an earlier reign as part of the Izumo cycle of legends, and the trick is perpetrated against a younger brother by his wicked elder brother, who is killed on the Emperor's orders when the news of his deed is reported at Court. In *Kojiki*, where the Sino-Confucian influence is far less strong, the ruse was attributed to the brave Yamato as an example of his resourcefulness. Of course it does not conform to the popular image of the hero and is not included in school-book versions of his life.

1.14   *Nihon Shoki*, ed. Nihon Koten Zensho (Tokyo, 1953), II: 164. Unless otherwise noted, this edition is the one cited.

1.15   The sword, originally discovered by the tempestuous god Susanoo in the tail of a giant dragon, was presented by him to Amaterasu Ōmikami, the sun goddess. Revered as one of the three imperial regalia, it (or a reasonable facsimile) is now enshrined in Atsuta near Nagoya. The regalia are religio-magic (Shinto) symbols and it is significant that the hero should have received the sword, not from his father, the Emperor, but from the High Priestess of Ise, the supreme representative of religious power in Japan. It was only when the hero foolhardily divested himself of the magic sword (see p. 7) that he became pregnable. Cf. the magical sword Excalibur, given to Arthur by the Lady of the Lake and returned to her by Sir Bedivere at the King's death. Yamato Takeru's visit to his aunt is probably a legendary representation of historical visits by early Japanese military leaders to female shamans, who provided them with amulets and ritual reinforcement. In terms of Campbell's universal myth it represents the stage of "supernatural aid," which follows "the call to adventure" and precedes "the crossing of the first threshold."

Yamato Takeru comes close to succumbing to a "refusal of the call" (Campbell, *Hero*, p. 59) but loyalty to the Emperor and to his own destiny prevails. In the universal myth (*Hero*, pp. 72–73) the hero's first encounter in his journey is with a protective figure, who provides him with amulets and other useful paraphernalia. In the Irish myth of the Prince of the Lonesome Isle (*Hero*, p. 105) the heroic youth is given advice by a *supernatural aunt*, whom he meets on his way to get three bottles of water from Tubber Tintye. On the "road of trials" the hero is exposed to a series of supernatural tests and ordeals. Yamato Takeru's first such test takes place in the marsh of Sagami. He manages this and subsequent challenges, but is finally downed by the mountain god (see p. 8).

1.16   *Kojiki*, p. 140. *Matsurigoto* ("sacred mission"), the word later used for "government," originally referred to religious rites or worship. Any important task performed for the Emperor, such as Yamato Takeru's subjugation of the Emishi, was *ipso facto* a religious mission.

1.17 *Nihon Shoki*, II: 170. "Azuma" is still used as a poetic designation for the eastern part of the main Japanese island, but of course the etymology is spurious.

1.18 *Nihon Shoki*, II:170.

1.19 In China and Japan (and even in Scotland) garlic was used to ward off evil spirits, witches, and other disagreeable creatures; and of course it is still eaten in many countries to prevent colds and infections of all kinds. After Yamato Takeru's adventure, people crossing Shinano Pass chewed garlic and smeared themselves and their animals with it "so that they would not be harmed by the god's breath" (*Nihon Shoki*, II:171). The legend is typically illogical since we have already been told that the hero killed the god.

1.20 *Kojiki*, p. 142.

1.21 *Nihon Shoki*, II:174.

1.22 *Ibid.*

1.23 *Kojiki*, p. 142.

1.24 The *Kojiki* account is full of quaint etymologies. The Plain of Tagi, for example, is related to *tagitagishiku* ("wobbly") and Tsuetsuki Slope to *mi-tsue wo tsuki* ("thrusting a stick").

1.25 More literally, "he became sober" *(sametamaiki)*. These details are typical of the "magic flight" in the universal heroic adventure. Campbell, *Hero*, p. 200.

1.26 Four poems are recorded in *Kojiki*; *Nihon Shoki* gives three of the poems and attributes them to Emperor Keikō, who is said to have written them during a stay in Kyushu many years earlier. The farewell message is strongly Chinese in style and appears only in *Nihon Shoki* (II:174–75).

1.27 "The last act in the biography of the hero is that of the death or departure. Here the whole sense of the life is epitomized. Needless to say, the hero would be no hero if death held for him any terror; the first condition is reconciliation with the grave." Campbell, *Hero*, p. 356.

1.28 Twenty-nine in the Western count. According to Professor Takeda, however, he was actually 32 (31 in the Western account), *Nihon Shoki*, II:173.

1.29 *Ibid.*, 175

1.30 "A white bird of eight fathoms" (i.e., a giant white bird) according to *Kojiki* (p. 143).

1.31 "And [the disciple] stooping down, and looking in, saw the linen clothes lying; yet went he not in. Then cometh Simon Peter following him, and went into the sepulchre, and seeth the linen clothes lie, and the napkin that was about his head, not lying with the linen clothes, but wrapped together in a place by itself" (St. John 20:5–7). Early Japanese religions attached little importance to what happened to the spirits of great men (emperors, warriors, etc.) after their death. Yet Yamato Takeru, the archetypal Japanese hero, is described as having risen from the dead like Jesus of Nazareth, leaving nothing in the coffin but his clothes and headdress. This is not the only instance of possible Christian influence in *Nihon Shoki*. The story of Shōtoku Taishi (late 6th century) includes an annunciation, a birth in (or near) a stable, and an empty tomb whose occupant, a sort of Lazarus figure, has risen from the dead. The Nestorian Church expanded to China from the 7th century, and it is possible that by 720, when *Nihon Shoki* was completed, fragments of the story of Christ had somehow reached Japan and been incorporated into the legends of native heroes. In this case the white bird may be related to the dove that traditionally symbolized the Holy Ghost.

1.32 A typical anachronism: Court caps, which designated official rank, were not introduced until about the year 600.

1.33 Kuroita Katsumi, *Kokushi no Kenkyū* (Tokyo, 1936), I:47.

1.34 In Japanese myth and legend white animals are frequently endowed with magical powers (cf. the white dog on p. 21, the white snake or boar on p. 7).

1.35 See p. 9.

1.36 See pp. 22–24 concerning "sincerity."

1.37 See p. 5.

1.38 Azuma no Kuni-miyakko. In fact no such post ever existed in Japan and, even if it had, the old man's lines,

> As I place them side by side,
> Of nights there are nine nights
> And of days there are ten days,

were hardly of a brilliance to merit any such reward. As it happens, this peculiarly prosaic exchange with the old man was subsequently regarded as the literary ancestor of linked verse *(renga)*, which in late mediaeval times became an immensely popular form of poetry, being dignified by the name of *Tsukuba no Michi* ("The Way of Tsukuba") in reference to its supposedly heroic origins.

1.39 *Kojiki*, p. 142.

1.40 *Ibid.*, p. 143. See n. 1.26 above.

1.41 This of course refers to Kusanagi, the sword that he had foolishly left with his wife before proceeding on his last mission (see p. 8). For the Japanese warrior the sword was to become an almost religious object of veneration.

1.42 Campbell, *Hero*, p. 207. In a book written for foreign readers (whom one would not expect to share the Japanese penchant for heroic failure) Mrs.

Theodora Ozaki rewrites the ending of the Yamato Takeru legend and manages to transform him into a successful Western-type hero:

When he got back he began to feel ill and to have burning pains in his feet, so he knew that the serpent had poisoned him. So great was his suffering that he could hardly move, much less walk, so he had himself carried to a place in the mountains famous for its hot mineral springs, which rose bubbling out of the earth, and almost boiling from the volcanic fires beneath.

Yamato Take bathed daily in these waters, and gradually he felt his strength come again, and the pains left him, till at last one day he found with great joy that he was quite recovered. He now hastened to the temples of Ise, where you will remember that he prayed before undertaking this long expedition. His aunt, priestess of the shrine, who had blessed him on his setting out, now came to welcome him back. He told her of the many dangers he had encountered and of how marvellously his life had been preserved through all—and she praised his courage and his warrior's prowess, and then putting on her most magnificent robes she returned thanks to their ancestress the Sun Goddess Amaterasu, to whose protection they both ascribed the Prince's wonderful preservation.

Here ends the story of Prince Yamato Take of Japan. (*The Japanese Fairy Book* [Tokyo, 1903], pp. 35-36.)

1.43   According to one version, after his banishment by the gods Susanoo was obliged to go to Korea—an appalling fate for a Japanese deity. *Nihon Shoki* describes him wandering about wretchedly in the fierce wind and rain and begging shelter from the various gods. All refused him because of his wicked conduct, and he was obliged to wrap himself in the straw coat and braided hat of the homeless traveller. This is the legendary origin of the ancient *ryūribanashi* or *sasuraibanashi* (stories of heroes who wander alone in a strange country or region) as later exemplified in the legends of Yamato Takeru, Yoshitsune, etc.

1.44   E.g., tearing up the boundaries between rice fields, polluting a sacred place with excrement, committing incest with his sister.

1.45   It is true that the campaign launched by Yamato Takeru in the Kantō region culminated eventually in the total subjugation of the Emishi and of the deities they worshipped (see p. 2). In this sense he was a "posthumous success," unlike the typically Japanese defeated heroes, who (since they supported losing causes) became "permanent failures." What firmly established the legend of Yamato Takeru as the prototype of Japanese heroism is the emotional tone and overwhelming importance of the way in which his life ended.

Chapter 2

2.1   Cf. the famous opening words of *Budō Shoshin Shū* by the samurai-scholar, Daidōji Shigesuke (1639–1730): "The warrior must keep the thought of death uppermost in his mind from the dawn of New Year's Day until the year comes to its end. . . ."

2.2   See n. 1.27 concerning the attitude of the Western hero to death.

2.3   Daidōji Shigesuke, *Budō Shoshin Shū*, p. 54.

2.4   From *Hagakure* (see n. 10.126). It is not only for the historical samurai that death is the ultimate criterion of sincerity, but even for the plebeian heroes and heroines of popular dramas (like those of Chikamatsu Monzaemon in the early 18th century), whose brief lives acquired their dignity and meaning by death, in particular by the courageous, self-sacrificial manner of their dying in double suicides.

In the words of a modern writer: "Death is not a mere end of life for the Japanese. It has been given a positive place in life. Facing death properly is one of the most important features of life. In that sense, it may well be said that for the Japanese death is within life." Kishimoto Hideo, *The Japanese Mind* (Honolulu, 1967), p. 119.

2.5   Here, incidentally, we have the principal explanation for the brutal treatment of Allied prisoners of war captured by the Japanese during the Second World War.

2.6   Concerning the Japanese attitude to suicide see pp. 316–17.

2.7   The great suicides of classical antiquity like Socrates and Seneca were of course *obliged* to kill themselves by superior political authority.

2.8   So powerful was the appeal of Thanatos to the Japanese warrior that in mediaeval warfare samurai frequently killed themselves before it was necessary, that is, before the battle was really lost.

During the course of the centuries the suicide ethos filtered down from the ruling samurai class to lower strata of society, including the urban bourgeoisie. For the heroes and heroines in Chikamatsu's plays (and their counterparts in real life) suicide represented the only honourable escape from the conflicting obligations of duty and humanity *(giri-ninjō)*.

2.9   Note, for example, the suicide of Admiral Ōnishi in 1945 (see pp. 331–32). Normally the warrior who committed harakiri was promptly beheaded by a comrade or attendant. The disembowelment was in fact a deliberately painful preliminary to death rather than its actual cause (see n. 5.61).

2.10 *Nihon Shoki*, ed. Nihon Koten Zensho (Tokyo, 1953), IV:192. (Unless otherwise noted, this is the edition cited.) The particle *no* in aristocratic names corresponds roughly to the European *von, de*, etc. *No* is preceded by the clan or family name and followed by the given name.

2.11 Possibly he refers to the Sogas' lack of military tradition; in the eyes of a Mononobe warrior the Sogas were mere civilians, and Umako looked absurd with a sword. It is not clear whether Moriya's trembling was the result of an illness or of his powerful emotions at the Emperor's death; in either case, Umako's suggestion (that he should have bells tied to his arms and legs so that they would ring when he shook) was in dubious taste.

2.12 Professor Naoki in *Kodai Kokka no Seiritsu* (Tokyo, 1965), pp. 26–27, compares the Mononobes to the Tokkō Keisatsu (Special Political Police) during the ultra-nationalist period in prewar Japan. Though this seems far-fetched, their role under Emperor Yūryaku was certainly concerned more with police duties than with religious ceremonial, the latter having been largely taken over by the Nakatomi and Imibe clans.

2.13

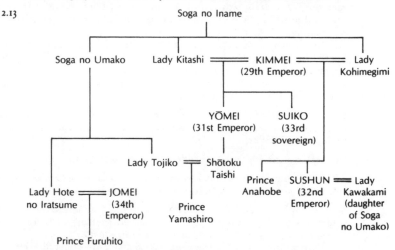

The double solid lines indicate marriages

2.14 The word *shintō* ("way of the gods") did not come into use until well after the introduction of Buddhism, and it was formulated in contradistinction to the word *butsudō* ("the way of the Buddha"). Shintoism, as Sansom says, is not a religion or a system of thought but an expression of the national character (George Sansom, *Japan, A Short Cultural History* [New York, 1962], pp. 49–53), and before the introduction of foreign ideas it had been so integral a part of Japanese sentiment that it did not require a special word. It was the arrival of Buddhism that made the native religion self-conscious.

2.15 A definitely "foreign" flavour attaches to the Sogas, as opposed to the Mononobes and other ancient Yamato clans, and it is quite probable that they were one of the clans that emigrated to Japan from the Korean peninsula, perhaps as recently as in the 4th century A.D.; but in the official genealogies they, like all the other great clans, are represented as descending directly from the Japanese gods.

2.16 Our main primary source for this period is the *Nihon Shoki*, which wished to give the impression that Japanese emperors were defenders of the faith from the outset. According to an account in *Gangōji Engi* (early 7th century), however, Emperor Bidatsu was a ruthless persecutor of Buddhism, and Yōmei did nothing to encourage it.

2.17 *Nihon Shoki*, II: 209.

2.18 One cryptic passage in the *Nihon Shoki* (II: 209) suggests that Moriya's defeat was due to female treachery: "[When they heard the news] people said to each other, 'Lord Umako's wife is the sister of the Great Chieftain, Mononobe no Moriya. It was she who plotted the Great Chieftain's destruction and Lord Umako foolishly followed her plan and killed him.' " Commentators suggest that Moriya's sister may have wished to acquire his property. It is possible that she helped Umako in his designs, but obviously the conflict between the Mononobes and the Sogas was based on more fundamental issues than this.

2.19   As it happens, the Sogas themselves were the first major victims of the Reform movement, but this was mainly because Umako's successors were too blatant in usurping certain imperial functions and even gave the impression (perhaps a correct one) that they aspired to become emperors themselves. A decisive Mononobe victory in 587 would almost certainly have delayed, and might possibly have prevented, the type of political and cultural reform carried out by Umako, Shōtoku Taishi, Prince Naka no Ōe, Nakatomi no Kamatari, and their Sinicizing successors.

2.20   Totoribe (Bird-Catchers' Guild) was one of the numerous *be*, hereditary corporations of workers which were attached to the different clans and which constituted by far the most numerous class in ancient Japan. Members of the Totoribe were traditionally responsible for capturing wild birds and raising them in captivity. Yorozu's *be* was attached to the imperial clan, and it appears that Yorozu had been personally presented by one of the emperors to Mononobe no Moriya to serve as his attendant. It is not clear whether Yorozu himself had ever engaged in the avian duties that were hereditary in his guild. Judging by his military prowess in 587, one would imagine that, rather than tending birds, he had spent a good part of his life as one of Moriya's armed retainers.

2.21   Strange meteorological disturbances often accompany the execution of heroes (cf. the "darkness over all the earth" in the Crucifixion and the sudden storm when Nichiren was about to be beheaded in 1263).

For the magic significance of white animals see n. 1.34. The role of animals in the stories of Yamato Takeru and Yorozu suggest Jungian overtones:

> . . . Neither for the primitive nor for the unconscious does [his] animal aspect imply any devaluation, for in certain respects the animal is superior to man. It has not yet blundered into consciousness *nor pitted a self-willed ego against the power from which it lives;* on the contrary, it fulfills the will that actuates it in a wellnigh perfect manner. . . . Again and again in fairy tales we encounter the motif of helpful animals. These act like humans, speak a human language, and *display a sagacity and a knowledge superior to man's.* In these circumstances we can say with some justification that the archetype of the spirit is being expressed through an animal form. (Carl Jung, *Psyche and Symbol* [New York, 1958], p. 217. Italics added.)

2.22   *Nihon Shoki*, II: 209–10.

2.23   *Makoto, magokoro*, and *shisei* are virtually interchangeable. The first two are "pure" Japanese compounds, in which *ma* = "genuine, pure, true," *koto* = "things," *gokoro* = "heart, spirit." *Shisei* is a Chinese-type compound, in which *shi* means "exceeding, utmost" and *sei* is the Sino-Japanese reading of *makoto.*

2.24   Concerning "movement of the times" *(jisei)* see note 6.105.

2.25   Kurt Singer, *Mirror, Sword and Jewel: A Study of Japanese Characteristics* (New York, 1973), p. 16.

2.26   Quoted by Naramoto Tatsuya in *Mainichi Shimbun*, Rekishi to Jimbutsu (no. 5), 19th February 1971.
       After a hectic, failure-studded career Yoshida Shōin (the martyr in question) committed his final blunder in an abortive plot against the shogunate in 1859 and was executed for treason at the age of twenty-nine.

> He was full of high ideals, grand visions and ambitious projects, yet he failed in almost all his undertakings large and small, for want, one would say, of common sense. It is not easy for a foreign student to understand why he so strongly influenced the minds of his contemporaries and was so extravagantly praised by later generations. It is clear that there is something in his life which appeals to the emotions of his compatriots. . . . (Sir George Sansom, *The Western World and Japan* [London, 1950], p. 284).

This "something," of course, was precisely *makoto.* Shōin's sincere impetuosity doomed him from the outset. Owing to his wild talk and indiscreet letters, his plot was discovered by the authorities before he came even close to attaining his objective. The intended victim (a high shogunal official) successfully obtained the imperial sanction for the conclusion of foreign treaties that Shōin had frenetically opposed, and returned safely to Edo. Shōin also went to Edo; but his destination was the common gaol, where he languished for three months before being decapitated. Sansom describes his final writings:

> In the last two days in gaol awaiting execution he scribbled in prose and verse what he called the Record of an Uneasy Spirit, the tale of his unsatisfied wishes and his uncompleted plans. The prison diaries of those days are vivid pieces of historical evidence, and Shōin's is among the most pathetic. He knew that he was a failure and he expressed a kind of proud repentance; but the best thing that he said justified all his efforts, for he declared: "I would rather be wrong in giving than wrong in receiving. I would rather be wrong in dying than wrong in living." (*Western World*, p. 289.)

This last statement of Shōin's can be read as a manifesto of all Japanese heroic sincerity, as can his famous precept, "It is unworthy of a samurai to be much concerned with the consequences when the action itself is virtuous." (Quoted by John Roberts, *Mitsui* [New York, 1973], p. 61.) Despite his repeated setbacks and dismal end, Yoshida Shōin was a posthumous success, becoming established as the brave, self-sacrificing precursor of the triumphant Meiji Restoration.

2.27   Naramoto (see n. 2.26) describes Shōin as a paragon of sincerity who acted with "pure selflessness" *(junsui muga ni yatte)*. "Most people," he continues, "act only after they have judged the practical situation, but this man totally lacked a utilitarian spirit *(kōrishin)*."

2.28   For a full discussion of *action* as a criterion of sincerity see chap. 8 (Ōshio), pp. 197–98.

2.29   Concerning the objective value of the hero's cause see p. 65.

Nezumi Kozō Jirōkichi, the most illustrious thief in Japanese history, was arrested, paraded through the streets, beheaded, and his head publicly gibbeted in Edo in 1832. Later his life was dramatized in numerous stories and Kabuki plays and he became a folk hero owing to his reputation for stealing from wealthy merchants and, in the style of Robin Hood, giving his haul to poor people. "Though I may have stolen," he declared after his arrest, "I have never committed injustice." Quoted in "Seigi no Mikata," *Mainichi Shimbun*, 15th February 1971. "The secret of Nezumi Kozō's lasting popularity," concludes the writer, "is his final execution [by the authorities]."

2.30   See p. 67 concerning the parabola of the heroic career.

2.31   As Hilaire Belloc observed in *A Moral Alphabet* (*Cautionary Verses* [London, 1949], p. 9) with somewhat un-Japanese jocularity:

> Decisive action in the hour of need
> Denotes the Hero but does not succeed.

2.32   The underlying dichotomy between sincerity and realism in the Japanese tradition can be schematized as follows:

SINCERITY	REALISM
emotional spontaneity leading to dangerous action	calculating intellect leading to judicious restraint
uncompromising idealism	level-headed pragmatism
human compassion *(nasake, ninjō)*	coldness, lack of human feeling *(hijō)*
selflessness, self-sacrifice	egoism, greed, pursuit of self-interest
sympathy with the loser *(hōganbiiki)*	awe for worldly power and success
defiance of unjust power	submission to authority as reflected in such typical sayings as *Nagai mono ni wa makareyo* ("Yield to the powerful!"), *Sawaranu kami ni tatari nashi* ("Leave the powerful alone and they will not harm you!"), *Deru kugi wa utareru* ("A nail that sticks out is hammered on the head"), *Tsuyoi mono gachi* ("The powerful will always prevail").

For a detailed (though somewhat confusing) discussion of the various value-systems in Japanese thought, see Kawabara Hiroshi, *Saigō Densetsu* (Tokyo, 1971), pp. 56–60.

2.33   Though Soga no Umako was the leader of the loyalist forces, the chronicles make it clear that he would not allow mere devotion to the Emperor —or, indeed, mere devotion to the great religion of nonviolence—to block personal and family ambitions. Emperor Sushun, the Soga candidate who came to the Throne after the defeat of the Mononobes, was to be allowed to reign but not to rule. The tension between Sushun and his overbearing uncle, Sumako, mounted steadily. In 592, when the head of a wild boar was presented to the Emperor, he rather pointedly asked when the head of his great enemy would be cut off in the same way. This rash remark was reported to Umako who, realizing exactly what the Emperor meant, promptly ordered his assassination, thus giving Sushun the distinction of being the only sovereign in Japanese history to have been murdered while actually on the Throne. Rather in the style of Macbeth, Umako followed up this murder by himself killing the man whom he had ordered to assassinate Sushun on the pretext that this man had seduced Lady Kawakami, the imperial consort (see n. 2.13). Unlike Macbeth, however, Soga no Umako continued to live and pursue his career as Chief Minister for another 34 years, a typical example of the successful survivor who appears again and again in Japanese history as a foil to the defeated hero.

2.34   Even if a specific individual like Yorozu actually existed in 587, it is almost unthinkable that he would have called himself "the Emperor's shield." As a warrior his loyalty would surely have been directed to Moriya, the leader of the clan that he served. In studying the concept of the Japanese hero, however, what is important here is that the official chronicle should have attributed loyalist sentiments to a member of the rebel forces and, above all, that the great hero of the battle should have been on the losing side.

The phrase "the Emperor's shield" (ōkimi no mitate) recurs in a patriotic poem which is included in the 8th-century anthology, Manyōshū (xx: 4373), and which became popular among soldiers in the second World War:

> From this day forth
> I will never turn back home—
> I who have set out to serve
> As the Emperor's shield.

When Mishima organized his private force in 1967 "to protect the Emperor from his enemies," he named it the Shield Society (Tate no Kai) in reference to this ancient image.

Chapter 3

3.1   "Il est assez puni par son sort rigoureux; et c'est être innocent que d'être malheureux." La Fontaine, writing in 1661 about the fall of Fouquet in Élégie aux Nymphes de Vaux.

3.2   *Arima no Miko* (Tokyo, 1961), published in *Bungakukai*. The archfiend in Mr. Fukuda's villain-filled play is the scheming ambitious Soga no Akae, who is represented as having an affair with Prince Arima's mother.

3.3   Thus in 643 Soga no Iruka (Umako's grandson) decided that Prince Yamashiro, a likely successor to the Throne, had to be removed from the scene in order to protect Soga interests. The Prince was attacked and he and his family were forced to commit suicide.

3.4   See p. 18.

3.5

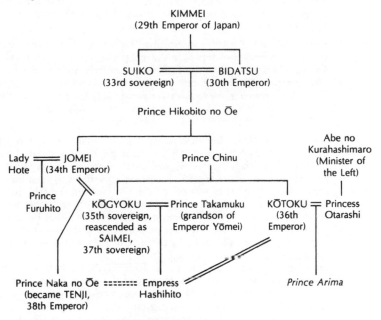

The double solid lines indicate marriages

The double dotted lines indicate illegitimate unions

IMPERIAL REIGNS	OTHER DATES	
Emperor Jomei 629-41	10th July 645	the Soga leaders are killed
Empress Kōgyoku 642-45	12th July 645	Emperor Kōtoku comes to the Throne
Emperor Kōtoku 645-54	14th July 645	Prince Naka becomes Crown Prince
Empress Saimei 655-61	28th Sept. 645	Prince Furuhito executed
Emperor Tenji 668-72	12th May 649	Soga no Ishikawamaro kills himself
	14th May 655	Empress Saimei ascends the Throne with Prince Naka as Crown Prince
	9th Dec. 658	Prince Arima arrested
	12th Dec. 658	Prince Arima executed

3.6   For example, Kuroita Katsumi, the famous prewar historian, writes:

> If he had become emperor, he would have had to assume numerous ceremonial and religious responsibilities that would make it impossible to devote himself to matters of domestic and foreign policy. In order to carry out the great reform movement, it was far better [that he should remain Crown Prince]. (*Kokushi no Kenkyū* [Tokyo, 1936], I:130.)

3.7   This personal explanation is not given by Kuroita or any of the other prewar historians, who would no doubt have regarded it as scandalous. For detailed discussions see Yoshinaga Minoru in *Nihon Kodai no Seiji to Bungaku* (Tokyo, 1956), and Naoki Kōjirō, *Kodai Kokka no Seiritsu* (Tokyo, 1965), pp. 222–43.

3.8   *Nihon Shoki*, ed. Asahi Shimbun Sha (Tokyo, 1956), p. 51. The eulogistic thumbnail sketches of Japanese sovereigns are based on Chinese models and should not be taken too seriously. The reference to the Emperor's kindly nature *(yawaraka)*, however, is unusual and may be significant: a man with a rougher, more assertive personality (like Emperor Yūryaku) would have been unlikely to tolerate his wife's affair with Prince Naka.

3.9   Until the middle of the 8th century capitals were usually moved at the beginning of each reign, partly for strategic reasons, partly because of matrilocal marriage practices, and partly because it was believed that ritual pollution ensued from an Emperor's death. Until a semipermanent centre of imperial rule was established in Nara in the 8th century, the word "capital" should be understood in a purely technical sense. The pre-Nara capitals were a collection of primitive wooden buildings, centred about the Emperor's residence, and most of them were in a state of virtual collapse by the end of a reign. Until the growth of an elaborate Chinese-type administration and the consequent proliferation of government offices as a result of the Great Reform, the capitals were more like encampments than cities, and the move from one to another was a fairly painless operation, especially since almost all the early centres were built in a small radius in the Yamato region. "Palace" may also give an exaggerated impression: the early imperial residences were simple wooden, thatch-roofed structures with none of the stately grandeur that the word "palace" conveys in the West.

3.10   *Nihon Shoki*, ed. Nihon Koten Zensho (Tokyo, 1953), IV:122. (Unless otherwise noted, this is the edition cited.) A similar movement of rats, in this case *towards* Naniwa, is recorded at the beginning of Emperor Kōtoku's reign. In both instances "old people" *(okinatachi)* are said to have commented that the movement of the rats presaged a change of capitals. *Nihon Shoki*, IV: 126.

3.11   *Nihon Shoki*, IV: 126.

3.12   *Ibid.*

3.13   Since the Emperor's wife was now openly ensconced with her brother-lover in Asuka, the question could only be rhetorical, and certainly it elicited no reply. The following free gloss by Professor Yoshinaga spells out the meaning of the Emperor's last poem: "Has some other man stolen you from me—you whom I cherished so dearly? Have you abandoned me and gone to another man?"

3.14   In her second reign she is known as Empress Saimei. The two-character, Chinese-type names of the sovereigns (Kō-toku, Kō-gyoku, Sai-mei, etc.) which are used to identify them in all the history books are posthumous designations. During their lifetimes they had long names pronounced in pure Japanese (e.g., Empress Kōgyoku/Saimei was Ame Toyo Takara Ikashi Hi Tarashi Hime no Sumera Mikoto), though there was usually a taboo against speaking or even writing the name of a living sovereign.

3.15   Naoki, *Kodai Kokka no Seiritsu*, p. 227.

3.16   In ancient Japan it was perfectly acceptable for a woman to remarry after her husband's death and become the consort of a new Emperor. Thus Empress Kōgyoku had been married to Emperor Yōmei's grandson, Prince Takamuku, before she became Emperor Jomei's consort (see n. 3.5).

3.17   For example, in the 6th century Emperor Bidatsu was able to marry Empress Suiko even though they were both the children of Emperor Kimmei (see n. 3.5).

3.18   A famous precedent, which may well have been in Prince Naka's mind, occurred in the 5th century when Emperor Ingyō's resplendent son, Crown Prince Karu, fell desperately in love with his beautiful half-sister. We are told that his passion was so violent that he was on the point of death; finally he decided that it would be pointless to die in this way and that he had better consummate his love, however sinful it might be to have intercourse with his mother's daughter. The couple was secretly united and the Crown Prince recovered his composure. Shortly afterwards Emperor Ingyō's soup froze and turned into ice. This culinary setback was interpreted as a sign that there had been some illicit relationship in the Palace, and the Emperor was informed about his son's incestuous liaison. As a result Prince Karu was removed from the line of imperial succession and banished to Iyo where, according to one version, he committed suicide after writing two final love poems to his sister-mistress.

3.19   Opposition to the Reform movement eventually came to a head in the Jinshin Uprising (A.D. 672), the most desperate and extensive struggle of its kind to date, in which all the conservative forces that had been antagonized by the reforms arose in support of Naka's younger brother, Prince Ōama. Kuroita (*Kokushi no Kenkyū*, pp. 142–43) compares this antagonism with the opposition to the Meiji reforms twelve centuries later when a movement in favour of "preserving national characteristics" (*kokusui hozon*) arose as a reaction against the government's policy of Westernization. A similar reaction against excessive foreign influence occurred in Japan after the American Occupation.

3.20   *Nihon Shoki*, IV: 129. In the Asuka region of Yamato, not far from the new capital. The canal must have been a good ten miles long.

3.21   Or "They referred to it as 'the Insane Canal' and said. . . ."

3.22   *Nihon Shoki*, IV: 132. According to an interlinear gloss in the chronicle, these criticisms were made while the work was actually in progress. They do not seem to have deflected the government from its course, for the very next sentence informs us that work was promptly started on a new palace in Yoshino.

3.23   Kuroita, *Kokushi no Kenkyū*, p. 142.

3.24   *Nihon Shoki*, IV: 133.

3.25   Members of the imperial family had recently started visiting hot springs for rest and recreation. Prince Arima's father had particularly enjoyed his stays in Arima Spa (near present-day Kobe), and there is a theory that the Prince's name, which was originally written with the same ideograms, derived from this place.

   Why should Prince Arima have chosen Muro rather than one of the nearer spas like Arima that were usually favoured by imperial visitors? There are many possible explanations other than the sinister one implied by the chronicle. If, as I believe, his mental illness was authentic, he may well have wished to avoid a more fashionable type of resort; a seaside spa like Muro may also have been a better place for a cure than Arima Spa, which was mountainous. In addition, as Professor Naoki points out (*Kodai Kokka no Seiritsu*, p. 235), Shioya no Muraji Konoshiro, who appears to have been the Prince's only close companion, was in charge of the public salt enterprises in the Muro region (his name means something like Lord Salt-House Herring) and he may have recommended these remote hot springs to his unhappy young friend.

3.26   *Nihon Shoki*, IV: 134.

3.27   *Ibid.*, IV: 139–41. I have inserted the additional account (from p. 141 of *Nihon Shoki*) between ". . . conspired together" and "This year I have come to the age," which seems to be the only logical place for this important passage. Prince Arima's remark that he is now old enough to lead troops in battle makes little sense where it is now placed (i.e., as a response to Akae's criticism of the government) but fits fairly well after the comment that he is still too young to carry out his plans. All dates are given according to the Julian calendar.

3.28   It is interesting that the government's three "mistakes" should all be of an economic nature. The first two refer to new taxes that had been levied as part of the Great Reform system: *so* was a produce tax payable in rice or other grains, while *yō*, a far more onerous burden, was payable in labour. Though Soga no Akae refers to the Empress *(sumera-mikoto)*, his criticism (or pretended criticism) is actually directed against Prince Naka and his colleagues who were responsible for the reforms.

3.29 It seems typical that Soga no Akae should have used ordinary labourers (*yoboro*) to capture Prince Arima rather than official guards or soldiers, and that three days should have elapsed before he was officially arrested.

3.30 This execution was a form of garrotte and involved strangulation with a cord. Among the types of punishment stipulated in the Chinese codes it was one degree less disgraceful than beheading. Tajii no Osawa no Muraji Kuniso presumably did not perform the grim operation himself but was in charge of the proceedings.

3.31 In other words, "Please spare me so that I may continue working for the good of the country" (not, as Aston charmingly translates the passage, "I request that my right hand may be made a national treasure"). Konoshiro's final request was naturally not granted.

3.32 See p. 11.

3.33 The second verse is obscure. It can also (see Nippon Gakujutsu Shinkōkai, ed., *The Manyōshū* [Tokyo, 1940], p. 9) be taken as a complaint by the Prince that during the present uncomfortable journey his rice is being served on oak leaves (*shii no ha*) rather than in proper boxes (*ke*) as at home. But then the poem becomes a mere self-pitying whine rather than a poignant statement of continued devotion to the gods.

3.34 Professor Takahashi suggests (Naoki, *Kodai Kokka no Seiritsu*, p. 240) that Prince Arima's friend, Shioya no Muraji Konoshiro, was to use his position in the salt enterprises to mobilize local fishermen and form a blockading fleet; but this seems fanciful.

3.35

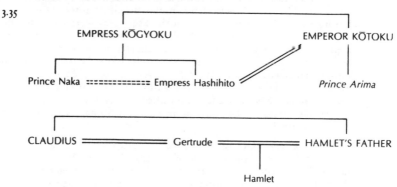

The double solid lines indicate marriages
The double dotted lines indicate illegitimate unions

3.36 ". . . the heart of America is good, the character of America is strong and we are going to continue to be a great nation." President Nixon, speaking in Huntsville, Alabama, 18th February 1974 (*New York Times*, 19th February 1974).

3.37   For "The Tales of the Tairas," see pp. 68–69. Concerning "Fires on the Plain" as a modern example of the literature of disaster see my introduction to the Penguin edition, New York, 1969, pp. viii *ff.*

3.38   Ivan Morris, *The World of the Shining Prince* (London and New York, 1964), pp. 196–98.

3.39   "Characters like these [i.e., the failed heroes] inspire us with an especially poignant sense of impermanence *(mujō)*." Kawabara, *Saigō Densetsu* (Tokyo, 1971), p. 50.

3.40   Concerning the symbolism of cherry blossoms, see n. 10.4.

Chapter 4

4.1   He also became the god of thunder and the patron deity of those who suffer injustice because of their sincerity.

4.2   . . . the Fujiwara leaders were firmly opposed to bloodshed of any kind. They did not believe in violent solutions. They achieved their own ends by planning and persuasion, and here they were prudent as well as moderate, for once they admitted the argument of force their own supremacy would be shattered. They favoured civilian virtues and were impressed by scholarship so long as scholars did not seek political advancement. (Sir George Sansom, *A History of Japan to 1334* [London, 1958], p. 150.)

    The Fujiwaras' leniency towards their enemies also had an ideological basis. This was a period when the Buddhist interdiction against killing was still influential; most of the Fujiwaras were good Buddhists and would not (unless it was absolutely unavoidable) risk the spiritual degradation involved in taking life. An equally powerful motive was the fear of *onryō*, the unappeased spirits of one's defeated enemies who might return to torment one after their death. As the story of Michizane shows, even a defeated enemy who had been allowed to end his days in peaceful retirement could become a lethal foe after he was dead. How much more dangerous would be the spirit of an enemy who had been executed or cruelly treated!

4.3   In Murasaki's novel, Genji is recalled to the capital and acquires political ascendancy at the expense of the Fujiwaras. In actual history, however, no pardoned exile was ever able to challenge their hegemony. Most of the historical models traditionally ascribed for Prince Genji were political exiles who had antagonized the ruling family. By far the most likely contender is Korechika, the popular young nobleman who was ousted from the capital by the ruling Fujiwara leader in 996 and appointed to the Government Headquarters in Kyushu (Morris, *The World of the Shining Prince,* [London and New York, 1964], pp. 56–57); Korechika, like Genji, was pardoned within two years, but his political career had been permanently blasted. Many of the *Genji* commentaries, starting with

Kakaishō in the 14th century, give Sugawara no Michizane as one of the models for Prince Genji, and *Shika Shichiron* in the 18th century states that he is *the* model. The attribution seems far-fetched. The only important points shared by the two men is that they had strong cultural interests and that both became political exiles; and this was hardly a rare combination in Heian times. What is important for a study of Japanese heroes, however, is that scholars through the centuries have *believed* that the historical models for the most illustrious hero in Japanese fiction were exiles, in other words, men who had suffered worldly failure.

4.4   The four branches of the vast Fujiwara clan were descended from Nakatomi no Kamatari, who had been given the cognomen of Fujiwara by his friend and associate, Emperor Tenji (see n. 3.5, above), in memory —or so tradition goes—of the wistaria arbour *(fuji-hara)* where they had discussed their plans to overthrow the Sogas.

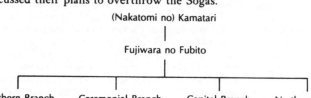

(Nakatomi no) Kamatari

Fujiwara no Fubito

Southern Branch   Ceremonial Branch   Capital Branch   Northern Branch

After a prolonged struggle the "northern" branch triumphed over the others in the early 9th century.

4.5   For the policies used by the Fujiwaras to secure their control over the government, see Morris, *Shining Prince*, pp. 200–12.

4.6   According to the Chinese-type hierarchy established in the Great Reform (see pp. 27–28), the administration of the country was controlled by the Great Council of State, which was directly responsible to the Emperor. The Great Council consisted of the Prime Minister; Ministers of the Left, Right, and Centre; Major, Middle, and Minor Counsellors; and Privy Counsellors (or Imperial Advisers). The post of Prime Minister was usually not filled. As a rule there were four Major Counsellors, three Middle and three Minor Counsellors, and eight Privy Counsellors. See Ivan Morris, *The Pillow Book of Sei Shōnagon*, II: Appendix 7, for factual details concerning Heian administration, and *Shining Prince*, chap. 3, for a description.

4.7   These Reform measures, which were initiated under Emperor Uda, were known as Kampyō no Seiji (politics of the Kampyō year-period) and led to the major Engi administrative reforms in the reign of his son, Emperor Daigo. Essentially these were conservative measures aimed at preserving the Taika *ritsuryō* system, which had been badly impaired by innovations in central administration, by the weakness of provincial government, and above all by the collapse of the official system of land distribution. Among the practical measures in the Kampyō Reform were: (a) the despatch of investigators (Momikushi) to the provinces to hear the complaints of farmers about local abuses, to check the drift of population from certain parts of the countryside, and to reestablish the local authority of centrally-appointed officials; and (b) an effort to cut the expenses of central government by amalgamating certain offices and bureaus and by reducing the personnel of the Imperial Guards.

4.8   Elderly, that is, by Heian standards. When Uda came to the Throne at 21, Michizane was precisely double his age.

4.9   *Nihon Sandai Jitsuroku*, one of the great literary accomplishments of the age, was commissioned by Emperor Uda but not completed until the reign of Emperor Daigo. Tokihira and Michizane were among the main collaborators and, by a typical irony, the 50-volume work was presented to the Court only a few months after Tokihira had forced Michizane into exile. *Ruijū Kokushi* was presented by Sugawara no Michizane in 892; of the original 200 *kan* only 61 have survived. Another important work by Michizane was his 28-volume collection of Chinese poetry by a grandfather, his father, and himself. He also wrote an erudite preface to a treatise on Buddhism by a famous contemporary, the priest Ennin. In 893 Emperor Uda commissioned Michizane to compile a new anthology of Japanese poems entitled *Shinsen Manyōshū*. The attribution both of this collection and of *Ruijū Kokushi* have been questioned by some modern scholars.

4.10   The legendary ancestor of the Sugawaras was Nomi no Sukune whom Emperor Suinin (*c.* 3rd century A.D.) summoned from the western province of Izumo to engage in a wrestling bout with the current champion. Nomi no Sukune killed his opponent by powerful kicks in the ribs and loins, and he was rewarded with all the dead man's lands and property. This rough encounter is said to be the origin of present-day *sumō*, a far more elegant (and safer) type of fighting. Some twenty years after his triumph Nomi no Sukune showed a gentler side of his nature when, so tradition goes, he proposed that clay figures instead of living retainers should be buried with the corpses of famous people.

4.11   See n. 1.6

4.12   Michizane appears to have taken a warm interest in the welfare of his students, even the least promising ones. We have an interesting collection of 10 Chinese poems written by Michizane in 882, one addressed to each of the students graduating from the Imperial University. In a poem to a student from the scholarly Wake family, Michizane refers to the fact that he has failed 13 times before finally passing—"So pray let me see your melancholy face relax its frown this day." Another gentleman (a Tachibana) was an "eternal student" who had taken some 20 years to pass. The following is from *Nihon Shoki* (ed. Nihon Koten Zensho [Tokyo, 1953], XVII: 150):

> Not till the age of forty-one
> Have you been free to leave these halls.
> [But do not grieve—]
> For great brains ripen late.

Among Michizane's more successful students from the Bunshōin (the private school of the Sugawara family) many rose to important positions in the government, and according to one theory it was they who first helped establish his posthumous reputation. From the point of view of the Fujiwaras the support of these former pupils for their old master was a potential source of danger, and several of them were exiled after Michizane's fall from power in 901.

4.13 According to Professor Kuroita (*Kokushi no Kenkyū* [Tokyo, 1936], I:255), Emperor Uda had to make haste in appointing Prince Atsuhito as his successor, since he could not risk the danger that his other consort, Atsuko (the daughter of Fujiwara no Mototsune) might have a son who, in line with Fujiwara "marriage politics," would automatically take precedence over any other possible successors; he also wished to name his heir before Tokihira, the new Fujiwara leader, had time to entrench himself too firmly. This might also help explain why Emperor Uda abdicated so precipitously a few years later when he was only 31 years old and his successor a mere 13.

4.14 According to one of the legends, however, Michizane actually did go to China and was there converted to Zen. Certain monks in the 15th century declared that during the Sung Dynasty, Michizane had visited China to study under a Zen master—this despite the fact that the Sung Dynasty did not come into existence until well after Michizane's death. A famous picture of Michizane called "The Heavenly Deity Who Crossed to China" *(Totō Tenjin)* shows the great scholar dressed in the robes of a Zen priest and carrying a branch of the plum blossom that had become symbolically associated with his legend. Sakamoto Tarō, *Sugawara no Michizane* (Tokyo, 1956), pp. 162–63.

4.15 A notable exception is Kibi no Makibi (693–775), a brilliant, energetic scholar, who is credited among other things with having invented the *katakana* phonetic syllabary. He visited China from 716 to 735, and on his return to Japan is said to have introduced the *biwa* lute, the art of embroidery, and the game of *go*. In 766 Makibi was appointed to be Great Minister of the Right, and he exerted considerable influence at Court until he was outmanoeuvred by the Fujiwaras, who had now started on their slow rise to ascendancy. On the whole, Makibi's contributions to Japanese culture far surpassed Michizane's; but, not having had the privilege of dying in exile, he never achieved the status of hero.

4.16 For another possible motive of Uda's abdication see n. 4.13, above.

4.17 Kuroita, *Kokushi no Kenkyū*, p. 255.

4.18 The Fujiwaras had come to depend on the Minamoto clan as their "claws and teeth" who would provide them with such military power as they might need when gentler methods failed.

4.19 Towards the end of 900 Kiyotsura gave a lecture to the Court concerning the dangers of the following year (901) which was Kanoto Tori, the 58th in the Chinese sexagenary cycle and therefore a year of crisis and change.

Kiyotsura warned Michizane that, since he had risen so rapidly in the hierarchy, his position would be particularly parlous during the forthcoming year of crisis and that therefore he should resign while there was still time. His prediction, whatever its motive, turned out to be entirely justified.

4.20

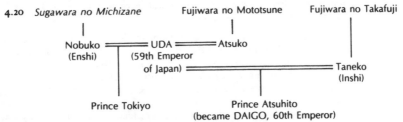

The double solid lines indicate marriages

4.21   The government is said to have done its best to make the journey uncomfortable for Michizane by preventing local officials from providing him with food, lodging, and other amenities. On one occasion when he found no shelter for the night he was obliged to sit on a piece of coiled rope. This is the origin of the famous Tsunaza Tenjin (the Heavenly Rope-Seated Deity), which depicts the old Minister seated in the middle of the coil, with a look of rage on his face and a baton in his hand. Such fierce images of the hero were common during the early period of his divinity, and are connected with his role as thunder god, a deity whom it is dangerous not to worship.

4.22   Translated by Burton Watson and Donald Keene, *Anthology of Japanese Literature* (New York, 1955), p. 165.

4.23   The tree is the *prunus mume*, commonly but incorrectly known as the Japanese apricot. Its small white *ume* (or *mume*) blossoms are traditionally respected in the Far East as symbols of fortitude because they appear in winter before any other flowers. Burton Watson in "Michizane and the Plums," *Japan Quarterly* XI, no. 2 (1964): 217–20.

4.24   *Kitano Tenjin Engi Emaki*, the first of many illustrated scrolls depicting Michizane's life, was produced in 1219. It is essentially a religious work designed to explain the origins and significance of the Kitano Shrine, where his spirit was enshrined about half a century after his death. The first section is a pictorial biography of the famous scholar; the second and more important part shows him in the process of becoming a god-hero. Michizane's poignant career was a popular subject for painters of the Tosa school from the 14th to the 17th centuries. The most readily available reproduction from the 13th-century hand-scroll can be found in Bradley Smith, *Japan—A History in Art* (New York, 1964), pp. 67–71.

4.25   Sugawara no Michizane, *Shosaiki*, quoted in Ikeda Kikan, *Heian Jidai no Bungaku to Seikatsu* (Tokyo, 1967), p. 72.

4.26   The site of the former Government Headquarters in Kyushu is about an hour's hideous drive from the modern industrial city of Fukuoka.

4.27   From *Kanke Kōsō*, quoted by Kitayama Shigeo, *Heian Kyō* (Tokyo, 1965), pp. 352–53. The third poem is translated by Burton Watson, "Michizane," p. 219.

4.28   Cf. p. 10.

4.29   But Tokihira had not reckoned with the lethal effects of Michizane's ghost; see p. 60.

4.30   On the anniversaries of Thomas à Becket's death in 1240 and 1241 a tower being built in London by Henry III collapsed, and it was reported that Sir Thomas's ghost had been seen standing on the battlements knocking down the stones with a staff. In 1242 the King ordered that the tower be rebuilt; but this time he named it after the martyr and it remained standing safely. Sir Thomas's Tower even managed to survive the Blitz.

4.31   Kitayama, *Heian Kyō* (Tokyo, 1965), p. 354. It was owing to this apparition that Michizane was originally worshipped as the thunder god (Raijin). Only after his spirit had finally been appeased was it possible to ignore his terrifying, vindictive aspect and to concentrate on his gentle, cultural attributes; at this stage he was transformed from being the angry god of thunder to being the kindly god of learning and literature as well as the patron deity of honest people who suffer from injustice. In this latter capacity he was identified with Kannon, the Buddhist goddess of mercy. Sakamoto, *Michizane*, p. 160.

4.32   Among other famous failures in Japanese history whom the government tried to appease after their deaths by erecting shrines are Fujiwara no Hirotsugu in the 8th century and Taira no Masakado in the 10th. Both men rebelled against the central government and were defeated by the imperial troops. Hirotsugu's vindictive spirit began taking revenge almost immediately after his death; Masakado's spirit was comforted by a shrine before it had a chance to start any mischief.

4.33   Burton Watson has described the shrine as follows:

The main building of the present shrine was built some three and a half centuries ago and is in the florid style typical of late Momoyama architecture; beautiful as it is, with its intricate roofs and splashes of red and gold, it conveys a somewhat false impression of the antiquity of the shrine, which is actually much older, dating from the middle of the tenth century. Clustered around the main building is an assortment of smaller shrines, monuments, and stone lanterns of all shapes, and among these grow the flowering plums for which the shrine is famous. Small trees, alarmingly bent and hollowed, they give the impression of having been subjected to almost intolerable buffeting and strain, which is why, when their scattering of delicate white flowers emerges each year from the blackened trunks to face the cold, they present such a poignant symbol of a modest but dogged determination to go on living. (Watson, "Michizane," p. 217.)

4.34   In the 17th century the Tokugawa government dedicated an important new shrine in their capital of Edo (Tokyo) for the worship of Michizane, whom the Shoguns particularly respected for his Confucian scholarship.

4.35   *Ōkagami* ("The Great Mirror"), quoted in *Shiryō ni yoru Nihon no Ayumi*, Kodai-hen (Tokyo, 1960), p. 139.

4.36   *Sugawara Denju Tenarai Kagami* (more literally "The Mirror of the Initiation-into-the-Secrets of Sugawara's Calligraphy") was a puppet play written in 1746 by Takeda Izumo. For a detailed synopsis in English see Aubrey Halford, *The Kabuki Handbook* (Tokyo, 1956), pp. 306–21.

4.37   Tokihira was the prime mover in the Reform movement from Yasunori's death in 895 until his own in 909. He was especially active in economic reforms, notably the regulation of the *shōen* (manors) and the improvement of the *handen* (allotment) field system.

4.38   Professor Burton Watson, one of the rare foreign scholars to have translated Michizane's Chinese poetry, provides a valuable assessment in "Michizane," pp. 217–18:

Michizane excelled all of the other men of his time in composing Chinese verse, which is to say that he was able to go beyond the stereotyped themes and sentiments expected of a court scholar—"Farewell to the Envoy from Pohai," "Viewing Chrysanthemums at an Official Banquet," etc.—and to use the medium to depict the actual scenes around him and the emotions they evoked. . . .

4.39   *Kokinshū*, nos. 272 and 420, in the *Nihon Koten Zensho* edition, pp. 85, 112. No. 420, a congratulatory poem written on the occasion of ex-Emperor Uda's excursion to the country in 898, is known to almost every schoolchild in Japan because of its inclusion in the famous *Hyakunin Isshu* anthology.

4.40   See Morris, *Shining Prince*, pp. 183–85.

4.41   It was not until the Tokugawa period (some seven centuries after his death) that Michizane came to be popularly worshipped as god of calligraphy. It is significant that in the famous puppet play of 1746 he figured not as a poet or a scholar but as a calligraphy master.

4.42   See n. 4.9.

4.43   "It is doubtful whether any person in Japan has been so popular for so long a time as Sugawara no Michizane." *Short Biographies of Eminent Japanese in Ancient and Modern Times* (Tokyo, 1890, anonymous and unpaginated).

4.44   Of all Japan's eminent failed heroes the only other man to have lived to an advanced age was also a civilian, namely Sen no Rikyū (1521–91), the most eminent of all tea-ceremony masters, and even he ended by having to kill himself. Michizane is unique among the historical failed heroes in having had a nonviolent death.

4.45   In the Christian experience there has always been the problem of what a pure mind and spirit must render unto Caesar, and despite frequent ecclesiastical compromises (e.g., by the Vatican during the Second World

War) the difficulty has never been resolved. The Japanese failed-hero mythology actually expresses the oil-and-water nature of world vs. spirit more fully and satisfactorily than Western efforts to discern God's Providence working through history.

4.46 See p. 39.See p. 39.

4.47 Descendants of Fujiwara branch families like the Konoe have in fact been important in the Japanese Court until modern times, and they even continued the old Fujiwara "marriage politics" by offering their daughters as imperial consorts.

4.48 See p. 25.

4.49 See pp. 11,35.

Chapter 5

5.1 As in most countries the majority of historical heroes in Japan are military men, the great difference, of course, being that so many of them fought on losing sides. For us who belong to a late or post-industrial age it is hard to obtain any clear picture of the character of a mediaeval knight, let alone a *Japanese* knight, and the available records concerning famous samurai are remarkably unhelpful when it comes to personal and psychological detail.

No doubt Emerson's description of "a rude race, all masculine, with brutish strength" applies to the generality of Japanese warriors as well as to their Western counterparts. Their style of life certainly epitomizes the harsh, violent side of the Japanese tradition; and, in case we are in danger of glamourising the mediaeval samurai, Professor Varley does well to remind us that they were "rough, unlettered men engaged in a brutal profession." (H. Paul Varley, *Japanese Culture* [New York, 1973], p. 173.)

Yet for all the ferocity, treachery, and sickening cruelty that blot the annals of the samurai through the centuries, their savagery was often mitigated by a genuine sensibility that manifested itself in a love of culture, especially poetry, a respect for "sincerity," and a feeling for "the pathos of things." These and the other positive qualities of the Japanese warrior are all epitomized in the historico-legendary composite of Yoshitsune, and recur in most of the later military heroes like Masashige and Saigō Takamori.

If superpatriots misuse the figure of the samurai, we should not let this taint an exquisite achievement . . . daring blended with delicacy, firmness allied to lightness, transport to taste. . . . The world is not rich enough in dreams of knighthood to make light of such images. (Singer, *Mirror, Sword and Jewel* [New York, 1973], p. 167.)

5.2 The *locus classicus* for the phrase appears to be a haiku by an early 17th-century poet, Matsue Shigeyori, who evokes the beauty of defeat as exemplified in nature by cherry blossoms scattering in the springtime wind:

Yo ya hana ni   literally: "Ah, the world to the blossoms
Hōganbiiki   Hōganbiiki (sympathy with loser)
Haru no kaze   Spring wind!"

Sympathy with the loser and a fascination with the heroic parabola are clearly related to the sense of *mujōkan* and *mono no aware* discussed on pp. 38–40, and belong to the "sincerity" side of the dichotomy outlined in n. 2.32.

In the legends of Yamato Takeru and Yoshitsune, as in the actual history of the modern hero, Saigō Takamori, a sensational series of victories is followed by cataclysmic defeat; in every case the pathos of their downfall is accentuated by the glory of their preceding success, and it is the nature of their *ending* that gives them their greatest appeal as heroes. As Mr. Kudō observes, "It is essential that [the hero] rise to a pinnacle and then fall." Kudō Yoroshi, "Tenraku-kei no Nihon Eiyū-zō," in *Shūkan Asahi* 6–8 (1973): 116.

5.3 E.g., Yoshitsune's visit to the supernatural regions. See Helen McCullough, *Yoshitsune, A Fifteenth-Century Japanese Chronicle* (Stanford, 1966), pp. 38ff. Professor McCullough's book contains an excellent study of the Yoshitsune legend followed by a translation of *Gikeiki.*

5.4 According to Mircea Eliade, myth can actually be "truer" than reality in that it makes the real story "yield a deeper and richer meaning, revealing a tragic destiny." Eliade gives an example of a recent accident in a Balkan village which was promptly embellished and turned into a myth; the local peasantry regarded the mythical version of the story as far more authentic than the events they had witnessed with their own eyes. (Eliade, *Cosmos and History* [New York, 1959].) In my description of Yoshitsune's career I have combined legendary and historical accounts, indicating (whenever it seems necessary) whether a particular event is true or fictitious. Indeed, throughout these chapters I have freely drawn on mythico-legendary sources that have no credibility as "objective" history yet provide valuable insights into the psychology of Japanese hero-worship. "Myth," as Professor Chadwick has written, "is the last— not the first—stage in the development of a hero." N. Chadwick, *The Growth of Literature* (Cambridge, England, 1932), p. 278.

5.5 *Hōgan-mono* ("plays about Yoshitsune") is the largest single subcategory in the Nō repertory. This reflects the vast appeal of the losing Yoshitsune during Muromachi times, the main creative era of Nō drama. The Yoshitsune legend continued to inspire writers through the Tokugawa period: Chikamatsu Monzaemon, the brilliant puppet and Kabuki dramatist, wrote no less than sixteen plays about Yoshitsune. For details about Yoshitsune literature and all other matters concerning his legend, by far the most valuable single source is Shimazu Hisamoto's *Yoshitsune Densetsu to Bungaku* (Tokyo, 1935), a veritable encyclopaedia of information about the hero.

5.6

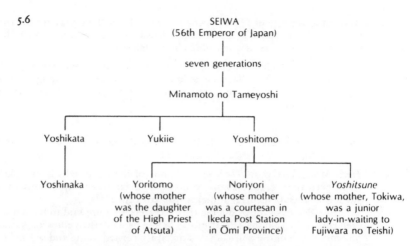

SEIWA
(56th Emperor of Japan)

|

seven generations

|

Minamoto no Tameyoshi

Yoshikata   Yukiie   Yoshitomo

Yoshinaka   Yoritomo   Noriyori   Yoshitsune
             (whose mother   (whose mother   (whose mother, Tokiwa,
             was the daughter was a courtesan in was a junior
             of the High Priest Ikeda Post Station lady-in-waiting to
             of Atsuta)   in Ōmi Province)   Fujiwara no Teishi)

5.7   Yoritomo's mother was the daughter of a Fujiwara aristocrat who was the Chief Priest in the important Atsuta Shrine; she was by far the most distinguished among Yoshitomo's many consorts.

5.8   According to the famous Koshigoe letter (see pp. 85–86), Yoshitsune specifically referred to himself as an orphan (jitsu naki no ko to nari).

5.9   The story is the basis of the famous Nō play, Hashi Benkei, translated by Arthur Waley in The Nō Plays of Japan (London, 1921).

5.10   See n. 1.6.

5.11   "You should have no difficulty in recognizing [Yoshitsune]. He is a little man with a fair complexion, and his teeth stick out slightly." Heike Monogatari, ed. Koten Nihon Bungaku Zenshū (Tokyo, 1966), p. 345.

5.12   See n. 5.46 concerning the hero's sexuality. Also see n. 5.70 about Yoshitsune as an Adonis figure.

5.13   McCullough, Yoshitsune, p. 5.

5.14   In the campaign against his cousin, Yoritomo also used his uncle, Yukiie, and his half-brother, Noriyori (see n. 5.6 for genealogy).

5.15   Yoshinaka's dazzling young wife, Tomoe Gozen, has a heroic role in the epic analogous to that of Yoshitsune's famous mistress, Shizuka (n. 5.48). She was endowed with legendary beauty and courage, and accompanied her husband on all his campaigns. Traditional depictions show her seated on a white charger in full samurai uniform commanding squadrons of eastern warriors. At the catastrophic battle in 1184 when Yoshinaka met his death, she was attacked by a herculean warrior named Uchida Ieyoshi but defeated him in single combat and sliced off his head. There are various traditions about what happened to this dazzling young amazon after her husband was killed. The usual version is that she retired to a convent at the age of 28 and spent the rest of her days praying for the repose of Yoshinaka's spirit; a rather less edifying account is that she became the mistress of one of his chief enemies.

5.16   When Yoshitsune left the capital at the end of 1185, he prevented his men from committing the pillage and arson that were common among departing troops. This greatly impressed members of the Court and the anxious citizenry of Kyoto.

5.17   See p. 80.

5.18   *Heike Monogatari*, p. 353. The Sacred Sword (Kusanagi) apparently· sank to the bottom of the sea and was never recovered.

5.19   *Heike Monogatari*, p. 11. *The temple bell:* one of the eight bells in the Hall of Impermanence at Jetavana Monastery, a famous temple built in a garden in Kosala (central India) in the 5th century B.C.
    The *sāla* trees: huge double-trunked trees that are said to have towered round the Buddha's death-place. When he died, the yellow blossoms on one of each of the pairs of trees instantly turned white and withered.

5.20   Varley, *Japanese Culture*, p. 66.

5.21   Wakamori Tarō, *Yoshitsune to Nihonjin* (Tokyo, 1966), p. 151. In the polygamous matrilocal society of early Japan, half-siblings with different mothers were brought up in the respective maternal households and usually had very little, if any, connexion with each other.

5.22   Those familiar with Turkish history will note certain striking similarities between Yoshitsune and the 15th-century failed hero, Cem, an elegant youth noted as a poet and painter but above all as a mighty warrior. He too was bedeviled by his elder half-brother, who had been brought up separately. The elder brother, a capable administrator who later became the Sultan Bayezid II, figures in the tradition as a wicked, jealous villain who treacherously compasses the hero's death. According to one version, Cem was murdered at his brother's behest in the Vatican by a treacherous barber wielding a poisoned razor; in another (more Japanese) version Cem committed suicide in despair over his unjust treatment. I am indebted to the young Turkish Japanologist, Selcuk Esenbel, for calling my attention to this interesting parallel.

5.23   See p. 72.

5.24   Yoritomo himself was outraged by Goshirakawa's tergiversations, which he no doubt regarded as typical of a corrupt and unreliable aristocracy. On one occasion he described the former Emperor as "the real devil" (*tengū*). In line with his general policy towards the Court, however, he continued to pay him the outward marks of respect.

5.25   Thus, according to the legend, it was Kajiwara who was responsible for Yoritomo's cruel treatment of Shizuka and her baby. One version of the legend compounds his fiendishness by making him suggest that Shizuka's stomach be ripped open in order to kill both mother and baby. Kajiwara's role in the Yoshitsune story is analogous to that of Soga no Akae in the tragedy of Prince Arima (see pp. 37–38): in each case the central villain is abetted by a socially inferior super-villain.

5.26   *Heike Monogatari*, pp. 329–30.

5.27   *Ibid.*, pp. 344–45.

5.28   *Ibid.*, p. 345.

5.29   It appears that about this time Yoshitsune was in fairly close association with his incompetent uncle, but there is no evidence that he had any plans for actually joining forces against Yoritomo. It was not until after Yoritomo had actually sent an assassin from Kamakura to Kyoto that Yoshitsune, realizing that an open clash was inevitable, turned to his uncle for support. Wakamori, *Yoshitsune*, p. 147.

5.30   According to a later form of the legend, the Koshigoe letter was actually written by Benkei on Yoshitsune's instructions. This is part of the tendency to give Benkei an increasingly active part in the events as the hero himself becomes a passive victim.

5.31   There are no important differences between the various texts of the Koshigoe letter. I have based my translation on the version given in the late Kamakura history, *Azuma Kagami*, ed. Nihon Shiryō Shūsei (Tokyo, 1963), p. 164.

5.32   . . . *soi wo noburu* (Koshigoe letter) means literally "to tell my true intentions." Yoshitsune wishes his brother to know that he has been motivated exclusively by a loyal desire to serve him and that he has never had any political ambitions of his own.

5.33   The Court had appointed Yoshitsune and Yukiie to be stewards of all the *shōen* estates in Kyushu and Shikoku respectively; this was a source of great potential wealth but did not provide the all-important manpower for a campaign against Kamakura.

5.34   Quoted by Ishii Susumu in *Kamakura Bakufu* (Tokyo, 1965), pp. 188–89.

5.35   Kadokawa Genyoshi, "Gikeiki no Seiritsu," *Kokugakuin Zasshi* LXV, nos. 2, 3 (1964): 79–100.

5.36   Nogami Toyoichirō, *Yōkyoku Zenshū* (Tokyo, 1935): V: 51.

5.37   *Ibid.*, pp. 54–55. "Portable altar" would probably be a more accurate translation of *oi* than "pannier." It was a large wooden box with legs used by travelling pilgrims to carry Buddhist altar fittings, vestments, and other accessories.

5.38   *Ibid.* p. 63.

5.39   *Ibid.*, pp. 67–68.

5.40   *Ibid.*, p. 72.

5.41   Togashi's conflict is made far more patent in *Kanjinchō*, which actually shows him stealing a look at the subscription list and realizing that it is bogus; his subsequent interrogation of Benkei is designed entirely to hoodwink the guards. The Kabuki version (1840) states what the Nō simply suggests, and also reflects the Edo period's preoccupation with the theme of *giri-ninjō* (duty *vs.* human emotion); *Ataka* (late 15th century) is imbued with the Nō aura of *aware* and *mujōkan* (transience).

5.42   Cf. the change in Yamato Takeru's character in the second part of his career.

5.43   It is significant that *Ataka* and *Funa Benkei*, the two most famous Nō plays about Yoshitsune during his downhill period, should both place Benkei in the central *shite* role and relegate his master to a subordinate part.

5.44   Wakamori, *Yoshitsune*, pp. 215–16, suggests that the relationship between Yoshitsune and Benkei as pictured in the late Kamakura and Muromachi versions of the legend reflects a nostalgia for a past age when relations between master and retainer were supposedly based on simple, personal bonds of loyalty and affection rather than on the type of cool self-interest that came to dominate lord-vassal relationships in later feudal times.

5.45   Benkei as he emerges in the later legends is just as fictitious a figure as Sancho Panza. Rambunctious mountain priests were standard characters in adventure dramas of the time, and Yoshitsune's servant belongs to a well-established tradition. At the same time it is possible that one or more monks accompanied Yoshitsune on his flight to the north and that Benkei is a composite figure based on actual *yamabushi*. He functions in the legendary structure as a sort of "foil hero" created so that Yoshitsune may continue on his flight and fully develop the *mono no aware* side of the failed hero's persona; in this sense the two of them (Yoshitsune-Benkei) combine to represent the quintessential Japanese hero.

5.46   Though Shizuka is the principal heroine in the Yoshitsune legend, she was far from being the only woman to accompany him on his retreat to the west. According to "The Chronicle of Yoshitsune," the hero had been on intimate terms with at least two dozen ladies during his short stay in the capital, and he had evidently made such an impression that no less than 11 of them embarked with him on his ship in the Inland Sea. Yoshitsune's reputation as a womanizer, which is again reminiscent of Prince Genji, is attested by numerous other sources and appears to have been one of the reasons that Yoritomo suspected his seriousness and reliability. The hero's amorousness became part of his legend. In a collection of prints by the late Tokugawa artist, Kunisada (1786–1865), he is pictured in a series of erotic encounters with different young ladies of the capital and endowed with genitals that are enormous even by the exaggerated standard of Japanese "spring pictures." The contrast between Yoshitsune's virile sexuality and the delicate, effeminate quality that is emphasized in the later legends is typical of Japanese romantic heroes and reflects Yoshitsune's dual nature.

5.47   According to *Azuma Kagami*, the famous dance took place *before* the birth of the child. In this instance the later, legendary version seems more plausible: women in an advanced stage of pregnancy do not usually make good dancers, and Shizuka's performance in Kamakura is reputed to have been one of the finest in her brilliant career.

5.48   Both Shizuka and Benkei appear to be composite figures and belong to a different level of historicity from Yoshitsune, about whom we have verifiable historical facts. Yoshitsune, in his turn, is far less "solid" historically than Yoritomo, since almost all the extant accounts about his life are heavily weighted on the side of legend. These distinctions, however, are mainly the concern of scholars; most Japanese regard Benkei, Shizuka, Yoshitsune, Yoritomo, and the other people in the story as having more or less the same degree of reality.

Shizuka is the outstanding female character and can be accepted as one type of failed heroine, a semifictitious counterpart to her tragic lover. Whenever I have asked Japanese people about failed heroines in the history of their country, they have mentioned the name of Shizuka. For another failed heroine of the period see Tomoe Gozen (n. 5.15).

Mainly owing to the prolonged period of military hegemony, during which women of the samurai class tended more and more to be kept in a position of irremediable inferiority, there are relatively few heroines (failed or otherwise) in Japanese history—except, of course, for culture-heroines like Ono no Komachi and Murasaki Shikibu.

Among the samurai a wife's relationship to her husband paralleled his relationship to his overlord and was therefore based on total, unquestioning loyalty and subservience. This relationship is succinctly described and justified by Nitobe (see n. 5.62):

Woman's surrender of herself to the good of her husband, home, and family, was as willing and honourable as the man's self-surrender to the good of his lord and country. Self-renunciation, without which no life-enigma can be solved, was the keynote of the loyalty of man as well as of the domesticity of woman. She was no more the slave of man than was her husband of his liege-lord, and the part she played was recognized as *naijo*, "the inner help." In the ascending scale of service stood woman, who annihilated herself for man, that he might annihilate himself for the master, that he in turn might obey Heaven. (Nitobe, *Bushido: The Soul of Japan* [Rutland, Vt., and Tokyo, 1969; first published 1905], pp. 146–47.).

Such heroines as did emerge during the long period of military rule (mid-12th to mid-19th centuries) rarely stand on their own, but are linked to their husbands or other close male relations, whose valour and glory they reflect in the same way that a vassal, however courageous, can only aspire to reflect the prestige of his lord. Thus the most illustrious women in the 12th century, Tomoe (see n. 5.15), Shizuka, and Masako, derived the possibility of heroic stature from their husbands, Yoshinaka, Yoshitsune, and Yoritomo respectively. Similarly, the famous 16th-century heroine Oichi no Kata (whom legend pictures, like Shizuka, as the most beautiful woman of her time) valiantly defied her brother, the prepotent Oda Nobunaga, and joined her husband, Shibata Katsuie, in the famous Götterdämmerung suicide in Kita no Shō Castle (1583); but the prime mover in the climactic act of heroism was Katsuie, not his wife. Again,

Yamanouchi Kazutoyo no Tsuma (1557–1617) was one of the most admired women of her time; yet, as we can gather from her very name ("The Wife of Yamanouchi Kazutoyo"), it was essentially through her husband that she acquired fame. Gracia Hosokawa (1563–1600), the famous Christian convert, is one of the few heroines in Japanese history who actually outshines her husband in self-sacrificial nobility and fame (see n. 7.71).

5.49   From *Gyokuyō*, the diary of Fujiwara no Kanezane (1149–1207).

5.50   Yoshitsune's flight to the northeast as a hunted outlaw belongs to the ancient legendary tradition of *sasuraibanashi* (see n. 1.43) and is typical of the Japanese romantic hero in distress.

5.51   See p. 73.

5.52   Ōshū had existed as a virtually independent state since the long northern wars in the 11th century, and its capital at Hiraizumi had become an impressive centre, in certain ways rivaling Kyoto itself. The vast Chūson Temple complex was noted for its lavish use of gold (quarried from the rich Ōshū mines), and some of the greatest artists of the late Heian period had contributed to its decoration. By comparison, Yoritomo's headquarters in Kamakura was a crude military encampment.

5.53   *Gikeiki* ("The Chronicle of Yoshitsune,"), ed. Koten Nihon Bungaku Zenshū (Tokyo, 1966), p. 209.

5.54   It appears that for various superstitious and religious reasons it was impossible for Yoritomo himself to attack his brother at this particular time. The ideal arrangement was to persuade Yoshitsune's hosts to do the job for him. Watanabe Tamotsu, *Yoshitsune* (Tokyo, 1966), p. 214.

5.55   In the legend, Yasuhira figures as another super-villain (see n. 5.25 about Kajiwara), unfilial, treacherous, cowardly, and brutal. He is reputed, inter alia, to have murdered his younger brother and his paternal grandmother.

5.56   The 11 other warriors in the Koromo stronghold appear to have deserted their master in his hour of need. This reduced Yoshitsune's force by 50 percent but did little to change the odds of the battle.

5.57   According to "The Chronicle of Yoshitsune," this wife was the daughter of Minamoto no Michichika, a government official and famous poet; but in fact her identity is dubious, and the tradition that she accompanied her hero-husband on his long flight to Ōshū is almost certainly legendary. The various accounts of Yoshitsune's female companions tend to be vague and contradictory (see n. 5.46).

5.58   *Gikeiki*, p. 216.

5.59   "Mere eastern retainers," as he describes them (*Gikeiki*, p. 212). Yasuhira, who (despite his villainy) would have made a socially respectable opponent, did not take part in the battle, presumably because he did not dare to incur any risks to his personal safety.

5.60   Yoshitsune's death poem expresses the wish that he may be reunited with Benkei in the next world.

5.61   *Gikeiki*, pp. 217–18.

5.62   *Ibid.*

The practice of self-disembowelment probably started during the fierce provincial fighting in the northeast during the 11th century, but the first recorded instance of harakiri is dated less than 20 years earlier than Yoshitsune's. This is the suicide of Minamoto no Tametomo, a gargantuan archer (seven feet in stature and having the strength of four men) who, when he was attacked by government forces in 1170 and all his followers had been killed, slashed open his stomach and died at the age of 33, later becoming the hero of numerous Kabuki plays (see n. 5.70).

Why did this particular form of self-immolation become established in the samurai class, not only as the standard way of avoiding disgrace and vindicating one's honour *(setsujoku)*, but as an official punishment prescribed by superior authorities, the method of suicide of an attendant on the death of his lord *(junshi)*, and the ultimate manner of remonstrating with an erring superior *(kanshi)*? In the first place, it was chosen as an excruciatingly painful form of self-mutilation, being in fact a gratuitous infliction of torture preceding the actual death-blow, which was normally administered by a sword-wielding second known as the *kaishaku-nin*. This choice of extreme suffering was no doubt related to the strain of self-mortification in Zen (which became the samurai's religion par excellence) and also to the idea that it was incumbent on members of the elite warrior class to display their unique courage and determination by undergoing an agonizing ordeal that mere commoners (or women) could not possibly endure. Referring to the defeated members of the League of the Divine Wind (1876), Mishima writes: "They knew that poison was the most effective way to commit a hasty suicide, but they spurned this womanish means of putting an end to life." Mishima Yukio, *Runaway Horses* (New York, 1973) (Gallagher trans.), p. 95; for the League of the Divine Wind, see n. 9.177.

In psychological terms a man's desire for pain reflects both an extreme assertion of the will and his anticipation of the respect he will receive for having chosen the most agonizing form of self-sacrifice; like suicide in general, it involves the transformation of a sadistic fantasy into a masochistic one. For a full discussion of the sadistic basis of suicide and self-inflicted suffering of all kinds see Theodor Reik, *Masochism and the Modern Man* (New York, 1941), esp. pp. 7–67.

But why disembowelment rather than some other form of self-torture? *Hara* (abdomen), apart from being the physical centre of the body, was traditionally regarded as the locus of a man's inner being, the place where his will, spirit, generosity, indignation, courage, and other cardinal qualities were concentrated. In this sense the word is analogous to the rather crude English "guts" (as in "he's full of guts"), but it has a far wider and more dignified sense, appearing in numerous idioms like *hara ga ōkii* ("large-stomached" = generous, magnanimous), *hara wo tateru* ("to raise one's stomach" = to become indignant, take offence), and *hara wo kimeru* ("to fix one's stomach" = to be settled in one's resolution). To rip open one's stomach in the act of *harakiri* was therefore a manner of suicide (or rather, pre-suicide) in which the samurai used his sword, the outer symbol of his spirit, to cut into the very core of his most precious emotions.

When Nitobe Inazō composed his famous *Bushido: The Soul of Japan*, partly in an attempt to explain and justify his country's military traditions to conventional Christian readers in Europe and America, he was at pains to discover Western parallels for seemingly bizarre Japanese customs like harakiri:

When Moses wrote of Joseph's "bowels yearning upon his brother," or David prayed the Lord not to forget his bowels, or when Isaiah, Jeremiah, and other inspired men of old spoke of the "sounding" or the "troubling" of bowels, they all and each endorsed the belief prevalent among the Japanese that in the abdomen was enshrined the soul. (Nitobe Inazō, *Bushido*, pp. 112–13.)

By far the best treatment of the subject in a Western language is "An Account of the Hara-Kiri" by A. B. Mitford (later Lord Redesdale) in *Tales of Old Japan* (London, 1883), Appendix A. Mitford includes (pp. 355–60) a description of a harakiri execution that he himself witnessed in Kobe in 1868 as official representative of the British Government. He ends his gruelling account with the following comment:

The ceremony . . . was characterized throughout by that extreme dignity and punctiliousness which are the distinctive marks of the proceedings of Japanese gentlemen of rank. . . . While profoundly impressed by the terrible scene, it was impossible at the same time not to be filled with admiration of the firm and manly bearing of the sufferer, and of the nerve with which the kaishaku [-nin] performed his last duty to his master. Nothing could more strongly show the force of education. The Samurai, or gentleman of the military class, from his earliest years learns to look upon the *hara-kiri* as a ceremony in which some day he may be called upon to play a part as principal or second. In old-fashioned families, which hold to the traditions of ancient chivalry, the child is instructed in the rite and familiarized with the idea as an honourable expiation of crime or blotting out of disgrace. If the hour comes, he is prepared for it, and bravely faces an ordeal which early training has robbed of half its horrors. In what other country in the world does a man learn that the last tribute of affection which he may have to pay to his best friend may be to act as his executioner? (Mitford, p. 359.)

The rationale of stomach-cutting was summed up in the following explanation to a foreign newspaper correspondent by Mishima Yukio, who typically related it to the concept of *makoto* ("sincerity"):

I cannot believe in Western sincerity because it is invisible, but in feudal times we believed that sincerity resided in our entrails, and if we needed to show our sincerity, we had to cut our bellies and take out our *visible* sincerity. And it was also the symbol of the will of the soldier, the samurai; everybody knew that this was the most painful way to die. And the reason they preferred to die in the most excruciating manner was that it proved the courage of the samurai. This method of suicide was a Japanese invention and foreigners could not copy it. (Quoted by Henry Scott-Stokes, *The Life and Death of Yukio Mishima* [New York, 1974], p. 14.)

The date was 1966, four years before Mishima put his theory into sanguinary practice.

From the late 17th century, by a typical Japanese process of ritualization, it became customary for the *kaishaku-nin* to strike off the principal's head before he had time to start disembowelling himself; this was especially true of executions, in which the prisoner merely went through the semblance of disembowelment, sometimes a mere scratch on the stomach, before his *kaishaku-nin* struck the fatal blow. The full process of self-torture, however, was never completely abandoned: both Vice-Admiral Ōnishi (1945) and Mishima (1970) resolutely disembowelled themselves according to the ancient ritual followed by Yoshitsune, Masashige, and other early heroes.

5.63   Sources differ about the identity of Yoshitsune's children who were killed in this bloodbath. According to many versions, there was only one child, a daughter of three.

5.64   "The Chronicle of Yoshitsune," pp. 219-20.

5.65   The characteristically Japanese word *wakajini* ("death at a young age") evokes a keen sense of "the pathos of things," and it is certainly no coincidence that so many of the most beloved heroes in Japanese history died very young:

> They shall not grow old,
> As we that are left grow old.
> Age shall not weary them nor the years condemn.

Mishima Yukio was appalled by the idea that he should still be alive at the indecent age of 45 and realized that there was little time to be lost if he wished to qualify as a Yamato hero.

5.66   Yasuhira's act of treachery turned out to have been useless. Only a few weeks after Yoshitsune's death, the Lord of Kamakura attacked and totally destroyed the "northern Fujiwaras" in a brief campaign, thus bringing to an end several generations of their glory. The vast Ōshū domains were incorporated with his own territory or distributed to his vassals as rewards. With this final victory Yoritomo emerged successfully from a decade of civil war, and in the following year (1190) he made his first triumphal entry into Kyoto, where his arrival was anxiously watched by the Retired Emperor and the high Court nobles. Yasuhira himself managed to escape to the north, but was betrayed by a retainer and killed. It has been suggested that Yasuhira's attack on Yoshitsune was not only treacherous but stupid, since it eliminated the one commander who might have organized a successful defence against the inevitable onslaught from Kamakura. This is unlikely. Yoshitsune's military talents were unsuited to the type of prolonged defensive operations that would have been necessary to withstand Yoritomo once he had decided to invest Ōshū with his overwhelming forces.

5.67   It is nowhere stated why Yoritomo himself did not inspect Yoshitsune's head. He was engaged in various religious observances at the time and was probably afraid of incurring ritual pollution; it is also possible that he did not relish the idea of examining the decomposing remains of a brother for whose death he was directly responsible.

5.68   Though the survival theories are all fanciful fabrications, it must be admitted that the identification of the hero's head cannot have been very reliable. The messenger from Ōshū had taken some six weeks to reach Koshigoe, and his arrival had been further delayed owing to an important religious ceremony in Kamakura. In the hot summer weather Yoshitsune's head must have been in an advanced state of decomposition despite the sweet *sake*, and it is theoretically possible that even people like Kajiwara who had known him well might have been deceived by a substituted head.

5.69   In Ainu lore he is said to have been known as Okikurumi. The Hokkaido theory, which is reported in the vast Tokugawa history, *Dai Nihon Shi*, and also incorporated in Chikamatsu's *jōruri* play, *Yoshitsune Shōgikei*, established a long-lasting connexion between the Yoshitsune legend and the northern island. During the Meiji period, steam engines in Hokkaido were sometimes named after people who figured in the legend, and Emperor Meiji himself during his state visit to Sapporo travelled in a train that was pulled by an engine called "Yoshitsune." Other engines in Hokkaido were called "Shizuka" and "Benkei"; it is significant that none was ever named after the successful Yoritomo.

5.70   A similar survival-legend concerns Saigō Takamori, who is said to have escaped from the battlefield in Kyushu and made his way to Russia (see p. 226). There is also a legend that Sugawara no Michizane left his place of exile in Dazaifu and went to China (Wakamori, *Yoshitsune*, p. 37). Another failed hero of the 12th century, Minomoto no Tametomo, was finally defeated in a naval battle (1170) and disembowelled himself; according to the legend, however, he fled to the Ryukyu Islands, where he founded a new dynasty of sovereigns. All these stories, in which the death of a historical hero is followed by his supernatural survival or resurrection, reflect a typically Japanese blending of real and fictive worlds. Yoshitsune was a famous historical figure who played an important part in the actual events of the 12th century; yet as his story developed during subsequent centuries he increasingly came to fit into an archetypal pattern of the mythical hero whose destruction guarantees the survival and stability of society. In many respects he is analogous to the tragic figure of the beautiful, childlike youth, Adonis, who was sacrificed (gored to death by a boar) and resurrected as a symbol of the yearly cycle of vegetation. Just so, the handsome young Yoshitsune was done to death by his elder brother (the evil force of destruction) and then returned to life in Hokkaido or on the Asian mainland.

The mythical victim-hero is endowed with supernatural powers (e.g., Yoshitsune's miraculous swordsmanship, his visit to the underworld, etc.), yet eventually he is defeated as an inevitable part of the natural cycle: through the periodic sacrifice of the life principle, the gods, fate, etc. are appeased and the continuance of the natural cycle is assured. The "wild child" of Mount Kurama is reminiscent of the youthful, vigorous Adonis; and it is also archetypal that Yoshitsune should be a virtual orphan. Finally the scapegoat must be sacrificially pure: in the case of Yoshitsune this takes the form of moral sincerity and a refusal to be corrupted by worldly intrigue.

As we know from J. G. Frazer and his successors, the ritual destruction of the hero or king is a seminal theme in many parts of the world. Whereas in the West the archetypes belong almost entirely to myth, in Japan they are projected onto actual historical figures. The numerous dramas about Yoshitsune invariably give precedence to nonhistorical and essentially mythical elements as opposed to actual events; since Yoshitsune is the archetype of the youthful sacrificial victim, this means that the plays deal with the downhill part of his career rather than with his military victories. The Japanese form of the death-rebirth myth places the emphasis entirely on the hero's sacrifice rather than on his rebirth; except in the legend of Yamato Takeru, where magical elements predominate (e.g., his posthumous transformation into a white bird), the theme of resurrection is unimportant.

5.71 In the basic sincerity-realism dichotomy (see n. 2.32) Yoshitsune clearly contravened the "law" by defying his elder brother, the chieftain of the Minamoto clan, and from a cold, realistic viewpoint *(bijō)* he amply deserved his fate. But judged by the emotional criterion of *nasake* this insubordinate young outlaw was unquestionably in the right.

5.72 Even after the defeat of the Tairas, Yoritomo continued his policy of playing potential Minamoto opponents off against each other. In 1185 Yoshitsune was ordered to attack his uncle, Yukiie, and it was only when he balked that Yoritomo realized he could no longer use his young brother in this particular way and turned against him violently.

5.73 After Hidehira's death the issue of whether to continue protecting Yoshitsune caused a weakening split among the Ōshū leaders, which apparently facilitated the conquest of their territory by the Kamakura forces. Wakamori, *Yoshitsune* p. 214.

5.74 Yoritomo died in 1199 and his direct line became extinct in 1219, partly owing to his proclivity to killing off his own close relatives; but the great shogunal families of later centuries (the Ashikagas and the Tokugawas) descended from Yoritomo's family.

It is interesting to speculate about what might have happened if Yoshitsune had somehow prevailed in the struggle with his elder brother. In all likelihood this would have meant an aggravation of the endemic disunity and disorder in the country, abetted by the continued influence of the Retired Emperor, who would presumably have tried to keep leading factions of the military class divided among themselves in order to increase the relative power of the Court.

5.75 Many of the legends represent Yoshitsune as a skilled flautist. This is connected with his role as an elegant courtier, and it also helps to explain his success with women. Above all, the lonely, plaintive, evanescent sound of the Japanese *fue* comes to symbolize the pathos of Yoshitsune's brief life. Yoshitsune's flute plays an important part in the romance from which the entire art of *jōruri* ballad-drama took its name. In this famous story Yoshitsune charms Lady Jōruri and her companions by the sound of his flute. She becomes his mistress, but he is obliged to leave her in order to continue his journey to the north.

Chapter 6

6.1 One interesting version, mentioned by Henri Joly in *Legends in Japanese Art* (London, 1908; reprinted Tokyo, 1967), p. 309, shows the hero seated on a coil of rope with a mariner's compass in his hand. The coiled rope is reminiscent of the depiction of the furious Michizane on his way to exile in Kyushu (see n. 4.21).

6.2 *Aa chūshin nanshi no bo.*

6.3 H. Paul Varley, *Imperial Restoration in Medieval Japan* (New York, 1971), p. 186.

6.4 Kublai Khan's invasions of 1274 and 1281 were the first such attacks in Japanese history, yet apart from the Hōjō Regent, Tokimune (1215–84), not a single important figure, historical or legendary, emerged from the struggle. In fact, the only real hero was an impersonal force of nature, the Kamikaze or Divine Wind, that destroyed the invading fleet at the crucial moment and ensured a Japanese victory. Perhaps the very totality of the Mongol collapse was unpropitious for traditional Japanese heroism; a military defeat might well have produced its crop of heroic failures.

6.5 The famous Scroll of the Mongol Invasion, one of the best sources of information about the first Mongol attack, illustrates the brave deeds of a certain warrior named Takezaki Suenaga. The main reason for producing the scroll was to substantiate Suenaga's request for a reward: it was in fact a sort of pictorial affidavit. Suenaga travelled all the way from Kyushu to Kamakura to press his claims and, owing to his persistence, he eventually received the stewardship of an estate.

Half a century later the failure to provide adequate rewards for Godaigo's supporters was one of the immediate reasons for the failure of the Kemmu Restoration (see pp. 127–28.) It is against this rather unidealistic background that Masashige's supposedly selfless devotion to the imperial cause stands out so impressively.

6.6 Traditional writers, who wish to draw ethical lessons from history, stress the moral decline of the later Hōjōs as the real reason for their collapse. They are thus fitted into the Confucian historiographic pattern of the corrupt, cruel, degenerate rulers who lose the sanction of Heaven and bring a dynasty to its end. The full repertory of "bad" qualities is attributed to Hōjō Takatoki, the last of the Hōjō Regents. In fact, no such moral reasons are required to explain the fall of the Hōjōs, which was due largely to economic and political difficulties.

6.7 Sir George Sansom gives the best detailed account of the succession dispute in English. See *A History of Japan to 1334* (London, 1958), pp. 476–84.

6.8 Godaigo's predecessor was Emperor Hanazóno, a grandson of Gosaga's elder son, Gofukakusa. He had come to the Throne at the typical age of 11 and abdicated in favour of the Junior Line (represented by Godaigo) when he was 21. His grandfather, Emperor Gofukakusa, had started his reign at the precocious age of 3 and abdicated when he was 16.

6.9 The Office of the Retired Emperor (Inchō), where much of the imperial business had been conducted since the late 11th century, was officially abolished a few years after Godaigo came to the Throne, and thereafter he concentrated all the remaining imperial powers in his own hands.

6.10 See p. 81.

6.11 Owing to the astute politics of his father, Retired Emperor Uda, Daigo managed to reign for 33 years (897–930) without the interference of a Regent or Chancellor. For this reason he is glorified as one of the greatest emperors in Japanese history, but in fact he never really succeeded in breaking the hold of the prepotent Fujiwaras, and after his death they reasserted themselves with a vengeance. In Godaigo's time the Hōjō Regents occupied a role analogous to that of the Fujiwaras in the 10th century, and if power was to be restored to the imperial family it was essential that they be put in their place. As it turned out, the Hōjōs were effectively ousted from power, but only to make way for a new line of military rulers. In the shuffle Godaigo himself was removed from the Throne and his descendants (the Junior Line) were permanently debarred from it. Thus his policy was, if anything, even less successful than that of the 10th-century predecessor from whom he took his name. But it is precisely for this failure that Godaigo is loved.

6.12 Burei Kō—so named because the conspirators wanted their meetings to seem like informal social gatherings.

> They would sit and drink in extreme dishabille, without their hats, their hair loose and their clothes rumpled—those who were monks discarded their robes and sat in their long shirts. They were waited upon by a score of beautiful girls of about seventeen, in diaphanous garments, serving delicacies of all kinds and pouring wine as if from a spring. All present enjoyed singing and dancing. But in the midst of these riotous pleasures only one thing was discussed—how to destroy . . . the warriors of Kamakura. (George Sansom, *A History of Japan, 1334–1615* [London, 1961], pp. 6–7.)

6.13 Since this is an unusually complicated period in Japanese history, the following chronology may be useful. I have divided it into four parts: (1)

1331–33 Godaigo *vs.* the Hōjōs, (2) 1333–35 Godaigo supported by Takauji: Kemmu Restoration, (3) 1335–36 Godaigo (in Kyoto) *vs.* Takauji, (4) 1336–92 Godaigo (in Yoshino) and his successors *vs.* Takauji and his successors: the period of the two Courts.

(1)

1331   Godaigo's plan to overthrow the Kamakura Bakufu is revealed, and in the 8th Month he is forced to fly to Mount Kasagi, where he is joined by Kusunoki Masashige.

Bakufu forces attack and capture Mount Kasagi; Godaigo is taken prisoner; Emperor Kōgon is enthroned and the imperial regalia (or copies thereof) are surrendered to him (9th Month).

Bakufu forces attack and capture Masashige's headquarters at Akasaka Castle (10th Month).

1332   Godaigo is exiled to the Oki Islands in the 3rd Month.

Masashige and Prince Morinaga conduct guerrilla raids against the Bakufu forces, and in the 12th Month Masashige recaptures Akasaka Castle.

1333   Akasaka Castle is again seized by Bakufu forces (2nd Month).

Battle of Chihaya Castle (2nd-3rd Months).

Godaigo flees from his island (2nd Month).

Ashikaga Takauji, a general serving the Hōjōs, changes sides and supports Godaigo (4th Month).

Loyalist forces under Nitta Yoshisada attack and capture Kamakura; Hōjō Takatoki (the Regent) commits suicide; fall of the Hōjōs (5th Month).

(2)

Godaigo returns to Kyoto, where he appoints Prince Morinaga as Shogun, Takauji as Commander-in-Chief of the eastern provinces, and Masashige as Governor of Settsu and Kawachi provinces (6th Month).

Godaigo opens the Records Office and Settlements Board.

1334   Kemmu year-period starts. Godaigo orders the rebuilding of the Imperial Palace.

Prince Morinaga is arrested and sent to Kamakura (10th Month).

1335   Hōjō Tokiyuki (Takatoki's son) captures Kamakura; Prince Morinaga is executed (7th Month).

Takauji recaptures Kamakura and disregards Godaigo's orders to return to Kyoto (8th Month).

(3)

Godaigo sends Nitta Yoshisada to "chastise" Takauji in Kamakura (11th Month).

Takauji defeats Nitta Yoshisada and marches on Kyoto (12th Month).

1336 Takauji's forces enter Kyoto, and Godaigo flees to Mount Hiei; shortly thereafter loyalist forces under Nitta Yoshisada and others oblige Takauji to flee to the west, and Godaigo returns to the capital (1st Month).

Takauji reaches Kyushu (2nd Month).

Takauji leaves Kyushu and proceeds east (4th Month).

Battle of Minato River: Nitta Yoshisada and Masashige are defeated by the Ashikagas, Masashige commits suicide; Godaigo flees again to Mount Hiei, Takauji recaptures Kyoto (5th Month).

(4)

Takauji puts Emperor Kōmyō (Senior Line) on the Throne (6th Month).

Godaigo returns to Kyoto (10th Month) and surrenders the imperial regalia (11th Month).

Godaigo flees to Yoshino (12th Month): beginning of the period of the two Courts.

1338 Emperor Kōmyō appoints Takauji as Shogun: beginning of the Muromachi (Ashikaga) Bakufu.

1339 Godaigo dies in Yoshino; the civil war continues.

1358 Takauji dies in Kyoto; he is succeeded as Shogun by his son.

1383 Loyalist resistance comes to an end.

1392 The two Courts are unified, but the imperial succession remains in the Senior (Northern) Line.

6.14 In recent times Mount Kasagi, some 50 miles from Osaka, has become a popular tourist resort. Only one of the many temples remains from the time of Godaigo's escape. The mountain is noted for its huge rocks, some of which have carvings attributed to Kūkai and other early Buddhist saints, but it is mainly famous as the place where the nationalist hero, Masashige, first joined Godaigo.

6.15 The dream and the encounter are described in *Taiheiki* ("The Chronicle of the Great Peace," for which see n. 6.27), ed. Nihon Koten Bungaku Taikei (Tokyo, 1960), I: 96–98.

6.16 In China and Japan the Emperor or other chief dignitary traditionally sat in a position facing south.

6.17 Lit. "that I shall again cultivate the virtue of the southern side" (see n. 6.16). The two Bodhisattvas, whose names literally mean Splendour of the Sun and Splendour of the Moon, were attendants of Yakushi Nyorai (Bhaisajya-guru), the Buddha of healing. In Godaigo's dream they were transformed into a pair of weeping children—weeping, of course, because of the sorrowful state of the loyalist cause.

6.18 Usually the dreams of emperors and other important people were explained by professional dream-analysts *(yumetoki)*, but no such experts were available in the wilds of Mount Kasagi and Godaigo had to do his own interpretation.

6.19 Warrior: lit. "a wielder of the bow and arrow." Mount Kongō was the highest peak of a mountain range on the border of Kawachi and Yamato provinces some thirty mountainous miles southwest of the Emperor's present headquarters (see map pp. x–xi). Masashige's famous stronghold of Chihaya was in the western foothills of the mountain.

6.20 Tachibana no Moroe (683–757), one of the most eminent statesmen of his time, descended in the 5th (not the 4th) generation from Emperor Bidatsu (reigned *c.* 570–585). He was born as Prince Kazuraki, but later given the name of Tachibana, which became one of the great aristocratic families in early Japan. In 743 Moroe was appointed to the top governmental post of Minister of the Left, and for a time he actually rivalled the Fujiwara family, but after his death the Fujiwaras rapidly reasserted themselves. In fact, it is extremely doubtful whether Masashige had any such distinguished ancestry.

6.21 This is not quite as confusing as it may seem. Mount Shigi in northern Kawachi Province is the site of Bishamon, a famous Shingon temple usually known as Chōgosonshiji. The temple, gloriously situated on the eastern cliffs, is a popular resort for pilgrims and tourists. It is dedicated to Bishamonten, one of the Four Heavenly Guardians of Buddhism, who protects people living in the north and who in Japan is also regarded as one of the Seven Gods of Good Fortune. Bishamonten is also known as Tamon, which implies something like "the message of good fortune heard in all directions," and this (rather inappropriately) became part of Masashige's name.

6.22 *Zehi no shian ni mo oyobazu:* lit. "without going into considerations of right or wrong." This important phrase emphasizes the selfless, spontaneous, uncalculating way in which, at least according to tradition, Masashige dedicated himself to the loyalist cause when Godaigo's fortunes were at their lowest ebb.

6.23 "Eastern barbarians" *(tōi)* refers to the Hōjō rulers in Kamakura. It is not clear why they have been guilty of any recent rebellion *(kinjitsu no daigyaku)*; presumably Masashige is referring to their suppression of the anti-Bakufu plot in the capital *(le bête est méchant: il se défend).*

6.24 These were the two eastern provinces where the Hōjōs had their main strength. Masashige's point is that brute force will not suffice to defeat the military usurpers; artifice *(chibō)* and stratagems *(hakarigoto)* are essential for a loyalist victory. He justified this opinion in his subsequent engagements against the Hōjōs when his cunning tactics so frequently triumphed over vastly superior numbers. This is a reflection of the traditional heroic idea that skill and "sincerity" *(makoto)* are more powerful than mere brawn.

6.25 Lit. "Since such is the way of battles . . ." Masashige warns the Emperor not to be disheartened by possible defeats along the way; it is the final victory that counts. In an ironic sense his prediction was correct, since his death at Minato River was fatal to the loyalist cause.

6.26 *Jakkan jijitsu no katakage wo tsutaeru mono ka mo shirenai.* Uemura Seiji, *Kusunoki Masashige* (Tokyo, 1963), p. 124.

6.27 The single most detailed source of information about Masashige and his period is *Taiheiki*, which was completed in its present form about 1370. The title of this vast historical romance (*Taiheiki* = "Chronicle of the Great Peace") is splendidly inappropriate since the book deals almost entirely with warfare and other forms of violence. Though often weak as history and poor in describing character, the work became immensely popular and for many centuries was regarded as the best account of the period. Its famous passages were chanted by wandering ballad-singers *(biwa-bōshi),* who accompanied their recitations on the lute (cf. "The Tales of the Tairas," pp. 68–69). The authors of "The Chronicle of the Great Peace" are naturally sympathetic to Godaigo and his supporters, and this is the first work to establish Masashige as the principal loyalist hero of his time. It accepts the idea that Godaigo's cause is hopeless and that Masashige's efforts are doomed to failure; but this of course makes them all the more laudable and appealing.

Though the book was largely debunked by historians in the late 19th century as being full of romantic fabrications, the recent trend has been to rehabilitate it. "Most [present-day] scholars," writes Professor Varley, "accept [*Taiheiki*] as generally reliable and discount its hyperbole as essentially stylistic." (Varley, *Imperial Restoration,* p. 128.) For a partial translation see Helen McCullough, *The Taiheiki,* (New York, 1959); for a critical evaluation and study of the period see Varley, *Imperial Restoration.*

Far less famous than *Taiheiki* but generally sounder as history is *Baishōron,* which was written in 1349. Being pro-Ashikaga, it helps correct the strong loyalist bias of the later work and for this reason was abominated by prewar nationalists.

6.28 Most prewar textbooks give 1294 as the year of his birth; but this is pure conjecture based on an early 19th-century history *(Nihon Gaishi)* which says that Masashige was 42 when he died. According to a Muromachi source *(Taiheiki Hyōban),* "Though Masashige lived to be fifty, he always regarded Yoshitsune as his teacher." If this is correct, he would have been born about 1286. See Uemura, *Masashige,* p. 195, for a discussion of these dates.

6.29 See n. 6.20.

6.30 The document in question is dated 1335, by which time Godaigo was reestablished on the Throne and Masashige had become a respectable member of the imperial government. It is quite possible that he had assumed Tachibana ancestry as being appropriate to his position in the

Imperial Guards; alternatively it may have been his father or grandfather who made the genealogical boast in order to enhance the family's position in their province. Uemura, *Masashige*, p. 31.

6.31   A certain warrior named Kusunoki accompanied Yoritomo on his triumphant entry into Kyoto in 1190, but it is not certain whether he belonged to the same family as Masashige. Another genealogical titbit (discovered in 1957) is that Masashige may have been the uncle of the first great Nō dramatist, Kanami. Kuroda Toshie, *Mōko Shūrai* (Tokyo, 1965), p. 456.

6.32   Recent research suggests that Kusunoki Kawachi no Nyūdō may actually have been Masashige's grandfather rather than his father. The more we examine the hero's background and career, the more dubious become the particulars in the traditional accounts. His father's name is usually given as Masayasu, but other sources have Masatō and Masakuro. In any case the element *masa* ("righteousness") appears consistently in the name of his immediate family, including his brother, Masasue, and his sons, Masatsura and Masanori.

6.33   E.g., ". . . the aura of the *akuto* hovers about Kusunoki Masashige." Kuroda, *Mōko Shūrai*, p. 457.

6.34   Quoted by Uemura, *Masashige*, pp. 44–45.

6.35   *Ibid.*, p. 36.

6.36   *Kōgon Tennō Shinki*, quoted by Uemura, *Masashige*, p. 25.

6.37   *Taiheiki* ("The Chronicle of the Great Peace"), ed. Nihon Koten Bungaku Taikei (Tokyo, 1960), p. 112. Rokuhara was the headquarters of the military government in Kyoto. Cf. the sentiment of this passage with the opening lines of "The Tales of the Tairas" (see p. 77). The pathos *(aware)* inherent in the evanescence of human glory is a recurrent theme in the Japanese tradition: in the hour of his failure even the most haughty man can become a poignant and appealing figure.

6.38   Subsequently Godaigo insisted that the regalia (mirror, jewel, and sword) which he surrendered to Kōgon in 1331 were false and therefore had no sacred significance. The entire question of the authenticity of the imperial regalia remains moot.

6.39   Dogō, Godaigo's place of exile, is in the Oki group of islands (see map, pp. x–xi). Again the Hōjōs were acting according to precedent. About one century earlier Emperor Gotoba had been banished to the neighbouring island of Dozen for having attempted to resist the rule of Kamakura. It was this contumelious attitude of the Bakufu towards the Imperial House that so infuriated loyalists like Chikafusa and Masashige.

6.40   There had been no sign of such popular loyalist feelings at the time of Gotoba's exile (see n. 6.39) when the Hōjō rulers still had great prestige in the country.

6.41   Though it is possible that this worthy gentleman never existed at all and was a creature of fiction, invented to fit into the pattern of the failed hero, Kojima has been admired by Japanese traditionalists through the centuries. The sincerity of his emotions as expressed in the famous carving on the cherry tree is far more important than any practical help he might have given to Godaigo; and the collapse of his plan to rescue the Emperor, far from being a regrettable fiasco, serves to confirm his noble stature. Kojima Takanori was one of the heroes of Mr. Yamaguchi, the young ultra-nationalist who assassinated the head of the Japan Socialist Party (Mr. Asanuma) in 1960 and afterwards committed suicide in prison.

6.42   Kuroda, *Mōko Shūrai*, p. 469.

6.43   *Ibid.*, p. 482. There is good reason to connect Masashige's outlaw *(akuto)* aspect with his success as a guerrilla fighter, but this of course is *not* part of the legend.

6.44   40,000 men according to current estimates, but see n. 6.47 concerning such figures.

6.45   This was a sad departure from tradition, because in earlier days the Bakufu would have scorned to bribe their warriors in this open way; and to announce a reward for the murder of an Imperial Prince, as was done at the same time, was an offence against tradition unthinkable to the Bakufu in its prime. (Sansom, *History of Japan, 1334–1615*, p. 13.)

6.46   The word *shiro* ("castle") gives an exaggerated impression of places like Akasaka and Chihaya. In fact, the "castles" of this period were often mere fortified positions surrounded by palisades and shields rather than massive, elaborate structures serving as permanent military headquarters. It was always the position that counted, not the buildings.

Godaigo's adherents . . . were forced to rely upon strongholds to which they could retreat to escape annihilation, and from which they could contain vastly superior attacking armies. Such a stronghold, or castle, was not an imposing bastion of the European type. It was primarily an area, a place easy to defend and hard to attack, such as the top of a steep mountain. The buildings in the area, if any, might be nothing more than the halls of a Shinto shrine or Buddhist temple, commandeered because of their strategic location. If time permitted, the defenders sowed the approaches with simple obstacles made from trees felled in the neighborhood, threw up wooden walls (sometimes plastered even with mud as a defense against fire arrows), dug ditches, and constructed flimsy towers which served as lookouts and vantage points for archers. In some cases, cliffs were substituted for walls. (McCullough, *The Taiheiki*, p. xxxvi.)

6.47   "The Chronicle of the Great Peace," our main source of information about the battles of Akasaka and Chihaya, vastly exaggerates the strength of the Kamakura forces in order to enhance the achievements of its hero. In describing the first attack against Akasaka Castle it refers to "300,000 horsemen" confronting some 5,000 of Masashige's defenders. Such scanty evidence as is available, however, suggests that during most of the fighting in 1332–33 Masashige was in fact outnumbered about 10 to 1.

6.48   Numerous *yagura* (towers, turrets) were erected in the gates and walls of the so-called castles to serve as observation posts and as places from which missiles could be hurled at (or dropped on) the attacking enemy.

6.49   *Taiheiki*, I: 114.

6.50   Famous generals who served Emperor Kao Tsu of the Former Han Dynasty (early 3rd century B.C.). The quotation is adapted from a speech attributed to Kao Tsu. "The Chronicle of the Great Peace" is replete with Chinese references, which are intended to give added grandeur to the people and events of 14th-century Japan. Masashige's achievements become all the more impressive by being compared with those of famous Han generals.

6.51   This brother was later known as Masasue (see n. 6.32). I have not established the identity of Wada Gorō Masatō (nor do I expect to do so).

6.52   Kusunoki Masashige's crest was the *kikusui*, a floating chrysanthemum flower half submerged by the waves. Saigō Takamori and his followers used *kikusui* as their password (see p. 272), and in 1945 the name *kikusui* designated the kamikaze attacks in Okinawa (see p. 303).

6.53   I.e., for the local populace, who were able to collect what the soldiers had abandoned. This is one of the only passages in the entire book that refers to the common people, who otherwise are entirely obscured by their pugnacious superiors. *Taiheiki*, I: 114–16.

6.54   *Taiheiki*, I: 116.

6.55   *Ibid.*, 118.

6.56   The hero is too sincere to indulge in any coy modesty. Literally the sentence begins, "Since from the outset I went ahead of the [other] warriors in this land and aimed at the meritorious deed of inauguration. . . ." "Inauguration" *(sōsō)* generally means a new and better order of things in the country; here it refers specifically to Emperor Godaigo's restoration to the Throne.

6.57   A quotation from the *Analects* of Confucius, which was no doubt familiar to every illiterate soldier in the castle.

6.58   *Taiheiki*, I: 118–19.

6.59   *Ibid.*, 120.

6.60   The belief in the overriding power of the spirit in warfare is not, of course, limited to Japan, but it lasted there far longer than in the West and strongly influenced the thinking of government and military leaders as recently as 1945 (see p. 285). In the Western tradition the *locus classicus* demonstrating the superiority of spirit over matter in battle is probably the following passage from the apocryphal books of Maccabees, which was widely quoted in the Middle Ages (*inter alia* by Chaucer):

Wher. Seron, who commanded the army in Syria, heard that Judas had mustered a large force, consisting of all his loyal followers of military age, he said to himself, "I will win a glorious reputation in the empire by making war on Judas and his followers, who defy the royal edict." Seron was reinforced by a strong contingent of renegade Jews, who marched up to help him take vengeance on Israel. When he reached the pass of Beth-horon, Judas advanced to meet him with a handful of men. When his followers saw the host coming against them, they said to Judas, "How can so few of us fight against so many? Besides, we have had nothing to eat all day, and we are exhausted." Judas replied: *"Many can easily be overpowered by a few; it makes no difference to Heaven to save by many or by few. Victory does not depend on numbers; strength comes from Heaven alone.* Our enemies come filled with insolence and lawlessness to plunder and to kill us and our wives and children. But we are fighting for our lives and our religion. Heaven will crush them before our eyes. You need not be afraid of them."

When he had finished speaking, he launched a sudden attack, and Seron and his army broke before him. They pursued them down the pass of Beth-horon as far as the plain; some eight hundred of the enemy fell, and the rest fled to Philistia. (*I Macc.* 3: 13–24 [New English Bible, italics added].)

In the Japanese tradition the concept of "sincerity" takes the place of the Judaeo-Christian "Heaven."

6.61 See p. 74 and n. 5.16.

6.62 Uemura, *Masashige,* pp. 97–98.

6.63 As Sansom points out (*History of Japan, 1334–1615,* p. 14), the opposing armies at Austerlitz numbered only 80,000 men each.

6.64 *Taiheiki,* I: 221.

6.65 "If Chihaya had surrendered, it is probable that the loyalist resistance would have collapsed, and therefore Kusunoki's strategy may be regarded as one of the finest achievements in the military history of Japan." (Sansom, *History of Japan, 1334–1615,* p. 124.) It was the defection of Takauji (the traditional villain) rather than the resistance of Masashige (the hero) that led directly to the defeat of Kamakura and Godaigo's return to power. But, if Masashige had been defeated at Chihaya, Takauji would probably never have changed sides.

6.66 The Hōjōs were a collateral branch of the Tairas; the Ashikagas descended from Minamoto no Yoshiie. According to an account in *Nan Taiheiki* (1402), Yoshiie prophesied that after seven generations Japan would be ruled by his descendant. Ashikaga Ietoki (Takauji's grandfather) descended from Yoshiie in precisely the 7th generation, but the Hōjōs were totally in control and there seemed no chance that his ancestor's prophecy would be fulfilled. He accordingly prayed to the Great Bodhisattva Hachiman (the god of war), who was the tutelary deity of the Minamotos, and, having offered his life so that the oracle might be fulfilled in three generations, he committed ritual suicide. Yoshiie's prophecy may be spurious but the suicide is a historical fact and Ietoki's self-sacrifice may well have been one factor that spurred Takauji to decisive action against the Hōjō rulers.

6.67 As a precaution in case the envoys were captured by Kamakura forces, Takauji ordered that the messages be written on small pieces of paper and concealed in the men's topknots or in the seams of their clothes.

6.68   This lack of idealism in Takauji's adherence to the Emperor is far from being unique among Japan's military leaders, who throughout history have tended to disguise less impressive motives by claiming to be loyal supporters of the Throne. Takauji's tergiversations may have been somewhat more blatant than most, but his attitude towards the imperial family was the rule rather than the exception among the military.

6.69   "The Chronicle of the Great Peace" comments on the fall of the Hōjōs in terms that are reminiscent of the opening passage of "The Tales of the Tairas" concerning the fall of the Tairas a century and a half earlier (see p. 77):

> Foolish indeed were these eastern warriors! For many long years they had ruled everything under heaven and spread their power to each corner of the land. Yet, since they lacked the proper spirit for governing the country, their strong armour and sharp weapons were now beaten down by mere canes and whips, and in an instant they were totally destroyed. From ancient times until the present the proud ones of this world have been cast down while the modest have survived. . . . (*Taiheiki*, I: 388.)

Despite the similarities, the tenor of this passage is far more didactic and moralizing than that of the opening lament in "The Tales of the Tairas," which has a melancholy, Buddhist tone.

6.70   Godaigo's chief intellectual mentor was the famous aristocrat-statesman-scholar-warrior, Kitabatake Chikafusa (1292–1354), who ranks with Masashige as one of the two greatest loyalist figures of the period. Chikafusa's seminal work, "A History of the True Succession of the Divine Monarchs" (*Jinnō Shōtōki*), written while he was immured in a castle under siege by his Ashikaga enemies, was not presented to the Court until 1339, the year when Godaigo died in Yoshino, but his socially conservative ideas and stress on the importance of legitimate succession and loyalty had a considerable influence on the Restoration movement. The famous opening lines of his book, which have been much quoted by nationalists since the 18th century, stress the idea that the uniqueness of Japan lies in the divine descent of the reigning emperors and call for unquestioning loyalty to them:

> Great Yamato is a sacred land. Our divine ancestors laid its foundations, and through the ages it has been ruled by descendants of the Sun Goddess. This is true of our country alone; it has never happened in any foreign country. For this reason Japan is called The Divine Land. . . . Every man born in the imperial land must devote himself loyally to the Emperor, even if it means sacrificing his life. Let no man believe that he deserves the slightest credit for so doing! (*Jinnō Shōtōki*, ed. Iwanami Shoten [Tokyo, 1936], pp. 17,19.)

6.71   Kitabatake Chikafusa (see n. 6.70) was among those who most resented the appointment. Godaigo, on the other hand, not only wished to reward Takauji for his timely adherence to the loyalist cause, but recognized him as a man of unusual ability who should be kept on his side. At this time Takauji was energetically restoring order in and near the capital, where he ruthlessly punished plunderers, free-booters, and other lawbreakers.

6.72   *Taiheiki*, p. 370. Accounts of Masashige in prewar textbooks often give the impression that the great loyalist hero captured Kyoto almost single-handedly from the Hōjōs, and Takauji's role in the victory is carefully played down.

6.73   Masashige was well rewarded for his service—but not well enough according to his later admirers. "It was tragic," wrote Rai Sanyō (1780–1832), "that Go-Daigo should have been so foolish as to fail to reward Masashige with titles and honours worthy of the great services he had rendered, for thereby he laid the way for the wicked Ashikaga Takauji to stain the history of the Throne by seizing power." W. G. Beasley, ed., *Historians of China and Japan* (London, 1961), p. 261.

6.74   Masashige was one of Godaigo's four close personal advisers known as the Three Trees and One Grass from their names which were Yū*ki*, Kusuno*ki*, Hō*ki*, and Chi*kusa* (*ki*=tree, *kusa*=grass).

6.75   George Sansom, *History of Japan, 1334–1615*, p. 287.

6.76   Even "The Chronicle of the Great Peace," despite its strong pro-Daigo bias, waxes indignant concerning the chaos of the rewards policy and Godaigo's "government by caprice." It comments, for instance, on the fact that of a number of generals who fought for the Emperor "with outstanding gallantry and loyalty," only one had received confirmation of a land holding, and that even he had been deprived of his post as constable *(shugo)*.

6.77   Prince Morinaga was killed on Tadayoshi's orders when the Ashikagas were retreating from Kamakura in the 7th Month of 1335. Perhaps because of the rather ignominious nature of his death, Morinaga was never accorded the same heroic stature as a man like Masashige, who committed suicide rather than suffer disgrace.

6.78   Presumably because Godaigo's treatment of Prince Morinaga reflected a sharp decline in moral standards. I am thinking of this passage in "The Chronicle of the Great Peace":

People discussed the matter among themselves and said, "It was [Prince Morinaga's] great deeds in battle that brought the war to an end and enabled the Emperor to return to his Throne. If His Majesty found fault with the Prince over some trifling matters, he should have admonished and forgiven him. Instead he heedlessly delivered him into the hands of his enemies and allowed him to be sent into distant banishment. Is this not a sign that once again the Court will bow down before the might of the military?" And indeed after Prince Morinaga was killed the whole country rapidly entered the age of the Shogun's [i.e., Ashikaga] rule. (*Taiheiki*, I: 431.)

6.79   Government mismanagement was of course only a proximate reason for the endemic disorders in the provinces. The fundamental cause was that Japan was undergoing a crucial period of change in conditions of land-holding and power relations. The old order based on the manorial *(shōen)* system of land tenure was finally breaking down, and throughout the country the military were engaged in a desperate struggle for control of their respective provinces. As Sansom remarks (*History of Japan, 1334–1615*, p. 18), the country would hardly have continued in a state of turmoil for

50 years if the issue had simply been which of two imperial lines should occupy the Throne.

6.80   The shields were so designed that they could be lined up along the ground to form a breast wall several hundred yards long and then hastily removed when the time came to attack. Uemura, *Masashige*, p. 170.

6.81   This was probably not the first time that Masashige's advice to the Emperor had been ignored. According to *Baishōron*, Masashige had always recognized Takauji's strength and in the spring of 1336 had suggested that he himself should serve as a peace envoy and take advantage of the recent loyalist victory to make a lasting, satisfactory settlement with the Ashikagas. If the account is to be believed, Masashige insisted that the real enemy was not Takauji but Yoshisada, and this certainly accords with what we know about the poor relations between the two loyalist commanders. Masashige's plan would at least have postponed the catastrophe; but the Court, being flushed with success, refused to take it seriously. (For details see Satō Shinichi, *Nambokuchō no Dōran* [Tokyo, 1965]. Professor Satō believes that the *Baishōron* account of Masashige's plan to make peace with Takauji is authentic.) Since the enmity between Masashige and Takauji is such an important part of the legend, the plan is rarely mentioned in prewar accounts of the story.

6.82   The ostensible reason for rejecting Masashige's advice was that it would be damaging for loyalist morale if Godaigo had to leave his capital and retreat to Mount Hiei twice in the same year (Uemura, *Masashige*, p. 182). Masashige was too loyal to disagree openly with the Emperor and, according to traditional accounts, he blamed everything on the "curtain government," which he accused of being Godaigo's worst enemy. A certain presumptuous courtier named Kiyotada is reported to have been particularly influential in opposing Masashige's advice. After the disaster at Minato River he was ordered to commit harakiri. Subsequently his furious ghost haunted the imperial family and the Court until it was finally pacified by a princess carrying a lantern filled with fireflies.

According to Professor Watsuji Tetsurō, the Emperor's rejection of Masashige's advice can be regarded as a sort of betrayal of faith. Watsuji suggests that the authors of "The Chronicle of the Great Peace" wished to connect the failure of Godaigo's Restoration with his refusal to follow the advice of his staunchest loyalist general (Varley, *Imperial Restoration*, p. 140). According to this point of view, Masashige incarnated the spirit of the loyalist movement and, when he (or rather, his advice) was rejected, the movement was morally doomed.

6.83   The historicity of the farewell scene was first questioned by two iconoclastic Meiji historians, Professors Shigeno and Kume, who pointed out, *inter alia*, that the episode is mentioned only in "The Chronicle of the Great Peace" and that Masatsura was far older than 10 when the alleged parting took place. The general Japanese public was shocked to be told that this famous story about their hero was fictitious (it was as if an English historian announced that Nelson's last words about duty were spurious), and Professor Shigeno was given the unflattering epithet of

Massatsu Hakushi ("Dr. Debunker"). In a study of Japanese heroism, however, what matters is not the story's authenticity but its existence.

6.84   *Taiheiki*, II:151.

6.85

青葉茂れる櫻井の

落合直文作詞
奥山朝恭作曲

（新興輯集部輯曲）

Ochiai Naobumi, "Aoba Shigareru Sakurai no," in *Nihon Shōka Shū* (Tokyo, 1953), pp. 60–61. The poem is typical of late 19th-century sentimental poetry and could be appropriately included in an Oriental version of *The Stuffed Owl* (the Lewis-Lee "anthology of bad verse"). When sung in Japanese, however, it has an unmistakable dignity and power.

Hototogisu in the last verse is often translated as "cuckoo," but there is no evocative resemblance between the two birds. The pervading sense of pathos is emphasized in the last two lines by the repetition of the word *aware*:

Tare ka aware to kikazaran
Aware chi ni naku sono koe wo.

6.86 The date of the main engagement was the 25th day of the 5th Month, which corresponds to 4th July in the western calendar. Sansom provides an excellent description of the battle (*History of Japan, 1334–1615, pp. 50–52*), but I believe that he is mistaken about the date, which he gives as July 5.

6.87 Takauji is said to have made a careful study of Yoshitsune's campaign at the Battle of Dannoura. Though he had no experience in naval warfare, he managed to maintain complete control of the sea throughout the engagement.

6.88 As Sansom points out (*History of Japan, 1334–1615*, p. 52), Yoshisada's retreat was a fateful blunder, since it left Masashige up in the air; but even without this setback Masashige's defeat was never in doubt.

6.89 *Taiheiki*, II: 159. The phrase *shichishō hōkoku* ("to serve the Emperor for seven lives") became a famous patriotic slogan, often being misattributed to Masashige himself (e.g., Yokota Yutaka, *Suicide Submarine!* [New York, 1962], p. 44). Shichishō Butai units were part of the kamikaze operations during the Pacific war (see p. 276 and n. 10.127).

In 1960 Mr. Asanuma's youthful assassin wrote the slogan in toothpaste on the wall of his prison cell shortly before hanging himself (see n.6.41). It was also much quoted by Mishima Yukio, and in 1970 when he and his followers were about to perform their culminating deed in the Self-Defence Headquarters the hachimaki bands that they tied round their heads were emblazoned in black ink with the Chinese characters, SHICHI SHŌ HŌKOKU.

6.90 *Taiheiki*, II:159.

6.91 See p. 101.

6.92 The intersection of the Sixth Avenue (Rokujō) with Kamo River was the principal execution grounds in Kyoto, and this is also where the severed heads of enemies were exposed on pikes.

6.93 It is tempting, but probably incorrect, to interpret this comment as ironical.

6.94 I.e., a hero shows his superiority to common mortals even when he is still a child.

6.95 *Taiheiki*, II:169–71.

6.96 *Ibid.*, II:171.

6.97 *Ibid.*

6.98 The Ashikaga shogunate theoretically lasted until 1597, being passed down in the family for 15 generations, but its power was rapidly eroded in the 15th century as part of the breakdown of national order.

6.99 "Though my bones will be buried in these southern hills, my spirit will always long for the Palace to the north." *Taiheiki*, II: 342–43.

6.100   According to the legend, the young hero, knowing that the odds against him were hopeless and that he was bound to lose his life in the forthcoming battle, visited Godaigo's tomb and wrote a poem on the door together with the names of his companions who would die with him.

6.101   Only a single member of the Kusunoki family ever went over to the Ashikagas, and his defection was temporary. This is an impressive record in an age of shifting allegiances. Satō, *Nambokuchō no Dōran,* p. 401.

   A final sensational attempt by supporters of the southern line was made in 1443, long after the Yoshino Court had ceased existing. Again it was led by a descendant of Masashige and, predictably enough, it failed, though at one point the insurgents actually managed to seize the imperial regalia.

6.102   But who were the legitimate emperors from 1336 to 1392? The problem was debated for many years and came to a head in 1910, when it almost brought down the Katsura government. In 1911 it was officially decided that the "southern" (Yoshino) Court had been the sole legitimate government during the 56 years in question. It is rather as if the American government, one century after the Civil War, declared that Jefferson Davis had been the legitimate President of the United States.

   After Japan's defeat in 1945 a number of "southern" pretenders came on the scene, all claiming to be direct descendants of Emperor Godaigo and therefore (according to the 1911 decision) the legitimate occupants of the Throne. The most conspicuous of them was a certain Mr. Kumazawa Kandō, who addressed his claim in a letter to General MacArthur. "Emperor Kumazawa," as he styled himself, generated a good deal of publicity and amusement of a type that would hardly have appealed to Masashige and the other loyalist martyrs.

6.103   According to Professor Hall, Godaigo's effort was not only useless but counter-productive: ". . . as an ill-conceived effort to regain imperial power, Go-Daigo's failure measurably weakened the imperial house, reducing much of its economic resources and police powers within the city." John Hall and Jeffrey Mass, ed., *Medieval Japan: Essays in Institutional History* (New Haven, 1974), p. 26.

6.104   The chapter about Masashige's death ends as follows:

   From ancient times until the present there has never yet been a man who so combined the three virtues of wisdom, humanity, and courage, or who met his death while so resolutely treading the path of righteousness. After Masashige and his brother had killed themselves, His Majesty again lost his kingdom and once more the rebels held sway. . . . (*Taiheiki,* II:160).

6.105   Cf. the posthumous worship of Michizane, Yoshitsune, and other failed heroes. "But most glorious of all," according to Rai Sanyō (1780–1832),

   was the Kusunoki family. By supporting the Throne and even giving up his life for it at a time when it was at its weakest and most discredited, shunned by almost everyone else for fear of the overwhelming power of the Hōjō, Kusunoki Masashige had set a shining example of supreme loyalty and heroism. (Beasley, *Historians of China and Japan,* p. 261.)

As a stalwart Confucianist, Rai Sanyō was faced with something of a dilemma when confronting his country's 14th-century history, when the "good" so conspicuously failed and the "bad" succeeded. He overcame the difficulty (at least to his own satisfaction) by introducing the notion of *jisei* ("movement of the times"), a force that frequently doomed heroes to defeat. This served as a useful bridge between conventional Confucian notions of rectitude and traditional Japanese ideals of "sincerity":

> Though Sanyō . . . used the orthodox Confucian framework of praise and blame in presenting his particular view of the Japanese past, he could scarcely use it in the orthodox Confucian way, for in those terms his thesis was simply not tenable. He could hardly make out that "good" rulers brought peace and prosperity and "bad" ones turmoil and decline, if most of the persons he wished to praise had been remarkable for their failures and early deaths, while those on whom he heaped most abuse had been rather conspicuously successful as rulers and long-lived as dynasties. He was hence constrained to look for some explanation of historical causation other than the usual one of the moral character and conduct of individual rulers. This he found in an idea which he called alternatively *jisei*, *jiun*, *sedō*, or *sei*, a "force" or "movement of the times," comparable to water bursting through a dike, against which mere human effort, however moral, glorious, or heroic, was powerless. It was owing to this irresistible force, he could then make out, that all his heroes had been failures and all his villains successes. The initial rise to power of the military class and decline of the Throne, deplorable and tragic though these had been, were yet inevitable because of *jisei*. The emperors Go-Toba and Go-Daigo had failed in their attempts to restore the Throne to its rightful power, for the reason that *jisei* was weighted against the Throne at those particular times. Inevitable for similar reasons was the defeat and death of Nitta Yoshisada, good and loyal though he was, and the strength and long-lasting success of the Ashikaga family, bad and disloyal though they were. (Beasley, *Historians of China and Japan*, pp. 261–62.)

In this formulation *jisei* and "sincerity" represent the matter-and-spirit dichotomy. In the "real" world matter triumphs over spiritual values (see n. 6.112).

6.106   Masashige was especially venerated by two heroic rebels, Yui Shōsetsu (1605–51) and Yoshida Shōin (1830–59), who conspired against the Tokugawa Bakufu and who, having failed in their attempt, were put to death. Shōin's *Shichishō Setsu* ("Views on the Seven Rebirths," 1856) is a tribute to Masashige in which he compares his own objectives with those of the 14th-century hero. He recognizes that he has failed just as Masashige did, but "hopes that [his] eternal heart may serve to stimulate later generations, and that [he] also may have seven lives to devote to this purpose." David Earl, *Emperor and Nation in Japan* (Seattle, 1964), p. 188.

6.107   Most of the structures in the hero's shrine were burnt down in the bombing of Kōbe during the Second World War, but they have now been securely rebuilt in reinforced concrete.

The "worship of Kusunoki" even extended to Western observers. Professor Varley quotes the comments of William Griffis, an American who worked in Japan during the early Meiji period. In 1876 he wrote as follows:

Of all the characters in Japanese history, that of Kusunoki Masashige stands pre-eminent for pureness of patriotism, unselfishness of devotion to duty, and calmness of courage. The people speak of him in tones of reverential tenderness, and, with an admiration that lacks fitting words, behold in him the mirror of stainless loyalty. I have more than once asked my Japanese students and friends whom they considered the noblest character in their history. Their unanimous answer was "Kusunoki Masashige." Every relic of this brave man is treasured up with religious care; and fans inscribed with poems written by him, in facsimile of his handwriting, are sold in the shops and used by those who burn to imitate his exalted patriotism. . . . I make no attempt to conceal my own admiration of a man who acted according to his light, and faced his soldierly ideal of honour, when conscience and all his previous education told him that his hour had come, and that to flinch from suicidal thrust was dishonour and sin. (Varley, *Imperial Restoration*, pp. 153–54.)

6.108 See p. 303.

6.109 See n. 6.83.

6.110 E.g., see Satō, *Nambokuchō no Dōran*, Appendix, pp. 1–6, and Uemura, *Masashige*, p. 139. For a discussion of Masahige's possible *akuto* background, see pp. 113–14.

6.111 See p. 113.

6.112 Quoted by Uemura, *Masashige*, p. 194. Masashige's reputed flexibility and ability to improvise are similar to an artist's imagination. His heroism becomes apparent in the separation between the desires of his spirit (loyalty, self-sacrifice, etc.) and the limitations of practical reality (inadequate military force, corruption at Court, etc.). Masashige's imaginative powers, which lead to the famous ruses and stratagems, fill the void of his objective weakness.

The constant emphasis on morale, sincerity, etc. can be similarly interpreted: here the hero's imagination is creating its own world in the vacuum between what *is* and what *ought to be*. A typical Japanese hero in kabuki, *chambara* films, etc. is the lone warrior who defeats hundreds of bloodthirsty opponents with his single shining sword, which symbolizes his pure sincerity. In the popular Zatōichi films, for example, the blind swordsman-hero, though attacked by hordes of fierce fighters, is invincible because he alone is armed with sincerity. Mere numbers are powerless against such spiritual strength. In the story of Masashige, the Bakufu, despite its overwhelming material force, is vulnerable because it lacks a "spiritual" leader who can mobilize its supporters by imagination and sincerity. Masashige secures victory for the loyalists, but once he has reinstated Godaigo on the Throne he loses his spiritual *raison d'être*. The legendary hero has no real place in a history that concerns economic and political facts: propitious resolutions exclude him (see p. 126). He does not reemerge as a central figure in the story until the loyalist cause is again in danger. When finally the Emperor rejects Masashige's advice, his cause loses its spiritual power and is doomed (see n. 6.82).

In this legendary sense Masashige represents an ideal vision of sincerity which, though it may illuminate the world for a while like a flash of lightning in a dark sky, is bound to be extinguished by impure reality. Takauji, of course, is the perfect exemplar of compromise, realism, political calculation, and success.

6.113   E.g., the incident recounted in *Kikuchi Taketomo Shinjō* in which Masashige tried to convince Godaigo that the "number one loyalist" *(chūkō daiichi)* in the land was not himself but Kikuchi Taketoki, who had actually given his life for the cause. Uemura, *Masashige*, p. 139.

6.114   According to Professor Satō, Masashige combined "flexible thinking" with "passionate judgment" *(Satō, p. 256)*. Professor Uemura emphasizes Masashige's "resistance to authority" *(kenryoku ni taisuru hankō no seishin)* as his consistent motive and implies that in opposing the Bakufu the hero somehow represented "the will of the people" *(Satō, p. 42)*. The idea that Masashige was something like a modern Resistance hero leading his Maquis against oppressive military rulers may make him attractive to many present-day Japanese readers, but it is hard to reconcile with his support of a reactionary autocrat like Godaigo.

6.115   Thus in a sense it is the tradition of *hōganbiiki* ("sympathy with the loser") that helped ensure the subsequent popularity and legitimization of the southern Court. If Takauji and Kōgon had been decisively defeated in 1336, they (rather than Masashige and Godaigo) might have become the heroes in later centuries and the northern Court would have had the nostalgic charm and prestige that Yoshino acquired.

6.116   After his defeat at Minato River, Nitta Yoshisada continued the fight against the Ashikagas and their allies until he was killed in battle at the age of 38.

6.117   Masashige has been compared to various foreign heroes. E.g., "Masashigué [*sic*] peut être comparé à Bertrand de Guesclin en France pour sa fidélité à l'Empereur et pour sa bravoure." (Daidōji Yuzan, *Budō Shoshin Shū* [Tokyo, 1965], p. 7L) The legendary Breton hero, however, was on the *winning* side in the war against the English.

   Also he has often been called the "Bayard of Japan" (e.g., Joly, *Legends*, p. 306), in reference to *le chevalier sans peur et sans reproche*. Yet Bayard, though he eventually died in battle, succeeded in saving France from an imperial invasion; to find a significant comparison one would have to identify a popular hero who not only was killed but who had supported a losing cause—and in the West that is indeed a *rara avis*.

6.118   See n. 6.98.

6.119   With a great sigh the Military Governor [Takauji] lamented, "Alas, due to slander and flattery by those close to the Throne, I am consigned to the fate of an ignominious rebel without any chance to explain my innocence." Indeed his grief was no perfunctory display, but without nurturing any bitterness in his heart he devoutly gave himself over to spiritual reflection and pious works, fervently praying for the enlightenment of the Emperor and eventually constructing . . . this great monastery for the practice of Buddhism. (Musō Kokushi, *Taishō*

Daizōkyō, LXXX: 463–64; quoted by Wm. Theodore de Bary *et al.*, eds., *Sources of the Japanese Tradition* [New York, 1958], p. 257.)

6.120 Takauji possesses three great virtues. The first is his courage. Although he has been near death in battle many times, he has invariably remained cheerful and has shown not the slightest trace of fear. Takauji's second virtue is his compassion: he hates no one and has on many occasions shown vengeful enemies the same leniency he would show children. Third, Takauji is magnanimous and not in the least niggardly. He makes little distinction among material things; and when he bestows weapons, horses, and the like, he does not even try to match the gift to the recipient but simply passes things out as they come to hand. (Quoted by Varley, *Imperial Restoration*, p. 133.)

6.121 See p. 107.

6.122 Quoted by Sansom, *A History of Japan: 1334–1615*, p. 98.

6.123 Quoted by Beasley, *Historians of China and Japan*, p. 261.

6.124 See n. 6.68. Even Masashige himself may have started his loyalist career as a turncoat (see p. 114).

6.125 De Bary, *Japanese Tradition*, pp. 256–57.

6.126 Sansom, *History of Japan: 1334–1615*, p. 100.

Chapter 7

7.1 The banner, which is probably authentic, is now in a private collection in Tokyo. In order to prevent its being acquired by a foreign buyer and exported from Japan, the government in 1964 named it an Important Cultural Property. For a reproduction and detailed discussion see Nishimura Sada's essay, "Shimabara Ran no Kirishitan Jinchū Hata to Yamada Emonsaku" in *Nihon Shoki Yōga no Kenkyū* (Tokyo, 1958). Professor Nishimura supports the traditional attribution of the painting to Yamada Emonsaku, the ex-Jesuit lay acolyte, for whose ambiguous role in the rebellion see pp. 174–75. It appears that the other banners carried by the insurgents were all made of cotton.

7.2 "When we regard him as a fictitious character, we find that historical documents give clear proof of his reality; but, when we try to find out about him from those documents, there are hardly any positive clues about his existence." Okada Akio, *Amakusa Tokisada* (Tokyo, 1960), Introduction, p. 1.

Though Amakusa Shirō led the greatest religious uprising in Japanese history, and though he lived almost a hundred years later than Martin Luther, his existence remains shadowy—so shadowy, indeed, that he stands in little danger of the type of psychiatric diagnosis that has been attempted with the great Protestant hero.

7.3 For the original text see *Shōgun to Daimyō*, no. 12 in the Nihon Rekishi Shirīzu (Tokyo, 1967), p. 40.

"All other faiths": lit. "the three faiths" *(sankyō)*, i.e., Buddhism, Confucianism, and Taoism. These (and presumably Shintoism to boot) would all be swept aside by Christianity. Opinions were divided among Japanese Christians about whether this would literally take place as a historical event (e.g., like the official acceptance of Buddhism in the 6th century) or whether it would be part of the program for an apocalyptic Last Day of Judgment. In either case the final resolution was close at hand.

7.4   In the recent "autobiography" of Amakusa Shirō by Mr. Sano Mitsuo (see pp. 146–47) the hero reiterates that he is *not* a "Son of God" or a Child of Heaven, but that the role was foisted on him by his supporters and that in the end he assumed it willy-nilly and even cooperated by staging what appeared to be miracles. In other words, he became a god despite himself.

7.5   Francis Xavier was so encouraged by the spread of Christianity since his arrival in 1549 that he praised the Japanese as the "delight of my heart." Other enthusiastic missionaries described Japan as a gift that God had given to the Church in return for their having lost the great island kingdom of the West to Protestant heresy.

7.6   After 1945 "feudal" *(hōkenteki)* became a vogue-word, being feely used as a pejorative for people who seemed to represent the bad old days of Japanism and repression. Thus a strict parent, a paternalistic employer, or a demanding teacher might all scornfully be described as "feudal." In this sense the repressive Tokugawa regime was regarded as the quintessence of feudalism, and the leaders who rebelled against it were naturally heroes. One verse in the "Song of Amakusa Shirō" (see p. 145) goes, more or less literally, "The Bakufu with its tough policy of suppression and exclusion *(sakoku)* is terror-stricken by Amakusa's rebellion; this fight, imbued with the lifeblood [of the rebels], [will last] for all eternity. Amakusa Shirō! Ah, the resistance of tomorrow!"

7.7   Cf. p. 93, above, concerning the feminine depictions of Yoshitsune on the stage. There are no contemporary paintings or descriptions of Amakusa Shirō. I am indebted to Donald Keene for calling my attention to an oil painting of him in a Buddhist temple in Takayama. The work is attributed to Shiba Kōkan (1724–1818), one of the first artists in Japan to have cultivated realistic methods of Western painting. That the portrait of a Christian rebel should have been painted during the anti-Christian Tokugawa period and that it should be hung in a Buddhist temple is typical of the incongruities surrounding Amakusa Shirō. Another oil portrait (in the Shimabara Castle museum) depicts the hero against an ocean background with his hands clasped in prayer and a look of mystical devotion on his boyish face. He is dressed in a white silk blouse and crimson singlet, and wears an elaborate, Portuguese-style ruff about his neck. Appropriately he is accoutred with the incongruous combination of a gold crucifix and a samurai sword.

7.8 See n. 7.4. The first installment, *Hōki* ("The Uprising"), appeared in the March 1972 issue of *Rekishi to Jimbutsu*, a publication of Chūō Kōron.

Amakusa Shirō is the subject of no. 51 in the popular Jimbutsu Sōsho series of books, in which each volume is devoted to a famous figure in the history of Japan (see n. 7.2). He is also the hero of no. 73 in the Nihon no Bushō ("Generals of Japan") series. See Ebisawa Arimichi, *Amakusa Shirō* (Tokyo, 1967).

7.9 See also n. 7.6

7.10 A simple wooden cross on a tall white pillar faces Shimabara Bay in a remote part of the peninsula and commemorates the site of the Christian fortress.

7.11 The persecution of Christianity in Japan from about 1614 to 1640 is one of the most ghastly stories in the world's long history of officially organized cruelty. Yet most of the Japanese horrors could be matched in contemporary Europe, where the Holy Inquisition was busy torturing and killing those whom it believed to be the enemies of the true Church. Suspected heretics in countries like Spain and Portugal were often subject to the very same torments that were being applied to Roman Catholics in Japan (see n. 7.17). On both sides of the world the men who supervised the tortures and executions were not thuggish brutes from the underworld but respectable government officials or ecclesiastics who were convinced that their severities were morally justified.

7.12 Professor Boxer quotes a typical oath of apostasy signed by a Japanese Christian and his wife. It is worth noting that the sanctions invoked in most of these apostatical oaths were based on the very beliefs that were being renounced.

> We have been Christian believers for many years. Yet we have found out that the Christian religion is an evil religion.... We hereby witness this statement in writing before you, worshipful magistrate. Hereafter we shall never revoke our apostasy, not even in the secret places of the heart. Should we ever entertain the slightest thought thereof, then let us be punished by God the Father, God the Son, and God the Holy Ghost, St. Mary, and all Angels and Saints. Let us forfeit all God's mercy, and all hope like Judas Iscariot, becoming a laughing-stock to all men, without thereby arousing the slightest pity, and finally die a violent death and suffer the torments of Hell without hope of salvation. This is our Christian Oath.... (C. R. Boxer, *The Christian Century in Japan*, 1549–1650 [London, 1951], p. 441.)

7.13 See pp. 176–77.

7.14 According to one version of the story, only the two brothers were arrested and executed.

7.15 There are numerous varying accounts of this particular incident (e.g., *Shōgun to Daimyō*, pp. 41–42, and Okada, *Amakusa*, pp. 3–4). In general outline it is probably authentic, but many of the details may be spurious and it is unlikely that (as is often suggested) this particular act of defiance led directly to the main rebellion.

7.16   "Au mois d'août [1638] à Omoura, Duarte Correa, familier du Saint-Office et affilié à la Compagnie de Jésus, après deux ans de captivité, fut torturé cruellement, et finalement brûlé à feu lent." Léon Pagés, *Histoire de la réligion Chrétienne au Japon depuis 1598 jusqu'à 1651* (Paris, 1869–70), II:850.

7.17   Boxer, *Christian Century in Japan* pp. 377–78. Correa's account, *Relaçam do alevatamento de Ximabara, e de seu notavel cerco, e de varias mortes da nossos Portuguezes po la Fé,* can be found on pp. 403–11 of Pagés, *Réligion Chrétienne au Japon.* It has been translated into Japanese (Tokyo, 1949), but not, so far as I know, into English.
        "Those who are intrigued by life's little ironies," notes Professor Boxer (*Christian Century in Japan*, p. 497), "may care to know that the original draft [of Correa's manuscript], when printed in 1643, was dedicated to the Inquisitor-General of Portugal, Dom Francisco de Castro, a notorious Jew-baiter and burner, Correa himself having been roasted to death over a slow fire in August, 1639."

7.18   Pagés *Réligion Chrétienne au Japon*, pp. 842–43.

7.19   The *tozama* were daimyo (feudal lords) in Kyushu and elsewhere who had not submitted to the Tokugawas until the victory at Sekigahara in 1600. They were always treated with more suspicion than the hereditary vassals, and the Bakufu did its best to curb their economic and military strength.

7.20   Tsuji Tatsuya, *Edo Bakufu* (Tokyo, 1966), p. 323.

7.21   Translated by James Murdoch in *A History of Japan* (reprinted London, 1949), II:650.

7.22   Okada, *Amakusa*, p. 17.

7.23   Pagés, *Réligion Chrétienne au Japon*, p. 405. "Bailiff" *(ministro de justiça* in the Portuguese) presumably refers to the local *daikan.*

7.24   The statement is dated 17th February 1638. Murdoch, *History of Japan*, p. 660.

7.25   It is interesting that, despite the religious nature of the revolt, not a single Catholic priest was found among the insurgents after the fall of Hara Castle, whereas several *bateren* (padres) had been immured in Osaka Castle during the great siege of 1615. Despite all the Portuguese slogans, the Shimabara Rebellion was a purely Japanese affair.

7.26   See p. 149.

7.27   The eldest child, a daughter baptized Regina, was born in 1615, the youngest, a girl called Man [*sic*], was 10 years younger than Amakusa Shirō. There must have been two other children older than Shirō (whose name denotes "fourth child"), but there is no record of them and they probably died young.

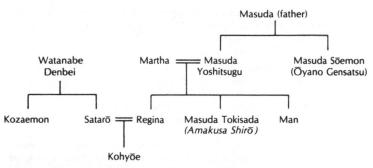

The double solid lines indicate marriages

7.28 See pp. 144–45.

7.29 More literally, he saw that this was "a child in whom the world could have hope." Okada, *Amakusa*, p. 89.

7.30 The hero's correct name is Masuda Tokisada; but he came to be known popularly as Amakusa Shirō or Amakusa no Shirō, "Shirō of Amakusa" (in which of course "Amakusa" is analogous to "Arabia" in "Lawrence of Arabia"), and I have consistently used that name in my discussion. Duarte Correa, the Portuguese chronicler, calls him Maxondanoxirô (Pagés, *Religion Chrétienne au Japon*, p. 406), which I suppose to be a Portugese corruption of Masuda no Shirō. Pagés (p. 844) writes, "Le chef des insurgents était un jeune homme, de dix-huit ans à peine, nommé Jérôme Machoudano Chicô, né de parents nobles, et originaire du Fingo." "Machoudano Chicô" is presumably a corruption of the Portuguese "Maxondanoxirô" a *c* having been mistakenly substituted for the *r*; "Fingo" refers to the Kyushu Province of Higo. Though the hero's father was of samurai stock, *parents nobles* is something of an exaggeration.

7.31 According to the "autobiography" (see n. 7.8), Amakusa Shirō was elected by the rebel leaders after endless meetings during which the various factions were deadlocked.

7.32 ". . . his son Shirō . . . being a brilliant young man *(saichi aru yoshi nite)*, was chosen as leader of the rebellion." Quoted by Okada, *Amakusa*, p. 85.

7.33 In view of the frequent misuse of the term in recent journalistic writing, it may be worth while to recall Max Weber's description, which clearly fits the case of Amakusa Shirō and of many other failed heroes in Japanese history:

> Personal authority also may have a source in the very opposite of tradition. The power of command may be exercised by a *leader*—whether he is a prophet, hero, or demagogue—who can prove that he possesses *charisma* by virtue of magical powers, revelations, heroism, or other extraordinary gifts. The persons who

obey such a leader are *disciples* or *followers* who believe in his extraordinary qualities rather than in stipulated rules or in the dignity of a position sanctified by tradition. (Reinhard Bendix, *Max Weber: An Intellectual Portrait* [New York, 1962], p. 295)

7.34   One intriguing possibility is that the choice of Amakusa Shirō to lead the rebellion was inspired, at least partly, by the knowledge of Dom Sebastião, the young Portuguese ruler who came to the Throne as Sebastian I. He was well known by Japanese Christians in Kyushu, and in 1562 the Christian daimyo of Bungo Province sent him a valuable sword as a mark of esteem.

From his early youth Dom Sebastião, a weak, sickly child who had been brought up by Jesuits, was imbued with fanatic religious fervour and viewed himself as a heroic Christian knight who would win glory by conquering the Moslem infidels in Africa. In 1578, at the age of 24, he landed in Morocco and rode forth to battle on his white horse. Like Amakusa Shirō he lacked practical military experience. He was promptly defeated at Alcazarquivir; his army was wiped out; he himself was killed; and the Portuguese Throne passed to the Spanish Crown. It was an unmitigated disaster, but Dom Sebastião became the centre of a heroic legend. It was rumoured that instead of being killed he had been captured by the Moors, and that in due course he would return to lead his unfortunate people to victory. (Summarized from *Columbia Encyclopedia*, 3rd ed. [New York, 1963], p. 191.)

This strange Messianic legend, which persisted for hundreds of years and came to be known as Sebastianism, was undoubtedly familiar to Christians in 17th-century Japan. Possibly (though of course this is pure conjecture) Amakusa Shirō was selected to lead the rebellion as a sort of reincarnation or revenant of the young Portuguese hero. It may be significant that when Mr. Couckebacker, the Dutch factor, wrote his diary of the events in Shimabara, he recorded the rumour, which was then current in Edo, that Amakusa Shirō had in fact not been killed at Hara Castle but had made a miraculous escape (cf. the legend about Yoshitsune's escape from his burning mansion), presumably so that he might return to save his people at some later time. See also p. 175, about the 13-year-old Christian boy who was associated with a suspected uprising near Nagasaki in 1657–58.

7.35   Okada, *Amakusa*, pp. 76–77. For Kozaemon, see n. 7.27.

7.36   But see p. 161, concerning these estimates.

7.37   Quoted by Tsuji, *Edo Bakufu*, p. 403.

7.38   The gory suppression of the Shimabara Rebellion is also reminiscent of the hideous executions of the slaves captured by the Roman troops after the Servile Rebellion 72 B.C. In both cases the authorities were determined to instil the masses with terror and in both cases they succeeded.

7.39   Okada, *Amakusa*, p. 49. The adviser was the famous warrior-minister, Sakai Tadakatsu (1587–1662).

7.40   See pp. 166–67.

7.41   Amakusa Shirō's role in the abortive attack on Tomioka is not confirmed by any contemporary records and may simply be part of the heroic legend. His headquarters are said to have been at Futae, the nearest port to the tip of Shimabara Peninsula.

7.42   It is hard to see how an attack on Nagasaki with a mere 12,000 men could possibly have succeeded; but, if the Christian population of the city had helped the rebels acquire the necessary weapons (especially the great cannon), they might have held out at Hara Castle for several months longer than they did.

7.43   The figure given by Dr. Ludwig Riess in "Der Aufstand vón Shimabara 1637–1638," *Mittheilungen der Deutschen Gesellschaft für Natur und Völkerkunde Ostasiens*, vol. V, Heft 44 (1890), is 20,000, but this seems far too low. My own tentative estimate would be about 30,000. Lacking rebel archives, however, we shall always be in the dark.

7.44   The main source for the theory that there were five *rōnin* leaders under Amakusa Shirō was the turncoat artist Yamada Emonsaku, but his testimony may well be suspect. According to Yamada, these five leaders were all in their fifties and had all been retainers of the Christian daimyo, General Konishi. For their names and further particulars see Tsuji, *Edo Bakufu*, p. 396, and Okada, *Amakusa*, p. 21.

7.45   Tsuji, *Edo Bakufu*, p. 396.

7.46   One of the accounts of the final attack on Hara Castle describes the appearance of the defenders. Most of them had no proper armour, though many carried swords, bows, and spears. They were mainly dressed in white cotton robes and close-fitting trousers. Some of them had round hats with cords tied under their chins; others wore homemade helmets consisting of iron hoops filled with straw and attached round the ears.

7.47   Among the defenders' battle-cries was *Masuda no Shirō Shōgun* ("Generalissimo Masuda Shirō") (see n. 7.30).

7.48   Though Couckebacker participated in the attack on the castle, he was evidently much impressed by the defenders. "If any of the rebels had subsequently been captured," he adds to the present passage, (quoted by Okada, *Amakusa*, p. 130), "and if any noblemen or priests had been found among them, I should have liked to make their acquaintance."

7.49   Okada (*Amakusa*, p. 253) quotes some rollicking verses, in the vein of "Onward, Christian Soldiers!" that were sung to the accompaniment of drums shortly before the final attack on the castle. The song was loud enough to be heard in the besiegers' camp, where (in view of the defenders' desperate state) it caused considerable surprise.

7.50   Pagés estimates that the number of official troops by the end of March was 200,000 (*Réligion Chrétienne au Japon*, p. 847), but this is probably an exaggeration. Official Japanese sources give the suspiciously precise number of 100,619 for late March, and say that by the end of the campaign a total of 124,000 had been thrown into the engagement. The total cost to the government was estimated at 400,000 ryō of gold (about seven million pounds sterling in 1975 values).

7.51   The occupants were able to communicate with Christian supporters in the hills outside the castle by using children's kites (Okada, *Amakusa*, p. 256), but there was no possibility of getting supplies from them.

7.52   *Ibid.*, p. 195.

7.53   Tsuji, *Edo Bakufu*, p. 405, and Okada, *Amakusa*, p. 206.

7.54   Okada, *Amakusa*, p. 209. One of these huge cannon balls has been preserved on a concrete emplacement in Nagasaki where, rather incongruously, it is surrounded on all sides by iron crucifixes.

7.55   Okada, *Amakusa*, pp. 254–55.

7.56   It is often suggested that Matsudaira was sent as a substitute for General Itakura, in whom the Bakufu had lost confidence. This seems unlikely. When Matsudaira left Edo in mid-January, the rebels were still not entrenched in Hara Castle and the government had no reason to doubt Itakura's efficacy. In fact, Matsudaira was sent, not to replace the earlier general, but to help him clear up the rebellion as rapidly as possible. Itakura, however, certainly interpreted Matsudaira's appointment as a threat to his own command.

7.57   Okada, *Amakusa*, p. 157.

7.58   *Ibid.*, p. 138. Their jibes contain a play of words on *semeru* = (*i*) to torture, (*ii*) to attack.

7.59   Okada (*Amakusa*, p. 161) quotes the poem but doubts its authenticity.

7.60   *Ibid.*, pp. 200, 204.

7.61   Several daimyos, for instance, had been using the rebellion as an excuse for not paying their commercial debts.

7.62   Two Dutch ships were at anchor in Nagasaki, but Couckebacker, no doubt wishing to minimize his involvement, hurriedly sent the other one to Formosa and informed Matsudaira that only *de Ryp* was available for the bombardment.

7.63   There, after we had inspected the situation on shore as well as at sea, we saw clearly that we could do nothing important with our guns, as the houses are merely made of straw and matting, the parapets of the lower works of defence being made of clay and the upper-most fortress being surrounded by a good high wall, built with heavy stones. . . . It was evident that it was not much use to fire guns from the batteries of the [shogunal] army, nor from our batteries. (Quoted by Murdoch, *History of Japan*, II: 657.)

Obviously Couckebacker did not want to be regarded as responsible for killing fellow Christians in Japan; but see n. 7.65.

7.64   Originally Matsudaira insisted that the Dutch dismount their cannons and leave them behind for the use of the attacking forces, but Couckebacker finally got permission to relinquish only one of them.

7.65   Boxer, *Christian Century in Japan*, p. 381. The French historian Léon Pagés compared Nicolaus Couckebacker to Pontius Pilate himself: "Comme un autre Pilate, après avoir essayé d'y demeurer étranger, à la dernière heure il céda lâchement." Pagés, *Réligion Chrétienne au Japon*, p. 846.

7.66   Pagés, *Réligion Chrétienne au Japon*, p. 846.

7.67   Okada, *Amakusa*, pp. 230–43.

7.68   Ebisawa, *Amakusa Shirō*, pp. 190–96.

7.69   Okada, *Amakusa*, p. 258.

7.70   No less than 16 warriors belonging to different daimyo forces claimed to have been the first to enter Hara Castle (*ichiban-nori*), and afterwards there was prolonged controversy among the various forces to decide who was most responsible for the capture. The main documentation concerning the attack is the Hosokawa Family Records, which obviously stress the Hosokawas' role in the final victory. The leader of the Nabeshima forces (the Lord of Saga) was put under house arrest by the Bakufu for having prematurely stormed the castle in advance of the shogunal representative, Lord Matsudaira.

7.71   Letter from Hosokawa Tadatoshi, Lord of Kumamoto and leader of the Hosokawa forces at Shimabara, written to his father directly after the fall of the castle. (Okada, *Amakusa*, p. 282.) There is a certain irony in the fact that Tadatoshi (1586–1640) had himself been baptized as a Christian when he was nine years old. Later he submitted to Tokugawa Ieyasu's orders and banished all Christians from his domains, and at the age of 52 he became a leading general in the suppression of the Christians at Shimabara. His mother was the famous Gracia Hosokawa (1563–1600), the beautiful daughter of Akechi Mitsuhide (Nobunaga's assassin), who was converted to Christianity, baptized under the name of Gracia in 1587, and much admired by the Jesuits as "Princess Gracia of Tango." Her husband, Hosokawa Tadaoki (1563–1645), one of the most powerful daimyos of the time, told the Jesuits that he himself would become a Christian were it not for the Sixth Commandment, which he could not possibly observe in good faith. (Boxer, *Christian Century in Japan*, p. 185.) When Ishida Mitsunari tried to take Gracia hostage in 1600 in order to prevent her husband from supporting Ieyasu, she gallantly resisted arrest and killed herself rather than submit to the enemy. Gracia is popularly admired as a paragon of feminine fortitude who sacrificed herself for her ideals. There can be no doubt about the lady's courage, but her death was certainly no act of Christian martyrdom.

7.72   Okada, *Amakusa*, p. 292.

7.73   Ebisawa, *Amakusa Shirō*, pp. 219–23.

7.74 According to an alternative version (Ebisawa, *Amakusa Shirō*, p. 223), the hero walked out of the hut attired in his splendid robes and was decapitated at the entrance. In yet another account (*ibid.*, p. 217), we are told that, while the Hosokawa warriors were running about the inner citadel searching for the rebel leader, Amakusa Shirō mounted a 10-foot platform which had been built with white stones and, looking up to heaven, prayed for divine succour. Then a dark cloud appeared near the platform. Amakusa Shirō was about to mount the cloud and escape when someone shot a single white-feathered arrow into the cloud, which instantly dissolved. A Hosokawa retainer by the name of Nagaoka Tatewaki took advantage of the young man's bewilderment and, letting out a great battle cry, killed him with one thrust of his spear. This is the last of the miracles attributed to Amakusa Shirō and it is typical that it should have been a total failure.

7.75 In another version the identification was carried out by the painter Yamada Emonsaku, who, despite his treacherous intentions towards his former leader, burst into tears on seeing the severed head. (Ebisawa, *Amakusa Shirō*, p. 221.)

7.76 Though Sasaemon evidently had no idea of Amakusa Shirō's identity when he killed Amakusa, he was handsomely rewarded by a *chigyō* (fief) of 1,000 *koku*. Subsequently Lord Hosokawa expressed the regret that the rebel leader had not been captured alive. (Ebisawa, *Amakusa Shirō*, p. 223.)

7.77 *Erāo tantos, que me emfadava de os contar.* (Pagés, *Réligion Chrétienne au Japon*, p. 1410.)

7.78 Ebisawa, *Amakusa Shirō*, p. 231. With neat economy the spikes were cut from the wooden poles that had been used to build the attackers' palisades.

7.79 Okada, *Amakusa*, pp. 145, 258, 300; and see n. 7.1, above, concerning the painting of Amakusa Shirō's banner.

7.80 Murdoch, *History of Japan*, II: 661.

7.81 According to one ingenious but improbable theory (Okada, *Amakusa*, p. 302), Yamada's "betrayal" was in fact a plan concocted by Amakusa Shirō so that, in case of disaster, there would be at least one survivor to tell the heroic tale of the rebellion and thus encourage others to carry on the good cause.

7.82 The hero's father, Jimbei, and his uncle, Gensatsu, were killed in the castle but it is not clear whether their heads were identified.

7.83 Tokugawa law responded as harshly as ever to farmers in Kyushu and elsewhere who presumed to complain about excessive taxation. Typical is the case of Sakura Sōgorō, the headman of Kōzu village (Shimōsa Province), who in 1645 was crucified with his entire family for having presented a petition to the central government in protest against his overlord's severe taxation of the local peasantry; Sōgorō's courage and his tragic end made him a folk hero and the subject of numerous *Yagi-bushi* ("ballads from Yagi"). Patia Isaku, *Japanese Folk Songs*, unpublished manuscript, 1974.

7.84   Tsuji, *Edo Bakufu*, p. 410. One interesting result of this forced migration is that to this very day different accents can be identified in Shimabara depending on whether the family descended from prerebellion inhabitants or from migrants who moved there from other parts of Japan after 1638.

7.85   *Ibid.*, p. 407. The new *danka* (parishioner) system, according to which everyone in Japan had to be registered as a parishioner of a Buddhist temple, was a particularly effective form of control.

7.86   Some Christian families in the Nagasaki region continued to practise their faith secretly until the proclamation of religious freedom after the Meiji Restoration. This remarkable achievement, however, had no general effect: for all intents and purposes Christianity in Japan was wiped out by 1660, the rate of arrests falling rapidly between 1639 and 1658 as the number of survivors dwindled. In 1865 about 100 "secret" Christians were discovered in the Nagasaki region. They were arrested by the local magistrate and put to the torture, as a result of which most of them apostatized. Paul Akamatsu, *Meiji 1868* (London, 1972), p. 214.

7.87   Boxer, *Christian Century in Japan*, p. 395.

7.88   *Ibid.*

7.89   Though Amakusa Shirō is present throughout the story, he appears more as an idea or an icon than as a concrete historical individual. The positive heroism in the Shimabara Rebellion (as in the kamikaze operations three centuries later) was exemplified by a *collectivity*, namely the lieutenants and other supporters who struggled and died in the castle; the actual leader comes down as an impassive, disembodied figure, who is encased in the activity of his followers.

7.90   Matsudaira Nobutsuna was rewarded for success at Shimabara by being appointed Lord of Kawagoe Castle near Edo with a fief of 60,000 *koku*. A few years later he again proved his value to the government by destroying the conspiracy of Yui Shōsetsu, another failed hero of the Tokugawa period, who had mounted a sort of Guy Fawkes plot against the government and disembowelled himself rather than be captured by the police. In 1657 Matsudaira organized the highly successful relief and reconstruction of Edo after the great fire that destroyed half the city. An able, resourceful Minister, he came to be known as Chie Izu ("the wise Lord of Izu"). Yet it is the failures like Amakusa Shirō and Yui Shōsetsu who are affectionately remembered today in songs, films, plays, and books. Lord Matsudaira, like Fujiwara no Tokihira and so many other "survivors," had the disadvantages of being realistic, practical, and successful.

7.91   The Roman Catholic Church recognized some 2,000 martyrs in Japan between 1614 and 1645. Amakusa Shirō, however, was not included among them, and this can perhaps be regarded as still another aspect of his failure. It may seem strange that the heroic leader of a great Christian rebellion should not have been accorded the laurels of martyrdom. Possibly there were too many uncertainties about the identity of Amakusa Shirō to make him acceptable as an official martyr. The unorthodox socioeconomic aspects of the rebellion may also have helped to disqualify him: an uprising that was, at least in part, a protest against economic injustice would hardly have recommended itself to a conservative Catholic hierarchy in 17th-century Europe. Fr. Michael Cooper, S.J. of Sophia University, Tokyo, to whom I am indebted for many valuable suggestions, has the following comment on the failure of Amakusa Shirō to be officially recognized as a martyr:

> . . . in fact there were and are a lot of rules and regulations about candidates for beatification—e.g. he or she must have died in *odium fidei* and without offering resistance. In any attempt to make any of the people slain at Shimabara "official martyrs," the *advocatus diaboli* would have had a field day on these two points alone, and on both counts they could not be recognized as official martyrs. (Letter to the author, dated 7th May 1974.)

7.92   The 13th-century religious hero Nichiren was persecuted by the Kamakura government and condemned to death (though the sentence was commuted at the last moment). This persecution, however, was motivated by political, not religious, considerations. In all Japanese history there is not a single Buddhist (or Shinto) leader who suffered martyrdom for his faith.

Chapter 8

8.1   Mishima Yukio, "Kakumei no Tetsugaku to shite no Yōmeigaku," *Shokun*, September 1970, pp. 23–45.

8.2   *Ibid.*, pp. 30, 38–39.

8.3   Hsin-hsüeh or Learning of the Mind; also known as the School of Intuition or Mind *(shin)* as opposed to Chu Hsi's School of Reason or Principle *(ri)*. For a discussion of these two main schools of neo-Confucianism in China and Japan, together with a translation of representative texts, see Wm. Theodore de Bary, ed., *Sources of the Chinese Tradition* (New York, 1960), pp. 344–92.

8.4   Mishima, "Kakumei no Tetsugaku," p. 40.

8.5   Mishima, "Kakumei no Tetsugaku," p. 36. Mishima's scorn of the "safe way" reminds me of a taxi journey that I suffered some years ago in Tokyo. The chauffeur was a young man of the type popularly known as "kamikaze drivers." Like a mediaeval samurai charging into an enemy fortress, he raced into the centre of the city at an insane speed, zigzagging between cars, buses, and pedestrians and totally ignoring traffic lights and other conventional impediments. After about ten minutes of this suicidal progress I asked the driver to stop and let me out of the taxi, explaining that I had just remembered an errand that I had to do on the way. Still driving at full speed, he turned round with a pitying expression and asked, "Why do you cling so much to life? [*Inochi wa sonna ni oshii no ka*]." I now realize that, in one respect at least, this young driver belonged to a well-established Japanese heroic tradition, and I am sure that both Ōshio Heihachirō and Mishima would have found an emotional kinship.

8.6   General Nogi Maresuke (1849–1912), the hero of the Russo-Japanese War, committed harakiri on the day of Emperor Meiji's funeral so that he might accompany his master to death; Madam Nogi, the perfect samurai wife, also killed herself. This is generally regarded as the last instance of the ancient Japanese custom of *junshi* (self-immolation of a retainer on the death of his lord)—the last, that is, until Mishima's chief follower, Mr. Morita Hisshō, committed harakiri immediately after his leader's death. General Nogi was an ardent believer in Wang Yang-ming's philosophy, whose tenets he expounded when serving as tutor to the Crown Prince (the future Emperor Taishō). Nogi's suicide was widely praised in prewar Japan and held up as evidence that the country's ancient tradition of nobility had survived into the 20th century. The following poem by Kuroiwa Ruiko, editor of the *Yorozu Chōhō*, is quoted by Katō Genchi in *Shinto in Essence* (Tokyo, 1954), p. 12:

> Falsely, I thought him
> An old soldier:
> Today, I confess him
> God Incarnate.

8.7   Mishima notes that the eminent intellectual historian, Professor Maruyama Masao, in his monumental work on Japanese thought (*Nihon Seiji Shisō Kenkyū Shi*), gives only a single page to Yōmeigaku (Wang Yang-ming philosophy). After the Meiji era, writes Mishima, Marxism took the place of Yōmeigaku among intellectuals, in much the same way that "humanism" took the place of Shushigaku (Chu Hsi philosophy, see n. 8.3). Mishima, "Kakumei no Tetsugaku," pp. 23–24.

8.8   He refers both to Saigō's writings and to the self-sacrificial action that brought his amazing life to its culmination.

8.9   The young man's text is Professor Inoue Tetsujirō's "The Philosophy of the Japanese Wang Yang-ming School."

8.10   Cf. Wang's dictum, "Knowledge is the beginning of conduct; conduct is the completion of knowledge." See Edwin Reischauer and John Fairbank, *East Asia, the Great Tradition* (Boston, 1958), p. 309, for a discussion of the political implications of this philosophy.

8.11   Mishima, *Homba*, pp. 373*ff.*

8.12 Mishima's letter is quoted *in extenso* in *The Eloquence of Protest*, ed. Harrison Salisbury (Boston, 1972), pp. 137–38. The letter was written in English and I have made a few minor corrections (e.g., changing "very seldom persons" to "very few people").

8.13 Kawabara, *Saigō Densetsu*, p. 26. See n. 5.70, n. 7.34.

8.14 Ref. Hugh Borton, *Peasant Uprisings in Japan of the Tokugawa Period* (2nd ed., New York, 1968).

8.15 Heihachirō-sama. Tetsuo Najita, "Ōshio Heihachirō (1793–1837)," in Albert Craig and Donald Shively, eds., *Personality in Japanese History* (Berkeley, 1970), pp. 155–79.

8.16 Kitajima Masamoto, *Bakuhansei no Kumon* (Tokyo, 1966), p. 426.

8.17 Mishima had a particular admiration for this League (Shimpūren) and he devotes a good part of *Homba* to describing their catastrophic coup and its influence upon his young hero, Isao.

8.18 See chap. 9 below.

8.19 *Senshindō Satsuki*, compiled in 1833. See Mishima, "Kakumei no Tetsugaku," p. 25.

8.20 The "movement for freedom and people's rights" (*jiyū minken undō*), though aimed at parliamentary government and legal democratic reform, was often marked by a type of violent activism that belongs to the Japanese samurai tradition (represented by such men as Ōshio and Saigō) rather than to analogous 19th-century movements in the West. A "people's rights" newspaper in 1876 had articles with captions like "Freedom must be bought with fresh blood" and "Tyrannical officials must be assassinated," which could easily have been drafted forty years earlier by Ōshio himself. See John Fairbank, Edwin Reischauer, Albert Craig, *East Asia, the Modern Transformation* (Boston, 1965). The authors note (*op. cit.*, p. 284) that "Ōkubo, the most powerful figure in the government, was killed in May 1878 by extremists who had the curiously mixed motives of avenging Saigō's death and defending 'people's rights.'"

8.21 These large-scale uprisings against the spiralling cost of food mainly took the form (as in 1837) of attacks against rice merchants; sometimes, however, the violence was directed against the police, and army regiments had to be summoned to crush the dissidents. (Abe Shinkin, "Ōshio Heihachirō," in *Nihon Jimbutsushi Taikei* [Tokyo, 1959], IV: 280.) Abe refers to a book by Ishizaki Tōkoku *(Ōshio Heihachirō Nempu)* in which Ōshio figures as a hero for the rice rioters.

8.22 E.g., Nakano Seigō, a member of the Diet and leader of the Greater East Asia League (Dai Tōa Remmei) and other ultra-nationalist societies, who committed harakiri in 1943 following a dispute with General Tōjō. Nakano believed in "strong action" and favoured a Japanese attack on Russia in order to help China. See Richard Storry, *The Double Patriots* (London, 1957), p. 150.

8.23   See Storry, *Double Patriots*, and Ivan Morris, *Nationalism and the Right Wing in Japan* (London, 1960), Appendix IV. As a rule the coups, notably that of February 1936, played directly into the hands of the conservative military establishment, who used them to suppress opposition.

8.24   See Abe, "Ōshio Heihachirō," pp. 279–80, for some titles.

8.25   See n. 8.6.

8.26   *Ōshio Heihachirō* by Mori Ōgai was originally published in 1914. It is a fascinating study of the hero, but must be used with some caution as a historical source. According to Mishima, "Kakumei no Tetsugaku," p. 30, Ōgai's "Apollonian" approach made it difficult for him to empathize with the activist Ōshio, who was "Dionysian" through and through. It is only after Ōshio's rebellion fails and he is obliged to assume the victim's role (i.e., to become like the later Yoshitsune) that the engrained Japanese "sympathy with the loser" *(hōganbiiki)* makes Ōgai regard his hero with any real affection.

8.27   See p. 5.

8.28   See pp. 86–87.

8.29   See pp. 130–31.

8.30   See p. 261.

8.31   The uprising started at 7 A.M. on 19th February (1837); the drum for retreat was beaten shortly before noon. The most detailed account is in Kōda Shigetomo, *Ōshio Heihachirō* (Osaka, 1942), pp. 181–213; see also Mori Ōgai, *Ōshio Heihachirō*, ed. Iwanami Shoten (Tokyo, 1960), pp. 36–37.

8.32   The fullest biographical account is Kōda Shigetomo, *Ōshio Heihachirō*.

8.33   At the time of Ōshio's insurrection the population of Osaka was about 337,000, as compared with over 400,000 in the late 17th century. The shogunal capital of Edo had well over a million inhabitants.

8.34   See pp. 176–77.

8.35   The name of the hero's father was Atobe Ichirō; from the little we know about this gentleman he appears to have been a conservative, Establishment figure who performed his duties conscientiously but entirely lacked his son's brilliance. Heihachirō was adopted first by the Shioda family, then by the Ōshios, whose name he used during the remainder of his life. For a genealogical chart see Mori Ōgai, *Ōshio Heihachirō*, pp. 68–69.

8.36   Mishima, "Kakumei no Tetsugaku," p. 32. "We have no information concerning little Martin's cleanliness [i.e., toilet] training," writes Erik Erikson with ill-concealed regret (*Young Man Luther: A Study in Psychoanalysis and History* [New York, 1962], p. 248). We are hobbled by a similar dearth of crucial information concerning Ōshio Heihachirō and the other Japanese heroes. See n. 7.2.

8.37   See frontispiece of Kōda Shigetomo, *Ōshio Heihachirō*.

8.38   Mori, *Ōshio Heihachirō*, p. 26.

8.39   For Saigō's attempt at suicide, see pp. 234–35. For a description of Ōshio's experience on Lake Biwa see Mishima, "Kakumei no Tetsugaku," pp. 33, 38; Mishima refers to it as *ryōchi e no shimpiteki taiken* ("a mystical experience [that led Ōshio] to intuitive knowledge").

8.40   Quoted from *Senshindō Satsuki* by Mishima, "Kakumei no Tetsugaku," pp. 33–34.

8.41   *Ibid.*, p. 34. One wonders how much the illiterate rustics gleaned from Ōshio's talks about *kitaikyo* and *chiryōchi*, but they were no doubt flattered at receiving such attention from an eminent samurai-scholar.

8.42   Mori, *Ōshio Heihachirō*, p. 28, gives a list of Ōshio's principal writings.

8.43   Mishima, "Kakumei no Tetsugaku," p. 34.

8.44   See Abe, "Ōshio Heihachirō," p. 293, for details.

8.45   The gurnard *(lepidotrigla miscroptera)* is a sea-fish with large head, mailed body, and three pectoral rays. It is full of bones and prickles that would be inedible for anyone except an enraged hero.

8.46   See p. 181.

8.47   Concerning the influence of Yōmeigaku (Wang Yang-ming philosophy) in Japan see pp. 181–83. Among the noted adherents during the past century were Yoshida Shōin (see n. 2.26), Saigō Takamori, General Nogi, and Mishima Yukio—all, most eminently, men of action.

8.48   de Bary, ed., *Sources of the Japanese Tradition* (New York, 1958), p. 379.

8.49   See n. 8.3.

8.50   For a fuller discussion see Najita, "Ōshio Heihachirō," passim, in Craig and Shively, *Personality in Japanese History*, and de Bary, *Japanese Tradition*, pp. 378–92. In addition to the Japanese sources cited above I am indebted to both these works for my summary of Wang Yang-ming's philosophy and its manifestations in Japan.

8.51   There is a clear dichotomy in the Japanese tradition between the "conformist" approach, represented, for example, by official Heian Buddhism of the Tendai and Shingon sects and by Chu Hsi neo-Confucianism, and reflected in proverbial sayings like *deru kugi wa utareru* ("A nail that sticks out is hammered") or *nagai mono ni wa makareyo* ("Yield to the powerful!") and the individualistic, heterodox, "eccentric" approach as seen in Nichiren's iconoclasm, certain forms of Zen, and Wang Yang-ming neo-Confucianism. Most of the failed heroes are naturally exemplars of the latter approach.

8.52   I have avoided the more literal translations of *taikyo* as "Great Emptiness" or "Absolute Void," since they have misleading nihilistic connotations.

8.53   Chu Hsi dualism stressed distinctions between

reason	matter
knowledge	action
self	objects
active	passive
past	present
life	death
positive	negative
superior	inferior
male	female
	etc. etc.

In Ōshio's metaphysics (*mono no tai nashi*, "there is no opposition between things") we can reach the truth only by perceiving the unity of all these seemingly exclusive categories.

Ōshio's insistence on the need to transcend conventional categories is by no means peculiar to Yōmeigaku philosophy. In this respect his *taikyo* is analogous to the "will of God" in the Old Testament, though of course it is a far more abstract concept: " . . . man cannot measure the will of God, which derives from a center *beyond the range of human categories. Categories, indeed, are totally shattered by the Almighty* of the Book of Job, and remain shattered to the last" (italics added). (Campbell, *The Hero with a Thousand Faces* [New York, 1956], p. 148.) As Campbell points out (*Hero*, pp. 148, 152, 171, etc.), moral virtues are not the criterion of the hero; what is needed is the culminating insight, the transcendent force, which goes beyond all pairs of opposites and demolishes all categories. In the West this force (or "destiny") normally leads to practical success, whether in the hero's lifetime (Luther, Washington, etc.) or posthumously (John Huss, Jeanne d'Arc, etc.); in Japan, however, "sincerity" operating in a corrupt worldly setting tends to stand in the way of pragmatic achievement.

8.54   Quoted by Mishima, "Kakumei no Tetsugaku," p. 36.

8.55   *Inochi wa kōmō yori mo karoshi.* Ref. Suzuki and Hirota, *Koji Kotowaza Jiten* (Tokyo, 1956), p. 83. See also n. 10.134.

8.56   Mishima, "Kakumei no Tetsugaku," p. 42.

8.57   *Ibid.*, p. 29. Ōshio's image is reminiscent of the biblical "through a glass darkly," but St. Paul was of course referring to spiritual salvation by *caritas* rather than to self-knowledge.

8.58   These are the opening lines of *Tzu Ching*, the "Three-Character Classic."

8.59   *Kyōsha no gotoshi.* Najita, "Ōshio Heihachirō," p. 163. Over six centuries before Ōshio's time the Buddhist recluse, Kamo no Chōmei, had written, "If we follow the ways of the world, things are hard for us; if we refuse to follow them, we appear to have gone mad *(kyō seru ni nitari)*." Kamo no Chōmei, *Hōjōki*, ed. Yūseidō (Tokyo, 1963), p. 54.

8.60   Lytton Strachey, "The End of General Gordon," in *Eminent Victorians.* (London, 1948), p. 251.

8.61   Mishima, "Kakumei no Tetsugaku," pp. 29–30.

8.62   *Ibid.: Sbitte okonawazaru wa imada kore sbirazaru nari.*

8.63   Miyake Setsurei (1860–1945) was the founder of a nationalist society and of an influential magazine which opposed Westernization in favour of a return to Japanism. His comments on Ōshio are discussed by Najita, "Ōshio Heihachirō," p. 159: "High tribute indeed for one [Ōshio] who died leading an abortive, and in many respects, miserable, rebellion."

8.64   Once Ōshio had launched himself on his mission he adopted the view that his primary allegiance must be to the Emperor, as the embodiment of eternal Japanese values, rather than to the Bakufu, which was a temporal, secular power. The union between the Emperor and his people was an absolute moral virtue that took precedence of any worldly obligations. According to Ōshio, the Bakufu's "betrayal" of the Imperial House had become especially outrageous since Takauji's villainous *volte-face* in 1335 (see Najita, "Ōshio Heihachirō," p. 171). In this sense Ōshio was a precursor of the loyalist movement that was represented later in the century by leaders like Ōkubo and Saigō, and he is sometimes pictured as a proto-Restorationist. The aim of Ōshio's forlorn fight against the authorities, however, was not to "restore the Emperor" (he never evinced the remotest interest in Ninkō Tennō, the actual Emperor of the time), but to "save the people" *(kyūmin)*, in particular the economically oppressed citizens of Osaka; and it is anachronistic to regard his revolt as an attempt to overthrow the political status quo in favour of centralized imperial rule.

8.65   In justifying his stand against the Bakufu authorities, Ōshio frequently used historical analogy. Many of his lectures referred to those late Ming heroes who followed Wang Yang-ming's philosophy and defied the government's authority in their efforts to bring justice to the empire and to help the weak and poor. Fiercely loyal to the old Ming Dynasty, these heroes gave their lives in a futile resistance to the Manchu "usurpers," who, in Ōshio's view of Chinese history, were analogous to the Tokugawa Bakufu. Najita, "Ōshio Heihachirō," p. 68. The fact that the Ming loyalists were clearly backing a hopeless cause and were bound to be destroyed confirmed the heroic sincerity of their motives.
        Among modern Western heroes who stressed the importance of sincere action regardless of conventional loyalties or practical consequences, and who (like Ōshio Heihachirō and Saigō Takamori) risked obloquy and death in pursuit of a greater loyalty, was the Irish patriot Sir Roger Casement. He too had served with great distinction in the government to which he eventually turned traitor and by which he was relentlessly destroyed. In his speech from the dock of the Old Bailey

immediately before he was sentenced to be hanged in June 1916, Casement declared, in words that might easily have been spoken by an Ōshio or a Saigō, " . . . my 'treason' was based on a ruthless sincerity that forced me to attempt in time and season to carry out in action what I said in word." (Brian Inglish, *Roger Casement* [New York, 1973], p. 345.) In their "ruthless sincerity" and in their failure (Casement referred to himself as an "individual Irishman who may have tried and failed," *ibid.*, p. 406) they were all alike; the great difference, of course, is that Casement has never become an *English* hero.

8.66   See p. 185.

8.67   For a detailed discussion see Borton, *Peasant Uprisings in Japan of the Tokugawa Period* (New York, 1968). As Professor Borton points out, the usual *ikki* were concerned with correcting specific, local injustices and not with changing the general system (*ibid.*, p. 95). Ōshio's uprising had a broader theoretical basis than any of the others, but only in the vaguest sense of the word can it be described as "revolutionary."

8.68   Najita, "Ōshio Heihachirō," p. 177.

8.69   Maeda Ichirō, "Ōshio Heihachirō," in *Nihon Rekishi Kōza* (Tokyo, 1952). The "four social estates" *(shimin)* were samurai, farmers, artisans, and merchants.

8.70   Najita, "Ōshio Heihachirō," pp. 177, 170.

8.71   This was recognized by Ihara Saikaku in the 17th century, and most of his later *chōnin* stories deal with the economic plight of the poorer townsmen:

Already towards the end of the century . . . there were signs of economic stagnation, and mercantile capitalism no longer seemed to offer its earlier opportunities. The more unfortunate *chōnin* families seemed to be unable to extricate themselves from their morass of poverty, however hard they worked. "Things have changed," Saikaku wrote. "Now it is only silver that can produce more silver. In these times it is not so much intelligence and ready wit that bring a man profit, but simply the fact of already possessing capital." Saikaku's later works accordingly deal with the gloomier side of *chōnin* life. For the first time he turns his attention from the upper bourgeoisie, which had either inherited or earned wealth, to the middle and lower strata of townsman society, from the individuals who used money to those who were used by it. Saikaku provides one of the only existing records from the seventeenth century of the lives of the indigent townsmen who, far from profiting from the rise of the merchant class, were engaged in a constant struggle for the bare necessities of life. (Ivan Morris, *The Life of an Amorous Woman* [New York, 1963], pp. 28–29.)

8.72   Akamatsu, *Meiji 1868* (London, 1972), p. 26.

8.73   Borton, *Peasant Uprisings*, pp. 35–36.

8.74   *Ibid.*, pp. 44–45. The uprising took place in the northeastern district of Aizu (near present-day Fukushima) in the fief of Lord Matsudaira Narisada. Typical is the following order issued after the suppression of an uprising in 1836 in the desperately poor mountain-province of Kai:

Whereas these individuals were leaders in the uprising over the question of the difficulty of purchase of rice, and having wrecked the cereal stores . . . and having threatened to burn down an official's residence if he did not open his gate, and causing the various villages . . . to become rebellious . . . and being the leaders during the march and carrying banners: they shall be crucified.

Ibid., p. 92; and Kōda, *Ōshio Heihachirō*, p. 130, give details.

8.75 In 1830 one *koku* of rice cost 88.5 *momme* of silver. The price rose to 119.9 *momme* in 1833, 155.7 in 1836, and 294 in 1837. (By 1840 it had fallen to 63.4.) Borton, *Peasant Uprisings*, pp. 208–209, contains a translation of Professor Honjō's useful chart of rice prices from 1616 to 1866.

8.76 Borton, *Peasant Uprisings*, p. 88.

8.77 For some examples of Ōshio's *kanshi* see Abe, "Ōshio Heihachirō," pp. 290–91, 298. Cf. Michizane's "social" poems, p. 48.

8.78 According to an alternative account, the appeal to Atobe was made by Ōshio's adopted son, Kakunosuke; when Kakunosuke reported the official refusal, Ōshio is said to have burst into one of his violent rages. In fact there is no documentary evidence whatsoever on this subject, and the entire story of the appeal may be part of the heroic legend that developed after Ōshio's death. Kōda, *Ōshio Heihachirō*, p. 144. The sale of his library, however, seems to be an incontestable fact.

8.79 Abe, "Ōshio Heihachirō," p. 302. See *ibid.*, pp. 299–300, for a summary of Ōshio's *Gekibun*. Chinese was the language of Confucianism and official government documents. According to Professor Abe, copies of the Summons were distributed mainly to nearby villages along the banks of Yodo River and reached only a small proportion of the audience that Ōshio had intended. It is significant of Ōshio's rural orientation that there was no organized distribution within the city itself.

8.80 Ōshio's call for a "return to Jimmu" (the legendary first Emperor of Japan) and his frequent invocations to the sun goddess, Amaterasu Ōmikami, hardly denote a revolutionary approach (see n. 8.64).

8.81 Ōshio gives the examples of Taira no Masakado, who rebelled against the Fujiwara-controlled government in the 10th century, and of Akechi Mitsuhide, who assassinated Oda Nobunaga (the first of the great national unifiers) in the 16th century. These were both men of heroic stature, but they failed (according to Ōshio) because they were motivated by political ambition. Concerning the Ming heroes, see n. 8.65.

8.82 The two Commissioners were Atobe of the Eastern Magistracy and Hori, who had been appointed to the Western Magistracy (Nishi Machibugyō) on 8th March and who was now making his first official inspection of the city.

8.83 Borton, *Peasant Uprisings*, p. 29, refers to the paucity of *rōnin* support for insurgent peasants. This was due partly to their traditional disdain for the lower orders and partly to their lack of common grievances.

8.84   Owing to Ōshio's blithe disregard for practical affairs, he and his family had been in straitened circumstances ever since his retirement in 1830 and he frequently had to depend on financial support from his disciples.

8.85   Kitajima Masamoto, *Bakuhansei no Kumon* (Tokyo, 1966), p. 425.

8.86   For an hour-by-hour account of the events of 25th March, see Mori, *Ōshio Heihachirō*, pp. 66–67.

8.87   See p. 186.

8.88   The news was reported to the chief shogunal minister, Mizuno Tadakuni, on 1st April 1837.

8.89   The list of their names is given by Kōda, *Ōshio Heihachirō*, p. 216.

8.90   Mori, *Ōshio Heihachirō*, p. 47.

8.91   *Ibid.*, p. 75.

8.92   For a detailed map of Gorōbei's house and the sanguinary events of 1st May, see Kōda, *Ōshio Heihachirō*, opposite p. 236.

8.93   *Ibid.*, p. 236.

8.94   See J. C. Hall, "Japanese Feudal Laws," *Transactions of the Asiatic Society of Japan* XLI, pt. 5 (Tokyo, 1913) for a translation of "The Edict in 100 Sections" *(O Sadamegaki Hyakkajō)* prescribing the procedure and legal rules to be followed by magisterial tribunals in the Edo period. The application of the fierce penal codes, and particularly the use of torture, became more severe during the later part of the Tokugawa shogunate, possibly as a result of the increasing number of uprisings, and "The Edict in 100 Sections" contains some of the most bloodcurdling examples of judicial cruelty in the world's legal literature.

8.95   See Abe, "Ōshio Heihachirō," pp. 292 *ff.* for details. Gorōbei, the towel-merchant, was condemned to imprisonment *(gokumon)*, which for a man of his age was equivalent to a death sentence.

8.96   The full text of the decree is quoted by Kōda, *Ōshio Heihachirō*, pp. 268–70. Section 103 of *O Sadamegaki Hyakkajō* specifies that

> Ordinarily the punishment of crucifixion is to be carried out either at Asakusa or Shinagawa; but there may be cases in which the culprit should be sent for punishment to the place where he committed the crime. A placard recording the facts of the crime and the punishment is to be exhibited for three days near to the corpse, which is to be handed over . . . to the Eta (pariah) attendants for inhumation. Whether or not the criminal is to be led around for public exposure previous to being crucified depends on the circumstances of the case. . . . (Hall, "Japanese Feudal Laws," p. 791.)

8.97   Mori, *Ōshio Heihachirō*, p. 83. Seventeen of the main offenders had succumbed to ill-treatment in prison and six had managed to commit harakiri. Only one of the 20 offenders sentenced to crucifixion was still alive when attached to the cross.

8.98   The only exception was a farmer named Nishimura, whose body had decomposed despite the pickling; the Bakufu officials therefore decreed that his grave should be destroyed (*fumbo-hakai*). Kōda, *Ōshio Heihachirō*, p. 240.

8.99 Sakamoto Gennosuke was a brave and efficient officer and undoubtedly the most impressive fighter on the government side. In many other countries it would have been he, rather than Ōshio, the ineffectual loser, who would have figured as the hero of 1837; yet in Japan his name is unknown except to scholars. Interestingly enough, Sakamoto was an old friend of Ōshio's, and he even wrote a secret work in praise of him. Abe, "Ōshio Heihachirō," p. 279, and see Mori, *Ōshio Heihachirō*, p. 41.

8.100 Mishima, "Kakumei no Tetsugaku," p. 51.

8.101 Unlike, for instance, Yoshida Shōin (see n. 2.26).

8.102 Quoted by Akamatsu, *Meiji 1868*, p. 62.

8.103 The Tempō Reforms were carried out from 1841 to 1843 under the rōjū, Mizuno Tadakuni (see n. 8.88). Tadakuni may well have been galvanized into action by Ōshio's uprising, but he hardly seems to have been inspired by his principles. In any case the Tempō Reforms were an unmitigated failure, and there were no further such attempts during the Tokugawa period.

8.104 By 1863 the price of one *koku* of rice had risen to 325 *momme* (see n. 8.75) and two years later it reached 1,300 *momme*.

8.105 See Borton, *Peasant Uprisings*, pp. 94–95.

8.106 Tanaka Sōgorō, *Saigō Takamori* (Tokyo, 1958), pp. 276–77.

8.107 In "The Mindful Peasant: Sketches for a Study of Rebellion," *Journal of Asiatic Studies*, August 1973, pp. 579–89, Professor Irwin Schneider refers to Ōshio's influence on peasant rebellions in the early Meiji period. Thus in the Nosé "world renewal" rebellion the peasant leaders proclaimed that Ōshio had provided direct inspiration for their own acts and referred to him as Yonaoshi Daimyōjin ("The Great World-Renewal Deity"). As Professor Schneider points out, Ōshio gave the peasant rebels inspiration but not a program or an ideology. In particular they were attracted by his idea of a restoration of the Age of the Gods (*jindai fukkō*) in which they would be freed from exploitation by local officials, money-lenders, monopoly merchants, and others who preyed on them in their weakness. It is especially significant for an understanding of the Japanese heroic tradition that the leaders of these rebellions did not expect victory (*ibid.*, p. 587) and accepted their martyrdom, destroying themselves "for society to let the world know our anger."

8.108 I cannot agree with Professor Borton when he writes (*Peasant Uprisings*, p. 93), "[Ōshio's] revolt was to fail, not because of a lack of courage on the part of its leader, but through the treachery of one of his followers."

8.109 Professor Abe's explanation is typical of postwar Japanese historians. According to Abe, Ōshio's failure to organize the "anti-feudal" elements in the country doomed his movement from the outset (Abe, "Ōshio Heihachirō," p. 283). He also points out (*ibid.*, p. 304) that Ōshio's main support came from landlords (*jinushi*) and other members of the traditional ruling class in the villages (*dentōteki sonraku shibaisha*) and that this limited the possibility of acquiring mass support for his revolt. It is true that Ōshio's samurai background may have impeded him from organizing effective popular backing, but the history of the hundreds of other failed *ikki* suggests that the idea of an "anti-feudal" mass rising in Tokugawa Japan is something of an anachronism.

8.110   See p. 185.

8.111   Abe, "Ōshio Heihachirō," p. 276.

8.112   Mishima, "Kakumei no Tetsugaku," p. 33.

8.113   Ōshio's reckless impracticality was recognized by his contemporary, the famous philosopher-historian Rai Sanyō (1780–1832). When he visited Ōshio's study a couple of years after his retirement from public service, Rai wrote a poem praising Ōshio as a true child of Wang Yang-ming but adding, "I fear only that you will bring misfortune on your extraordinary talent; I pray you sheath your sword after polishing it; Observe [this] poem on the wall." Quoted by Najita, "*Ōshio Heihachirō*," p. 175.

8.114   See p. 102.

8.115   *Times Literary Supplement*, December 1, 1972, p. 1445. The reviewer's reference is to Don Quixote, the hero in Western literature who in so many ways (e.g., the ironic gap between intentions and results) comes closest to the Japanese type of heroic failure.

Chapter 9

9.1   Plans for a statue were first formulated in 1883, six years after Saigō's suicide, the main sponsor being Fukuzawa Yukichi (1834–1901), who wrote a prospectus and publicized the scheme in his newspaper. The project was abandoned owing to fear of the government (for whom Saigō was still a proscribed rebel), and it was not resumed until after the promulgation of the Meiji Constitution in 1889. Following a successful appeal for popular financial support, which produced over 25,000 subscribers, the commission to build a statue was given to the Court artist, Takamura Kōun (1852–1934), who finished his work in 1898.

9.2   Sakamoto, "Nanshū-Ō" (see n. 9.8, below), p. 46.

9.3   This contemporary appellation (Daisaigō) referred to Saigō's physique as well as to his heroic stature; it was also used to differentiate him from his brother, Tsugumichi (1843–1902), who, though he ended his government career as a brilliant worldly success, could never have been designated as "great."

414 NOTES

9.4 *Tenchi irezaru chōteki.* Itagaki Taisuke (1837–1919), quoted by Kawabara Hiroshi, *Saigō Densetsu* (Tokyo, 1971), p. 68.

9.5 From an account by Kawakami Takeshi, quoted by Mushakōji Saneatsu, *Saigō Takamori* (translated and adapted by Sakamoto Moriaki in *Great Saigō, The Life of Takamori Saigō* [Tokyo, 1942]. My citations refer to Professor Sakamoto's version, which is hereafter abbreviated as "Mushakōji."

9.6 See p. 266.

9.7 Article from *Hōchi Shimbun*, quoted on p. 180 of *The Tokio Times*, 29th September 1877. *The Tokio Times*, an American weekly, was one of the earliest English-language newspapers in Japan. It took a strong anti-Saigō stand in reporting the Satsuma Rebellion. In contrast, the rival British newspaper in Japan, *The Japan Mail*, consistently supported Saigō's cause; this reflected the special British ties with Satsuma that developed after Sir Harry Parkes's visit to Kagoshima in 1866, and also Saigō's own pro-British sentiments.

9.8 The preface by Soejima Taneomi (1828–1905) of the Saga fief is quoted by Sakamoto Moriaki in his Foreword to "Nanshū-Ō's (Saigō Takamori's) Posthumous Words," unpublished manuscript (hereafter referred to as Sakamoto, "Nanshū-Ō)," p. 23. I am indebted to Sakamoto Moriaki (formerly professor at Kagoshima University) for supplying me with voluminous material about Saigō Takamori, with whom his family had close connexions (his father and three uncles having fought on the side of the rebels in 1877, and two of the uncles having been killed). Concerning Saigō's popularity among enemies like clansmen of the Shōnai fief, Professor Sakamoto writes: "Is there any example similar to this in any country of the world? Have the nations vanquished by Napoleon edited Napoleon's posthumous works into a book? Have the Jews [persecuted] by Hitler edited Hitler's posthumous works?" (Unpublished notes sent to the author.)

9.9 I realize that the left-right dichotomy is particularly simplistic in Japanese politics, where the two extremes come together at many points, and where people often switch from "left" to "right" and vice versa (see my *Nationalism and the Right Wing in Japan* [London, 1960], especially Appendix V, "Political Attitudes in Japan"). For a study of Saigō's influence, however, it is useful to divide his followers on the basis of whether they made him a symbol primarily of popular, liberal values or of a traditional, "Japanist" approach. By this division I do not intend to imply that, e.g., the "people's rights" movement (see n. 8.20) was in any useful sense of the word "left" wing.

9.10 Kawabara, *Saigō Densetsu*, p. 79. Thus Nakae Chōmin (1847–1901), an eminent writer and editor, who started the "Freedom News" (*Jiyū Shimbun*) and who introduced Rousseau's *Le contrat social* to Japan, publicly urged the hero to lead a "people's rights" movement against the government —a preposterous notion for someone with Saigō's political views. Many of these pro-Saigō "people's rights" advocates were imprisoned and harshly treated by the government of Ōkubo and his successors.

9.11   *Teichū Kōron* by Fukuzawa Yukichi, cited by Kawabara, *Saigō Densetsu*, p. 72. According to Fukuzawa, Saigō Takamori, who until a few years previously had been revered as a second Kusunoki Masashige, was now officially regarded like the arch-traitor Taira no Masakado (d. 940).

9.12   Sakamoto, "Nanshū-Ō," pp. 4, 31. And see n. 9.1, above.

9.13   How do Saigō's opponents dare call him a traitor? . . . He is just as sincere in his reverence for the Emperor as the high officials in the government. Since the Satsuma Rebellion his opponents have been abusing him severely, yet none of them has imputed craftiness or insincerity to him: when it comes to sincerity, they can find no fault in Saigō. Thus it is clear that Saigō is no traitor to the Emperor, but rather a man who respects His Majesty more than anyone in the world. Saigō may have behaved incorrectly towards the Ōkubo government but never towards the country as a whole. (Fukuzawa, cited by Kawabara, *Saigō Densetsu*, p. 72.)

9.14   Sakamoto, "Nanshū-Ō," p. 4.

9.15   Uchimura Kanzō (1861–1930), *Daihyōteki Nihonjin* (Tokyo, 1907). See also Kawabara, *Saigō Densetsu*, p. 144.

9.16   Uchimura, *Daihyōteki Nihonjin*, pp. 17–20.

9.17   E.g., Uchimura, *Daihyōteki Nihonjin*, p. 50. Nitobe Inazō (1862–1933), the famous Christian convert, who as an official of the League of Nations became an eloquent advocate of international peace, succumbed to a similar temptation when he presented the great Japanese hero as a Christian *malgré lui*. In *Bushido: The Soul of Japan* (Rutland, Vt., and Tokyo, 1969 and 1972; first published 1905), Nitobe writes in his sonorous Victorian prose:

Still another instance I may cite from Saigō, upon whose overhanging brows "Shame is ashamed to sit":—"The Way is the way of Heaven and Earth; Man's place is to follow it; therefore make it the object of thy life to reverence Heaven. Heaven loves me and others with equal love; therefore with the love wherewith thou lovest thyself, love others. Make not Man thy partner but Heaven, and making Heaven thy partner do thy best. Never condemn others; but see to it that thou comest not short of thine own mark." Some of these sayings remind us of Christian expostulations, and show us how far in practical morality natural religion can approach the revealed. Not only did these sayings remain as utterances, but they were really embodied in [Saigō's] acts. (Nitobe, *Bushido: Soul of Japan*, [Tokyo, 1972 ed.], p. 78.)

9.18   Kawabara, *Saigō Densetsu*, pp. 87–91. Kōtoku Shūsui was executed in 1911 at the age of 40. He became established as a hero for members of the Japanese left, and inasmuch as his career ended miserably and the immediate result of his death was the collapse of the socialist movement for which he had struggled, he may be classed as a sectarian failed hero.

9.19   *Ibid.*, p. 89.

9.20 Concerning the opinions of Tōyama Mitsuru (1855–1944), see Kawabara, *Saigō Densetsu*, pp. 108–10.

9.21 Kawabara, *Saigō Densetsu*, pp. 140–42. Though Kita Ikki (1884–1937) never came close to acquiring the status of a national hero, a study of his personality and life suggests certain interesting similarities with Saigō Takamori. Both men combined an apparent purity and sincerity of motive with a hatred of the "corrupt politicians" who were too timid to adopt a strong stand in foreign affairs; both were exceedingly energetic and active, yet ultimately they showed poor judgement in practical matters and became involved in the ill-conceived outbreaks initiated by their fanatic young followers which brought them both to their final ruin.

Another great admirer was the right-wing politician Nakano Seigō (1886–1943), the founder of the Tōhō Kai (Eastern Association) and Secretary-General of the Imperial Rule Assistance Association, who committed harakiri as the final outcome of his long feud with General Tōjō. When his corpse was discovered, a book of Saigō's was lying open on his desk.

9.22 Kawabara, *Saigō Densetsu*, p. 145. Saigō was especially popular among officers of the dissident Imperial Way Faction (Kōdō Ha) of the army. His rebellious, nonconformist nature made him somewhat suspect among certain members of the Establishment officers in the rival Control Faction (Tōsei Ha). Their leader, General Tōjō Hideki, was one of the few eminent Japanese before 1945 who actually voiced strong disapproval of the hero for having defied the legal government of his day. Sakamoto, "Nanshū-Ō," p. 49.

9.23 Jean Stoetzel, *Jeunesse sans chrysanthème ni sabre: Étude sur les attitudes de la jeunesse japonaise d'après guèrre* (Paris, 1953), p. 233. The poll was conducted in 1949.

9.24 Tōkei Sūri Kenkyūjo (Institute of Statistical Mathematics), *Nihonjin no Kokuminsei* ("The National Character of the Japanese"), (Tokyo, 1961). Not surprisingly both Saigō Takamori and Kusunoki Masashige rank highest on the lists compiled by people over 50 years old and lowest on the lists of people in their 20s (who gave first place to Noguchi Hideyo, the bacteriologist); they are highest on the lists compiled by labourers and farmers, lowest on those by teachers and other professional people (who again put Dr. Noguchi first). Despite the shift in attitudes (before the war a hero like Saigō would certainly have ranked far higher), not a single woman was included in any of the lists.

The Librarian of the National Diet Library has published a study concerning the popularity of Japanese statesmen and military figures since the 16th century on the basis of the number of books about them. In post-1945 publications Saigō easily heads the list with 64 books (compared with 24 books for the next contender, who is Saigō's great admirer, Nakae Chōmin, see n. 9.10). Saigō also has the largest number of pre-1945 books (153, compared with 110 for his runner-up, General Nogi, see n. 9.189). Ōyama Gōtarō, in *Kōshin*, no. 225 (April 1973), and Kokkai Toshokan, ed., *Jimbutsu Bunken Sakuin* (Tokyo, 1972).

9.25   See Sakamoto Moriaki, "A Tragic Hero of Modern Japan: The True Phase of Saigō the Humanist," unpublished manuscript (hereafter referred to as Sakamoto, "Saigō"). More recently another authority has written a book entitled "The Humanism of Saigō [the Great]," where he classes the hero among the outstanding "humanists" of the world like Lincoln and Gandhi—Yoda Noritaka, *Nanshū-Ō no Hiyūmanizumu* (Tokyo, 1965).

The repeated comparisons with Lincoln, a much esteemed figure in postwar Japan, are reminiscent of the way in which enthusiastic publishers write blurbs likening their authors to Melville, Kafka, and other voguish writers. Professor Sakamoto (see n. 9.8) has for many years been preparing a work entitled *Saigō Takamori, the Lincoln of Japan,* in which he attempts to prove, *inter alia,* that Saigō's downfall resulted from his having antagonized the Satsuma authorities by promoting the central government's antifief policy, and that Ōkubo's "despotism" was a distant cause of the Pacific war of 1941–45.

9.26   Sakamoto, "Nanshū-Ō," p. 46. The author was the famous Kabuki playwright, Kawatake Mokuami (1816–93), and the work was entitled *Okige no Kumo Harau Asagochi* (lit. "The clearing of the clouds and the morning breeze in the southwest [Kyushu]"). The first performance, on 7th June 1878, was attended by government officials, foreign representatives, and other notables—an impressive audience considering that Saigō's rebellion had ended only nine months earlier and that his great enemy in the Meiji government, Ōkubo Toshimichi, had been assassinated only a few weeks before. The part of Saigō was played by the great Danjūrō himself.

9.27   The author of this famous *Battōtai* ("The Brigade of Unsheathed Swords") song was Toyama Masakazu (1848–1900), a professor at Tokyo Imperial University who later became Minister of Education and was responsible, among his many other worthy achievements, for introducing the patriotic *banzai sanshō* (three *banzai* cheers), the Japanese equivalent to "Hip hip hurrah!" "No place in Heaven or on earth" refers to Itagaki's denunciation (see p. 219).

9.28   Quoted by Kawabara, *Saigō Densetsu,* p. 46. The identity of the poet is uncertain (Kawabara suggests Nishi Dōsen or Fusō Kan), but it was certainly *not* written by Saigō himself, as was widely believed at the time.

9.29   This lute-ballad *(biwauta)* was composed by the former Bakufu official and Meiji statesman Katsu Kaishū (1823–99), who had been appointed Minister of the Navy five years before the rebellion. He is said to have taken four years to write the ballad, which he dedicated to the spirit of Saigō Takamori. It is included in *Shikon* ("The Spirit of the Samurai"), (Kagoshima, 1970), pp. 105–107.

9.30   Yet there is not a single photograph or first-hand statue or portrait (see n. 9.46).

9.31   Kawabara, *Saigō Densetsu,* p. 27. The American zoologist Edward Morse, who was living in Japan at the time of the Satsuma Rebellion, wrote as follows in his journal: "On my walk I find the people crowded before the picture-shops where there are many-coloured war-pictures hung. . . . One picture shows a star (Mars) hanging in the sky, in which General Saigō is. The General is a rebel chief but all the Japanese love him. After Kagoshima was occupied, he and his disciples (officers out of office) committed harakiri. Many people believe that Saigō is in the star that has recently begun to sparkle very brilliantly." *Japan Day by Day* (Boston, 1917), p. 66.

9.32   E.g., see p. 101 concerning Yoshitsune. Similarly, Toyotomi Hideyori (1593–1615), who, though not exactly a hero, gained popular appeal owing to his unfortunate life and tragic end, was said to have escaped from Osaka Castle and to have made his way through the surrounding Tokugawa forces, eventually reaching Satsuma with a small band of devoted followers.

9.33   Kawabara, *Saigō Densetsu*, pp. 28–32.

9.34   For details see Kawabara, *Saigō Densetsu*, p. 28. According to a variant theory, Saigō would be returning aboard the Japanese warship *Unebi*, which was due to arrive shortly after the Russian crown prince. In a satirical article written in 1891 Fukuzawa Yukichi commented that, if Lord Saigō actually were to return to Japan, he would be so horrified by the chaotic state of affairs that he would promptly leave in order to cultivate his farmland in the other world! Quoted in *Rekishi Kenkyū*, June 1972, trans. Professor Moriaki Sakamoto.

9.35   Kawabara, *Saigō Densetsu*, pp. 28–29. In his "Freedom News" (see n. 9.10), Nakae Chōmin, who had recently resigned from the Imperial Diet, declared that if this rumour about Saigō's return was true it would be the greatest possible blessing for Japan. (*Nihon no Rekishi* XX [Tokyo, 1966], *Taidan*, p. 1.)

In April 1891 "A Record of Saigō Takamori's Survival" (*Saigō Takamori Kun Seizon Ki)* provided a full account of the current theories and canards. Later in the same year a further flurry of excitement was caused by a rumour that the government was about to redeem the private banknotes that had been issued by Saigō Takamori during his rebellion. Large quantities of these banknotes were still extant, but unfortunately for the owners this rumour proved to be as false as all the others. See Kawabara, *Saigō Densetsu*, pp. 26, 37, for further details.

9.36   *Hokushin Shimbun* (Niigata Prefecture), 9th April 1891, quoted by Kawabara, *Saigō Densetsu*, p. 38.

9.37   Inoue Kiyoshi, *Meiji Ishin* (Tokyo, 1966), p. 440.

9.38   Kawabara, *Saigō Densetsu*, p. 122.

9.39   *Ibid.*, p. 123.

9.40   The usual derivation of the word *hayato* is from *hayashi* ("swift," "nimble").

9.41   This social pride has been connected with Saigō's supposedly "reactionary" tendencies. E.g., Tanaka, *Saigō Takamori* (Tokyo, 1958), p. 3.

9.42   The following chronology gives the main dates in Saigō's life interspersed [in square brackets] with important events in contemporary Japanese history:

1828	(23 Jan.) born in Kagoshima
1839	(aet. 11) enters the clan school
1844	(aet. 16) leaves school and is appointed *kōrikata-kakiyaku* (Magistrate's Assistant Clerk), continuing in the post until 1853
[1849	succession crisis in the Shimazu clan; Saigō supports Nariakira]
[1851	Shimazu Nariakira becomes daimyo of Satsuma]
1852–53	(aet. 24) both Saigō's parents and also his paternal grandfather die
[1853	Commodore Perry arrives in Japan]
[1854	the first Japanese ports are opened to Westerners]
1854	(aet. 26) travels to Edo in Nariakira's suite
1855–58	(aet. 27–30) serves as Nariakira's agent in Edo, Kyoto, etc.
[1856	Townsend Harris is appointed Consul-General to Japan]
[1857	the Shimoda Convention regularizes American trade relations]
[1858	other foreign treaties are signed by the Tokugawa Bakufu]
[1858	Shimazu Nariakira dies, and is succeeded as ruler of Satsuma by Hisamitsu, his half-brother]
1858	(aet. 30) attempts to commit suicide with his friend Gesshō.
[1858–59	the "Ansei purge"]
1859	(aet. 30) sent into exile
[1860	Ii Naosuke, the chief shogunal Minister, is assassinated]
1862	(aet. 34) returns from his first exile
1862	(aet. 34) exiled for the second time
[1863	the British navy bombards Kagoshima]
1864	(aet. 36) is pardoned and returns from exile; appointed to be the chief Satsuma emissary in Kyoto and aide-de-camp to the daimyo
[1864–65	successful campaigns against the dissident Chōshū clan]
[1865	Sir Harry Parkes arrives in Japan as the first British Minister; establishes close relations with Satsuma]
1865	(aet. 37) married to his official wife, Itoko
[1866	Satsuma-Chōshū alliance against the Bakufu]

1866   (aet. 38) receives Sir Harry Parkes in Kagoshima

[1867   death of Emperor Kōmei; succeeded by Emperor Meiji]

[1868   3 Jan. Imperial Restoration proclaimed under Emperor Meiji]

[1868   7 Apr. Edo Castle surrenders to the loyalist troops: collapse of the Tokugawa Bakufu]

1868   (aet. 40) returns to Kagoshima and works in the local administration as Clan Counsellor

1871   (aet. 43) goes to Tokyo and joins the central government, becoming Chief Counsellor of State

[1871   the government announces the abolition of fiefs and the formation of prefectures under central control: official end of feudalism]

[1871   the Iwakura Mission leaves for Europe; Saigō, Ōkuma, and Itagaki become heads of a "caretaker" government]

1872   (aet. 44) appointed Commander-in-Chief of the Imperial Bodyguards and Field Marshal.

1872   triumphal return visit to Satsuma with Emperor Meiji

[1873   the government announces universal military conscription]

[1873   the Iwakura Mission returns to Japan]

1873   (aet. 45) resigns from the government following the Korean crisis; returns to Kagoshima and in 1874 (aet. 46) establishes a private school there

[1874   Samurai uprising in Saga]

[1876   the government abolishes the right to carry swords and other samurai privileges]

[1876   Samurai uprisings in Kumamoto and Hagi]

1877   17 Feb.   (aet. 49) leads the Satsuma Rebellion (Seinan Sensō)

1877   24 Sept.   (aet. 49) defeated and commits suicide in Kagoshima

[1889   Meiji Constitution proclaimed]

1890   (13 years after death) reappointed to 3rd Court Rank

1898   (21 years after death) bronze statue erected in Ueno Park

9.43   The Saigō family descended from the Kikuchi, a loyalist clan that had fought for the Southern Court in the 14th century, belonging to the same losing side as Kusunoki Masashige. Takamori's father descended in the 9th generation from an ancestor who about 1700 had become a vassal of the Shimazus, the hereditary lords of Satsuma. He belonged to the category known as *hirazamurai* ("middle samurai"), which W. G. Beasley defines as follows: "Retainer of full samurai status; clearly superior to *ashigaru* ['foot soldier'] but not belonging to the small group of upper samurai who were close to the daimyo." W. G. Beasley, *The Meiji Restoration* (Stanford, 1972), p. 428.

Here is a compact genealogy:

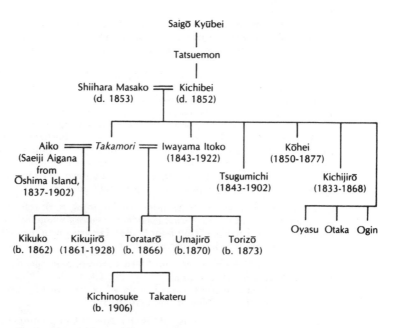

The double solid lines indicate marriages

9.44 See p. 217.

9.45 Ernest Satow, *A Diplomat in Japan* (London, 1921), p. 181.

9.46 Tanaka, *Saigō Takamori*, p. 1. This undocumented report concerning Saigō's virile endowment may be part of a heroic tradition (see n. 5.46). It might be supposed that the physical descriptions of Saigō are part of legendary exaggeration, but his baggy, outsize army uniform (formerly in the Yasukuni Shrine Museum, now in a private collection) can be measured accurately and confirms the dimensions that have been traditionally attributed to the hero.

One remarkable fact, which adds to the legendary quality of Saigō Takamori and puts him more in the category of a Yoshitsune or a Masashige than of famous contemporaries like Kido and Ōkubo, is that he would never be photographed, either in groups or alone, and even refused Emperor Meiji's request for a photograph. He lived at a time when the Japanese craze for cameras had already started, and all the other famous Meiji figures appear in numerous photographs. Saigō is conspicuous by his absence from group photos of government leaders between 1871 and 1873. Nor is there a single portrait, sketch, or statue made from life. All the contemporary paintings and sculptures of Saigō Takamori, including the famous one by Eduardo Chiossone (1832–98; the Italian artist who disseminated the technique of oil painting in Japan), were executed by people who had seen him often quite briefly, but for whom he had never posed. As a result we do not even know whether Saigō wore a beard or a moustache. Most of the Meiji prints give him a hirsute countenance, but the official portraits and statues show him clean-shaven.

Why this strange reluctance to be preserved in a visual medium? Simple modesty hardly explains it, since he was far from shunning public attention. It is possible that he was embarrassed by his corpulence, or that he preferred to be known for his achievements and character than for his physical attributes, or that he was influenced by his belief in "selflessness" (jiko-fuchūshin-shugi) (see pp. 243–44). Perhaps there was also a more subtle and unconscious factor, namely, a profound sense of moral shame and personal unworthiness—the same motive that made him eschew titles, awards, and other worldly honours, the same motive, indeed, that may have inspired his will to die (see p. 232).

9.47   Uchimura Kanzō (Daihyōteki Nihonjin [Tokyo, 1970], p. 21) refers to him as a "dense, reticent youth" (noroi mukuchi no shōnen), whom many of his schoolmates regarded as a "simpleton" (ahō). He was given the nickname udo, which refers to a large, useless fellow.

9.48   Tanaka, Saigō Takamori, p. 296, and Marius Jansen, Sakamoto Ryōma and the Meiji Restoration (Princeton, 1961), p. 189. Cf. Luther's "inarticulate stubbornness" and "secret furious inviolacy" as discussed by Erik Erikson, Young Man Luther (New York, 1962), p. 83.

9.49   In a "psychohistorical analysis" of Ōkubo, Albert Craig points out that a certain amount of boisterous mischief was encouraged among the samurai youth of Satsuma as a sign of manliness. (Craig and Shively, eds., Personality in Japanese History, pp. 269, 274, 278.) The ideal Kyushu warrior (Satsuma hayato) was prepared to break rules for a good cause.

9.50   Mushakōji, Great Saigō, p. 86, and see n. 9.62, below. This particular incident (which is reminiscent of the Ōshio fish-eating story, see p. 192) may be apocryphal, but it is typical of anecdotes about the hero's ardent nature.

9.51   Mushakōji Saneatsu (b. 1885). Great Saigō, p. 341.

9.52   The diplomat was Ernest Satow, whose impressions of Saigō are quoted in Taidan (see n. 9.35), p. 6.

9.53   Craig and Shively, Personality in Japanese History, p. 274.

9.54   Uchimura, Daihyōteki Nihonjin, p. 21.

9.55   Mushakōji, Great Saigō, p. 8.

9.56   These are the poems:
(a) Takazaki Gorōemon (1865) (lines 1–2),
(b) Gūsei (c. 1870) (lines 3–4),
(c) Gūsei (1874).

9.57   Letter of 4th April 1863, to Toku Tōchō.

9.58   Quoted by Tanaka, Saigō Takamori, p. 298.

9.59   Mushakōji, *Great Saigō*, p. 4.

9.60   For a Westerner's assessment of Saigō's hero, Shimazu Nariakira (1809–58), see William Elliot Griffis, *The Mikado's Empire* (New York, 1913), pp. 136–37:

> Notably preeminent among the Southern daimios, in personal characteristics, abilities, energy, and far-sightedness, was the Prince of Satsuma (Nariakira Shimazu). Next to Kaga, he was the wealthiest of all the daimios. Had he lived he would doubtless have led the revolutionary movement of 1868. Besides giving encouragement to all students of the ancient literature and history, he was most active in developing the material resources of his province, and in perfecting the military organization, so that, when the time should be ripe for the onslaught on the Bakufu, he might have ready for the Mikado the military provision to make his government a complete success. To carry out his plans, he encouraged the study of the Dutch and English languages, and thus learned the modern art of war and scientific improvement. He established cannon-foundries and mills on foreign principles.
>
> The renown of this prince extended all over the empire, and numbers of young men from all parts of the country flocked to be his pupils or students. Kagoshima, his capital, became a centre of busy manual industry and intellectual activity. Keeping pace with the intense energy of mind and hand was the growing sentiment that the days of the bakufu were numbered, that its fall was certain, and that the only fountain of authority was the Mikado. The Satsuma samurai and students all looked to the prince as the man for the coming crisis, when, to the inexpressible grief of all, he sickened and died, in 1858.

9.61   Saigō's first interview with Fujita Tōko, the great sage of the Mito School, took place in May 1854. Tōko died in the following year at the age of 49.

9.62   Nariakira's principal aim was to secure the succession of Tokugawa Yoshinobu (Keiki). The plan failed in 1858, but in 1867 Yoshinobu became the fifteenth and last Shogun of the Tokugawa line. It should be noted that at this stage the main political power in the Bakufu government was held, not by the Shogun himself, but by the Tairō (Regent); from 1858 this crucial post was occupied by Ii Naosuke (1815–60), the man whose assassination provoked Saigō's violent outburst (see pp. 229–30).

9.63   In 1858, for example, he travelled as follows:

Jan.   arrived Edo (from Shimonoseki)
Apr.   Edo to Kyoto
May   Kyoto to Edo
June-July   Edo to Kagoshima (20 days)
July-August   Kagoshima to Fukuoka (8 days), to Osaka (10 days), to Kyoto
Sept.-Oct.   Kyoto to Edo (10 days), to Kyoto
Oct.-Dec.   Kyoto to Fushimi to Osaka to Kyoto to Osaka to Kagoshima (11 days), into exile

For a detailed account of Saigō's movements see Sakamoto Moriaki, "Chronological Table of the Life of Saigō Takamori" (unpublished manuscript).

9.64   Mushakōji, *Great Saigō*, pp. 47–48. Gesshō (1813–58), a member of the

Hossō sect of Buddhism, was a leading cleric in Kiyomizu Temple (Kyoto). An ardent loyalist, he cooperated with members of the imperial aristocracy to overthrow the Tokugawa Bakufu and "restore" the Emperor. This led to an order for his arrest, his flight to Satsuma, and his dramatic death.

9.65 Sakamoto, "Nanshū-Ō," pp. 10, 39. Saigō's descendants have preserved Gesshō's two poems and Saigō's own poem about the suicide, and they still hold a memorial in honour of the documents each year on the anniversary of the drowning.

9.66 The clan authorities had succumbed to Bakufu pressure by refusing to give Gesshō sanctuary in Satsuma and by banishing him to the western frontier of the province; on arrival at the border of Hyūga he would almost certainly have been killed by his escort (James Murdoch, *A History of Japan* [London, 1926], III: 716) or arrested and put to death by the Bakufu police. According to Sakamoto (*Shiroyama Kanraku*, pt. II [Kagoshima, 1963], p. 36), he decided to kill himself because he had been unable to keep the promise to save Gesshō's life that he had made to the priest's patron, Prince Konoe.

9.67 Uchimura, *Daihyōteku Nihonjin*, pp. 22, 28.

9.68 See p. 231.

9.69 Mishima Yukio, "Kakumei no Tetsugaku to shite no Yōmeigaku," *Shokun*, September 1970, p. 38.

9.70 Quoted by Sakamoto, "Nanshū-Ō," p. 18. Saigō paid regular visits to Gesshō's tomb in Kagoshima.

9.71 Most writers about Saigō Takamori tend to skirt the psychological implications of their hero's failed suicide, and often the incident is omitted entirely. Surprisingly many people in Japan are unaware that Saigō ever made the attempt. For Mishima Yukio, of course, Saigō's effort to kill himself was of the greatest significance, and in his last essay he compares its spiritual significance with that of Ōshio Heihachirō's near-drowning on Lake Biwa.

9.72 Mishima, "Kakumei no Tetsugaku," p. 43, and Kawabara, *Saigō Densetsu*, p. 96. A similar sense of "having already died" has been expressed by kamikaze survivors (see p. 322).

9.73 The so-called Ansei purge, which lasted from 1858 to 1859, was ordered by the Bakufu Regent, Ii Naosuke, to curb the growing dissident movement in the provinces. Nariakira himself would probably have been forced to retire from his post of daimyo if he had not anticipated this setback by dying (ref. Beasley, *Meiji Restoration*, p. 137). Saigō's banishment was a decision by the Satsuma authorities, i.e., by Shimazu Hisamitsu and his associates. It is true that the main pressure to remove the troublesome young samurai and men of his kind from public life came from Edo, but, as Beasley remarks (*ibid.*, p. 141), many of the daimyos were all too ready to emulate the Regent by meting out punishments to

opponents of the Bakufu; in addition there was a strong personal antagonism between Saigō and his new overlord.

9.74 Hisamitsu (1817–87), Nariakira's younger brother, governed the province
of Satsuma in the name of his son (Tadayoshi) from 1858 until 1868. In the
traditional accounts of Saigō's career, Hisamitsu figures as "a bad thing"
in contrast to his virtuous older brother.

9.75 Saigō's first place of banishment (1859) was Ōshima. In 1862 he was sent
to Tokunoshima; later he was moved to the islet of Okinoerabu. The
Ryūkyū chain of islands had been Satsuma territory since early in the
17th century.

9.76 Mushakōji, *Great Saigō*, p. 116.

9.77 *Ibid.*, pp. 116–17.

9.78 Tanaka, *Saigō Takamori*, p. 136.

9.79 Mushakōji, *Great Saigō*, p. 88.

9.80 *Ibid.*, pp. 88–89.

9.81 When he left for the island of Ōshima, Saigō is said to have taken along
over 1,200 books, mostly works of Chinese history and philosophy. In a
letter dated May 1863 he wrote to a friend: "Since I am a prisoner, many
people evidently think that I am in a bad way. Not so—I am devoting
myself to books so that I may become 'a worthy scholar.' " Quoted by
Sakamoto Moriaki, *Saigō Takamori* (Tokyo, 1971), p. 10.

9.82 *Moshi un wo hiraku naku tomo i wa makoto wo osamu.* (Sakamoto, "Nanshū-Ō," p. 14.) This poem, which Saigō wrote in 1862, was engraved in
stone by Katsu Kaishū (see n. 9.29) and can be seen near Senzoku Pond
in Tokyo.

9.83 See n. 9.43 for a genealogy. Saigō's eldest son, Kikujirō (1861–1928) left the
island for Kagoshima in 1869; from the age of 11 he spent two years
studying in the United States. In the rebellion of 1877 he fought on his
father's side and lost one leg in the final battle of Shiroyama. Later, when
Saigō was posthumously rehabilitated, the government honoured Kikujirō by appointing him Mayor of Kyoto for six years.

Saigō married his first wife before his banishment, but they soon
became divorced and we do not even know her name. His island-wife was
of too lowly status to be officially recognized, and in 1865, after he had
returned from his exile, Ōkubo persuaded him to marry the daughter of
a Satsuma official, by whom he had three boys. On the whole, he seems
to have taken little interest in any of his wives or children. One of the
few poems that refers to his family is the famous *Kankai* (1868), in which
he affirms his single-mindedness and integrity by declaring that he will
not, like most successful men of his day, buy good rice fields to bequeath
to his sons and grandchildren (*jison no tame ni biden wo kawazu*)
(Sakamoto, "Nanshū-Ō," p. 19), a decision which he resolutely put into
practice (see p. 246). As a typical failed hero Saigō was, until the very end,
too engaged in the momentum of his own dramatic rise and fall to have

time to spare for cozy domesticity. After the heady wine of heroism other potions are bound to seem insipid.

9.84   Sakamoto, "Saigō," p. 16.

9.85   *Masateru shi ni ryūbetsu su* ("On Parting with Mr. Masateru"), Sakamoto, "Nanshū-Ō," p. 15. The poem starts:

> Like a dream this parting, like a cloud. . . .
> Once more I turn my tear-drenched face towards you,
> But find no words to speak my thanks
> For all the goodness [*jinon*] that you showed me in these exile years.

Ten years later, after his final resignation from the government, he wrote a poem with this remarkable line: "While in prison, I knew Heaven's will; while in office, I lost the moral sense" (literally: "the way of the heart").

9.86   W. G. Beasley in his monumental study of the Meiji Restoration points out that it was the final alliance of Satsuma and Chōshū that finished off the Tokugawa Bakufu: "The alliance of the two domains early in 1866 completed this realignment, symbolizing a marriage of *tōbaku* ["Destroy the Bakufu!"] with *fukoku-kyōhei* ["Enrich the country, strengthen the army"], an association of anti-Bakufu politics with the pursuit of national strength." Beasley, *Meiji Restoration*, p. 410.

9.87   In preparation for Sir Harry's visit, Saigō had written to his friend Ōkubo in Kyoto urgently requesting that he find vols. 1–2 of Macaulay's *History of England* and send them to Shimazu Hisamitsu so that he might be better prepared for his meeting with the foreigner. Mushakōji, *Great Saigō*, p. 218.

9.88   For Satow's impression of Saigō Takamori, see p. 228. Satow's suggestion during the meeting in Kobe was that English support for Satsuma would help offset the assistance that France was giving to the Bakufu.

9.89   E.g., see Uchimura, *Daihyōteki Nihonjin*, p. 27.

9.90   Professor Sheldon gives a conjectural total of 10,000 killed in the 24 major battles that constituted the so-called Bushin War. *Journal of Asian Studies*, Feb. 1974, p. 315.

9.91   Quoted by Mushakōji, *Great Saigō*, p. 246.

9.92   A recent study by Paul Akamatsu entitled *Meiji 1868: Revolution and Counter-revolution in Japan* (London, 1972), is no. 3 in "The Great Revolution Series." My review-article challenging the idea that the Meiji Restoration should be classed as a revolution appeared in *History Today* (London), July 1972.

9.93   Professor Beasley concludes his opus (see n. 9.86) as follows:

> . . . I am reluctant to call the Restoration a revolution in the full meaning of the term. In part, this is because what happened in Japan lacked the avowed social purpose that gives the "great" revolutions of history a certain common character. But it is also because of the nature of the society to which the Restoration gave

rise, in which "feudal" and "capitalist" elements worked together in a symbiosis dedicated to acquiring national strength. . . . What then is left, when none of these standard categories satisfactorily apply? Only to call it a nationalist revolution, perhaps, thereby giving recognition to the nature of the emotions that above all brought it about. (*Meiji Restoration*, pp. 423–4.)

9.94   *Kono inakamono no yajin ni wa nan no yaku ni mo tatanu.* Quoted by Tanaka, *Saigō Takamori*, p. 274.

9.95   According to Tanaka (*Saigō Takamori*, p. 278), this was due not so much to any official recognition of his talents as to a desire to remove him from Satsuma, where he might become a focus for antigovernment dissidents. This certainly appears to have been Saigō's own understanding. In a letter written a few months earlier (see n. 9.150) he said that so long as he lived freely in retirement the government was afraid that he might have some dangerous plan afoot and so they tried to tie him with "golden cords" (i.e., a salary).

9.96   The poem ends:

> The sacrificial ox, tied to his stake,
> Awaits the next day when he will be killed and boiled.

Here Saigō refers to Chuang-tzŭ's refusal to serve the King of Chu despite all the valuable rewards that were being offered. If he was foolish enough to accept, he would be like the sacrificial ox (*gigyū*) who, having been royally treated for many years, awaits his imminent slaughter and wishes that he were a young pig. (Unlike Chuang-tzŭ, however, Saigō did not reject the sacrificial role.)

9.97   The other principal members were: Prince Sanjō (Prime Minister), Prince Iwakura (Minister of the Right), Ōkubo (Minister of Finance), and Kido, Ōkuma, and Itagaki (Counsellors).

9.98   Sakamoto, "Chronological Table," p. 28.

9.99   Tanaka, *Saigō Takamori*, pp. 287–88.

9.100   *Nanshū Ikun* (see n. 9.8).

9.101   Uchimura, *Daihyōteki Nihonjin*, p. 22. Concerning Wang Yang-ming's form of neo-Confucianism and its influence in Japan, see pp. 193–98.

9.102   Sakamoto, "Saigō," p. 4.

9.103   Mishima, "Kakumei no Tetsugaku," pp. 38–39. For Absolute Spirit and its central significance in Wang Yang-ming's philosophy, see pp. 195–98.

9.104   Sakamoto, "Nanshū-Ō," p. 28.

9.105   . . . *waga makoto no tarazaru wo tazunubeshi.* Kawabara, *Saigō Densetsu*, pp. 175–76.

9.106   Sakamoto, "Nanshū-Ō," p. 32.

9.107   Uchimura, *Daihyōteki Nihonjin*, p. 43.

9.108   Sakamoto, "Nanshū-Ō," p. 31.

9.109   Uchimura, *Daihyōteki Nihonjin*, p. 44, and Mushakōji, *Great Saigō*, p. 123. "Self-love leads to defeat" *(mizukara aisuru wo motte yabururu zo)*. (Uchimura, *ibid.*) This refers, of course, to moral (not practical) defeat.

9.110   Quoted by Uchimura, *Daihyōteki Nihonjin*, p. 44.

9.111   First four lines of *Shitei ni shimesu*, quoted by Sakamoto, "Nanshū-Ō," p. 20.

9.112   Sakamoto, "Nanshū-Ō," p. 33.

9.113   From "The Great Learning": "What truly is within will be manifested without. Therefore the superior man must be watchful over himself when he is alone." Trans. James Legge, *The Four Classics* (Hongkong, 1957), p. 9.

9.114   For the connexion between Zen and Wang Yang-ming philosophy, see pp. 194–95.

9.115   *Hito wo aite ni sezu ten wo aite ni seyo.* Quoted by Kawabara, *Saigō Densetsu*, pp. 175–76. For a more impressive, Victorian-style translation, see n. 9.17.

9.116   Uchimura, *Daihyōteki Nihonjin*, p. 43, refers to the law and the prophets. For Nitobe's comments, see n. 9.17.

9.117   *"Bushi no nasake"*—the tenderness of a warrior—had a sound which appealed at once to whatever was noble in us [Japanese]; not that the mercy of a samurai was generally different from the mercy of any other being, but because it implied mercy where mercy was not a blind impulse, but where it recognised due regard to justice, and where mercy did not remain merely a certain state of mind, but where it was backed with power to save or kill. . . . Benevolence to the weak, the downtrodden or the vanquished was ever extolled as peculiarly becoming to a samurai. (Nitobe, *Bushido*, pp. 42–43.)

9.118   A contemporary account describes their hovels as being less than 20 feet square and looking more like stables than human dwellings. *Satsuma Keiiki*, quoted by Kawabara, *Saigō Densetsu*, p. 123.

9.119   In one of Saigō's Submissions (a remarkably outspoken document for a samurai official) he criticized the cruelty of the authorities and noted that many of the hard-pressed inhabitants had tried to escape the province, abandoning all their cattle and farm tools, and were brought back forcibly by the hundreds. Kawabara, *Saigō Densetsu*, p. 123.

9.120   Ref. Akamatsu, *Meiji 1868* (London, 1972), pp. 304–305; Tanaka, *Saigō Takamori*, pp. 136–37, 288; Kawabara, *Saigō Densetsu*, p. 126; and Inoue, *Meiji Ishin* (Tokyo, 1966), pp. 4–6, 146–47. In the view of Professor Inoue and some other modern scholars, Saigō became a "counter-revolutionary" after the Restoration. The term is entirely inappropriate in the historical context; but certainly Saigō opposed anything like a social revolution and his later attitude towards the Satsuma peasantry is reminiscent of Luther's opposition to the Peasants' Revolt in 1524–25.

9.121   Quoted by Kawabara, *Saigō Densetsu*, p. 133.

9.122   The symbol of all Western-style luxury became the Rokumeikan (the

Hall of the Baying Stag), a club in Tokyo designed in the style of an 18th-century German palace. This was the incongruous setting where Meiji leaders arranged parties, receptions, and balls for their foreign guests. Among Saigō's nationalist successors the Rokumeikan became an object of particular loathing, a Sodom and Gomorrah where the very people who should protect the Japanese spirit were vitiating it by aping foreign ways. Writing in 1891, Fukuzawa Yukichi pointed out that "the cost for a single guest at a party in the Rokumeikan or a single dish served at the Imperial Hotel is more than Lord Saigō's entire living expenses for a month." Quoted in *Rekishi Kenkyū*, June 1972 (trans. Prof. Sakamoto Moriaki).

9.123 ". . . children were brought up with utter disregard of economy. It was considered bad taste to speak of it, and ignorance of the value of different coins was a token of good breeding." Nitobe, *Bushido*, p. 98. Compare Ōshio's attitude to money (see n. 8.84).

9.124 Uchimura, *Daihyōteki Nihonjin*, p. 39. After the adoption of the gold standard, the yen was valued at half an American dollar.

9.125 *Ibid.* In accordance with his principles (see n. 9.83), Saigō offered nothing to his wife or children, and he made no provision for them after his death.

9.126 Kawabara, *Saigō Densetsu*, pp. 132–33.

9.127 Roberts, *Mitsui: Three Centuries of Japanese Business* (New York, 1973), p. 96.

9.128 Uchimura, *Daihyōteki Nihonjin*, p. 41.

9.129 A typical food incident occurred in 1872 when Saigō was participating in war games with the Imperial Guards in Etchōjima. At lunchtime all the generals took out their dainty, lacquered lunchboxes. Meanwhile, Saigō's aide-de-camp, knowing his master's simple tastes, handed him a large rice-ball. As Saigō was opening the paper wrapping, he accidentally let the ball fall on the ground where it rolled into a patch of sand. Saigō nonchalantly picked up the rice-ball, wiped off the sand, and started munching away. We are told that the soldiers observing the scene were deeply impressed by their general's "humble conduct." The story is told by an eyewitness, Yamamoto Ieyoshi, in *Nanshūō Itsuwa Shū* (Tokyo, 1903), p. 87.

9.130 Uchimura, *Daihyōteki Nihonjin*, p. 42.

9.131 See pp. 241–42.

9.132 In 1871 the samurai were "allowed" to cut off their traditional topknots and go without swords; 5 years later an edict forbade everyone, except army officers and members of the police, from carrying swords.

9.133 See Inoue, *Meiji Ishin*, p. 428, and Tanaka, *Saigō Takamori*, p. 214.

9.134 Mishima quotes the following impassioned argument that a certain Kyushu samurai presented to the government in 1876 as part of "A Petition Concerning the Proclamation of the Edict Prohibiting the Wearing of Swords":

In my view, the bearing of swords is a custom that characterized our Land of Jimmu even in the ancient era of the gods. It is intimately bound up with the origins of our nation, it enhances the dignity of the Imperial Throne, solemnizes the rites of our gods, banishes the spirits of evil, puts down disorders. The sword, therefore, not only maintains the tranquillity of the nation but also guards the safety of the individual citizen. Indeed, the one thing essential to this martial nation that reveres the gods, the one thing never to be put aside even for an instant, is the sword. How, then, could those upon whom is laid the burden of fashioning and promulgating a national policy that honors the gods and strengthens our land be so forgetful of the sword? (*Homba*, trans. Michael Gallagher [New York, 1973], pp. 75–76.)

9.135   Inoue, *Meiji Ishin*, pp. 344, 346.

9.136   Beasley, *Meiji Restoration*, p. 363. Saigō characteristically insisted that the *spirit* of the army, which of course depended on the inculcation of traditional samurai values, was more important than mere numbers or technology:

The number of a standing army must be restricted by finance. No vain show of power should be made. Raise a picked army by giving a stimulus to the military spirit, and even a small number of troops will be enough to resist foreign attack and hold foreign contempt in check. (Mushakōji, *Great Saigō*, p. ix.)

9.137   Inoue, *Meiji Ishin*, pp. 144, 340.

9.138   Tanaka, *Saigō Takamori*, p. 263.

9.139   Beasley, *Meiji Restoration*, p. 259; Sansom, *The Western World and Japan* (London, 1950), pp. 339–40; and Akamatsu, *Meiji 1868*, p. 295.

9.140   According to Fukuzawa Yukichi, the policy of abolishing the fiefs could never have been accomplished as easily as it was without Saigō's assent. *Teichū Kōron*, in *Fukuzawa Yukichi Zenshū* (Tokyo, 1925–26), VI: 536.

9.141   Sakamoto, "Nanshū-Ō," p. 26.

9.142   This bombardment, which was the result of righteous British indignation about the death of a Mr. C. L. Richardson, who was killed near Yokohama by some Satsuma retainers, destroyed about one-third of the city of Kagoshima, including Shimazu Nariakira's industrial establishment, Shūseikan, the pride and joy of the Satsuma modernizers. For details, see Beasley, *Meiji Restoration*, pp. 199–200.

9.143   In much the same way, America's near-destruction of Japan, culminating in the atomic bombardment of August 1945, far from turning Japan away from the West and its values, inaugurated the most intense period of Westerization and adulation of all things foreign since the early Meiji decades.

9.144   Sakamoto, "Nanshū-Ō," pp. 24–25.

9.145   *Ibid.*, p. 24.

9.146   Sakamoto Moriaki, *Saigō Takamori*, p. 93. The high-minded samurai was Yokoyama Shōtarō whose younger brother (Mori Arinori) subsequently became the first Minister of Education in Japan.

9.147 Mushakōji, *Great Saigō*, pp. 312, 313.

9.148 *Ibid.*, p. 314.

9.149 See p. 232.

9.150 "... When the opportunity comes to correct the evils [in the govern-ment], I shall certainly not remain an idle spectator." On the following page Saigō described the officials of the central government as "thieves" and remarked that anyone who suggested that he join such a government must regard him as a fit companion for thieves. The letter, which was written in September 1870 to retainers from the daimyo of Shōnai, is quoted *in extenso* by Sakamoto Moriaki, "Chronological Table," pp. 19–21.

So far as actual corruption was concerned, Saigō's fulminations against the new rulers were somewhat exaggerated; for the first real scandal, the Hokkaido colonization project, did not occur until several years after his death.

9.151 Mutsu Munemitsu, quoted by Kawabara, *Saigō Densetsu*, p. 126. Mutsu (1844–97), a samurai of the Kii fief, was active in the Meiji Restoration and received several official appointments in the new government. Like Saigō, however, he became dissatisfied with its policies and at the time of the Satsuma Rebellion he assisted a similar uprising in Tosa. He was discovered and punished, but later became an important member of the government and took a leading part in revising the unequal treaties. Thus his career ended successfully—and unheroically.

9.152 The legendary Saigō came to be respected as a basically *unpolitical* man. Politics is the world of cold facts, realism, compromise, and material success (see n. 2.33); Saigō occupied an entirely different sphere. Good politicians are traditionally regarded as *rikōsha*, "clever people," and in Japanese the word has all the derogatory connotations of its equivalent in England. In this sense Saigō was definitely not clever; the purity of his nature doomed him to be worsted in politics by the careful, calculat-ing type of leader exemplified by Ōkubo Toshimichi.

9.153 During the Tokugawa period diplomatic missives from Japan were signed with the title of Ōgimi or Taikun (Great Lord). After the Imperial Restoration the Japanese began to use the title of Kōjō (His Majesty the Emperor), which the Koreans would traditionally accept from no one but the ruler of China. Mushakōji, *Great Saigō*, p. 343.

9.154 Sakamoto Moriaki, *Shiroyama Kanraku*, pt. 2, p. 9.

... Saigō risked his life in similar sacrificial missions in 1864 when he visited the fief of Chōshū at a time when he was regarded as their greatest enemy and in 1868 when he entered Edo Castle unarmed. Sometimes it must have seemed to Saigō that death was deliberately evading him. (Sakamoto, "Chronological Table," p. 34.)

9.155 E.g., Inoue, *Meiji Ishin*, pp. 343–44.

9.156 *Ibid.*, p. 346.

9.157 In the remote past the southern regions of the Korean Peninsula had been far closer to Japan, both politically and psychologically, than areas like Hokkaido or even the northeast of the main island. At various times during her history, notably in the late 16th century, Japan's rulers had tried to recover a territory which they were convinced had once been part of their kingdom and which, in addition, was the natural gateway to the continent.

9.158 Uchimura, *Daibyōteki Nihonjin*, pp. 32ff. See also Kawabara, *Saigō Densetsu*, p. 134, who describes Saigō as an "unwavering symbol of continental expansionism" *(yuruginai tairiku shinshutsu no shinboru).*

9.159 Wm. Theodore de Bary *et al.*, eds., *Sources of the Japanese Tradition* (New York, 1958), p. 656. The letter was addressed to his fellow Counsellor, Itagaki Taisuke, who had been fiercely criticizing the government for its pusillanimous attitude towards Korea. In another letter to Itagaki a few weeks later he wrote:

> If, on the other hand, we send an envoy to tell the Koreans that we have never to this day harbored hostile intentions, and to reproach them for weakening the relations between our countries, at the same time asking them to correct their arrogance of the past and strive for improved relations in the future, I am sure that the contemptuous attitude of the Koreans will reveal itself. They are absolutely certain, moreover, to kill the envoy. (de Bary, p. 656.)

9.160 *Dai Saigō Zenshū*, III: 1201.

9.161 Prince Sanjō, the somewhat indecisive Prime Minister, was opposed to war in Korea but did not wish to confront Saigō without the backing of the members of the Iwakura Mission. Ōkubo returned from Europe in May (1873), Kido in July, and Prince Iwakura and Itō in September.

9.162 The principal advocates of war against Korea (or of steps that might lead to war) were: Etō Shimpei (Saga), Gotō Shōjirō (Tosa), Itagaki Taisuke (Tosa), Saigō Takamori (Sastuma), and Soejima Taneomi (Saga). The main opponents were: Itō Hirobumi (Chōshū), Prince Iwakura (Court noble), Kido Kōin (Chōshū), Ōkubo Toshimichi (Satsuma), Ōkuma Shigenobu (Saga), and Prince Sanjō (Court noble). It will be noted that the members of the Iwakura Mission all belonged to the latter category.

9.163 Inoue, *Meiji Ishin*, pp. 352–53.

9.164 *Ibid.*, p. 363.

9.165 The letter (to Itagaki) is quoted by Inoue, *Meiji Ishin*, p. 360, and Uchimura, *Daibyōteki Nihonjin*, p. 34. Saigō had been suffering from another bout of his chronic filiariasis.

9.166 Sakamoto, "Chronological Table," p. 30.

9.167 Mushakōji, *Great Saigō*, p. 359.

9.168 Sakamoto Moriaki, "Saigō Takamori's Poems and Posthumous Words" (unpublished manuscript), p. 8.

9.169   The crisis [of 1873] determined the nature of the Meiji government and its policies for the next two decades. In the first place, it marked the final stage in the disintegration of the loose and widely based Restoration alliance of Court nobles, feudal lords, and samurai of every rank and region, leaving in its stead a small nucleus with a relatively coherent view of the country's future. Saigō's resignation split the Satsuma contingent, more than half of which withdrew to Kagoshima. Since this included many army men, the army became more of a Chōshū preserve than ever. (Beasley, *Meiji Restoration*, p. 376.)

9.170   Sakamoto, "Nanshū-Ō," p. 18.

9.171   *Ibid.*

9.172   Uchimura, *Daibyōteki Nihonjin*, p. 48.

9.173   "Saigō disliked talking to treacherous Japanese," wrote Miyake Setsurei (1860–1945), an ultra-nationalist journalist and one of Saigō's great admirers, "and preferred his faithful dogs." Quoted by Sakamoto, "Nanshū-Ō," p. 22.

9.174   Sakamoto, "Saigō," pp. 47–48.

9.175   Sakamoto, "Nanshū-Ō," p. 32.

9.176   It was ordered that photographs of Etō's severed head be displayed in government offices throughout the country. Sakamoto ("Chronological Table," pp. 38–39; "Saigō," pp. 43–47) gives a detailed account of the events leading up to the trial and execution, which he presents as a blatant miscarriage of justice instigated by the egregious Ōkubo.

9.177   The League of the Divine Wind plays a major part in one of Mishima's last books, *Homba (Runaway Horses*, see n. 5.62), in which he inserts a detailed account of the 1876 rebellion as a sort of novel within a novel. According to Mishima's record, which is a brilliant pastiche of Meiji style, the Kumamoto patriots regarded all foreign innovations, even telegraph wires, as defilements of their sacred land. When obliged to walk under electric power lines, they covered their heads with white fans, and if they so much as glimpsed a man dressed in Western clothes they would purify themselves by scattering salt. They named their league in memory of the "divine wind" *(kamikaze* or *shimpū)* that was supposed to have saved Japan at the time of the Mongol invasion in the 13th century, and prepared for the day when they too would rescue their country from foreign intrusion. The last straw was the edict in which the government forbade samurai from carrying swords.

         In their attack on the imperial garrison, members of the League refused to use guns or other Western weapons, and were rapidly mowed down by government firepower. This suicidal decision is explained by Mishima in the following passage:

         . . . what the men of the League had been willing to risk by renouncing the use of firearms had clarified their intent. Divine aid was to be theirs, and their very purpose was to challenge the Western arms hateful to the gods with swords alone. Western civilization would, as time went by, search out weapons still more terrible, and would direct them at Japan. And then might not the Japanese themselves, in their anxiety to counter these, fall into bestial fighting and lose all hope of restoring the ancient worship . . . ? To rise to the combat bearing only the sword, to be willing to risk even crushing defeat—in no way but this could the fervent aspirations of each man of the League take expression. Here was the essence of the gallant Yamato Spirit.

The "purity of resolve" *(junsuisei)* exemplified by the League of the Divine Wind was a powerful inspiration for the sacrificial hero of Mishima's novel—and no doubt for Mishima himself.

9.178   These peasant risings were of course inspired more by economic discontent than by ideology and belonged to the tradition of *byakushō ikki* (see p. 200). Government repression was severe. After the defeat of a peasant rebellion in Mie Prefecture in 1875, no less than 50,000 participants were punished. Inoue, *Meiji Ishin*, p. 435.

9.179   Mushakōji, *Great Saigō*, pp. 393–94.

9.180   Inoue, *Meiji Ishin*, p. 441.

9.181   Mushakōji, *Great Saigō*, p. 407.

9.182   Sakamoto Moriaki, *Shiroyama Kanraku*, pt. 2, p. 15, and "Chronological Table," p. 52.

9.183   Mushakōji, *Great Saigō*, p. 408. The son was Kikujirō (1861–1928). Saigō's realization that he could now do nothing to prevent disaster is a typical situation in the career of the Japanese failed hero (see p. 186).

9.184   *Jibun no seimei wa shokun ni ageru.* Quoted by Inoue, *Meiji Ishin*, p. 442, and Mushakōji, *Great Saigō*, p. 409.

9.185   According to Uchimura (*Daihyōteki Nihonjin*, p. 37), the rebellion was an act of frustration and despair resulting from Saigō's knowledge that the Meiji Restoration had produced the opposite results from those he had intended. We must of course remember that Saigō never consciously planned the rebellion even though its outbreak did satisfy both psychological and ideological needs. In Professor Sakamoto's view ("Chronological Table," p. 31 *et passim*) the political basis of the war was the long-standing rift between the two major Satsuma factions, i.e., between the high-ranking "conservative" group centred about Shimazu Hisamitsu's favourite, Ōkubo Toshimichi, and the lower-ranking "reformist" group led by Hisamitsu's old enemy, Saigō Takamori. According to this conspiracy theory, Saigō's political setbacks were all ultimately a result of manoeuvres by Hisamitsu, who (acting through Ōkubo) used the Korean crisis as a pretext to remove Saigō from power.

9.186   *Tenchi no zainin.* The letter was addressed to Prince Arisugawa, the Commander-in-Chief of the Imperial Expeditionary force and is dated 3rd March 1877. (Sakamoto, "Nanshū-Ō," pp. 49–50.) Saigō's letter, writes Professor Sakamoto, makes it clear that he did not expect to win the war, "but he thought it was his duty for the good of humanity to let the Imperial government know right from wrong." (Sakamoto Moriaki, *Shiroyama Kanraku*, pt. 2, p. 26.) Also on 3rd March Saigō wrote a letter to the Governor of Kagoshima saying that, if the government forces attacked him with an Imperial Prince at their head, he would strike him down as he marched on Tokyo. *(Ibid.)* Clearly Saigō's "sincerity" took precedence over any respect for imperial personages or fear of being charged with lèse-majesté.

9.187 On 7th February Ōkubo wrote to Itō Hirobumi that he "secretly shouted with joy" when he heard about the Satsuma uprising, since it was "a happy event for the Imperial Court." Sakamoto, "Chronological Table," p. 53.

9.188 Advanced, not marched: because of his obesity Saigō had to be carried almost the entire way in a chair. Sakamoto, "Chronological Table," p. 54.

9.189 Among the government casualties during the fighting in Kumamoto were the Imperial Colours of the 14th Regiment, which was commanded by Major (later General) Nogi. These colours were captured by a Satsuma battalion on 22nd February and sent to Saigō's headquarters. Despite Nogi's glorious military career, this disgrace is said to have weighed heavily on him during the rest of his life. One reason given for the general's suicide in 1912 is that he felt responsible for the loss of the Imperial Colours 35 years earlier and wanted to demonstrate his deep appreciation for the leniency shown by Emperor Meiji when he had so graciously refrained from punishing him.

9.190 The enormity of Saigō's blunder was recognized at the time. The following is from a contemporary article in the *Hōchi Shimbun* included in *The Tokio Times* of 29th September 1877:

The Satsuma [ex-samurai], chosen instruments of Saigō, were the most formidable warriors of the old regime. So when he led them to Kumamoto . . ., many were in doubt as to which would be successful—the Imperial troops or the insurgents. But when Saigō wasted many days in laying siege to Kumamoto castle, then those who had some knowledge of the science of war began to say:—"Ah, he has made a mistake, and has clearly done what he ought not." And doubtless the mistake then committed was the foundation of the complete and final disaster which has now resulted in his overthrow and death. If he had entirely disregarded Kumamoto castle, had marched straight on to Fukuoka in Chikuzen, sent another force into Bungo, and after such a beginning, had followed up the struggle with the same valor and energy which he exhibited during the closing weeks of the rebellion, the result might have been today far different from what we now behold. But Saigō's strategy was sadly at fault, for with the best and bravest soldiers in the country under his command he could not extend the insurrection beyond four out of the nine provinces of his native island. . . .

The writer sums up his discussion by pointing out that, although Saigō was "in some respects a remarkable man" (a daring statement for the time), the insurrection provided "abundant proof of his lack of skill and generalship."

9.191 Mushakōji's account (*Great Saigō*, pp. 457–58) probably exaggerates the jubilation of the populace at the return of the defeated general. It should be remembered that Saigō's private schools had no close connexions with the ordinary inhabitants of the town, and also that, however much they might admire Saigō in his glorious defeat, few citizens would dare cooperate with a man who was being attacked by imperial forces as a rebel.

9.192 The letter is quoted *in extenso* in Mushakōji, *Great Saigō*, pp. 471–76.

9.193 The poems (by Nakajima Takehiko and Hashiguchi Harumine) are quoted by Mushakōji, *Great Saigō*, p. 477. It may seem strange to the Western reader that an officer who had been leading troops against the imperial forces should believe that he had actually been fighting for the Emperor's cause *(Kimi ga tame omoi)*, but the writer and his companions, having been motivated by "pure sincerity," were probably not aware of the slightest inconsistency.

9.194 There seems to be little doubt that he was hit in the groin (Inoue, *Meiji Ishin*, pp. 447–48), but traditional accounts say that he was wounded in the thigh and the abdomen, which are presumably regarded as more dignified parts of the anatomy.

9.195 Not surprisingly there are several versions of these last words. Most of the books I have consulted give *Shindon mō koko de yo ka. Shin* is an abbreviation of Shinsuke, and *don* is a term of endearment in Satsuma dialect. Inoue, *Meiji Ishin*, p. 448, and Mushakōji, *Great Saigō*, p. 479.
      The mood of the scene could hardly be more different than that represented by Admiral Nelson's parting injunction, "Kiss me, Hardy!" —nor could Beppu's final act for his master.

9.196 E.g., see pp. 101, 133–34.

9.197 This was General Miyoshi Shigeomi. See Uchimura, *Daihyōteki Nihonjin*, p. 38.

9.198 *Ā okina no kaoiro nanzo sore onko taru ya*, quoted by Uchimura, *Daihyōteki Nihonjin*, p. 38.

9.199 *Hōchi Shimbun* (see n. 9.190).

9.200 *Ibid.*

9.201 Robert Scalapino, *Democracy and the Party Movement in Prewar Japan: The Failure of the First Attempt* (Berkeley, 1953), p. 61.

9.202 E.g., p. 222.

9.203 In his concluding remarks on the government's "wealth and strength" *(fukoku kyōhei)* policy, Beasley *(Meiji Restoration*, p. 412) explains the extent of the resistance (in which the Satsuma Rebellion was, of course, the culminating event) and points out that "the leadership's success in resisting this challenge set the pattern of Japan's history for the next few generations."

9.204 "[Ōkubo] could compromise when compromise was the only alternative, even compromise principle. He wrote in 1873, 'endure shame, give up what is right, but achieve our goals.' " Craig, *Personality in Japanese History*, p. 291. It is hard to imagine any statement of views that would be so repellent to Saigō Takamori.

The following are typical of Ōkubo's arguments that led to Saigō's political defeat at the time of the Korean crisis:

If we permit the initiation of such a great venture, blithely and with no consideration for [eventualities], we shall in all probability have cause for much regret in
the future. . . . I consider such a venture entirely beyond comprehension, as it
completely disregards the safety of our nation and ignores the interests of the
people. It will be an incident occasioned by the whims of individuals without
serious evaluation of eventualities or implications. These are the reasons why I
cannot accept the arguments for the undertaking of this venture. (de Bary, *Japanese
Tradition*, p. 662.)

9.205   See 8.20.

9.206   See Inoue, *Meiji Ishin*, p. 353, for a typical formal portrait of Ōkubo
Toshimichi. Craig, *Personality in Japanese History*, pp. 291–96, discusses his
personality and appearance.

9.207   The "core of coldness" in Ōkubo's personality to which Beasley refers
(*Meiji Restoration*, p. 156) is amply supported by contemporary descriptions. Fukuchi Genichirō, a fellow member of the Iwakura Mission,
wrote that encountering Ōkubo was "like meeting an iceberg in the
Arctic ocean" and "all my friends felt the same way." Similarly
Yamamoto Gombei wrote, "Overwhelmed by his dignity, we were
struck silent and became smaller." We are told that, when Ōkubo entered
the Council of State, his fellow Counsellors would "lower their voices
and adjust their dress." Craig, *Personality in Japanese History*, p. 293.

9.208   See p. 229.

9.209   *Ikazuchi Shimbun*, 4th April 1891, quoted by Kawabara, *Saigō Densetsu*, pp.
45–46. This need for a national hero is discussed by Kawabara Hiroshi:

. . . the functions that the Meiji Government had undertaken were of national
scope . . . and demanded that national unity and cohesion be strengthened. For
this purpose a human symbol was necessary. They [i.e., leaders like Itō and
Yamagata] had to find a symbolic figure who, having started as a member of the
clan government *(hanbatsu)* had gone beyond both clan and class and could become a symbol representing closer national cohesion *(yori kimmitsu na kokuminteki
ittaisei wo hyōgen suru shinboru)*. Kawabara, *Saigō Densetsu*, p. 128.

9.210   Kawabara stresses the value of legends in indicating a people's cultural
and political characteristics, and his study of Saigō Takamori is specifically concerned with such legends and their significance for understanding the Japanese tradition. Kawabara, *Saigō Densetsu*, p. 13 *et passim*.

9.211   Saigō Takamori belongs squarely to the tradition of the defiant *shishi*, the
"men of spirit," who became conspicuous in the 1860s as activists in the
movement to "honour the Emperor and expel the barbarian." (Beasley,
Meiji Restoration, p. 430.) The prototype of the Meiji *shishi* was the samurai loyalist, Yoshida Shōin (see n. 2.26). The early *shishi* were, according
to the somewhat idealized image, fervent young patriots prepared to
offer their lives in opposing unjust authority. They lived on a high
emotional level (like the members of the League of the Divine Wind) and
were endowed with considerable romantic appeal. Kawabara (*Saigō Den-*

setsu, pp. 105*ff.*) traces a psychological line of descent from the *shishi* of the Restoration period through the *sōshi* ("bravoes") of the "people's rights" movement to the right-wing swashbucklers *(tairiku rōnin* and *uyoku sōshi)* and finally the "young officers" *(seinen shōkō)* of the 1930s. Though these groups differed in many ways, their common heroes were rebels like Ōshio Heihachirō, Yoshida Shōin, and Saigō Takamori, who had all met violent deaths in their confrontation with the government of the day. Saigō was a particular favourite: members of patriotic societies often adopted his name as a cognomen, and Tōyama Mitsuru was described as "Present-day Saigō" (Ima Saigō). (Kawabara, *Saigō Densetsū,* p. 137.) Many of the later *sōshi* and rightist bullyboy types, whom Saigō would have thoroughly despised, used to swagger about the streets of Tokyo in what came to be known as a "Saigō pose" and tried to copy his clothing and mannerisms in an undignified caricature of their hero.

9.212   Mushakōji, *Great Saigō,* p. 23.

9.213   Kawabara, *Saigō Densetsu,* p. 23.

9.214   de Bary, *Japanese Tradition,* p. 655.

Chapter 10

10.1   *Kike Watatsumi no Koe* (Tokyo, 1963), p. 38. The pilot was Sublieutenant Okabe Heiichi of the Shichishō Butai.

Of the many thousands of suicide fighters who died during the Pacific war the following appear in the course of this chapter; unless otherwise stated, they all had the rank of Lieutenant or Sublieutenant (Chūi or Shōi):

1. *Adachi* Takuya, True Spirit Special Attack Unit, killed at the age of 22.

2. *Arima* Masafumi, Rear Admiral, commander of the 26th Air Flotilla, killed in October 1944 in the Philippines area.

3. *Doi* Saburō, Ōka Jinrai Attack Unit, killed in April 1945 in the Okinawa area.

4. *Hayashi* Ichizō, (Mt.) Tsukuba Unit, killed in April 1945 in the Okinawa area at the age of 23.

5. *Iguchi* Yonosuke, 201st Air Group, killed in December 1944 in the Philippines area.

6. *Ishibashi* Nobuo (Mt.) Tsukuba Unit, killed in April 1945 in the Okinawa area at the age of 25.

7. *Kaijitsu* Susumu, Seven Lives Unit, killed in February 1945 in the Okinawa area at the age of 22.

8. *Kanno* Naoshi, 201st (and, later 343rd) Air Group, killed in June 1945 in the Okinawa area.

9. *Kuno* Yoshiyasu, 201st Air Group, killed in October 1944 in the Philippines area.

10. *Matsuo* Isao, Heroes' Special Attack Unit, killed in October 1944 in the Philippines area at the age of 23.

11. *Matsuo* Tomio, Ōka Jinrai Attack Unit, killed in April 1945 in the Okinawa area at the age of 21.

12. *Miyanoo* Bumbei, killed in April 1945 in the Okinawa area.

13. *Nakano* Kunitame, 201st Air Group, killed in January 1945 in the Philippines area.

14. *Nomoto* Jun, White Heron Special Attack Unit, killed in 1945 at the age of 23.

15. *Nonaka* Gorō, Lieutenant Commander, 5th Naval Air Fleet, killed in March 1945 in the Okinawa area.

16. *Oda* Hiroyuku, 2nd Army Air Squadron, killed in May 1943 in the New Guinea area.

17. *Okabe* Heiichi, Seven Lives Unit, killed in February 1945 in the Okinawa area at the age of 22.

18. *Seki* Yukio, Shikishima Unit, killed in October 1944 in the Philippines area.

19. *Suga* Yoshimune, True Spirit Special Attack Unit, killed at the age of 23.

20. *Ugaki* Matome, Vice Admiral, commander of the 5th Naval Air Fleet, killed in August 1945 in the Okinawa area.

21. *Yamaguchi* Teruo, 12th Air Flotilla, killed in 1945 at the age of 23.

22. *Ōnishi* Takijirō, Vice Admiral, commander of the 1st Naval Air Fleet, later Vice Chief of Naval General Staff, committed harakiri in Tokyo in August 1945 at the age of 54.

10.2 Plaque on 3rd floor of Science Museum, Exhibition Road, South Kensington, London, S.W. 7.

10.3 The German V-1 flying bomb, which was produced in the same year as the Ōka, is described as a pilotless midwing monoplane with a span of 17′8″, a length of 25′4 1/2″, warhead of 1,870 lbs., and a range of 150 miles. Technically a far more sophisticated weapon than the Ōka, it entirely lacked the heroic implications of the little Japanese craft. For its psychological effect, see p. 329.

10.4 ". . . the Samurai have chosen for their truest symbol the fragile cherry blossom. Like a petal dropping in the morning sunlight and floating serenely to earth, so must the fearless detach himself from life, silent and inwardly unmoved." Eugen Herrigel, *Zen in the Art of Archery* (New York, 1971), p. 106.
    Ōka is the "Chinese" reading of *sakurabana*, the cherry blossom, which in due course became a general symbol for all suicide operations. The full name of the manned bomb was *Ōka Jinrai*, in which *jinrai*

("divine thunder") is related to the image of *kamikaze* ("divine wind").

The idea of producing manned bombs in order to save the large aircraft was already being discussed in 1943, and in the summer of that year plans for a rocket-driven projectile which could be loaded under a Mitsubishi land bomber were submitted to the Naval Aeronautical Department at Yokosuka. The prototype of the Ōka suicide craft was completed in August 1944—several months *before* Vice Admiral Ōnishi initiated the first kamikaze unit in the Philippines (see p. 281). A Divine Thunder Unit (Jinrai Butai) was formed under (Navy) Captain Okamura in September 1944 for purposes of testing and training, and the weapon was first used in the following March. Several models of Jinrai Ōka were produced (the one exhibited in the Science Museum is an *Ōka II, Yokosuka MXY.8*); most of them were painted light green above and grey below, and were emblazoned with a chrysanthemum outlined in red.

10.5   "Baka bomb." *Baka, banzai,* and *harakiri* were among the small repertory of Japanese words generally known among the American military during the Pacific war. The selection is significant.

10.6   See p. 315 concerning the "madness" of heroism.

10.7   For Divine Thunder Unit (Jinrai Butai) see n. 10.4. For details of the attack see Inoguchi Rikihei and Nakajima Tadashi, *Shimpū Tokubetsu Kōgekitai no Kiroku* (hereafter abbreviated as *Shimpū*) (Tokyo, 1963), translated (by Roger Pineau) as *The Divine Wind: Japan's Kamikaze Force in World War II* (hereafter abbreviated as Inoguchi) (Annapolis, 1958), pp. 141–46; also Bernard Millot, *L'Epopée Kamikaze* (Paris, 1970), pp. 221–23.

10.8   Inoguchi, pp. 142–43.

10.9   For a photograph of the unit and its pennant, see *Shimpū*, photograph no. 13.

10.10   Inoguchi, p. 144. For the cataclysmic Battle of Minatogawa see pp. 132–33.

10.11   For the traditional connotations of weeping in Japan see Ivan Morris, *The World of the Shining Prince* (London, 1964), pp. 145–46.

Au Japon . . . les pleurs sont l'expression d'une émotivité naturelle et intrinsèque de la sensibilité nippone. Les larmes ont alors, en dehors de la manifestation du chagrin, une signification d'émotion intense, qui n'exclut pas, ce qui semble paradoxal, une froide résolution et un parfait sang-froid. (Millot, *L'Epopée Kamikaze*, p. 296n.)

10.12   Commander Nakajima of the 5th Air Fleet was on duty in Kanoya airbase (southern Kyushu) on 12th April, the date of the present attack.

10.13   Inoguchi, p. 152.

10.14   *Ibid.,* p. 153.

10.15   Six were shot down after making their release, and one presumably developed engine trouble and crashed on the return journey.

10.16   Yokota Yutaka, a Kaiten (suicide-torpedo) pilot, describes the last night aboard the mother submarine before his attack:

I could picture every detail in my mind as clearly as though all those things were actually happening right at the moment. Now I would rest, making sure to get a good night's sleep. Tomorrow I would be bursting with strength. No enemy would be able to stop me. For once I was able to go right to sleep. Even the uncomfortable berth had no effect on me. The next day found me full of vigour (Yokota, *Suicide Submarine!* [New York, 1962], p. 177.)

Such last-minute naps, in which warriors refreshed themselves so that they might be totally alert for their final challenge, appear to have been common among kamikaze fighters and can lead to interesting speculations—especially for chronic insomniacs. Millot, *L'Epopée Kamikaze*, p. 298, comments as follows:

La nuit fut paisible et tous les hommes dormirent comme si le lendemain allait être un jour de routine sans autre incident que l'accomplissement des tâches quotidiennes. Cette particularité du tempérament nippon était générale et provenait du fait qu'à partir du moment où une décision, quelle qu'elle soit, était prise, il ne convenait plus de se torturer l'esprit. La suite et les conséquences de cette décision appartenaient, dès lors, à une volonté supérieure dont les hommes étaient les instruments.

While sharing Millot's admiration for such self-mastery, I suggest that serene, joyful dedication to a chosen task was more important than any *volonté supérieure*.

A young kamikaze pilot, Lieutenant Ishibashi, in a cheerful letter written to his parents on the morning of his fatal flight says, "I slept soundly last night and did not even have any dreams. My head is clear and my spirits refreshed." *Shimpū*, p. 177.

10.17   The destroyer *Stanley* was the only ship reported to have been damaged by a suicide bomb on 12th April. Inoguchi, p. 154n., and John Toland, *The Rising Sun* (New York, 1970), p. 700.

10.18   The vast majority of kamikaze planes used in the war were conventional aircraft. Altogether only about 100 Ōka flying bombs were ever actually launched (Millot, *L'Epopée Kamikaze*, p. 358), and their effect was far more psychological than practical (see p. 328).

10.19   Already on 6th October the Japanese knew (from the Russians, as it happens) that the next major American assault would be against the Philippines, and they had plenty of time to prepare for the challenge. Millot, *L'Epopée Kamikaze*, pp. 58, 96.

10.20   Admiral Yamamoto Isoroku, Combined Fleet Commander-in-Chief from 1941 to 1943, was by far the most popular of Japan's military leaders during the Pacific war—this not so much because of his success in organizing the Pearl Harbor attack but because of his inspiring personality and his widespread reputation for purity and sincerity. Despite his initial opposition to the war (*Shimpū*, p. 191), he came to be regarded as the very symbol of the Imperial Navy, and his sudden death in April 1943, when his plane was shot down by an American fighter over Bougainville, was a doleful omen. Fearing the terrible effect that the news would have on Japanese morale, the government kept it hidden from the public for more than a month. The destruction of Admiral Yamamoto's plane had a further unhappy implication for the Japanese, since it suggested that the Americans had probably deciphered their code.

Though Ōnishi's reputation never approached that of Yamamoto (who was his superior in age, rank, and—no doubt—talent), the characters of the two men had much in common (see p. 282).

10.21 "He favoured men of action," writes Captain Inoguchi, "men who could be counted on to put words into deeds. He was opposed to men who merely talked and argued on paper without accomplishing anything. In talking with him one always had the feeling that his penetrating gaze was fathoming one's innermost thoughts." (Inoguchi, p. 182.)

10.22 Rear Admiral Takagi Sōkichi dubbed him "The Foolish Admiral" (Gushō), and until the end of the war this unflattering nickname was frequently used by his opponents in high naval circles. (Kusayanagi, Tokkō no Shisō [Tokyo, 1972], p. 21.) Ōnishi's disrespectful, unorthodox approach is also said to have provoked the suspicion of the Prime Minister, General Tōjō. (Kusayanagi, p. 25).

10.23 Inoguchi, pp. 180–81.

10.24 For readers who are too young (or too old) to recall the general military situation in late 1944 the following note may be useful. From the triumphant outset at Pearl Harbor until the Battle of Midway (June 1942) the war had gone almost absurdly well for the Japanese—better, indeed, than anticipated in their most optimistic forecasts. Within six months they were in control of a vast area stretching from the Aleutian Islands in the north, to New Guinea in the south, the Indian-Burmese border in the west, and the Gilbert Islands in the east.

The defeat at Midway (so appropriately named) was the turning point. In a single engagement the Imperial Navy lost no less than four aircraft carriers and it never recovered from the blow. Thereafter the enemy tended to be successful in engagement after engagement, though often at the most hideous cost. While the true facts were hidden from the people until the end, government and military leaders were obviously aware that the built-in material discrepancy between them and the enemy was leading Japan in a disastrous direction. As the situation in the Pacific deteriorated month by month, it was realized that an all-out stand would have to be made at some point. The point chosen was the Philippines, which the Americans were poised to invade at the end of October 1944. The defence of the Philippines was crucial: quite correctly Japan's leaders concluded that to lose strategic islands was tantamount to losing the Pacific war.

On 17th October, the very day of Vice Admiral Ōnishi's arrival in the Philippines, the spearhead of U.S. invasion forces had landed on Suluan Island at the entrance to Leyte Gulf; meanwhile a huge American armada had gathered in the Philippine seas to reconquer the islands. To forestall the enemy initiative a powerful task force under Admiral Kurita directed an attack against the American ships in Leyte.

The Battle of Leyte Gulf, a vast clash consisting of four major engagements, was one of the fiercest sea battles in world history (see

Samuel Eliot Morison, *Leyte* [Boston, 1958]). It started in mid-October and produced the very opposite effects of those intended. Admiral Kurita's 2nd Fleet, which contained Japan's main naval strength in the area, was decimated. As if to symbolize the disaster, the *Musashi*, one of Japan's two giant battleships from which so much had been hoped, was fatally damaged; as it slowly began to sink, the commanding officer, Admiral Inokuchi, committed harakiri in atonement for the loss.

This epic battle witnessed the first use of organized kamikaze units, which took off from Mabalacat on the 25th; but they were far too late to affect the outcome. At early dawn on the 25th the Japanese lost two more battleships, and during the course of the day all four of their aircraft carriers were wiped out, together with numerous cruisers and destroyers.

The Japanese catastrophe at Leyte Gulf marked the effective end of the Imperial Navy as an operative fighting force and this, together with the rapid exhaustion of petrol reserves and the pitiful shortage of aircraft, meant that the home islands were in danger of successful invasion for the first time since Kublai Khan, and convinced men like Ōnishi and Ugaki that only unconventional, i.e., suicide, tactics could counter the overwhelming American forces.

10.25   Inoguchi, p. 7. Concerning the genesis of the Special Attack units see also Hayashi Shigeru, *Taiheiyō Sensō* (Tokyo, 1967), p. 463, and Millot, *L'Epopée Kamikaze*, pp. 106–7.

10.26   Inoguchi, p. 7.

10.27   *Ibid.*, p. 9.

10.28   *Ibid.*

10.29   18th January 1945, in Tainan. Inoguchi, p. 123. At about the same time he had remarked to a newspaper correspondent that, even if Japan could not win the war, the memory of the young men who had sacrificed themselves for their country *(seinentachi ga kokunan ni junjite)* would prevent Japan and the Japanese from perishing. Kusayanagi, *Tokkō no Shisō*, p. 17.

10.30   Inoguchi, p. 70, and Millot, *L'Epopée Kamikaze*, p. 143.

10.31   *Shimpū*, p. 94. The Japanese phrase, *tōsotsu no gedō* (lit. "a deviation from generalship") has been translated as "unorthodox command" (Inoguchi, p. 70) and, more freely, *un procédé monstrueuse* (Millot, *L'Epopée Kamikaze*, p. 143).

Like Ōnishi himself, Captain Inoguchi had been appalled by the idea of suicide tactics when they had been proposed earlier in the war and had declared that "such an inhuman thing will have to be answered for in heaven." (Inoguchi, p. 170.) Now, however, he believed that the method was justified, since there was no other solution to Japan's predicament.

Commander Nakajima, who personally ordered many of the kamikaze sorties from Mabalacat, never lost sight of the extraordinary nature of the tactics. "My ordering the sorties," he writes "was but a function within the system, and my presence in the system was almost as defiant of rationality as the system itself." (Inoguchi, p. III.) But, as we know from the history of Japanese heroes, reason is far from being the ultimate criterion in times of crisis.

10.32   Kusayanagi *Tokkō no Shisō*, pp. 37–39. Concerning the mixed reactions of the High Command to the pilots' enthusiasm for the kamikaze idea, Millot comments as follows: "Ce volontariat spontané était à la fois sublime et inquiétant. Sublime parce qu'il demontrait une foi patriotique et une détermination admirables, toutes deux réconfortantes en ces temps difficiles. Il était aussi inquiétant parce qu'il risquait de déborder les structures hiérarchiques." (*L'Epopée Kamikaze*, p. 264.)

In a newspaper interview in 1968 Lieutenant General Watanabe Sei, who during the war had served as a Lieutenant Commander in a Naval Special Attack unit, said that in the beginning the military were much opposed to kamikaze tactics: "We saw no reason to waste lives and expensive equipment. . . . The kamikaze pilot was born out of necessity." *Stars and Stripes*, 20th July 1968.

10.33   See n. 10.169 concerning American reactions.

10.34   Millot, *L'Epopée Kamikaze*, p. 264.

10.35   Inoguchi, p. 10.

10.36   Inoguchi, pp. 11–12.

10.37   *Ibid.*, p. 68, and Millot *L'Epopée Kamikaze*, pp. 122, 148–49.

10.38   Inoguchi, p. 19, and *Shimpū*, pp. 48–49. "Hundred million" had become established as a hyperbole with powerful patriotic associations. Cf. the favorite wartime slogan of the perfervid General Araki: "a hundred million hearts beating as one" *(ichioku isshin).*

10.39   Kusayanagi, *Tokkō no Shisō*, pp. 15–16. When the notes (totalling about ¥2,000) reached the Munitions Ministry in Tokyo, the Minister, Mr. Fujiwara, held one of them in his hands and wept uncontrollably.

10.40   For details and a photograph see Morison, *Leyte*, p. 302 and opp. So fierce were the explosions of torpedoes and bombs aboard the *St. Lo* that great sections of the flight deck and entire airplanes were hurled hundreds of feet into the air.

10.41   For descriptions and some extraordinary photographs see Inoguchi, pp. 57–61. The kamikaze attack of the 25th was part of the gigantic Battle of Leyte Gulf. Ōnishi had vainly tried to delay the ill-fated sortie of Admiral Kurita's task force on the 24th until kamikaze planes had a chance to strike the enemy; but the following day it was too late to avert disaster (Inoguchi, p. 71). In his account of the Battle of Leyte Gulf, Toland (*Rising Sun*, pp. 546–72) writes (p. 568), "Ōnishi's *kamikaze* group was created specifically to support Kurita's raid on Leyte Gulf." This is somewhat misleading, since Ōnishi created numerous such groups, and his realization that suicide tactics represented Japan's only remaining hope had far wider implications than any specific engagement in the Philippines or elsewhere.

10.42   Inoguchi, p. 64. I have slightly altered the translation of the Emperor's message, from which the rather important word "but" has been omitted in Mr. Pineau's version. The Imperial message is quoted in *Shimpū*, p. 90, as follows: SONO YŌ NI MADE SENEBA NARANAKATTA KA. SHIKASHI YOKU YATTA.

10.43   "That night," writes Commander Nakajima (Inoguchi, p. 64), "I was told by my friend Captain Inoguchi, who had just arrived from Manila, 'Admiral Ōnishi was completely upset when he heard the Imperial words at Manila. I think that the Admiral interprets His Majesty's comment as criticism of the commander responsible for these tactics.' "

10.44   Cf. General Nogi's lifelong feelings of guilt towards Emperor Meiji (see n. 9.189).

10.45   *Taiatari, nikudan, jibaku.* An early term for "suicide pilot" was *jibaku kōgeki hikōshi* ("self-blasting attack pilot").

10.46   The suggestion was made by Captains Inoguchi and Tamai. Inoguchi, p. 13.

10.47   Kublai Khan's invasion of 1281 (which came seven years after a previous abortive attempt) was carried out by combined armies of about 150,000 men, the largest overseas expeditionary force that the world had ever seen. Many factors contributed to its failure (e.g., the inability of the Chinese and Korean troops to form a single front after they had landed in Kyushu and the effectiveness of the Japanese defence wall), but the typhoon was certainly a culminating blow to the Mongols. Japan's religious institutions, both Shinto and Buddhist, immediately claimed credit for the divine intervention, which they represented as an answer to all the prayers offered at the shrines and temples during the critical years. But "danger past, fear forgotten," and the Kamakura Bakufu was niggardly in its rewards. At the height of the crisis the former Emperor, Kameyama, had prayed at the Great Ise Shrine and is said to have offered himself as a sacrifice if this could ward off the national danger; he was never reminded to make good on his offer.

The *locus classicus* for the phrase "divine wind" is a passage in *Nihon Shoki*, the first official chronicle (A.D. 720), which includes a poem by the legendary Founding Emperor, Jimmu Tennō:

> Kamukaze no
> Ise no umi no
> Ōishi ya. . . .
> ("On the great rocks
> Of the Divine Wind sea of Ise. . . .")

Here *kamukaze* is a *makura kotoba* (pillow word or conventional epithet) associated with Ise. In the late 13th century the Great Ise Shrine became particularly important as a centre for prayers to save the country from the Mongol invaders, and it is probably for this reason that the decisive typhoons were given a name *(kamukaze, kamikaze)* that was traditionally connected with Ise.

10.48   When the Imperial Army organized suicide units, they differentiated them from their naval equivalents by using the term *shimbu* ("brandishing the sabre") which, though similar in sound, is written with two entirely different Chinese characters. Since suicide units remained primarily a navy weapon, the term *shimpū* has always been far more familiar.

10.49   It may be a comment on changing values in Japan that more recently the term *kamikaze* is being used to designate ventures that seem foolish and quixotic rather than dangerous. An editorial article in the *Asahi Shimbun* (30 August 1973) headed "Japanese Search at Loch Ness" criticizes a large-scale expedition, including a submarine, sonars, and underwater television, to determine whether the monster really exists: "If they are going to spend 150 million yen, can they not think of something a little more intelligent? To have a *kamikaze* search party with a mountain of equipment come from far-away Japan for publicity purposes must be very annoying and embarrassing for the residents of Loch Ness."

10.50   The dichotomy is almost exactly the same as that between the vulgar *harakiri* and the solemn *seppuku*. In my own descriptions I have preferred to use *kamikaze* and *harakiri*: since these words are familiar to Western readers and have even become part of our vocabulary, it seems pretentious to insist on *shimpū* and *seppuku*.

Some writers (e.g., Nagatsuka, *J'étais un kamikazé* [Paris, 1972], p. 215) have suggested that the term *kamikaze* was first popularized by *nisei* soldiers in the American army, but I have found no evidence to support the theory.

10.51   Inoguchi, p. 13. But I have changed the translation of *tai* from "unit" to "force."

10.52   The term *tokkō* was first used by Captain Jō Eiichirō, an early advocate of suicide tactics. Captain Jō, who had served as naval attaché in Washington and later as aide-de-camp to the Emperor, was in command of the carrier *Chiyoda* when it was sunk by American planes on 25th October 1944, and he went down with his ship.

10.53   Inoguchi, p. 13.

10.54   The *tanka* by Motoori Norinaga (1730–1801) is as follows:

> *Shikishima* no
> *Yamato*gokoro wo
> Hito towaba
> *Asahi* ni niou
> *Yamazakura*bana

10.55   Nagatsuka, *J'étais un kamikazé*, p. 217.

10.56   See n. 10.4.

10.57   Millot, *L'Epopée Kamikaze*, p. 275.

10.58   See p. 321.

10.59   Nagatsuka, *J'étais un kamikazé*, pp. 258–59.

10.60   See n. 10.16.

10.61   Inoguchi, p. 204. The last letter of Lieutenant Hayashi is included in *Shimpū*, pp. 177–79; a translation appears in Inoguchi, pp. 203–207.

10.62   *Shimpū*, p. 185.

10.63   A photograph (no. 3 in *Shimpū*) shows Vice Admiral Ōnishi himself pouring a ceremonial cup of *sake* for a young pilot, who stands with his hands raised in a reverential attitude, while the other pilots solemnly await their turn.

   During the final months of the war, as conditions became more chaotic, plain water was often substituted for *sake*, and frequently the ceremony had to be omitted entirely owing to pressure of time. *Shimpū*, p. 187.

10.64   Inoguchi, pp. 203–207.

10.65   Nagatsuka, *J'étais un kamikazé*, p. 245.

10.66   E.g., *Shikkari yatte kure. Shimpū*, p. 180.

10.67   An Imperial Navy anthem whose sombre words come from a poem by Ōtomo no Yakamochi (d. 785). See Inoguchi, p. 50.

10.68   Inoguchi, p. 85.

10.69   The reason for this change in procedure was that the mechanism frequently stuck at the last moment and could not be activated in time; it also appears that several pilots, in their excitement about the forthcoming plunge, actually forgot to arm their bombs and therefore crashed uselessly. (Millot, *L'Epopée Kamikaze*, p. 163.) . . . "It is likely," writes Captain Inoguchi, "that the pilot's very concentration on scoring a telling hit made him forget that one vital step toward his goal." (Inoguchi, p. 96.) In addition, the critical scarcity of oil during the last period of the war led to a decision that kamikaze planes should be loaded with sufficient fuel for only a one-way flight.

10.70   Toland, *Rising Sun*, p. 716.

10.71   In a high-altitude attack the pilot started his dive from about 20,000 feet; in a low-level approach he skimmed about 35 feet over the water, then rose to about 1,300 feet and crashed into the ship. Sometimes, in order to confuse the enemy, both types of attack would be used by different planes in the same formation. A medium altitude, which would have allowed for greatest accuracy, was impossible because of interception and antiaircraft fire. Inoguchi, pp. 91–92.

10.72   E.g., *Shimpū*, p. 176.

10.73   Millot, *L'Epopée Kamikaze*, pp. 163–64.

10.74   The members of the Shikishima Unit were promoted by Admiral Toyoda on 12th November 1944; thereafter, posthumous promotions became routine for all kamikaze pilots who had died in attack missions. The fact that they *and no others* were automatically given such promotions confirms that these men were officially recognized as heroes irrespective of whether their missions succeeded or failed.

10.75   Inoguchi, pp. 111–13.

10.76   Millot, *L'Epopée Kamikaze*, p. 192. Most of these documents, including Ōnishi's personal papers, were destroyed in the subsequent bombing.

10.77   For Ōnishi's parting speech to the kamikaze pilots in Taiwan, see p. 284.

10.78   Despite the frenzied efforts of Ōnishi and his pilots, not a single American ship was sunk, or even "claimed sunk," by suicide pilots from Taiwan, and only three ships were damaged. Inoguchi, p. 223.

10.79   Nagatsuka, *J'étais un kamikazé*, pp. 147–48.

10.80   Toland, *Rising Sun*, p. 406, and Nagatsuka, *J'étais un kamikazé*, pp. 69–70.

10.81   Toland, *Rising Sun*, p. 568*n*. Equally unsuccessful was the first navy kamikaze pilot, Rear Admiral Arima Masafumi, who took off from the Philippines on 15th October 1944, intending to crash his plane into an aircraft carrier, but was shot down before hitting his target, the U.S.S. *Franklin*. Arima's heroic example was broadcast on Radio Tokyo and, according to the Imperial Navy, it "lit the fuse of the ardent wishes of his men." Cf. Morison, *Leyte*, p. 166; Kusayanagi, *J'étais un kamikazé*, pp. 35–36; Millot, *L'Epopée Kamikaze*, pp. 101–4.

10.82   Fearing the effect on public morale, the Japanese government waited for nine days before announcing the fall of Saipan.

10.83   Among the few "prisoners" were a number of children who had become separated from their families. The American marines, having witnessed their parents' horrifying deaths, treated these orphans with particular kindness. Millot, *L'Epopée Kamikaze*, pp. 73–75.

10.84   Address by Koiso Kuniaki to the Imperial Diet on 21st January 1943, quoted by Toland, *Rising Sun*, p. 630. Cf. the Emperor's observation (see p. 330) that the war had "developed not necessarily to Japan's advantage."

10.85   Toland, *Rising Sun*, p. 630.

10.86   For details about the *shinyō* and also the suicide-frogmen (*fukuryū*), see Millot, *L'Epopée Kamikaze*, pp. 267–71.
         In Okamoto's film *Nikudan* ("Flesh Bullet"), the hero, who belongs to a last-ditch kamikaze unit in Kyushu, almost literally "goes to sea in a tub"—a rusty tin cylinder lashed by ropes to a huge torpedo, which he is supposed to direct against an American ship as it approaches the coast during the last days of the war. In his final frenzy he aims it at a Japanese garbage-scow, which he mistakes for an American aircraft-carrier; and, to compound the irony, the torpedo turns out to be a dud. This particular weapon appears to have been fictitious, but it is typical of the many makeshift suicide devices that were improvised during the final months.

10.87   By far the most detailed description of Kaiten operations is *Suicide Submarine!* by Yokota Yutaka (New York, 1962). The Kaiten carried 3,000 lbs. of high explosive, had a range of 40 nautical miles, and travelled at about 30 knots. From the beginning they were cursed with mechanical troubles and most of them exploded before coming close to their targets. Though Japanese Imperial Headquarters believed that Kaiten had sunk some 40 Allied ships, including aircraft-carriers and battleships, the only Allied navy ship actually destroyed by a Kaiten during the entire war was the U.S. tanker, *Mississinewa*, which was attacked in Ulithi Atoll in November 1944. The Japanese, on the other hand, lost almost all their Kaiten craft, as well as eight mother submarines and their crews.

   Concerning the "sure death" aspect of the Kaiten, Yokota explains:

   Though Kuroki and Nishina [the inventors] had designed into the Kaiten, as ordered by the Naval General Staff, a device which could cast the pilot free while he was still 150 feet short of the target, no one intended to use it. And no one ever did, in all the Kaiten missions carried out. A man could only be positive of a sure hit when he met sure death. Abandoning the Kaiten might allow it to go off course. The best method was to take it on, all the way. (Yokota, *Suicide Submarine!*, p. 50.)

10.88   Millot, *L'Epopée Kamikaze*, pp. 253, 263, and Yokota, *Suicide Submarine!*, pp. 45–46, 138.

10.89   Millot, *L'Epopée Kamikaze*, p. 251, describes the farewell ceremonies aboard an I-49 submarine as it approached its targets off Ulithi in November 1944. For a further description of the "last meal," see Yokota, *Suicide Submarine!*, p. 170.

10.90   Many of the Kaiten men continued reading and studying in their cramped quarters until the very last moment. (Yokota, *Suicide Submarine!*, pp. 161, 170.) Among the many homely touches mentioned by Yokota is the following: "The Kaiten men enjoyed their trip with Captain Orita, and were particularly fascinated with the submarine's toilet, a complicated arrangement of valves and handles that could truly embarrass the man who did not know how to operate it properly, or was careless in doing so." Yokota, *Suicide Submarine!*, p. 46.

10.91   Yokota, *Suicide Submarine!*, pp. 254–55, discusses Operation Kongō. Named after Masashige's mountain headquarters, this was one of the major Kaiten efforts of the war and involved a combined attack on American ships in Guam, Ulithi, Hollandia, and other islands.

10.92   Yokota, *Suicide Submarine!*, p. 255.

10.93   Over 100 Nakajima Ki.115B Tsurugi suicide craft were produced between March and August 1945. For details and pictures, see Millot, *L'Epopée Kamikaze*, pp. 347–50.

10.94   Launching sites, facing the Pacific Ocean, were to be established on mountains from Hokkaido to Kyushu, and the catapult devices were all to be installed by October 1945, just in time for the expected invasion. For information about this particular kamikaze venture I am indebted to my colleague, the eminent Buddhist scholar, Professor Y. H., who was himself trained for this type of attack. During his time on Mount Hiei he decided that in case the war ended before he was propelled on his mission he would become a Buddhist priest; and so it turned out—much to the benefit of myself and his many other friends and students.

10.95   Inoguchi, p. 169.

10.96   Jean Mabire, *Les Samouraï* (Paris, 1971), p. 369.

10.97   Quoted by Millot, *L'Epopée Kamikaze*, pp. 295–96.

10.98   Millot, *L'Epopée Kamikaze*, pp. 311–12, goes so far as to suggest that the Imperial Navy Command was aware from the outset that the attack could not succeed and that they actually intended the disaster. If his interpretation is correct, this last sortie by the Imperial Navy perfectly exemplified the nobility of failure.

10.99   The 6th April attack (Kikusui No. 1) from Kanoya base in Kyushu comprised:

NAVY

80 kamikaze planes of various types
8 mother planes carrying Ōka craft
145 other attack planes
116 escort fighters and "evaluation" planes
23 scout/patrol planes

ARMY

133 planes of various types, mainly kamikaze.

Of the kamikaze planes that participated in the combat 162 failed to return. Millot, *L'Epopée Kamikaze*, p. 287.

10.100   Millot, *L'Epopée Kamikaze*, pp. 137–38, 147. These older pilots frequently implored their commanding officers to assign them to kamikaze attack planes, but they were almost invariably refused on the grounds that their services were more valuable elsewhere.

10.101   Quoted by Inoguchi, p. 181.

10.102   Nagatsuka, *J'étais un kamikazé*, pp. 261–62.

10.103   In the postwar years, studies were made among families who had contributed one of their members to kamikaze units, and it was found that in almost every case the young man who had joined the Special Attack forces was "the finest son"—the most affectionate, best educated, least troublesome, the one, in short, who had given his parents the greatest joy. Here, of course, we must make due allowance for romanticism and idealization in hindsight.

10.104   Inoguchi, p. 43; Nagatsuka, *J'étais un kamikazé*, p. 224.

10.105   E.g., *Shimpū*, p. 186. By signing with his own blood *(keppansho)* the supplicant emphasized the sincerity of his request, and such petitions were hard to refuse.

Though the families of kamikaze pilots obviously suffered great anguish in anticipation of the fatal news they were bound to receive, there was also pride in the knowledge that their sons had been chosen as "living gods." A unit commander in Taiwan who had realized that one of his pilots was an only son and should therefore not be used for a suicide mission unless it was absolutely essential informed the young man's mother accordingly; but like so many kamikaze mothers she turned out to be a veritable *matrona Romana*, and in the impassioned style of a Volumnia implored the commander not to deprive her son of the honour that was his due and that he himself so ardently desired (*Shimpū*, p. 187). Commander Nakajima relates the following story in a similar vein:

One day early that spring [1945] a lady paid a call on the 765th Air Group, based at Kijin, in Formosa. She was met by the group commander, Captain Masuda Shogo, who learned that she was Mrs. Kusanagi Misao, the wife of a judge in the Taihoku Higher Court. She handed a muffler and a lock of hair to Captain Masuda, asking that one of the special attack pilots might carry them into battle. Her son, a student pilot, had died of illness before completing his flight training. She felt that her son's desire would be fulfilled if these mementoes of him could go into battle. A message was written on the muffler and signed with the mother's name. It read:

I pray for a direct hit.

MISAO

Captain Masuda accepted these tokens and when the special attack unit of his air group moved from Kijin to a forward base, he presented them to the leader. This group leader himself carried the mementoes when he later dived into an enemy ship. (Inoguchi, p. 128.)

10.106   Millot, *L'Epopée Kamikaze*, pp. 266–67. Yokota records a similar speech by a commanding officer who was offering him and his fellow pilots the opportunity to join a Kaiten unit:

If any man among you burns enough with the desire to save his country, to board this new weapon and take part in our great offensive against the approaching enemy, he may volunteer. I cannot tell you any more about it, except that it will have more power than any aeroplane you might fly. Now listen carefully to what I say next. Your squadron leaders are to hand each of you a piece of paper. If you are particularly anxious to volunteer for this new weapon, write your name and squadron number at the top of the paper, and make . . . two circles below it. I repeat, two circles if you're really eager to go. If, however, you do not have a truly deep desire to go, but are willing to make this sacrifice for your country if called upon, inscribe only one circle. This is most important, so I repeat—two circles if you feel very strongly that you must go, but only one circle if you are merely willing to do this duty. Those who don't want to go at all, but wish to continue with flight training, are to destroy their papers. . . .

One last thing must be added before the papers are handed out. I must tell you that this weapon is of such a nature that whoever mans it on a mission against the enemy is not expected to return alive. He will surely be able to inflict a great hurt on our enemy during his mission, but he will give his life in doing so. Therefore, think carefully before you decide. Be absolutely sure you want to go, before volunteering. Most of all, be sure you will not be concerned later with what you leave behind. Your minds will have to be absolutely clear at all times, so you will be able to give full concentration to the job ahead of you. (Yokota, *Suicide Submarine!*, p. 11.)

10.107   Inoguchi, pp. 158–59.

10.108   Millot, *L'Epopée Kamikaze*, pp. 330–31, 367*ff*.

10.109   Nagatsuka, *J'étais un kamikazé*, pp. 231–34.

10.110   On this vexed question of whether the kamikaze missions were voluntary in the proper sense of the word, Nagatsuka comments as follows:

> On pose très souvent une question au sujet des circonstances dans lesquelles nos pilotes s'incorporaient dans les corps d'attaques-suicide: "Étaient-ils vraiment volontaires ou désignés d'office?" . . . En ma qualité de témoin qui a vécu cette mission, j'affirme que notre désir concordait d'une façon parfaite avec l'ordre donné par le haut commandement. Du moins, était ce mon cas. . . . Evidemment, des groupes entiers d'aviateurs se présentèrent pour ces missions par suite de circonstances urgentes, et d'autre part personne ne peut rendre compte d'un état d'âme, sauf les intéressés. . . . Volontaires ou contraints, la question n'est pas là. Je puis affirmer en ma qualité d'ancien pilote-suicide rescapé, que *tous mes camarades étaient prêts à accepter volontairement l'ordre ou à demander leur mission.* (*J'étais un kamikazé*, p. 234); (italics added.)

This seems as balanced an answer as one is likely to receive from someone who actually participated in the drama.

10.111   After the Pacific war, Mr. Ōmi Ichirō made a pilgrimage on foot to the homes of kamikaze pilots throughout the country. During the course of this journey, which lasted almost five years, he collected large numbers of letters and mementoes, mostly written by reserve naval officers from civilian colleges who had joined Special Attack units after brief periods of training. A sample of this material is included in *Shimpū*, pp. 174–88, and translations are given in Inoguchi, pp. 196–208. The most famous of many such collections to be published was *Kike Wadatsumi no Koe* ("Hearken to the Ocean Voices!" Tokyo, 1952), in which the first item is a testament by an Army Special Attack pilot who was killed in Okinawa at the age of 22. The book had an enormous sale in Japan, and its title even entered the language as a set phrase with the general implication of "Lest we forget!" In 1963, as memories of the war began to recede, a second volume was published with the same title. A valuable collection of diaries by university students killed in the war was edited in 1951 with the title *Haruka naru Yamagawa ni* ("To Distant Mountain Streams") and includes material by kamikaze pilots. These and similar books continue to appear in new editions and often become best sellers.

10.112   *Shimpū*, pp. 183–84, translated in Inoguchi, p. 199.

10.113   E.g., "Dear Father: As death approaches, my only regret is that I have never been able to do anything good for you in my life." Letter from Yamaguchi Teruo, quoted by Inoguchi, p. 198.

10.114   *Shimpū*, pp. 181–82, translated in Inoguchi, p. 202.

10.115   *Watakushi wa kono utsukushii chichihaha no kokoro, atatakai ai aru ga yue ni*

Kimi ni junzuru koto ga dekiru. Kore de watakushi wa chichihaha to tomo ni tatakau koto ga dekimasu. Shimpū, p. 183.

10.116 *Shimpū*, p. 181, translated in Inoguchi, p. 197.

10.117 *Shimpū*, p. 176, translated in Inoguchi, p. 200.

10.118 Nagatsuka, *J'étais un kamikazé*, p. 162.

10.119 *Ibid.*, p. 272.

10.120 Quoted in Kudō Yoroshi in "Tenraku-kei no Nihon Eiyū-zō" ("The Japanese Hero-Image [and] the Pattern of Falling"), *Shūkan Asahi* 6–8 (1973): 114–17.

10.121 Quoted in *The Mainichi News*, 29th September 1968, from a book of poems entitled (in translation) "My Life Burns in the Light of the Moon."

10.122 *Shimpū*, p. 180, translated in Inoguchi, p. 207.

10.123 *Ibid.*

10.124 Yokota, *Suicide Submarine!*, p. 161.

10.125 Nagatsuka, *J'étais un kamikazé*, p. 149.

10.126 The most important single philosopher to expound the samurai ethos was Yamaga Sokō (1622–85), a Confucian nationalist and an expert on military tactics and lifestyle. The most influential book on the subject was the 11-volume compilation known as *Hagakure* (or *Nabeshima Rongo*) which was produced in 1716 and became a primer for Japanese military men. Concerning the influence of *Hagakure* on kamikaze fighters, see Mishima Yukio, *Eirei no Koe* (Tokyo, 1970), pp. 48*ff.*

10.127 For "seven lives" (*shichishō*) see p. 133; *shichishō* was commemorated in the names of several kamikaze units, and *shichishō* cloths were often tied round the heads of suicide fighters as they left on their missions. Thus Yokota describes his departure for a Kaiten attack:

> I was the last to be called. Lieutenant Hamaguchi, division officer for the maintenance section, who was calling out the names, took up the sixth *hachimaki* and tied it round my head. Written on it in graceful brush strokes were the characters for *"Shichi shō hōkoku,"* signifying Kusunoki Masashige's loyalty to his Emperor centuries before. My *hachimaki* carried the slogan, "Reborn seven times to serve the nation." (Yokota, *Suicide Submarine!*, p. 137.)

> P. 303 discusses the use of Masashige's Kikusui emblem for kamikaze operations in Okinawa. *Kikusui* crests were also painted on the conning towers and hulls of Kaiten mother submarines (Yokota, *Suicide Submarine!*, pp. 43, 125).

10.128 *Shimpū*, p. 176, translated in Inoguchi, p. 200. Concerning "the Emperor's shield," see the statement by the prototypic hero, Yorozu, on p. 20.

10.129 Inoguchi, pp. 79–80. Concerning Masashige's last instructions to his son, see p. 131.

10.130 See n. 10.126.

10.131   *Bushidō wa shinigurui nari. . . . Heizei hito ni norikoetaru kokoro nite nakute wa narumajiku sōrō.* Mishima, *Eirei no Koe* (Tokyo, 1970), p. 48.

10.132   "An Irish Airman Foresees His Death," *The Collected Poems of W. B. Yeats* (New York, 1956), p. 133.

10.133   *Kike Wadatsumi no Koe* (Tokyo, 1963), I: 231.

10.134   See n. 8.55. The *locus classicus* is Ssu-ma Ch'ien's famous letter to Jen An in 98 B.C.:

> A man has only one death. That death may be as weighty as Mount T'ai, or it may be as light as a goose feather. It all depends upon the way he uses it. . . . It is the nature of every man to love life and hate death, to think of his relatives and look after his wife and children. Only when a man is moved by higher principles is this not so. Then there are things which he must do. . . . (Wm. Theodore de Bary, ed., *Sources of Chinese Tradition* [New York, 1960], p. 272.)

10.135   Quoted by J. Seward, *Hara-Kiri* (Tokyo, 1968), p. 86.

10.136   In *The Japanese Cult of Tranquillity* (London, 1960), Karlfried Graf von Dürkheim describes the kamikaze pilots as "a supreme expression of the true Japanese outlook" and as the greatest modern exponents of "life through death." "There is a manner of dying," writes von Dürkheim, "which transcends the antithesis 'life and death' and which might be termed 'already existing in another life.' Such a frame of mind—and of body also—enables a man to face the most arduous task of his life and even death itself without flinching. He has attained perfect tranquillity without inner resistance, having sacrificed his ego-self, and he now surrenders himself simply to the demands of the moment."

The letters, diaries, and poems of the kamikaze pilots are certainly infused with this type of tranquillity; yet to identify it as "the true Japanese outlook" is surely overstating (and therefore weakening) the case.

10.137   Nagatsuka, *J'étais un kamikazé*, p. 197. For Fujisaki's last letter before his own suicide attack in Okinawa, see Nagatsuka, *ibid.*, p. 249.

10.138   Inoguchi, p. 80. Yokota (*Suicide Submarine!*, p. 113) mentions similar jokes about Yasukuni among a group of Kaiten volunteers: "We used to tease sometimes, saying, 'I will arrive at Yasukuni before you do, and will therefore be senior.' We'd talk then about all the awful things we planned to do to the later arrivals."

10.139   From the moment they entered the Special Attack units, all of them knew that they were "living corpses." Lieutenant Kanno, who joined the kamikaze forces in the Philippines, dramatized this realization by awarding himself the usual posthumous promotion *before* his death and by inscribing on his pilot's bag the words "Personal effects of *the late Lieutenant Commander Kanno Naoshi.*" Inoguchi, p. 34.

10.140   Nagatsuka, *J'étais un kamikazé*, p. 258.

10.141   Millot, *L'Epopée Kamikaze*, p. 299. Stories that suicide pilots were given alcohol or drugs to provide them with the necessary courage for their last flight, or that they were chained into their cockpits in case they decided to bail out at the last moment, are entirely apocryphal. They run counter to all that we know about the kamikaze psychology and were presumably fabricated by Western journalists in an effort to explain (or denigrate) Japan's suicide tactics.

Even more ludicrous are popular fantasies about bacchanalian feasts on the eve of departure, when the young pilot-victims were allegedly distracted with wine, women, and song to console them for their forthcoming sacrifice, and stories that they later went into battle like priests in hooded robes (Toland, *Rising Sun*, p. 714).

A kamikaze survivor, Lieutenant General Watanabe Sei, writes, "I think most Americans think of the kamikaze as a reckless daredevil with suicidal tendencies. They were anything but that." He describes as "sheer nonsense" the popular belief of Americans that kamikaze pilots had wild parties on the eve of their flights or were drunk or doped to give them the necessary courage for their final mission. *Stars and Stripes*, 20th July 1968.

10.142   "My [fellow pilots,]" writes Yokota concerning his companions who were shortly to embark in their suicide-torpedoes, "were friendly to everyone, as well as to one another. None wore sad looks, nor overly proud ones, as you really could expect of people who were the best trained of any Kaiten men up to that moment. In addition to all these things, they laughed a lot and said many humorous things to make other people laugh." *Suicide Submarine!*, p. 121.

10.143   Photograph no. 7 in *Shimpū*.

10.144   Yokota, *Suicide Submarine!*, p. 159. Yazaki Yoshihito, one of the inventors of the Kaiten, had suffocated to death during a Kaiten training exercise, and Yokota resolved to take along his ashes in an urn when the time came for a suicide attack. Yokota, p. 113.

10.145   *Sukkari atatakaku natte, seikatsu mo jitsu ni raku ni narimashita. . . . Shimpū*, pp. 182–83.

10.146   *Shimpū*, pp. 177–79, translated in Inoguchi, pp. 205–206.

10.147 $\bar{A}$ *tama to kudaken. Shimpū*, p. 176, translated in Inoguchi, p. 201.

10.148   Pilots in sure-death craft like the Ōka bombs and Kaiten torpedoes were of course spared the risk of survival; after the change in arming procedures and fuel loads for conventional planes (see p. 294), such "failures" became impossible for them also.

10.149   "As the evening progressed," writes Commander Nakajima in his description of the last party in Cebu base (see p. 318),

I started to leave the party. Two or three pilots followed me to the door and even outside, pleading to be chosen soon for a special attack. Some of their colleagues who heard these entreaties shouted, "Unfair! Unfair! No special favours!" And these strange words mingled with and were lost in the sound of general good cheer that finally faded from my hearing as I walked thoughtfully to my quarters. (Inoguchi, p. 80.)

10.150 Inoguchi, pp. 164–68. Vice Admiral Ugaki's attack took place on 15th August, *after* the Emperor's surrender broadcast; it therefore had no conceivable military motive, and was purely an act of sincere defiance. Four of the 11 bombers in his attack force were foiled by engine trouble; the other seven succeeded in making suicide plunges but there is no record that any American ships were hit. Before crashing his own plane, Ugaki transmitted the following final message:

I alone am to blame for our failure to defend the homeland and destroy the arrogant enemy. The valiant efforts of all officers and men of my command during the past six months have been greatly appreciated.

I am going to make an attack at Okinawa where my men have fallen like cherry blossoms. There I will crash into and destroy the conceited enemy in the true spirit of *Bushido*, with firm conviction and faith in the eternity of Imperial Japan.

I trust that the members of all units under my command will understand my motives, will overcome all hardships of the future, and will strive for the reconstruction of our great homeland that it may survive forever.

Long live His Imperial Majesty the Emperor! (Inoguchi, p. 168.)

Ugaki's last diary entry ended with the statement, "I too have made up my mind to serve our country forever with the spirit of Kusunoki Masashige." Toland, *Rising Sun*, p. 853.

10.151 *Time*, 19th August 1966, p. 26. Also attending the reunion were about 50 middle-aged women who during the war had been local high school girls assigned to washing down the kamikaze planes. Many had become friendly with the young pilots, and one of them recalled that when the squadron got its flying orders "we felt like the wives of samurai sent off to battle in old Japan."

A group of kamikaze pilot survivors has been organized in Tokyo and meets annually for dinner. One of their members is Mr. Ono Takashi, manager of the Grand Palace Hotel, who kindly invited me to his office during a visit I made to Japan in 1973 and vividly described his wartime experiences and emotions. He himself had been prepared to leave for an attack but had been frustrated by engine trouble, and the war ended before a new plane became available. A fellow pilot of his, who had recently been married, informed his wife that he would shortly be leaving on a suicide flight and promised to let her know when the precise time came. Having received his flying orders, he notified his wife accordingly, but his plane (like Mr. Ono's) proved to be earth-bound; a few days later, before a replacement could be brought in, kamikaze sorties were suspended at his base. He rushed to the house of his wife's family in Osaka, having first sent a telegram with news of his survival, but arrived only in time to see her funeral cortege leaving the front door. After receiving the first news about her husband's sortie, she had seated herself in front of his photograph and his fatal letter, and had slashed her carotid artery. The telegram (like Friar Laurence's letter to Romeo in Mantua) had miscarried and could not prevent the tragedy. Stunned by his wife's death and his own survival, he subsisted for many years in a virtually cataleptic state before slowly returning to life.

10.152   Sakai Saburō, *Samurai* (New York, 1957), p. 319.

10.153   *Stars and Stripes*, 20th August 1970. In 1968 Watanabe Sei became a Lieutenant General in Japan's Air Defence Force.

> The soft-spoken general enjoys a quiet life and likes to spend time in his garden at home. He says about the only real excitement he gets nowadays is when he rides into Tokyo. "Have you ever seen those crazy kamikaze drivers?" Then he smiles and says, "I think you Americans gave them that name."

10.154   *Stars and Stripes*, 8th August 1963, describes the reunion between the American officer and the three kamikaze fighters who had been so reluctant to survive.

10.155   Concerning Aoki's rescue, see Toland, *Rising Sun*, pp. 714–17.

10.156   Aoki became a model prisoner and was sent back to Japan in 1946. (Toland, *Rising Sun*, p. 717.) The horror of survival is also evoked by Yokota Yutaka, the young suicide-torpedo volunteer, who describes how he and a companion returned from an abortive attack:

> Shinkai felt as badly as I did. He, who had been always so jolly, was deep in gloom. We both felt like outcasts. We dreaded returning to our barracks. We were sure no one would speak to us. Six Kaiten men had gone out, and four had been launched. Shinkai and I were now returning for the second time. People would think there was something wrong with us, we thought, and would turn their faces away. As soon as we could be free of the submarine we went to our old room and stayed there, secluding ourselves as much as possible. We avoided contact with other people. We hoped the earth would suddenly open and swallow us into its depths. (Yokota, *Suicide Submarine!*, p. 193.)

Later he asked his commanding officer for help:

> [Death had] again refused to turn her head in my direction and hold out welcoming arms to me. I felt helpless, without strength. I discussed this with Ensign Sonoda.
> "Sir," I asked, "what am I to do? I cannot possibly return to the base again. You know that."
> All he could say then was, "You are right, Yokota." He was at a loss for words. (Yokota, *Suicide Submarine!*, p. 212.)

The end of hostilities brought no surcease:

> [I could not] again face the world, from which I had so completely withdrawn. I was miserable, and thought of committing suicide, but I was too proud to do it. My life had been measured as worth one American aircraft carrier, I reminded myself. How could I surrender it now to a small pistol bullet? . . . My soul was in agony, so I stayed at Otsujima [base], doing little more than lie around for two weeks. I pondered the special Imperial Rescript issued after the surrender announcement to members of the military, in which the Emperor ordered us to "conquer a thousand difficulties, and endure the unendurable." That I could not do. Though I had decided not to die, I could not boldly enter life again. I became inanimate, waiting to see what the future would hold. I felt like one of our *bonsai*, the miniature trees that do not grow, but simply age. (Yokota, *Suicide Submarine!*, p. 250.)

10.157   Nagatsuka, *J'étais un kamikaze*, pp. 269–79. The American task force was about 300 miles from the airbase, and about 150 miles from the present position of the kamikaze attackers. Since they had fuel for only 350 miles of flight, they either had to turn back at once or crash into the ocean. The procedures of Nagatsuka's unit did not call for arming the bombs until the planes approached their target, but a bad landing would almost certainly cause them to explode.

10.158   See p. 291, concerning Nagatsuka's preparations for departure on the previous evening. Like Lieutenant Kanno (see n. 10.139), Nagatsuka had already awarded himself a posthumous promotion, but in his case the hubris of anticipating fate was harshly punished.

10.159   "Sacred words" referred to the Imperial Precepts to Soldiers and Sailors (1882), in which the following famous passage must have had particular relevance for the disgraced pilots: ". . . with single heart fulfil your essential duty of loyalty, and bear in mind that duty is weightier than a mountain, while death is lighter than a feather. Never by failing in moral principle fall into disgrace and bring dishonour upon your name." Wm. Theodore de Bary, ed., *Sources of Japanese Tradition* (New York, 1958), p. 706.

The agony of such public humiliation was not limited to returning kamikaze pilots. Yokota describes a similar screed when he returned from an unsuccessful Kaiten mission:

The new executive officer slammed his bamboo pointer down on a table. "You should be ashamed of yourself, Nomura!" he shouted. "As for the rest of you, it is no wonder that one or two of you come back from each mission without being launched at a target. What is your *hachimaki* for? And your sword! Doesn't it mean anything at all to your spirits? And the big send-off given you by all hands when you leave on a mission. These things are not done so that you can turn round and come back again! Once at sea, you must overwhelm the enemy! If anything goes wrong with your Kaiten, fix it! If the propeller won't spin, turn it with your bare hands! Crash into the enemy, no matter what! That's what the Kaiten is for!" Yokota and his companions are overwhelmed with the same shame that tormented Nagatsuka: "If someone had reproached me privately on returning from a mission, I might have been able to endure it. Or if someone had teased me, in a friendly way, I would have accepted it. But this public accusation levelled at myself and other men who had offered their lives, some more than once, was simply unjust! I wanted no more of Otsujima, the place I had once thought so highly of. All I wanted now was to get away to sea. I would never come back." (Yokota, *Suicide Submarine!*, pp. 220, 201.)

10.160   ". . . There was a fundamental difference in the heroism of the opposing warriors," writes C. R. Brown (Vice Admiral, U.S. Navy). "The Japanese resolutely closed the last avenue of hope and escape, the American never did. To the Western mind there must be that last slim chance of survival—the feeling that, though a lot of other chaps may die, you yourself somehow are going to make it back." Inoguchi, pp. v–vi.

10.161   Commenting on these earlier suicide attacks, Admiral Suzuki Kantarō, who himself had led a group of torpedo boats in a "death-defying" *(kesshi)* assault during the Sino-Japanese War, wrote,

The daring attempt to blockade Port Arthur during the Russo-Japanese War was a fair chance of rescuing the participants. Their only aim was to sink boats at the

entrance to the harbour, but the commanding officer refused his permission for
the operation until he was assured that rescue boats would be provided. . . . In
the midget submarine attack on Pearl Harbor . . . Admiral Yamamoto would not
authorise that part of the operation until it was shown that there was at least some
chance of retrieving the small two-man submarines. (Quoted in Inoguchi, pp.
189–90.)

   Government propagandists gave considerable publicity to the
"Three Bombs," the name attached to three soldiers who, early in the
China Incident, had rushed forward and blown themselves up to make
a hole in the enemy defences; but this of course had been a spontaneous
act of self-sacrifice and not part of any planned strategy.

10.162   Nagatsuka, *J'étais un kamikazé*, p. 254.

10.163   Millot, *L'Epopée Kamikaze*, p. 172.

10.164   *Philippines:*   6 carriers and battleships claimed sunk, }
                          2 carriers actually sunk;   }
                          31 other ships claimed sunk,   }
                          14 other ships actually sunk. }

         Okinawa: 20 carriers and battleships claimed sunk, }
                          0 carriers and battleships actually sunk; }
                          77 other ships claimed sunk,   }
                          16 other ships actually sunk. }

(Inoguchi, pp. 114, 160.) One of the principal naval officers involved in the
operations admitted after the war that the Japanese figures "may well be
in excess of the actual results achieved." Inoguchi, p. 160.

10.165   Nagatsuka, *J'étais un kamikazé*, p. 140, and Millot, *L'Epopée Kamikaze*,
         p. 200.

10.166   Most of the estimates I have seen vary between 4,000 and 5,000. The
         names of 4,615 kamikaze pilots who lost their lives in the Pacific war (2,630
         navy *shimpū* and 1,985 army *shimbu*) are inscribed in the Kannon Temple
         in Tokyo, popularly known as the Special Attack [Forces] Temple
         (Tokkō Kannon). (Kannon is the Buddhist goddess of mercy; for the
         implied incongruity see p. 317.) The figure of 4,615 does not, of course,
         include the vast numbers of "living grenades" and others who died in
         suicide operations on land; nor does it take into account those who were
         killed in other "special" operations like Kaiten, *kairyū*, and *shinyō*.
            On 18th November 1973, a monument in memory of some 1,000 navy
         suicide pilots killed in the Pacific war was unveiled in a Shinto ceremony
         at Kashiwara Shrine near Nara. Among the 700 people in attendance
         were the Emperor's brother, Prince Takamatsu, and relatives of the
         pilots. *Agence France-Presse* (18 Nov. 1973).

10.167   "If we take an overall view of the entire operation," writes Captain
         Inoguchi Rikihei in a report after the termination of hostilities, "the
         regrettable fact is that both [conventional] kamikaze planes and piloted
         bombs exerted little practical power [*kōdōryoku shō narishi*]." (Quoted in
         Shimpū, p. 190.) Cf. Vice Admiral Brown, ". . . the key question for the

pragmatic military man must be—was it a successful tactic? My answer is an unqualified *no.*" Inoguchi, p. vii.

A recapitulation of kamikaze aerial operations from 13th October 1944 to 30th June 1945 gives a total of 34 vessels destroyed, among which the only major ships were the carrier escorts, *St. Lo* (Philippines area, 25th October), *Ommaney Bay* (Philippines area, 3rd-4th January), *Bismarck Sea* (Okinawa area, 21st February). By far the largest number of ships sunk (13) were destroyers. In the same period 288 vessels were damaged in kamikaze attacks.

The total number of Japanese killed in the Battle of Okinawa was about 130,000, over ten times the American figure of 12,300. Estimates of the number of suicide pilots killed in the battle vary considerably, and the precise figures will never be known. A conservative estimate would be 2,000. We are also uncertain about the number of suicide planes used in this savage struggle. According to official Japanese records, 2,944 kamikaze planes were lost (2,055 navy and 889 army); the official American estimates are somewhat smaller.

10.168 According to Mishima Yukio, the ultimate failure of the kamikaze was marked, not by Japan's surrender in August 1945, but by the Emperor's declaration of nondivinity five months later. In *Eirei no Koe* ("Voices of the Fallen Heroes") he writes that the "irrational deaths" *(higōri na shi)* of the kamikaze heroes had a significance only if these men's lives had in fact been dedicated to an Emperor-god *(kami naru Tennō no tame ni).* If this belief of theirs ever proved untrue, it would mean that they had killed themselves in a "foolish sacrifice" *(oroka na gisei).* Hirohito's denial of imperial divinity in January 1946 ("The ties between us and our people have always stood upon mutual trust and affection. They do not depend upon mere legends and myths. They are not predicated on the false conception that the Emperor is divine . . . .") was therefore an ultimate betrayal of the kamikaze heroes. The Emperor's declaration was far more significant than any defeat in battle, for it meant that the failure of the kamikaze was irremediable. By dismissing the principle for which they had sacrificed themselves as a "false conception," he posthumously sullied their deaths (Mishima, *Eirei no Koe*, p. 59). Mishima ends with the lament, "Why did His Majesty make himself into a human being?" *(Nadote Sumeragi wa hito to naritamaishi).* (Mishima, *Eirei no Koe*, p. 62.) With all respect to Mishima, I submit (p. 308) that the motives of the kamikaze volunteers may have been considerably less straightforward and more complex than this threnody implies.

10.169 Western reactions to kamikaze tactics were a great deal more complicated than this summary would suggest, and included not merely anger and disgust, but (especially after the first shock had worn off) curiosity, bewilderment, and even pity for the young pilots who were believed (quite incorrectly) to have been dragooned into the suicide operations. I recall that my own reactions as a young sailor (who in 1944 was liable to be confronted with the kamikaze in a rather direct and unpleasant way) were mainly surprise and a sense of strangeness.

Some eminent foreign scholars managed to draw simplistic conclu-

sions; thus Ruth Benedict identified the kamikaze spirit as "an illustration of the power of mind over matter." (Quoted by Inoguchi, p. 194.)
Other observers regarded the operations as an example of how young
men could be transformed into fanaticized robots, or as a manifestation
of the "fierce, brutal side of the Japanese character" which co-exists with
the "polite, refined, sensitive side." Millot, *L'Epopée Kamikaze*, p. 14.

A detailed discussion of American and British reactions to this first
full, direct encounter with the totally alien tradition of Japanese heroism
might provide a useful case-study of cultural incomprehension, but
would be far beyond the scope of this study. Suffice it to illustrate some
typical Western misunderstandings by translating extracts from an interview in March 1946 between a member of the U.S. Strategic Bombing
Survey and a number of former Japanese naval officers who had been
attached to the 205th Special Attack Force in Taiwan (*Shimpū*, pp. 186–88):

Question: There is a diametrical difference in thinking about kamikaze strategy
between your country and ours. In America a single human life is immensely
precious, but in Japan you were prepared to sacrifice large numbers of pilots
for suicide missions. What was your reason?

Answer: The idea behind the Special Attack Forces has its origins in ancient
Japanese traditions *(Nihon korai no mono de)*, and it recurs throughout our
history. In the recent war we realized that such attacks had become essential
because of the military situation. They were never imposed on us from
above. . . .

Question: Was the recruitment for the Special Attack Forces voluntary or compulsory?

Answer: It was completely voluntary. There were, however, cases in the Philippines and elsewhere in which an entire unit would adopt these tactics because
of the military situation at the time. . . .

Question: If one thinks of Americans in their twenties, it is totally impossible to
understand the spirit of [Japanese kamikaze fighters]. It is inconceivable that
young Americans would be ready to commit suicide like that for their country or for an Emperor. Surely you must have used high-powered methods of
indoctrination in the Special Attack Forces to train young men to think in
that way.

Answer: No, we never organized any particular form of indoctrination. . . .

Question: Did members of the Special Attack Forces participate so that their spirits
might be worshipped in Yasukuni Shrine?

Answer: If that is what someone wanted, he had no need to volunteer for the
Special Attack Forces. . . .

10.170 The moral case against dropping the atom bomb on Japan has rarely been
stated more eloquently than by the distinguished American officer, Admiral William Leahy, who regarded it as "an inhuman weapon to use on
a people that was already defeated and ready to surrender." "The Americans," he said, "had adopted an ethical standard common to the barbarians of the Dark Ages." Toland, *Rising Sun*, p. 798.

10.171 Operation Olympic, the invasion of Kyushu, was to be followed by
Operation Coronet, the conquest of Honshu. Both would have involved
fearful losses for the Allies. In addition, far more Japanese would have

been killed than actually died in Hiroshima and Nagasaki, though that was hardly the paramount consideration among American leaders at the time.

10.172 There is a great discrepancy in estimates of the death toll, this being one of the rare cases in which an attacking power deliberately minimized the degree of its "success." According to the Americans, the "Fat Man" killed 35,000 people in Nagasaki; Japanese officials give a figure of 74,800. The numbers of casualties in Hiroshima three days earlier was far greater: according to Japanese experts 200,000 people died as a result of the bomb dropped by the *Enola Gay;* here again official American estimates were far smaller.

10.173 Quoted by Ivan Morris, *Nationalism and the Right Wing in Japan* (London, 1960), p. 24.

10.174 Concerning Ōnishi's futile efforts to avoid surrender, see Inoguchi, pp. 171–74; Toland, *Rising Sun,* p. 828; Hayashi, *Taiheiyō Sensō,* p. 463, and Millot, *L'Epopée Kamikaze,* p. 364.

10.175 Inoguchi, p. 172.

10.176 The nationalist activist, Kodama Yoshio, is discussed in Morris, *Nationalism,* pp. 204, 227, 257, 269, 307, 330, 377, and there is a biographical note on pp. 443–44. Mr. Kodama's autobiography, which includes information about his distinguished naval friend, has been translated into English with the title, *I Was Defeated* (Tokyo, 1951).

10.177 The ill-cutting sword is displayed in the Yasukuni Shrine Museum (Tokyo) below a photograph of the Admiral and a scroll of his calligraphy with the characters WAKŌ ("subdued brightness").

Kusayanagi, *Tokkō no Shisō,* pp. 9–13, gives further details concerning Ōnishi's suicide.

10.178 Concerning other acts of harakiri by military men on, or shortly after, 15th August, and also mass suicides by civilian groups, see Morris, *Nationalism,* pp. 26–28.

10.179 Kodama, *I Was Defeated,* p. 173.

10.180 For the full text and a reproduction of the calligraphy, see Kusayanagi, *Tokkō no Shisō,* pp. 12–13; the translation is from Inoguchi, p. 175.

10.181 Lit. "My reputation will not be established [even] after my coffin is covered. A hundred years from now there will [still] be no friend [to understand me]." (Quoted by Kusayanagi, *Tokkō no Shisō,* pp. 19–20. See also *Shimpū,* p. 172.) The proverb in Japanese is *kan wo ōite koto sadamaru (Koji to Kotowaza Jiten* [Tokyo, 1956], p. 241).

10.182 *Shimpū,* p. 173, translated in Inoguchi, p. 187.

10.183 31-syllable poem by Vice Admiral Ōnishi Takijirō presented to his staff after the organization of the first kamikaze units. Quoted by Inoguchi, p. 187.

Glossary

Akasaka

Mountain stronghold established by Kusunoki Masashige in Kawachi Province. It was captured by Bakufu forces in 1331, recovered by Masashige in 1332, and recaptured by the Bakufu in 1333. In 1382 it was finally destroyed by troops of the "northern" (pro-Ashikaga) dynasty.

Amakusa Shirō

1620–38. Youthful Christian martyr who occupied a central, through somewhat mysterious, role in the disastrous Shimabara Rebellion of 1637–38. He was chosen to head the 37,000 insurgents in their epic defence against the massed forces of the Tokugawa Bakufu and their allies. See chap. 7, *passim*.

Arima no Miko

640–58. Unfortunate young prince (son of the 36th Emperor, Kōtoku) who fell foul of his politically astute cousin, Prince Naka no Oe, and was executed at the age of 18 on a dubious charge of treason. See chap. 3, *passim*.

Ashikaga Family

Branch of the Minamoto family; it came to power after the overthrow of the Kamakura Bakufu, and established its military headquarters (Bakufu) in Kyoto. Fifteen members of the family became successive Shoguns of Japan, from Takuji in 1338 until Yoshiaki, who held the position from 1568 until 1573, the end of the Ashikaga Bakufu.

Ashikaga Takauji

1305–58. Founder of the Ashikaga shogunate, which tried to rule Japan during a period of almost constant disorder from 1338 until 1573. Having first changed sides from the Hōjōs to Emperor Godaigo, he subsequently turned against Godaigo and was the leading general in the successful campaign to oust him from the capital and to establish an Emperor of the "northern" line in his place. When Takauji died of cancer in Kyoto and was succeeded as Shogun by his son, widespread fighting was underway between adherents of the "northern" and "southern" Courts. Despite all his impressive attributes and achievements, Takauji (the "successful survivor") figures in the legend as a treacherous villain, and statues of him were decapitated by loyalist zealots in the 19th century.

Asuka

Region in Yamato Province, some 20 miles south of Nara. Many of the ancient Japanese capitals (i.e., Imperial Courts) were situated here, and it gave its name to an important period in art history (552–645).

Ataka

Famous barrier by the Japan Sea where the fugitive Yoshitsune barely escaped detection and capture thanks to the resourcefulness of his follower, Benkei, and to the compassion of the officer in command, Togashi.

Aware

See *Mono no aware.*

Bakufu

"Tent government," name given to the military regime first established by Minamoto no Yoritomo *c.* 1190. Successive Bakufu regimes (Minamoto, Ashikaga, Tokugawa) governed Japan with the theoretical authorization of the Imperial Court until the Meiji Restoration, such delegation of power being a typical feature of Japanese institutional history.

Benkei

D. 1189. Burly priest-warrior who became Minamoto no Yoshitsune's most loyal follower and stayed with him until the sanguinary end at Koromo River. In the legend he figures as a sort of Sancho Panza. Endowed with cunning, resourcefulness, humour, and superhuman strength, Benkei provided his master with invaluable moral and physical support during the downhill part of his career.

Biwa, Lake

The most famous lake in Japan; 180 miles in circuit, it is situated near Kyoto at the eastern foot of Mount Hiei.

Chihaya

Site of a famous stronghold in Kawachi Province near the capital where Kusunoki Masashige established his headquarters in 1333 after the final fall of Akasaka. It was besieged by a vast Bakufu force, and Masashige's brilliant defence was an important practical and psychological factor in the eventual downfall of the Kamakura regime.

Chikafusa

See Kitabatake Chikafusa.

Couckebacker, Nicolaus

Chief of the Dutch factory at Hirado from 1633 to 1639. Having been ordered by the Japanese authorities to assist them in destroying the Christian rebels at Shimabara, he bombarded their stronghold in Hara Castle during February/March 1638 from the Dutch ship *de Ryp.* Couckebacker's participation in the assault was, according to his own reports, both reluctant and ineffective; but he obviously had good reason to say so.

Daigo, Emperor

885–930. 60th Emperor of Japan (reigned 897–930). The son of Emperor Uda, he helplessly presided over the downfall of his Minister, Sugawara no Michizane. Though Daigo managed without a Fujiwara Chancellor, almost all his principal officials were members of that prepotent family. His reign is associated with the Engi period (901–23), which later came to be viewed as a model for imperial rule in Japan.

Daimyo

"Great name." Feudal lords, ranking from commanders of castles up to governors of provinces. Later, in the Tokugawa period, the term was used to designate all members of the military class with revenues over 10,000 *koku* (50,000 bushels) of rice p.a. At the outset of the period their total number was 262.

Dannoura

Site of one of the most famous and evocative battles in Japanese history. It was here, in the Inland Sea, that Yoshitsune led the Minamotos in inflicting a culminating defeat upon the Tairas in 1185. During the course of this engagement, the climax of the upward part of Yoshitsune's meteoric career, the hero is said to have leapt over eight boats to reach an enemy.

Emishi

Backward groups of Japanese tribesmen in the eastern and northern provinces of the main island, many of whom resisted central imperial authority until the 9th century. They were of the same racial stock as the Japanese, but had been left behind technologically and culturally.

Fujiwara Family

Large, immensely powerful family, descended from Nakatomi no Kamatari. With various ups and downs they directed Japanese politics from the late 8th century until the middle of the 12th century. The Fujiwaras depended mainly on peaceful methods of control, notably their close connexions with the imperial family, their monopoly of certain crucial offices like those of Regent and Chancellor, and their skill in extruding rival families and individuals (like Michizane) from the centre of power.

Fujiwara no Hidehira

Warlord and leader of the "northern Fujiwaras" in their powerful Ōshū territory. (The "northern Fujiwaras" were of Emishi descent and unrelated to the main Fujiwara family.) Hidehira protected the fugitive Yoshitsune from the wrath of his elder brother, Yoritomo; the death of the old chieftain in 1187 sealed the hero's fate.

Fujiwara no Mototsune

836–91. Head of the Fujiwara family and leading political figure from 873 until his death. During this time he served as Chancellor and Regent, doggedly resisting all attempts to challenge the power of his clan.

Fujiwara no Tokihira

871–909. Son of Mototsune, he became leader of the Fujiwaras and served as Minister of the Left from 899 until he died. Tokihira represented the Fujiwara family in their successful effort to remove Sugawara no Michizane from power, and in 901 he encompassed his rival's ruin. Though a vigorous, capable statesman, Tokihira is represented in the legend as an ambitious, unprincipled villain—a typical "successful survivor."

Fujiwara no Yasuhira

1155–89. Son of Hidehira, the chieftain of the "northern Fujiwaras" in Ōshū. Violating his father's dying wishes, he attacked the fugitive Yoshitsune in 1189 and impelled the hero to kill himself. Despite this valuable service, Yoritomo subsequently annexed the Ōshū territory, and the treacherous Yasuhira himself became the victim of treachery, being put to death by one of his own retainers.

Fukuzawa Yukichi

1834–1901. Eminent liberal thinker and writer, who founded Keiō (University) and probably did more than any other person in Japan to introduce Western ideas like political democracy. He started an influential newspaper in which he advocated parliamentary government, and his books emphasized individualism, self-respect, and the elimination of old feudal patterns of thought and behaviour.

Genji, Prince

Hero of the first 40 books *(kan)* of *The Tale of Genji*. His name became a byword for male charm, beauty, talent, and sensitivity, and he is sometimes known as "the Shining Prince."

Gesshō

1813–58. Loyalist priest of the Hossō sect who became a close friend of Saigō Takamori and who fled from Kyoto to Kagoshima in 1858 to avoid arrest by the Bakufu authorities. He and Saigō jumped into the sea off Kagoshima in an unconventional form of double suicide. Saigō was rescued, but his priestly friend drowned.

Godaigo, Emperor

1288–1339. 96th Emperor of Japan (reigned 1318–39). Planned to overthrow the Kamakura Bakufu and return to the benign state of affairs that supposedly existed in the 10th century under Emperor Daigo by ousting the military "usurpers" and restoring real power to the imperial family. At first he was unsuccessful and the Bakufu exiled him to the Oki Islands (1332), but in 1334 his loyalist supporters succeeded in restoring imperial rule temporarily in the so-called Kemmu no Chūkō (Kemmu Restoration), which proved to be an extraordinarily inept effort at turning back the clock. The revolt of Ashikaga Takauji brought Godaigo's brief period of power to an end in 1336 and forced him to flee south to Mount Yoshino, where he instituted a "southern" Court and carried on the civil war until his death.

Goshirakawa, Emperor

1127–92. 77th Emperor of Japan (reigned 1156–58); a shrewd, scheming politician, he played a key role in Kyoto during the reigns of his three immediate successors and managed to survive the rapid shifts in power during the second half of the 12th century.

Hachimaki

Headband worn by kamikaze pilots, student demonstrators, Olympic athletes, and others in preparation for energetic or decisive action. The practical aim is to protect the eyes from sweat and hair, but symbolically the *hachimaki* indicates determination and sincerity in pursuit of some important (or supposedly important) undertaking.

Hara Castle

Abandoned castle at the southern tip of Shimabara Peninsula. It was the headquarters of the Christian rebels in 1637–38, when it housed some 37,000 men, women, and children. In the end they were all slaughtered by Bakufu and daimyo troops and the castle was razed to the ground.

Harakiri

"Belly cutting," an excruciating form of self-mutilation (more properly known as *seppuku*) which among members of the warrior class became the conventional means of avoiding capture or other forms of disgrace.

Hashihito, Empress

D. 661. Consort of Emperor Kōtoku and mistress of Prince Naka no Ōe, her half-brother. In 653 she abandoned the Emperor and started to live openly with her princely lover. Kōtoku wrote a plaintive poem referring to her illicit liaison, and in the following year followed this up by dying.

Heian Kyō

Imperial capital of Japan from 794 until 1868; later known as Kyoto. It gave its name to the era from the late 8th to the mid-12th centuries.

Heian Period

Long and, on the whole, remarkably peaceful period in Japanese history, lasting from the late 8th century until the mid 12th, when political power was in the hands of the Court aristocracy and concentrated in the capital city of Heian Kyō (Kyoto). One of the most important eras for the development of indigenous Japanese culture.

Hidehira

See Fujiwara no Hidehira.

Hiei, Mount

Mountain range northeast of the capital; site of Enryaku Temple, the headquarters of the Tendai sect of Buddhism. Most of the terrifying raids on the capital by warrior monks started from here; later it became a convenient place of refuge for Emperor Godaigo and other less eminent gentlemen when conditions in the capital became uncomfortable.

Hōganbiiki

Literally, "partiality for the Lieutenant." "Lieutenant" (Hōgan) refers to Minamoto no Yoshitsune, and the phrase became established in the Japanese language to denote sympathy with the loser, the *locus classicus* being a poem in which the beauty of defeat is exemplified by the scattering of blossoms.

Hōjō Family

Family, related to the Tairas but closely associated with the Minamotos, whose successive leaders, under the title of Shikken (Regent), were the actual rulers of Japan during most of the period from the death of Yoritomo in 1199 until the fall of Kamakura in 1333.

Hosokawa Gracia

1563–1600. Wife of the powerful Kyushu daimyo, Hosokawa Tadaoki, she was converted to Christianity at the age of 24 and baptized under the name of Garashiya (Gracia). She was much admired by the Jesuits as "Princess Gracia" and later acquired national renown as a paragon of feminine courage when she sacrificed her life rather than fall hostage to her husband's enemy.

Hosokawa Tadatoshi

1586–1640. Warrior, Lord of Kumamoto, and apostate. Baptized as a Christian at the age of nine, he later submitted to the orders of his overlord, Tokugawa Ieyasu, and banished all Christians from his domains in Kyushu. He was also a leading general in the suppression of the Christian insurgents at Shimabara (1638), and one of his retainers had the honour of capturing the head of the young rebel insurgent, Amakusa Shirō.

Ichinotani

Site of Yoshitsune's brilliant victory over the Tairas in 1184 by the shores of the Inland Sea.

Ikki

Rising, insurrection, revolt. As economic conditions deteriorated towards the end of the Tokugawa period, these insurrections became increasingly frequent, not only in rural areas but in the growing cities. Ōshio Heihachirō's hopeless rebellion in 1837 was by far the largest of the urban *ikki*.

Ise

Site of the Great Ise Shrine, some 50 miles east of Nara; dedicated to the sun goddess (Amaterasu), the shrine is the principal place of Shinto worship in Japan.

Itagaki Taisuke

1837–1919. Loyalist samurai from Tosa (in Shikoku) who was appointed to be Counsellor in the early Meiji government but resigned at the same time as Saigō (1873) owing to dissatisfaction with its policies. Thereafter he became the leader of the Liberal Party (Jiyū Tō), an ancestor of the present ruling party in Japan.

Itakura Shigemasa

1588–1638. Warrior and personal attendant to Tokugawa Ieyasu, he was ordered to suppress the Shimabara Rebellion in 1637 but perished in the attempt after writing a gloomy farewell poem.

Iwakura Mission

Mission to Europe and America from 1871 to 1873 by some 50 high-ranking Meiji government officials, including Prince Iwakura and Okubo Toshimichi, but notably excluding Saigō Takamori.

Izumo

Important region in the west of the main island of Japan, which retained a degree of political and religious autonomy until about the 4th century A.D. In mythology it is associated with the rule of the storm god, Susanoo no Mikoto.

Junshi

Ancient samurai practice of committing suicide at the death of one's overlord as an ultimate token of loyalty. A famous instance was that of General Nogi, who committed harakiri in 1912 on the demise of Emperor Meiji; not to be outdone, his wife, Shizuko, also killed herself.

Kaiten

Suicide torpedoes (named from an old word meaning "to remedy an unfavourable situation with a single blow"); they were launched from mother submarines in 1944–45, each torpedo carrying one suicide pilot, in a hopeless effort to avert defeat by destroying American warships.

Kajiwara no Kagetoki

D. 1200. Senior retainer of Minamoto no Yoritomo; he is said to have become fiercely jealous of Yoshitsune's military success and to have traduced him in a series of damaging reports sent to Kamakura. In the legend he figures as the arch-villain who is mainly responsible for turning Yoritomo against his devoted young brother.

Kakunosuke

See Ōshio Kakunosuke.

Kamakura

Small town in eastern Japan, 30 miles from present-day Tokyo, where Minamoto no Yoritomo established his military headquarters (Bakufu). After Yoritomo was appointed to be Shogun in 1192, the town became the *de facto* centre of power in Japan, and in the 13th century its population is said to have exceeded one million. It declined rapidly after the defeat of the Hōjōs in 1333, but was later rebuilt and regained some of its former military importance.

Kamikaze

"Divine wind," name taken from the immense typhoons that (at least according to tradition) saved Japan from the fury of the Mongols in the 13th century.

It came to designate the organized suicide tactics in 1944–45 which, it was vainly hoped, would have a similar effect in preserving the nation from disaster. (During the Pacific war the word was *shimpū*, the Sino-Japanese reading of the characters for *kamikaze*.)

Kasagi, Mount

Mountain west of Nara, where Emperor Godaigo took refuge in 1331 after being forced to flee Kyoto by the Kamakura Bakufu. Soon afterwards Kasagi was occupied by Bakufu forces and Godaigo taken prisoner.

Keikō, Emperor

One of the founding emperors of Japan (4th century A.D.); father of the legendary hero, Prince Yamato Takeru.

Kemmu Restoration

Kemmu no Chūkō (1334–36). Abortive effort by Emperor Godaigo and his loyalist supporters to wrest political power from the military class and "restore" centralized imperial rule to Japan under a Court aristocracy.

Kikusui

Famous crest of Kusunoki Masashige: a floating chrysanthemum flower half submerged by the waves. In subsequent Japanese history it became a patriotic symbol and was used by loyalist heroes, including Saigō Takamori and many kamikaze units during the Pacific war.

Kitabatake Chikafusa

1292–1354. Aristocrat-statesman-scholar-warrior, who ranks with Kusunoki Masashige and Nitta Yoshisada as one of the preeminent loyalists of this troublous period. He was the author of the most influential nationalist treatise on Japanese history, *Jinnō Shōtōki* ("A History of the True Succession of the Divine Monarchs").

Kiyomori

See Taira no Kiyomori.

Kōgon, Emperor

1313–64. Member of the "northern" line, enthroned by the Kamakura Bakufu in 1331, at the age of 18, after Godaigo had been forced to flee the capital. On Godaigo's triumphant return two years later, Kōgon was himself forced to leave and, after his brief period of uneasy glory, he spent the rest of his life in a temple.

Kojima Takanori

C. 1330. Loyalist chieftain who made an abortive attempt to rescue Emperor Godaigo on his way to exile in 1332, and who tried to comfort his sovereign by carving a poem on a cherry tree. According to tradition, Kojima persevered until his death in the futile struggle for the loyalist cause, and he became established as a minor failed hero.

Kongō, Mount

Mountain on the border of Yamato Province; Kusunoki Masashige built his famous "castle" of Chihaya on its western slope.

Koromo River

Site of Yoshitsune's residence during his fugitive period in Ōshū. This is where Benkei and his other companions were killed and where he himself committed suicide in 1189.

Koshigoe

Post station about a mile from the eastern military headquarters at Kamakura. Yoshitsune waited here disconsolately for permission to enter Kamakura and see his brother, Yoritomo; four years later, after Yoshitsune's defeat and suicide, his severed and sadly decomposed head was exposed in this same place.

Kōtoku, Emperor

596–654. 36th Emperor of Japan (reigned 645–54), father of the unfortunate Prince Arima; during his later years he appears to have suffered acutely from the liaison of his wife, Empress Hashihito, with her half-brother, Prince Naka no Ōe.

Kumano

Region south of Nara; it is the site of three famous shrines and a traditional place of pilgrimage.

Kumaso

Backward, dissident tribes in the west of Japan (mainly Kyushu) who were brought under central, imperial rule by Yamato Takeru and other conquering heroes of the semilegendary period. Though at one time the Kumaso were identified as descending from a separate race of "southern" immigrants, they were in fact of the same ethnic strain as other Japanese.

Kurama

Site of a famous temple in the wild, mountainous region north of Kyoto. It was here that the young Yoshitsune was immured as a *bonze* from the age of six and secretly learnt the arts of war. He remained until 1174 when he managed to escape to the northeast and prepare for his fight against the Tairas.

Kusanagi

The "grass mower," famous sword given to Prince Yamato Takeru by his shaman-aunt in Ise; it became one of the Three Imperial Regalia, and is worshipped in Atsuta Shrine (Owari).

Kusunoki Masashige

1294–1336. Paradigm of the Japanese loyalist hero. He brilliantly supported the losing cause of Emperor Godaigo and committed harakiri after being decisively defeated at the Battle of Minato River. See chap. 6, *passim.*

Kusunoki Masasue

D. 1336. Younger brother of Masashige. He fought with him in the loyalist campaign against the Ashikagas until their final defeat at Minato River. As the two brothers were both about to commit harakiri, Masasue is said to have made the famous *shichishō* ("seven lives") declaration, "Would that I could be reborn seven times into this world of men so that I might destroy the enemies of the Court!"

Kusunoki Masatsura

1326–48. Eldest son of Masashige. He was ten years old when he parted from his father "at Sakurai's leafy ford" on the eve of the fatal Battle of Minato River. In obedience to the paternal behest he pursued the struggle against the Ashikaga "usurpers," but the odds were hopelessly against him and at the age of 22 he died with all his followers. According to tradition, he visited Emperor Godaigo's shrine before setting out on his last battle and carved a patriotic *tanka* on the door together with his name and those of his loyalist companions.

League of the Divine Wind

Shimpūren, society of nationalist samurai zealots in Kyushu who fiercely but hopelessly opposed the Meiji government's policy of encouraging Westernization. In 1876 they mounted a desperate uprising in Kumamoto, but after some preliminary successes were exterminated by government forces, who were armed with superior modern weapons.

Makoto

"Sincerity," the cardinal quality of the Japanese hero, denoting purity of motive, a rejection of self-serving, "practical" objectives, and complete moral fastidiousness.

Manyōshū

"The Collection of a Myriad Leaves," the oldest (and most impressive) poetic anthology in all Japanese literature, consisting of 20 books *(kan)* and containing some 4,500 poems, mainly *tanka* but also many long poems *(chōka)* of a type that virtually disappeared in later centuries. About 500 writers are represented, and the works cover the period from *c.* 400 to *c.* 660, the date of compilation.

Masashige

See Kusunoki Masashige.

Masasue

See Kusunoki Masasue.

Masatsura

See Kusunoki Masatsura.

Matsudaira Nobutsuna

1596–1662. Warrior and statesman, who led the Bakufu forces in suppressing the Shimabara Rebellion, broke up the conspiracy of Yui Shōsetsu, and served as close adviser to the young Shogun, Tokugawa Ietsuna. His talents were widely recognized and he came to be respected, though not loved, as Chie-Izu ("the wise [Minister] from Izu").

Matsukura Shigemasa

D. 1630. Originally a vassal of Toyotomi Hideyoshi, he switched to the side of Tokugawa Ieyasu and played a distinguished part in the Battle of Osaka (1614–15), as a result of which he became the Lord (daimyo) of Shimabara, a fief of 43,000 *koku*. He was famous for his fiendish persecution of Japanese Christians, a tradition that was pursued with sadistic enthusiasm by his tyrannical son, Shigeharu.

Michizane

See Sugawara no Michizane.

Mifune Toshirō

B. 1920. The most eminent film actor in postwar Japan, he is especially noted for his portrayal of brave, independent, outrageous, sincere samurai types.

Minamoto Family

Outstanding samurai family descending collaterally from the 9th-century emperor, Seiwa. The Fujiwaras relied on them for military support, especially in the provinces. In the 12th century the Minamotos, under Yoritomo, became the predominant power in the country and established a proto-feudal administration in Kamakura.

Minamoto no Noriyori

D. 1193. Warrior who joined the revolt against the Tairas under the direction of his half-brother, Yoritomo. In due course he fell out with Yoritomo (as did almost every other close relation) and burnt himself to death in order to escape capture.

Minamoto no Yoritomo

1148–99. Warrior and statesman; son of Yoshitomo and elder brother of Yoshitsune; leader of the Minamoto clan and founder of the Kamakura Bakufu. He was one of the most brilliant successes in all Japanese history, but figures in the Yoshitsune legend as a cold, ruthless, scheming politician who hounded his young brother to an untimely death.

Minamoto no Yoshinaka

1154–84. Cousin of Yoritomo and famous as a fierce mountain warrior. After helping defeat the Tairas, he occupied Kyoto with his unruly troops, but the former emperor, Goshirakawa, plotted with Yoritomo to destroy him and he was run to ground near the capital.

Minamoto no Yoshitomo

1123–60. Father of Yoritomo and Yoshitsune, he was defeated by the Tairas and murdered by one of his own retainers, who sent his head to Kyoto. Yoshitsune vowed to avenge his death—and did so.

Minamoto no Yoshitsune

1159–1189. 9th son of Minamoto no Yoshitomo and younger brother of Yoritomo. After a series of coruscating military victories, which secured the triumph of the Minamotos over the Tairas, he fell foul of his jealous elder brother, Yoritomo, and was finally forced to commit harakiri after all his followers had been killed. His worldly failure became the basis of his lasting popularity as the great romantic hero of Japanese history, and his memory is fixed in the Japanese language with the word *bōganbiiki* ("sympathy with the loser"). See chap. 5, *passim*.

Minamoto no Yukiie

D. 1186. Brother of Yoshitomo and uncle of Yoshitsune, he feuded with Yoritomo (as did almost every other important member of the Minamoto family). Having joined forces with the losing side in the Yoritomo–Yoshitsune struggle, he was done to death on Yoritomo's orders.

Minato River

River near present-day Kobe; site of a sanguinary and decisive battle fought one hot day in 1336 when the loyalist forces under Kusunoki Masashige and Nitta Yoshisada were defeated by Ashikaga Takauji; sometimes used as a Japanese equivalent of "Waterloo."

Mishima Yukio

1925–70. Illustrious and wildly energetic novelist, playwright, essayist, film actor, *chansonnier*, etc., etc., who committed harakiri in the Self-Defence Headquarters in Tokyo following the failure of his so-called private army (the Shield Society) to gain military support for changing Japan's postwar Constitution and giving power to the Emperor.

Mongol Invasions

The first (and last) military invasions in recorded Japanese history. Mounted in 1274 and 1281 under the direction of Kublai Khan, they were decisively defeated owing—or so tradition has it—to the "divine winds" *(kamikaze)* that providentially destroyed the Mongol fleets.

Mono no aware

Central theme in traditional Japanese sensibility and aesthetics, corresponding to *lacrimae rerum*, the pathos of things. An understanding of *mono no aware* is reflected, among other things, in an instinctive sympathy with the fate of the failed hero, whose defeat dramatically and poignantly exemplifies the confrontation of all living creatures with adversity, suffering, defeat, and death.

Mononobe

Ancient clan *(uji)* whose leaders served successive Emperors in carrying out Shinto (and, subsequently, judicial and police) functions. After their defeat in A.D. 587 they lost pride of place to the more forward-looking Sogas.

Mononobe no Moriya

D. 587. Leader of the ancient Mononobe clan, who was defeated by his great enemy, Soga no Umako, in the battle of A.D. 587.

Mori Ōgai

1862–1922. Man of letters, novelist, literary editor, and translator, who started his career as a doctor, studied in Germany, and was appointed Surgeon-General to the Imperial Army in 1907. A prolific writer of fiction, he moved from works in the German romantic tradition to historical novels dealing mainly with samurai heroes like Ōshio Heihachirō who exemplified his idea of the Japanese spirit.

Morinaga, Prince

1308–35. Son of Emperor Godaigo, he played an impressive role in the loyalist struggle against the Kamakura Bakufu and was appointed Shogun in 1333. Morinaga followed up his early success by heroic failure when he was suddenly arrested in Kyoto and banished to Kamakura, where he was executed by the Ashikagas. Despite all Morinaga's contributions to the loyalist cause, Godaigo did nothing to save his son from disaster.

Naka no Ōe, Prince

626–72. Crown Prince who eventually ascended the Throne as the 38th Emperor of Japan (reigned 661–72). He was a leading figure in the movement to overthrow the Soga clan, restore power to the imperial family, and reform Japan on modern, Chinese lines. He enjoyed almost uninterrupted political success, partly owing to his acumen in disposing of potential rivals like Prince Arima.

Nakae Tōju

1608–48. Confucian samurai scholar from Ōmi Province who espoused the doctrine of Wang Yang-ming and stressed the priority of personal action over abstract learning. He exemplified his filial piety (the supreme Confucian virtue) by resigning a promising official position in order to look after his aged mother in her village near Lake Biwa which she refused to leave. Tōju often addressed himself to the humbler members of society, who were neglected by more orthodox Confucian scholars, and he was much revered by the villagers, who referred to him as Ōmi Seijin (the Holy Man of Ōmi).

Nakatomi no Kamatari

614–69. Close associate of Prince Naka no Ōe in directing the Great Reform and the anti-Soga conspiracy that led up to it, his objective being to help modernize and centralize Japan on Chinese lines. Ancestor of Japan's future rulers, the Fujiwara family.

Nasake

Compassion, fellow-feeling: an ability (shared by all sincere samurai) to perceive the suffering inherent in the human condition and to sympathize with the weak and helpless. It is reflected in a reluctance on the part of heroes like Masashige to inflict suffering on peasants and other helpless, swordless folk.

Nitta Yoshisada

1301–38. Originally a retainer of the Kamakura Bakufu, but switched to the loyalist side and led the forces that captured Kamakura in 1333. Though for a time he cooperated with Ashikaga Takauji, he became his mortal enemy after Takauji's break with Emperor Godaigo. He survived the disaster at Minato River in 1336 and continued to resist the Ashikagas; but during a surprise attack he was wounded by an arrow and avoided capture by committing suicide. In Fujishima Shrine, erected on the spot where he died, Yoshisada is honoured as one of the supreme loyalist heroes of Japan.

Nobo, Plain of

Plain in Ise Province, some 40 miles east of Kyoto. This is where Prince Yamato Takeru met his lonely death at the age of 30 after failing to return to the capital and make his last report to his father, Emperor Keikō.

Nogi Maresuke

1849–1912. Military commander who participated in the campaign against the Satsuma Rebellion and later established a brilliant reputation during the Sino-Japanese and Russo-Japanese wars. He led the Third Army, which captured Port Arthur from the Russians. Determined to follow his master, Emperor Meiji, into death, General Nogi committed suicide (*junshi*) in 1912. This culminating act established him as a model of self-sacrificing loyalty and served as proof that the ancient samurai ideals were still alive.

Ōka

"Cherry Blossom," name given to manned suicide bombs, carried by mother planes and used by the Japanese in 1944–45 with the principal objective of sinking American aircraft carriers; in the event, not a single carrier or other capital ship was destroyed by an Ōka.

Ōkubo Toshimichi

1830–78. Samurai from Satsuma who, like Saigō Takamori (his childhood companion), took a leading role in the overthrow of the Tokugawa Bakufu and the "Restoration" of the Emperor. Thereafter he became a leading member of the Meiji oligarchy with the ranks of Counsellor and Minister. After Saigō's resignation in 1873, Ōkubo was the dominant figure in the regime until his assassination five years later. Though generally respected for his attainments in helping Japan to modernize and survive as a nation, and despite his violent and untimely death, Ōkubo was too cold and political a figure to acquire real popularity.

Ōnishi Takijirō

1891–1945. Vice Admiral, Commander of the 1st Naval Air Fleet, Vice Chief of Naval General Staff, organized the first kamikaze units in the Philippines in 1944 and took a leading part in kamikaze tactics until the end. He committed harakiri and died in Tokyo on the day following the surrender of Japan.

Ōshio Heihachirō

1796–1837. Fervent Police Inspector and Confucian scholar of the Wang Yangming school, who stabbed himself to death after the failure of his abortive uprising in Osaka to protest against the conditions of the esurient populace. See chap. 8, *passim*.

Ōshio Kakunosuke

1811–37. Adopted son and close supporter of Ōshio Heihachirō. He died with his father when their hiding place in Osaka was discovered by the police. A year and a half later the Court ordered that his pickled corpse, together with Heihachirō's, be publicly exposed and crucified.

Ōshū

Remote territory in the northeastern part of the main island, where Yoshitsune took refuge with the "northern" Fujiwaras and met his sanguinary end in 1189.

Rokuhara

Section in the southeast of Kyoto where the representatives of the Kamakura Bakufu resided from 1220; these military headquarters were totally destroyed by the loyalists in 1333.

Rōnin

Lit. "wave man." A disenfeoffed or masterless samurai who was no longer attached to any daimyo. In the Tokugawa period many of them became soldiers of fortune and swashbucklers, offering themselves and their sharp swords to anyone who needed (and could pay for) the services of daring warriors.

Saigō Takamori

1827–77. Statesman, soldier, poet, and failed hero who, having risen from a poor samurai family in the west of Kyushu to become Chief Counsellor of State (1871) and Commander-in-Chief of the Imperial Bodyguards and Field Marshal (1877), fell out with Ōkubo and other leading members of the Meiji oligarchy in 1873, returned to his home province of Satsuma, and in 1877 became the leader of a catastrophic rebellion which ended with his suicide. See chap. 9, *passim*.

Sakurai

Site of the parting scene between Kusunoki Masashige and his eldest son in 1336 on the eve of the cataclysmic Battle of Minato River; it is the title of a famous patriotic song.

Samurai

Lit. "one who serves." In general, any member of the military class; more specifically, the retainer of a daimyo.

Satsuma

Proud, pugnacious, "outside" province in southwestern Kyushu, which clung tenaciously to national, samurai traditions. The second largest province in Japan, it remained the most independent, closed, and clannish. Satsuma was the birthplace of Saigō, Ōkubo, and other Meiji leaders.

Satsuma Rebellion

The last important national insurrection in Japan (until the February Incident of 1936). It broke out in February 1877 when Saigō Takamori led an army of about 15,000 supporters who captured Kagoshima (the capital of Satsuma) and then marched north. Foiled in their attempt to take Kumamoto in central Kyushu, the rebels fell back on Kagoshima, where they were wiped out by overwhelming government forces.

Sekigahara, Battle of

Major battle in Japanese history. It was here in 1600 that Tokugawa Ieyasu gained a decisive victory over his enemies; this led to the establishment of the Tokugawa Bakufu, which ruled Japan for over two and a half centuries.

Shimabara

Peninsula in western Kyushu, site of the Christian rebellion of 1637–38, which ended in the greatest bloodbath of the Tokugawa era.

Shimazu Family

Hereditary rulers (daimyo) of Satsuma Province; they had been defeated by the Tokugawas in 1600 and were traditionally inimical to the ruling shogunate.

Shimazu Hisamitsu

1817–87. *De facto* ruler of Satsuma Province after the death of Shimazu Nariakira in 1858, he tried to effect a reconciliation between the Court and the Bakufu. Following the Restoration, he became important in the new government and was appointed Chancellor and Minister of the Left, but, disgruntled with "over-hasty" centralization and other national policies, he retired to Satsuma in 1874 in high dudgeon. Hisamitsu survived his much resented retainer, Saigō Takamori, became a Prince in 1884, and received a grand state funeral on his death.

Shimazu Nariakira

1809–58. Daimyo of Satsuma from 1851 until his death. A devoted loyalist, he did his best to establish close relations between Satsuma and the Court, and also to encourage a reconciliation between the Court and the Bakufu. In addition he was active in reforming his own domains and during his brief period in power he imported modern military and other technology from the West to Kagoshima. He was adulated by Saigō Takamori, and Saigō's attempt at suicide in 1858 has been interpreted as an act of *junshi* on the death of his lord.

Shiroyama

"Castle Hill" in Kagoshima where Saigō Takamori took refuge from the imperial forces during his last days and where he finally committed harakiri on 24th September 1877. It gave its name to a famous ballad about the hero.

Shishi

"Men of spirit" who became conspicuous in the 1860s in the patriotic movement to "honour the Emperor and expel the barbarian." The prototype was

Yoshida Shōin, the defiant samurai loyalist; Saigō Takamori belongs squarely to this activist tradition, which survived (though with a certain moral decline) into the 1930s.

Shizuka Gozen

Beautiful dancing girl of Kyoto. The mistress of Minamoto no Yoshitsune during his stay in the capital, she became one of the most illustrious legendary heroines of Japan. During her lover's fugitive period she was captured by Yoritomo's forces and sent to Kamakura, where she was forced to dance before Yoshitsune's enemies. On this occasion she courageously improvised a song in praise of Yoshitsune. Yoritomo ordered that her infant boy (Yoshitsune's son) be murdered, and later she was sent back to Kyoto where she spent the rest of her life as a nun.

Shogun

Abbreviation of Seii Taishōgun ("barbarian-subduing generalissimo"), originally a title given to the general who suppressed the dissident Emishi in the early 9th century. Later the Shoguns became hereditary, *de facto* military rulers of Japan, theoretically appointed by the Emperor to keep the peace, but in fact the real political hegemony of the country during a large part of its history. The first line of prepotent Shoguns was established by Minamoto no Yoritomo in 1192.

Shōtoku Taishi

574–622. Served as Regent from 593 until his death and is universally recognized as one of the "good things" in Japanese history, being credited with a dazzling series of achievements, notably in the fields of culture (especially Buddhism and Confucianism) and foreign (i.e., Chinese) relations. He worked closely with Soga no Umako to promote the advance of Japanese civilization under a central imperium and paved the way for the Great Reform movement, which started some twenty years after his death.

Soga Family

A clan (*uji*) which had strong Buddhist and continental connexions and which developed close ties with the imperial family; after the defeat of the Mononobes in 587 the Sogas became the most powerful political unit in Japan and kept this position for almost 60 years until they were destroyed by Prince Naka no Ōe, Nakatomi no Kamatari, and other leaders of the Great Reform movement. In many of their political techniques they anticipated the Fujiwara family, but they made the mistake of aspiring (or appearing to aspire) to the Throne itself, and they were undone by their hubris.

Soga no Umako

D. 626. Leader of the prepotent Sogas, who led his clan to victory in the battle against the Mononobes in 587 and remained a dominant political figure in Japan for some four decades: recognized as a success, but not as a hero.

Sugawara no Michizane

845–903. Scholar, calligrapher, poet, and statesman who in 901 was exiled from the capital owing to Fujiwara power politics and who died during his forlorn exile in Kyushu, later becoming venerated as the god of poetry and scholarship, the tutelary saint of failures, etc. See chap. 4, *passim.*

Susanoo no Mikoto

Rambunctious Shinto deity of wind and storm, brother of the sun goddess (Amaterasu); he was disgraced among the gods and banished forever from the Plain of High Heaven.

Taiheiki

"Chronicle of the Great Peace," a 41-volume chronicle which (despite its title) concentrates on intrigue and violence during the sanguinary period from 1318 to 1368; attributed to the priest Kojima (d. 1374) of Mount Hiei.

Taira Family

Warrior family, descended collaterally from Emperor Kammu (d. 806); they achieved hegemony in 1159 as the first in a line of military rulers, but their brief period of glory came to an end when they were decisively crushed by the Minamotos in 1185. Their evocative failure gave rise to the saying, "Even the proud Tairas did not last for long."

Taira no Kiyomori

1118–81. Warlord and statesman, known for his energy, pride, and arrogance. He led his clan to the height of military and political power, but lived to see the resurgence of the Minamotos, who were to bring the Tairas to ruin four years after his death.

Takamori

See Saigō Takamori.

Takauji

See Ashikaga Takauji.

Tanka

31-syllable (5–7–5/7–7) poem, which was established as the standard form of elegant verse throughout most of Japan's history.

Togashi

Vassal of Minamoto no Yoritomo, he was appointed to guard the strategic barrier of Ataka but, owing to his sympathy with the loser *(hōganbiiki),* allowed Yoshitsune and his companions to cross safely and make good their escape to the north.

Tokihira

See Fujiwara no Tokihira.

Tokiwa, Lady

C. 1160. Minor lady-in-waiting whose association with Minamoto no Yoshitomo led directly to the birth of Yoshitsune. According to the legend, Taira no Kiyomori was so overcome by her beauty that he made her his concubine and agreed to spare the lives of her three young children, including Yoshitsune—an act of humanity that he was to regret most bitterly.

Tokugawa Period

Period from 1600 to 1868, when the Tokugawa Bakufu harshly and, on the whole, efficiently kept the peace from their headquarters in Edo (Tokyo). The Tokugawa family, who came to power as hereditary Shoguns following Ieyasu's victory at Sekigahara, claimed descent from the 9th-century emperor, Seiwa, via the Minamotos and Nitta Yoshisada.

Uda, Emperor

867–931. 59th Emperor of Japan (reigned 887–97). Having come to the Throne as a learned and ambitious young man, he tried to resist Fujiwara political hegemony, especially by giving a share of the power to "outsiders" like Sugawara no Michizane. His efforts proved nugatory when the Fujiwaras succeeded in forcing Michizane's removal from the capital in 901.

Ugaki Matome

Vice Admiral in the Imperial Japanese Navy and Commander of the 5th Naval Air Fleet; he was closely involved in kamikaze tactics since 1944. Ugaki ended his life in a final suicide attack on 15th August 1945 *after* the Emperor had made his surrender broadcast.

Umako

See Soga no Umako.

Wang Yang-ming

1472–1529. Chinese scholar-official who founded the Idealist School of Ming Confucianism. His activist philosophy had a powerful influence on many well-known figures in the history of modern Japan (where it is known as Yōmeigaku); these men include Ōshio Heihachirō, Saigō Takamori, General Nogi, and Mishima Yukio.

Yamada Emonsaku

D. 1655. The first well-known painter of Western style in Japan, he was baptized by the Jesuits at an early age and served as one of Amakusa Shirō's chief captains in the Shimabara Rebellion. His role in the drama is somewhat murky, but the scant available evidence suggests that he tried to betray his young master to the enemy. His plan was discovered by the rebels and he was sentenced to death. While Yamada was awaiting execution, the castle was captured by government forces and he was rescued, thus becoming the only known survivor of the catastrophe. The practical advantages of treachery were confirmed when he later became established in Edo, and still later in Nagasaki, as a successful artist.

Yamagata Aritomo

1838–1922. Samurai from Chōshū who, after distinguishing himself in the battles against the shogunal army, became a leading figure in the Meiji government. He worked to establish a new military system that led to national conscription; played a leading part in crushing Saigō Takamori's rebellion. Later he served as Prime Minister (twice), Privy Counsellor, and elder statesman *(genrō)*. He was responsible for assuring a strong political role for the military, and received a state funeral on his death.

Yamamoto Isoroku

1884–1943. Admiral, Combined Fleet Commander-in-Chief (1941–43), and the most popular military leader during the Pacific war. He opposed Japan's entry into the war, but once the decision was made, he took the lead in organizing the attack on Pearl Harbor. Yamamoto was killed when his plane was shot down by an American fighter over the Solomons. He was posthumously promoted to the Supreme Military Council and given a state funeral in May 1943.

Yamato

One of the five "inner" provinces. Until the end of the 8th century almost all the capitals of Japan (including Nara) were in this province, which lies about 25 miles south of Kyoto. The name is also used poetically and patriotically to describe Japan in general.

Yamato Takeru no Mikoto

"The Princely Brave of Japan," a composite, legendary hero, the son of Emperor Keikō (4th century A.D.). Having successfully conquered various dissident tribes on behalf of the Yamato Court, he was finally defeated by a malignant mountain deity near Lake Biwa and died alone on the Plain of Nobo at the age of 30 before he was able to return to the capital and make his report to the Emperor. See chap. 1, *passim*.

Yashima

Site of a famous battle in Shikoku between the Tairas and the Minamotos, in which Yoshitsune, the Minamoto commander, scored a decisive victory.

Yasuhira

See Minamoto no Yasuhira.

Yōmeigaku

See Wang Yang-ming.

Yoritomo

See Minamoto no Yoritomo.

Yorozu

D. 587. Historical prototype of the Japanese failed hero. An obscure warrior who fought on the losing side in the culminating battle between the Sogas and the Mononobes and who committed suicide with great bravura rather than endure the ignominy of capture. See chap. 2, *passim*.

Yoshida Shōin

1831–59. Samurai scholar and loyalist hero who was executed for treason after the discovery of his hopeless anti-Tokugawa plot. He gained posthumous success with the downfall of the shogunate in 1868.

Yoshinaka

See Minamoto no Yoshinaka.

Yoshino

Magnificent mountainous region forming the southern half of Yamato Province. It was here among the famous cherry blossoms that Emperor Godaigo established his "southern" Court in 1338 after he had been obliged to abandon Kyoto, and Yoshino remained the centre of "southern," loyalist resistance until the settlement of 1392.

Yoshisada

See Nitta Yoshisada.

Yoshitomo

See Minamoto no Yoshitomo.

Yoshitsune

See Minamoto no Yoshitsune.

Yui Shōsetsu

1605–51. Military strategist and heroic rebel who organized a hopeless anti-Tokugawa conspiracy (a sort of Guy Fawkes plot). He committed suicide when the plot was discovered; his followers and their families were hideously tortured and crucified on the orders of the chief shogunal adviser, Matsudaira Nobutsuna.

Yukiie

See Minamoto no Yukiie.

Bibliography

ABE SHINKIN. "Ōshio Heihachirō." *Nihon Jimbutsushi Taikei* IV (1959).

AKAMATSU, PAUL. *Meiji 1868.* London, 1972.

Azuma Kagami [The Mirror of the East]. Nihon Shiryō Shūsei edition. Tokyo, 1963.

BEASLEY, W. G., ED. *Historians of China and Japan.* London, 1961.

———. *The Meiji Restoration.* Stanford, 1972.

BORTON, HUGH. *Peasant Uprisings in Japan of the Tokugawa Period.* New York, 1968.

BOXER, C. R. *The Christian Century in Japan, 1549–1650.* London, 1951.

CAMPBELL, JOSEPH. *The Hero with a Thousand Faces.* New York, 1956.

CHADWICK, N. *The Growth of Literature.* Cambridge, England, 1932.

CRAIG, ALBERT, AND SHIVELY, DONALD. *Personality in Japanese History.* Berkeley, 1970.

DAIDŌJI SHIGESUKE (Yūzan). *Budō Shoshin Shū* [Elementary Readings on the Way of the Warrior]. Tokyo, 1965.

DE BARY, WM. THEODORE, CHAN, WING-TSIT, AND WATSON, BURTON. *Sources of the Chinese Tradition.* New York, 1960.

DÜRKHEIM, KARLFRIED GRAF VON. *The Japanese Cult of Tranquillity.* London, 1960.

EARL, DAVID. *Emperor and Nation in Japan.* Seattle, 1964.

EBISAWA ARIMICHI. *Amakusa Shirō.* Tokyo, 1967.

ELIADE, MIRCEA. *Cosmos and History.* New York, 1959.

ERIKSON, ERIK. *Young Man Luther: A Study in Psychoanalysis and History.* New York, 1962.

FAIRBANK, JOHN, REISCHAUER, EDWIN, AND CRAIG, ALBERT. *East Asia, the Modern Transformation.* Boston, 1965.

FUJIWARA NO KANEZANE. *Gyokuyō* [Leaves of Jade]. Kokusho Kankō Kai edition. Tokyo, 1906–7.

FUKUDA KŌSON. *Arima no Miko* [Prince Arima]. Tokyo, 1961.

FUKUZAWA YUKICHI. *Teichū Kōron* [The Discussion of 1877]. In *Fukuzawa Yukichi Zenshū* [The Collected Works of Fukuzawa Yukichi], vol. VI. Tokyo, 1925–26.

Gikeiki [The Chronicle of Yoshitsune]. Nihon Koten Bungaku Zenshū edition. Tokyo, 1966.

GRIFFIS, WILLIAM ELLIOT. *The Mikado's Empire.* New York, 1913.

HALL, J. C. "Japanese Feudal Laws." In *Transactions of the Asiatic Society of Japan* XLI, no. 5 (1913).

HALL, JOHN, AND MASS, JEFFREY, ed. *Medieval Japan: Essays in Institutional History.* New Haven, 1974.

HAYASHI SHIGERU. *Taiheiyō Sensō* [The Pacific War]. Tokyo, 1967.

Heike Monogatari [Tales of the House of Taira]. Koten Nihon Bungaku Zenshū edition. Tokyo, 1966.

HERRIGEL, EUGEN. *Zen in the Art of Archery.* New York, 1971.

Hitachi Fudoki. [The Hitachi Topography]. Musashino Shoin edition. Tokyo, 1956.

IHARA SAIKAKU. *The Life of an Amorous Woman and other Writings.* Translated by Ivan Morris. New York, 1963.

IKEDA KIKAN. *Heian Jidai no Bungaku to Seikatsu* [Literature and Life in the Heian Period]. Tokyo, 1967.

INOGUCHI RIKIHEI AND NAKAJIMA TADASHI. *Shimpū Tokubetsu Kōgekitai no Kiroku* [Records of the Divine Wind Special Attack Force]. Tokyo, 1963. Translated by Roger Pineau, as *The Divine Wind: Japan's Kamikaze Force in World War II.* Annapolis, 1958. Japanese edition cited in Notes as *Shimpū.* English edition cited in Notes as "Inoguchi."

INOUE KIYOSHI. *Meiji Ishin* [The Meiji Restoration]. Tokyo, 1966.

ISHII SUSUMU. *Kamakura Bakufu.* Tokyo, 1965.

JANSEN, MARIUS. *Sakamoto Ryōma and the Meiji Restoration.* Princeton, 1961.

JOLY, HENRI. *Legends in Japanese Art.* Tuttle & Co. edition. Rutland and Tokyo, 1967.

KADOKAWA GENYOSHI. "Gikeiki no Seiritsu" [How the Chronicle of Yoshitsune Was Put Together]. In *Kokugakuin Zasshi* LXV, nos. 2–3 (1964): 79–100.

KAGOSHIMA-SHI GAKUSHA RENGŌKAI [League of Kagoshima City Institutes]. *Shikon* [The Spirit of the Samurai]. Kagoshima, 1970.

KAMO NO CHŌMEI. *Hōjōki* [An Account of My Hut]. Yūseidō edition. Tokyo, 1963.

KATŌ GENCHI. *Shinto in Essence.* Tokyo, 1954.

KAWABARA HIROSHI. *Saigō Densetsu* [The Saigō Legend]. Tokyo, 1971.

KEENE, DONALD. *Anthology of Japanese Literature.* New York, 1955.

KISHIMOTO HIDEO. *The Japanese Mind.* Honolulu, 1967.

KITABATAKE CHIKAFUSA. *Jinnō Shōtōki* [A History of the True Succession of the Divine Monarchs]. Iwanami Shoten edition. Tokyo, 1936.

KITAJIMA MASAMOTO. *Bakuhansei no Kumon* [The Agony of the Bakufu-Fief System]. Tokyo, 1966.

KITAYAMA SHIGEO. *Heian Kyō.* Tokyo, 1965.

KŌDA SHIGETOMO. *Ōshio Heihachirō.* Osaka, 1942.

KODAMA YOSHIO. *I Was Defeated.* Tokyo, 1951.

Kojiki [Record of Ancient Matters]. Nihon Koten Zensho edition. Tokyo, 1963.

Kokin Waka Shū [Collection of Old and New Poems]. Nihon Koten Zensho edition. Tokyo, 1956.

KOKKAI TOSHOKAN [National Diet Library]. *Jimbutsu Bunken Sakuin* [Index of Personality Documents]. Tokyo, 1972.

KUDŌ YOROSHI. "Tenraku-kei no Nihon Eiyū-zō" (The Japanese Hero-Image [and] the Pattern of Falling). In *Shūkan Asahi* 6–8 (1973): 114–17.

KURODA TOSHIO. *Mōko Shūrai* [The Mongol Invasions]. Tokyo, 1965.

KUROITA KATSUMI. *Kokushi no Kenkyū* [A Study of History], vol. I. Tokyo, 1936.

KUSAYANAGI DAIZŌ. *Tokkō no Shisō—Ōnishi Takijirō Den* [The Philosophy of the Special Attack Force: A Biography of Ōnishi Takijirō]. Tokyo, 1972.

LEGGE, JAMES. *The Four Classics.* Hongkong, 1957.

MABIRE, JEAN. *Les Samouraï.* Paris, 1971.

MAEDA ICHIRŌ. "Ōshio Heihachirō." In *Nihon Rekishi Kōza.* Tokyo, 1952.

Manyōshū [The Collection of a Myriad Leaves]. Edited by Nippon Gakujutsu Shinkōkai. Tokyo, 1940.

McCULLOUGH, HELEN. *The Taiheiki.* New York, 1959.

———. *Yoshitsune, A Fifteenth-Century Japanese Chronicle.* Stanford, 1966.

MILLOT, BERNARD. *L'Epopée Kamikaze.* Paris, 1970.

MISHIMA YUKIO. *Eirei no Koe* [The Voices of the Fallen War Heroes]. Tokyo, 1970.

———. *Homba,* Tokyo, 1969.

———. "Kakumei no Tetsugaku to shite no Yōmeigaku" [Wang Yang-ming Thought as a Revolutionary Philosophy]. In *Shokun* (September 1970), pp. 23–45.

———. *Runaway Horses.* Translated by Michael Gallagher. New York, 1973.

MITFORD, A. B. *Tales of Old Japan.* London, 1883.

MORI ŌGAI. *Ōshio Heihachirō.* Iwanami Shoten edition. Tokyo, 1960.

MORISON, SAMUEL ELIOT. *Leyte.* Boston, 1958.

MORRIS, IVAN. *Nationalism and the Right Wing in Japan.* London, 1960.

_____. *The World of the Shining Prince: Court Life in Ancient Japan.* London and New York, 1964.

MORSE, EDWARD. *Japan Day by Day.* Boston, 1917.

MURDOCH, JAMES. *A History of Japan,* vols. II–III. Routledge & Kegan Paul edition. London, 1926 (reprinted 1949).

MUSHAKŌJI SANEATSU. *Saigō Takamori.* Translated and adapted by Sakamoto Moriaki in *Great Saigō, The Life of Takamori Saigō.* Tokyo, 1942.

NAGATSUKA, RYŪJI. *J'étais un kamikazé: Les chevaliers du vent divin.* Paris, 1972.

NAOKI KŌJIRŌ. *Kodai Kokka no Seiritsu* [The Establishment of the Ancient State]. Tokyo, 1965.

NARAMOTO TETSUYA. "Rekishi to Jimbutsu" [History and Personalities]. In *Mainichi Shimbun,* no. 5, 19 February 1971.

NIHON REKISHI SHIRĪZU [Japanese Historical Series]. *Shōgun to Daimyō* [Shogun and Daimyos]. Tokyo, 1967.

NIHON SEMBOTSU GAKUSEI SHUKI HENSHŪ IINKAI [Committee to Edit the Notes of Japanese Students Killed in Combat]. *Kike Wadatsumi no Koe* [Hearken to the Ocean's Voice!]. Tokyo, 1968.

Nihon Shoki [The Chronicles of Japan]. Nihon Koten Zensho edition. Tokyo, 1953.

NISHIMURA SADA. "Shimabara Ran no Kirishitan Jinchū Hata to Yamada Emonsaku" [Yamada Emonsaku and the Banner in the Christian Camp during the Shimabara Rebellion]. In *Nihon Shoki Yoga no Kenkyū.* Tokyo, 1958.

NITOBE INAZŌ. *Bushido: The Soul of Japan.* Tuttle & Co. edition. Rutland and Tokyo, 1969.

NOGAMI TOYOICHIRŌ. *Yōkyoku Zenshū* [Collected Nō Plays], vol. V. Tokyo, 1935.

OCHIAI NAOBUMI. "Aoba Shigareru Sakurai no" [At Sakurai's Leafy Ford]. In *Nihon Shōka Shū,* pp. 60–61. Tokyo, 1953.

OKADA AKIO. *Amakusa Tokisada.* Tokyo, 1960.

ŌOKA SHŌHEI. *Fires on the Plain.* Translated by Ivan Morris. Penguin Books edition. New York, 1969.

PAGÈS, LÉON. *Histoire de la réligion Chrétienne au Japon depuis 1598 jusqu'à 1651.* Paris, 1869–70.

REIK, THEODOR. *Masochism and the Modern Man.* New York, 1941.

RIESS, DR. LUDWIG. "Der Aufstand von Shimabara, 1637–1638." In *Mittheilungen der Deutschen Gesellschaft für Natur- und Völkerkunde Ostasiens* V. no. 44 (1890).

ROBERTS, JOHN. *Mitsui: Three Centuries of Japanese Business.* New York, 1973.

SAKAI SABURŌ. *Samurai.* New York, 1957.

SAKAMOTO MORIAKI. "A Tragic Hero of Modern Japan: The True Phase of Saigō the Humanist." Unpublished manuscript.

_____. "Chronological Table of the Life of Saigō Takamori." Unpublished manuscript.

_____. "Nanshū-Ō's (Saigō Takamori's) Posthumous Words." Unpublished manuscript.

_____. *Saigō Takamori.* Tokyo, 1971.

_____. "Saigō Takamori's Poems and Posthumous Words." Unpublished manuscript.

_____. *Shiroyama Kanraku* [The Fall of Shiroyama]. Kagoshima, 1963.

SAKAMOTO TARŌ. *Sugawara no Michizane.* Tokyo, 1956.

SANO MITSUO. "Hōki" [The Uprising]. In *Rekishi to Jimbutsu.* March 1972.

SANSOM, GEORGE. *A History of Japan to 1334.* London, 1958.

_____. *A History of Japan, 1334–1615.* London, 1961.

_____. *Japan, a Short Cultural History.* New York, 1962.

_____. *The Western World and Japan.* London, 1950.

SATŌ SHINICHI. *Nambokuchō no Dōran* [The War between the Northern and Southern Courts]. Tokyo, 1965.

SATOW, ERNEST. *A Diplomat in Japan.* London, 1921.

SCALAPINO, ROBERT. *Democracy and the Party Movement in Prewar Japan: The Failure of the First Attempt.* Berkeley, 1953.

SCHNEIDER, IRWIN. "The Mindful Peasant: Sketches for a Study of Rebellion." In *Journal of Asian Studies* (August 1973): 579–89.

SCOTT-STOKES, HENRY. *The Life and Death of Yukio Mishima.* New York, 1974.

SEI SHŌNAGON. *The Pillow Book,* 2 vols. Translated by Ivan Morris. London and New York, 1967.

SEWARD, JOHN. *Hara-Kiri.* Tokyo, 1968.

SHELDON, CHARLES. Review of *Boshin Sensō* and *Boshin Sensōshi.* In *Journal of Asian Studies* (February 1974): 314–16.

SHIMAZU HISAMOTO. *Yoshitsune Densetsu to Bungaku* [Yoshitsune Legends and Literature]. Tokyo, 1935.

Short Biographies of Eminent Japanese in Ancient and Modern Times, 2 vols. Tokyo, 1890. (Anonymous.)

SINGER, KURT. *Mirror, Sword and Jewel: A Study of Japanese Characteristics.* New York, 1973.

STOETZEL, JEAN. *Jeunesse sans chrysanthème ni sabre: Étude sur les attitudes de la jeunesse japonaise d'après guerre.* Paris, 1953.

STORRY, RICHARD. *The Double Patriots.* London, 1957.

Taiheiki [The Chronicle of the Great Peace], vol. I. Nihon Koten Bungaku Taikei edition. Tokyo, 1960.

TANAKA SŌGORŌ. *Saigō Takamori.* Tokyo, 1958.

TŌKEI SŪRI KENKYŪJO [Institute of Statistical Mathematics]. *Nihonjin no Kokuminsei* [The National Character of the Japanese]. Tokyo, 1961.

TOLAND, JOHN. *The Rising Sun.* New York, 1970.

TSUJI TATSUYA. *Edo Bakufu.* Tokyo, 1966.

TSUNODA RYUSAKU, DE BARY, WM. THEODORE, AND KEENE, DONALD. *Sources of Japanese Tradition.* New York, 1958.

UCHIMURA KANZŌ. *Daihyōteki Nihonjin* [Representative Japanese]. Tokyo, 1970.

UEMURA SEIJI. *Kusunoki Masashige.* Tokyo, 1963.

VARLEY, H. PAUL. *Imperial Restoration in Medieval Japan.* New York, 1971.

———. *Japanese Culture.* New York, 1973.

WAKAMORI TARŌ. *Yoshitsune to Nihonjin* [Yoshitsune and the Japanese]. Tokyo, 1966.

WALEY, ARTHUR. *The Nō Plays of Japan.* London, 1921.

WATANABE TAMOTSU. *Yoshitsune.* Tokyo, 1966.

WATSON, BURTON. "Michizane and the Plums." In *Japan Quarterly* XI, no. 2 (1964): 217–20.

YAMAMOTO IEYOSHI. *Nanshūō Itsuwa Shū* [A Collection of Anecdotes about Saigō Takamori]. Tokyo, 1903.

YODA NORITAKA. *Nanshūō no Hiyūmanizumu* [The Humanism of Saigō Takamori]. Tokyo, 1965.

YOKOTA YUTAKA. *Suicide Submarine!.* New York, 1962.

YOSHINAGA MINORU. *Nihon Kodai no Seiji to Bungaku* [Ancient Japanese Politics and Literature]. Tokyo, 1956.

Index